Modern England

*or, How Things Came to be
the way they are*

*History as growth of choices
or options (for living, being,
thinking)*

The United Kingdom: Physical

MODERN ENGLAND

From the Eighteenth Century to the Present

Second Edition

R. K. WEBB

UNIVERSITY OF MARYLAND, BALTIMORE COUNTY

1817

HARPER & ROW, PUBLISHERS, New York
Cambridge, Hagerstown, Philadelphia, San Francisco,
London, Mexico City, São Paulo, Sydney

Sponsoring Editor: John Michel
Project Editor: Claudia Kohner and Jo-Ann Goldfarb
Senior Production Manager: Kewal K. Sharma
Compositor: Ruttle, Shaw & Wetherill, Inc.

Art Studio: J & R Technical Services, Inc.
Cover Art: The Bettmann Archive

**MODERN ENGLAND: From the Eighteenth Century to the Present,
Second Edition**

Library of Congress Cataloging in Publication Data

Webb, Robert Kiefer.
  Modern England.

  Includes bibliographies and index.
  1. Great Britain—History—18th century.
  2. Great Britain—History—19th century.
  3. Great Britain—History—20th century.
  I. Title.
DA470.W4 1980   941.07   79-19829
ISBN 0-06-046974-9

To the Memory of Howard Robinson

Contents

Preface   *xi*

Introduction   Early Eighteenth-Century England   *1*

    SOME GEOGRAPHICAL CONSIDERATIONS   *1*
    ENGLISH SOCIETY   *5*
    ENGLISH POLITICS   *40*
    SELECTED READINGS   *71*

PART I
THE OLIGARCHY CHALLENGED:
REFORM AND INDUSTRIALISM, 1760–1832   *77*

1   "The Present Discontents," 1760–1789   *79*

    THE POLITICS OF THE SIXTIES   *79*
    BRITAIN OVERSEAS, 1770–1782   *86*
    THE EMERGENCE OF REFORM, 1776–1789   *94*
    SELECTED READINGS   *104*

2   The World and the Spirit, 1760–1830   *107*

    THE ECONOMIC REVOLUTIONS   *107*
    THE REVOLUTIONS IN UNDERSTANDING   *122*
    SELECTED READINGS   *131*

3   The French Revolution, 1789–1815   *134*

    VERSAILLES TO AMIENS, 1789–1802   *134*
    AMIENS TO VIENNA, 1802–1815   *143*
    SELECTED READINGS   *155*

4   The Emergence of Liberalism, 1815–1832   *157*

    RECONSTRUCTION, 1815–1820   *157*
    NEW DIRECTIONS, 1820–1830   *168*
    THE CONSTITUTIONAL REVOLUTION, 1828–1832   *186*
    SELECTED READINGS   *203*

PART II
THE EXPANDED OLIGARCHY:
EARLY VICTORIAN ENGLAND, 1832–1867

207

5 The Impact of Reform, 1832–1848   209

POLITICS AND THE CONSTITUTION   _210_
THE DEMANDS OF THE MIDDLE CLASSES   _222_
RELIGION   _228_
THE CONDITION OF THE WORKING CLASSES   _236_
SELECTED READINGS   _254_

6 Peel's Decade, 1841–1850   259

SOCIAL REFORM   _259_
THE ECONOMY   _267_
THE TURNING POINTS   _277_
SELECTED READINGS   _282_

7 Consensus, 1850–1867   285

THE LIBERAL TRIUMPH   _285_
PALMERSTON   _301_
NEW DIRECTIONS, 1859–1867   _316_
SELECTED READINGS   _331_

PART III
THE CLAIMS OF DEMOCRACY, 1867–1918

337

8 The Great Rivalry, 1868–1886   339

THE WORKING-OUT OF REFORM   _339_
BRITAIN OVERSEAS, 1870–1886   _352_
SELECTED READINGS   _372_

9 The Erosion of the Liberal Consensus, c. 1873–1900   375

THE GREAT DEPRESSION, 1873–1896   _375_
THE LABOR MOVEMENT   _386_
A CHANGING MIDDLE-CLASS CULTURE   _399_
INTELLECTUAL LIFE   _409_
SELECTED READINGS   _415_

10 Politics and Empire, 1886–1911   421

THE NEW FORMS OF POLITICS   _421_
THE TORY HEGEMONY, 1886–1905   _428_
THE LIBERAL RESURGENCE, 1900–1911   _454_
SELECTED READINGS   _466_

11 The End of Victorian England, 1911–1918   *469*

THE EDWARDIAN INTELLECT   *469*
REVOLT, 1911–1914   *472*
ARMAGEDDON, 1914–1918   *481*
SELECTED READINGS   *491*

PART IV
THE TRIALS OF DEMOCRACY   *493*

12 Between the Wars, 1918–1940   *495*

RECONSTRUCTION AND REACTION, 1918–1923   *495*
TOWARDS LABOUR, 1918–1924   *511*
TOWARDS A CRISIS, 1925–1931   *520*
THE NATIONAL GOVERNMENT, 1931–1940   *531*
THE LEGACY, 1918–1940   *549*
SELECTED READINGS   *562*

13 Brave New Worlds   *565*

THE SECOND WORLD WAR, 1940–1945   *565*
THE POSTWAR ERA IN PROSPECT   *573*
THE FORTUNES OF THE PARTIES   *588*
THE POSTWAR ERA IN RETROSPECT   *612*
SELECTED READINGS   *626*

Appendix 1 The Kings and Queens of England, 1688–1980   *629*

Appendix 2 Titles, Honors, and the Peerage   *630*

Appendix 3 The Church of England   *637*

Appendix 4 The English Courts   *644*

Appendix 5 Local Government   *654*

Appendix 6 English Money   *656*

Appendix 7 Additional Reading   *658*

Index   663

Maps
THE UNITED KINGDOM: PHYSICAL   *ii*
THE UNITED KINGDOM: COUNTIES   *4*
THE UNITED KINGDOM: PRINCIPAL CITIES   *6*
INDIA PRIOR TO THE MUTINY (C. 1856)   *312*
SOUTHERN AFRICA BEFORE THE BOER WAR   *358*
EGYPT AND ITS SURROUNDING AREAS IN THE LATE
   NINETEENTH CENTURY   *362*

Preface

In 1945, and for some years after, Britain was still perceived as a great power. Now, the Empire is gone in name and in all but the most vestigial fact; the Commonwealth is a famous shadow. In one part of the world after another, the British military presence has disappeared, and a United Nations founded today would probably not find the British a permanent seat on the Security Council. In other countries one usually seeks in vain, even in the most encyclopedic of newspapers, for news of what is happening in Britain, unless there is a general election, a royal wedding, a spectacular trial, or some new burst of quaintness or eccentricity. Britain figures less prominently than was once the case in the curriculums of schools and colleges, and so the citizens of other countries, knowing little of what goes on in England today, are also less aware of the legacy from Britain (or, more strictly, England) — in law, institutions, and the economy — that still shapes the lives of many of them.

At the same time, new kinds of awareness have emerged. The "swinging London" of the sixties profoundly altered styles, as the Beatles and their successors have affected popular culture. Increasing tourism has meant a wide familiarity with the delights of the English countryside and with at least the most famous historical monuments. The export of some remarkable British television series may have awakened a new interest in and sympathy with at least parts of Britain's past. The country has been an irresistible magnet to immigrants from former colonies seeking a better life, and the inhabitants of even the most prosperous of European and American countries seem to sense that somehow a country that by ordinary standards is impoverished, beset by problems, and in decline has retained, or acquired, a degree of ease and civility not to be found elsewhere.

The falling-off in general awareness of Britain and its history has not deterred the historians, in Britain, across the Atlantic, or across the Channel; indeed, Britain's altered status has provoked a whole new range of questions. While activity in the much-ploughed but still fertile historiographical fields of the Middle Ages and the sixteenth and seventeenth centuries has not slackened, increasing attention has been given to the past two centuries. In that period Britain secured and lost its ascendancy, established (and again lost) its primacy as an industrial and financial power, and coped with the consequences of a populous, urban, industrial society by adapting old political structures and shaping a welfare state that retains its fascination for foreigners, even though their own countries may now offer more generous benefits than the British provide for themselves. These two hundred years have increasingly taken on a kind of unity. The long political reorientation of the nineteenth century and the ultimate transition to democracy were triggered by the clashes and crises early in the reign of George III. The loss of one empire was followed by the building of another. The economic departures of the late eighteenth century created the first industrial society and, by reaction, all other industrial societies. The modern cultural context is rooted in the eighteenth-century emergence of Romanticism, in the revival of religious concern, and in the faith in rational and scientific methods confirmed in these same decades — all developments in which England played a disproportionate role.

This book is an attempt to encompass the whole sweep of that period in a single volume. The first edition was completed in 1966–1967. A dozen years until a revision is a long time, but the delay was less than fatal in part because the mid-sixties caught the subject on a historiographical plateau. The great work of Sir Lewis Namier still seemed largely unassailable and carried conviction for many decades before and after the narrow period — the 1750's and 1760's — to which his own researches were confined. Administrative historians had created a virtual subfield in nineteenth-century studies, as they pursued the welfare state to its real or assumed origins. Four marvelous syntheses that still dominate our historical awareness were then new: W. L. Burn's *The Age of Equipoise*, G. Kitson's Clark's *The Making of Victorian England*, Phyllis Deane's and W. A. Cole's *British Economic Growth, 1688–1959*, and E. P. Thompson's *The Making of the English Working Class*. The reinterpretation of mid-Victorian Liberalism by J. R. Vincent and the more extensive recasting of our views of Disraelian Conservatism by Robert Blake, Maurice Cowling, F. B. Smith, and Paul Smith appeared in time to be noticed at least in the English edition of this book, but not soon enough to be taken fully into account. For the period after 1876 the landmarks were few, a circumstance that goes some distance to explain the boldness of my treatment of the last hundred years, which a few reviewers were kind enough to notice.

By now most of the historical scene is in ferment once more. The Namierite spell has been broken, and the eighteenth century is again a period for lively exploration. The years between 1880 and 1940 are changed out of all recognition, while in thirty years of the postwar era we can see both unities and surprises that were less in evidence at twenty years' distance from 1945. This revision has, therefore, been very extensive, in substance where the work of historians has compelled it and to some extent in style throughout. Because some teachers have found the book uncomfortably foreshortened for courses that begin in 1688 or 1714, I have added two extensive sections of political narrative that will, I hope, increase the usefulness of the book without distorting an introduction I continue to regard as preliminary to the main business starting round about 1760. Bibliography has been differently treated. I have not counted, but I have the impression that the books of note published since 1967 outnumber all the books I had to consider for the original version. The quantity of titles needed for a decent sampling and acknowledgment suggested removing them from footnotes at the most relevant places to essays at the ends of chapters.

The appendices continue, as before, to be essential, so much so that it makes sense to read them first. To the list of monarchs and the explanations of peerage, church, and law courts I have had to add (rather grumpily) two

. of the reorganization of local government in the more — a brief made the structure and many names that will be familiar to 1970's, which different from what we must use for the period covered by future; and an explanation of the old system of English money, now sunk this most without a trace by the decimalization that Victorian rationalists began to agitate for in the 1850's but that was not achieved until the 1970's. Birth and death dates continue to be given in the index, to avoid cluttering the page. Titles of peers, being subject to change, are used in the form appropriate to the period under discussion: thus, Lord Ashley becomes Lord Shaftesbury after 1851, and the Marquess of Salisbury appears only after earlier incarnations as Lord Robert Cecil and Lord Cranborne. Once William Pitt becomes Earl of Chatham, I follow the custom of using his title, partly to avoid confusion with his son, the younger William Pitt; but most politicians, like Disraeli, who were ennobled late in life may have the honor noted but will retain their humbler and more famous surnames throughout the book.

I remain unrepentant about having written a history of England. Although the term Britain (and the adjective British) is used for general references to the United Kingdom after its creation in 1707. Scotland and Ireland — like the Empire and Commonwealth — appear in these pages only when they impinge on English developments. With some violation of chronology, the catching up is done at these points; the index and headings in the table of contents should help in tracking them down as needed. The basic structure of the book remains unaltered, except for small variations in the introduction and the last chapter on postwar Britain. More readers than was the case a decade ago may find the rooting of that structure in politics to be irrelevant, as economic history has moved on towards becoming a separate, highly technical discipline and as social historians have opened up new ranges of inquiry and have found novel methods of dealing with them. But, in my judgment, matters have not yet progressed enough to warrant a general history of England conceptualized on the basis of these new departures. I hope that I will have alerted readers sufficiently to what is happening on the frontiers of historical inquiry, though the prospect of stumbling on yet another historiographical plateau is remote, as is the possibility of satisfying everyone when synthesis, even for a couple of hundred years in a single country, is now almost beyond the accomplishment of one person.

I dedicated this book to Howard Robinson, my first English history teacher, and a learned, lively, enthusiastic, skeptical, engaged, and marvelously funny man. He died early in 1977, at the age of 91, after a career and a retirement of astonishing productivity. The new version, sadly, must be a tribute to his memory, as fresh in my mind (and the minds of his other students) as it was when I first encountered him in a classroom in a crazy Gothic building in Oberlin almost forty years ago.

I want to thank once again those colleagues and friends whose advice and criticism, or whose painstaking and stern reading of typescript and proofs, were of so much importance in the original version: Geoffrey Best, J. H. Buckley, Peter Gay, J. F. C. Harrison, Richard W. Lyman, and Gordon Wright, to whose names I must add those of two fine historians who have since died, tragically early — David Joslin, of Cambridge, and David Owen, of

Harvard. Substantial parts of the present version were rea~
and Stephen Koss, and the whole was read by David Spring; ~heila Biddle
like their friendship, are invaluable. Pamela Greeff did much rety~dings,
an accuracy and good humor astonishing to one aware that his typing ~ith
lowing his handwriting into illegibility. So thanks to all and responsibility to
none, save me, with one exception: Stephen Koss persuaded me to restore a
minor joke I had taken out in the editing; he is entirely unanswerable for
that.

In 1841, a worthy though not quite eminent Victorian, the distinguished
civil servant Sir Arthur Helps, published a book called *Essays Written in the
Intervals of Business.* The original version and the revision of this book were
written in the same way. The business has not suffered from it, but my wife
and daughters have; mere thanks cannot repay that debt.

RKW

Modern England

Introduction
Early Eighteenth-Century England

SOME GEOGRAPHICAL CONSIDERATIONS

A visitor coming to Britain for the first time from a continental country must adjust to a very different geographical scale. Illinois and Indiana together are slightly larger than the whole island of Great Britain; England and Wales cover an area about the size of New England. England would go twice into Italy, four times into France. By comparison with the larger continental countries, such as Russia, India, Canada, or the United States, England seems almost insignificant. One can just manage an overnight train journey in Britain, say, from Aberdeen, the farthest north of large cities, to London, but could easily be in Penzance, at the southwestern extremity, by the next evening.

Nearly everything the visitor sees makes the same point. Rivers are little, fields are little, freight cars are little. Not even in the mountains of Scotland or Wales will one find true grandeur. The whole country is, as has often been said, human-sized. In a well-known verse, the early twentieth-century writer G. K. Chesterton suggested that

1

"the rolling English drunkard made the rolling English road," but the countryside was not subdued and ordered by such seemingly casual human effort. Long and heavy labor created the present face of England—from the raising of the monoliths at Stonehenge to medieval forest clearances to the cuts and tunnels of the Victorian railways; such works are less than awesome only when set against what has been done in larger, harsher lands that challenge even modern technology.

Britain is a country in miniature. It is not small as a piece of another country is small; it is rather as though a much larger country had been shrunk in every dimension. Here is a second adjustment the continental visitor must make—to the astonishing variety one will find. At home one might travel for days through landscape changing not at all in character and sometimes hardly in details. In England a few hours' journey will most likely take one through wide variations in terrain, vegetation, and agricultural practice—from bleak, open moorland, to narrow almost mountainous valleys, to gently rolling parkland; from heather to grass to cultivated fields; from dry stone walls outlining fields to hedges to ragged mounds of earth. Industry in Britain is concentrated in and around cities such as Manchester or Birmingham—the region north of the latter has long been known as the Black Country—or near the ports, but from time to time in one's travels, one encounters, in the midst of gentle agricultural land or even in places of some scenic splendor, a cluster of mills, a chain of brickworks, or the pyramidal refuse heaps of coal mines, reminders of the advantages Britain derived in an age of rudimentary transportation from mineral and power resources concentrated in a small area within easy reach of navigable water.

Some of this variety derives from history—from the ebb and flow of conquest and immigration, from successive field systems, from royal or aristocratic whim or policy, from the demands and opportunities of industrialism. The interplay of such determinants underlies the agricultural characteristics of the country, the pattern of place names so quaint and colorful to tourists and so informative to historians, the variation in physical types and, perhaps most striking, the extraordinary richness of dialects and accents which come so close to defeating foreigners who unwarily assume that the English they hear on the BBC or learn in school is, as it is called, standard.

This variety begins with the land itself. The division between highland and lowland Britain is generally said to follow a line that runs uncertainly from the mouth of the Tees in the northeast to the mouth of the Exe in the southwest. This distinction helps to explain many phenomena: the survival of Celtic races, languages, and practices in the highlands, the pattern of loyalty during the Civil War in the seventeenth century, the alteration of the economic map of the country with the industrial revolution.

The highland zone is the modest remnant of a very old chain of mountains. But though grandeur and terror are lacking in this landscape, the country is rugged, complicated, and often inhospitable. Nearly everywhere the rainfall exceeds forty inches a year; hard rock impedes drainage; the cloud formation reinforces the chill and the bleakness. Agricultural life is poor and uncertain, and even cattle or sheep farming is sometimes a gamble, as the sparse vegetation and the upland cold are liabilities unknown to the richer grazing lands to the east and south. But the highlands have also been the source of most of Britain's mineral wealth—tin, copper, and china clay in Cornwall, lead in the Mendips, coal in Wales and the northeast, iron in the Forest of Dean and the Cleveland Hills. Early exploitation of these resources often changed the way of life of the nearby inhabitants but, usually because of the peculiar social organization of the country, brought little improvement in living standards. That had to wait for more recent times, and it is at least arguable that local populations in still backward parts of the highland regions have benefited less from their mineral wealth than from the diffusion of consumer-goods industries and the growth of marketing and services since the late nineteenth century. They have benefited greatly, too, from the recently discovered and appreciated resource of their natural beauty: At vacation time the town dwellers of Britain flock to Cornwall, North Wales, the Lake District of the northwest, and Scotland, though it should be added that cloud and rainfall in those areas make the life of a tourist as much of a gamble as the life of a farmer.

Lowland Britain is flat only along stretches of the east coast and in scattered places inland, say in the Thames valley immediately west of London. But this lovely rolling country, rising gently towards the highland zone, did not always show its present order and attractiveness. In prehistoric times and throughout a large part of the Middle Ages, much of the land was heavily forested; only in the sixteenth century did a shortage of timber begin to worry English policymakers and ironmasters. Although the rainfall in the lowlands is nearly always less than the forty inches of the highlands, excess water remains a problem over much of the country, especially in areas with heavy soils or in that region inland from the Wash on the mid-east coast and stretching north into Yorkshire, where within historic times sluggish, meandering rivers turned low-lying land into the swampy Fens. Only the development of modern agricultural and drainage techniques since the seventeenth century has made much of this land useful.

Our continental visitor would probably have been well prepared

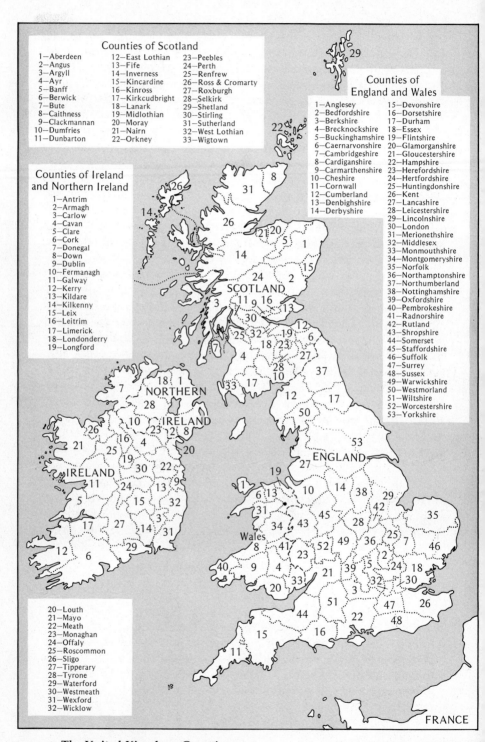

Counties of Scotland

1—Aberdeen	12—East Lothian	23—Peebles
2—Angus	13—Fife	24—Perth
3—Argyll	14—Inverness	25—Renfrew
4—Ayr	15—Kincardine	26—Ross & Cromarty
5—Banff	16—Kinross	27—Roxburgh
6—Berwick	17—Kirkcudbright	28—Selkirk
7—Bute	18—Lanark	29—Shetland
8—Caithness	19—Midlothian	30—Stirling
9—Clackmannan	20—Moray	31—Sutherland
10—Dumfries	21—Nairn	32—West Lothian
11—Dunbarton	22—Orkney	33—Wigtown

Counties of England and Wales

1—Anglesey	15—Devonshire
2—Bedfordshire	16—Dorsetshire
3—Berkshire	17—Durham
4—Brecknockshire	18—Essex
5—Buckinghamshire	19—Flintshire
6—Caernarvonshire	20—Glamorganshire
7—Cambridgeshire	21—Gloucestershire
8—Cardiganshire	22—Hampshire
9—Carmarthenshire	23—Herefordshire
10—Cheshire	24—Hertfordshire
11—Cornwall	25—Huntingdonshire
12—Cumberland	26—Kent
13—Denbighshire	27—Lancashire
14—Derbyshire	28—Leicestershire
	29—Lincolnshire
	30—London
	31—Merionethshire
	32—Middlesex
	33—Monmouthshire
	34—Montgomeryshire
	35—Norfolk
	36—Northamptonshire
	37—Northumberland
	38—Nottinghamshire
	39—Oxfordshire
	40—Pembrokeshire
	41—Radnorshire
	42—Rutland
	43—Shropshire
	44—Somerset
	45—Staffordshire
	46—Suffolk
	47—Surrey
	48—Sussex
	49—Warwickshire
	50—Westmorland
	51—Wiltshire
	52—Worcestershire
	53—Yorkshire

Counties of Ireland and Northern Ireland

1—Antrim	
2—Armagh	
3—Carlow	
4—Cavan	
5—Clare	
6—Cork	
7—Donegal	
8—Down	
9—Dublin	
10—Fermanagh	
11—Galway	
12—Kerry	
13—Kildare	
14—Kilkenny	
15—Leix	
16—Leitrim	
17—Limerick	
18—Londonderry	
19—Longford	
20—Louth	
21—Mayo	
22—Meath	
23—Monaghan	
24—Offaly	
25—Roscommon	
26—Sligo	
27—Tipperary	
28—Tyrone	
29—Waterford	
30—Westmeath	
31—Wexford	
32—Wicklow	

The United Kingdom: Counties

beforehand for suffering a damp climate, and except in rare seasons he would not have been misinformed. As one might expect of an island in the Atlantic, there is much cloudiness, and while many countries with a less fearsome climatic reputation have much more rainfall, precipitation in the British Isles comes more gently over longer periods. But the oceanic climate offers important compensation in that the Atlantic currents sweeping across from the Caribbean warm a land that shares its latitude with Hudson Bay, Labrador, and Moscow. Britain has never known wide variations between winter and summer. This temperateness has made possible a vigorous life, without serious interruption from snow and ice (persistent only in the extreme north or on the highest land) or from excessive heat or drought. It affects Englishmen's clothing, their sports, and the construction of their houses, most notable to foreigners for the idiosyncrasy of the heating arrangements.

Finally, there is the sea. No part of England is more than seventy miles from salt water, and the jagged coastline, with its many small harbors and estuaries, has for centuries helped the sea to provide an ease and unity for English life. In earlier centuries, once the prehistoric land link had sunk below the surface, the North Sea and the English Channel had been readily traversed by men, goods, and ideas: Britain was an integral, though lately acquired, province of the Roman Empire, part of a Scandinavian, then of a great Anglo-Norman kingdom, and a not insignificant member of the universal Christendom of Rome. But in early modern times, though trade and traffic across the Channel increased, England withdrew from Europe to a political and emotional isolation that has not yet been fully overcome. Since the sixteenth century and the contest with Spain, England has treasured a naval and imperial heritage so thoroughly linked with the sea that oceans can seem less difficult to bridge intellectually and spiritually than the short distance to the Continent. Whether the sea has served as highway or barrier, the basic geographical fact in English history is that Britain is an island.

ENGLISH SOCIETY

The Aristocracy and Gentry

In 1696, Gregory King completed his *Natural and Political Observations and Conclusions upon the State and Condition of England,* a set of ingenious calculations that has made him today the most famous of the late seventeenth-century practitioners of "political arithmetic" or, as we should say, statistics. But King was probably known to most of his contemporaries not as a political arithmetician but as

The United Kingdom: Principal Cities

6

holder of the offices of Rouge Dragon and Lancaster Herald. From 1677 to his death in 1712, that is, he was one of the country's leading experts in genealogy and heraldry, the complex chivalric code that had grown up in the Middle Ages, symbolizing the part played in society by a few men of surpassing military and political importance. To their descendants at the end of the seventeenth century, Gregory King's profession of heraldry would have made much more sense than his strange hobby of counting and calculating.

The best-known fragment of King's work—a table giving the numbers, ranks, income, and expenditure of English families—has recently been severely criticized. King's sources were inevitably imperfect and his methods were insufficient to bridge the gaps. Moreover, King was an extreme conservative; it is significant that he chose to date his estimates in 1688, the watershed between a society of which he approved and a newer, more mobile and monied society he disliked. Yet the categories of the table, writes King's critic, must be seen for what they are, "a monument to a static, and in some ways anachronistic view of a pre-war society," still valuable to us "in the sense that they reflect how the pre-industrial Englishman of a traditionalist cast of mind preferred to think his social order was constituted."* The number of such traditionalists was legion in eighteenth-century England, and King's classification can serve as a revealing first introduction to the nature of that society. For all its faults, historians have as yet produced little that is more helpful.

Of the five and a half million people who, according to King's estimates, were living in England and Wales in 1688, some sixteen thousand were of the rank of gentleman or higher; with their families, dependents, and servants (all considered as part of the family) they made up something under 3 per cent of the population and accounted for 13 per cent of the national income. Technically, "gentleman" was a term restricted to those entitled to bear arms, to display, that is, the distinctive heraldic devices that once had been worn on shields or emblazoned on banners; hence, as a general term, it could be applied over a broad gradation from mere gentlemen to the greatest noblemen. But the "gentlemen of England" were very conscious of the barriers that marked them off from each other within that broad category of gentility. Above the mere gentlemen came the esquires and the knights, terms that descend from medieval military organization; above the knights came the baronets, the proud possessors of hereditary knighthoods that had been created early in the seventeenth century to make money from the socially ambitious for a

*G. S. Holmes, "Gregory King and the Social Structure of Pre-industrial England," *Transactions of the Royal Historical Society*, 5th ser., vol. 27, p. 64 (1977).

royal treasury perpetually short of it. In law, everyone in these ranks was a commoner; in ordinary parlance, they were summed up as the gentry.

Above the baronets came the ranks of the peerage, ranging from barons at the bottom to dukes at the top and set off from commoners by legal privileges of some importance: they sat in the House of Lords, not the House of Commons, and could be tried for serious crimes only by their fellow-peers. More to the point, however, the peers and a small number of wealthy and prominent gentry had easy access to a degree of social and political privilege that lesser gentry could rarely aspire to. The rewards of politics came more readily and regularly to them than to their less exalted neighbors, as did political office, with the attendant income that was so important a means of increasing a family's fortune; they were assured of patronage appointments for their relatives or clients and of advancement in rank for themselves. Many country gentlemen who could not claim these rewards prided themselves on their immunity to such temptations, or, as they put it, on their independence. They preferred to exercise their power locally and disdained giving up an ancient name for the obscurity of a new title. But that pride may have been only compensation for failure to attain the impossible.

Foreign visitors found the mobility in the upper ranks of English society one of the most striking characteristics of the country. Few noble families could trace their titles back beyond the sixteenth century, and those who could genuinely claim descent from the companions of William the Conqueror were rarities. The fortunes of war had wiped out a good many older noble families; the fortunes of politics, in an age when life and death were the stakes in the political game, eliminated others. Still, service to the Crown, in war or in peace, was the normal way to rise, either into the peerage or within it. Wealth was a prerequisite to title, but it too could come from such service and clinch a claim that mere landed income would not support. A few of the most able and favored lawyers and an occasional soldier could in a lifetime earn enough or gain sufficient status and respect to rise from obscurity into the peerage; but only at the very end of the eighteenth century did a new peer emerge from the ranks of commerce—and he was a banker, one of the aristocrats of trade. Extinctions and recruits balanced fairly nicely, and the size of the peerage was well under 200 until the very end of the century. Of the 160 "temporall lords" in Gregory King's tables, thanks to old age, minorities, or other disqualifications, an active part in ruling England was taken by, say, 125 or 130 peers and a few prominent gentry, a group of men who knew each other and who acted and ruled on the basis of well-understood if rarely articulated assumptions.

For all the importance that the age attached to rank—and social competitiveness increased in the course of the century—perhaps, both for contemporaries and for us, the most meaningful distinctions were founded on differences in wealth. Gregory King put down the yearly income of mere gentlemen at £280 and temporal lords at ten times that amount; many, of course, were much richer, rising, it was said, as high as £40,000 a year, a sum that, allowing for the differences in the value of money, would readily qualify its recipient as a millionaire by any modern standard. And differences in income brought many other differences. The most striking way to display one's wealth was by building or rebuilding a country house. Blenheim Palace was built for the Duke of Marlborough by a nation grateful for his victories in the War of the Spanish Succession, a gratitude strengthened, no doubt, by his close and mutually dependent relationship with the Whigs in power; but other noblemen built their palaces without such subsidies (or such obvious subsidies). The many country houses built or rebuilt in the eighteenth century reflected the general rise in landed incomes. Architectural design moved with fashions in taste, from baroque extravagance early in the century to the balanced Palladianism of fifty years later, and in abandoning the formal settings copied from the Continent, the English by the middle of the century made their greatest contribution to the art of landscape gardening, a carefully planned naturalness associated with the designer "Capability" Brown. But less wealthy aristocrats and well-to-do gentlemen built too, as their tastes and incomes allowed; and the indefatigable traveler Celia Fiennes, herself a member of landed society, carefully and approvingly noted the many modern houses or modernizations of old houses in which she stayed at the turn of the century.

Differences in wealth could also mean differences in taste, cultivation, and style of life. Some upper-class children continued to be tutored privately; for a clergyman to become a tutor to the son of a prominent political family was a nearly certain way to advancement in the church hierarchy, once his charge had access to patronage. But more and more families among the nobility and the wealthier of the gentry were sending their sons to the so-called public schools, certain old foundations originally intended to educate poor boys for the Church but which since the fifteenth and sixteenth centuries had been gradually transmuted into boarding schools for the aristocracy. Of the small number of upper-class boys who spent some time at Oxford or Cambridge, the two English universities—where they enjoyed many privileges attaching to their rank, such as special gowns and dining at the high table—still fewer remained to take a degree. As with the public schools, the principal attainments were certain formal and conventional modes of behavior and some ability to refer to or quote from the classical authors who were so important a staple of political oratory.

A somewhat larger number of the sons of landed families spent some time at one of the Inns of Court, corporations that had grown up in the Middle Ages for the training of lawyers. Although the Inns were no longer important as teaching institutions, exposure to what lectures were given and attending the law courts could be of some practical use to young men who would have to spend their lives coping with the intricacies of the land law and governing their localities as justices of the peace. The wealthiest families would probably send at least the eldest son on the Grand Tour, an extended stay of a year or two on the Continent, to learn the social graces and the latest dances, to practice French, and to admire ancient monuments and more modern works of art. With some lack of discrimination, rich Englishmen brought home increasing quantities of that art to proclaim their taste and to enrich their own more provincial culture.

The children of the poorer gentry or of gentry in more backward parts of the country received no such education and could claim no such cultural authority. In a famous chapter on English society on the eve of the Glorious Revolution, the nineteenth-century historian Thomas Babington Macaulay scandalized many respectable members of Victorian country families by suggesting that their ancestors among the country gentlemen in the time of James II were little more than boors. He was saying no less than the truth, about some of them at least. But while many who by rank were deemed gentlemen were ignorant, drunken, and violent, others had reached a remarkable degree of refinement, discrimination, and responsibility. In *Tom Jones,* Henry Fielding caught the two types as Squire Western and Squire Allworthy; in the eighteenth century the victory lay increasingly with Squire Allworthy.

Despite the differences that divided the upper ranks of society, there were more characteristics binding them together. Nearly all landed gentlemen played some role in local government, and though political power might vary, peers and gentry shared a common interest in national politics and the affairs of Parliament. Their recreations—field sports, and hunting in particular—were an even more obvious bond, and during the early eighteenth century they guaranteed their monopoly by exacting steadily more savage laws for the protection of game. But the most important tie that joined the upper classes in English society together was their basic dependence on land.

A gentleman did not work for his living. He lived on the income from his land, and that income came, not from direct exploitation of his holdings, but from rents derived from letting his land to others. Here was a major barrier to upward mobility, particularly for the ambitious townsman or professional man for whom the ultimate felicity was to enter the ranks of landed society. The capital cost of procuring an estate which could support a gentleman's family without recourse to continuing income from the trade or profession that was left behind was perhaps twenty times the annual gross income. A thousand pounds a year would place one in the middling gentry; putting together a fortune of twenty thousand pounds or more in a lifetime took luck or lucky marriages and a favorable rate of interest. It usually meant patient and diplomatic husbanding of resources over three or four generations, a span of time that could absorb the stains of plebeian origin. In the sixteenth century, Lord Burleigh, Queen Elizabeth's great minister, had argued that "gentility is but ancient riches"; the maxim held, all but universally, two centuries later.

While the need for husbanding capital slowed down social ascent, failure to attend to it could make descent rapid and disastrous. Among the aristocracy in the sixteenth and early seventeenth centuries, there seems to have been much wastefulness and irresponsible ostentation, an astonishing carelessness about the morrow. That attitude had largely passed away by the late seventeenth century. Still, nothing could be more damaging to a family than a spendthrift, a compulsive gambler, or an overenthusiastic builder; hence the close attention paid to ways of keeping estates intact.

In the Middle Ages, the lawyers and the courts had worked out a device known as entail, which ensured that the landed property essential to the support of a great family would not be sold or sacrificed. In the early seventeenth century, however, circumstances had turned against the holders of large landed estates and made it increasingly necessary to sell land, and ingenious ways were found to bar entail so that land could be sold. By the late seventeenth century, when the economic and political crises had passed, the preservation of estates again became essential. The lawyers now devised the strict settlement, which in the eighteenth century came to control about half of the land in the country. Under its terms, a landowner was in reality only a tenant for life, deprived of the freedom to alienate any settled part of his inheritance for a period beyond his lifetime. Usually at the time of the marriage of his eldest son, the landowner would agree with his son that the son would inherit the estate and that it would in due course pass to the yet unborn grandchildren; the settlement would include the appointment of trustees who would be able legally to protect the interests of the grandchildren. Then, when the eldest grandson came of age or married, his father would negoti-

ate a new settlement similar to that between his father and himself. It
was always possible *not* to settle, but the pressure of general expectation and of family and friends made it fairly certain that a settled estate became at least once in each generation the subject of a complex
renegotiation that guaranteed the integrity of the inheritance. Once a
settlement was concluded, only a private act of parliament could
break its hold.

But these settlements had other purposes too. The son had to be
provided with income until he came into possession; a jointure had
to be arranged to provide income for his bride, should he predecease
her and for his widowed mother if she survived. Since, under the
rules of primogeniture, estates passed wholly to the eldest son, capital sums called portions had to be set aside for younger sons and
daughters. A daughter's portion would go to make up the dowry that
went to her husband when she married. For younger sons, the existence of portions contributed greatly to freedom of movement within
the society; they could use this inheritance to launch or subsidize a
career in the professions or in trade, though perhaps more used it to
support a life of indolence. There was, therefore, a steady outflow
from the landed classes into other parts of society; and because association with trade and supplementing income from commerce were
not guarantees of social disgrace—however undesirable trade may
have been as a sole source of income—there never existed in England
the sharp distinction between landed society and the world of business that existed in nearly all Continental countries.

The eighteenth century saw extensive efforts to expand estates.
If a family wanted to increase its political power, the acquisition of
more land was an excellent way of bringing more voters under one's
sway and so of increasing one's claims on those with favors to grant
to faithful allies. To some extent, expansion was simply good business; the age was beginning to respect rational, capitalistic calculation much more than it had been valued—at least among the aristocracy—a century before: estates were rounded off or consolidated,
their organization improved, and their yield increased. The cost of
land purchase was usually met by borrowing on mortgage. The rate
of interest was low in the eighteenth century, and expanded income
and good management could make it possible to carry a heavy burden of debt.

Much of this land was acquired from smaller landown-
ers—gentlemen who had fallen on hard times and had to sell their estates, or, more important, the freeholders or small owner-occupiers,
who owned and farmed their own land and who are often, loosely,
called yeomen. Some owner-occupiers had supplemented their incomes by farming additional land leased from neighboring land-

ESTIMATED NUMBERS AND RELATIVE ECONOMIC IMPORTANCE OF ENGLISH LANDED SOCIETY ABOUT THE YEAR 1790

	NUMBER OF FAMILIES	RANGE OF INCOME £	AVERAGE INCOME £	PROPORTION OWNED OF CULTIVATED LAND IN ENGLAND AND WALES
I. Great landlords	400	5,000-50,000	10,000	20–25%
II. Gentry				
(a) Wealthy gentry	700-800	3,000-5,000		
(b) Squires	3,000-4,000	1,000-3,000		50–60%
(c) Gentlemen	10,000-20,000	300-1,000		
III. Freeholders				
(a) Better sort	25,000	150-700	300	15–20%
(b) Lesser sort	75,000	30-300	100	

Taken from G. E. Mingay, *English Landed Society in the Eighteenth Century* (1963), p. 26. Reproduced with the permission of Routledge and Kegan Paul, Ltd., London and the University of Toronto Press.

lords; but the policy of consolidating estates cut into this source of additional income, a development that, coupled with heavy taxation on landowners, could make the temptation for the small owner to sell out very attractive. How far this class of small owners disappeared or survived in the eighteenth century is a complicated question. Many survived into the nineteenth century, and the precise timing of the disappearance of others—occasionally to a better life, more often to a poorer—depended on a complex of local and personal factors. One thing is sure: the times favored the big landlord and the big tenant.

In the seventeenth century, France had dominated Europe, socially as well as politically, and it was to be a good many decades before English gentlemen considered themselves in every respect equal or superior to their analogues across the Channel. But in time they did, thanks to the increasing solidity and extent of their landed and movable wealth, their increasingly confident political control at home, and some unprecedented victories in war. As their confidence grew when they looked abroad, so their assumptions became more firmly entrenched at home. By the middle of the eighteenth century, the aristocracy and the landed gentry were the real rulers of England. In 1752, Henry Fielding defined "No Body" as "all the people in Great Britain except about 1,200," and those 1,200 saw no reason at all why anything should challenge their supremacy.

Towns and Trade

The late Professor T. S. Ashton has described the eighteenth century, at least as the economic historian sees it, as an age given over to measuring, weighing, and calculating. "If men may be judged by their utterances, the educated no longer troubled their minds over-much with high matters of doctrine and polity: they were exercised less with the purpose of life than with the art of getting a living, less with the nature of the state than with the means of increasing its opulence. In 1700 there were fewer men searching the Scriptures and bearing arms than there had been fifty years earlier, and more men bent over ledgers and busying themselves with cargoes. There were fewer prophets and more projectors, fewer saints and more political economists. And these economists were concerned less with principles of universal application than with precepts derived from experience, less with what was ultimately to be wished for than with what was immediately expedient."*

This worldly outlook was not unknown among landed classes, but it was more likely to be found in the kingdom's towns. English gentlemen, preferring the country, might have looked on the towns with some aesthetic distaste, but they were not hostile to their inhabitants, at least the better sort among them. Indeed, except for the occasional merchant who was too pushful in trying to establish a claim to the status of gentleman, towns were a source of legitimate pride on the part of England's rulers, for they contributed in no small degree to her growing prosperity and strength.

London apart, only two towns at the beginning of the century—Bristol and Norwich—had more than twenty thousand inhabitants; in the new century they were quickly joined and surpassed by the villages of Liverpool, Birmingham, and Manchester, on their way to becoming towns and, in time, great cities. Bristol (again leaving London aside) was the principal port through which Britain's overseas trade was carried on; Norwich was the leading center for the manufacture of woolen cloth.

From Bristol the first English voyages for North America had gone, and the fisheries of the North Atlantic, the forests of Nova Scotia, the tropical islands of the West Indies, and the tobacco plantations of Virginia and the Carolinas all remained vital to her prosperity. But the town did not look westward alone. There was little enough trade with France, the perpetual enemy in the eighteenth century; there was more with Spain; and in 1703 the Methuen Treaty

*T. S. Ashton, *An Economic History of England: The 18th Century* (1955), p. 1. Reproduced by the courtesy of Methuen and Co., Ltd., London.

with Portugal—England's "oldest ally"—by giving a highly favorable preference helped to convert the English taste for the claret of southwestern France into the eighteenth-century liking for port. *wine*

Though the bulk of England's trade was with Continental Europe, the country was more in need of goods from Europe—wines, luxury goods, naval stores, timber, and Swedish and German iron—than Europe was in need of English exports, by all odds the most important being woolen cloth. England had, therefore, to finance essential European imports by re-exporting tropical products and other goods carried from elsewhere in the world. Hence the importance of the west coast of Africa. There English merchants found buyers for printed cotton cloth from India and for English metal goods and gin; in return they got ivory and gold that could be sent to the Far East in exchange for cottons, silks, spices, and tea, and they procured slaves for the West Indies and the southern colonies of North America, a trade on which much of the prosperity of Bristol, and to a lesser extent Liverpool, was based. *Eng. needed Europe more than Europe needed England* *slave trade*

During the eighteenth century, England's trade with the Continent fell off; the gap was filled by increased trade with the rest of the world. The East and West Indies remained the most valuable sources of goods for English consumption and for marketing in Europe, but trade with the North American colonies rose as well. This increase was due on the one hand to the growing English demand for tobacco and cotton, the latter the raw material of a new English industry that was to underpin the prosperity of the port of Liverpool. By the middle of the century, the North Atlantic trade was being helped by the rapid growth, through immigration and natural increase, of the North American population, mostly English settlers who continued (even after they broke away) to buy English goods in larger and larger quantities. The mainland colonies paid for their imports from the mother country by selling supplies to the West Indies, which of course had got English money for sugar and rum. But mercantilists viewed the northern colonies, economically so similar to England, less favorably than the West Indies; and the efforts of English statesmen to prevent the growth of what then seemed an unhealthy rivalry helped to create a divergence of views on the two sides of the Atlantic that in time had some singular consequences.

In the early centuries of English overseas enterprise, merchants banded together into so-called regulated companies. Each company enforced rules on its members and divided up the trade among them; the members continued, however, to trade on their own account. As voyages grew longer and risks greater, the regulated company began to give way to the joint-stock company, created by Crown charter and trading as a corporate unit, with the risk spread widely over *joint-stock chartered companies* many stockholders. By the early modern period, the export of wool to the Continent, which had been confined in the Middle Ages to the regulated Merchants of the Staple, had sunk to insignificant proportions; the monopoly on the export of woolen cloth, in the hands of the Merchant Adventurers, another regulated company, was broken in 1689. But the sixteenth and seventeenth centuries saw the creation of many famous joint-stock companies for more distant and dangerous commerce: the Muscovy Company, the Levant Company, the Africa Company, the East India Company, and the Hudson's Bay Company. In time, particularly in the East, interlopers came to infringe on these monopolies; and by the middle of the eighteenth century only the East India Company and the Hudson's Bay Company remained as active trading organizations. As merchants grew wealthier, the need to share risks was no longer so great, and the risks themselves declined with longer experience, better ships and seamanship, improved insurance, and growing British control of the seas. The word *merchant* continued to be general in its application, for merchants usually dealt in the most miscellaneous goods—at wholesale, not retail—and engaged as well in widely varying activities: banking, for example, was a frequent adjunct of a successful mercantile business. But there was an increasing tendency to concentrate on particular products, certain parts of the world, or one or another branch of overseas trade: thus, shipowning and insurance by the eighteenth century had come to be separated from actual trading.

While freedom made inroads on the organization of overseas trade, it made little headway so far as government regulation was concerned. Certainly the cluster of policies and prejudices that we sum up retrospectively as mercantilism had advanced considerably in sophistication since the middle of the seventeenth century; but merchants and statesmen alike agreed—and in a preindustrial world there was good reason for it—that the amount of trade in the world was limited and that England could benefit only at the expense of some other country. In the seventeenth century, the Dutch (their Protestantism notwithstanding) had been the target of three commercial wars; in the eighteenth century, rather more in line with English religious prejudice, the French were the chief rivals. The Navigation Laws known to the eighteenth century stemmed from a Cromwellian statute enacted in 1651. Retained at the Restoration, that law was expanded by later statutes into a complex code of regulations that governed the ownership and manning of English ships, asserted an English monopoly of the coastal trade and (with exceptions) of the colonial trade, and determined whether foreign ships might or might not carry certain products to and from England and

Ireland. The rationale behind the Navigation Laws went beyond
mere avarice or concern for national prosperity: the merchant fleet
and, even more, the fishing fleet were looked upon as "nurseries of
seamen," ready for use in naval warfare. When the country was at
war, English ships and sailors were occupied with more vital matters
than commerce, and the carrying of cargo was left to foreigners.

It would be difficult to overstate the importance of foreign trade
to the gradually diffusing prosperity of eighteenth-century England
and to the revolutionary future developments of the British economy.
By opening wider markets, foreign trade enabled England to escape
from the limitations of her own slowly expanding but still circumscribed demand, and so stimulated specialization and improved
technology; it increased the supply and reduced the costs of essential
raw materials; it gave other countries the purchasing power necessary to buy British goods; it helped to provide a surplus that could be
used as capital for new or enlarged ventures at home; and it encouraged an improved structure of business organization. When the
elder William Pitt made expansion of the Empire the keystone of his
policy, he captured popular imagination, above all in the towns. Men
knew where to find the key to the promise they were beginning to
feel.

If Bristol can stand as a symbol for English foreign trade, so
Norwich, the other large provincial town in the early eighteenth century, can typify the woolen industry and, beyond that, English industry in general. The manufacture of wool, once widely scattered
about the country, had gradually become concentrated in three
regions: East Anglia, with Norwich increasingly dominant; the west
country, particularly Wiltshire, Somerset, and Gloucester; and the
West Riding of Yorkshire, with its twin centers of Leeds and Bradford. As an ancient industry — England had perfected clothmaking
techniques in the late Middle Ages — the woolen manufacture had
been subjected to the closest regulation both by the state and by
elaborate, custom-ridden combinations of masters and workmen. In
the eighteenth century, much of the state's regulation existed more in
name than in fact, but traditional ways and attitudes were so deeply
ingrained in the old manufacturing centers that the attainment of virtual laissez-faire brought with it little that was expansive or stimulating: the woolen industry was revolutionized in the nineteenth century, not in centers like Norwich but in the West Riding, where the
trade, diffused among small masters, was less regimented and more
open to innovation, and where the traditional concentration on
cheap rather than fine cloth made it possible to compete with the
rapidly growing cotton industry. But throughout the eighteenth cen-

tury Norwich remained a bustling, thriving city, on whose prosperity a notable local culture was built. No one there knew that their world was crumbling beneath them.

Such geographical concentration was increasingly characteristic of all English industry. To a considerable degree, of course, it was dictated by the availability of raw materials. The woolen trade, having long outgrown local supplies of wool, drew on the spreading pastures of all England and on Spain as well. But other raw materials were less easy to transport, and industry had to go to them, or at least to navigable water on which heavy goods could be easily and cheaply carried. Thus the cutlers of Sheffield relied on northern Europe for high-quality iron and steel, imported through Newcastle and Hull; the rushing streams in the hills west of town turned their grinding wheels. Birmingham and the Black Country to its north made iron from nearby Shropshire and Worcestershire into tools and hardware. The location of the extractive industries was necessarily determined by natural resources. In Cornwall, where the tin mines that had attracted the Romans to Britain were declining, the Cornish miners were able to turn to copper. The lead-mining industry in the Mendip Hills, south of Bristol, however, had died out; by the eighteenth century England's lead came chiefly from the Pennines. The iron industry was steadily on the move, not only in search of easily available ore but seeking the remaining forests to make the charcoal needed for smelting; only slowly in the eighteenth century did ironmasters learn to use coal (as coke) for smelting and so find it practicable to stay in one place. Subsurface coal mining moved from place to place until crude steam engines at the beginning of the eighteenth century made it possible to build larger, more permanent installations; if the engines could do little else, they could pump water from deep mines.

Much English industry had attained a high degree of capitalist organization. Mining and the iron industry required large amounts of capital to provide shafts and tunnels, pumps and furnaces. A few industries in large towns, London especially, were being organized on a scale that, for the time, was gigantic; the brewing and distilling trades became "factory" industries very early. But even in the textile trade, where the main work was still done in the cottages of spinners and weavers, capitalist organization was essential. The subdivisions of the woolen industry were highly complex: to route the raw and semifinished wool through a maze of specialties required both managerial skill and financing. The very dispersion of manufacture, even in the simpler textiles, meant that someone had to ride out to the villages to distribute raw materials, oversee the completion of orders, and bring back and market the finished products; wheels, looms, and stocking frames had to be rented out; the domestic workers had to be staked to their wool, flax, or yarn and supported by advances until the work was done.

Whole counties or regions thus became tied to the dominant town or towns, as Norfolk outworkers were to Norwich or as workers in Leicestershire and the neighboring counties were to the masters of the knitting industry based in Leicester. Such entrepreneurs needed skill, energy, and resources; they had to judge the state of the market, the fickleness of fashion, the quality of raw material, the niceties of pricing, and, in addition, had to cope with hundreds of often inefficient and cagily dishonest workmen, who had no steady supervision. This highly articulated, interdependent, and complex organization worked well enough for a country with a modest export trade and a steady domestic market. But it could not easily cope with a large upsurge in demand at home and abroad; one by one, domestic industries, seeking more efficient and cheaper production, had to discover new technologies and new forms of organization. But no one could have foreseen that in the middle of the eighteenth century.

London was the one great city of the kingdom, with over half a million people in the early eighteenth century. To its west lay Westminster, the capital, to which the aristocracy and gentry came regularly for Parliament and for "the season" in late spring. London profited from its proximity to the seat of government, both in supplying the great men of the kingdom and in catering to the financial needs of government. London was a port, the busiest in the kingdom, not only because of its foreign trade, but because its huge population had to be supplied; given the sorry state of inland transport, that was done largely by water. This ancient responsibility had produced highly complex and restrictive commercial and labor organizations, best illustrated perhaps in the exquisite organization of the trade in "sea coal," shipped by a monopoly from the northeastern coal fields to meet the insatiable London demand.

In the course of the seventeenth century, and particularly in its last decade and in the first decade of the new century, London developed its financial hold over the rest of the country: it was then that the phrase "The City" came to mean, as it still does to Englishmen, what "Wall Street" means to an American. It was in London that the great overseas companies had their headquarters; there, too, the new insurance underwriters began to transact business in Mr. Lloyd's coffeehouse. From the early years of the Restoration, banking developed rapidly. At first, certain tradesmen accustomed to dealing in valuables—goldsmiths in particular—took deposits for safekeeping; in time they and other merchants with established reputations learned that they could lend the money deposited with them, so long as they kept sufficient reserves to meet normal calls for funds from their customers; they developed both the banknote and the check. Some banks in operation in England today can be traced back through a succession of firms to these original goldsmith bankers. By the eighteenth century certain bankers had begun to specialize: some handled funds and loans for the aristocracy; others concentrated on industry and trade, served as agents for country banks, or concerned themselves with government finance. Organized as partnerships, London banks were not large enough to need to call on the wider resources that could be mustered selling shares to the public.

The most notable departure in banking history occurred in 1694, when a favored group of London merchants were incorporated as the Governor and Company of the Bank of England. The country was at war with France and—as is always the case in wartime—in need of funds. In return for a loan of £1.2 million to the government, these merchants were allowed to form a bank—that is, they could receive deposits, make loans, and issue notes. They were later given a monopoly of joint-stock banking in the country: only the Bank of England was to be allowed to grow beyond the resources of a partnership. In this purely political bargain no one had any notion of the function of a central bank, controlling the machinery of credit of the country and giving its main attention to the public interest. The proprietors of the Bank of England were in business to make money for their stockholders, no more. In its early years, the Bank had little to do with the country outside of London, and only gradually did it take over as the government's chief financial agent—lending to it for short periods of time, negotiating the terms of large public loans, and managing the public debt, which was established in the 1690's as a consequence of a decision to finance the war by long-term borrowing, with the payment of interest guaranteed by Parliament.

The growth of the great financial, trading, and insurance companies extended the influence of the City of London around the world. In the early eighteenth century, London still shared its financial power with Amsterdam, which had dominated international finance in the seventeenth century. Dutch capital remained important in English calculations throughout the early eighteenth century: the two countries had, after all, come into close political collaboration after the Dutch *stadholder* mounted the English throne as William III following the Glorious Revolution. But by mid-century, the victory of London was assured.*

The founding of these famous institutions must not, however,

---

*Professor Ashton has estimated that of 810 merchants who kissed the hand of George III after his accession in 1760, at least 250 were of foreign origin.

be taken as indicating any high degree of sophistication in understanding the operation of financial machinery. Not until the nineteenth century did most bankers begin to have any very clear ideas as to what loans were or were not safe, about the need to keep their position sufficiently liquid, or about the desirable ratio between loans and deposits. A chance to make money could lead to disastrous speculation which there was neither machinery nor ingrained prudence to control. There was enough sense of economic promise in the last decade of the seventeenth century to bring about a large flotation of companies for a variety of purposes, some sound, some with not the slightest chance of success; and many investors in these joint-stock enterprises suffered. But hope sprang eternal. In 1713, in the Treaty of Utrecht, Great Britain gained the asiento, the monopoly of supplying slaves to the Spanish colonies in the New World — a prize of moderate value that was wildly inflated in public imagination. With the asiento Great Britain also gained the right to send one small ship a year to the Spanish colonies, a trifling concession that seemed to promise a break in the mercantilist wall around the Spanish Empire, which until then the British had been able to penetrate only by smuggling.

Among the principal beneficiaries of this excitement was the South Sea Company, ostensibly a company aiming at a monopoly of trade to the Spanish Empire but in actual fact a finance company determined to rival and defeat the Bank of England. Founded in 1711, the South Sea Company established itself in government and public confidence, and by 1718 was secretly proposing to the government that it take over the whole of the national debt, at a lower rate of interest, in exchange for confirmation of its trading monopoly. The official announcement of the government's endorsement of the scheme early in 1720 touched off a new speculative boom in the shares of scores of doubtful companies launched on this wave of optimism. The shares of the South Sea Company themselves increased ten times in value and then, inevitably, fell; the crash brought companies and thousands of people down in ruins.

The South Sea Bubble inculcated a deep distrust of joint-stock organization and of company speculation. For more than a hundred years after 1720, the Bubble Act of that year forbade joint-stock organization except by the protracted and costly process of securing a royal charter or a private act of Parliament. For the next century and a half, partnerships were sufficient for nearly all but those few gigantic enterprises that required immense amounts of capital — docks, say, or turnpikes, canals, and (after 1830) railways. The absence of temptation to speculate in company shares may well have saved eighteenth-century England from some serious crises.

Nothing, even at the time of the South Sea Bubble, threatened land as the most important, respected, and desirable form of investment; but in the early eighteenth century, men with capital to spare became more and more accustomed to investing in government loans —the funds, as they were called. The now certain security of the Hanoverian succession and the cautious and sensible management of the government's finances gave investors such confidence in its obligations that the government was able to reduce the rate of interest sharply in the course of the century.

When the government decided to borrow money, the terms of the loan were worked out with the Bank and certain London merchants in the confidence of the ministers. Once the terms were agreed upon, a syndicate of merchants would be formed to buy the government's securities in the first instance and then, in turn, to sell them to investors. Obviously, the merchants in such syndicates stood to make large profits. To guarantee their place at the trough, it was important to attract and hold the notice of ministers; and for this reason—as well as for access to government contracts and other financial dealings with the state—wealthy merchants, particularly those in London, sought to enter the House of Commons and there to earn favor by systematic loyalty in voting for the government. Merchants were an increasingly important element in a House that had hitherto been largely a monopoly of the land; but most of them were there to pursue their own concerns and to form what pressure groups they needed to form; they were not there to assert a rightful say over national policy on all matters whatsoever. Though the country gentlemen hated the growth of the money power and the corruption they feared it brought to politicians and to society generally, the threat was more apparent than real, and on balance the country benefited from this hard-headed but limited alliance between merchants and politicians.

For centuries London had held a privileged position in the kingdom: it could exclude royal agents from its boundaries, and the Lord Mayor, always one of the great merchants of the city, played an important ceremonial and symbolic role, not just in London but nationally. The Corporation of the City of London that he headed was made up of two bodies: the popularly elected Court of Common Council, and the Court of Aldermen, popularly elected too, but for life. The aldermen, therefore, tended to be the wealthiest merchants and those most likely to be tied in interests and sympathies to the government; the Court of Common Council was a more genuinely popular organ. The two bodies were constantly at loggerheads, and in 1725, Walpole's government, siding with its natural allies, carried

an act giving the force of law to a customary veto exercised by aldermen over the Court of Common Council. It was bad enough, as the
lesser merchants and artisans of the City saw it, that the aldermen
were so rich; they were also hand in glove with the government, and
the government was far from popular with London's more democratic elements.

Small merchants, tradesmen, and artisans disliked taxation, of
course, and they disliked privilege. But they particularly disliked the
government's foreign policy. The Treaty of Utrecht, which, as we
shall see, provided such impressive gains for the Empire, was highly
unpopular because some of the spoils of the war had been returned
to France; and in every subsequent war, the government (with an understandable eye to international political realities) made peace
without the full victory that vocal elements in the country wanted.
Middling opinion in London and much of the country was, to borrow a late Victorian term, "jingoistic": it was a truculent, often ignorant, prideful, patriotic emotion in which can be seen the origins of
what one day would come to be called "public opinion." Throughout
most of the early eighteenth century, this crude and simpleminded
opposition to government was impotent, even when it broke out, as
it did from time to time, in riots. It was without influential parliamentary spokesmen; opposition politicians played on it only to embarrass the ministers in the hope of turning them out, but without
any intention, once in office, of implementing a policy more acceptable to the vociferous townsmen. Their day was to dawn after 1760.

Meanwhile, their unmeasured opinions reflected a measured
optimism, prosperity, and hope. Life, even in the murderous towns,
was getting better for many Englishmen, with steady prices and a
long succession of good harvests in the thirties and forties. The
measuring and calculating and attention to business were spreading
widely. Many townsmen still bore the sober imprint of seventeenth-
century puritanism, a kind of seriousness and moral pride that no
doubt lent additional force to their sense of national superiority.
They found their literary spokesman in Daniel Defoe. With a keen
eye to the rewards of authorship, Defoe published a series of *Tours* in
the 1720's. This is how he saw one east-coast port, important for the
Holland trade: it was, he said, "a Town of Hurry and Business, not
much of Gaiety and Pleasure, yet the Inhabitants seem warm in their
Nests, and some of them are very Wealthy. . . ." Defoe was not one to
see, or at any rate to publicize, the less attractive features of his country, but his comment on Harwich can be taken, without too much fal-
sification, as a valid report on what was most significant in the life of
towns in the early eighteenth century.

The Poor

Except for the small owner-occupiers, who were being squeezed out in the changing patterns of land organization, the English families who have so far appeared in this analysis experienced modest but fairly steady growth in prosperity, comfort, and optimism, an emphasis justified if one is looking for the circumstances and attitudes that carried the significant burden of the future. Still, life was, to a remarkable degree, as Thomas Hobbes a century earlier had described life in the state of nature—poor, nasty, brutish, and short. The shortness held for everyone, rich and poor alike. Doctors surely killed more people than they saved; there was little knowledge of the principles of sanitation; infant mortality was the rule, rather than the exception, and survival to old age rare testimony to an unusually tough constitution. Plague, which had decimated European populations periodically since the Middle Ages, did not reappear after the terrible year 1666, but other scourges remained, not least smallpox, which killed its hundreds of thousands and disfigured many more. The modern comforts that Celia Fiennes so proudly noticed did not much soften the dismal prospect of long, cold, damp winters, even for the rich; and the further down one moves on the social scale the greater was the nastiness and brutishness, compounded by isolation in the country and by overcrowding in the towns. A growing population had swamped and defeated the relatively rigid institutions of rural life in the seventeenth century, and the even more inadequate institutions of the towns could not cope with those who had managed to escape from the countryside. The vast majority of Englishmen lived on the edge of violence, starvation, degradation, and sudden death.

This blanket description of the uncertainties of life for the bulk of England's people must not be understood to imply that there was merely a mass of undifferentiated poor. Indeed, the social range below the comfortable and respectable levels of society was, if anything, more complex than it was above. Gregory King's roughly functional classification of what later generations came to call the working classes consisted of "artizans and handycrafts," common seamen, laboring people and outservants, cottagers and paupers, common soldiers (significantly ranked well below the seamen), and vagrants. Other observers would have classed them differently, and a breakdown of "laboring people" would turn up wide variations in importance, incomes, and self-estimates of their social position in relation to those above or below them. The ground for generalizing about the disheartening quality of their life is that, no matter how useful many, perhaps most, of these poorer Englishmen were, they could be plunged into misery by illness, old age, drunkenness, the fluctuations of the economy, or the arbitrary decisions of authority. No man of sound appearance and reasonable age could ever feel secure, for example, against the "press gang," authorized to seize men in the streets or taverns and carry them off to man His Majesty's ships in time of war.

Beneath what is often called the surface of society, below those who were relatively settled and comfortable, poverty bred turbulence, a turbulence caught, in either its latent or actual state, in the paintings of William Hogarth. But this turbulence was tamed or diverted in a variety of ways. In the countryside, where the sway of the landed classes was more or less complete, a natural, expected deference complemented the accepted rightfulness of the rule of superior over inferior, enforced, when it did not work automatically, by the judicial power of the gentlemen of England in their guise as justices of the peace. Nor was such legitimate influence unknown to the towns, in transmuted forms. But when Parliament was moved by representations from interests in the country that were in one way or another threatened by violence or crime—machine-breaking, say, or stealing of cloth left to bleach in the sun—the makers of policy could rise to little more than the imposition of savage penalties, often death, for minor crimes. Such vindictiveness only increased desperation and often made it worth a criminal's while to commit a greater crime, since the penalty risked was no worse.

There was only sporadic focus or direction to this discontent. To some extent, no doubt, brute energy was harmlessly drawn by the many opportunities to expend it in customary ways that were little questioned even by respectable men. Drunkenness was endemic as a means of escape from squalor and frustration; in the early eighteenth century it grew worse, as some little surplus accrued to the poor in good times and found its way into purchasing the oblivion of gin, made cheaper by newly lowered duties and by the efficiency of the burgeoning distilling industry. The Gin Mania of the thirties and forties was a social fact of the first order and a factor of no mean importance in keeping down the increase in population. Gambling was another outlet, often associated with violent recreations, of which cockfighting and bearbaiting were the tamest. Elections and local ceremonies often became excuses for license and riot.

Rioting was a characteristic of the age: indeed, G. M. Trevelyan, the great twentieth-century historian, described eighteenth-century England as "aristocracy tempered by rioting." Riots were sometimes encouraged by men of high position, to pursue religious or political vendettas, or they could be spontaneous outbursts of popular fury, against impressment or the shortage of food and consequent high prices or any one of a hundred grievances. The mob, as it was coming

the mob

to be called (from *mobile vulgus*), was by no means composed merely of the dregs of society; rioting was a way of demanding redress for small tradesmen, artisans, and laborers as well. But once the tumult was over, whether redress was obtained or not (and it sometimes was), the thrust was blunted; having been expressed, perhaps the grievances were not so likely to fester.

Throughout the latter part of the seventeenth century and into the eighteenth, there was little that respectable people or the forces of order could do but endure the risks of rioting; since the abolition of the Court of Star Chamber, that once popular engine of "Tudor despotism," in 1641, disturbance of the peace was left to the common law, which on this subject was highly defective. In 1715, Parliament passed the Riot Act, an extraordinary yet characteristic statute. Its

Riot Act

purpose was to give strengthened powers to local authorities to apprehend rioters, once they had been duly warned to disperse, so that they might be prosecuted as felons. Even more important perhaps, the act indemnified the enforcers of the law should rioters be hurt or killed: under the common law it was possible to prosecute them for assault or murder. When a body of men were "riotously or tumultuously assembled together," a magistrate came as close to them as he safely could and read, in the name of the king, a proclamation set down in the act ordering the rioters to disperse; but even this "reading the Riot Act" could not take place before an hour had elapsed, an hour in which much damage could be done, say, to hedges around a new enclosure or to the windows of a miller suspected of hoarding grain in order to mulct the poor. The Riot Act was the main statutory weapon of the scattered, amateur enforcement officers who (with ultimate resort to the use of soldiers) bore the responsibility for keeping England peaceful until the establishment of professional police in the nineteenth century.

One further provision by the state was of the utmost importance in maintaining the social fabric: the poor law. A good deal of sixteenth-century experimenting in coping with the threat posed by underemployed and wandering poor had culminated in the great Elizabethan Poor Law, the "43rd of Elizabeth,"* a statute passed in

poor law 1601

1601. That law gave the parish the responsibility to relieve its poor and empowered the local authorities to levy a rate, or tax, to meet the cost of that relief. The provision was not, nor was it meant to be, generous. Not much was done between the middle of the seventeenth century and the latter years of the eighteenth to carry out one of the original injunctions—to find work for the able-bodied paupers.

---

*So-called from the legal form of citation for statutes by the year of the reign; thus the poor law is "43rd Eliz., c[hapter]2."

What care was given to those who were paupers because they were ill, old, or orphaned often depended on whether the parish in fact had a workhouse or poorhouse and on how that dismal establishment was run. The casual administration of the law that followed the abandonment of attempts at centralized control after the Restoration made its good effects haphazard, and generalization becomes nearly impossible.

In one respect, however, the Restoration period tightened up the law, again to the detriment of the poor. A statute of 1662 provided that settlement in a parish could be gained only by birth or apprenticeship or, for a woman, by marriage to a man of that parish. It could also be acquired by paying parish rates or renting a house worth ten pounds a year—neither a very likely way for a poor man to qualify. Finally, settlement could be gained by giving written notice of an intention to do so, but the parish authorities were free to decide that any applicant might become a burden upon the parish and to refuse settlement, just as they could expel paupers or potential paupers who had no settlement. As a consequence, a poor man would be likely to move only short distances or not at all; though many took the chance, to move away from a parish where one had a settlement was to tempt fate. But whatever the shortcomings of the poor law, there is no gainsaying its importance as an engine of social police. By giving the poor a right to relief, it made the difference (however niggardly) between life and death for many of the aged, orphaned, sick, and mad; and few Englishmen who lived close to the borderline of subsistence (that is, the great majority of them) did not at one time or another in their lives have to resort to its harsh mercies.

No one in the eighteenth century thought that poverty could be abolished or even much reduced: the belief in a naturally ordered society of high and low was strongly ingrained and reinforced by Biblical assurances that the poor will always be with us. The first half of the eighteenth century did, however, see a spread of humanitarian feeling. It stimulated a wider exercise of personal charity—sometimes effective, sometimes ignorant, always intermittent—and the founding of a new range of institutions to relieve or improve the lot of men on this earth, from the charity schools for the poor that were founded with such enthusiasm from the early years of the century to the hospitals that were the most important charitable enterprises of mid-century. But the trickle of philanthropy became a flood only in the later eighteenth century and the nineteenth. A scattered and insulated society could tolerate the chaos to which the poor contributed and of which they in turn were victims. A few broken windows or burnt hayricks, even occasional terrorization, were part of the price paid by the English oligarchy for the decentralization that

Tudor and early Stuart monarchs and their councils had tried to overcome with their centralizing statutes: the liberties of Englishmen
were not without their cost. But this willingness to accept near-
anarchy and a vast extent of degradation is also powerful testimony
to the fact that the eighteenth-century poor posed no concerted threat
to the rulers of England.

A Society in Transition

In the past fifteen to twenty years study of the social history of
England has taken a quantum leap, stimulated to a considerable extent by the work of French scholars committed to "total history" but
also by an insistence (in part, at least, political) that history must
become less concerned with powerful, literate, and recordkeeping
groups in society and pay more attention to the largely silent or inar-
ticulate who make up the overwhelming majority of mankind. To
discover the undiscovered, new ranges of historical sources have
been ransacked. Sometimes these forays turn up striking individual
glimpses of greater or lesser typicality; more often they yield large
masses of information that can be quantified and manipulated in objective, verifiable, and presumably more scientific ways. Demog-
raphers have led the way in technical matters, sociologists and anthropologists in theory; and social historians have followed, filling in
the chinks with an increasing grasp of historical observation and offering generalizations—always (if not always admittedly) tentative—
about the nature of that society.

In England the central social institution, the family, had undergone a fundamental transformation long before the eighteenth
century. The extended patriarchal family known to readers of the
Bible, to anthropologists, and to medieval historians had been modified over several centuries to become the cohesive nuclear family we
still know. Within that institution there have, of course, been
changes. Though the extent of instability or shattering of eighteenth-
and twentieth-century families is probably fairly constant, its causes
are now to be found increasingly in institutional arrangements, such
as divorce, instead of in the terrible finality of sudden, mostly
unexplained death. By the same token, the average age of the population has gone up, the number of children relative to other age groups
has fallen, and the number of aged has risen, though the old were, by
and large, left as much apart from ordinary family life two centuries
ago as they are now. But the average number of children to a family
has not changed greatly, no matter what social level one examines;
there is evidence of rational planning of family size, though the
means have shifted from late marriage to sophisticated methods of

birth control. Until very recently, servants or (in the trades) apprentices were assimilated temporarily to a family, and in grand aristocratic households the number of retainers gave at least an appearance of medieval social arrangements well into the era of the new dispensation. But, at any rate, in the upper-class families historians have studied most closely, the core of a husband, a wife, and a relatively small number of children—especially in a context of increasing prosperity, better diet, and greater life expectancy—seems to have encouraged freer and more open emotions, greater equality among family members, more autonomy, and an increased concern for privacy.

The microhistorical social unit has remained fairly constant, then, throughout the period covered by this book. Not so the larger groupings by which contemporaries and historians since have understood that society. Here we confront the crucial question of analysis in terms of class, given universality and emotional and sociological justification by Karl Marx and a host of commentators since. The notion of a society divided into two or three classes, in conflict with each other and joined internally by common economic interests, is one that attained reality in nineteenth-century England and that has offered a highly productive mode of social analysis in the Victorian era and since—though even in the heyday of class a century ago, give or take a little, there were phenomena that class cannot explain and structures and dynamics that contradict the dominant perceptions of contemporaries and historians. In the eighteenth century, however, the concept of class had just been invented within a fascinating group of Scottish students of society; it passed from Adam Smith, a member of that circle, to his followers, the political economists, from whose lexicon it entered Marx's. Latent, as Professor Perkin observes, in eighteenth-century society, class can be at times a useful construct for understanding isolated phenomena. It is more likely to be misleading than helpful in understanding how society worked as a whole.

Eighteenth-century society was a matter of status, of hierarchy, of ranks and orders. Each social unit and each individual stood in a distinct and accepted relationship to other units and individuals ranged above or below—a pattern that, despite the mobility experienced by a few favored and more unfavored individuals, carried with it the sense of immutability and divine ordinance. The key substantive notion within this hierarchy was property: land, capital, a stock of goods, tools were obvious kinds of property; but so was office; so even, in a way, was personal liberty. Kind and extent of property fixed one's position in the social scale, though in no simply measurable way. Bonds of obligation held the parts together and communicated between them. In theory, and to some extent in actuality, obligation was embodied in deference in one direction, and in protection and charity in the other; it was enforced, when the moral bonds were insufficient, by coercion from the top or by riot and sullenness from below. The most helpful metaphor is organic: preachers and moralists constantly harped on the relevance of the physical body to the body politic, whose parts were hierarchically arranged as head and members in a whole that could be altered only at the risk of disorder and death. It is significant that the word *organization* prior to the end of the eighteenth century carried only a biological meaning and that the currently dominant structural or institutional meaning of the word emerged only after a mechanistic view of society began to supplant the organic.

Intellectual and Religious Life

The intellectual and religious life of England in the eighteenth century was dominated to a remarkable degree by the figure of Sir Isaac Newton. Like his lesser contemporary Gregory King, Newton faced both ways; ironically, he set more store by his avocation of theology than he did by his profession of science or, as it was called then, natural philosophy. His admirers did not follow him in that; they were overwhelmed by his scientific accomplishment. For one thing, Newton's work embodied a novel, even revolutionary, "philosophical modesty." The vast and intricate metaphysical questions that had occupied earlier seventeenth-century thinkers were set aside; Newton and his followers concentrated instead on what could be known and experimentally or mathematically verified: it was a signal triumph of the empiricism and practicality for which England has become so famous. Moreover, Newton's enunciation of the principle of gravitation and his work on optics allowed men to understand the working of the universe as they had never done before, and in a way that challenged them to try to comprehend all other phenomena — natural, human, even divine — by a similar exercise of reason. It has been argued, in fact, that English science was held back in the eighteenth century by the very immensity of Newton's achievement: certainly leadership in mathematics passed to the Continent, and the Royal Society, which had contributed so much to the scientific revolution in the generation or so after its founding in 1662, displayed little originality, declining into a pleasant scientific refuge for gentlemen, a mission it fulfilled comfortably for more than a hundred years. On the other hand, perhaps it is wiser to look on the eighteenth century as a time of scientific consolidation: it was an imposing legacy to absorb.

It would be going too far to say that English art and literature were Newtonian, though Newton was much admired by both artists and writers.* There are, however, some suggestive parallels in temper and concern. Instead of metaphysical speculation, the scientists pursued empirical truth, and gave unity to their discoveries by the elaboration of principles they called laws of nature. It may not be entirely fanciful to see a similar movement in architecture: the late seventeenth century and the years of Queen Anne were dominated by the style known as English Baroque. The genius of the movement was Sir Christopher Wren, who superintended the rebuilding of the City of London, along with many other projects, after the Great Fire of 1666. To fifty-odd enchanting, imaginative, and to a considerable degree experimental churches in the City, Wren added his masterpiece, St. Paul's Cathedral. His younger associates, Nicholas Hawksmoor and Sir John Vanbrugh—the latter a playwright who suddenly turned architect by designing Castle Howard for the Earl of Carlisle—escaped Wren's preoccupation with what he called the "true Latin" language of classically ornamented surfaces. Frankly confronting the challenge of manipulating the mass of large-scale planes and volumes, which had never really interested Wren despite his ingenuity in handling them, the younger architects added to the bold individuality that characterizes Baroque. But to a still later generation, their buildings seemed heavy and threatening:† in the reigns of George I and George II, the preferred style came to be an ordered classicism that ran back to the early seventeenth-century court architect Inigo Jones, through him to the Renaissance architect and writer Palladio, and ultimately to the Roman authority Vitruvius, where those architectural principles were indelibly enshrined. The finest exemplars of the new fashionable "Whig" style were the Earl of Burlington, who trained himself to be an architect in Italy, and his humbler but equally brilliant associate, the painter turned architect William Kent; they in turn were succeeded by the neoclassicists of mid-century. Meanwhile, books explaining the principles and their application allowed provincial and colonial craftsmen to build "correctly," and to give a graceful consistency to houses and towns in both England and America through the style we now call Georgian. The typical expression of this English Palladianism was to be found (appropriately) in the country house and the city square, not in churches or public buildings.

*Thus Alexander Pope: "Nature and Nature's laws lay hid in night./God said, 'Let Newton be!' and all was light!"
†Some wit wrote a famous mock epitaph for Vanbrugh: "Lie on him heavy, Earth, for he/Laid many heavy loads on thee!"

So too the writers, who turned from the ultimate questions that had occupied many minds in the preceding century to explore the ethical and social problems confronting men in this life. It was an age of the brilliant political pamphlet, the moral essay, the instructive tale; and one need only compare Milton's *Paradise Lost,* which towers over the poetry of the seventeenth century, with Alexander Pope's *Essay on Man,* perhaps the poetic masterpiece of the eighteenth-century, to appreciate the revolution that had taken place over seventy years. Pope's humane involvement in this life has echoes of the worldly pragmatism that has been noted as characteristic of so many ordinary Englishmen of the time, while his elegantly stated perceptions shared an equally characteristic spirit with the elegant profundities of Newton's formulations. Less, no doubt, than the architects, but still significantly, the poets held to principles rooted in the classical models that had been so admired in the late seventeenth century. Even Samuel Johnson, that passionate egoist who, larger than life, dominated the English literary scene in the middle of the eighteenth century, was deeply imbued with the classical axioms of his age. Novelists, to be sure, were popularizing a literary form that could not be tied to classical rules and precepts, but the novel was not yet the dominant form that it became in the nineteenth century.

Among philosophers, John Locke stood beside Newton in the pantheon. In Locke's *Essay Concerning Human Understanding* lay the source of the psychological tradition that ruled English philosophy virtually unchallenged into the last third of the nineteenth century and that, in many ways, still affects it deeply: the questions Locke asked and answered—about perception, the relation of simple to complex ideas, the qualities of objects, the connection between the mind and the external world—remain very much alive. But the knowledge of the universe that the early eighteenth century owed to Newton and the understanding of the mind that it owed to Locke had their most stunning impact on theology.

That impact came at a time when the religious passions of the seventeenth century had worn themselves out in stalemate. The revulsion men felt against the concerns and forms of argument of their predecessors arose as well from a renewed and expanded interest in the affairs and promise of this world. But the nature of that world was being changed out of all recognition by the discoveries of the astronomers and the explorers.

"The revelation" wrote Sir Leslie Stephen in 1876, "finally clenched by Newton's astonishing discovery, that the world was an atom in space, whirling round the sun, itself, perhaps, another atom, utterly crushed the old imaginations which still survive in Milton's poetry. The scenery had become too wide for the drama. It was possible, indeed, verbally to promote the Jewish deity to rule over the vast territory which had thus sprung into existence. . . . But though the traditionary mythology was not forced by a clear logical necessity to postulate a limited earth and heavens, it became more shadowy and dim when confronted with the new cosmology. Through the roof of the little theatre on which the drama of man's history had been enacted, men began to see the eternal stars shining in silent contempt upon their petty imaginings. They began to suspect that the whole scenery was but a fabric woven by their imaginations. Another doubt was already dawning."*

The way to meet this new challenge seemed to lie along the rationalist lines set out by the seventeenth-century theologians. Almost no one as yet could go so far as to conceive a world without God, and few could admit that ultimately science and religion might conflict. Newton himself had been sure that purging Christianity of the superstitious accretions of centuries would make it stand forth as a simple, rational faith that no man could deny. That obscurity made atheists was an almost unchallenged article of faith among the exponents of rational religion. In 1695, Locke published his *Reasonableness of Christianity*; the following year an unabashed deistic pamphleteer, John Toland, published *Christianity Not Mysterious*; and in a short time, both in the Church of England and in the Dissenting sects, the puzzling doctrine of the Trinity was being warmly debated. Few could go beyond the so-called Arian position, that Jesus was not coequal with God the Father, but by mid-century it was a short step to a denial of His divinity altogether. That step could be taken openly only outside the Church, though there were men in the Church who must have concealed a Unitarian tendency; certainly after mid-century some left the Church because of it.

Religion, moreover, was proclaimed to be natural as well as rational. God's existence was evident from His works: the eye, the hand, "the spacious firmament on high" (to borrow from Joseph Addison's famous hymn) proclaimed His majesty, benevolence, and ingenuity. From such security it was easy to go on to assume that religion could be nothing but cheerful, that evil could be explained away, and even that God was excluded from any active intervention in this world. The latter point was taken up by the Deists in the 1720's and maintained against a host of shocked clerical critics. The many answers to the Deists contradicted each other with such completeness that the Deists, at this distance, seem to have emerged the easy winners.

*Sir Leslie Stephen, *History of English Thought in the Eighteenth Century* (1876, reprinted 1962), I, 69.

The complacency, optimism, and civilized worldliness of much early eighteenth-century theology were paralleled by the attitude of Churchmen towards the Church of England as an institution. The seventeenth-century English had quarreled and even gone to war over questions of theology and Church government. At the Restoration in 1660 — a restoration of both king and Church — the returning Anglicans were determined to settle old scores with the Puritans, despite the king's promise of "a liberty to tender consciences." The Savoy Conference in 1661 showed that there would be no concessions, even to the Presbyterians who had done so much to bring about the Restoration, and in 1662 several hundred ministers were ejected from their livings because they could not in conscience unreservedly accept the services and rubrics of the Book of Common Prayer, as they were required to do by the Act of Uniformity of that year. The old Elizabethan ideal of comprehension had been abandoned. Around the ejected ministers grew up a body of believers known as Dissenters or Nonconformists, who for over two centuries were to play a highly important part in English history.

Though it had purged itself of its most obvious enemies, the Restoration Church was not to have an easy time of it. Understandably, most Anglicans at the time were believers in the divine right of kings, with its corollary of passive obedience, however tyrannical the ruler. But when James II came to the throne, determined to restore England to Catholicism, the Anglicans were put in a cruel dilemma: was complete submission required when the end of it would be the destruction of the Church? Most Anglicans accepted the dismissal of James in the Glorious Revolution and, less happily, the accession of William and Mary; a few — the so-called Nonjurors — including the then Archbishop of Canterbury swallowed the first but rejected the second and so were deprived of their posts. But uneasiness about the dynastic question and hatred of the Dissenters among devout Anglicans at all levels of society provided support and passion for the Tory party, intensely for nearly half a century and recognizably for much longer.* From the High Anglican standpoint the accession of the Hanoverians in 1714 was a disaster. Not only was their link to the Stuarts remote, but political reaction against the Tory and High Anglican stance of Anne's last government ensured that the Hanoverian bishops would be Whig in political sympathies and, to a very large degree, liberal, or latitudinarian, in their theology.

To the more conservative High Churchmen, excluded from the bench of bishops and mostly isolated in country parishes, the eighteenth century was a far from happy time. Even the Church's legisla-

*See below, pp. 42–45.

tive body, the Convocation of the Clergy, in the lower house of
which the parish clergy were represented, was taken away from
them. In theory, Convocation was the organ on the religious side of
English society equivalent to Parliament on the secular side; but just
after the Restoration, the clergy had lost the power to tax themselves,
and so the last real reason for the king to keep Convocation in existence had vanished. Thereafter, it usually met only to be immediately
prorogued; on the few occasions when it was allowed to meet for
business, the upsurge of conservative protest forced a hurried end to
the session. After a particularly acrimonious Convocation in 1717,
when conservative elements in the Church moved to attack Benjamin
Hoadly, Bishop of Bangor, for his extremely latitudinarian views,
Convocation was again prorogued, never to meet again for business
until 1855. Only in the nineteenth century did the High Church
tradition, which in the meantime sank into a serious, not quite sullen
quietism, reassert itself in a radical guise that transformed the
Church. The eighteenth century belonged to the Whigs and the latitudinarians.

The Church of England was, and is, an established church. This
means that the Church is deeply embedded in the fabric of national
life; in the eighteenth century it was much more firmly entrenched
than it is today. The Act of Settlement in 1701 had made it certain that
the king would be an Anglican. The bishops sat in the House of
Lords and were appointed by the government. The clergy received
no financial support from the state—except for the grants from
Queen Anne's Bounty, established in 1704 to distribute the first
fruits and tenths, ecclesiastical revenues that had gone to the king
since the Reformation, for improving the income of poor clergymen.
But the secular power stood ready to enforce the collection of tithes, a
portion of the produce of agricultural land that formed one of the
main sources of Church income, and to uphold other Church privileges. The Church was in full control of education, at least of most education with any pretension to excellence, and at the university level
subscription to the Thirty-Nine Articles, the basic doctrinal statement of the Church, was required for matriculation at Oxford and for
graduation from Cambridge. Prayers were said for the king in
churches, and all public and official religious observance was Anglican. It was, however, at the parish level that the Church meshed most
significantly with lay society. Many churches were, as the phrase has
it, in the gift of laymen; because they were patrons or had succeeded
to the right of appointment (called advowson) of pre-Reformation
monastic corporations, many landowners in the eighteenth century,
as before and after, could rely completely on the parish clergymen in
the government of their dependencies. In earlier centuries, parish

clergymen were often ill-educated and socially inferior; in the eighteenth, many of them were rising to the status of gentlemen and
could be companions and almost the equals of the squires. An important symptom of this development is the steady rise in the number of clerical justices of the peace.

Two aspects of this close tie between Church and state have
been subjects of much misunderstanding and even scorn by critics in
the nineteenth century and since. One concerns the place of Dissenters. In the Restoration period the Dissenters were subject to sporadic
persecution, not so much by national policy as by local prejudice;
they had been tainted with disloyalty and rebellion, and there were
occasional signs even after 1660 that they were not to be trusted: their
Whig allies were involved in the attempts to exclude and overthrow
King James, and some Dissenters were willing to accept the Declaration of Indulgence issued by James in favor of Catholics as a means of
escaping from their own disabilities. But in 1689 the Toleration Act
recognized their right to practice their religion. Not that the concession was made in any generous spirit: Dissenters' meeting houses
had to be licensed, they were forbidden to meet behind closed doors
(something few of them would have wanted, but the suggestion that
at bottom they were all conspirators rankled), the privileges of the act
extended only to Trinitarians, and Dissenters continued to be subject
to a great many civil disabilities. They were obliged to support the
Church of England financially; they could be married only by clergymen of the Establishment and could be buried in parish churchyards
with Anglican rites or none; they were excluded from the universities; and they were forbidden, under the Corporation Act of 1661, to
hold municipal office and, under the Test Act of 1673 (aimed primarily at Catholics), to hold office under the Crown.

Both of the latter prohibitions were evaded regularly after 1689,
either by open violation or by the practice of "occasional conformity," i.e., taking communion according to the Anglican Prayer Book
once a year. After 1727, in most (though not all) years an indemnity
act was carried to remit the penalties for those persons who served in
municipal corporations in violation of the Corporation Act. By the
reign of George II, then, the Dissenters had much of the substance of
equality, though they were far from equal. But, at least in the first
half of the eighteenth century, few of them hoped for more. They
were jealous of the privileges that had been conceded to them, and
the Dissenting Deputies were set up as a representative body in 1733
to guard against the revocation or erosion of those privileges. But
they did not press for the expansion of privileges or for disestablishment of the Church, goals so dear to their Victorian descendants. Indeed, few groups in the kingdom were more loyal. With their eco-

nomic and social roots largely in the towns and in the busy world of commerce and industry, the Dissenters shared in the spreading prosperity and were not yet sufficiently confident or outward-looking to pose any threat to the established order.* Theologically the distinctions that had grown up in seventeenth-century Puritanism between Presbyterians, Independents (or Congregationalists), and Baptists — the three main denominations — tended to blur, and the leading ministers, like Dr. Philip Doddridge, were looked on with respect by all Dissenters; indeed, in the latitudinarian spirit of the times, there was considerable contact with the more liberal Churchmen. But the theory of Church and state remained virtually unquestioned: England was a single religious and civil society, and whoever chose to withdraw from the religious side of that society could not claim full citizenship on the civil side.

The other misunderstanding about the close tie between Church and state concerns the worldliness of the Church in the eighteenth century. There is much ground for this misunderstanding, or criticism, especially if one brings to it a sense of values and priorities derived from the nineteenth-century religious revival. The political involvement of the Hanoverian bishops, the extent to which the higher positions in the Church were being filled in the eighteenth century by younger sons of aristocratic and gentry families, and the grossly disproportionate incomes from one Church post to another led to many abuses: nonresidence, in which the incumbent would draw the income and pay a curate (often poorly) to conduct the services; pluralism, or the holding of more than one Church appointment at the same time for the sake of the income; nepotism and favoritism; and what was very like political servility. The last charge lies particularly heavily against the bishops, understandably enough when episcopal incomes could vary from £450 per year in Bangor to £5,000 in Winchester, £6,000 in Durham, £4,500 in the archbishopric of York, and £8,000 in the archbishopric of Canterbury. Translation — being moved from one diocese to another — was earned, and an uncomfortably outspoken bishop, such as Bishop Watson of Llan-

---

*Quakers are not properly identified at this time with the main body of Dissent. They had won a number of special privileges, and while they shared many social characteristics with the Presbyterians, Independents, and Baptists, they kept themselves apart. Roman Catholicism in England, never a part of Dissent, survived among some aristocratic and gentry families; gaining and losing converts among the English, the Catholics numbered perhaps 80,000 in 1770. Unhampered in the practice of their religion, they suffered few of the legislated indignities visited on their coreligionists in Ireland. Most English Catholics were anxious to demonstrate their loyalty and to live down Catholic involvement in treason in the time of Elizabeth.

daff, could stay in his ill-endowed diocese for an entire career. But bishops had always been deeply concerned with politics; in the Middle Ages, indeed, a bishopric was more likely to be earned by working for the king than by saintliness or service in the Church. It is to the credit of Walpole and Newcastle that they took good advice and appointed men of scholarship and piety as well as political soundness, and most of the bishops worked hard at the business of their dioceses—a bishopric was no small administrative task. Still, the fact remains that in the House of Lords, their dependable progovernment votes were an important element in political calculations.

The structure and spirit of the eighteenth-century Church was in many ways an accidental product of history: had Convocation not been thrust into the background, had the Nonjurors not left for a principled obscurity, had the seventeenth-century advocates of comprehension (or, as we might say, reunion) been able to make themselves heard above the political din, the eighteenth-century Establishment might have worn a very different look. But to most men, the ecclesiastical arrangements of the early eighteenth century seemed to be set firmly in the natural order as a dictate of God's will. Religious intensity, so recently escaped from, was deeply distrusted, whether it was "enthusiasm" to the left or "superstition" (i.e., popery) to the right. The Church steered confidently between the shoals, and most Churchmen preached a correspondingly complacent doctrine.

Latitudinarianism does not exhaust the religious thought of the age. Within the Church itself, three writers fed very different traditions. In 1728, William Law, a Cambridge scholar who had refused to take the oaths to George I, published his *Serious Call to a Devout and Holy Life*, one of the finest works of piety in any language; he ended his life as a mystic. George Berkeley, Bishop of Cloyne (in Ireland), starting from Locke's postulates, solved the problem of knowledge of the external world by emphasizing the all-embracing knowledge and constant interposition of God, a conclusion far removed from Deism or the skepticism soon to be advanced by David Hume. And in 1736, Joseph Butler, a future bishop of Bristol and then of Durham, published his *Analogy of Revealed Religion*, a most original defense of orthodoxy against the Deists. While working thoroughly within the assumptions of his time, Butler not only wrestled with the problem of evil but cast doubt on the efficacy of reason to unravel the mysteries of either nature or revelation; he found his certainty in a conviction of the existence of a moral order under God's governance. Perhaps no eighteenth-century writer so much appealed to the men of the religious revival (and even of the reaction against it) in the nineteenth century.

But the most important exception to the latitudinarian and passive confidence of so much of the Church was an Anglican whose increasingly uneasy relationship with his beloved Church led his followers into gradual separation as the Methodists. John Wesley was born into the High Church tradition in a remote Lincolnshire rectory in 1703. He went to Oxford, where in 1729 with his brother Charles he founded a "Methodist" society devoted to systematic exercises in piety (hence "Method") and good works among the poor of the town. From 1733 to 1738 he was a missionary in Georgia; there he made his first acquaintance with the Moravians, a German pietistic sect. While attending a Moravian meeting after his return to London in 1738, he felt his heart "strangely warmed" — the crucial turning point of conversion, the profound psychological upheaval that became the central experience of the personal religion he soon began to preach. Emphasizing the sense of sin, the need for complete reliance on the goodness of Jesus the Redeemer, and the restoration through belief and good works of the "diseased will," and discounting theology and even learning, Wesley's sermons appealed particularly to those whose lives were bleak and uncertain. The confident simplicities and mechanistic philosophizing of the latitudinarians were incomprehensible to such men and women; the dry scholastics of ordinary High Churchmen repelled them. But Wesley, his brother Charles, and George Whitefield and Howell Harris preached a brand of religion they could grasp. It appealed so powerfully to some of them that conversion completely changed the direction of their lives.

Methodist preaching and the circumstances of the meetings brought on extreme examples of those psychological manifestations so often associated with religious revivalism — public confessions of unnamable sins, shouting and groaning, fits and delusions. To alarmed and orthodox Anglicans, this was proof, if it were needed, that Wesleyanism was enthusiasm of the worst kind. Denied access to more and more pulpits, with great reluctance Wesley finally began to preach in the fields. Huge crowds came to hear him; so also did magistrates, parsons, and troublemakers who on many occasions, with no small encouragement from their superiors, set upon Wesley and his associates. But he was not silenced, and to many working people, lesser tradesmen, and artisans, he brought color and solace, discipline and hope. Methodists are said virtually to have civilized the backward, still almost tribal principality of Wales, and, even discounting the miraculous stories Wesley himself tells in his *Journals* of sudden reformations of whole communities of sinners, there is no doubt that he and his movement were one of the great cultural facts of the century.

ENGLISH POLITICS

From Revolution to Stability

A dark memory lay submerged in the eighteenth-century conscious-ness: in the 1640's Parliament had rebelled against and then executed King Charles I, subverting the monarchy and opening the way to the military despotism of Oliver Cromwell and his Puritan followers.* But a happier event, the Glorious Revolution, was the ground on which the politics of Britain were invariably justified in the century or so prior to the Reform Act of 1832. The restoration of Charles II in 1660, joyfully welcomed by most of the politically perceptible parts of the country, soon turned sour: the shattering of the unity of the Church of England by the ejection of the Dissenters and the casual absolutism, self-indulgence, and deceitfulness of the returned mon-arch undermined the loyalty that had been his for the taking. The king's brother, James II, a convert to Catholicism, came to the throne in 1685 bent on furthering absolutism on the Continental model and determined to secure full equality for his coreligionists. He set out to attain these goals by direct assault on the institutions of the country — particularly on municipal organizations in his efforts to get a com-pliant Parliament — by manipulation of the law, and by using a declaration of indulgence in favor of Catholics to gain urban, Dis-senting support against the fervently Anglican oligarchs in the gentry and aristocracy.† Tolerable so long as the king remained childless, James's impolitic (but not unsuccessful) maneuvering be-came unacceptable when a son was born to him and his second wife in 1688. James, however, had two daughters by his first marriage; both were unshakably Protestant. The older of them, Mary, was the wife of William of Orange, *stadholder* of the Netherlands and cham-pion of Europe's Protestants in the wars against Louis XIV of France. Eager to detach England from its mercenary alliance with Louis and to bring it into the Protestant camp, William asked for and got an in-vitation to come to England; it was signed by an impressive array of leaders across the whole spectrum of English politics. Favored by a persisting east wind, William landed in the West Country, at Torbay near Plymouth, in mid-November 1688 at the head of a force of some 15,000 men. Careful to make no public commitments, he moved

---

*The memory of that radical episode surfaced impressively in nineteenth-century radical rhetoric and argument. See a report on the collaboration of many historians in gathering evidence for the continuity in T. W. Mason, "Nineteenth-century Cromwell," *Past and Present*, no. 40, pp. 197–191 (July 1968).
†See above, p. 36.

steadily towards London, as more and more of the king's subjects brought the invader their allegiance. James fled for France on December 21; captured by some fisherman and returned to London, he was allowed to escape once again.

A parliament can exist only when a king calls it; lacking that summons, the Lords and Commons who assembled in Westminster on February 1, 1689, are known as a convention. Agreement in an unprecedented situation was difficult. When, in defiance of all constitutional logic, it was declared that the throne was vacant, following James's "abdication," the question of succession was resolved by William's refusal to serve as regent for James or to play a subordinate role to his wife; he would return to Holland if his new subjects insisted that he be less than king. But he agreed that the crown could be held jointly, and so, until Mary's death in 1694, it is the reign of William and Mary; thereafter, the widowed king ruled alone. On accepting the throne, the new monarchs also accepted a Declaration of Rights, drawn up by the Convention in 1688 and converted by Parliament the next year into the Bill of Rights. The king's right to suspend laws was abolished; his right to exempt particular individuals from penalties attending violation of the law, the so-called dispensing power, was condemned "as it hath been exercised of late." A number of civil rights — freedom from cruel and unusual punishments and from excessive bail, for example — were guaranteed.

The Declaration had also stated broader grievances against James II, and in time legislation took care of some of them. The Triennial Act, passed in 1694, required parliamentary elections every three years, while other reforms were accomplished by securing Parliament's control over supply. Thus the resentment that had grown throughout the Restoration period against a standing army under royal control ended with its virtual abolition, to be replaced by an army dependent on annual appropriations and on a limited, renewable Mutiny Act, which was the basis of army discipline. One clear gain in 1689 was the passage of the Toleration Act, which allowed Dissenters to practice their religion, subject to certain minor but still demeaning regulations. Another more ambiguous improvement was the decision in 1694 not to renew the Licensing Act of 1662, which had permitted censorship of the press. Since then, it is always said, England's press has been free, and so it was, in comparison to more absolutist countries and so far as restraints prior to publication were concerned. But, once something was published, authors and publishers were left to the not-so-tender mercies of the law of libel, which has remained especially stringent in England.

William III inherited a political system whose central reality was the bitter rivalry between the Whig and Tory parties. The names, originally terms of abuse with obscure Scottish and Irish origins, were applied in the late 1670's to those who wanted to exclude the future James II from the throne and those who insisted on his right to succeed. The Tories were thus the court party, supporters of a divine-right monarchy and a narrow, exclusive Anglicanism, while the Whigs were more loosely attached to the Church of England, sympathetic to Dissenters, and particularly concerned with limiting royal power—indeed, in Monmouth's Rebellion in 1685 and in other plots, many Whig leaders were tainted with treason, and some were executed. The Revolution of 1688 intensified these divisions by giving toleration to Dissenters and by adding a dynastic problem, with James II, to many Tories still the legitimate king, and his male heir across the water and with the throne in England occupied by a female heir and a foreign prince.

The Revolution had been the work of men from both parties, and, while William III intended to rule himself, his early appointments reflected his obligations in both directions. In the Convention, however, the Whigs proved to be extremists still, determined to drive out their old Tory enemies and to pare down a royal power that William was equally determined to maintain. William soon found it more comfortable to rely on Tories like the Earl of Danby, Charles II's long-time minister who had signed the letter of invitation, or even the Earl of Sunderland, an adventurer who had remained loyal to James almost to the end. But to politicians the attractions of office are irresistible, and the Whigs soon learned their lesson. By 1694 most of their leaders had come to moderate their demands and offered William a cohesive body of support, for himself and for his war. They did so, however, at the cost of alienating many old followers in the country party—Country Whigs, or Old Whigs, as they were known—who inclined increasingly to Toryism, which, a few elder statesmen apart, opposed the Court, its war, and its dalliance with Dissent.

When William III died in March, 1702, he was succeeded by his wife's sister Anne, a conscientious but intellectually limited woman, devoted to the Church of England and dependent on favorites, first Sarah Duchess of Marlborough, the partisan and self-centered wife of John Churchill, first Duke of Marlborough and the great English commander in the wars against France; then after 1708 on Abigail Masham, the duchess's cousin and the queen's dresser, whose personal likes and dislikes took on considerable political importance in the later years of the reign. The dynastic problem that exacerbated the party struggle had been worsened by the passing of the Act of Settlement in 1701. Anne had borne many children, but the only child to survive infancy died in 1700 at the age of eleven. To forestall a restoration of the main Catholic Stuart line on Anne's own death, the new act settled the crown on the Electress Sophia of Hanover, who was descended from the marriage in 1613 of the daughter of James I to the Elector Palatine of the Rhine. For insurance, the act also required that English kings be in communion with the Established Church.

The issues between the parties were real, elections (under the Triennial Act) were frequent and widely contested, and political tension was perhaps greater than at any time with the possible exception of the period 1910–1914. Despite Tory majorities in the constituencies, Anne could rely for most of her reign on men who professed to be above party, or who found it easy to trim their sails as the exigencies of power required. Sidney, Lord Godolphin, a commissioner of the treasury under James II, had switched sides in time to carry his financial expertise into the same post under William III; under Anne he became sole occupant of the office of Lord Treasurer, the post most likely then to be held by the leader of government. Godolphin had established a firm working relationship with Marlborough, whose Tory inclination was suppressed in a higher interest: successful prosecution of the War of the Spanish Succession after 1702, for which the principal support came from Whigs. Another moderate party man was Robert Harley, descended from a Presbyterian family that had sided with Parliament during the civil war; Harley entered Parliament in 1689 as a Whig, but made the gradual Country-Whig pilgrimage into Toryism. He entered Anne's government in 1704 as secretary of state, hoping to soften the obstreperousness with which his party had come to be identified in its opposition to the war and to Godolphin and Marlborough whose war it was.

The fanatical Tories would not, however, be mollified. In 1709 Dr. Henry Sacheverell, a combative High Churchman and fellow of Magdalen College Oxford, preached a sermon, by invitation, before the lord mayor and aldermen of London at St. Paul's Cathedral. *The Perils of False Brethren, both in Church and State* had been preached before in Oxford, to no great surprise, where Sacheverell's high-flying sentiments were well known. But it was another matter to preach in London against Dissenters and the ministers who deferred to them and in favor of the old divine-right doctrine of nonresistance — and on Guy Fawkes Day, when the nation commemorated its delivery from a Catholic plot to blow up King James I in his parliament a century earlier. By publishing his sermon, Sacheverell committed a seditious act. In a disastrous (though understandable) error in judgment, the government proceeded against him with the weapon of impeachment. Tried before the House of Lords, Sacheverell was convicted, but only by a narrow majority, and no more than minor penalties were applied. The rioting and turmoil brought on by the prosecution in March 1710 was more violent than any in the century before the Gordon Riots of 1780.

The government lost credit from the episode. Godolphin was dismissed, and Harley, out of office since 1708, returned as lord treasurer, seconded as secretary of state by Henry St. John, soon to be created Viscount Bolingbroke. Bolingbroke was a brilliant, immensely hard-working politician who had been recruited by Harley to a minor ministerial post in 1704; if he had any religious inclination at all, it was deistic, but he calculatedly made himself the principal advocate of the High Church position. Bolingbroke's version of coherent party rule clashed with Harley's moderate views, a clash exacerbated by personality differences that in time falsified St. John's repeated protestations of loyalty.

The government of 1710–1714, the first since 1688 to have a distinct Tory cast, realized some old Tory and High Anglican ambitions. The war was brought to an end in the Treaty of Utrecht, though protests from Whigs and the commercial interests of the country were so severe that the treaty was carried in the Lords only by creating twelve new Tory peers. On the religious side, an act in 1711 outlawed occasional conformity, the practice by which Dissenters excluded by law from government posts had routinely qualified to hold them, and in 1714 Bolingbroke carried the Schism Act, forbidding Dissenters from keeping schools; the Schism Act never became law, however, because Queen Anne died before the royal assent could be given. Shortly before her death Anne had dismissed Harley (now Earl of Oxford) as Bolingbroke had long urged her to do; but on her deathbed, distrusting Bolingbroke, she made the less partisan Earl of Shrewsbury her lord treasurer, thus assuring the peaceable succession of George I, the son of the Electress Sophia. The six weeks that elapsed between the queen's death and the time George I arrived from Hanover to take up his new inheritance were virtually without incident. The Tories were shattered, and some of them turned extreme. But even Bolingbroke was aware that the insistence of a few doctrinaires that James III be proclaimed king had little support in the country: true to his inheritance, the Pretender refused to renounce Catholicism. In the autumn of 1715 an abortive rising of Jacobites—as partisans of James II and his son were called—revealed the political bankruptcy of his English supporters.* But if Tory lead-

---

*James II died in 1701. His son, whose birth had touched off the train of events that led to the Revolution of 1688, was known to Jacobites as James III and to others as "The Pretender" or, in time, "The Old Pretender." He survived until 1766. His son, Charles Edward, "The Young Pretender," or "Bonnie Prince Charlie," a wonderfully romantic figure, led the cause in the more serious rising of 1745.

ers had little chance at power for the next forty years, the principle concerns that had motivated them remained alive, as did Toryism itself in the constituencies and in parsonages across the land.

The new reign did not mean an end to party strife. The Whigs had old scores to even. Oxford and Bolingbroke were both accused of treason, for contacts with the Pretender, though most politicians, Whigs among them, had maintained some connection with the exiled court in St. Germain as a hedge against a turn of political fortune. Oxford escaped serious punishment but had no further political career. Bolingbroke, who had fled to France where he briefly entered the Pretender's service, was convicted and stripped of his title and estates. Pardoned, he returned to England in 1725; though without his peerage or a public career, he helped to direct, and to some extent inspired, opposition to the rule of Sir Robert Walpole and his successors and in his writings left to posterity a controversial reputation as a political philosopher.

The victorious Whigs quarreled not only with Tories, but among themselves. The dominant politician in the quick succession of reshuffled governments after 1714 was Lord Stanhope, who steered a skillful diplomatic course in a treacherously shifting European situation following the death of Louis XIV in 1715. But at home little beyond political maneuvering was accomplished until 1718. In that year — the four-year delay emphasizes the ambiguity of the Whig triumph — the Occasional Conformity and Schism Acts were at last repealed; and, more portentously, the Triennial Act of 1694 was replaced by a Septennial Act, because the Whigs did not feel confident about facing a mandatory election in that year: extending the permissible life of a parliament from three to seven years may have reduced public accountability, but it also helped to reduce the political temperature, which frequent elections in troubled times had kept at a high level. In 1719, Stanhope and his colleagues moved to limit the peerage: they saw the creation of twelve Tory peers in 1712 to carry the Treaty of Utrecht as a crass political maneuver that was also a precedent for diluting the aristocracy; the proposed limitation of new creations to the replacement of peerages that failed for want of heirs would have guaranteed Whig predominance in the upper house. But members of the House of Commons saw in the bill a nearly insurmountable barrier to their own social ambitions; in rejecting it, they assured that their own class, already established on the land, would remain the principal source from which until very recent times members of the House of Lords were recruited.* The

*For subsequent occasions on which the creation of peers, or the threat to do so, had important political effects, see below, pp. 201–202, 465.

Whigs had scarcely recovered from the bitter internal divisions created by this bill when they were plunged into the disaster of the South Sea Bubble.*

That the Whigs and the nation came through the new crisis so well is owing to one man, Sir Robert Walpole, who now moved to the center of the political stage. A country squire from Norfolk, Walpole had entered Parliament in 1701 and attached himself to Godolphin and the Whigs, becoming secretary at war in 1708, where his effectiveness as a minister quickly became apparent: he was chosen as manager of the impeachment proceedings against Sacheverell. But Walpole could not long survive Harley's coming to power. He was dismissed early in 1711, as a move in Harley's attack on the Duke of Marlborough with whom Walpole had worked closely. In 1712 Walpole was impeached for alleged corruption, found guilty, imprisoned in the Tower of London, and expelled from the House of Commons. He re-entered the House the next year and, with the Hanoverian succession, quickly moved into positions of prominence, where his skill at finance was demonstrated; he conducted the Whig vendetta against Oxford and Bolingbroke. Going into opposition at the beginning of 1717, when his brother-in-law Lord Townshend was maneuvered out of government, he was the principal spokesman for the Commons in opposition to the peerage bill.

Because he was out of office, Walpole was not implicated, as many ministers were, in the South Sea scandal. When he returned to office in mid-1720, his financial acumen quickly restored both the company and the country to soundness, and his political skills bought the time needed to recover confidence. Though Walpole moved up quickly through the financial offices of the state—from paymaster-general to chancellor of the exchequer to first lord of the treasury—his ascendancy was not automatic. To those still seeking scapegoats for the Bubble, he was the "skreenmaster general" who covered up the involvement of those in high places, and only the sudden deaths of Stanhope in 1721 and of the Earl of Sunderland in 1722 left him without immediate rivals. He made certain, however, that no other Whig politicians—notably the brilliant Lord Carteret, an ally of Sunderland's—would emerge as serious challengers, and he quickly set about the further discrediting of the Tories. Francis Atterbury, bishop of Rochester and the most outspoken and principled advocate of the Stuart cause in England, was brought to trial for treason, convicted, and exiled; spies, rumors, and plots were used to tag as Jacobites any other Tory leaders who dared to show their heads. But the vindictive and scheming side of Walpole was far less

*See above, p. 21.

important in securing his ascendancy than two other considerations.
One was his personality: bluff yet sensitive, easygoing and congenial
yet remarkably astute and perceptive, he mirrored the prejudices of
his countrymen on a heroic scale and charmed most of political
England into his grasp. And by constructing a political system to
maintain that grasp, he brought stability to a country that had had
enough of political warfare and created the pattern in which the government of England was fixed for the remainder of the century and
even beyond.

[margin note: Walpole as architect of new political system]

A convincing claim can be made that Walpole was England's
first prime minister, a term neither Walpole nor any of his eighteenth-century successors used. To them as well as to opponents who
abused them with it, "prime minister" conjured up memories of
such "over-mighty subjects" as Cardinal Wolsey in the early sixteenth century or Lord Strafford in Charles I's time. The distrust
inspired by one man who arrogated power to himself is shown by
what happened to the exalted office of Lord Treasurer, held by
Godolphin and Oxford under Queen Anne. After 1714 that office was
invariably "put into commission," that is, its powers were diffused
among five commissioners called lords of the Treasury; one of the
commissioners was always the chancellor of the exchequer, responsible for immediate supervision of the financial administration, while
the first lord of the Treasury ranged over the whole area of government and is the formal office held by prime ministers today. Theoretically, the prime minister is only first among equals in the cabinet, an
institution that in these same years was emerging as an inner group
of ministers better adapted to transacting daily business than the
larger, unwieldy, and increasingly formal Privy Council or Cabinet
Council, although many customs now associated with cabinet government—the necessity of unanimity, say, or the practice of collective responsibility and resignation as a group upon defeat—were
fixed only at the end of the eighteenth century or early in the nineteenth. But the natural tendency of one man to dominate a government, however worrisome it was to contemporaries, was confirmed
by Walpole's twenty-one-year tenure of office and by his political
mastery.

[margin note: emergence of cabinet]

The Forms of Eighteenth-Century Politics

A key concept in eighteenth-century culture—whether in theology,
morals, architecture, poetry, or physics—was balance. The idea is
inescapable in politics too. The notion of a mixed government of
monarchy, aristocracy, and democracy goes back to Aristotle and was
still in men's minds in the eighteenth century. But much more rele-

vant to that century was the mixed or balanced constitution that Charles I had defended against the claims of the Commons to control him and which remained the way men thought about their government down to the middle of the eighteenth century. It was a mixture of king, Lords, and Commons.

So far in our analysis of eighteenth-century society, little has been said about the king. Indeed, the monarchy to which George I succeeded in 1714 was already at a discount, in decline since the Restoration. Though the claim of George I to the throne by descent was real, it was remote, and he was, if anything, even more alien than William III. Like William, he brought with him foreign advisers whose power was disliked and whose rewards were resented, and he added a couple of German mistresses who were scarcely to his subjects' taste. Although George did not speak English well, the communication problem that once was invoked to explain a less active royal role was not serious. More relevant were his German prejudices and his dislike for much in English institutions and society, views shared by his son George II. And the two Hanoverian kings in turn were looked on condescendingly by the great Whig aristocrats who, considering themselves the natural rulers of England, traditionally favored limitations on the monarchy and found their constitutional ideal in the aristocratic Venetian republic, where the doge reigned but did not rule.

The kings of England did not merely reign, however; they ruled. The Glorious Revolution did not at a stroke create modern limited monarchy, although some of the ill-defined powers inherent in English kingship were removed or restricted. Under the Bill of Rights of 1689, the king's prerogative powers in law had been sharply limited, and his control of the army was made dependent on parliamentary authorization.* The power to tax, which had been brought under increasing control during the seventeenth century, was now thoroughly circumscribed by the necessity of parliamentary consent; never again would large revenues be granted to the king for life, as had been done with the Customs at the beginning of the reign of

---

*The small professional army, maintained in this hand-to-mouth way, was supplemented for home defense and internal security by a militia, which was the subject of intense dispute during the Restoration period but which had little more than the status of a joke during the early eighteenth century. Both before and after its reform in 1757, the militia was county-based, recruited under a quota and headed by the lord-lieutenant. It was closely identified with local government and the structure of county society; officers' ranks were much sought after as signs of social prestige. But as a fighting or police arm, it numbered more failures than successes through most of the century.

James II. Finally, the Act of Settlement of 1701 contained two sweeping limitations. Since then judges have held their offices "during good behavior" and not at the pleasure of the king; they can be removed only on a joint address of both houses of Parliament. Sir Francis Bacon, James I's famous Lord Chancellor, had called the judges "lions under the throne": they were so no longer. And in settling the crown on the Electress Sophia of Hanover and her descendants, the act confirmed what the Glorious Revolution had strongly suggested: that the king held his title by what was, in effect, the consent of Parliament. Monarchy by divine right, which Queen Elizabeth had quietly assumed, about which James I had lectured his subjects, and which had become popular dogma after the Restoration, was dead.

In time, rather by circumstance than legislation, royal powers were still further reduced. Queen Anne was the last English monarch to veto a bill passed by both houses, just as she was the last monarch to touch for the "king's evil," scrofula, a bit of magic that had survived from the medieval belief in the "thaumaturgic powers" of a king who was part god. More day-to-day business was transacted in the Cabinet without significant royal participation. But, despite these limitations, the king remained a powerful figure. He was the source of all honor—the conferring of peerages, for example. The entire civil service, to use a modern term, were his servants. High office was in his gift, and, while the king often appointed men whose qualifications lay rather in political circumstances than in his own preference, he could insist on consultation on all issues, and he could dismiss even the most popular or politically powerful minister. The king was not above politics. The king's government was the king's.

The House of Lords, the second element in the balance of the constitution, is more difficult to characterize. Though it could not be taken for granted, it rarely made trouble for the king's ministers. The peers were dependent on royal favor, for themselves and their clients, and were reluctant on both personal and public grounds to oppose the king's government openly. Moreover, the twenty-six bishops formed an almost solid phalanx in support of the government, once Anne's Tory appointees died. So did the sixteen Scottish peers who had sat in the House since 1707, and whose election as representatives of the Scottish nobility was controlled by the government. At the same time, the House of Lords included the most powerful men in the country, in terms of wealth, social position, and political influence, and was the source from which most holders of important offices came. But the inevitable rivalries among these noble politicians were less dependent on the disposition of the House of Lords than on the play of faction in the House of Commons.

Probably the oldest justification of the power of the House of Commons lay in its role as "grand inquest of the nation," charged with finding out what was wrong and asking that it be set right. With one exception, any direct exercise of that power had disappeared; the exception was the very lively right of the subject to petition Parliament for redress of grievances; though restrictions had been imposed by an act in 1664 against "tumultuous petitioning," adopting a petition to Parliament remained the standard justification for holding a public political meeting. Much more telling was the power of the House of Commons in finance. The House had established its sole right to originate money bills in the fifteenth century; in the 1670's it had been made clear that the House of Lords could not amend a money bill, but only accept or reject it. In 1712, to be sure, a standing order of the Commons provided that such a bill could be introduced only on a motion by a minister; but the House had to be reckoned with once such a bill was introduced, as it did on any bill. Hence it was considered essential that someone "lead" the House. The Speaker, the presiding officer, was still to some extent an agent of the government; his rulings on procedure or his power during debate to recognize a member or not could be of inestimable value to a hard-pressed government. But the actual leadership was confided to a minister, usually, for obvious reasons, one of the ministers especially concerned with finance.

Another justification of the Commons' claim to power lay in its representative function — a somewhat abstract notion, for the Commons represented many of the interests or districts of the country only under the then standard theory of "virtual representation." The House had 558 members in the eighteenth century. Almost 86 per cent of them sat for English constituencies, 489 as against 24 from Wales and 45 from Scotland. Eighty of the English members represented counties, each of which returned two members; county members were almost certain to be men of substance in their county, and these seats carried the greatest prestige. The remaining English members included four members for the two universities of Oxford and Cambridge, and 405 members for parliamentary boroughs — cities and towns, mere villages, or decayed towns that were boroughs in name only and by virtue of their having been created as such. There were 204 boroughs in all, London returning four members, five boroughs one member each, and the remainder the customary two members. The geographical distribution was astonishingly uneven. The small county of Cornwall returned, in all, 44 members, and the five counties in the southwest of England returned a quarter of the House. The explanation of some of this inequity lies in the history of towns: many boroughs, once perhaps prosperous ports, had fallen on evil times since their creation as parliamentary boroughs, while villages, quite properly overlooked in the sixteenth century, had grown to be sizable towns. Thus Manchester and Birmingham returned no members, and Old Sarum—the inhospitable site from which the medieval townsmen had moved to found modern Salisbury—still sent its two members to Westminster, although it had no inhabitants at all: it was the classical "rotten borough." The imbalance was made worse in the sixteenth century. It became increasingly clear to the landed gentry and aristocracy that membership in the House of Commons not only put one at the center of things but was a good way to attract notice; in an Elizabethan court that was, as Sir John Neale has put it, "exquisitely organized for powerful begging," the creation of parliamentary boroughs to take care of ambitious families was important business. It was then that "the country gentleman and his cousin, the lawyer . . . captured the House of Commons."*

This transformation accounts for the fact that landed gentlemen far outnumbered true townsmen in the House of Commons, although the high proportion of borough seats might suggest the reverse. Country gentlemen or noblemen were often patrons of towns near their estates and could presume on that relationship; in other cases they offered to serve for nothing and so to relieve the townsmen of the onerous burden of paying the expenses of their representatives. By the eighteenth century members of Parliament were no longer paid. In fact, men eager to get into Parliament were willing to bid high for the privilege, by promising (or being asked for) and securing benefits and favors or, more crudely, by bribery and fighting expensive elections. When merchants and bankers, with an eye to their businesses, tried to enter the Commons, money alone was usually what counted; the gentry could count at least in part on their prestige or influence. It was a system that made corruption a normal expectation. "Political bullying starts usually from above, the demand for benefits, from below; the two between them made eighteenth-century elections."†

How were members chosen? Here again, the variety is extraordinary. In the counties, there was a uniform franchise: the possession of lands worth forty shillings a year. In 1415 when this limitation was imposed, it had been intended to confine the franchise to respectable landowners; but the fall in the value of money had given the counties fairly wide electorates, ranging in mid-century from some 600 in the

*J. E. Neale, *The Elizabethan House of Commons* (1949), pp. 145–148.
†L. B. Namier, *The Structure of Politics at the Accession of George III* (1929), vol. 1, p. 128.

tiny county of Rutland to perhaps 15,000 in Yorkshire. In Anne's reign genuine political issues divided the country and, as the Triennial Act was in operation, elections were frequent and bitterly contested. When those issues disappeared after 1720 and the country entered a period of stable and unadventurous rule, counties seemed either too large to bribe or too expensive to canvass, and so there were not many contests. Usually, the leading landed families agreed informally who their members would be, most likely the eldest sons of resident peers (who were commoners at law) or one or two of the largest landowners among the commoners, and no one would oppose them. Elections were fought only when the leadership of the county was in dispute, and when the challenger thought he had sufficient strength to risk the expense.

Some boroughs had virtually universal suffrage; such were the so-called pot-walloper boroughs, where everyone could vote who had his own hearth, on which he could boil a pot, and who controlled his own doorway; there were no more than a dozen such boroughs and some of them were very small. In other boroughs, the vote went to those who were resident and paid "scot and lot," certain small local taxes. Such boroughs could be small or large, the largest being Westminster, with about 9,000 voters in 1761. In some places, the corporation of the town—the governing body, usually co-opted—chose the burgesses to sit in Parliament; in still others the vote was conferred on freemen, those who had qualified as members of one of the guilds. London was a freeman borough, with some 6,000 voters in 1761, but some boroughs had begun to create honorary freemen, an expensive though useful way of padding the rolls of voters at election time. Finally, there were the burgage boroughs, in which the franchise was vested in the owners of certain pieces of property; this was the characteristic arrangement of the rotten, or pocket, boroughs, and by 1760 most of them were owned by single individuals who were the sole voters in their constituencies. In 1761 only twenty-two of the more than 200 boroughs numbered over 1,000 voters; well over a hundred constituencies belonged in the category of "close," rotten, or pocket boroughs.

Men entered the House of Commons for a wide variety of reasons. The House contained many men who would not be found there now, who are in fact excluded by law because of the posts they hold: civil servants and officers in the Army and Navy, all of whom found it useful to their careers to demonstrate their political loyalty or (in some cases) to ward off inquiries. To lawyers and merchants, favorable notice from the court and the ministry could mean riches and high position; for bankrupts and men whose fortunes did not bear looking into (like the wealthy nabobs back from India), being in the House promised immunity from inquiry or arrest, and an occasional bastard could gain respectability. Some members were what Sir Lewis Namier called "the inevitable Parliament men," the eldest sons of important peers, the younger sons of a few of the greatest men in the kingdom, and those landed gentlemen who, by reason of extensive holdings and their local power, were the natural representatives of their communities. Many country gentlemen, proud of their "independence," believed they were in the House of Commons to vote as the interests of the country and their locality dictated, no matter what the politicians said.

This boast of "independence," the refusal to accept the dictates of politicians or the corruption of the court and the system identified with the king's chief minister, was characteristic of the country outlook and was likely to mask adherence to Tory principles—still, despite Whig victories, a considerable force in the country. Loyal to the Church and to the king on most matters, these country gentlemen opposed his government on others. Their principal political demands, if realized, would have made effective government impossible: they wanted taxes lowered or eliminated; they disliked the connection with Hanover, which the Hanoverian kings or their ministers could scarcely abandon; and to guarantee the independence of the House from ministerial influence, they regularly called for place acts, to prevent holders of certain offices under the Crown from sitting in the House of Commons as a dependable nucleus of government support.* They maintained their sense of loyalty and consistency by insisting that on these points the king was badly advised. And opposition politicians, Whigs though they might nominally be, could always muster some independent support by giving voice to these very grievances—until they entered office, when their views miraculously changed.

Parliamentary politics, then, resulted from the interaction of three large blocks: placemen, who invariably voted with the government in power, whatever its makeup; the country gentlemen, most of them loyal on most issues but able to be swayed against the government on certain popular causes; and the professional politicians.

*Customs and excise officers were forbidden to sit in the House. In the Act of Settlement of 1701 a clause, not to come into operation until the queen's death, forbade anyone holding office under the Crown from sitting in the House—a provision that would have produced a separation of legislature and executive like that in the United States. A new place act in 1707 repealed this clause, limiting the prohibition to holders of "new" offices and certain offices already in existence. Members of parliament appointed to other "old" offices had to resign on appointment but could be re-elected, giving their constituents a chance to approve or disapprove.

Most political leaders could count on "connections" of relatives, friends, dependents, and others attracted to them by interest or conviction. Stable at the center and decreasingly so towards the outer edges, where a slight or a tactical bid from another leader might detach an occasional hanger-on, connections were important in calculating the likely result of a vote in the House of Commons, for, as Sir Lewis Namier pointed out, in any vote (or division, as it is called in the House of Commons) there are only two sides, aye or nay; if two of the great blocs were likely to vote on opposite sides, the way the third divided would make the difference.

Walpole, in some ways the creator and certainly the master of the system, was secure in possession of the confidence of the Crown— always his first consideration; he was careful to muster the necessary votes among the bishops in the Lords; placemen and merchants were bound to him by interest. But, despite all these certainties, he had continually to manipulate the patronage to assure the majorities that would keep him in power, whether majorities in the House of Commons or majorities in the country, for in general a government could control the outcome of elections. To speak of winning or losing elections is meaningless in the eighteenth century. After an election the government's political managers might have to recalculate its strength in the Commons and perhaps redirect the flow of patronage; but the life of a government did not depend on the country's giving its voice in an election. For more than forty years, under Walpole and later without him, the chief wirepuller was a strange, timorous man, the Duke of Newcastle, himself able to control elections to twelve seats (as patron or by virtue of one or another official position), and many more by his constant maneuvering. Much of Newcastle's vast fortune was sunk in politics, so that an estate that brought in £27,000 a year in the 1730's yielded only a third of that sum when the duke died. It was a costly, troublesome game.

The Forms of Administration

Below the political level, the historian faces a different kind of problem. The administrative structure of English government had grown rapidly at the end of the seventeenth century and in the reign of Anne, thanks largely to the demands of war. But once this period of growth was over, little changed until nearly the end of the century. Understanding the eighteenth-century constitution is in good part a problem in tracing often obscure evolution; the difficulty in understanding eighteenth-century administration lies rather more in trying to master a complex of stable institutions, where description is nearly as hopeless as it is tedious. Eighteenth-century administration was a confused legacy from at least eight hundred years of improvisation and adaptation. In the Middle Ages, the nation had been governed from the king's household; for centuries no distinction was made between public money and the king's private fortune or between the duties of officers who served him personally and the tasks of running the nation which were confided to these same men. Thus the attendants in the king's chamber and wardrobe — literally his bedroom and the adjoining apartment — gradually developed machinery for administering the treasure that the Anglo-Saxon kings had kept close by their persons. Similarly, the chancellor, in charge of the king's chapel, became the keeper of his writing office (because churchmen were literate) and, since that office issued the writs by which lawsuits were instituted, the chancellor emerged in time as the head of the legal system of the kingdom.

chancellor

In one after another area of medieval government, the pressure of business led to the growth of small bureaucracies; as they came to follow more and more formal procedures, they found it more convenient to stay in one place rather than to travel with the king's household, which in the Middle Ages was constantly on the move. In the twelfth century, a part of the financial administration "went out of court," becoming, so to speak, a public office apart from the Royal Household; it was called the Exchequer, because its accounting was done, on the abacus principle, at a table covered by a checkered cloth. In the twelfth and thirteenth centuries, those officials who specialized in legal administration settled down at Westminster to become the king's courts. The balance between such institutionalized arms of government and the officials who remained in the Royal Household fluctuated from reign to reign or even from year to year, as circumstances or royal desires dictated. The Household was still a lively competitor in the early sixteenth century, when Henry VII found it a more flexible instrument of government than the more formal and elaborate routines of the "public" offices. By the middle of the sixteenth century, however, the great officers of state had all gone "out of court," the last to do so being the king's secretary; that office carried such wide-ranging responsibilities that in time it had to be divided into two.

Exchequer

Westminster

In the early eighteenth century the principal ministers were the First Lord of the Treasury, the Chancellor of the Exchequer (these two offices sometimes held by one man), the Lord Chancellor, the Lord President of the Council, the Lord Privy Seal, and the two secretaries of state. These were the ministers who usually formed the small inner cabinet; they could meet together informally and with greater assurance of secrecy (and in all likelihood agreement) than would be possible with the larger and now quite formal Privy Council or Cabinet

Council. Except for the Lord President of the Council and the Lord Privy Seal, these ministers each headed a department. The Treasury and its accounting office, the Exchequer, had established their control over financial administration. The Lord Chancellor, who also presided in the House of Lords, headed the Court of Chancery, which had grown up at the very end of the Middle Ages to provide equity through a more flexible system of law than was to be found in the highly complex and rigid structure of the English Common Law, then administered in the three royal courts of Common Pleas, King's Bench, and Exchequer (separated from the financial office of the same name). The responsibilities of the two secretaries of state were divided between the Northern and Southern Departments, a rough dividing line that applied both within England and to their oversight of diplomatic relations with Northern and Southern Europe. Since the seventeenth century it had been clear that these ministers were responsible in a way to Parliament as well as the king, but the implications of that joint responsibility were by no means clear.

It is surprising to a modern observer to learn how few men were involved in the actual administration of the nation's business. The secretaries of state, for example, charged with all the domestic, foreign, and military affairs of the country, except for finance and law, had a combined staff of only twenty-four persons, including menial help. Historians who use their letters must be grateful that ministers had to take care of so much of their correspondence themselves, but many routine matters that would now be dispatched by subordinates had to be dealt with by men who could usefully have been freed to concentrate on broad questions of policy. But there were few men available who could carry out administrative tasks competently. A good "man of business" below the ministerial level was such a rarity that as a rule he would carry over from administration to administration.

Below this small number of highly responsible offices at the top was a vast and complicated assortment of offices—in the Royal Household and outside it, in England, Ireland, and Scotland, in the diplomatic and colonial services. Some of these offices were important for administration; others were justified only by their political utility. High places at court conferred great honor and so were restricted to the most exalted aristocrats; they offered a useful way for the political managers to keep the most powerful people in the country in line. Many others were sinecures, carrying a handsome stipend but few or no duties. They were often held by the placemen in the Commons, sometimes merely to assure ministerial majorities, sometimes to support members who played an active but subordinate role in steering legislation through the House; or they might be used to provide pensions for ministers who had retired or for members of their families, whose fortunes might well have been reduced by the extremely high costs of a political career. The supply of offices ranged down to the humblest posts in Customs or Excise; the award of one of these might produce some political gratitude from a member of Parliament or a country gentleman who had recommended one of his dependents for it.

The wars in the late seventeenth century had forced reforms at the Treasury, but after that, this chaotic and wasteful administrative machine creaked on with little change. Its importance in providing patronage precluded any tampering in the interests of efficiency or economy, but it is perhaps equally important that no stimulus was forthcoming within administration itself. Although the money to support this machine came from a parliamentary grant of certain revenues to the king for the Civil List—a grant made for the reign but strictly limited since the Revolution—many officials continued to be paid by fees, an almost certain guarantee that efficient administration would be hampered by forcing business to go through as many steps as possible. Perhaps the most remarkable survival of ancient practices was in the Exchequer itself, where clerks still used Roman numerals and where cutting wooden tallies—notched sticks that had served as receipts in a preliterate age—was still a part of the standard routine.*

The indispensability and the relentlessness of this cumbersome machinery of government point to an assumption of first importance that underlay the whole structure of national politics. Parliament, ministers, and placemen were there to serve one overriding purpose —carrying on the king's government. The obligations were few— protecting the country from foreign enemies and promoting English interests abroad; the maintenance and support of local authorities in keeping order at home; and raising the revenue to keep these functions and the court in operation. What was desired was not change, not bringing a better life to the people of England, but merely to keep things moving in the way in which they had always moved. Parliamentary legislation was aimed almost exclusively at expediting this narrow range of activities: thus the Riot Act of 1715 strengthened the hand of local law enforcement officers and clarified the law under which they operated; the Septennial Act of 1716 increased the life of a Parliament from three to seven years, to provide greater political sta-

---

*When this archaic procedure was finally abolished in the nineteenth century, it was decided to dispose of the stock of tallies. They were burned in a stove under the House of Lords; the stove overheated and burned down both Houses of Parliament on October 16, 1834.

bility and to cut down on expense and public turmoil; an act of 1722 gave parishes or groups of parishes the authority to build poorhouses for the better administration of relief, though it was adopted in relatively few places; new navigation laws looked to the improvement of revenue or control. Those great objects of nineteenth-century legislation for social improvement or the wide range of subjects that today make up a political party's program were simply beyond eighteenth-century imaginations.

diff bet~ 18th + 19th c.

Local Government

At the national level, then, government was limited and unadventurous. The creative impulses of the Tudor and early Stuart periods, when well-meaning ministers had tried, however ineffectively, to use the state machinery to promote national unity and well-being, had been lost. The government of which most Englishmen were aware, however, was not that run from the Palace of Westminster and the offices around the nearby street known as Whitehall, but government in their locality—the government of parish, county, and town.

Whitehall

The parish was originally a unit of ecclesiastical administration attached to each church; it had become a unit of civil administration as well. Its governing body was the vestry—sometimes elected, sometimes co-opted, sometimes including virtually all the residents, sometimes a narrow oligarchy. If the churchwardens, who were in charge of maintaining the church building and churchyard, found that their expenses exceeded their revenues, they could ask the vestry to levy a church rate, or tax. Few parishes could avoid levying a poor rate, to provide funds for those parish officers known as overseers of the poor. All the inhabitants of the parish were expected to turn out to work on the roads, when summoned by the surveyor of highways. These parish officers were unpaid and held their posts for a year or until a successor was chosen, a provision made necessary by the fact that men were not eager to be saddled with the onerous duties involved and resorted to many ingenious ways of escaping office. Not many people would object to serving as churchwardens, certainly, but to be an overseer, a surveyor, or a constable was to expose oneself to expense, abuse, frustration, and even prosecution.

parish + vestry

parish officers voluntary

In rural England, the government of the county was closely entwined with that of the parish. At the head of the county was the lord-lieutenant, usually the greatest nobleman of the county, chosen for his post by the Crown. He led the militia and controlled the patronage. Below him came the justices of the peace. Resident noblemen were likely to be too busy to serve, so the justices were usually country gentlemen, with an increasing number of clergymen. Justices of the peace had been created in the fourteenth century for the

County lord-lieutenant + j.p.'s

better enforcement of the law; successive generations had piled, as
one sixteenth-century writer put it, "stacks of statutes" on them,
making them administrative officers as well. They were the key figures in local government; they received neither salary nor fees, but
holding the post was an honor, and for a man of position this natural
obligation was not without its more intangible rewards. Single justices could dispose of many matters, with no one to check them at all:
fining drunkards or blasphemers or committing offenders for trial.
Two justices sitting together had wider powers. Four times a year the
justices of a county came together in Quarter Sessions, or General
Sessions. Here much important administrative business was transacted; Quarter Sessions were also full-scale courts, complete with
juries, and could deal with the most serious crimes, although by custom capital cases had come to be reserved for trial by the king's justices when they came on regular circuit from Westminster to hold Assizes. When parish officials failed to act, the justices of the peace took
over their responsibilities: they would, for example, supersede decisions made by the overseers of the poor in the granting of relief in
particular cases. They had extensive power to grant or withhold
licenses for fairs, taverns, hawkers, and certain other businesses.
With the power to declare "a common nuisance" and to make
bylaws, they could serve as a virtual legislature for their locality,
making regulations that they would themselves enforce as judges.
But in rural England, few would question openly the overriding authority of men who were, by virtue of their wealth and social standing, the natural leaders of their communities.

　　Justices in towns and metropolitan areas did not have so lofty a
reputation. Where there were no resident gentry or no gentry willing
to take on the much harder task of governing in and around large
towns, the posts sometimes fell into the hands of petty tradesmen
who used them to make money or merely for the pleasure of tyrannizing; the "trading justices" of Middlesex, London's county, were
bywords in the eighteenth century for meanness and corruption.
Town governments themselves had to a considerable degree declined into self-serving and unresponsive oligarchies. They had once
been composed of leading merchants and tradesmen, and their regulations had had the best interests of the town in view. But in the
eighteenth century, few corporations were either active or responsive to needs, and few were representative. The Corporation Act of
1661, as we have seen, excluded Dissenters; the extent to which they
had been allowed to enter into town government by disregarding the
law varied from place to place, but mostly they were excluded from
any significant role. Moreover, in the reign of James II, town charters
had been revoked wholesale by the King in a foolish attempt to gain
support for his pro-Catholic policies. The effect of the new charters

was, in the first place, to cement a Tory monopoly that, even after Toryism declined, remained stodgy and unadventurous. At the same time, a horror of tampering with the charters gave men, as G. M. Trevelyan put it, a superstitious reverence for sheepskin. No one raised the possibility of reforming the corporations, even though rapidly growing towns faced problems for which the old institutions were totally inadequate, especially when the members of the corporations saw themselves as custodians of the town's property and little else.

The characteristic of local government in both town and country that most strikes us today is its complexity, the chaos of adaptations and survivals—in some places, Manchester for example, the old institutions of the manor still provided the main forms of government. Almost as striking, in the towns at least, was the lack of relevance of local government to the problems of a growing and changing society. There were, however, two further characteristics that do not come quite so immediately to view; one of them compounded the difficulties of doing any more than was done, the other pointed a way out of the morass.

The procedure of modern government is bureaucratic; it makes use, that is, of officials, usually salaried, who are appointed or elected to carry out, either directly or through paid agents, a set of obligations; they work according to established procedures, and failure or inefficiency brings corresponding penalties: reprimand, demotion, or dismissal. In the eighteenth century, such procedures were not normal in local government. Medieval forms of government had invariably been organized as courts; in local government, procedure remained judicial rather than bureaucratic. When the amateur and unpaid officers failed to perform their duties, instead of being discharged or subjected to some form of administrative discipline, they were indicted, tried, and, if found guilty, fined. As Sidney and Beatrice Webb have said, ". . . at the Assizes and Quarter Sessions, the county, the Hundred, and the parish, together with most of the unpaid and compulsory serving officers, were, one or other of them, always in the dock as defendants to criminal indictments, on which they were perpetually being fined."* The fine was then, normally, used to pay for doing the neglected work.

Modern administrative methods were, however, beginning to take hold, and new institutions were being created to deal with troublesome social problems. Concerned and enlightened citizens of a

---

English Local Government (1966), I, 308. The hundred, a term of obscure origin, was applied to a medieval unit of local government. It survived as a vestigial remnant of governmental machinery in a few places into the nineteenth century.

town, whose corporation was corrupt or unresponsive, might form a
body of improvement commissioners, charged with laying sewers,
paving and lighting the streets, and constructing other amenities to
make life in the town safer or more tolerable. A chronic poor-law
burden, insoluble by the old procedures, might lead to a plan for
making a town, rather than its constituent parishes, the unit of poor-
law administration, for incorporating the guardians of the poor and
providing professional, salaried administration. Groups of men, seeing the frustration of the parish administration of highways and not
unaware of profits to be made from improved transportation, formed
turnpike trusts to build toll roads. The rapid growth of such ad hoc
bodies contributed to the administrative confusion of eighteenth-
century England, but they also made possible some creative social
experiments that in the next century found their way into national
legislation.

    Such new organs of local government could not, however, sim-
ply be set up by interested men without further ado. They might find
it necessary or wise to circumvent the established local authorities,
but they still had to obtain the necessary legal powers. That meant
resort to Parliament. A private bill would be introduced that, if
passed, would confer the requested powers on the body mentioned;
the act would not apply, as a public act did, to the entire country.
Private bill legislation still forms a part of the parliamentary process
today, but it is much less important than it was in the eighteenth
century. Then the private bill was the only way to accomplish certain
things now done by routine administrative or judicial action: incorporation, naturalization, or divorce, for example. A private bill was
necessary to alter the settlement of a landed estate, to enclose land, or
to acquire rights of way for a canal or railway. Finally, the private bill
was the principal means by which social legislation was accomplished. In the seventeenth century the initiative in social administration had passed to the landed gentlemen and the town oligarchies.
Sometimes they used it routinely, without imagination; sometimes
they perverted and abused it; sometimes they used it creatively. To
do the latter, they had to seek authority from a Parliament of like-
minded men. Such local requests formed the bulk of the business
that came to Westminster. One can only understand what was happening at the center of eighteenth-century English government by
first understanding the localities.

The Victories of Oligarchy

The system of which Walpole was the master could work well only in
the absence of profoundly divisive issues, and Walpole did his best
to keep the country quiet, internally and externally. But his domi-

writing
against
Walpole

nance bred enemies. Isolated Tory leaders like Bolingbroke and
many country gentlemen were instinctively hostile, and a phalanx of
able writers entered the lists against him: Jonathan Swift, the famous
Irish churchman and pamphleteer; Alexander Pope, the leading poet
of his time; John Gay, who wrote *The Beggar's Opera*; and the great
novelist Henry Fielding. Men in or near power grew restive, too:
leaders whom Walpole shut out as potential rivals—Lord Carteret the
most important—and more ordinary politicians who disliked a system that made them mere cogs in a machine. Still, Walpole faced no
serious threats to his supremacy until 1733. In that year he proposed
a sensible reform of the excise, a system of taxes on various kinds of
goods that had worked well since the reign of Anne. His plan to extend the system to wine and tobacco gave opposition politicians the
opportunity they had been waiting for. They insisted that the proposal was a step toward a general excise tax on all products, that it
would vastly increase patronage by creating hordes of inspectors,
that the liberties of Englishmen would be undermined by those same
inspectors who might pry anywhere to find contraband goods. So
convincing were these largely specious arguments, and so alarming
were the demonstrations in the streets, that Walpole had to withdraw
the bill.

Today a government that suffered such a defeat would resign.
Walpole did not. It was the business of the king's government to
carry on until it either lost the king's confidence or could no longer
manipulate the House of Commons successfully. Neither circumstance was true in 1733. Newcastle pulled off his usual success in the
general election of 1734, and the next year Bolingbroke once more left
England for France. But Walpole's command was never quite so
secure again. The solidity of his position in court was eroding. In
1737 Queen Caroline died; Walpole's staunch ally, this intelligent
woman had helped to keep a petulant, erratic, and increasingly irascible George II in line. Moreover, Frederick, Prince of Wales was
keeping an alternative court at Leicester House—fathers and eldest
sons in the House of Hanover lived in mutual detestation—where
opposition politicians gathered, sure that sooner or later Frederick
would become the source of power and patronage. What finally
drove Walpole from office, however, was his sense that he could no
longer control the Commons, and that came about because of the
issue he most dreaded: war. Britain's expanding trade, particularly in
the Americas, continually ran afoul of Spanish claims; repeated
Spanish searches of British ships inflamed the rough patriotism of
the English, who found a new and thrilling voice in the maverick
politician William Pitt. So vocal did public opinion become that in
1739 Walpole was forced to declare war on Spain: this was the "War

war w/
Spain

of Jenkins's Ear," so called after the celebrated Captain Jenkins, who, when his ear was allegedly cut off by a Spanish coast guard in the mid-thirties, "committed his soul to God and his cause to his country," later, at the height of the war fever, producing his preserved ear to horrify the House of Commons. With the war and politics going badly, Walpole resigned early in 1742, on the pretext of a defeat over an election petition.

The new government was largely made up of Walpole's old colleagues, with one marked difference. At last Carteret, much admired by the king, had his chance. The military situation did not improve, however; the French joined the war against England in 1744, and Carteret proved ineffective. Newcastle and his brother, Henry Pelham, insisted to a reluctant king that Carteret (now Earl Granville) must go. And so he did, leaving the king to fulminate and intrigue against an unwanted government, the Broad Bottom ministry, as it was called, because it took in a wide political spectrum, including some country Tories in minor posts. When the king's interference proved intolerable, the Pelhamites resigned in a body, leaving Granville to form a ministry that lasted a mere two days. The triumphant return of the Pelhams gives a premature impression of one of the modern conventions of cabinet government: that the king must accept ministers who are in command in the House of Commons. It was, however, a false dawn, an accidental circumstance that perhaps a stronger king might not have yielded to. Stamp his foot though he might, George even gave in to accepting William Pitt—who had spoken loudly against Hanover—in a minor post in 1746.* The Pelham ministry continued until Henry Pelham's death in 1754, when his brother Newcastle succeeded as its head. Thus, in a militarily unsuccessful and politically lackluster way the system proved durable: the internal stability into which Walpole had so skillfully and unscrupulously maneuvered a divided nation was not dependent on one man's will.

Eighteenth-century England was a limited monarchy, a free and internally peaceful country. The tributes of her foreign admirers (like Voltaire) were conclusive. And, having gained all these felicities, Englishmen found their growing sense of superiority borne out by a quite different order of triumphs—over the world outside. By the middle of the century, she was the most powerful nation on earth.

The first and most lasting of these victories was the union with Scotland in 1707. In 1603, after centuries of enmity and war between the two neighboring countries, James VI of Scotland became James I

---

*For the constitutionally crucial return of a dismissed government, see below, pp. 216–217.

of England, and the two crowns were united; but Scotland kept its separate government and parliament, and the two cultures continued in very different paths. Scotland's role in the Civil Wars of the seventeenth century was ambiguous. Charles I's difficulties had been precipitated by his impolitic decision to impose episcopal institutions on the strongly Presbyterian Scots, to whom bishops were anathema. But, after cooperating initially with the English parliamentary rebels, the Scots found it impossible to accept the growing radicalism of the Puritans; they sided with the King and had to be beaten into submission by Cromwell in 1650 and 1651. The Restoration in Scotland brought restoration of the bishops too; coupled with brutal misgovernment, this Stuart policy produced a revolution in Scotland in 1689 far more bitter and partisan than that in England. Many Episcopalians remained north of the Border, but bishops were abolished, and the Scottish parliament was liberated from an enforced subservience to the Crown.

This liberated parliament now became the focus of a growing Scottish nationalism. A touching and dramatic proof of Scottish ambition towards separate nationhood was the Darien Scheme, launched at the end of the seventeenth century to establish a Scottish colonial empire in the Caribbean. Even had the plans to set up a colony in what is now Panama, in the very heart of the Spanish Empire, been well conceived, success in such a grandiose enterprise would have been beyond the financial resources of so poor a country. But the emotional commitment was intense, and Scotland was deeply embittered when England not only intrigued against the Darien Company at home and abroad but refused to help survivors of the ill-fated expedition. It was as much an expression of exasperation as of a vestigial loyalty to their native dynasty that led the Scots to pass the Act of Security in 1704 as an answer to the English Act of Settlement three years earlier: on Anne's death, the Scottish crown was to pass to someone other than the English king. The island seemed about to be divided again into two hostile nations.

While these tensions grew, some forward-looking men on both sides of the Border were negotiating terms for a union; in 1707 it was brought about, most generously. There was to be a single parliament for the new United Kingdom of Great Britain. The extinction of their parliament was not, however, balanced by a major role for the Scots in the new legislature. With one sixth the population of England, Scotland got a mere forty-five seats in the Commons and sent sixteen elected representative peers to speak for the Scottish nobility in the House of Lords; both delegations were rubber stamps for the English ministry. But while the Union robbed Scotland of a parliamentary life, she got a great deal else that may have mattered more. The Scots gained free trade with England and full access to the Empire; they kept their own legal system (as they still do) and their own established church — today when the queen goes north to Scotland she worships as a Presbyterian, not as an Anglican. The financial settlement was more than fair: England absorbed the Scottish national debt, the Scottish share of taxation was fixed at a mere one-fortieth of England's, and a sum of nearly £400,000 was paid by the English in recognition of the larger burden of debt that Scottish taxpayers would now have to shoulder; most of it went, as intended, to reimburse investors in the ill-fated Darien Scheme.

The Union was one of the great acts of statesmanship in English history. It was the making of Scotland, too, for it opened wide opportunities at home and south of the Border for men at all levels of Scottish society. Despite an archaic land system and the power of the landlords, Scotland, thanks to her Calvinism and a remarkable system of parish schools, developed an impressive democratic tradition, within which men were not only literate and educated but accustomed to enterprise and its rewards in social mobility. The Scots were, as a result, increasingly well prepared to take advantage of the opportunities offered to them by the Union. At first, the advantages of the Union accrued largely to the Presbyterians in the southern Lowlands; much disaffection remained in some still Episcopalian regions and particularly in the Highlands, where tribal organization had survived almost intact. The exiled Stuarts became the focus for this romantic sentiment and, helped by archaic ambitions and rivalries among some Scottish nobles, the disaffection burst out in two Jacobite rebellions, in 1715 and again in 1745. But they were easily defeated,* and the opening of the Highlands after 1745 helped to break down the isolation in which such dangers could breed.

Across the Irish Sea, the story was not so happy. In the twelfth century, Ireland had been "conquered" — a conquest that was and remained for centuries little more than a toehold around Dublin — and had to be reconquered periodically thereafter. As new leaders appeared, or as English difficulties gave the opportunity, the Irish rose in rebellion: under the Earl of Tyrone in the 1590's, on the eve of the English Civil War in 1642, against the Cromwellian regime, and again at the time of the Glorious Revolution. Each time the rebellion was put down savagely, and each time further measures were taken to keep the Irish in submission, measures that merely strengthened Irishmen in their hatred for England, contempt for the law, and willingness to go to any lengths to get revenge or independence.

---

*Particularly in 1745 there were some doubts in England as to the outcome. The national anthem, "God Save the King," dates from that time.

There were two aspects to the English attack on Irish life and institutions, each of them clearly involved with English vested interests. First was religion. The great majority of Irishmen had remained loyal to Rome at the time of the Reformation, and persisted in that loyalty with a fierceness that has given the Irish priesthood an authority unmatched in any other Catholic country. The penal laws against Irish Catholics were far more severe than laws against English Catholics; in the settlement after William III's victory over James II at the Battle of the Boyne in 1690, they reached an extreme of degradation. Catholics were not permitted to bear arms, to hold office, or to sit in the Irish parliament. No Catholic could purchase land. No Catholic could inherit land from a Protestant, and Catholic land could descend intact only to a Protestant, being compulsorily divided if it went to Catholics. Nor was the penal code restricted to important matters: no Catholic was allowed to own a horse worth more than five pounds; a Protestant had merely to produce the money and he could take any horse that struck his fancy. Moreover, the Irish had to contribute to the support of a Protestant, Episcopal, established Church of Ireland, a vast apparatus of archbishops, bishops, and parish priests that ministered indifferently to the small Anglican communities and that served primarily as a valuable supplement to English patronage. Members of the Church of Ireland were not, however, the only Protestants in Ireland. Many Scots had been encouraged to settle in Ireland, particularly in the northern province known as Ulster. They were subject to the same disabilities as English Dissenters, and, even after their heroic resistance to Catholic armies in 1689, the Irish Dissenters had to wait until 1719 to get toleration.

The other side of English policy was concerned with the economy. Each of the reconquests of Ireland had involved some confiscation of land held by the Catholic Irish and its transfer to successive waves of English landlords, speculators, or farmers: Scottish immigrants in the early years of the seventeenth century, Cromwellian soldiers, royal favorites, and deserving politicians. By 1700, native Irish landlords held little more than an eighth of the land in the country. The English landlords, who increasingly monopolized ownership of Irish land, were often absentees; and the mode of exploitation of the land was wasteful, inefficient, and — especially once the population began to rise — so subdivided as to make even the barest subsistence for the peasants doubtful. The English Parliament also applied the Navigation Laws to Ireland with increasing severity: a colony on the doorstep was much more likely to be looked to than one across the Atlantic. Precluded from trading in many commodities, with England or with other countries, the Irish fell back on what was permitted; but as soon as a branch of Irish trade flourished enough to threaten English interests, Parliament devised new restrictions. Much of this limitation had been brought about under the Restoration — Irish cattle, for example, could not be shipped to England. But in 1699 the export of woolen cloth was forbidden: it meant the destruction of the largest Irish industry, and an industry in Protestant hands at that. When Irish resistance once more broke out, at the end of the eighteenth century, the lead was taken by Protestant landowners and merchants.* England's ingratitude to those who could have been her best friends and allies seems almost willful; it is proof of the blindness that affected English policy and attitudes towards Ireland throughout the disastrous history of the connection.

The Irish Parliament had been hamstrung since the end of the fifteenth century by Poynings' Law, which gave the English Parliament power to legislate for Ireland, no matter what the Irish Parliament had done, and which gave the English government a veto over what remaining initiative the Irish Parliament chose to exercise. The Irish government was, of course, completely under the domination of Westminster, and, saddled as it was with a huge apparatus of useless offices of much interest to the administrators and beneficiaries of English patronage, that government was utterly inefficient. Only the army could hold the country together and deal with the endemic terrorism which was all the Irish could do to protest. Throughout most of the eighteenth century there was no public attack on English supremacy. The Irish were thoroughly beaten down. The better off among them were grateful for small mercies — English governments after 1714 tended not to enforce the worst features of the penal laws against Catholics. Some of the best potential leaders had taken service abroad with the French armies fighting against England. Whatever the explanation, eighteenth-century Englishmen did not have to pay much attention to Ireland. It was a triumph of sorts.

The Glorious Revolution was a watershed in the history of English foreign relations. In Elizabeth's time, the great Catholic power of Spain became the principal enemy. But James I and Charles I had kept the peace with Spain and, except for a short time, with France. After the middle of the seventeenth century, Spain was no longer so important: Cromwell's forces profited from the decline of that Empire by seizing Jamaica in 1655, a gesture in a neo-Elizabethan foreign policy beloved of Puritans. But Spain could not be dismissed; she still offered a lure to English traders, either through smuggling or through the assurance that one day the barriers would fall or open freely. Spain continued to bedevil English foreign policy because the

*See below, pp. 141–143.

childless and enfeebled Spanish king, Charles II, took forty years to reach his deathbed. The question of who was to inherit his kingdom and (more to the point) his Empire did not become crucial until 1700.

Elizabeth had cautiously aided the Dutch in their rebellion against Spain in the sixteenth century. But, Protestant though this ally was, English policy towards Holland fluctuated during the seventeenth century. Even Cromwell found himself fighting a commercial war against Holland and adopting the Navigation Act of 1651 as an instrument to wrest commercial supremacy from his highly efficient coreligionists. Charles II fought two more wars against the Dutch, but during a brief interval of friendliness following the second, he permitted the marriage of Princess Mary to William of Orange, with consequences that we have seen for England's constitutional and political development and for the balance of Catholic and Protestant in Europe. The war that England entered on the Protestant side, following William III's accession to the throne, was not simply a religious war. France had come to occupy the place that had made both Spain and Holland competitors and threats to England in times past: she was the leading imperial and commercial power. She confronted the English around the world, in North America, the West Indies, and India, and now threatened, through a candidate from the French royal house, to claim the succession to the Spanish throne.

The War of the League of Augsburg, into which William brought England, ended inconclusively in 1698; but the War of the Spanish Succession, which broke out in 1702, following the death of Charles of Spain, was of the first importance in the diplomatic and colonial history of England. English troops were committed heavily on the Continent, and the Duke of Marlborough won some famous victories. It was also the first war in which British naval strategy became deeply involved in the Mediterranean, as it has continued to be ever since. In 1704 the English seized Gibraltar and Minorca as bases, and England has retained Gibraltar to this day.

The Treaty of Utrecht, won by tortuous but impressive diplomacy in 1713, had its greatest effect on the British Empire. There were some minor gains in the Caribbean; Spain ceded Gibraltar and Minorca and also transferred, as we have seen, the asiento to Britain, giving her the right to furnish slaves to the Spanish colonies and to send one ship a year to trade in those colonies. Although Spanish pride was wounded by the cessions—grievances that brought her into conflict with England in the eighteenth century—the old standing hostility had come to an end: Spain was minor, both as a nuisance and as an opportunity. The victory over France was another matter; though established firmly in Canada, to the north of the English colonies, France was forced to yield her claims to the vast island of Newfoundland, except for some ill-defined fishing rights on certain uninhabited shores, and to give up Acadia (now Nova Scotia), a colony that developed a particularly close relationship with New England. The treaty was unpopular in England because it did not gain more, and much of what it did gain was promise rather than actuality; but it is usual and not incorrect to take it as the beginning of the modern history of the Empire.

When the desultory war with Spain into which Walpole was forced in 1739 merged into a French war in 1744, New Englanders, looking northward, attacked the threatening French fortress at Louisburg, on Cape Breton Island, northeast of Nova Scotia; it was given back, to colonial outrage, in 1748, in a characteristic treaty that restored the *status quo ante bellum* everywhere. It is perhaps worth noting that in one battle in that war, at Dettingen in Germany in 1743, George II personally led his army, the last English monarch to do so; but the battle is less important as an indication of the changing functions of the monarchy than it is revealing of the entanglements into which the Hanoverian connection seemed perpetually to drag England.

The man who was able to play most successfully on the frustration with the traditional ends of Continental diplomacy and on the hope of gain from breaking France's foreign trade was William Pitt, the grandson of Thomas Pitt, who had made a fortune as an interloping merchant in India.* Like his grandfather, William Pitt was ambitious, immensely energetic, and proud; he was also lonely, withdrawn, and an impossible colleague. A member of the ministry but not the cabinet after 1746, Pitt criticized the ineffectiveness of his colleagues with increasing venom, and in 1755 he was dismissed, freeing him to be even more critical. In October 1756 he was back in office, and in November he formed his own ministry. A few months later he was once more dismissed: the King and his colleagues had found him too difficult and not successful enough to be tolerable. Within a few weeks, however, he was given the freedom of the city by nearly every important town in the kingdom; at the end of June he was back in office, in alliance with Newcastle whom he had so often derided, and firmly in control.

Contemptuous of the petty business of politics and hating faction, Pitt was a threat to the eighteenth-century system; his appeal to opinion in the country was a portent of things to come: he was prob-

---

*Thomas Pitt bought what was then the largest diamond in the world, sold it to the Regent of France for eight times what he paid for it, and used the proceeds for, among other things, buying the pocket borough of Old Sarum.

ably the first demagogue in English history. But he was also a
brilliant war minister, with a magnificent grasp of strategy, the ability to perceive and reward talent, broad vision, and a capacity for administration perhaps unparalleled in any other British statesman,
before or since. In two years he gave his country a series of unmatched victories and left England poised, when he resigned in 1762,
on a nice question: whether the old system he so despised and into
which he fitted so badly could possibly absorb his victories without
shattering.

The European war, in which Britain participated largely through
subsidies, ended inconclusively; Britain's main attention was
directed overseas, where she was clearly victorious. But Pitt had little
to do with one of the most spectacular and significant of those victories. The East India Company, founded at the end of Elizabeth's
reign, had ever since been engaged more or less profitably in trade
with India; by the late seventeenth century the Company's activities
were centered on the three presidencies of Bombay (the dowry
brought to Charles II by the Portuguese princess Catherine of
Braganza), Madras, and Bengal, the last with its headquarters at Calcutta. With the steady disintegration of the Mogul Empire in the
eighteenth century, the Company found itself more and more drawn
into the governing of territories in which it traded, activities that
proved to be even more profitable than commerce. But from the late
seventeenth century the French moved into India with a much more
consistent and imaginative drive for domination, which by the
1740's had made her great governor Dupleix the virtual ruler of South
India.

British and French forces had not come into conflict in India
before 1714, but when the French and British went to war in the forties, sporadic fighting there was inevitable. In 1746 the French captured Madras; it was to regain that vital presidency that the British
were willing to sacrifice Louisburg, a wise bargain seen from other
vantage points than that of New England. Soon the British and
French were supporting rival candidates for the succession to the
Carnatic, the area surrounding Madras; and at Arcot in 1751 a young
clerk with the East India Company, named Robert Clive, demonstrated his remarkable military and political capacities by defeating
the French and helping to seal the fate of Dupleix, who was recalled
in 1754. On his next tour of duty in India, Clive was able to take advantage of an atrocity, the infamous Black Hole of Calcutta — in which
more than a hundred British retainers had been suffocated by imprisonment in a tiny guardroom — to mount an expedition against
the Nawab of Bengal; at Plassey in June 1757, with eight hundred Europeans and some two thousand Indian soldiers, Clive defeated the

Nawab's fifty thousand men. For placing a client ruler on the throne, he received a gift of £200,000 and later (from the same ruler) the annual rent paid by the Company for the site of Calcutta, some £30,000 a year; he returned to England the wealthiest of nabobs, and "astonished at his own moderation." A similar victory in the south in 1760 by Sir Eyre Coote did more to destroy the political and military role of the French in India, and Pitt's officers helped to consolidate the gains. In the Seven Years' War, Great Britain became the dominant power in India, with consequences that have not yet run their course.

The war that was more truly Pitt's was quite as dramatic and more far-ranging, and even though his successors sacrificed many of his gains, its consequences were surely as large. At one after another point around the world, British forces struck: they took Louisburg at last in 1758; and in 1759 alone, they put two French fleets out of operation, seized Dakar in West Africa and Guadeloupe and other rich sugar islands in the West Indies, and secured all of Canada, in a brilliant battle on the Heights of Abraham at Quebec. That miraculous year did not end the war; the end was to come less profitably four years later. But the "year of victories" marked the highest point to which British prestige had ever come, and fed the appetite for more. It was half a century before Britain rose so high again; and by then the whole setting—in the world and at home—in which Pitt's triumphs were won had changed. The old world, which at the end of the fifties seemed so secure and so victorious, did not survive the sixties unshaken.

Selected Readings

The best introductions to the ways in which the appearance and the use of the land of England have changed are W. G. Hoskins, *The Making of the English Landscape* (1957) and the somewhat more restricted but nontechnical book by Christopher Taylor, *Fields in the English Landscape* (1975). G. M. Miller, ed., *The BBC Pronouncing Dictionary of British Names* (1971) is essential for straightening out things that are not always what they seem. Cynthia Fansler Behrman, *Victorian Myths of the Sea* (1977) explores some fascinating consequences of Britain's history as an island.

The standard, detailed, but now rather elderly volumes covering the period of this Introduction in the *Oxford History of England* are G. N. Clark, *The Later Stuarts, 1660–1714* (2nd ed., 1955) and Basil Williams, *The Whig Supremacy, 1714–1760* (2nd ed., 1962). Two recent general accounts are J. B. Owen, *The 18th Century, 1714–1815* (1975) and, of particular value for this Introduction, W. A. Speck, *Stability and Strife: England, 1714–1760* (1977). See also H. T. Dickinson, *Liberty and Property: Political Ideology in Eighteenth-Century Britain* (1977), which is somewhat more broadly conceived than the title suggests. Dorothy Marshall, *English People in the Eighteenth Century* (1956) is still useful, though the kind of social history represented in it is now rather old hat. Useful for the broad context of the economy are Charles Wilson, *England's Apprenticeship, 1603–1763* (1965); B. A. Holderness, *Pre-Industrial England: Economy and Society from 1500 to 1750* (1976); and D. C. Coleman, *The Economy of England, 1450–1750* (1977). More directly applicable are T. S. Ashton, *An Economic History of England: The 18th Century* (1955) and Eric Pawson, *The Early Industrial Revolution: Britain in the 18th Century* (1979).

G. E. Mingay, *English Landed Society in the Eighteenth Century* (1963) is the standard survey of that central subject, but for developments in more backward parts of the country, see Edward Hughes, *North Country Life in the Eighteenth Century*, one volume of which (1952) is devoted to the Northeast, the other (1965) to the Northwest. Mark Girouard, *Life in the English Country House: A Social and Architectural History* (1978), which runs from the Middle Ages down to the Second World War, is fascinating, indispensable, and a delight; see also J. Jean Hecht, *The Domestic Servant Class in Eighteenth-Century England* (1956). The best edition of Gregory King's estimates is George E. Barnett, ed., *Two Tracts by Gregory King* (1936); the many encomiums of King are noted in an article that raises serious questions about his reliability: G. S. Holmes, "Gregory King and the Social Structure of Pre-Industrial England," *Transactions of the Royal Historical Society*, 5th ser., vol. 27, pp. 41–68 (1977). On legal aspects of landownership, see A. W. B. Simpson, *An Introduction to the History of the Land Law* (1961). Two articles (among others) by H. J. Habakkuk have provided the foundation of much conventional wisdom about the land market, the device of strict settlement, and the fate of the yeomanry: "English Landownership, 1680–1740," *Economic History Review*, vol. 10, pp. 2–17 (February, 1940), and "Marriage Settlements in the Eighteenth Century," *Transactions of the Royal Historical Society*, 4th ser., vol. 32, pp. 15–30 (1950). Habakkuk's views are now being criticized, the best instances being Christopher Clay, "Marriage, Inheritance, and the Rise of Large Estates in England, 1660–1815," *Economic History Review*, 2nd ser., vol. 21, pp. 503–518 (December, 1968); F. M. L. Thompson, "Landownership and Economic Growth in England in the Eighteenth Century," in E. L. Jones and S. J. Woolf, eds., *Agrarian Change and Economic Development: The Historical Problems* (1969), pp. 41–60; and Randolph Trumbach, *The Rise of the Egalitarian Family: Aristocratic Kinship and Domestic Relations in Eighteenth-Century England* (1978). G. E. Mingay's *The Gentry: The Rise and Fall of a Ruling Class* (1976) is a slight sketch, but it does cover the whole sweep from the Middle Ages down.

On British foreign trade, one must mention first the classic study of company organization, W. R. Scott, *The Constitution and Finance of English, Scottish, and Irish Joint-Stock Companies to 1720* (3 vols., 1910–1912). On ports other than Bristol and London, C. N. Parkinson, *The Rise of the Port of Liverpool* (1952) and Gordon Jackson, *Hull in the Eighteenth Century: A Study in Economic and Social History* (1972). Some admirable studies of individual merchants are Conrad Gill, *Merchants and Mariners of the 18th Century* (1961); Richard Pares, *A West-India Fortune* (1950), especially relevant for Bristol; and Lucy Sutherland, *A London Merchant, 1695–1774* (1933). Particularly useful for the origins and provisions of the navigation code is G. L. Beer, *The Old Colonial System, 1660–1754* (1912), while L. A. Harper, *The English Navigation Laws* (1939) is an interpretation of their effects. Among studies of particular industries may be mentioned J. U. Nef, *The Rise of the British Coal Industry* (1932); T. S. Ashton and J. Sykes, *The Coal Industry of the Eighteenth Century* (1929); W. H. B. Court, *The Rise of the Midland Industries, 1600–1838* (1938); J. H. Clapham, *The Woolen and Worsted Industries* (1907); Peter Mathias, *The Brewing Industry in England, 1700–1830* (1959); and R. G. Wilson, *Gentleman Merchants: The Merchant Community of Leeds, 1700–1830* (1971). On finance, Sir John Clapham, *The Bank of England, a History* (1945); D. M. Joslin, "London Private Bankers, 1720–1785," *Economic History Review*, 2nd ser., vol. 7, pp. 167–186 (December, 1954); Scott's volumes on joint-stock companies cited above and John Carswell, *The South Sea Bubble* (1960) for a good narrative of the disaster than struck them; and Charles Wilson, *Anglo-Dutch Commerce and Finance in the Eighteenth Century* (1940). On public finance, P. G. M. Dickson, *The Financial Revolution in England* (1967). On social and political attitudes and tensions in the capital, George Rudé, *Hanoverian London, 1714–1808* (1971), generally, and Lucy Sutherland, "The City of London in Eighteenth-Century Politics," in R. Pares and A. J. P. Taylor, eds., *Essays Presented to Sir Lewis Namier* (1956), pp. 49–74.

Two contemporary records (mentioned in the text) of the state of Britain and its civilization are Daniel Defoe's *Tour thro' the Whole Island of Great Britain* (1724–1727), and Celia Fiennes's tours a couple of decades earlier, the best edition being Christopher Morris, ed., *The Journeys of Celia Fiennes* (1947). A recent perspective on a little-explored part of English life is J. H. Plumb, *The Commercialization of Leisure in Eighteenth-Century England* (1973).

Moving further down on the social scale, Leslie Clarkson's *Death, Disease, and Famine in Pre-Industrial England* (1975) documents the terrible uncertainties of life. W. G. Hoskins, *The Midland Peasant* (1957), a history of the Leicester village of Wigston Magna, dramatically demonstrates the appearance of "the poor" — as well as the influx of stockingers (domestic outworkers in the hosiery trade) — in the seventeenth century. Dorothy Marshall's *The English Poor in the Eighteenth Century* (1926) can be supplemented by her article, "The Old Poor Law, 1662–1795," reprinted in E. M. Carus-Wilson, ed., *Essays in Economic History* (1962), vol. 1, pp. 295–305. A more extensive discussion of the provision of poor relief is volume 7, *The Old Poor Law* (1927), of Sidney and Beatrice Webb's celebrated *English Local Government*. On the earlier forms and impulses of philanthropy, W. K. Jordan, *Philanthropy in England, 1480–1660* (1959), and on newer forms, M. G. Jones, *The Charity School Movement* (1938) and, more generally, David Owen, *English Philanthropy, 1660–1960* (1964).

On town life, see particularly M. Dorothy George, *London Life in the Eighteenth Century* (1925) and George Rudé's *Paris and London in the Eighteenth Century: Studies in Popular Protest* (1971). Rudé's important essays supplement the older but still useful study by Max Beloff, *Public Order and Popular Disturbances, 1660–1714* (1938); an excellent impression of the frequency of rioting can be gained from the first chapter of Robert F. Wearmouth, *Methodism and the Common People of the Eighteenth Century* (1945). E. P.

Thompson has discussed the impulses to rioting in "The Moral Economy of the Crowd in the Eighteenth Century," *Past and Present*, no. 50, pp. 76–136 (February, 1971); from a broader standpoint, highly relevant to the discussion in the text are two other articles by Thompson: "Patrician Society, Plebeian Culture," *Journal of Social History*, vol. 7, pp. 382–405 (Summer, 1974), and "Eighteenth-Century English Society: Class Struggle Without Class," *Social History*, vol. 3, pp. 133–165 (May, 1978). Crime, too, may be seen as protest: Douglas Hay, Peter Linebaugh, and E. P. Thompson, eds., *Albion's Fatal Tree* (1975), and J. M. Beattie, "The Pattern of Crime in England, 1660–1800," *Past and Present*, no. 62, pp. 47–95 (February, 1974). On the side of enforcement, Leon Radzinowicz, *A History of the English Criminal Law and Its Administration*, vol. 1 (1948).

An excellent first approach to the demographic problem is M. W. Flinn's little pamphlet, *British Population Growth, 1700–1850* (1970), which may be followed by the articles in E. A. Wrigley, ed., *An Introduction to English Historical Demography* (1966). Wrigley has been the principal technical director of the Cambridge Group for the Study of Population and Social Structure, but the group's chief publicist has been Peter Laslett: *The World We Have Lost* (1965), *Family Life and Illicit Love in Earlier Generations* (1977), and an edited volume, parts of which apply to England, *Household and Family in Past Time* (1972). Lawrence Stone's confident and stimulating book, *The Family, Sex, and Marriage in England, 1500–1800* (1977) follows on his earlier studies of aristocratic families and their fortunes. H. J. Perkin, *The Origins of Modern English Society, 1780–1880* (1969) is an important interpretation of the emergence of a class society, which needs to be set against E. P. Thompson's more recent articles, cited above. For the structure of a society constituted on a different organizing principle, L. J. Saunders, *Scottish Democracy, 1814–1840* (1950), which, despite the dates in its title, has considerable retrospective importance.

Superb work has been done on the architecture and planning of towns: John Summerson, *Georgian London* (1946) and *Architecture in Britain, 1530–1830* (1953); Donald J. Olsen, *Town Planning in London: the Eighteenth and Nineteenth Centuries* (1964); and Steen Eiler Rasmussen, *London, the Unique City* (1937).

The confident rationalism of English secular and religious thought is dealt with in Roland Stromberg, *Religious Liberalism in Eighteenth-Century England* (1954); G. R. Cragg, *Reason and Authority in the Eighteenth-Century* (1964); and Basil Willey, *The Eighteenth-Century Background* (1940). Our knowledge of the eighteenth-century Church of England is peculiarly the creation of the great ecclesiastical historian Norman Sykes. His *Church and State in the Eighteenth Century* (1934) is the definitive exploration of that relationship within the assumptions of that century; in *From Sheldon to Secker* (1959) he traces the emergence of the institutional and doctrinal compromises from the Restoration to the mid-eighteenth century; and he wrote two biographies of statesmen of the Church: *Edmund Gibson, Bishop of London* (1926), and *William Wake, Archbishop of Canterbury* (2 vols., 1957).

Most of the extensive literature on Dissent is unsatisfactory. Following are some useful books on various aspects of the problem: G. R. Cragg, *Puri-*

tanism in the Age of the Great Persecution, 1660–1688 (1957); Olive Griffiths, *Religion and Learning* (1935), on intellectual developments within Presbyterianism, leading towards Unitarianism; C. G. Bolam, et al., *The English Presbyterians, from Elizabethan Puritanism to Modern Unitarianism* (1968); H. McLachlan, *English Education Under the Test Acts* (1931), on the Dissenting academies; Richard T. Vann, *The Social Development of English Quakerism, 1655-1755* (1969); and Norman Hunt, *Two Early Political Associations* (1961), on the Quakers and the Dissenting Deputies. John Bossy, *The English Catholic Community, 1570–1850* (1975) is a study of first importance.

On John Wesley himself, V. H. H. Green, *The Young Mr. Wesley* (1961) and parts of Msgr. Ronald Knox's idiosyncratic and brilliant interpretation *Enthusiasm* (1950). Stanley Ayling, *John Wesley* (1979) is a good brief life. The historiography of Methodism is in many ways dominated by the perceptions of the great French historian Elie Halévy, whose two early essays (1906) have been translated by Bernard Semmel as *The Birth of Methodism* (1971). For an authoritative appreciation of their influence and importance, John Walsh, "Elie Halévy and the Birth of Methodism," *Transactions of the Royal Historical Society*, 5th ser., vol. 25, pp. 1–20 (1975). See also Bernard Semmel, *The Methodist Revolution* (1973); Rupert Eric Davies and Gordon Rupp, eds., *A History of the Methodist Church in Great Britain* (1965); Robert F. Wearmouth, *Methodism and the Common People of the Eighteenth Century* (1945); and John Walsh, "Methodism and the Mob in the Eighteenth Century," in G. J. Cuming and Derek Baker, eds., *Popular Belief and Practice* (1972), pp. 213–227. Alan D. Gilbert, *Religion and Society in Industrial England: Church, Chapel, and Social Change, 1740–1914* (1976) is a useful introduction to a sociological approach to the interplay of religious forces.

On the watershed (if indeed it was) of 1688–1689, J. R. Jones, *The Revolution of 1688 in England* (1972); John Carswell, *The Descent on England* (1969); and Gerald M. Straka, *Anglican Reaction to the Revolution of 1688* (1962). Lucile Pinkham, *William III and the Respectable Revolution* (1954) is a controversial essay favorable to James II. For a biography of the victor, Stephen B. Baxter, *William III and the Defense of European Liberty, 1650–1702* (1966). G. H. Jones, *The Mainstream of Jacobitism* (1954) traces the fortunes of the losers. On the nature of politics under William III and Anne, J. H. Plumb, *The Growth of Political Stability in England, 1675–1725* (1967); Geoffrey Holmes, *British Politics in the Age of Anne* (1967); W. A. Speck, *Tory and Whig: The Struggle in the Constituencies, 1701–1715* (1970); Sheila Biddle, *Bolingbroke and Harley* (1974); B. W. Hill, *The Growth of Parliamentary Parties, 1689–1742* (1976); and, on the political ideas that informed the party struggle, J. P. Kenyon, *Revolution Principles: The Politics of Party, 1689–1720* (1977). The most dramatic incident of the reign is dealt with in Geoffrey Holmes, *The Trial of Dr. Sacheverell* (1973) and "The Sacheverell Riots: The Crowd and the Church in Early Eighteenth-Century London," *Past and Present*, no. 72, pp. 55–85 (August, 1976), in which Holmes demonstrates the concerted nature of these riots and the apparent respectability of many of the rioters, motivated by religious fervor.

Two volumes of J. H. Plumb's projected three-volume life of Walpole have appeared: *Sir Robert Walpole*, vol. 1: *The Making of a Statesman* (1956) and vol. 2: *The King's Minister* (1960). H. T. Dickinson, *Walpole and the Whig Supremacy* (1973) is a compact and useful political biographical study. For a biography of one of Walpole's chief victims, G. V. Bennett, *The Tory Crisis in Church and State, 1688–1730: The Career of Francis Atterbury, Bishop of Rochester* (1975). Most of the books cited in this and the preceding paragraph are important for understanding the political system under Walpole and after. On structure and political practice, the following books are indispensable, or nearly so: John M. Beattie, *The English Court in the Reign of George I* (1967) deals with organization and function. Central to an understanding of the historiography of eighteenth-century politics is L. B. Namier, *The Structure of Politics at the Accession of George III* (2 vols., 1929), a revolutionary work in its time and now a classic, though its applicability outside its stated period carries less persuasiveness than formerly. For a more detailed description of the electoral system, E. and A. Porritt, *The Unreformed House of Commons* (2 vols., 1903). On the organization and working of the Commons, P. D. G. Thomas, *The House of Commons in the Eighteenth Century* (1971); Sheila Lambert, *Bills and Acts: Legislative Procedure in Eighteenth-Century England* (1971); Betty Kemp, *King and Commons, 1660–1832* (1957); and Archibald S. Foord, *His Majesty's Opposition, 1714–1830* (1964). Romney Sedgwick, *The House of Commons, 1715–1754* (2 vols., 1970), a segment of the *History of Parliament*, is a biographical directory of members of the House. On the upper house, Corinne C. Weston, *English Constitutional Theory and the House of Lords, 1558–1832* (1965). E. N. Williams, *The Eighteenth-Century Constitution, 1688–1815* (1960) is a useful collection of documents, with a commentary. On defense, which was a political question, H. C. B. Rogers, *The British Army of the Eighteenth Century* (1977) and J. R. Western, *The English Militia in the Eighteenth Century: The Story of a Political Issue* (1965). Local government is still the almost exclusive domain of Sidney and Beatrice Webb, *English Local Government* (9 vols., 1906–1929).

The difficulties of Walpole's later years in office can be approached through Paul Langford, *The Excise Crisis* (1975) and Isaac Kramnick, *Bolingbroke and His Circle: The Politics of Nostalgia in the Age of Walpole* (1968). On Walpole's successors, J. B. Owen, *The Rise of the Pelhams* (1957); Reed Browning, *The Duke of Newcastle* (1975); and Ray A. Kelch, *Newcastle, a Duke Without Money: Thomas Pelham-Holles, 1693–1768* (1974). The "Great Commoner" has received a full-scale biography by Stanley Ayling, *The Elder Pitt, Earl of Chatham* (1976), while Erich Eyck, *Pitt versus Fox: Father and Son* (1950) chronicles a political duel that was repeated in the next generation.

On the union with Scotland, C. H. Dand, *The Mighty Affair: How Scotland Lost Her Parliament* (1972) and David Daiches, *Scotland and the Union* (1977). Accounts of the other great external victories of Britain must still be extracted from incidental coverage in books mentioned above or from yet more general studies, though mention should be made of Robert Garrett's biography, *Robert Clive* (1976). On the diplomatic context, D. B. Horn, *Great Britain and Europe in the Eighteenth Century* (1967).

Part I
THE OLIGARCHY CHALLENGED: REFORM AND INDUSTRIALISM

1760–1832

Chapter 1
"The Present Discontents"

1760–1789

THE POLITICS OF THE SIXTIES

Bute and Grenville

"I shall burn all my Greek and Latin books; they are histories of little people!" So wrote Horace Walpole, the son of the great minister, in 1762, when England's supremacy seemed permanently established. Twenty years later, he said despairingly that to call Britain "Great" was to make a bad joke, and he was not alone in his gloom. The national mood in the early eighties was anything but buoyant. An empire was lost, England had been threatened with invasion, and London had been in the hands of a mob for a week. With strange stirrings in distant places and in hitherto silent parts of society, the times seemed out of joint.

In such reversals, men look for scapegoats. No one had yet begun to make fundamental criticisms of the structure and purpose of English society. Very few could comprehend the long-term forces that determined these changes, while the creative impulses we can now trace back to those decades were not yet sufficiently in evidence to offer much hope. But though we may see more broadly and deeply than men of that time, they were not wrong in blaming the politicians and the King.

George III was twenty-two when he came to the throne in 1760. His father, Frederick, Prince of Wales, had died when George was twelve. Shielded from companions of his own age, George grew into manhood under the priggish criticism of his tutor, the Earl of Bute, an attractive but limited Scottish peer, from whom he absorbed a superficial clutter of political philosophy and a dislike for the political system of his grandfather's reign. George was determined that Bute would be his chief minister. Ministers were responsible to the king, not to Parliament, and everyone at the time expected changes. But the delicately balanced political structure into which Bute was intruded in March, 1761, was not capable of absorbing such a shock without breaking.

Newcastle, the "minister of numbers," could see little beyond politics: Pitt, the "minister of measures," a tyrant and a visionary, held politics in contempt, preferring to rely on the unorganized support of the independent country gentlemen in Parliament and on jingoistic public opinion out of Parliament. Though he could not say so openly, George wanted neither man. Newcastle was the embodiment of a political system by which the Whig aristocrats had steadily eroded royal power. George was determined to reverse that trend. His model was William III, not, as his enemies said, Charles I; his purpose was to reassert legitimate royal rights against a casual and unformulated perversion that had not had time to solidify into constitutional practice.

Pitt shared the King's contempt for political factions, but the war Pitt had so successfully waged was George II's, and so George III was determined to end it as soon as possible. As far as France was concerned, that could be done profitably; but no argument could persuade the King of the value of the Continental war and the alliance with Frederick of Prussia, who was much too close to the Hanover George II loved and George III despised. When George inserted in his first speech from the throne the famous assurance that he gloried in the name of Britain, he was declaring a policy of isolation from the Continent and making an effective appeal to the country gentlemen.

Within six months of Bute's entry into office, Pitt was out. Knowing that Spain was about to enter the war, he advocated attacking first, but was almost unanimously opposed by his colleagues and resigned. Early in 1762 the ministers reversed themselves and declared war against Spain; in August, Havana was seized, in October, the Philippines. Meanwhile the Continental war had grown more complicated because of strange doings in Russia. When the Czarina Elizabeth died in January, her successor, the Germanophile Peter III, promptly turned his back on his Austrian allies to cooperate with the Prussian enemy; his wife, Catherine the Great, overthrew him in July and continued, though not so enthusiastically, to dally with the Prussians. To George's ministers it seemed a good time to get out—to keep Britain's colonial acquisitions and to restore the crazy diplomacy of Europe to its prewar arrangements, an idea that hardly appealed to Frederick, who saw in the Russian alliance a chance for important territorial gains. Newcastle was nearly alone in thinking that Frederick should be supported; isolated on this point and increasingly uneasy about his slipping political control, he resigned—temporarily, he surely thought—never to return to real power. The political machinery he had managed so skillfully was put into the hands of the unscrupulous Henry Fox, who systematically purged the administration of Newcastle's men, destroying his political base. Contemporaries were shocked by the move, but it can be seen as an intelligent if ruthless attempt to get a loyal and reasonably unified administration. Lacking the institution of a nonpartisan civil service, there was no alternative to a spoils system.

Meanwhile, George's squabbling ministers managed to negotiate a peace treaty with France and Spain. From the latter, Britain got Florida in exchange for Havana and other conquered Spanish territories; with France—total victory was a concept unknown to eighteenth-century diplomats—an exchange of territories was negotiated in the West Indies, while the French were tolerated in India on condition that they recognize British supremacy. The greatest prizes won from France were the Louisiana Territory east of the Mississippi and all of Canada.* The treaty with France and Spain, arranged in Paris at the end of 1762 and proclaimed in March, 1763, forced the other European powers to come to terms, restoring the situation of 1756—seven years of fighting for nothing. In Continental eyes perfidious Albion had done it again, taking all the gains herself and leaving her allies in the lurch. Britain came out of the war the supreme colonial power, but she would have no friends in Europe when the French were ready to claim revenge.

Difficulties with the inevitable postwar financial problems and a campaign of personal vilification led by opposition politicians broke Bute's spirit; he resigned in April, 1763. As his successor the King chose George Grenville, an unpopular but honest and, within limits, able minister. Grenville did nothing to overcome his unpopularity. Determined to have command of his administration, he insisted not only on full control of the patronage but on an open show of support from the King. Having pedantically secured this intelligible end,

---

*A powerful segment of opinion in England held it a bad bargain to take a vast, useless, indefensible half-continent instead of the rich little West Indian sugar island of Guadeloupe. But Guadeloupe was returned to France, much to the relief of the English West India interests, who were not happy at the prospect of seeing the prices secured to them by their monopoly threatened by the output of a new and more productive island.

Grenville then set out, just as pedantically, to attain a foolish goal, the suppression of criticism in the country. His target was John Wilkes.

John Wilkes

[handwritten: jingoist critic of govt]

Wilkes was the son of a distiller, a good trade in the days of the Gin Mania. A thoroughgoing rake, whose arranged marriage to a wealthy older woman early became nominal, Wilkes spent most of his time and a lot of his money in the conquest of susceptible females (despite his physical ugliness) and in the rumored orgies of a high-living clique who called themselves the Medmenham Monks. A member of Parliament from 1757, Wilkes seemed little likely to become a symbol of a nascent agitation for reform. But in 1762, with his friend the poet Charles Churchill, he began to publish a paper called the *North Briton,* to which nothing was sacred; society was alternatively delighted and outraged by its irreverence and wit. Appealing to the growing anti-ministerial and jingoistic feeling in the country, the paper came to concentrate its hostility on the compromising Peace of Paris—like the peace of God, said Wilkes, "it passeth all understanding"—and in Number 45, the last issue of the paper to be published, he attacked the King's speech defending the treaty so disrespectfully that the government acted.

A general warrant was issued for the apprehension of all persons concerned in the paper's publication. Wilkes's house was broken into, his papers were seized, and he himself was thrown into the Tower. Wilkes claimed privilege as a member of Parliament and insisted besides that general warrants, in which no names were named, were illegal; on both grounds the Chief Justice of Common Pleas, Sir Charles Pratt, later to be famous as Lord Camden, agreed. Once released, and playing the martyr for liberty, Wilkes sued successfully for damages and then proceeded to republish Number 45. Having a press at his disposal, he could not resist trying to publish a private edition of an obscene poem called (in burlesque of Pope) *An Essay on Woman.* A regular warrant was issued against Wilkes both for seditious libel and for publishing pornography, and the House of Commons voted that privilege did not cover him. He fled to France, was expelled from the House, and, as he did not return to stand trial, was declared an outlaw. The government had won the first encounter.

The Colonial Problem

While disproportionately occupied with this ludicrous episode, Grenville's government was wrestling with the financial problems posed by a vast new empire that had to be garrisoned and maintained. Having had trouble getting a cider tax and wanting at least to hold the line on the land tax, Grenville cast about for alternative means of raising money. The logical place to turn was America, where two million subjects of the Crown were defended solely at British expense and allowed to violate trade regulations with impunity. Grenville decided to enforce the laws, to collect the duty on sugar, and to put a stop to smuggling. Popular at home and difficult to object to (though easy to resent) in the colonies, this move was followed by a disastrous financial innovation. England had long had (and still has) a stamp tax—on such formal documents as receipts, licenses, and land transfers; it then applied to newspapers as well. Now, in 1765, this tax was extended to the colonies, provoking the potent cry of "No taxation without representation" and alienating the most vocal groups in the colonies—printers and editors, lawyers, and tavern keepers. It even seemed possible that the colonies might overcome their inflexible separatism to act together against the hated tax.

Faced with incipient rebellion, ministerial quarrels, and a deteriorating relationship with the King, Grenville insisted on more and more guarantees of royal support and went on lecturing the sullen monarch. Finally, in July, 1765, a substitute ministry was patched together, and the tiresome Grenville was dismissed. The dominant element in the new mixture was drawn from the Rockingham Whigs. Based on the remains of the Newcastle connection and now headed by the Marquess of Rockingham, one of the greatest noblemen in the country, this group was soon to be distinguished by the presence of two men just entering politics in the mid-sixties: Charles James Fox and Edmund Burke. Fox, the son of Henry Fox, and one of the most popular and appealing of English politicians, formed the link between the Rockingham connection and the nineteenth-century Whig party. Burke, from an Irish middle-class background, became Rockingham's private secretary, making his way in English politics by a combination of great ability and sincere flattery of the aristocracy.* At the same time he was able to see the most niggling political transaction or problem in a broad philosophical context. With Rockingham he concerted a new and portentous view of the basis of politics, starting the transition from the eighteenth-century faction to the

---

*Burke wrote to the Duke of Richmond in 1782: "You people of great hereditary trusts and fortunes are not like such as I am, who, whatever we may be by the rapidity of our growth and even by the fruit we bear, and flatter ourselves that while we creep on the ground we belly into melons that are exquisite for size and flavour, yet still are but annual plants that perish with one season and leave no sort of traces behind us. You, if you are what you ought to be, are in my eye like the great oaks that shade a country, and perpetuate your benefits from generation to generation. . . ."

modern party. His general philosophical position, set out in a host of pamphlets on specific issues, has retained its power and appeal: no other eighteenth-century writer has made so important a contribution to our political consciousness today. But whatever the future of the Rockingham connection, their ministry of 1765–1766 was a weak makeshift, with just enough energy and cohesiveness to repeal the Stamp Act in 1766 and at the same time to pass a Declaratory Act asserting the power of Parliament to legislate for the colonies on all matters whatsoever. The figure of Pitt stood in the wings, and after much infighting among the factions, the King dismissed Rockingham in July, 1766, and called on Pitt, who was raised to the peerage as Earl of Chatham.

Though he entered office on his own terms, Chatham continued to be an impossible politician. His "broad-bottom" administration was united only by his personality; but, as he was dictatorial and given to deciding policy without consultation, Chatham often offended his colleagues. Moreover, his strokes of policy came to nothing: Prussia would not swallow its resentment of the Peace of Paris, and the Americans, deprived of the Stamp Act as a target, turned their agitation elsewhere. Suffering from a mental condition that kept him periodically immobilized for the rest of his life, Chatham withdrew early in 1767, leaving the government in the hands of his colleagues under the nominal leadership of the Duke of Grafton, a worthy but not very capable man. The ablest of the ministers, Lord Shelburne, Secretary of State for the Southern Department, was also the most distrusted — partly because he had risen under Bute, partly because he was an intellectual, partly for personal reasons — and after his department was reduced by the creation in 1768 of a third secretaryship for American affairs, Shelburne was dismissed. The Chancellor of the Exchequer, the bright, ambitious but erratic Charles Townshend, moved into the vacuum early in 1767 by imposing new revenue duties on the American colonies, a subject on which Townshend had always taken a strong line. The duties were ingenious because they were put forward as trade regulations, to which the Americans had said they did not object. But the duties raised little money and simply turned the colonists against trade regulation. Then, while the government staggered along without effective leadership, the seemingly impossible happened to bedevil its last two years — John Wilkes returned.

John Wilkes Again

Wilkes sought the immunity of a parliamentary seat to escape from his French creditors. In the general election of 1768, he was returned triumphantly for the rambunctious popular constituency of Middlesex. His arrest as an outlaw provoked riots, and when he was brought before Lord Mansfield, Wilkes was freed from the outlawry on an extraordinary technicality;* he was then tried and sentenced to jail for the libels of 1763. Imprisonment, for men of position in the eighteenth century, was not necessarily a hardship; certainly it did not interrupt Wilkes's political career. Expelled from the House of Commons on the ground that he had been an outlaw when a candidate, he was re-elected. The Middlesex electors were as adamant as the House of Commons. Four times in all, Wilkes was elected, and four times the Commons refused to have him, resolving after the last election to seat his leading opponent. Wilkes then stood for election as an alderman in the City of London and, when he was released from prison in 1770, moved rapidly up in the City hierarchy, becoming Lord Mayor in 1774. His most important accomplishment as a City official was his refusal in 1776, as alderman and magistrate, to allow the sergeant at arms of the House of Commons to arrest a printer who had published accounts of debates which the House still insisted were secret. By this time, the more lenient Lord North was in office, and the matter was dropped. The House thus tacitly admitted the right of the public to be informed of its proceedings, though it was to be another sixty years before the full implications of this concession were worked out.†

Wilkes was allowed to take his seat as M.P. when he was elected once more in 1774. By that time the increasingly vocal London radicals had returned a little band of "Wilkite" M.P.'s committed to the independence and even the reform of Parliament and also, portentously, to the notion that M.P.'s should vote as their constituents instructed them, a democratic doctrine opposed to the notion of virtual representation that was built into the structure of eighteenth-century politics.‡ Wilkes himself was not much interested in forcing through

---

*On the grounds that the writ read "at the County Court for the County of Middlesex" instead of "at the County Court of Middlesex for the County of Middlesex." The riots had presumably made Mansfield prudent.

†Accounts of more or less reliability had been published for a good many years, often fantastically disguised. Dr. Johnson had served in his youth as a clandestine parliamentary reporter and saw to it, as everyone knows, that the Whig dogs did not get the best of it. On the subsequent history of parliamentary reporting, see A. Aspinall, "The Reporting and Publishing of the House of Commons Debates, 1771–1834," in R. Pares and A. J. P. Taylor, eds., *Essays Presented to Sir Lewis Namier* (1956).

‡There are many eighteenth-century examples of instruction on specific points, but they do not make it the normal practice or expectation. Burke eloquently defended the autonomy of the M.P. in his *Letter to the Sheriffs of Bristol.*

his followers' program. Once he had got his expulsion stricken from the records of the House, he simmered down into quiescence. Perhaps he was frightened by the Gordon Riots of 1780,* perhaps he was just getting old and looking for comfort and self-indulgence. But if he was almost an apostate, he remains important as the symbol around which first coalesced the emerging political self-consciousness of the petty tradesmen and others of the middling classes who were his supporters.†

BRITAIN OVERSEAS, 1770–1782

The American Revolution

When Charles Townshend died in 1767, Lord North took over as Chancellor of the Exchequer; three years later North succeeded Grafton and began a twelve-year tenure of office. At almost the same time, in his magnificent *Thoughts on the Cause of the Present Discontents,* Burke advanced the argument for cohesive parties as the foundation of political order. North, however, achieved stability in another way, much as Walpole had done—by not making issues of things, Wilkes being a case in point. Beyond this sensible attitude, which came naturally to a man of his indolent temper, North displayed a real ability in finance and astuteness in controlling the House of Commons, both in political maneuver and in debate. At last there was a minister to the King's taste, and in ordinary times North's talents and the resulting calm might have been a welcome change. But the times were not ordinary.

To pacify America, North characteristically repealed the obnoxious duties Townshend had put on certain commodities. He kept the tax on tea, however, both to maintain the right of Parliament to legislate for the colonies as set out in the Declaratory Act of 1766 and to hold on to the rather sizable revenue. But in 1773, when the East India Company tried to solve some of its financial problems by selling surplus tea in America cheaply, the colonists protested against the tax by dumping one shipment into Boston harbor.

The Boston Tea Party was the last straw to many Englishmen who had hoped to conciliate the colonies. Punitive measures were undertaken against Massachusetts: the port of Boston was closed, the political structure of the colony was revised by making the upper

---

*See below, pp. 96–97.
†The government was under another embarrassing attack at this time in the form of the savage letters of "Junius," written for the press by someone with inside knowledge but whose identity remains a secret still.

house of the legislature appointive instead of elective, troops were quartered in the town, and the governor was given power to transfer trials to England. These "Intolerable Acts" backfired; far from isolating Massachusetts from the other colonies, they advanced the cause of intercolonial cooperation and led to the calling of the First Continental Congress.

The growing conviction among the colonists that Britain was intent on destroying their liberties illustrates strikingly how differing perspectives and diverging traditions can lead to irreconcilable interpretations of events. The colonists, who had read the great seventeenth-century English jurist Sir Edward Coke, responded to his notion that the law embodied certain prescriptive rights and privileges with which Parliament could not tamper; they had not caught up with the growing English belief in parliamentary supremacy, only recently enshrined in the *Commentaries* of Sir William Blackstone. Moreover, the colonists had drawn more radical conclusions than the English from John Locke's doctrines of natural law and the right of revolution. On a less theoretical level, financial measures that seemed inevitable or ingenious to British ministers looked like outrageous interference in the colonies.

Perceptions differed too on the problem of the American West. Faced with consolidating the territorial gains of the Seven Years' War and trying to balance the claims of Indians, fur traders, and land-hungry colonists, the Grenville ministry in 1763 had issued a proclamation that closed the trans-Appalachian West to settlement, at least for a time, in the hope of preserving a peaceful trading empire there, while diverting settlers to the newly acquired territories of Florida and Canada. Badly drawn in some details and poorly presented, this step—a statesmanlike and broadly conceived solution to a difficult imperial problem—was a powerful grievance to the Americans. Shelburne's attempts to mollify colonial opposition were defeated in the cabinet by the tough attitude of Townshend and his friends, but colonial policy was an area where, on occasion, real imagination was shown. Thus, the greatest monument of imperial statesmanship of the time was the Quebec Act of 1774.

Aimed in the first place at correcting some flaws in the settlement of 1763, the act recognized flatly that the French residents of Canada were not yet ready for the self-government promised in 1763 as a lure to English settlers who never came. It provided for an authoritarian constitution, recognizing the Roman Catholicism of the French and permitting them to live under French civil law, though the English criminal law was retained. These concessions to the culture of a non-English people were remarkably forward-looking. But the American colonists to the south, feverishly anti-Catholic and oversensitive to any step that might seem to violate English liberties, saw this remarkable statute as only another and possibly the worst of the Intolerable Acts.

The Declaration of Independence was a logical and natural result of this estrangement. But most Englishmen could not see that inevitability, and the King and his ministers had no intention of giving up without a fight. The fight was not very impressive. The British military machine, operating at great distance from its bases, was hampered by difficulties of communication and supply. The economy drive of the preceding decade had destroyed much of the fighting potential of both the Navy and the Army. Generalship was mediocre. And the government was hopeless. North, adequate in peacetime, was a total loss as a war leader: his natural indolence became worse; he avoided decisions, did not answer letters, and was paralyzed by realizing his own incompetence. What force there was in the government came from Lord Sandwich at the Admiralty and Lord George Germain in the American Secretaryship. Germain, an adherent of the King before his accession, had been convicted by a court-martial for disobeying orders at the Battle of Minden in 1759. His disgrace had had political overtones, and his firmness once in office was not without psychological significance. Holding the King's confidence, he was a decent administrator by contemporary standards; but he was not the farseeing statesman that was needed. As if all these handicaps were not enough, Britain had to face the consequences of her diplomatic isolation.

In 1777 the British made an all-out effort to win the war, hoping to split New England from the other colonies by sending an army from Canada through the interior to link up with British forces based in New York. The Canadian force was under the command of General John Burgoyne, an able, clever, and intelligent man.* A victim of faulty communication, an unrealistic timetable, the wilderness, and an unfortunate diversion of the New York forces, Burgoyne was beaten at Saratoga. In the following year a commission under the Earl of Carlisle went to the colonies with instructions permitting them to concede almost everything short of outright independence. But armed with their victory at Saratoga and having just concluded an alliance with France, the Americans rejected the offer. The French, now seeing sufficient prospects of colonial success, came in against Britain and were joined a year later by Spain, the other defeated colonial power of 1763. The widening of the war brought it nearer home. An invasion of Britain by the French and Spanish fleets was avoided,

---

*Able, clever, and intelligent enough to have been made a central character in G. B. Shaw's play *The Devil's Disciple*.

but, lacking the spirit and readiness of the Elizabethans, when they were similarly threatened two hundred years earlier, the British might have fared badly, had not this new "armada" been so weakened by illness and poor preparation. British insistence on the right to search neutral ships brought Holland into the war against her in 1780, and in the same year Russia, Sweden, and Denmark (later joined by Prussia) concluded an "armed neutrality" to resist interference with their rights on the seas. Then, after a succession of military disasters in America, Cornwallis's forces, cut off at Yorktown by French and American troops, surrendered on October 19, 1781. Though not entirely decisive, the loss of a second army made it clear that the war could not be easily won. Coupled with the mood of depression at home, Yorktown simply killed the fighting spirit among all but a few.

At last, after repeated pleading, North was allowed to resign. He was succeeded by a coalition of Rockingham and Shelburne. Rockingham died within four months, and Shelburne, who had had the responsibility for peace negotiations, became the head of the government, staying in office just long enough to conclude the Treaty of Paris in 1783, which was left to his successors to ratify.* Shelburne's intentions, as became a man who found friends among some of the most advanced thinkers of his time, were imaginative but incomprehensible to less intellectual politicians. He hoped for a commercial and possibly a diplomatic union with an independent America. To that end, he was willing to grant the United States the territories west of the Mississippi, to keep the expansive new nation agricultural and so complementary to the industrial and commercial power of Britain. Parliament reluctantly agreed to accept the terms, along with a promising arrangement for settling commercial debts and an unpromising plan for compensating the large numbers of refugee loyalists who had suffered from the American victory. But, hammered at by vested interests, Parliament could not be persuaded to accept Shelburne's commercial proposals, which would have allowed the Americans full participation in the British system of trade.

France emerged from the war with no noticeable benefits; so did Holland. Spain had to content herself with regaining Florida, where, to the wry satisfaction of the British, she could be a nuisance to the Americans. Having put up so poor a show, Britain did well against the Continental powers, a triumph Shelburne secured by using favorable terms to detach the Americans from their allies. Perfidious Albion had bred an apt pupil.

---

*For the complicated and central domestic political history of this period, see below, pp. 97–100.

Reconstruction in Ireland

While the Americans were fighting to win their independence, the status of another part of the Empire was being drastically altered. Ireland did not benefit from the indifference that had allowed the transatlantic colonists to stray into a divergent path: she was too near for that, and too closely tied to the economic interests of the men who sat in the parliament in Westminster. But there were always some Irishmen to protest against injustice to their country. The steady undercurrent of violence against landlords among the suffering rural poor was acceptable to no respectable Irishman, including the leaders of the Roman Catholic Church. But for nearly thirty years in the first half of the century, Jonathan Swift, Dean of the Anglican Cathedral of St. Patrick in Dublin, had slashed at English presumption and injustice with searing wit and devastating invective. By the sixties, the nationalism foreshadowed by Swift was spreading rapidly among Anglo-Irish Protestants.

Their demands were basically for the liberties which, as Englishmen, they felt were denied them. They wanted a habeas corpus act, tenure for their judges, a septennial act as a first step in reforming the rotten and subservient Irish parliament, some break in the solid statutory wall of commercial prohibition and discrimination. The leaders, Henry Grattan and Henry Flood, respectable Protestant landowners, were unwilling to concede to the Catholics an equal role in their movement. Ultimately a drawback to the Irish cause, the exclusiveness of the Irish leaders, like their respectability, helped to assure them sympathy in England, where men like Chatham and Burke came to their support.

The government's primary concern was to get an increase in Irish troops (paid for by the Irish) to help garrison the newly acquired territories overseas;* they were willing to make some concessions, the most important being the Octennial Act of 1768, which guaranteed regular parliamentary elections in Ireland for the first time. The government had no intention of leaving the Irish to themselves, however. After the first election under the Octennial Act in 1768, the Lord Lieutenant and his officials used their power to get what they wanted from the Irish parliament; influence and an increasing resort to outright corruption soon discouraged Flood, who took a government post, abandoning the reform leadership to Grat-

*The Irish were asked, that is, to help defend colonies they had helped to conquer, but could not trade with. V. T. Harlow, in *The Founding of the Second British Empire*, I (1952), p. 512, comments that it was rather like asking a member of a club who is not allowed in the dining room for a donation to repair the roof.

tan. Then, with the outbreak of the American Revolution, the situation changed abruptly.

The war cut off the few markets the Irish had — linen goods to the colonies, exports to France, and the trade in ships' provisions, which in time of war the British government insisted on keeping for domestic use. The economic impact was therefore extremely serious, and its effects were worsened when North's plan to relax restrictions on Irish trade was defeated by the violent protests of English vested interests, who were not prepared to accept competition from their despised neighbors. Instructed by this display of truculent mercantilism, and seeing in 1778 that Britain was willing to make extraordinary concessions to the rebellious colonists, the Irish borrowed a couple of leaves from the Americans' book. They began, first, to refuse to import British manufactures, and then, to threaten the use of force. The first tactic brought quick results in a large installment of commercial freedom — access to American and African colonies, permission to export woolen goods and glass, and the right to trade with Turkey and the Near East. The second tactic was even more successful. The withdrawal of troops from Ireland for service in America left the country dangerously open to invasion, a particularly real threat when (as we have seen) the combined French and Spanish fleets came too close for comfort in 1779. All over Ireland there sprang up companies of Volunteers, who trained themselves as a militia; reluctantly, the government gave them arms. Unquestionably loyal against any potential foreign invasion, the Volunteers were still an ambiguous force. Catholics supported them and in time became Volunteers too. Moreover, the companies were quickly converted into instruments of nationalist agitation.

The government tried to use its weapon of influence, to no avail. Finally, in 1782, the Volunteers came together in a convention, which carried resolutions calling for full autonomy in internal affairs; the threat behind the resolutions was all too clear. The North government fell within a month, and the Rockingham ministry had little choice but to concede everything the Irish asked for. Through legislation in 1782–1783, the Irish parliament became independent and, with the king, sovereign — an overwhelming concession, though radical only by eighteenth-century standards. The Irish parliament was far from representative, and the concession did not grant, nor could men of the time have conceived of, what later generations called "responsible government" — the right, that is, of the legislature to choose the holders of executive power. After all, given the constitutional position of the king, that arrangement did not exist even in England. The Irish executive government still answered to London; Grattan and his friends considered the king, advised by his British ministers, as an essential partner in Irish legislation. The British still determined a unified commercial policy for the Empire, and the Irish parliament had little option but to agree to it. Britain remained in command of foreign policy and could commit Ireland to war or peace. Given all these points of control and the potent weapons of influence, it should have been easy to keep Ireland in line. Yet British ministers were uneasy; however respected Grattan might be, they thought gloomily about who might follow. No Irish politician could afford to make concessions to British fears, and no British government could offer a really satisfactory *quid pro quo,* so Ireland remained casually autonomous until 1801, when Pitt finally resolved the question by securing a legislative union.*

Mercantilist

The New Empire

The early decades of the reign of George III saw the founding of the "second British empire," launched on different and consistent principles long before the old empire collapsed at Yorktown and Paris. The new empire was to be primarily a trading empire. As such, it was more fully consistent with mercantilist principles and was presumably free from drains in finance and population and from the troublemaking that seemed an unvarying consequence of emigration and settlement. The new empire expanded into different parts of the world. This was an era of stupendous feats by British explorers in the Pacific, the most notable among them the voyages of Captain James Cook between 1768 and 1779. Pursuing the theory of a huge unknown southern continent, Cook laid claim to many islands in the South Seas, circumnavigated New Zealand, and discovered the fertile eastern coast of Australia, whose western coast had repelled earlier efforts at exploration. Although Australia and New Zealand ultimately became settlement colonies, this did not happen until long after their opening; the use of Australia as a penal colony did not contradict the selfish but consistent purposes that underlay the new imperial expansion. Throughout the Pacific and Indian oceans and along the route to India, the British worked to secure strategic and commercial advantages.

Cook's explorations were also notable for their scientific character. Not only was he charting unknown parts of the world and exploding a long-held geographical theory, but his first voyage was specially commissioned by the Royal Society to observe the transit of Venus in 1769; he took along the young Joseph Banks, later an emi-

*On Pitt's efforts, first to conciliate, then to absorb, Ireland, see below, pp. 102, 141–143.

nent naturalist and president of the Royal Society, whose observations of the plant and animal life along the way were of the first scientific importance. This kind of concern, so typical of the age, is also evident in the beginnings of close and sympathetic study of the languages, customs, and cultures of the people of eastern countries, especially India. Such activity found its most eminent exponent in the learned lawyer and orientalist Sir William Jones and received valuable encouragement from the great Indian governor Warren Hastings.

Imperial Theories

In this rethinking of imperial concepts and responsibility after 1763, the rationalization of the Empire played a large part. We have already seen the unexpected results of this reorientation in America and Ireland, and we shall see something of the largely successful efforts to regulate and subordinate the government of India.* But, Shelburne aside, ministerial attitudes remained halfhearted, empirical, and forced. Creative thought came from men outside politics. First in importance among them was the Scottish philosopher Adam Smith, whose *Inquiry into the Nature and Causes of the Wealth of Nations* was published in the fateful year 1776. Summing up a line of thought pursued through the previous fifty years by such writers as Bernard Mandeville and David Hume, Smith's book also stands as the fountainhead of the modern study of economics. Smith concluded that if men were left alone to pursue their own economic interests as they saw them, they would be "led by an invisible hand" to the result most advantageous to the common interest. Consequently, he attacked the colonial system as an artificial diversion of resources, creating unhealthy vested interests and distorting the natural pattern of trade. Smith was no fanatical dogmatist; just as he made exceptions to the doctrine of laissez-faire which many of his later disciples forgot, so he made exceptions in his criticism of colonialism. For example, he found the traditional argument for the Navigation Acts convincing: it was necessary to encourage a fleet and to train the sailors to man it, for in the last resort "defence is of much more importance than opulence." But this famous phrase does not affect his highly corrosive main argument. Smith had been anticipated in his anticolonialism by a hardheaded clergyman, the Dean of Gloucester Cathedral, Josiah Tucker. But Tucker had found few converts, and even Smith did not come into his own until after his death. One of Shelburne's stable of intellectuals, Smith managed to touch a few im-

*See below, pp. 99–100, 102.

portant publicists and politicians; but he himself saw no hope of converting British businessmen to his views. Indeed, their restrictionist and protectionist views led him to coin the phrase "the mercantile system."

At the same time that Smith formulated the economic argument against colonies, the political argument against them was being advanced by Major John Cartwright. Coming from an old landed family, Cartwright served as an officer in both the Navy and the militia, but spent most of his life as a political pamphleteer and a steadfast reformer. He lectured and wrote about what he saw as the happy days of Anglo-Saxon England when there had been true liberty; as a defender of the liberties of Englishmen he published his first defense of the Americans in 1774. Denying the newfangled doctrine of parliamentary supremacy, at least so far as the colonies were concerned, he also rejected schemes for imperial federation (which had attracted Smith) and, with a vision caught by few Englishmen for another hundred years, advocated an outright grant of independence, relying on the ties of common language and traditions to hold the two countries close in a "grand league and confederacy." It was as a carrier of its old libertarian civilization, not as a conqueror, that England should appear before the world. Cartwright caught his argument in the title of his pamphlet, *American Independence, The Interest and Glory of Great Britain.*

Another of Shelburne's protégés was the Dissenting minister Richard Price, a political thinker of note, an important theologian, and a mathematician whose work on actuarial statistics helped the late eighteenth-century growth of the life insurance business. Price, too, was in the field with a pamphlet in 1776, *Observations on the Nature of Civil Liberty,* in which he looked to the conversion of the Empire into a federation of autonomous states, with Britain serving only to arbitrate differences and to guide a common defense—notions that clearly underlay Shelburne's peacemaking. But Price was important far beyond his contacts with power. He was a spokesman for the awakening consciences and widening political concerns of the Dissenters, and the Dissenters, almost solidly on the side of the colonies against Britain, were closely linked to the nascent agitation for reform at home.

THE EMERGENCE OF REFORM, 1776–1789

Reforming Activity

The American Revolution and its aftermath made the United States the mecca and the touchstone of nearly all English radical reformers for a hundred years, and opposition politicians were quick to take advantage of its appeal. Burke, who had been an agent for the colony of New York, welcomed the American Revolution as a further development of the principles of 1688; Chatham's last efforts before his death were directed at conciliation; and it was no idle whim that led the citizens of Pennsylvania to name a town Wilkes-Barre, after two reforming heroes. The colonists' demands for their just liberties and the teachings of the new theorists of empire came together with the political challenges of the first two decades of the reign to force a clarification of ideas and programs at home and abroad. After all, the separation of powers, that cardinal principle of the American Constitution, simply carries out the hope of English reformers to make the House of Commons an effective check on an executive from which ideally, in their view, it would be quite independent. Revolution in America and reconstruction in Ireland were of a piece with reform in England.

The vaguely disreputable air about the Wilkite movement — stemming as much from Wilkes's own reputation as from the intervention of the mob — rapidly dissolved in the seventies. The American war and domestic difficulties converted most of the Dissenters to reform, led by Price and his friend Joseph Priestley, the foremost of Unitarian theologians, a controversialist of superb talents, a philosopher of considerable interest, and a scientist of the first rank. In 1776, Cartwright followed his American pamphlet with another, much more influential, called *Take Your Choice!* Arguing from ancient pre-Norman liberties, much as reformers in the early seventeenth century had done, Cartwright insisted that political reforms — universal male suffrage, annual elections, and the equalization of parliamentary constituencies — could resurrect the glories of old England. In 1780 he began to demand the abolition of property qualification for membership in the House of Commons and payment of members as well. These simple, purely political goals, for which Major Cartwright was to agitate for fifty years, remained even longer the central program of most working-class radicals and of a good many of their superiors.

The ideas of Price, Priestley, Cartwright, and a host of pamphleteers could not by themselves accomplish much, nor was widespread sympathy from Dissenters and other respectable people enough. What was needed was organization, and the appearance of systematically applied pressure outside Parliament — out-of-doors, to use the contemporary phrase — and even outside the traditional ruling classes made the impression that counted. One center of such agitation was the old Wilkite constituency of Middlesex, drawing on a sometimes raucous but increasingly respectable and focused London opinion. The Wilkite Society for the Defence of the Bill of Rights, founded in 1769, and Cartwright's and Horne Tooke's Society for

Constitutional Information, founded in 1771, were the chief propaganda organs.

But, though reform movements necessarily gravitated towards London, their most important development took place in Yorkshire, where the freeholders were stirred up by a remarkable Anglican clergyman, the Reverend Christopher Wyvill. Complaints about the high cost of government quickly turned into more general criticisms of the structure and influence of the executive and of the unrepresentative Parliament. In Yorkshire, and in other counties joined to Yorkshire by committees of correspondence, meetings petitioned for reforms, and by 1780 there was talk of refusing to pay taxes and of setting up an "association" of men of property to put pressure on a recalcitrant Parliament. The "county movement" was important because, unlike the Middlesex agitation, it drew support from the solid, middling landowners of the counties, precisely the kind of people who had always been eulogized as the most independent, sober, and honorable of Englishmen.

Opposition politicians, always seeking extraparliamentary support, took the movement cautiously to their hearts. One noble politician, the Duke of Richmond, believed that the power of the peers could survive only through the adoption of radical reform. But most of the politicians preferred the Rockinghams' plans for "economical reform," changes not in the economy but in the structure of the civil service, to make government cost less and to cut down the influence of the Crown that so effectively neutralized the hopes of the opposition. Early in 1780, Burke, in a memorable speech, proposed a number of specific reforms such as the abolition of the third secretaryship of state (for the American colonies) and the Board of Trade; but these and similar proposals got nowhere, at least in part because Parliament was not yet ready to interfere directly with the royal prerogative. In April, rather to everyone's surprise, an opposition spokesman, John Dunning, carried a trite but now famous resolution that "the influence of the Crown has increased, is increasing, and ought to be diminished." The opposition lacked the resources to follow up the victory, and it remained, dramatic but barren, the parliamentary peak of the reform movement down to 1780.

The Gordon Riots

North was saved, partly by his own parliamentary skill, partly by the weakness of the opposition, but mostly because the reformers were temporarily discredited by an outburst not at all of their own making. Their respectability and their able leadership in time might well have overcome such obstacles as the political opportunism of the

Rockinghams or the timidity of the M.P.'s where the royal prerogative was concerned, had it not been for the Gordon Riots. Lord George Gordon, a son of a leading Scottish nobleman, was an unstable young man who with a few fanatical followers organized a Protestant Association to petition against what they imagined was an increase in Catholic influence in the country. Able to point to the concessions made to Irish Catholics and to the recruitment of Irish troops, Gordon and his friends drew on the anti-Roman prejudices latent in large parts of the populace. Petitions were presented to the House of Commons, and on the evening of June 2 rioting broke out in London, mild enough by the standards of the time. By the next day the situation had got seriously out of hand, and for more than a week London was given over to the fury of mobs. Buildings were burned, private houses were looted, the Bank of England was threatened, prisons were broken open, and in a gruesome climax streams of alcohol flowing through the gutters from destroyed distilleries caught fire and burned some drunken and insensible rioters to death. The rioting seems to have remained at least partially anti-Catholic, directed against priests, schoolmasters, and wealthy papists, rather than against their poor coreligionists. But the mobs also turned on the authorities and to some extent simply on the wealthy and powerful. The resulting property damage was surprisingly small, but the riots left hundreds dead and a lasting scar on English memories.

The casual eighteenth-century attitude towards rioting did not survive the Gordon Riots. No longer could men think easily about turning disorders to their own benefit, political or otherwise. Perhaps most important of all, this terrible episode sprang to men's minds during the French Revolution. London's own terror was an ingredient in the fear of revolution that dominated men's consciousness throughout the first half of the nineteenth century.

Economical Reform

The riots gave North a reprieve. But, as we have seen, he could not survive the chill winds from Europe, Ireland, and America; in March, 1782, he resigned, able at last to convince King George that he was a necessary sacrifice to parliamentary opinion. The unhappy King was to spend two anxious years before he found another minister who could do what North could do, and more besides. In the meantime, he had to turn to a coalition of the Rockingham Whigs and Shelburne. He much preferred the latter, who did indeed become head of the ministry after Rockingham's death in July, 1782. But Shelburne was so occupied with the peace negotiations that he could not undertake the reforms to which he was committed by temperament and counsel. The Rockinghams managed, however, to carry through some of the program they had advanced before the Gordon Riots. Burke's proposals for economical reform, as now enacted, destroyed the unnecessary third secretaryship for colonies and (temporarily) the Board of Trade; many minor posts in the Royal Household were abolished and the Civil List was revised. Other measures struck at important channels of influence: revenue officers were disfranchised, government contractors were forbidden to sit in the House of Commons, and the Paymaster General was required to make a distinction between his own money and the government's and to pay the latter into an official account of the Bank of England, a practice soon generalized for other departments.* Another administrative reform in 1782 replaced the two secretaries of state for the Northern and Southern Departments by secretaries responsible for Foreign Affairs and for Home Affairs (and Colonies); thus the conflicts inherent in the old division of labor were done away with, and the way was paved for the appearance of additional secretaryships as new areas of administration claimed attention.

The Fox-North Coalition

Shelburne was brought down in February, 1783, by a combination of factions that seemed outrageous to the King and to most opinion at the time. Charles James Fox, the most popular member of the Rockingham connection and a man of great though sometimes wasted abilities, had withdrawn from the government when his leader died. Unable to work with Shelburne, and unable to stay in power without a coalition, he could only turn to Lord North, who, quite lacking in ambition, was willy-nilly the head of the connection with obligations to his followers. A Shelburne-North combination was made impossible by the flat refusal of Shelburne's Chancellor of the Exchequer, the young William Pitt, to have anything to do with

---

*The Paymaster Generalship was notorious for its profits. Henry Fox, first Lord Holland, the political manager who succeeded Newcastle in 1762, and the father of Charles James Fox, held the office from 1757 to 1765. When he gave it up, he simply kept about £500,000 in his own hands, half of which his executors still owed to the government twenty years later. This casualness in accounting extended all the way down the line. As late as the 1830's the remittance of taxes was handled by private individuals, not government officers; if the agents were bankers, as they frequently were, the money was often used for short-term investment while "in transit," an indirect contribution of government funds to the industrialization of Britain. See L. S. Pressnell, "Public Monies and the Development of English Banking," *Economic History Review*, 2nd ser., V, 378–97 (1953).

North, so the King, lacking any possible alternative, was forced to accept a Fox-North government, a pure example of the factionalism he had sworn to exterminate. Taking office in April, under the nominal headship of the Duke of Portland, the coalition lasted only until December, when the King had found someone to take over and a pretext for getting rid of Fox and North.

India

The King's pretext must lead us back a bit into the tangled involvement of the British in India. A preserve of the East India Company, India was secured by the great victory of Clive over the French at Plassey in 1757; Clive's gains were ratified in the Peace of Paris in 1763. For the next twenty years, while the Company was consolidating its rule in the eastern region of Bengal, the country was a happy hunting ground for adventurers who held poorly paid offices with the Company and made enormous fortunes by trading on the side. These nabobs returned to England to flaunt their wealth in what seemed alarming numbers. To indignation about nabobs were added a growing humanitarian concern for the exploited Indians and a lot of questioning about the state of the East India Company, which, in spite of its deep political entanglements, seemed continually in need of bailing out. Lord North had got through his Regulating Act in 1773, which provided for a loan to prevent bankruptcy. At the same time, the administrative problem was dealt with by a reform of the courts in India, by making the East India Company's government of Bengal at least theoretically supreme over the other presidencies of Madras in the southeast and Bombay in the west, and by establishing in Bengal a governor-general who, with a council, could reform the chaotic administration.

Defects turned up, and a new Indian act was needed. One proposal was Burke's bill in 1783. As a political theorist, Burke admired established corporations independent of government; as a politician, he was annoyed by the opportunities for patronage given to the government in North's act. Consequently, he was bound to oppose any supersession of the East India Company by direct British rule. The proposal he advanced in 1783 was ingenious and strikingly modern: to place the direction of the Company in the hands of a board of seven commissioners, appointed by the Crown and holding office for four years under a secure, quasi-judicial tenure. Below them would be nine assistant commissioners, named by the proprietors of the Company, to manage the commercial side of Indian affairs under the supervision of the board. Because the bill tied officials in India to close supervision by the commissioners in London — a provision that could not be effective before the era of modern communications—it was opposed by Warren Hastings, the governor-general since 1773. But a worse miscalculation was made on the political side. The sixteen men to fill the posts of commissioners and assistant commissioners for the first four-year term were actually named in the bill—and they were all loyal Foxites.

To an already aroused and feverish opinion out-of-doors, the bill seemed a flagrant piece of jobbery, worse for being perpetrated by the self-appointed enemies of influence. Propaganda swamped the good features of the bill, and the King, seeing his opportunity, let it be known, once the bill had passed the Commons, that he would consider any peer who voted for it a personal enemy. The ministers were promptly beaten in the upper house, and in December King George dismissed them, without even the courtesy of an interview.*

William Pitt $1784 - 1806$

The government was now confided to a younger son of the great Chatham, and the heir to his tradition through Shelburne. William Pitt was twenty-four when he became prime minister; he had been Chancellor of the Exchequer under Shelburne at an age when today only an extraordinary man can gain a seat in the House, let alone office. He represented a nonpartisan view of politics that King George found to his taste, and that made him acceptable to the independent members. Nevertheless, Pitt's political position was not promising. All the other members of his cabinet were in the House of Lords; unlike Fox or North, he had no stable connection in the Commons on which to rely. His opponents engineered defeat after defeat, and the fact that Pitt did not resign shows how important it still was to have the confidence of the king and how far the constitution was from the modern convention requiring resignation on any major sign of loss of confidence in the House.

Even after Pitt won a resounding victory in the general election he felt strong enough to call in March, 1784, his difficulties continued. But gradually, aided by the skillful management of his political lieutenants George Rose, John Robinson, and Charles Jenkinson, Pitt built up a connection of independent members interested in

*A strange postscript to the Whig defeat over India was the impeachment trial of Warren Hastings, which, managed by Burke and his friends, dragged on from 1788 to 1795. The faults in Indian administration, for which most of England was willing enough to blame Hastings, grew rather out of the misdeeds of his subordinates or out of a difficult colonial situation in which highhanded methods were inescapable. Hastings was finally acquitted, but he was ruined financially by the trial.

good government, of renegades from North's faction, and of men whose support he was able to buy by judicious use of patronage— though it is important to note that Pitt preferred to use impressive and inexpensive rewards of titles and honors rather than costly administrative liabilities such as pensions and places. Pitt came increasingly to dominate his cabinet, supplanting departmental government by a unified set of ministers reporting to the king only through the prime minister. This pattern of political control grew slowly and unevenly, and it was a long time before Pitt could afford to alienate any powerful figure. By the end of his first decade in office, however, a few persistently maverick ministers had fallen victim to the anachronism of their constitutional theory, the most notable being Lord Chancellor Thurlow in 1792.

The most serious political threat to Pitt's tenure of office was the regency crisis of 1788–1789. Shortly after his fiftieth birthday in June, 1788, the King fell ill; by autumn alarming symptoms had developed. Because the most prominent of them was an intermittent and violent delirium, he was treated as mad and subjected to unspeakable treatment by his physicians. The disease has now been established as porphyria, a hereditary condition that in acute phases can resemble madness. And once the illness threatened to become permanent, the question was raised of how the royal power would be exercised. If, as seemed logical to many, the Prince of Wales became regent, the crisis could well result in Pitt's dismissal, to be replaced by the Prince's friends, the Whigs, chief among them Charles James Fox. Aided by divisions among the Whigs and by their strategic miscalculations, Pitt played a waiting game and was rescued by the King's recovery. Not for another thirteen years was his hold on power seriously challenged—and then it was by the King, not by political opponents.

Pitt's gradual consolidation of political control did not, however, mean a radical change in the relation of the prime minister to questions of policy. The role of government still remained limited,* and Pitt's friends in Parliament continued to disagree about specific items of legislation—as Henry Dundas, Pitt's indispensable manager of Scottish affairs, opposed the abolition of the slave trade while Pitt's close friend William Wilberforce strongly advocated it. But the unification of administration and the new importance of the office of prime minister were giant steps towards a view of government that was to become dominant in the new century.

In legislation, Pitt's record was spotty, a fact fully explained by his political situation and his constitutional views. He had already acknowledged his obligation to the Yorkshire reformers and his

---

*See above, pp. 57–58.

belief in the necessity of some measure of parliamentary reform by raising the question twice as a private member in 1782–1783. The first time, he proposed a commission of inquiry; the second, the disfranchisement of corrupt boroughs to give their seats to London and the counties. In 1785, he introduced a bill to abolish (with consent) thirty-six rotten boroughs, with compensation to the voters, the seats to go to the counties and possibly to London. The suffrage was also to be extended to forty-shilling copyholders and certain leaseholders. But the effort was premature. The King, some of Pitt's colleagues, and many of his supporters opposed it as too drastic; Wyvill and the reformers took the defeat as a clear sign that further education of the country was needed. Pitt also failed to carry through Shelburne's grand scheme for an economic union with America, and, even more strikingly, failed to settle the Irish problem. In 1785 he proposed an economic union with Ireland, a threat to the mercantilist stranglehold over that island which accorded with his own belief in the teachings of Adam Smith and which was enthusiastically received in Ireland. But, again, Pitt was too far ahead of his time. Smith's gloomy predictions about the myopia of British manufacturers were borne out in the organization of a highly vocal opposition led by Josiah Wedgwood, the great pottery manufacturer, which forced concessions unacceptable to the Irish, who in turn forced Pitt to abandon the modified scheme.

On the credit side of the ledger, Pitt gained support for the Eden Treaty in 1786, a liberal commercial agreement with the French. He carried an India act in 1784, setting up a board of control, named by the government of the day; the board's orders were to be obeyed by the directors of the East India Company, and in emergencies it could even give direct orders to the Company's servants in India. Wrongdoing in India was to be answered for in British courts, and a check was maintained over the means of raising illegitimate fortunes. The act, amended two years later to increase the power of the governors-general over their councils, provided a form of authoritarian rule under parliamentary supervision that was to last for nearly seventy-five years. A similarly authoritarian act was applied to Canada in 1791. The country was divided into two provinces: Lower Canada (now Quebec), primarily French and Catholic; and Upper Canada (now Ontario), settled by loyalists who had fled from the rebel colonies to the south. Each province was given an elective assembly, but the governor-general (except in finance) could exercise wide powers free of legislative control; moreover, the act provided for the creation of a colonial aristocracy and the endowment of the Anglican Church. Pitt tried, in other words, to keep down any democratic tendencies by a firm executive hand and by the establishment of society on the

English model. The act was to lead to severe difficulties and ultimately to rebellion,* but at the time it was a characteristic and satisfactory solution.

Administrative Reform

The Canada Act and the India Act give a clue to the essential nature
of Pitt's rule. He was primarily an administrative reformer and
remained so throughout his life. The famous couplet of Alexander
Pope, written in 1773, "For forms of government let fools contest /
Whate'er is best administered is best," could easily serve as a motto
for Pitt. In that light, he does not appear merely as a minister who
abandoned reform for repression at the time of the French Revolution. Such a picture is easy enough to paint if one sees the late eighteenth century from the point of view of a Victorian overimpressed
with Parliament or from that of a modern democrat. It is more just to
see Pitt as a man with a different order of priorities, concentrating on
the steamlining and improving of the machinery of government. To
Pitt, questions of vast importance to later generations could seem irrelevant, obstructive, or, in time of war, dangerous.

As an administrative reformer, Pitt was brilliantly successful. A
superb finance minister, he carried through reforms that had begun
to be talked about during North's administration and on which
Rockingham, Shelburne, and the coalition had made some progress
— paying officials by salaries instead of fees, to speed up administrative processes and to reduce opportunities for corruption; abolishing
useless sinecures; reorganizing departments; providing more careful
supervision. None of this was done with the comprehensive sweep
of a doctrinaire; rather, Pitt abolished offices as their occupants died,
insinuated new, competent civil servants into old departments, imposed regulations for accounting and discipline that seemed to be
primarily devices for saving money and whose ulterior results were
barely evident. The Customs and Excise were reformed, and the yield
was increased by lowering duties and improving their collection.
Though Pitt multiplied new taxes, at least revenues now went into
one consolidated fund from which all disbursements were made; this
made possible a much simplified accounting procedure and, for the
first time, some awareness (not fully worked out until the middle of
the nineteenth century) of how the government stood financially.

By 1789, then, important changes were being made in the constitution, reflecting significant shifts in the structure of society and in
men's ideas about government. The placidity of the fifties had given

*See below, pp. 220–222.

way to a ferment of ideas and a flux in institutions, the end of which no one could foresee. But it is important to emphasize that these changes came about almost entirely in response to concrete and definable problems: the rebellion in America, unrest in Ireland, the exercise of royal influence and government patronage, the need for efficient and cheap government. As has so often happened, many Englishmen found their answers to these challenges in actual or imagined past experience: Major Cartwright in Anglo-Saxon England, Burke in a corporative view of society, a host of reformers in the traditional independence of the country gentlemen in the House of Commons as a barrier and guarantee against corruption. Even the administrative reformers, who seem now more modern than any of their contemporaries, were not likely to see much beyond their ledgers or their day-to-day problems. One might say that there were reformers aplenty but no radicals, that scarcely anyone in this still complacent age had gone to the root of things (the literal meaning of *radical*) to question the basic organization of society, to ask where it was all leading, or to think of drastic changes to make their world democratic, industrial, and progressive. These terms were unknown or largely meaningless to eighteenth-century men. In spite of the marked extension of political concern in these thirty years, those Englishmen who were not comfortable were hardly heard from, except in occasional rioting which, at least until 1780, could be easily defended as one of the essential liberties of Englishmen. But below the political level of society, with which we have been so far concerned, other currents were flowing whose manifestations to contemporaries did not reveal the patterns we can see. Their ultimate results, then unimaginable, were to help to create the very different world of today.

Selected Readings

Present understanding of George III's purposes at the beginning of his reign was established by Sir Lewis Namier in *The Structure of Politics at the Accession of George III* (2 vols., 1929) and *England in the Age of the American Revolution* (1930). The latter, which stops in 1762, is the only volume to appear of a projected multi-volume history. For anticipation of Namier's conclusions by other historians and for a criticism of his methods, Herbert Butterfield, *George III and the Historians* (1957). The most important recent general study is John Brewer, *Party Ideology and Popular Politics at the Accession of George III* (1976). The volume in the *Oxford History of England* that covers what, for all practical purposes, is the entire reign is J. Steven Watson, *The Reign of George III, 1760–1815* (1960).

Books on the political turmoil in the early years of the reign tend to be either biographies or detailed studies of ministries. The king himself is dealt with in two biographies: John Brooke, *King George III* (1972) and Stanley Ayling, *George the Third* (1972). On some of the "king's friends," Sir Lewis Namier and John Brooke, *Charles Townshend* (1964); Alan Valentine, *Lord North* (2 vols., 1967); Alan Valentine, *Lord George Germain* (1962); and G. S. Brown, *The American Secretary* (1963), the last two interestingly contrasted studies of a puzzling figure. For opposition leaders, Sir Philip Magnus, *Edmund Burke, a Life* (1938); and Ross J. S. Hoffman, *The Marquis: A Study of Lord Rockingham, 1730–1782* (1975). On ministries, P. Langford, *The First Rockingham Administration, 1765–1766* (1973); John Brooke, *The Chatham Administration, 1766–1768* (1956); and Ian R. Christie, *The End of North's Ministry, 1780–1782* (1958). Broader thematic interpretations include Richard Pares, *King George III and the Politicians* (1953); Frank O'Gorman, *The Rise of Party in England: The Rockingham Whigs, 1760–1782* (1975); and several important essays by Ian R. Christie included in his *Myth and Reality in Late-Eighteenth-Century British Politics and Other Papers* (1970).

Specific crises in the reign have also received close attention from historians. On the Wilkes imbroglio, in addition to Brewer's book already cited, Raymond Postgate, *That Devil Wilkes* (1929, rev. ed., 1956); Betty Kemp, *Sir Francis Dashwood* (1967); Lucy Sutherland, *The City of London and the Opposition to Government, 1768–1774* (Creighton Lecture, University of London, 1959); and George Rudé, *Wilkes and Liberty: A Social Study of 1763 to 1774* (1962) and "Wilkes and Liberty, 1768–9" (1957), a study of the riots, reprinted in his *Paris and London in the Eighteenth Century: Studies in Popular Protest* (1971). The American Revolution has of course produced an immense literature, much of it by Americans from the American side. Of particular interest for the British perspective are Ian R. Christie, *Crisis of Empire: Great Britain and the American Colonies, 1754–1783* (1966); C. R. Ritcheson, *British Politics and the American Revolution* (1954); Bernard Donoughue, *British Politics and the American Revolution: The Path to War, 1773–75* (1964); Bernard Bailyn, *The Ideological Origins of the American Revolution* (1967); Carl B. Cone, *Burke and the Nature of Politics,* vol. 1: *The Age of the American Revolution* (1957). A. Temple Patterson, *The Other Armada* (1960) is an account of the abortive invasion of Britain by her Continental enemies. On the negotiations that ended the war, Richard B. Morris, *The Peacemakers: The Great Powers and American Independence* (1965). The old and new empires are contrasted in the many sympathetically inclined volumes of L. H. Gipson, *The British Empire Before the American Revolution* (15 vols., 1936–1970) and V. T. Harlow, *The Founding of the Second British Empire, 1763–1793:* vol. 1, *Discovery and Revolution* (1952); vol. 2, *New Continents and Changing Values* (1964). The first volume of Harlow's study includes a superb account of the constitutional developments in Ireland. See also the magnificent biography of England's premier explorer, J. C. Beaglehole, *The Life of Captain James Cook* (1974). J. B. Brebner, *North Atlantic Triangle: The Interplay of Canada, the United States, and Great Britain* (1945) is a distinctive and suggestive study.

On the agitation for reform that arises in the late seventies, Caroline Robbins, *The Eighteenth-Century Commonwea thman* (1959) traces the descent of so-called "Real Whig" ideas from the seventeenth century to the reign of George III. Peter Brown, *The Chathamites: A Study in the Relationship Between*

Personalities and Ideas in the Second Half of the Eighteenth Century (1967) includes some of the reformers among the portraits. D. O. Thomas, *The Honest Mind: The Thought and Work of Richard Price* (1977) is an admirable study of one of the most fascinating of the reformers, and John W. Osborne, *John Cartwright* (1972) is a biography of a staunch radical whose career spans half a century of agitation with singular faithfulness. The Association movement is set in a wider context by Ian R. Christie, *Wilkes, Wyvill and Reform* (1962) and E. C. Black, *The Association: British Extraparliamentary Political Organization, 1769–1793* (1963). There is an important interpretation of the crucial years 1779–1780 in Herbert Butterfield, *George III, Lord North, and the People* (1949). Extending forward as well as back is John Cannon, *Parliamentary Reform, 1640–1832*, an especially valuable survey. A detailed, day-by-day account of the Gordon riots is given in J. Paul de Castro, *The Gordon Riots* (1926), while a fictional account of great power is Charles Dicken's *Barnaby Rudge*. George Rudé's "The Gordon Riots: A Study of the Rioters and Their Victims" (1956) is reprinted in his *Paris and London in the Eighteenth Century* (1971).

The Indian component of the political battles of the eighties can be traced in Holden Furber, *John Company at Work* (1948) and Lucy Sutherland. *The East India Company in Eighteenth-Century Politics* (1952), while the later history of the Company is authoritatively handled in C. H. Philips, *The East India Company, 1784–1834* (1940). Warren Hastings's posthumous reputation has been handsomely rehabilitated in Keith Feiling, *Warren Hastings* (1954) and Michael Edwardes, *Warren Hastings, King of the Nabobs* (1976). See also P. J. Marshall, *The Impeachment of Warren Hastings* (1965). John Cannon, *The Fox-North Coalition: Crisis of the Constitution, 1782–4* (1969) is definitive; John W. Derry, *Charles James Fox* (1972) is the best life so far of that complex and intriguing figure. Erich Eyck's *Pitt versus Fox: Father and Son* (1950), already cited, enters the second generation at this point. John Ehrman, *The Younger Pitt: The Years of Acclaim* (1969) brings Pitt's life authoritatively down to the French Revolution.

The question of the king's illness has at last been resolved by Ida Macalpine and Richard Hunter, *George III and the Mad-Business* (1969), which is also a valuable contribution to the history of the treatment of mental illness, the mistaken diagnosis. On the immediate political consequence, John W. Derry, *The Regency Crisis and the Whigs, 1788–9* (1963). On Pitt's administrative reforms, W. R. Ward, *The English Land Tax in the Eighteenth Century* (1953); J. E. D. Binney, *British Public Finance and Administration, 1774–1792* (1958); and A. Hope-Jones, *The Income Tax in the Napoleonic Wars* (1939). A useful summary of a more broadly constitutional aspect of the reforms is Archibald Foord, "The Waning of 'the Influence of the Crown,'" in Robert L. Schuyler and Herman Ausubel, *The Making of English History* (1952), pp. 410–413.

Chapter 2
The World and the Spirit

1760–1830

THE ECONOMIC REVOLUTIONS

The Problem of the Industrial Revolution

For nearly a century, most historians would have named the Industrial Revolution as the most important of the transformations that became apparent early in the reign of George III. The historian who in the 1880's brought the phase into general use chose 1760 for the beginning of his survey, and the author of one of the most famous short histories of the Industrial Revolution starts with the same year and ends with 1830. Hallowed by usage, these dates have become conventional, but in recent years research has extended the range of industrial and agricultural innovation in both directions.* The very concept of "revolution" has been questioned, as applied to the highly complex transformation of the economy extending over a century or more, a century in which old ways persisted side by side with new. Nevertheless, Britain when George III died was a very different

---

*The phrase was popularized by Arnold Toynbee (the uncle of the controversial universal historian of the same name) in his *Lectures on the Industrial Revolution in England* (1884).

society from what it was when he came to the throne, and economic change was a major factor in making it so.

Roads and Canals

In the first three decades of George's reign, some important inventions in a few industries began a profound alteration of the British economy, but their effect was obvious to few people at the time. Had a perceptive and widely traveled man been asked what was most novel in the economic life of the time, he would have pointed not to factories or machines but to the changes visible in the countryside. For the first time since the Romans, systematic efforts were being made to improve Britain's roads. The ancient obligation of parishes to maintain highways within their boundaries had accomplished little. Their inhabitants tried hard to avoid work and expense, and the only way of forcing them to take action — procedure by indictment at Quarter Sessions — was too cumbersome to be useful. From mid-century, however, concerned or canny men banded together locally to operate turnpikes, authorized by Parliament, financed with borrowed capital, and paid for by tolls levied on users. Built by engineers like Thomas Telford and J. L. Macadam, the turnpikes helped to provide at least parts of England with relatively smooth and rapid transportation, a development of no small economic importance. The concurrent development of the swift, lightly sprung stagecoach did much to unify the country by permitting men and ideas to move rapidly between London and the provinces.

Roads, even when improved, could not handle heavy loads. The cheapest solution to that problem was water transport. The coastal trade was large and indispensable. Not many places were more than a few miles from navigable water, and many towns and rivers that are now mere pleasure spots or sleepy backwaters have an almost forgotten commercial history. The water system was completed by the network of canals built largely in the last half of the eighteenth century — an economic development of the first order. The gracefully curving waterways — cutting through the changing levels of fields, altering the vegetation and wildlife in many areas, and accented by hundreds of humpbacked bridges — made it possible to bring heavy goods, (coal especially) cheaply to inland districts. Over two decades from the end of the fifties, the Duke of Bridgewater built a canal in Lancashire to join Manchester to the River Mersey and extended it to tap other developing industrial areas; although there were earlier examples of canal building and river improvement, Bridgewater's highly profitable project captured imaginations and inspired imitators. His canal was built by a former millwright with no formal education, James Brindley, one of the most striking of the humble men of genius who changed the face of Britain. Brindley and other engineers like Telford, the road builder, worked out methods of surveying, cutting, and tunneling that underlay the great task of building the railways in the next century. Contractors learned how to organize big undertakings and the labor of large numbers of workmen; and the men who did the back-breaking labor contributed their nickname, "navigators," to the English language: abbreviated to "navvy," it means those who do the hard, unskilled work of excavation.

Enclosures

The landscape was changing in other ways too. The look of rural England today — if one can overlook the spreading towns and villages and the ravages of the Dutch elm disease — was in good part created during the reign of George III. Much of England in the outlying counties, such as Kent, Suffolk, and Devon, had been enclosed — divided, that is, into separate fields — in medieval times; more enclosures, resulting from a shift from arable agriculture to pasture, were made in the fifteenth and sixteenth centuries, particularly in the Midlands. Some enclosure was always going on, as the landowners of a village agreed to it or as dominant men forced their smaller neighbors to give in. But about the middle of the eighteenth century, enclosure by agreement began to give way to enclosure by private act of Parliament. Helped on by a low rate of interest and a growing market for the produce of efficient farms, larger landowners began to apply for parliamentary approval of enclosure schemes. A private act would give owners of the majority of land in a village the means to cut through the resistance of small tenants and to redistribute land in blocks proportional in acreage to previous open-field holdings. In 1801 the first general enclosure act was passed to simplify the process. More and more land that had hitherto lain waste was brought into cultivation, particularly under wartime pressure on the food supply. In 1700, perhaps half of the arable land in England was in open fields; by 1830, that ancient system of cultivation had been displaced by enclosure almost everywhere.

These changes in the organization and exploitation of land had far-reaching effects. For the wealthier and more progressive landlords and farmers, enclosure meant the possibility of more specialized, intensive, and profitable farming, but smaller owners and tenants were not likely to be so fortunate. Although not all of them opposed or suffered from enclosure, the numbers of independent owner-occupiers, or yeomen, who farmed their own land, had declined drastically in the early years of the eighteenth century, as heavy wartime taxation, which fell on landowners rather than tenants, cut deeply into their profits. Yeomen who were good farmers might well be better off as tenants, for landowners were eager to find able men to run their farms; but the less enterprising owner-occupiers and tenants, their farms heavily mortgaged, were hard hit by a slump in agriculture after 1815 and by a heavy burden of local taxation. Facing an increasingly competitive commercial situation, they often gave up to go into other lines of work or declined into the rural laboring class. Small tenants and cottagers alike were hurt by the enclosure and ploughing up of commons and wastelands, which deprived them of land where they could pasture a cow or pig and gather fuel, vital adjuncts to their old way of life; and only the most humane landlords did anything about providing allotments for pasture or gardens for their small holders or laborers. It took more than a hundred years to create the typical pattern of Victorian rural society — large landlords, tenant farmers, and landless (or nearly landless) laborers — but the process has the look of inevitability about it.

Agricultural laborers had no easy lot, troubled as they were by their growing numbers, bad harvests, rising prices of food, and shortsighted poor-law administration; but, in spite of what is often said, their economic condition was not necessarily made worse by the process of enclosure itself. Indeed, good farming, where it was practiced, was more likely to create jobs than to destroy them. Wastelands had to be cleared, hedges planted, fences built and maintained, drainage ditches dug and kept open, buildings put up; and, until the effective mechanization of agriculture early in Victoria's reign, most of the sowing, cultivating, and harvesting had to be done by hand.

Agricultural Techniques

Historians a couple of generations ago were so impressed by the new agricultural techniques first suggested or practiced in the eighteenth century that they spoke of an agricultural revolution. But many of these techniques, such as the use of root crops and rotation to restore fertility to the soil, had been worked out in the late seventeenth century, while others were not and could not be put into general use until well into the nineteenth. For example, early in the eighteenth century, Jethro Tull recommended the drilling of seed and regular cultivation by the horse-drawn hoe, yet wooden drills were not very practical, and the use of metal drills had to wait until there was an engineering industry to build them. Again, after mid-century, Robert Bakewell worked marvels in breeding cattle; new breeds promised larger size and earlier maturity and so an increase in the nation's meat supply. But the general practice of selective breeding had to wait until enclosures made segregation possible. Figures for the weight of animals at provincial cattle markets were not so impressive as they were claimed to be in London; lacking transport, even cattle for London had to be brought overland in inefficient and weight-consuming cattle drives from as far away as Wales and Scotland, to be fattened in fields and stalls near the metropolis.* The eighteenth century had no scientific knowledge of soil chemistry or of the principles of fertilization. Drainage remained a nearly unsolved problem for heavy soils. And worse than the lack of knowledge was the sullen resistance to innovation almost everywhere. Too many farmers were sure the old ways were best, and ignorant or lazy laborers had less and less incentive to be anything else.

In certain areas—around Edinburgh or in the light, easily drained soils of Norfolk—agriculture was progressive and highly profitable, based on intelligent leasing policies and enforcement of soil-restoring crop rotations; the model estates of Coke of Norfolk at Holkham were visited by improvers from all over Europe. Agricultural publicists wrote, traveled, and propagandized widely—Arthur Young and Sir John Sinclair were the most important—and the King, "Farmer George," took the movement under his patronage. But travelers' accounts well into the nineteenth century are full of laments about bad farming. The advances of eighteenth-century agriculture, though ragged and uneven, were impressive: at the end of the century a vastly bigger population was still fed largely from England's fields. But the "agricultural revolution" —which may in reality have been two or three distinct "revolutions"—was completed only with the striking technical advances that characterize the "high farming" of the mid-nineteenth century.

Industrial Change

The course of significant innovation in industry runs well outside the boundaries of the conventional dates of the Industrial Revolution. Far into the nineteenth century British industry remained an amalgam of ancient and new techniques and modes of organization; in some ways it is so even today. A Quaker, Benjamin Huntsman, had invented the crucible-steel process in the 1740's, but not until more than a century later, after the introduction of a means of making

*Those whose awareness of the cattle business is conditioned by films dealing with the American West would do well to read A. R. B. Haldane's *The Drove Roads of Scotland* (1952); perhaps as many as 100,000 head of cattle were being driven annually from Scotland to England at the end of the eighteenth century. For further perspective, it might be recalled that London's geese and turkeys were also driven overland, often on foot, from East Anglia.

cheap steel in quantity, did the cutlery center of Sheffield, with its tiny workshops, find a better future as a factory town. In Norwich, where the flourishing textile trade had created great prosperity in the early and middle eighteenth century, manufacturers refused to adopt (or were prevented from adopting) the machinery that enabled rivals in the West Riding of Yorkshire to undersell them; the town simply declined until, again after the middle of the nineteenth century, its economy was rebuilt on the basis of the factory production of shoes, food products, and machinery.

In textiles, the domestic or putting-out system was under imminent sentence of death, but its death agonies were terrible. Because power spinning in the new cotton industry preceded power looms, many laborers in the last third of the eighteenth century were attracted into the easy-to-learn trade of handloom weaving. There were perhaps as many as a quarter million of them in the 1820's. But by that time power looms were making inroads on a trade where earnings were always erratic and often low; after the slump of 1825–1826, handloom weaving was clearly doomed. Some weavers moved to other work, but many did not. England was thus presented with its most dramatic — and most investigated — example of technological unemployment. In other trades, the domestic system, like Charles II, was an unconscionable time a-dying. There were still hand nailmakers in the Black Country northwest of Birmingham in the 1870's, and investigations by a concerned government in the 1840's into the condition of the framework knitters (who made the country's stockings and similar apparel) showed an industry whose essentials had changed little in 250 years; not until the sixties did significant mechanization begin.

There are many explanations of the unevenness of innovation: the scattering of industry, the difficulty of breaking tradition, a lack of scientific and technological knowledge and skill. The innovators themselves, who certainly deserved to be rewarded, sometimes slowed down diffusion of their inventions by maintaining their patents and refusing to license others in a backward industry. The expiration or breaking of certain patents mark important turning points in industrial history: the Lombes' silk-throwing patent in 1732, Arkwright's cotton-spinning patents in 1785, Watt's patents on the steam engine in 1800. Some idealists, like Josiah Wedgwood in the pottery industry or Sir Humphrey Davy, the inventor of the miners' safety lamp, refused to take out patents; and perhaps a few good words can be found even for those who pirated inventions. Secrecy, too, played a part: after stealing Italian designs for machinery to make silk thread, the Lombe brothers set up their mill on an island to prevent rivals from doing to them as they had done to others. But

more strictly economic explanations may be more convincing than
any of these. For example, early in the eighteenth century, Abraham
Darby, of Coalbrookdale in Shropshire, invented the coking process,
whereby coal was roasted to drive out impurities, thus making it a
more effective fuel for the smelting of iron ore; yet this vital contribution to modern industrial technology remained limited to Shropshire, while ironmasters elsewhere went on building charcoal furnaces. It now appears that it was not the Darbys' access to coal with
peculiar qualities or their secretiveness that accounted for their sin-
gularity; rather they perfected a means of casting thin-walled products that required the superior qualities of coke-smelted iron, and
that made it worthwhile for them to use what was in fact a more expensive smelting process. For other less specialized purposes charcoal remained a cost-effective method of smelting until a dramatic
fall in costs after 1750 made the new method profitable, while
demand grew so rapidly as to maintain or even increase prices in
spite of immense increases in output. It seems likely, then, that
canny entrepreneurs adopted newly perfected techniques as soon as
market conditions warranted capital investment that was often quite
high.

Where, then, amid change of great complexity and unevenness,
did the *revolution* lie in the reign of George III? In a few industries of
surpassing importance—iron and textiles—technological advances,
falling costs, and rising demand combined to produce revolutionary
effects. In a little over a century after 1750 the English iron industry
increased its output by about 250 times and was transformed from a
high-cost industry able to supply only about half the country's needs
to a low-cost exporting industry; iron became not only the material
from which pots and hardware were made but the basis for the modern engineering and transport industries. In textiles, the revolution
came about only slowly in the manufacture of woolen cloth, once virtually synonymous with the textile trade, partly because of vested interests that inhibited adoption of new techniques and partly because
it took a long time to perfect machines to deal with that tricky fiber.
The linen trade remained small, and the silk trade was insignificant,
surviving only because of stiff protective legislation to keep the British market, in good mercantilist fashion, out of the hands of more efficient French and Italian manufacturers.

Cotton was another matter altogether, a new industry with a
huge potential demand. First imported from India at the end of the
seventeenth century, colorful cotton calicoes quickly became so popular that an alarmed woolen trade got their import banned in 1701.
Concentrating mainly on cheap coarse goods, domestic cotton manufacturers had begun to print their own calicoes; with a few excep-

tions, they too were banned for home consumption in 1721. But the prohibitions were soon lifted—in 1736 for mixed cotton and linen fabrics, known as fustian, and in 1774 for printing on pure cotton. The cotton trade, already a booming export business, could then move even more rapidly ahead. Free from inherited traditions, interests, and regulations, it could easily respond to the growing demand by taking advantage of a series of remarkable inventions. John Kay's flying shuttle, invented about 1733 though not generally adopted until after 1760, speeded up and lightened the work of the handloom weaver. The spinning jenny of James Hargreaves, a domestic machine invented in the sixties, the factory-based inventions of Richard Arkwright (a former barber), and Samuel Crompton's spinning mule, invented in the eighties, made possible an enormous increase in yarn production, especially after Arkwright's patents were voided in 1785. The previous year Edmund Cartwright had invented a power loom. By 1835, more than six times as much cotton was being spun as in 1813; in 1844, output had increased by two-thirds over 1835. At the same time, costs dropped. One estimate put the average price per yard of cotton goods of all kinds in 1820 at just under thirteen pence, in 1844, at a little over threepence.* Small wonder that the export of cotton goods was more than four times greater by mid-century than in 1820, or that English cottons—carded, spun, woven, and printed by machinery—could be shipped to India to undersell native handmade calicoes, destroying that industry and the livelihood of hundreds of thousands of people.

The Factory System

Cotton was the first industry whose techniques of production were mechanized from beginning to end. A corollary of that innovation had far-reaching social effects. England had known large industries before, where hundreds of workmen labored under the same roof or in the same firm: naval dockyards and shipbuilding yards, armaments, some iron-works, some mines, breweries in London, and even a few textile "factories" where, for greater efficiency, weavers were brought together into one large shed. But the cotton factories of the late eighteenth century were integrated in a way unknown before. No longer were factories mere aggregates of workmen pursuing their separate tasks in close proximity; now the workmen had themselves become part of a vast machine, tied to a set routine, which began on the dot and ended (many too many hours later) on

*G. R. Porter, *The Progress of the Nation* (first published 1836–1843, ed. by F. W. Hirst, 1912), pp. 296–297.

the dot. Their pace was determined by a single source of power that moved the machinery at a steady speed to which the workers had to accommodate themselves.

At first the cotton factories depended on water power, with which England was fairly well provided. But mills had to be located near the source of power, often well away from readily available supplies of labor: in some seasons too, streams could be uncertain. Escape from this inconvenience and uncertainty was provided by the most important single invention in modern industrial history, the steam engine. The old Newcomen engines, used for pumping out mines, were inefficient: for each stroke of the piston, driven by the alternate injection and condensation of steam, the cylinder was first heated and then cooled, thus wasting a great deal of energy. James Watt, a Glasgow instrument maker, called in to repair a Newcomen engine, hit on the idea of condensing the steam in a separate chamber, with gains in both speed and efficiency. Financed by a Scottish ironmaster, Watt patented his engine in 1769. In 1774, his Scottish backer sold his share of the patent to the great Birmingham entrepreneur Matthew Boulton; from the resulting partnership developed the first modern engineering works.

Steam did not conquer overnight. At first the engines could be used only for pumping, and production remained small as Boulton and Watt assembled machines from parts made elsewhere. In the eighties, Watt perfected a reciprocating engine, the governor for smoothing the delivery of power, and, most important of all, a device for converting the lateral thrust of the piston into rotary motion, making it possible to drive spinning mules and other machinery. John Wilkinson, the testy ironmaster-inventor whose machine for boring cannon turned out cylinders for Boulton and Watt, devised ways of using steam power in blast furnaces, hammers, and rolling mills, opening wider markets for the output of the Soho Works, where increasingly the manufacture of engines was centralized. By 1800, after a quarter of a century, more than a thousand engines, of all kinds, were in use, particularly for pumping. Factory use was small until the new century, when most industries were transformed by the new form of power and the ingenuity of the engineers.

These innovations in technology and organization reduced costs and increased efficiency, results that in turn made possible the steady widening of the market at home and abroad. But the factory system was not the only way in which these desirable ends could be reached. Adam Smith had begun his great treatise of 1776, *The Wealth of Nations*, by describing the many stages in manufacturing so simple an article as a pin. He was calling attention to and praising the division of labor; subdividing processes increased both skill and output and occasionally led a highly specialized workman to discover some new technique to increase efficiency still further. This, rather than integration in large factories, was the course followed in the metal trades. In mid-century the great metal-working center of Birmingham was not dominated by factories like the cotton towns; it was a city of small, specialized workshops, an economic characteristic that gave a special flavor to its political radicalism, in contrast to the more proletarian radicalism of the factory towns around Manchester.

The factory drastically changed the way of life of those subject to it. At first, it was sometimes difficult to recruit factory workers. The rural people around a new water-driven factory distrusted and shunned it. Domestic workers did not find factory life attractive either. However bad conditions were in their cottages, however little they earned, even though they might well work longer hours at their loom than they would at a factory machine, they usually preferred to stick to their traditional ways—setting their own pace, tyrannizing over their own children, doing a little farming on the side, cheating their employer as they could not so easily do under the eye of the hated factory supervisor. Factory workers had to be on time; they had to work every day; they had to keep up with the machine; they had, in short, to accept a new and rigorous discipline—commonplace to us, but terrible to the easygoing creatures of a vanished world. Every industrializing society has had to make this painful transition, whether through the constant exhorting, regimentation, and possible banishment to labor camps in the Soviet Union, or the fines, beatings, and blacklisting in early industrial Britain.*

Faced with a reluctant and disruptive casual supply of adult labor, factory owners often turned to children. One source was London, where workhouse masters, with orphan children in large supply, were only too glad to send them off to the factory districts where they were housed in crowded and often unsanitary dormitories, raised in ignorance, and kept working for twelve hours a day. Shocking as the practice seems to modern susceptibilities, it outraged few contemporaries. Rural children went into the fields as soon as they were able to bind or to glean; weavers' children were put to work early, knotting breaks in the yarn. It was thought admirable that children should augment the family income, excellent that they could be kept off the streets and taught something useful. No one thought

---

*There were more subtle devices. The founder of British socialism, Robert Owen, when he was head of the progressive mills at New Lanark in Scotland, invented a "silent monitor"—a four-sided pyramid of wood, fixed to each worker's machine; a different-colored face was turned outward daily to indicate to other workers and to the foreman, who recorded it in a book, the quality of work—and the moral worth—of that worker.

they needed much education—enough to read a bit in the Bible perhaps—and they certainly were not expected to rise above their station in life.

Child labor had important advantages for the employer—cheapness, lack of organization, ease of recruitment and discipline—and, in cotton factories at least, the proportion of children under fourteen seems to have risen by 1835 to about 13 per cent of the labor force, nearly half of which was women and girls. That the system was subject to abuses soon became apparent, but the first, largely futile efforts at regulating it, beginning in 1802, brought a growing humanitarian concern into conflict with the argument of economic necessity. Effective regulation did not come until the 1830's.* ✓

Technological change in a few industries led, then, chiefly through the factory, to a social revolution. But it was a revolution of small proportions until well into the nineteenth century. In 1851—the year of the first census to give us some idea of the occupations of the British people—more than a quarter of all men over the age of twenty were still employed in agriculture. Twice as many men and women worked in domestic service as in the cotton trade, the largest of the industrial occupations. After 70 years of rapid industrial growth, there were barely 80,000 ironworkers. To our industrial age, the industrial problems of the past loom large; they seemed less important to the generation of the Industrial Revolution itself, while to many men charged with policymaking at the national and local levels they were remote and incomprehensible.

Population and the Growth of Towns

Factories and inventions were not the only, or even the principal, source of sweeping economic changes during the reign of George III. The basic fact of social history in these years is the unprecedented growth in population. In 1780, the population of England and Wales was perhaps 7½ million; by 1851 it was 18 million, about two and a half times as great. The first census was taken in 1801, but the sharp rise had begun before there were official figures to prove it, at least as far back as the middle of the eighteenth century.†

*See below, pp. 159, 243–245.
†Gregory King estimated that the 5½ millions in England and Wales in 1695 was about double the population in 1260; he predicted that the next doubling, to 11 million, would be accomplished in about 2300, and the next doubling after that—to 22 million—in 3500 or 3600 "in case the World should last so long." Then it would be capable of no further increase because there would not be enough land to support a larger population. In actuality, the first doubling had taken place by 1815 and the second within another forty years.

Few subjects of historical debate are so important or so uncertain as the causes of this startling development. The foundations and the conclusions of earlier interpretations have been effectively criticized: we know much more than formerly about the defects of the census figures and of the indicators and estimates available before the census. Forty years ago the leading explanation was a falling death rate, due largely to improvements in medicine, but confidence in that theory has been seriously shaken. Eighteenth-century discoveries may have begun the evolution of modern scientific medical practice, but, except for vaccination at the very end of the century, it is argued, the new doctors were not much better at saving life than were adherents of the older pragmatic medicine. Improvements in public health and sanitation certainly had a positive impact, but in the fifties and sixties, historians tended to look more to factors that contributed to lowering the age of marriage, to producing more children per family, to an increase in fertility and in the birth rate: the decline of apprenticeship; the changing social structure in the countryside, the operation of the poor law, changing preferences in family size. Now the pendulum has swung back once more, and skepticism about the causal role of mortality is less confident. But until more detailed local studies are undertaken and the methods of family reconstitution more widely applied, the debate about causes, and even about indicators must remain problematical.

The one thing certain is the fact of the population explosion itself. Small wonder that in 1798 a young clergyman named Thomas Robert Malthus formulated a law of population which predicted that population would increase in geometrical progression, while the food supply could increase only in arithmetic progression, thus putting a natural limit to the growth of population, for the oversupply would perish through vice and misery. In the second edition of his *Essay on the Principle of Population,* five years later, Malthus suggested a way out—the practice of "moral restraint," i.e., refraining from marriage and "irregular gratifications" until a family could be supported. But the gloomy conclusions of the first edition took hold in popular opinion (at least among the upper classes) and helped to transform economics, which had been suffused with Smithian optimism, into "the dismal science."

The larger population was also differently distributed. Historians earlier in this century, taking their lead from Karl Marx, saw the changes in agriculture as a necessary precondition of industrialism: enclosures made possible greater food production to feed the masses in the new towns and drove people from the land into the factories. The relationship between improving agricultural output and a growing population is far more complex than this simple explanation suggests, while enclosure did not necessarily produce an uprooted class. On certain kinds of soil, or where conversion to pasture was involved, it might do so; but, as we have seen, it could also multiply jobs. Studies of migration have shown that there was no wholesale transfer of population from the agricultural south to the industrial north. While in time the rural population grew beyond the capacity of the rural economy to absorb it, the surplus became chiefly a problem for the poor-law authorities and not a source for filling the towns and factories. When migrants came to towns—and some industrial areas drew more than others—they tended to come from the immediately surrounding and already tributary countryside; only London, always a consumer of workers, drew migrants from long distances. But even such short-range rural migration provided only a small proportion of town populations; despite the unhealthiness of town life, they grew primarily by their own natural increase. The only significant external immigration came from Ireland, where population had increased at an even more rapid rate than in England, and where the land system, by permitting almost perpetual subdivision, came close to imposing the stark alternatives of emigration or starvation. At first, the Irish came to England as migrant labor— for harvesting or for temporary employment in building canals. But more and more of them stayed, and, accustomed as they were to a lower standard of living and lower wages, they seemed to pose a terrible threat to English workers, who looked on them with hostility and contempt.*

Early in the eighteenth century, half a million people lived in London; only two other English towns—Bristol and Norwich—had more than 20,000 inhabitants; and no more than 13 per cent of the population of Great Britain lived in aggregates of more than 5,000 persons. Birmingham, a village in the seventeenth century, more than quadrupled its population between 1675 and 1760, and doubled it again by the end of the century; Manchester trebled its numbers in the thirty years before 1800; and, by 1851, half the population of the country lived in towns. In one town after another, this rapid growth strained inherited instruments for coping with men's needs—local government, the poor law, housing, sanitation, police. It helped to increase social tensions, and the more so in those towns (mainly port cities) where the Irish arrived and often stayed. Apologists for the early Victorian factory owners sometimes tried to stave off state regu-

*There was a small but important Jewish immigration in the eighteenth century. In 1734 the Jewish population of England was estimated at 6,000; by 1800 there were perhaps 15,000 to 20,000 Jews in London alone and 5,000–6,000 elsewhere.

lation by insisting that the real social problem of the country lay not in the factories but in the towns. If one can discount the self-interest that lay behind the argument, there was much truth in it: growing towns were the greatest challenge faced by modern Britain.

The Pattern of Economic Growth

The upsurge in population was not without its benefits. There seem to have been two periods of marked economic expansion in the eighteenth century—one in the 1740's and 1750's, the other (after which the impetus was sustained) in the 1780's; the correlation with upsurges in population is remarkably close. Increased numbers relieved the labor shortages that had worried informed Englishmen since the seventeenth century; but, more important, the larger population and its growing concentration in towns increased demand, not merely for the products of England's manufacturers and artisans, but for imported commodities. A rise in English imports, in turn, gave suppliers abroad the credits they needed to increase their purchases of English goods. The export trade had flourished throughout the early eighteenth century without bringing about any remarkable leaps forward in the English economy. But the growing export trade and the newly expanding domestic market after mid-century together stimulated the quest for higher production and lower costs and so contributed to technical and organizational innovation. Other factors besides population growth and its concomitants, of course, helped to determine the pattern of growth at any given time— agricultural improvement; the incidence of good and bad harvests and their complex effects on prices and incomes; the fluctuations of the economy; the rate of interest; and the distortions, scarcities, and opportunities that came with the French wars. The amalgam is difficult to analyze. But merely to list the forces at work is a healthy reminder that the Industrial Revolution grew as much from circumstances inherent in the eighteenth-century economy as it did from the impulses we tend to associate with a new industrial era.

The Entrepreneurs

The economic revolutions of the reign of George III were brought about through the decisions of thousands of individuals, weighing the present and future state of the country, and the prospects it held for them. The business practices of the late eighteenth century were very much of a piece with those of earlier decades. Joint-stock organization was forbidden by the Bubble Act of 1720, except by consent of Parliament or by royal charter; but, in any event, few enterprises were large enough to require sweeping so widely for capital. Most firms could be financed at the outset from savings, mortgages, or sales of land, or by pooling resources, often of men of moderate wealth, in partnerships. The organized capital market existed to serve commercial enterprises, not industry, though the rapid growth of country banks in the late eighteenth century provided a flexible means for bringing surplus capital into the hands of those who could put it profitably to work. Once in existence, firms could continue and expand by the same means, and perhaps most successfully of all by resolutely ploughing back profits.

In every industry there were a few big firms with great resources — the Strutt and Arkwright combinations in cotton, the Marshalls in flax, Boulton and Watt in engineering — but many more small firms operated on a shoestring. If the equipment of a small manufacturer was old and inefficient (it was often bought secondhand from a more progressive firm), the margin had to be made up by low wages and long hours. Working conditions like these did not seem unjust to the entrepreneur, who himself might well work sixteen or eighteen hours a day managing the plant, getting orders, trying to assess the state of the market or to guess the turn of fashion; even the wealthiest businessmen in England worked hard at such activities. When jobs were hard to get, the most tight-fisted employer was in some sense a benefactor of his workmen; for if a firm failed, there might be no place to go except the workhouse. And there were many failures. With narrow margins, with the state of trade uncertain, with the terrifying impact of the business cycle, many firms went under, some to be reborn in new combinations, some to disappear (with their owners' savings) forever.

The successful men showed it: they improved, retooled, and expanded their factories or extended their activities into allied, or even quite tangential, fields such as banking. Some of the more enlightened set up schools, model villages, recreation facilities, and chapels for their workpeople. More engaged in some sort of humanitarian or religious activity that could give them status in the eyes of their fellow citizens. They educated their sons to be gentlemen. In some towns they were able to penetrate the ruling oligarchy; in others they were contemptuously excluded. In a few cases, they helped to beautify their towns; more often, they made them uglier by building over open spaces and by the smoke and waste from their factories. It must be said, however, that given the need for housing, the shortage of capital, civic inaction, and a lack of urban transport, it is hard to see how they could have solved town-planning problems that we today, with infinitely greater resources, find almost insuperable.

Still, the very men who built or spoiled these towns did what they could to meet the challenges as they understood them. Pressing from the outside against entrenched and narrow oligarchies, manufacturers often formed alliances with the liberal element among the merchants to agitate for reform, not only to gain power and recognition but to do what they saw needed doing—light the streets, set up police, pave and drain, promote religion and culture, and make their towns something to be proud of. The reign of George III saw the multiplication in provincial towns of a curious assortment of institutions: some were political or administrative, such as improvement commissioners or sewer authorities; some were charitable, such as orphanages and dispensaries; some were cultural, such as literary and philosophical societies. These decades were the great age of provincial culture, when merchant wealth was extensive and settled, when ambitious men were making their way intellectually as well as economically, and when the towns were far enough away from London to be independent and proud enough to look up to no one. The makers of a new society, these men were quite sure of what they were doing: they had goals, ambitions, and a glimpse of indefinite progress. And their assumptions were simple enough to make these ends seem attainable.

THE REVOLUTIONS IN UNDERSTANDING

Hume and Bentham

Engineers, entrepreneurs, and overseers were not the only agents who brought a new quality or tone to British life during George's reign. Other men, many of whom never saw a factory or a mine—writers, artists, philosophers, and preachers—were finding new urgencies, new and radically different ways of looking at themselves and the world, and were communicating their discoveries throughout society. Historians, true to their labeling nature, have found memorable tags for different aspects of this transformation—the Romantic Revolution, the Evangelical Revival, and so on—names that often hide more than they reveal or that serve as substitutes for thought and analysis. Still, they reflect profound realities that did as much to determine men's thoughts and actions as any changes in the economy.

Intellectually, the eighteenth century, as we have seen, was dominated by the accomplishments of Sir Isaac Newton. Much of the scientific activity of the time amounted to little more than working out the consequences of his insights or (more fruitfully) trying to extend his methods to refractory areas of individual and social behavior. While physics rested complacently on its laurels of certainty, and the

Royal Society declined into a pleasant intellectual club for dilettanti, considerable advances were made in laying foundations for the study of economics and psychology. David Hume and Adam Smith were the major figures in the former, David Hartley in the latter. But for all the elegant simplicities and confident explanations of mid-eighteenth-century thought, its philosophers, following a rigorous logic from their assumptions, were critical not only of the jumble of inherited institutions and dogmas but of some of their own most cherished beliefs.

Beyond any question the most important single figure in mid-eighteenth-century British philosophy was the genial Scotsman David Hume. Able to turn his critical mind to almost every subject, from economics to morals to history, he was at his most devastating when applying his subtle intelligence to the apparent certainties in which most of his fellow critics found refuge—the comforting security of natural religion, and the reliance on causality that underlay the scientific faith of the time. Even when Hume refrained from making his skepticism explicit, it was impossible for his readers to miss its implications: it seemed as though he had demolished any grounds for intellectual certainty in either religion or science. Hume took his own corrosiveness placidly enough: in irrational characteristics like feeling and habit he found meaning in life and reasonable security that one social phenomenon would follow on another to which it seemed "causally" related; he simply did not need the comforts of religion. But it was not so easy for less securely planted people to accept his conclusions without protest.

Hume's effect on British (or, indeed, European) thought was rather like the impact of George III's intentions on English politicians or Grenville's imperial reforms on the Americans: he forced men to rethink their positions, provoking them into more effective restatements or into new and radical departures. The shock that Hume gave to an obscure German metaphysician named Immanuel Kant, leading him to undertake his seminal reconstruction in philosophy, was hardly less in Hume's own island, though his countrymen remained long immune to the solutions provided by the German philosophers. An important Scottish "common sense" school, led by Thomas Reid, broke with the Lockean tradition and turned to a kind of intuitionism of considerable influence in the nineteenth century. Other thinkers fell back on firmer reassertions of orthodoxy. But Hume did not have his sole effect in encouraging contrary views. Some men were ready to take up his critical attitude and carry it further.

The most important of these disciples was Jeremy Bentham. A child prodigy, Bentham was destined by his father for the law; but in his early teens, while he was a student at Oxford, his acute mind rebelled at the intellectual complacencies he was fed, most of all at the confident but intellectually slipshod panegyrics of Sir William Blackstone's *Commentaries on the Laws of England* (1765–1769), only recently published but already a classic. Casting about for intellectual support, Bentham raided the works of British, French, and Italian *philosophes* to produce an idiosyncratic amalgam which, in its ultimate effects, went far towards making the world a different place. From Hume, whose critical attitude he shared, he drew the essential test of utility as the basis for morals; but he went far beyond Hume in insisting that one need not accept the world as one found it. For Bentham was, as Hume was certainly not, a congenital reformer. He found the stimulus to this side of his thought in Continental writers, most notably Helvétius, a French philosopher who emphasized the central role of legislation, and Beccaria, an Italian penal reformer. Bentham was also a thorough devotee of the fashionable "associationist" psychology of Locke and Hartley. Believing that men acted as they did because they sought pleasure and avoided pain, he developed a view of human nature that was remarkably effective as a basis for reforming legislation, however oversimple or defective it may have been as a general moral philosophy.

His great aim in life was, as he would have said, to maximize happiness. His instrument was the law, guided by pleasure-pain psychology and the test of utility. Bentham's thought was thoroughly secular and ahistorical. Of every law and institution he asked, simply, does it work, does it contribute to "the greatest happiness of the greatest number," and if not, given the ways in which men inevitably act, what laws or institutions must be substituted? In his belief that the legislator holds the key to human happiness, Bentham stands in striking contrast to Adam Smith, who contended that men left to their own best interests would automatically bring about good—a contrast effectively summed up in two phrases of the great French historian Elie Halévy: the artificial identification of interests *versus* the natural identification of interests.

Bentham's direct influence was a long time in taking effect. Gifted with an extraordinarily restless and in some ways childlike mind, Bentham wrote much and published little in his early years. The *Fragment on Government* of 1776 was an attack on Blackstone, the *Introduction to the Principles of Morals and Legislation* of 1789 a preliminary statement of his views. But in pamphlets and through conversation he had gained by the early 1800's a powerful reputation among men interested in the reform of the law, and at his death in 1832 he was recognized as one of the most influential intellects of his time. The exact nature and extent of that influence remains a subject of controversy: but, whatever the outcome of that debate, he was one of the seminal minds of his time and perhaps our clearest reminder that much of the most creative thought of the new century and the new society was done — by Bentham and by people who, working from different sources and assumptions, reached similar conclusions — in obedience to eighteenth-century canons of enlightened thought.*

The New Sensibility *Romanticism*

At the same time, however, there was a growing rebellion against that way of thinking. Again one can see the roots of it in eighteenth-century thinkers themselves — in Hume's emphasis on feeling, for example. By the sixties a good many people found the rationality and resolute classicism of the preceding generation too cold and formal for their tastes. There grew up a "cult of sensibility," popularized in novels like Richardson's *Pamela* and *Clarissa Harlowe* or Mackenzie's *The Man of Feeling*. For a generation or more, strong men wept openly and embraced each other; ladies fainted and suffered from "excessive sensibilities." The "Gothic" novelists — Horace Walpole, "Monk" Lewis, and Mrs. Ann Radcliffe are the best known — appealed to other tastes by parceling out mystery, passion, and horror *Gothic* in medieval settings. More sophisticated men and women developed an awareness of and a sentimentalized respect for exotic people — Chinese and Indian sages, red and black savages, and noble peasantry. And at the same time, men responded with new emotion to wild, untended scenery. The early eighteenth-century preoccupation with the regularity and proportion that characterized "beauty" was supplemented, and at times almost submerged, by a new fascination with the picturesque and the "sublime" — the aesthetic category that encompasses awe and terror. Mountainous parts of the country once avoided as horrid and ugly became admired and fashionable: the pilgrimages to the highlands had begun.

This revolution in sensibility was intensified and carried further by developments in the arts. In architecture there was a revival of interest in Gothic, one aspect of a widening and sometimes eccentric eclecticism that showed itself in an enthusiasm for ruins (often carefully constructed by cooperative landscape gardeners) or in such individual fantasies as Horace Walpole's Gothic villa at Strawberry Hill, William Beckford's Fonthill Abbey, or the Prince Regent's improbably Oriental and oddly lovely pavilion at Brighton. Public building, however, remained loyal to classical forms, and such

*See below, pp. 181–186.

Gothic restoration as was done to cathedrals, most frequently by James Wyatt, the architect of Fonthill Abbey, was likely to be disastrous.

The reign of George III was a great period in British painting, dominated by the grand classical lines of portraitists such as Reynolds, Gainsborough, Romney, and Lawrence. But early in the new century, the East Anglian landscape painters, John Constable, John Crome, and J. S. Cotman, showed a growing concern with light and atmosphere paralleled and carried further in the work of J. M. W. Turner, the greatest nineteenth-century English painter, in whose later canvases forms quite dissolve into light and air. By the end of the reign classically oriented "historical" painting was vying—often in the same artists, most notably in the Scot Sir David Wilkie—with "genre" painting, scenes often from humble life, preparing the way for Victorian sentimentality.

Most striking of all were adventures into entirely new realms of artistic awareness, penetrating the recesses of consciousness to attain visions expressible only in private symbols—devices virtually unknown in painting since the time of artists like Hieronymus Bosch in the late Middle Ages. The work of the poet and painter William Blake reflects a new sensibility with an especial appeal to our own times. Hating England's "dark Satanic mills" and certain of the possibility of building a new Jerusalem in her green and pleasant land, Blake wholeheartedly rejected classicism, Newtonianism, and materialism for a mysticism of his own formulation and an absolute conviction in the rightness of his inner vision.

In literature a closely parallel development took place. In the sixties and seventies the preoccupation with the exotic and savage was reflected in Macpherson's poems, passed off as those of the legendary Celtic bard Ossian, and in Bishop Percy's famous collection of old ballads. The Scot Robert Burns and the East Anglian George Crabbe celebrated ordinary or ordinarily forgotten men in poetry, in Crabbe's case with an intensity and range of psychological implication that has made him of great interest to the twentieth century. In 1798 William Wordsworth and Samuel Taylor Coleridge, the most famous of the so-called Lake poets, in the preface to their *Lyrical Ballads*, issued a manifesto of the new poetry, concerned with a deeper appreciation of reality, perceived with an intense inner and individual awareness and expressed without the limitations of classical forms in a language free from the artifices and rhetoric so dear to the preceding generation.

The romantics looked backward and inward. Though his best work dealt with the eighteenth century, Sir Walter Scott, among the most professional and successful of writers, reconstructed medieval

England and sixteenth-century Scotland so powerfully that his genial
but morally serious "Gothicizing" became one of the most potent
cultural influences of the first half of the new century. The second
generation of romantic poets, headed by Keats, Shelley, and Byron,
carried the intensity of personal feeling yet further. Shelley and
Byron adopted a radicalism far beyond the innocent communism affected for a time by the Lake poets, and in Byron the romantic temper
culminated in a grandeur of action and a style of life that affected a
whole generation in Europe, as far afield as Russia.

In this feverish and creative confluence of artistic currents, much
of the promise and difficulty of the new world are evident. Men's
sensibility was immeasurably widened; ranges of natural and psychological facts and orders of truth, until then unknown, became apparent. Culturally, the new century was infinitely richer, headier,
and more exciting than the old. But, however widely extended the
new awareness and the new rhetoric, a great price was paid for this
richness and insight. The ordered world of earlier culture was lost.
External criteria gave way to internal; forms came not from tradition
but from the act of creation itself. And as order and security of taste
gave way, so did unity. A world being made more complex and interdependent by industry and science was, culturally, becoming more
diffuse and divided.

The revolutionary changes that we sum up in the term *romanticism* did not at once have such sweeping consequences. As with any
great change in cultural style, it took time for new ways of seeing
things to become assimilated — a generation perhaps before romantic
rhetoric reached down to the level of popular culture, and yet another
generation before the anarchic effects of a newly complex intellectual
life became obvious. But the importance of this revolution was
masked in another way — by the change in tone flowing from a
religious revival and by an accompanying seriousness that rapidly
penetrated into almost every corner of British life.

The Religious Revival

In 1760, John Wesley was at the height of his remarkable career.* His
emphasis on the sense of sin and on the necessity of personal conversion was responsible for a new intensity and sobriety among many
people in the lower-middle and working classes, but the revivalistic
manifestations and "enthusiasm" associated with the movement
continued to breed distrust or hatred among the more prosperous
and educated members of the Anglican Church with which Wesley

*On Wesley's early life, see above, p. 39.

still claimed communion. Even before Wesley's death in 1791, Methodism was beginning to separate itself from the Established Church, and the break became more nearly definitive after 1795 when the Wesleyan Conference authorized the administration of Holy Communion, which Methodists had until then always taken in an Anglican church. The Wesleyan Connection, the main branch under Wesley's successor Jabez Bunting, continued to insist on the irrelevance of politics and the sinfulness of trying to change institutions, an attitude which, it has been powerfully argued, was transmitted to a crucial portion of the population, helping to immunize them against revolutionary fervor. This argument has been criticized in detail, especially in view of the steady fragmentation of Methodism to the left, where new, politically radical sects appeared. But there is no question that the general effect of Methodist teaching was to concentrate the main attention of its adherents on their own lives and that, as a result, it made for discipline and good order—in striking contrast to the calumnies circulated about it by those complacent churchmen who could neither understand nor tolerate it.

An increasing number of adherents of the Church of England, however, could not take so superior an attitude, either to Methodism or to the profound spiritual problems it wrestled with. Within the Church of England, there grew rapidly in these years a movement to which the name Evangelical has been attached. Partly a response to the challenge of Methodism, partly a reaction against the easy and cold certitudes of official eighteenth-century religion, Evangelicalism, like Methodism, emphasized the sense of sin, the weakness of man without God, the profound psychological experience of conversion, and dedication to service.

The most famous group of Evangelicals was the Clapham Sect, named after the village southwest of London, where many of its leaders lived, especially the wealthy banking family of the Thorntons. The rector of Clapham, John Venn, was the spiritual leader of the Claphamites; they drew theological support from Cambridge scholars like Charles Simeon and Isaac Milner; and they included among them an important politician, William Wilberforce, a close friend of William Pitt and a young man of society who was converted in 1785. Wilberforce remained the chief Evangelical spokesman in Parliament down to 1825 and carried through the greatest social reform associated with them—the abolition of the slave trade in 1807. But other causes engaged their attention too: amendment of the law, education, strict observance of the Sabbath, the improvement of manners, and the suppression of vice. Conservative in political outlook—as became those to whom political questions could not be central—and accepting the hierarchical assumptions and prejudices of nearly all of the upper classes of their time, the Claphamites have not drawn

much sympathy from later generations: they have seemed too superior, too stiff, too callous when it came to other abuses of their time,
such as child labor. But we have learned in recent years to judge them
in their own context, to understand a narrowness of vision that few
could then have escaped, and to know that in this circle there was an
intellectual liberality and a sense of dedication that stand to the ever-
lasting credit of serious religion.

The same can be said of the activities of another evangelical,
Hannah More. A prominent blue-stocking, as the intellectual ladies
of her time were called, she wrote poetry and a couple of plays that
had considerable success. But in the eighties she was converted and
put the fashionable world behind her; with her four sisters, she
devoted herself to good works in the Mendip Hills south of Bristol—
relieving the poor, founding schools, and writing improving (and
rather dreary) tales and ballads to wean poor readers away from dangerous books. By the nineties, the Evangelicals had a friend in the hierarchy in the Bishop of London, Beilby Porteus; their activities and
organizations had grown apace with their numbers. The widespread
founding of Sunday schools, to teach the poor to read, was primarily
an Evangelical activity, dating from the 1770's. Evangelical organizations like the Church Missionary Society and the British and Foreign
Bible Society stimulated the reinvigoration and rivalry of older
Anglican bodies, the Society for Promoting Christian Knowledge
and the Society for Propagation of the Gospel in Foreign Parts, and,
through Bishop Heber, the Evangelicals made a vital contribution to
missionary enterprise in India.

At the same time that Evangelicalism was directly or indirectly
transforming the Church of England, a similar spirit was taking hold
in the Dissenting congregations. While the English Presbyterians
were rapidly turning Unitarian and advancing enlightened philosophical and religious views that were anything but Evangelical, the
Congregationalists and Baptists were turning away from their Cal-
vinistic heritage to a new brand (for them) of experiential religion,
akin to Methodism and Evangelicalism—fundamentalist in theology
and active in good works. There was considerable interdenomina-
tional cooperation, not merely to secure civil liberties or grants of
privilege, as had been the case earlier in the century, but for missionary enterprise, Bible and tract distribution, and agitation against
slavery. The Dissenters, however, suffered from political discrimination and a sense of social inferiority, and tended to remain apart
from the mainstream of English life, except in certain towns where
they had the advantage of numbers. Their time was to come in the
thirties and forties of the nineteenth century; meanwhile, the greatest changes in social tone were brought about by Methodists and
Evangelical churchmen.

The Reformation of Manners

Travelers returning to England in the nineties, after a long absence, professed surprise at the numbers of carriages driving to and from churches on Sunday mornings. It was easy to explain the phenomenon as a reaction to the French Revolution. But the eighteenth century had never been lacking in moral seriousness; strengthened by the steadily growing humanitarian impulse, this seriousness had produced, early in the reign of George III, the efforts of Captain Coram and Jonas Hanway to relieve the lot of orphans, foundlings, prostitutes, and chimney sweeps, and of John Howard to reform the wretched conditions in English prisons, which were among the worst in Europe. For a century to come, these men, Howard especially, and others like them had the stature of heroes to many worried, strenuously moral Englishmen.

The sexual obsession of Boswell or Wilkes, and the reckless gambling and drinking, endemic and even increasing among some of the upper classes, marked a way of life that was already seen to be passing by the last decade of the century. Smoking largely disappeared; people increasingly kept Sabbath; drunkenness, though it remained a national vice, seems to have declined. Early in the new century, wigs gave way to hair powder and then to natural hair; knee breeches were replaced by sober, utilitarian trousers. The days, two generations before, when women liked a "fatt storie" as much as men, were gone; and the new morality found its most extreme expression in the works of Dr. Thomas Bowdler, whose name has become the verb "bowdlerize," because in 1818 he published an expurgated *Family Shakespeare*. What we call "Victorianism" long antedates Victoria.

In *Orlando*, a tour de force by the twentieth-century novelist Virginia Woolf, a long metaphor describes a climatic change that came over England at the beginning of the nineteenth century — an all-pervading cold and damp that turned men inward, chilled their minds, bred hypocrisy, and ruined style in language and life. It is a stunning indictment by a writer, descended from a great evangelical family, who belonged to a generation that had broken away from a century of respectability and that hated what they had left behind. But it is possible, indeed necessary, to look at this cultural change more positively — to admit that much in the callousness and excess of eighteenth-century society was hateful and had to be swept away by a new seriousness, which, whatever its faults, carried with it a new humanity and an insistence on enforcing it. By 1789 many people had a glimpse of a better world, and they saw a multitude of competing ways to attain it. Some found the answer in politics, some in

fast & loose 18th c.
gives way to prim & proper 19th

religion, some in humanitarian activity, some in industry and trade. Ferment in a society may go on making gradual changes, or it may be suddenly speeded up by some external challenge or catastrophe. The latter happened in England, because of the revolution in France.

Selected Readings

T. S. Ashton's remarkable brief history, *The Industrial Revolution, 1760–1830* (1948, rev. ed. 1964) is still worth reading. More recent summary interpretations are Phyllis Deane, *The First Industrial Revolution* (1965) and Peter Mathias, *The First Industrial Nation: An Economic History of Britain, 1700–1914* (1969). David S. Landes contributed "Technological Change and Development in Western Europe, 1750–1914" to the *Cambridge Economic History of Europe*, vol. 6, part 1 (1965), pp. 274–585, and he later expanded this essay into a full-scale history, *The Unbound Prometheus: Technological Change and Industrial Development in Western Europe from 1750 to the Present* (1969). M. W. Flinn, *Origins of the Industrial Revolution* (1966) is both a valuable interpretative sketch and a historiographical commentary.

The improvements in Britain's roads are dealt with extensively in William Albert, *The Turnpike Road System in England, 1663–1840* (1972) and, from a geographer's perspective, in Eric Pawson, *Transport and Economy: The Turnpike Roads of Eighteenth-Century Britain* (1977). Canals have been even more fully examined of late. Two books by T. S. Willan deal with water transport in the pre-canal age: *River Navigation in England, 1600–1750* (1936) and *The English Coasting Trade, 1600–1750* (1938). The Duke of Bridgewater is the subject of Hugh Malet, *The Canal Duke* (1961), while the engineers figure largely in Anthony Burton, *The Canal Builders* (1972). J. R. Ward, in *The Finance of Canal Building in Eighteenth-Century England* (1974), examines the social, economic, and geographical sources of investment, while the impact on towns, old and new, is studied in J. Douglas Porteous, *Canal Ports: The Urban Achievement of the Canal Age* (1977).

The older sanguine and polemical view of the course of English agriculture is well put in Lord Ernle, *English Farming, Past and Present* (1912), which was brought out in a sixth edition, with extensive commentary to supply the necessary correction, by G. E. Fussell and O. R. McGregor in 1961. The most recent general assessment is J. D. Chambers and G. E. Mingay, *The Agricultural Revolution, 1750–1880* (1966), but it must be read in the light of the argument about periodization in F. M. L. Thompson, "The Second Agricultural Revolution, 1815–1880," *Economic History Review*, 2nd ser., vol. 21, pp. 62–77 (April 1968). R. A. C. Parker, *Coke of Norfolk: A Financial and Agricultural Study, 1707–1842* (1975) is a more detailed and accurate assessment of the contributions of that great landlord than earlier enthusiastic accounts.

The industrial revolution itself can be seen most strikingly in the history of two industries. M. M. Edwards, *The Growth of the British Cotton Trade, 1780–1815* (1967) is a valuable study, while the impact on a famous sector of labor is treated, with impressive revisionism, in Duncan Bythell, *The Handloom Weavers: A Study in the English Cotton Industry During the Industrial Rev-*

olution (1969). The most celebrated of the cotton masters are the subjects of R.
S. Fitton and A. P. Wadsworth, *The Strutts and the Arkwrights, 1758–1830*
(1958). On the other, very different industry, T. S. Ashton's classic *Iron and
Steel in the Industrial Revolution* (1924) has been qualified in an important
way in Charles K. Hyde, *Technological Change and the British Iron Industry,
1700–1870* (1977). On a very large *early* eighteenth-century iron business, M.
W. Flinn, *Men of Iron: The Crowleys in the Early Iron Industry* (1962). There are
many histories of other industries and industrial towns, which make clear
the varying characteristics in a complex picture, for example: T. C. Barker and
J. R. Harris, *A Merseyside Town in the Industrial Revolution: St. Helens, 1750–
1900* (1954); J. D. Chambers, *Nottingham in the Eighteenth Century* (1932); John
Prest, *The Industrial Revolution in Coventry* (1960); D. C. Coleman, *The British
Paper Industry, 1495–1860: A Study in Industrial Growth* (1958); W. H. B. Court,
The Rise of the Midland Industries, 1600–1838 (1938), on Birmingham and the
Black Country; Eric Roll, *An Early Experiment in Industrial Organization* (1930),
on the firm of Boulton and Watt. W. H. B. Court, "Industrial Organization
and Economic Progress in the Eighteenth-Century Midlands," *Transactions
of the Royal Historical Society*, 4th ser., vol. 28, pp. 85–99 (1946), reprinted in
his *Scarcity and Choice in Economic History* (1970), is an important explication
of an alternative to factory organization in the quest for industrial efficiency
and productivity. A. E. Musson and Eric Robinson, *Science and Technology in
the Industrial Revolution* (1969) not only has much to say about that problematical link but also devotes a number of chapters to the history of engineering. Other major firms in industrial history are dealt with in W. G. Rimmer,
Marshalls of Leeds, Flax-Spinners, 1788–1886 (1960); George Unwin, *Samuel
Oldknow and the Arkwrights* (1924); A. Raistrick, *Dynasty of Ironfounders: The
Darbys and Coalbrookdale* (1953), though on this subject see Hyde's book
mentioned above. Neil McKendrick's article, "Josiah Wedgwood: An Eighteenth-Century Entrepreneur in Salesmanship and Marketing Techniques,"
Economic History Review, 2nd ser., vol. 12, pp. 408–433 (April, 1960), and
reprinted in E. M. Carus-Wilson, ed., *Essays in Economic History*, vol. 3 (1962),
pp. 353–379, points to a departure that is not strictly industrial or technological. On all this, see the important retrospective cautions against too
ready generalization from the early industrial giants to all entrepreneurs in
P. L. Payne, *British Entrepreneurship in the Nineteenth Century* (1974), which
anticipates his chapter, "Industrial Entrepreneurship and Management in
Great Britain," in Peter Mathias and M. M. Postan, eds., *Cambridge Economic
History of Europe*, vol. 7, part 1 (1978), pp. 180–230.

The best brief introduction to the population factor is M. W. Flinn, *Brit-
ish Population Growth, 1700–1850* (1970). Some of the major articles that have
contributed to the debate are reprinted in part 2 of D. V. Glass and D. E. C.
Eversley, eds., *Population in History* (1965) or appear in E. A. Wrigley, ed., *An
Introduction to English Historical Demography* (1966). Arthur Redford, *Labour
Migration in England, 1800–1850* (1926, 2nd edn., 1964), remains indispens-
able, and on the relation between agricultural and industrial areas, see J. D.
Chambers, "Enclosure and Labour Supply in the Industrial Revolution,"
Economic History Review, 2nd ser., vol. 5, pp. 319–343 (1953), reprinted in
Glass and Eversley, cited above, pp. 308–327. Interpretation of the popula-

tion figures plays an important part in the patterning proposed by Phyllis Deane and W. A. Cole, *British Economic Growth, 1688–1959* (1962), a book that must be reckoned with for all of modern English economic history. On the approach to the industrial revolution, see also T. S. Ashton, *An Economic History of England: The 18th Century* (1955) and *Economic Fluctuations in England, 1700–1800* (1959), and Eric Pawson, *The Early Industrial Revolution: Britain in the 18th Century* (1979).

On the transformation of towns, C. W. Chalklin, *The Provincial Towns of Georgian England: A Study of the Building Process, 1740–1820* (1975), and the tentative assessment, in an international context, by M. J. Daunton, "Towns and Economic Growth in Eighteenth-Century England," in Philip Abrams and E. A. Wrigley, eds., *Towns in Societies: Essays in Economic History and Historical Sociology* (1978), pp. 245–277. Arnold Thackray examines the Literary and Philosophical Society of Manchester in "Natural Knowledge in Cultural Context: The Manchester Model," *American Historical Review*, vol. 79, pp. 672–709 (June, 1974), while an equally famous philosophical society is the subject of Robert E. Schofield, *The Lunar Society of Birmingham* (1963).

The key philosopher for the late eighteenth century is dealt with in Norman Kemp Smith, *The Philosophy of David Hume* (1949); J. A. Passmore, *Hume's Intentions* (1952); and Duncan Forbes, *Hume's Philosophical Politics* (1975), while Hume's transition from philosopher to historian is explored in Victor G. Wexler, *David Hume and the History of England* (1979). On other Scottish thinkers, Anand Chitnis, *The Scottish Enlightenment: A Social History* (1976) and S. A. Grave, *The Scottish Philosophers of Common Sense* (1960). The best introduction to Bentham is D. J. Manning, *The Mind of Jeremy Bentham* (1968), but the magisterial work remains Elie Halévy, *The Growth of Philosophic Radicalism* (1901–1904, trans. 1928).

The transformation in taste that contributed to the emergence of romanticism can begin with Edmund Burke's landmark in esthetic theory, *An Essay on the Sublime and the Beautiful* (1756), but modern writers who have dealt with it are Samuel Monk, *The Sublime: A Study of Critical Theories in 18th-Century England* (1935); Marjorie H. Nicolson, *Mountain Gloom and Mountain Glory: The Development of the Aesthetics of the Infinite* (1959); Esther Moir, *The Discovery of Britain: The English Tourists, 1590–1848* (1964); and Walter Jackson Bate, *Classic to Romantic: Premises of Taste in Eighteenth-Century England* (1946). Emery Neff, *A Revolution in European Poetry, 1660–1900* (1941) places the Romantic writers in a broad European context.

On Methodism, see the works mentioned in the bibliography for the Introduction. For its later course, Robert Currie, *Methodism Divided: A Study in the Sociology of Ecumenicalism* (1968). The most extensive, though still controversial, study of the Clapham Sect is Ford K. Brown, *Fathers of the Victorians* (1961). There are some admirable biographical studies: M. G. Jones, *Hannah More* (1952): Standish Meacham, *Henry Thornton of Clapham, 1763–1815* (1963); Robin Furneaux, *William Wilberforce* (1974); and John Pollock, *Wilberforce* (1977); while the novelist E. M. Forster has drawn an admirable picture of life in Clapham in his biography of his great-great-aunt, *Marianne Thornton* (1956). On the reformation of manners, M. J. Quinlan, *Victorian Prelude* (1941).

Chapter 3
The French Revolution

1789–1815

VERSAILLES TO AMIENS, 1789–1802

The English Reaction

The French Revolution began in May, 1789, when the British were still celebrating the centenary of their own revolution. It seemed only appropriate that the kingdom across the Channel should at last copy those English liberal institutions French writers had so long admired. But not all British reactions were complacent. Some men found the sweeping nature of French reconstruction exhilarating, proclaimed as it was in the ringing declarations of principle so attractive to eighteenth-century convictions. English reformers awoke to new activity. By 1791, Major Cartwright and his friends had again plunged into the work of the Society for Constitutional Information; early in 1792, Charles James Fox encouraged some young Whigs to form the Society of the Friends of the People, to work for liberal principles that he continued to defend to his death. Some strong spirits drew sterner morals from France. In a famous address given late in 1789, Dr. Richard Price, the liberal Dissenter, concluded that in gaining their liberties the French had underlined the lesson of 1689 — that the people, as the true source of power, reserved the right to choose their governors, "to cashier them for misconduct," and to institute a new form of government.

This interpretation of the English and French revolutions was attacked by Edmund Burke in one of the most brilliant political broadsides ever composed, the *Reflections on the Revolution in France*, published in November, 1790. Rejecting the simplistic contractual view of Price and the reformers, Burke invoked a more profound and mystical contract between past and future generations to justify a conservative interpretation of 1689 and to condemn the events in France. Burke's diatribe, at the time of its publication, expressed a distinctly minority view; yet the book was more than an alarmist tract. Building on his reverence for tradition and on his awareness of the deep complexity of society, Burke produced a statement of conservative political theory vital to all subsequent political thought. The more immediate political result was an open break with Fox in May, 1791, irreparably splitting the opposition group he had tried so hard to weld into a true political party. Before long, Burke's views gained more and more adherents. Mob violence in Paris reminded Englishmen of their own endemic unrest and of the Gordon Riots. When Louis XVI was executed, they were horrified, forgetting what had happened to Charles I a century and a half before; and highborn French refugees were in London, sedulously cultivating the makers of opinion and policy, and putting in the worst possible light events they could neither understand nor forgive.

More alarming to many upper-class Englishmen than what was happening in France was the spread of reform enthusiasm at home. No longer was it confined to liberal, noble Whigs, the inevitable Noncomformist radicals, or those propertied gentlemen who wanted reform to purge corruption. The demand for reform was beginning to be heard from new levels of society in a new way. The ebullience of London support for Wilkes had been transmuted into a serious, principled radicalism among the artisans who formed radical clubs in towns throughout the kingdom; these little groups were linked together by the London Corresponding Society, founded in 1792 by a shoemaker named Thomas Hardy. Never numbering more than a tiny minority, these societies seemed more threatening than they actually were. But their members read, thought, questioned, and planned; they held meetings, borrowed French rhetoric, and distributed propaganda with great enthusiasm. When in 1791–1792, Thomas Paine, who had made a reputation as a pamphleteer for the Americans fifteen years before, published his *Rights of Man* — a reply to Burke stating the radical case with superb clarity and with an equal brilliance of phrasing — over 200,000 copies were circulated, and in cheap editions it penetrated into parts of the country untouched by the agitations of the preceding decades. After issuing a proclamation against seditious publications, the government prosecuted Paine (who fled to France) and others for seditious libel.

 The government's shift to a repressive policy drew broad support in the country, support by no means limited to the upper classes. In July, 1791, occurred the terrible Birmingham riots, in which the Unitarian minister and philosopher, Dr. Priestley, saw his house and laboratory burned by a mob convinced that he was a danger to Church and king. Dissenters throughout the country found themselves suspected of the worst designs on the constitution, and men of liberal opinions were careful to disavow earlier compromising statements or to keep a discreet silence. In Scotland in 1793, savage sentences of transportation were passed on reformers who had come as delegates to a convention to agitate and possibly to prepare for drastic changes: to timid souls the very word was an ominous reminder of the revolutionary Convention across the Channel. Respectable citizens throughout the kingdom hastened to join loyalist societies like the Association for the Preservation of Liberty and Property against Republicans and Levellers; Priestley, and a good many others who thought like him, decided to emigrate to the United States. By 1794, both reformers and antireformers had turned extreme.*

Meanwhile, Pitt played a waiting game. At the outset, he commended the French for imitating the English constitution, while deploring their excesses. He naturally welcomed the irretrievable split in the opposition and the support he gained from Burke and his friends and, in 1794, from the Duke of Portland at the head of another fragment of the Foxite group. The concern of Pitt's new allies and the increasingly alarmist temper in the country led him to refuse all constitutional reform and even to defend abuses, in striking contrast to his own statements of less than a decade before. Pitt's policy was not,

*Lord Cockburn (pronounced Coburn), an eminent judge and a Scottish Whig, was a boy at the time of the Terror in France, "Grown-up people talked, at this time, of nothing but the French Revolution, and its supposed consequences," he recalled. "I heard a great deal that I did not comprehend; but, even when not fully comprehending, boys are good listeners, and excellent rememberers, and retain through life impressions that were only deepened by their vagueness, and by their not flowing into common occupations. If the ladies and gentlemen, who formed the society of my father's house, believed all they said about the horrors of French bloodshed, and of the anxiety of people here to imitate them, they must have been wretched indeed. Their talk sent me to bed shuddering." Quoted from *Memorials of His Time* (1856), p. 50, Cockburn's is a convincing explanation of the process by which the fear of revolution was transmitted to two generations.

however, the result of mere political necessity or opportunism. He was, as we have seen, an administrator first of all, and he had new and strange threats to deal with. From 1793, Britain was at war; by 1794, the country was threatened with invasion: events forced Pitt to view the issue starkly as one of national survival under the challenge of an enemy who broke all the rules.

The Course of the War

In 1792, France became a republic; early the next year, she executed her king. The rulers of Prussia and Austria went to war, but their aims were dubious, their performance was ludicrous, and Pitt wisely stood aside. Early in 1793, however, the French annexed the Austrian Netherlands; and Britain went to war, obedient to her centuries-old policy of keeping the Channel ports out of French hands.

Pitt and Henry Dundas (later Lord Melville), his principal associate, thought of the war in the traditional way. They raised some troops (not very effective ones) as best they could by organizing French refugees, hiring Hessian mercenaries, and allowing individuals to recruit their own companies. But Britain's primary task was to subsidize the fighting of her Continental allies—Prussia, Russia, Austria, Holland, Spain, and Sardinia—while herself picking up colonial territories to be used as bargaining counters. The allies, who felt little obligation to Britain beyond taking her pay, were half-hearted, incompetent, and devious; and the military expeditions to the Continent ended in disaster. The leisurely professionalism of eighteenth-century warfare could not cope with the new-style French army, a "nation in arms," unorthodox with its mobile tactics and an ideological zeal unknown since the seventeenth century. One by one the allies dropped away until in 1795 only Austria was left. By that time the genius of Napoleon was turning French ambitions towards Austria's possessions in Italy; utterly defeated, the Austrians made peace at Campo Formio in 1797, leaving Britain alone to face France and Spain, which had come into the war out of hardly surprising suspicion of Britain's colonial intentions.

In 1798, Britain managed to piece together a second coalition with Austria and Russia, compensating the former for the creation of an independent Netherlands by the promise of territorial gains in Italy, and enticing the Tsar with prospects of extending his influence over the important Mediterranean island of Malta (held independently by the ancient crusading order of the Knights of St. John) and over parts of Germany. But by 1800, Austria had suffered crushing defeats, the Netherlands refused to help an expedition designed to liberate them, and the Tsar capriciously defected to the French and set up a Baltic alignment whose "neutrality" was directed against British shipping.

Napoleon did not have it all his own way. Britain's fleet had kept the French from reinforcing their colonial garrisons; early in 1797, Sir John Jervis and Horatio Nelson defeated a much larger force of Spanish ships in the battle of Cape St. Vincent; and by the end of the year—despite two mutinies in the British fleet because of wretched pay and conditions—the enemy was shut up in its ports and the threat of invasion removed for the time being. Just before the formation of the Second Coalition, Napoleon took an army to Egypt as a first step towards substituting French for British domination in the East. Nelson moved into the Mediterranean and destroyed the French fleet in the Battle of the Nile at Aboukir Bay, forcing Napoleon to abandon his Egyptian project; the French army was later defeated by a British land force under General Abercromby. Nelson, now Lord Nelson, moved north to destroy the design of the Baltic "armed neutrality" by a brilliant and bloody raid into the harbor at Copenhagen in April, 1801.

Command of the seas could only mean a standoff with a formidable military power on the Continent. Yet the fiasco in Egypt and difficulties in Italy led Napoleon to put out peace feelers at the end of 1799. Pitt and his friends were by now convinced that a lasting peace was impossible without guarantees of the Channel coast and the Mediterranean and without a stable French government; so they refused to be drawn into negotiations and hoped for the best from the Austrians. What they got were two stunning defeats, at Marengo and Hohenlinden, after which the Austrians early in 1801 concluded a separate peace treaty at Lunéville. Despite her victories on the Baltic and Mediterranean fringes, Britain then had little choice but to enter into talks that resulted in the short Peace of Amiens in March, 1802. By that time, however, Pitt had fallen from power.

The Home Front

Faced with such disasters on the Continent, for which successes at sea and in the colonies were little compensation and barely relevant, Pitt realized that the war would have to be "total," at least so far as defeat of the French was concerned. For that he had to mobilize a country that had impressive economic resources, a firm spirit in adversity, and seriously defective governmental machinery. The organization of the armed forces was chaotic. Men were recruited for the Navy by press gangs that rounded up victims on the streets and in taverns and forced them into service. The Army got its men by paying bounties to recruits, often making them too drunk to know what they were doing. The militia was bogged down in the interests of the localities from which its units were drawn; they were ill-trained and limited to service within the country. There were, in short, almost no disciplined, effective, or willing troops. There was a considerable degree of professionalism in the Navy, but Army leadership was casual and amateur. There was no general staff, little planning, and no clear line of responsibility; the creation of the new office of Secretary of State for War in 1794 was only a halting step in the right direction. But Pitt can hardly be blamed for failure to deal more effectively with a military establishment that was to resist fundamental change for nearly another century.

Pitt was more successful on the financial side. Wisely refusing to rely entirely on borrowing, he imposed new direct and indirect taxes and raised existing rates; but he made his most important breakthrough by a complicated plan to do away with the land tax, so long the mainstay of British public finance, and to substitute an income tax, the administration of which was gradually brought to a strikingly modern and professional level.*

It is against the urgencies of an unsuccessful war, threatened invasion, administrative reconstruction, and the priorities they imply that we must see the steps taken by the government against the radicals. At best diversionary, at worst subversive, these newfangled demands and organizations had to be dealt with in a situation where war and politics, not abstract justice or visions of a bright future, were the essential ingredients. The government proceeded sternly but regularly. The proclamation against seditious publications in 1792 gave way to more serious legislation—the suspension of habeas corpus in 1794, and in the following year a new treason act that aimed to guarantee not only the safety of the king and the realm but also the immunity of Parliament and the constitution from both written and spoken criticism. The Seditious Meetings Act of 1795 forbade public lecturing and meetings of more than fifty people without permission of the magistrates.

These actions were perhaps more alarming in prospect than in actuality. The savage repression that took place in Scotland in 1793–1794 could not easily be transferred south of the Border, where the legal system was less authoritarian; in 1794, before the new treason act, Thomas Hardy, John Thelwall, John Horne Tooke, and others were prosecuted for high treason and acquitted of the unquestionably excessive charge by London juries. Encouraged by this

---

*The scheme was to declare the land tax permanent and then allow those liable to it to redeem their obligations by payments to the government on terms that constituted a profitable loan.

result and stimulated by the bad harvest and resulting distress in 1794–1795, the reform societies continued their activity and, even after the Seditious Meetings Act, managed to keep alive while complying with its provisions. Application of the acts, as was inescapable in the absence of central enforcing machinery, varied from place to place and with the incidence of distress.

In 1795, following a series of bad harvests, there were widespread food riots. One plan for dealing with the distress has since become famous, or infamous, among historians. The justices of the county of Berkshire met that year at the village of Speenhamland and worked out a scheme for supplementing insufficient wages by payments out of the poor rates, the subsidies varying according to the size of the applicant's family and the price of bread. Propagandists trying to make the poor content with their lot had repeatedly told them that the poor laws gave them a major advantage over the French peasantry, and the Speenhamland plan seemed to justify that argument, within the limits of what then passed for humanitarian views. The results, as we shall see,* were ambiguous and in some ways perhaps disastrous.

By 1796 and 1797, reform activity quieted down, though in the latter year Charles Grey, Fox's principal lieutenant and the man who as prime minister carried the Reform Act of 1832, courageously introduced a bill for the reform of Parliament. It was, needless to say, decisively defeated, and Fox for a time decided it was useless to attend a Parliament that seemed to be no more than a rubber stamp for his archenemy Pitt. In 1798, however, there was a resurgence of popular agitation, due to the high prices of food and other bad effects of the war on the home front, and a new form of protest became evident. The mutinies in the fleet the year before were a protest against the wretched conditions in which the sailors had to live and work; they were not directly associated with any of the reform societies, though the pronouncements of the mutineers borrowed French rhetoric and slogans easily ascribed to the reformers. The same can be said for the small trade unions — or combinations, as they were then called — that were springing up among workmen in the rapidly changing industrial structure of England.

When such developments were set against a background of repeated disasters in war and of a revolt in Ireland, it is hardly surprising to find a new rash of repressive legislation — an act of 1798 that put newspapers under the supervision of justices of the peace; an act of 1799 that outlawed the Corresponding Society and any other group with branches, oaths, or secret offices; and two acts in 1799

*See below, pp. 245–247.

and 1800, the famous Combination Laws, which forbade any combination in restraint of trade, whether of masters or men, though of course the major target was trade unionism. The Combination Laws represented no new principle, for combinations had been outlawed in specific trades on numerous occasions, and were in any event illegal at common law as conspiracies in restraint of trade. The acts were passed to intimidate and tighten control over workingmen who were threatening to break out of their expected subordination; they made possible speedier action in the common-law courts by allowing two magistrates to conduct summary trials of workers accused of combining.

Ireland

Ireland presented the most formidable domestic challenge to Pitt's government and eventually drove him from office. The concessions of the late seventies and eighties had gone some distance towards satisfying Irish ambitions, at least temporarily. The lot of Catholics had been made easier, the Irish were admitted at least partially to the British mercantilist system, and in the eighties, following the failure of Pitt's commercial proposals, an installment of tariff protection had helped Irish industry. Yet Irish independence, as we have seen, was more apparent than real. No one yet could imagine an autonomous Irish executive, responsible to an Irish legislature. Because the government in Dublin Castle took its orders from Whitehall, Irishmen could not go the whole distance they wanted to economic protection or to the religious concessions so generally abhorred by the Ascendancy (as the Irish Protestants were called) and the British.

Within this fundamentally unsatisfactory situation, the more radical among the Presbyterians in the northern province of Ulster— who, like Dissenters in England, suffered disabilities— set up the Society of United Irishmen in 1791. They quickly established close relations with the radical societies in England and with Roman Catholic agitators in the south, to whom they contributed ideas and direction and from whom they might, if necessary, get numbers and violence. Pitt's first step to deal with this two-pronged threat was to suppress the Ulster United Irishmen, using tactics similar to those applied to their collaborators in England. He then planned to make immediate concessions to the Irish Catholics. In 1793 they were given the parliamentary vote on the same basis as the English forty-shilling freeholders; they were allowed to serve on juries and permitted to hold minor offices and to bear arms. But Catholics, in England and Ireland, still could not hold major offices or be elected to Parliament: these were concessions that came to be known as "Catholic Emancipation." Pitt certainly intended to move in that direction, but his timetable was thrown off by the manifestly liberal attitude of Earl Fitzwilliam, who became Lord Lieutenant late in 1794; the King, alarmed, demanded Fitzwilliam's immediate dismissal. Thereupon the most radical United Irishmen fell victims to their own impatience. While Pitt was forced to mark time, the Ulster revolutionaries, and especially a young lawyer named Wolfe Tone, began to work for a French invasion.

An unhappy Ireland had always been a strategic weak point for Britain, and at this time it could not be foreseen how reluctant the French would be to take advantage of it. A little band of Frenchmen landed in Wales early in 1797 and was quickly captured, but the threat was enough to set off a firm repression of the Ulster movement. Desperation led to rebellion by early summer, 1798; the revolt was suppressed quickly, too quickly for any effective French assistance. Wolfe Tone returned from the Continent with a small French force and was captured; after being found guilty of treason, he committed suicide.

The rebellion underlined Pitt's growing conviction that the Irish constitutional arrangements were intolerable. The autonomy that had been granted in 1782 was to be done away with. An act of union was passed in 1800, and the Irish legislature was bullied or bribed into voting its extinction. On the first day of 1801 the United Kingdom of Great Britain and Ireland came into existence. The House of Lords was increased by four Irish bishops, chosen in rotation from the twenty-two, and by twenty-eight temporal peers, elected by the Irish peerage and holding office for life; one hundred Irish members were added to the House of Commons. The established churches of the two countries were united; Ireland was brought completely within the British mercantilist structure; debt charges on prior obligations remained separate; and the contributions of Great Britain and Ireland to the combined expense of the new kingdom were set for twenty years at a proportion of fifteen to two—a measure of Ireland's poverty, since the two populations stood in a ratio of nearly five to two.

Though the act did not go so far in making concessions as had the act of union with Scotland in 1707, Pitt intended a generous settlement. In his mind, the *quid pro quo* for union was to be Catholic Emancipation—allowing Roman Catholics to hold high office and to sit in Parliament. Knowing that too early an avowal of this plan would defeat the Union, he kept his counsel, expecting to use his political skill to extract the concession later. He had miscalculated. He failed to carry an important minority of his cabinet with him; they undercut him with the King and would have undercut him in Parliament. But it seems likely that, even with cabinet unanimity, he would have foundered on the insurmountable resistance of the King: George had no intention of violating his coronation oath to defend the Anglican Church. His policy ruined on an essential point, Pitt resigned on March 14, 1801, an action that emphasizes the king's continuing position as head of the government. George is often said to have mirrored the prejudices of the ordinary members of Parliament and their constituents, so when he denounced Pitt's proposal as "the most Jacobinical thing I ever heard of!" we may fairly conclude that he was demonstrating the muddled thinking as typical of the late eighteenth-century country gentlemen as the slovenly use of "communist" was to become of a good many of their twentieth-century counterparts.

AMIENS TO VIENNA, 1802–1815

Addington and Pitt

Pitt was succeeded as prime minister by Henry Addington, the Speaker of the House, a good administrator, eminently "safe," and quite lacking in the brilliance that had made Pitt at times almost as unpopular as his master Shelburne. Nor did Addington have a "party," even of the rudimentary kind emerging among "Mr. Pitt's friends," who gathered around their leader from the many political groupings that had dissolved under the stress of war and fear of revolution. Addington had a small following; so did some of his ministers. But he was able to attract broad support among the independent country gentlemen for his policies of peace at any price and retrenchment—including rapid demobilization and the abolition of the income tax. He took advantage of the brief period of peace after Amiens to institute some valuable administrative reforms, such as the payment of civil service salaries by Parliament directly, rather than from the king's Civil List. Addington was also the first minister to make the presentation of the annual budget the occasion—as it has been ever since—to review the state of the economy and to set out the principles that governed the administration's proposals.

Addington was to have little chance, however, to display his talents as a peacetime minister. Britain's extensive territorial concessions to France at Amiens—giving up nearly all her conquests—had been dictated by the urgent insistence on peace; they were tolerable only if the guarantees in the treaty worked to maintain the independence of the new republics Napoleon had erected in the Netherlands, Switzerland, and Italy. But it soon became clear that these were mere puppet states. France began to expand in all directions in violation of implicit understandings, if not specific provisions, and left England little choice, in view of obvious war preparations across the Channel, but to beat France to the punch. War was declared in May, 1803. For a year Addington survived, thanks largely to his predecessor's cooperative silence. He brought back an improved income tax and encouraged reforms in army recruiting and discipline, but the military situation was beyond him, and in May, 1804, he gave way to Pitt.

Trafalgar

At the head of an unstable coalition and regarded with suspicion by many former supporters, Pitt lacked the resources that had upheld him before his resignation. Some M.P.'s now distrusted him because he had favored Catholic Emancipation; others thought his resignation had been a mere sham and put the worst construction on his support of Addington. He was seriously hurt by charges of corruption (not upheld in the impeachment trial) made against his First Lord of the Admiralty, Henry Dundas, now Lord Melville. But Pitt surmounted these liabilities to form a third coalition with Austria and Russia by August, 1805, in time to draw off the large invasion forces Napoleon had mounted across the Channel at Boulogne.

The year 1805 saw only one British victory, and that tinged with tragedy. In the spring Lord Nelson, misjudging the intentions of the French fleet in the Mediterranean, had let it escape through Gibraltar to the West Indies. There, according to Napoleon's plan, his various fleets were to combine; then, having lured the British far from home, they were to sprint for the Channel to spearhead the invasion of Britain. But Nelson chased the French across the Atlantic and back, preventing the rendezvous and forcing Villeneuve, the French admiral, to retire to a Spanish port. He finally met Villeneuve's fleet off Cape Trafalgar, below Cadiz, on October 21, and, in smashing it, destroyed Napoleon's naval forces and removed the threat of invasion for good. Nelson himself fell in the action, to be mourned, as he is today remembered, as one of the greatest British heroes. Except for that costly victory, there was only disaster. The Russians and Austrians were defeated by Napoleon, now Emperor of the French, at Ulm in October and at Austerlitz in December. Austria had to give up again, and promptly signed the Treaty of Pressburg. The war claimed yet one more victim in January, 1806, when Pitt, worn out by strain and crushed by defeat, died at the age of forty-six.

Politics from Pitt's Death to the Regency

The King now had no choice but to swallow his distaste for Fox, who came into office with his friends under the nominal headship of Lord Grenville. Lord Grenville was the youngest son of George's second prime minister, one of Pitt's principal lieutenants down to 1801, and the leader of the opposition to Addington's administration. Addington, now raised to the peerage as Viscount Sidmouth, was there as a conservative balance. This coalition was somewhat grandiloquently named the "Ministry of all the Talents." Fox tried to make peace, only to learn that Napoleon had to be fought, not dealt with. Then in September he died, ending a checkered career that on balance was made noble by devotion to the cause of liberty, a cause he never had a real chance to serve as minister. He did not live to see the one great legislative monument of the ministry—the abolition of the slave trade—carried early in 1807, the first installment of a long campaign against slavery led by the Clapham Sect; Wilberforce had moved the bill. But a government effort to win Catholic Emancipation, a traditional goal of the Foxite Whigs, lost them the confidence of the King, who demanded that they promise never to raise the subject again—a clear invitation to resign. The ailing Duke of Portland then pieced together a ministry that picked its way amid quarreling factions until 1809.

One trouble with Portland's ministry was that no government was large enough to hold its two most able members. Lord Castlereagh, dour and sensitive, was a superb war minister and diplomat; in both his view of foreign policy and his support of Catholic Emancipation he had good claims to be considered the heir of Pitt. But that claim was disputed by George Canning, the Foreign Secretary, who, after gaining national fame for his literary brilliance while still a schoolboy at Eton, had headed a talented propaganda team for the government during Pitt's last years in office before 1801. His intrigues against Castlereagh led in 1809 to a duel between the two ministers, both of whom were then forced to resign. The long-range result was to create wide distrust for Canning—not lessened by snobbish contempt because he was the son of an actress and so "no gentleman"—which kept him in the political wilderness for years.

The government was further damaged by charges of corruption and inefficiency. One scandal involved the Duke of York, the King's second son, who had done much as commander in chief to improve Army organization; it was discovered that his mistress, Mrs. Clarke, had been selling promises of promotions in the service. The Duke was exonerated of direct complicity but had to resign. Allegations of electoral corruption led in 1809 to the passage of "Curwen's Act," which prevented the Treasury from giving financial support to the proprietors of parliamentary boroughs—a further blow at the influence of the Crown. Finally the evacuation of an ill-fated expedition to the island of Walcheren, at the mouth of the Scheldt in the Netherlands, completed the demoralization of the government. Portland resigned to die and was succeeded by Spencer Perceval, an able, courageous, but colorless man who held things together until, in 1812, he was assassinated by a bankrupt, who blamed the government for his disgrace. Perceval's successor was Lord Liverpool. As Robert Banks Jenkinson, he had been one of Pitt's chief "men of business," an administrator of first-class abilities; then (as Lord Hawkesbury) he was Foreign Secretary under Addington, Home Secretary under Portland, and War Secretary after Castlereagh's resignation in 1809.

This transfer of power was not accomplished without a great deal of faction-fighting and a number of unsuccessful attempts by other politicians to form a government. The only constitutionally important feature of this pulling and hauling, however, concerned the heirs of Fox—whom we can now begin properly to call merely Whigs, for Pitt's descendants were beginning to call themselves Tories, a term Pitt had never used. At the end of 1810, the King's illness returned. Early in 1811 a regency bill was carried naming the Prince of Wales as regent, to have the full powers of the king if his father did not recover in a year. This was the chance the Whigs had waited for. The Prince felt no more warmly toward George III than he had twenty-two years before, when the regency question had troubled the political world. He regularly consorted with the Whigs whom the King so detested, and although the Royal Marriages Act of 1772 forbade members of the royal family to marry without the king's consent, the Prince had violated the act in 1785 by secretly marrying a Roman Catholic widow, Mrs. Fitzherbert; he lived with her until 1803. Meanwhile, in 1795, he was forcibly married—the Fitzherbert match being contrary to law—to Caroline, a petty German princess of gross manners and unsavory appearance. The Prince, however decadent he became, was a man of taste; although the marriage was consummated, he refused to live with his bride, who spent her married life, in a grubbily promiscuous way, in Italy—until she became queen.*

The Prince had set up his court at Carlton House, and later in his fantastic pavilion at Brighton, a seaside resort he made fashionable. To Carlton House came the opposition politicians around Fox who had no hope of getting office from the King. Now, after so many years, and after Fox's flamboyant charm had vanished into the grave, it seemed as though their time had come—for the Regent remained as free to choose his own ministers as his father had been to choose Bute. But twice during 1812 the Whigs were disappointed. From George's point of view, now that he was regent, they had two fatal disqualifications: they were committed to Catholic Emancipation

*See below, pp. 167–168. On the earlier regency crisis, see above, p. 101.

and, in spite of Fox's disillusion over Napoleon in 1806, they were suspected of being lukewarm about carrying forward the war. But the Prince was not entirely without gratitude and made two attempts at coalition-building—one on his assumption of full royal powers in February, 1812, the other after Perceval's assassination in May, when Liverpool resigned to permit the formation of a more broadly based government.

None of the efforts succeeded: the Tory factions outside the government could not agree among themselves, and the Whigs, remembering the fate of the coalition of 1806, insisted on having a free hand to carry what measures they wanted. The right of a new government to implement its own program without hindrance from the king is now an assumption so automatic that it is difficult to put oneself back into the fluid constitutional situation of the early nineteenth century, when such a demand—though it followed logically from Fox's insistence in 1783 on having full control of his administration—seemed simply obstinate to many observers. It gave the Regent a pretext he was happy enough to take. Liverpool, his growing reputation for firmness and common sense further strengthened by the failure of these futile efforts at cabinetmaking, returned to office in June with Perceval's team—including Castlereagh and excluding Canning—to remain there for fifteen years.

The Continental System and the Peninsular Campaign

The war had gone badly. Austria was sunk in defeat after Pressburg; Prussia, goaded into war by Napoleon, was decisively beaten at Jena in 1806, and Russia at Friedland in the following year. The Treaty of Tilsit in 1807 not only humiliated the two defeated powers but, through the magic effect of Napoleon's personality on the impressionable Tsar Alexander I, brought Russia into the balance against Britain. When Nelson's victory at Trafalgar wrecked the chance of mounting an invasion, Napoleon turned to economic warfare. In the Berlin and Milan decrees of 1806 and 1807, he proclaimed a blockade of Britain—enforced against British ports, not by his own ships, which he no longer had in any quantity, but by closing Continental ports under his control to ships that had come from or stopped in Britain. The British replied by orders in council requiring that neutral shipping to and from the enemy be licensed, pay customs, and be checked for contraband in British ports—and Britain had the ships to enforce her demands. The first round of this blockade war ended in a draw. In 1808, Britain's exports and grain imports dropped dangerously; the country suffered real distress and the disturbances that automatically followed in those days. But the French and their satellites suffered severely too and soon were opening ports to neutrals under rather uncertain controls, which allowed an influx of British and colonial goods, either with tacit permission or through outright smuggling.

In 1810, Napoleon, now more firmly in control of the Baltic and occupying Spain, tried again; this time the effect on Britain was very serious. Moreover, Napoleon was able to turn resentment of the blockades to his advantage. The neutral that suffered most from the economic warfare was the United States—more at the hands of the British than the French, for the British stopped ships at sea to search them, a right the Americans refused to concede. Furthermore, the British, looking for deserters in the American ships, had forced a number of Americans into the British Navy, presuming them English because they spoke it and disallowing claims and even documentary proof of American citizenship. Though the French offer to repeal their decrees if the British withdrew their orders in council was no great concession—France needed American ships to bring her vital materials—it served to inflame American passions against England and forced President Madison to demand British concessions. Finally, after much jockeying, the British withdrew their orders, but too late to prevent an American declaration of war in June, 1812. This needless war could hardly engage the British deeply; that fact may account for their having done so badly. The government's efforts were bound to be directed to the calamities on the home front and to Europe, where the course of victory seemed at least to be set and where the stakes were higher than they were across the Atlantic.

In 1807, French armies, with Spanish complicity, had invaded Portugal. The British, loyal to their long-standing relationship with Portugal, sent troops to be used there or in Spain, as needed. The British expedition was commanded by Sir Arthur Wellesley, who had distinguished himself fighting in India when his older brother was viceroy. But a sudden change in command prevented him from following up his early victory at Vimeiro, and to the horror of many people at home (including William Wordsworth, who wrote a pamphlet on the subject), the French army, so thoroughly defeated, was allowed by the Convention of Cintra to return home with its arms intact. Meanwhile, Napoleon had pensioned off the contemptible Spanish royal family and put his brother Joseph on the throne, an action that touched off national resistance among the outraged Spaniards. A new French army captured Madrid in December, 1808, but was slowed in its advance to the south by a diversionary attack on its supply lines by a British force under Sir John Moore, which, after retreating with brilliant rear-guard fighting, was successfully evacuated by the British fleet at Corunna.

Early in the following year, Wellesley returned to Portugal. His plans were not spectacular: he relied on disciplined troops, carefully organized supplies, good mapping, efficient staff work, and a willingness to fall back again and again to prepared, invulnerable positions. When the chance offered, he would win in small engagements by striking where the French were weakest and by opposing his organized staying power to the mobile tactics of the French, who were unable to cope with situations that required standing still. His methodical campaign was a long time in bringing a decisive victory, but meanwhile he kept his army intact and tied down the French in huge numbers. Three years later Wellington—Wellesley had been made a viscount in 1809 after Talavera and an earl in 1812 after the capture of Ciudad Rodrigo—entered Madrid and began gradually to force the French northward. Meanwhile, Napoleon, determined to protect his Continental System, had launched an expedition against Russia, which was ending in disaster. By late 1812, though the war was far from won, the prospects were hopeful. The government, however, had much to concern it at home, developments that went much deeper than the immediately distracting struggles of political factions.

The Resurgence of Radicalism

The hard times that accompanied the two periods of effective enforcement of the Continental System, 1807–1808 and 1810–1812, exasperated more general economic developments. One of these was the rise in prices. The growing popular faith in paper money issued by banks throughout the country rested finally on the ability and willingness of those banks to exchange paper for hard coin, mostly gold, which was rapidly replacing silver as a monetary medium. Behind the country banks and the London private bankers stood the privately owned Bank of England, still far from exercising its modern responsibilities as a central bank. The Bank was the custodian of the nation's ultimate gold reserve, true, but it functioned as a commercial bank as well, lending to ordinary commercial clients as well as to other banks for which it discounted bills of exchange. The disruption of normal trading patterns, the necessity of sending large sums abroad as subsidies to the allies, the flight from Britain of privately held gold chasing the best advantage in abnormal price fluctuations, and the inevitable demands in periods of panic to convert paper into gold—all these factors, coming together in 1797, threatened the Bank of England's obligation to convert paper to gold. The government gave, and Parliament confirmed, permission to suspend specie payment.

In thus protecting its credit, the Bank dispensed with the automatic control, normally provided by the gold reserve, over the amount of money in the country. On the whole, the Bank did well in keeping a rein on its own issue of bank notes, though it was generous in discounting, i.e., making loans that increased the amount of available money and fed the inflation of the early years of the new century. Seeing unprecedentedly high prices, many critics quickly accused the Bank of having overissued paper money. The best economic analysis of the time, enshrined in the report of a Commons committee in 1810, agreed in blaming the Bank and called for a resumption of specie payments. Modern historians have pointed to other, certainly more important, causes of the inflation, among them the casual issue of paper money by country banks and the enormous demands of war on the nation's resources. Parliament refused to implement the report. Reversing an inflationary trend is always painful, and it could seem wise to wait until the reversal would not hamper the war effort. Indeed, the prime minister had said that he considered the report equivalent to a declaration that any peace terms should be accepted rather than continue the war.

The hard times of the latter years of the war could also be ascribed to the increasingly rapid and extensive changes in industry. In the textile trades, older skills were being made obsolete by mechanization; in other industries, where machinery was not yet making much headway, manufacturers frequently sought ways of economizing on labor by reorganizing the trade and introducing cheaper processes, like the mass-produced and inferior "cut-up" stockings so hated by the framework knitters. Hardest hit by these developments were certain woolen workers in the West Riding of Yorkshire, the framework knitters of the Midlands, and the hand-loom weavers in the cotton districts in Lancashire and Scotland. Confronted with the high cost of living and the rapid demolition of what remained of old paternalistic legislation, these workers rebelled —against the machines that outperformed them and, even more, against the masters who installed the machines and destroyed traditional ways. From 1811 to 1813, and sporadically for three or four years after, there was an epidemic of machine-breaking and rioting. These were the so-called "Luddite Riots," named for General Ludd or King Ludd, a mythical folk figure who was the avenger of the wrongs done to workingmen.

Some men in the ruling classes suspected the existence of a wide conspiracy and saw the French and French sympathizers behind it. Dismissing this explanation outright, historians have generally seen the riots as isolated responses to distress; the only connection between the scattered outbreaks may have been that rumors of success in one place emboldened men to try in another. Though they were deadly serious, involving widespread destruction of property, personal violence, and even murder, these disturbances, it was thought, were in no sense revolutionary. But it has been convincingly argued that, though diffused, these outbreaks were in fact highly organized protest movements, growing not only from an old tradition of machine-breaking, but from the political radicalism of the nineties and, especially, from the growing but frustrated trade-union impulse.

The Combination Laws had only partly accomplished their purposes. While there were frequent prosecutions—none was ever undertaken, of course, against a combination of masters—many combinations of workmen survived either through collusion with masters or with the understanding of an occasional magistrate or because the unions were not always easy to distinguish from "friendly societies" —clubs whose professed aims (such as sickness and burial benefits) were unexceptionable. These little organizations, though they rose and fell, kept alive a sense of solidarity and trained men to leadership, not only among the more prosperous skilled workmen to whom historians have usually confined their attention but in wider segments of the working class as well. The law forced them into a fabric of conspiracy, and when they turned to Luddism after 1811, the situation seemed almost Irish. Confronted with swift secret action they could not anticipate or prevent, and unable to discover the culprits, the government and local authorities fell back on spies and informers and on new and savage laws against machine-breaking, measures that were both provocative and ineffective. Luddism was tamed, not by prosecutions, but by the coming of better times and the diversion of working-class protest into political channels.

The political instrument was forged by a quite different group of radicals. Middle-class reformers, as we have seen, met much hostility during the nineties, especially if they were Dissenters. But, however prudent they may have become, they did not forsake their beliefs. Indeed for some of them, and particularly for the Unitarians who furnished so many of their social and intellectual leaders, radical premises were built into the very structure of their thought. Increasingly persuaded by a deterministic view of the world and its history propagandized by Priestley, the Unitarians of those days looked on their time of troubles as a temporary interruption of an inevitable trend to a reformed and enlightened society. In the new century many factors combined to strengthen the faith of these men and women. The more intellectual among them sharpened their principles and their wits in the growing number of libraries and literary societies. Businessmen who suffered from high taxes and the disruption of trade or whose old-fashioned forms were being threatened by innovators in other perhaps less traditional parts of the country agreed in lamenting the long continuance of the war and demanding that governmental policies (on which they cast all the blame) be reformed when peace came. Other businessmen who were able to take advantage of the war or who were on the winning side of industrial and commercial changes confidently looked forward to a time when they might claim their just share in ruling their towns and the country, and when society might be reshaped according to their criteria of efficiency, cheapness, and utility. Responsible, concerned citizens had plenty of chances to see in their towns not only what needed to be done but what forces of obstruction there were in the selfish, corrupt, and self-perpetuating oligarchies or in the apathy or ignorance of the mass of the people.

The place where radicalism attained its greatest wartime success was in the city of Westminster, the West End of the growing metropolitan complex of London. Westminster, where Parliament sat and much of the fashionable world lived, was especially well suited for radical leadership. It was a scot-and-lot borough, with some ten thousand electors, mostly small tradesmen and artisans with a leaven of more respectable merchants and professional men. For most of the eighteenth century, Westminster's representatives had been nominated by the Dean and Chapter of Westminster Abbey, following the wishes of the Crown; but after 1780 one of the members was Charles James Fox. When Fox died in 1806, the radicals tried unsuccessfully to put up the wealthy, radical member for the county of Middlesex, Sir Francis Burdett. In the general election of 1807, however, the Westminster radicals persuaded Burdett to become a candidate; they organized their efforts well and elected not only Burdett but the radical naval officer Lord Cochrane.*

Two men were responsible for this impressive result. One was a master tailor named Francis Place, who in the nineties, while a journeyman leather-breeches maker, had joined and profited greatly

*Blocked in the Navy, despite an outstanding record, because of his politics and his unorthodox naval ideas, Lord Cochrane was finally expelled from the Navy and from Parliament, having been involved in some questionable transactions on the stock exchange. Nothing daunted, he went off to command the Chilean navy in the fight for independence from Spain, then became an admiral in the Brazilian navy, and finally as an admiral in the Greek navy helped to win Greek independence from Turkey. When he succeeded to the earldom of Dundonald in 1831, he was, as it were automatically, purged of his "crimes" and reinstated in the Navy, where he was responsible for the adoption of steam power and screw propellers. He ended his distinguished career as a full admiral.

from a branch of the London Corresponding Society. Self-educated,
energetic, clever, and deadly serious, Place soon did well enough in
tailoring to retire from active business and spend the rest of his life
serving as a spokesman (not always with unanimous support) and
defender of English workingmen and as a bridge between them and
the middle-class radicals, especially those around Jeremy Bentham.
For the next forty years, the library in Place's shop in Charing Cross
was a gathering place of London radicals and a source of enlightenment for working-class leaders from all over the country. Place was
the manager of the Westminster election; he arranged the finances,
organized the canvassers and the voters, and pulled all the wires that
needed pulling.

Francis Place mouthpiece for working radicals

The chief propagandist was William Cobbett. Cobbett was a
Surrey farm boy who had enlisted and served in America. After his
discharge from the service, he became a patriotic bookseller and publisher; in 1792 he returned to the United States, where he set up in
business in Philadelphia as "Peter Porcupine," whose chief mission
was to combat anti-English ideas. In 1800, Cobbett returned to London as an anti-Jacobin propagandist. With quasi-official support he
founded the weekly *Political Register* in 1802 but, by 1805, the government found it had been nursing a viper. Cobbett was always at base
a Tory, devoted to an old, rural, idealized England, hating London,
stockjobbers, economists, Jews, and anyone who seemed to him to
be perverting England from his bluff, vigorous, old-fashioned ideals.
Perhaps no journalist writing on either side of the Atlantic has ever
expressed his hatreds and aspirations in such superb polemical
prose. But the invective he served up to the French and the reformers
was engaged with equal or greater fervor in the radical cause, which
he supported in his idiosyncratic way from 1805 until his death thirty
years later. The conversion, which never embarrassed him despite
the efforts of his enemies to turn it against him, was due largely to
his indignation at the sufferings he saw among farm laborers and
London artisans. He blamed his old enemies, but he now began to
attack paper money, the national debt, corruption, places, and sinecures: he labelled them, most unfairly, "the Pitt system." Having
hectored the voters of Westminster into giving the radicals the electoral victory of 1807, Cobbett went on to hector the nation.

In 1809, the Westminster reformers gained a new ally in the intellectual upper crust. Jeremy Bentham, whom we have met as a
seminal but still largely unknown legal philosopher, had become
convinced that only democracy could bring about the greatest good
of the greatest number. In association with his close friend and colleague James Mill, the Scottish writer and philosopher, Bentham
began a series of expositions of his political and methodological

views that gained him a wide audience and a wider reputation at all levels of society. Through him a powerful radical reformist philosophy was grafted onto a cluster of complementary traditions, and the resulting amalgam has set the tone of much British reform down to the present day.

The vast majority of the country remained untouched by these movements, though more and more people were aware of them. Some religious persons, particularly among the Methodists, were opposed on principle to political agitation and to trying to cure any ills but those in the souls of men. Many others were distracted by the war or more immediate problems; and, in a country where modern communications had not yet broken down isolation and where class lines provided effective insulation, there were always those who were barely aware even of the war, let alone the novel tactics of London radicals. But towards the end of the war, a ferment was working in British society that could no longer be ignored.

Peacemaking

The first order of business still remained winning the war and settling the peace. During 1813, Wellington pushed his way up through the Iberian Peninsula, at great cost and against a superbly led enemy, into southern France. Meanwhile, the other European nations that had previously done so badly against Napoleon found a new cohesive force in the nationalist fervor stimulated by French occupation. France had been drained of money, manpower, and will by her enormous efforts to subdue a continent. Peace terms were being negotiated from late 1813, under the direction of Austria's Prince Metternich, but were revised in Britain's favor after the personal intervention of the Foreign Secretary, Lord Castlereagh, early in 1814. The upshot of the talks was the Treaty of Chaumont, engineered in accordance with Castlereagh's principles, by which the great powers — Britain, Prussia, Russia, and Austria — were joined together in an alliance to arrange a general European settlement, and to win and guarantee the peace in Europe. By March, 1814, Metternich and Castlereagh had decided to expel Napoleon from France and to restore Louis XVIII, and on March 31, the victorious allied armies entered Paris.

It was not quite all over. Napoleon was sent to the island of Elba in the Mediterranean, but in March, 1815, before the peace terms were finally concluded, he escaped from exile and returned to rouse France against the unpopular Bourbon king. His plans were wrecked by an allied force led by Wellington and the Prussian general Blücher at Waterloo in Belgium, on June 18. Napoleon then surrendered to the British, to be imprisoned on the island of St. Helena in the South Atlantic, and the powers returned to Vienna to ratify the peace they had concluded a few days before the battle. France was confined to the boundaries of 1790 and was given back most of her colonial possessions. Future aggression was guarded against by the creation of buffer states on either side—the enlarged kingdom of Sardinia to the south, the new kingdom of the Netherlands (joining Holland to Belgium) to the north. Austria was compensated for her loss in the Netherlands by gaining Lombardy and Venetia in Italy. The complex of Germany was simplified into a confederation of thirty-eight states, but Castlereagh's hope to erect a strong independent Poland to separate Prussia and Russia foundered on the refusal of those two powers and Austria to undo the partition of that unhappy country. Britain got a pronouncement against the slave trade, kept the Channel coast in safe hands, and gained important way stations on the route to the East such as Malta and the Cape of Good Hope, which she had taken early in the war as a part of her successful colonial campaign. The map of Europe, thus remade, was to stand with few changes for a century. The conflict with the United States had been concluded the year before, with no significant gain for either side. Having at last come to the end of what is sometimes called the second Hundred Years' War, stretching from the end of the seventeenth century, Britain could now turn to the scarcely less arduous and much more puzzling problems of a hundred years of peace.

Selected Readings

For an overview of Britain in the Revolutionary period, we must still go back to P. A. Brown, *The French Revolution in English History* (1918). There is no recent period or monographic work on military history from the British perspective, but the naval side is covered in G. J. Marcus, *The Age of Nelson: The Royal Navy, 1793–1815* (1971). Until a second volume of John Ehrman's life of William Pitt appears, we are still dependent on J. Holland Rose, *William Pitt and the Great War* (1911). But other aspects of politics in the last decade of the century have been helpfully explored in recent years: F. O'Gorman, *The Whig Party and the French Revolution* (1967); L. G. Mitchell, *Charles James Fox and the Disintegration of the Whig Party, 1782–1794* (1971); E. A. Smith, *Whig Principles and Party Politics: Earl Fitzwilliam and the Whig Party, 1748–1833* (1975), a biography also important for Irish matters and the Act of Union; and the second volume of Carl B. Cone's *Burke and the Nature of Politics: The Age of the French Revolution* (1964). Radical activity in the 1790's is sympathetically treated in E. P. Thompson, *The Making of the English Working Class* (1963). The crucial constitutional change involving Ireland and encompassing Pitt's fall is dealt with in G. C. Bolton, *The Passing of the Irish Act of Union* (1966).

Pitt's successor has received a good biography in Philip Ziegler, *Adding-*

ton: *A Life of Henry Addington, First Viscount Sidmouth* (1965), and an administrative development in which Addington's administration is crucial is dealt with authoritatively in A. Hope-Jones, *Income Tax in the Napoleonic Wars* (1939). The great humanitarian reform of the period has attracted much rewarding attention. In addition to the biographies of Wilberforce, cited earlier, the background is impressively recounted in Roger Anstey, *The Atlantic Slave Trade and British Abolition, 1760–1807* (1975). Historical debate about abolition has turned on the question of whether West Indian slavery was prospering or declining in the generation preceding abolition. The influential book by the West Indian historian and politician Eric Williams, *Capitalism and Slavery* (1944), has been impressively rebutted, and the impact of humanitarianism given new force, by Seymour Drescher in *Econocide: British Slavery in the Era of Abolition* (1977).

The political history of the latter part of the period covered in this chapter remains spotty. Denis Gray, *Spencer Perceval, The Evangelical Prime Minister, 1762–1812* (1963) is valuable on the ministerial side; on the Whigs and the second Regency crisis, which so frustrated them, Michael Roberts, *The Whig Party, 1807–1812* (1939). The constitutional significance of the crisis and of the whole period is interpreted in Richard Pares, *King George III and the Politicians* (1953). The prophetic activity of the Westminster radicals and their allies needs more scholarly attention. For Francis Place, Graham Wallas, *The Life of Francis Place* (1898, 4th ed. reprinted 1951) is classic but dated. There are more recent studies of Cobbett: John W. Osborne, *William Cobbett: His Thought and His Times* (1966) and the admirable sketch in E. P. Thompson, *The Making of the English Working Class* (1963). Warren Tute, *Cochrane* (1965) recounts the life of a colorful and embattled radical. Thompson's book gives a full and important discussion of the Luddites, but see also Eric Hobsbawm, "The Machine Breakers," *Past and Present*, no. 1, pp. 57–70 (1952), reprinted in his *Labouring Men* (1964), pp. 5–23. On the economic context of the protests, F. Crouzet, *L'économie britannique et le blocus continental, 1806–1813* (2 vols., 1958), unfortunately not yet translated. A. Aspinall, *The Early English Trade Unions* (1949) is valuable as an account and also for the documents it contains.

For the military history of the latter years of the war, Elizabeth Longford, *Wellington: The Years of the Sword* (1969). On peacemaking and peacekeeping, Harold Nicolson, *The Congress of Vienna: A Study in Allied Unity, 1812–1822* (1946) and Henry A. Kissinger, *A World Restored: Metternich, Castlereagh, and the Problems of Peace, 1812–22* (1957).

Chapter 4
The Emergence of
Liberalism

1815–1832

RECONSTRUCTION, 1815–1820

England in 1815

Nearly a generation of war exaggerated rapid and fundamental changes that in origin were largely independent of the war. No one had yet learned to live with change of such magnitude. As always after a war, the overwhelming desire was to return to the world and the life the war had shattered. Even the most advanced reformers tended to think only of simple remedies for old problems, and the idea that continuing, guided, creative effort in a fluid society might come from an organically unified nation or from the rebuilt and extended machinery of the state was hardly imaginable.

The immediate goals were to try to undo the worst features of wartime and to conserve what advantages had been gained. In the former category one thing was agreed on by nearly everyone in the upper and middle classes: the income tax must go. By their standards it was heavy, it was "inquisitorial," and worst of all it was efficient. Over objections of a government that badly needed the revenue, the tax was abolished in 1816.* A Parliament of landowners moved even more swiftly to cushion the blow that peace seemed certain to give to agriculture. The war had forced a vast expansion of cultivated land, much of it poor and inefficient and needing high prices to keep it in production. The postwar slump in demand and the restoration of normal trading abroad brought a fall in prices and in the incomes of both landlords and farmers; and the prospect of land going out of cultivation alarmed ministers who still hoped to keep the country reasonably self-sufficient in food. The Corn Law of 1815, passed over strong public protest, was intended to keep foreign wheat out of the British market when the domestic price per quarter (eight bushels) fell below 80 shillings.† In 1817, to protect another branch of domestic agriculture, Parliament increased the duty on imported wool.

But those who had suffered most during the war, the working classes and the poor, did not fare so well in the reconstruction. Petitions for the fixing of wages got nowhere, nor did the Midland framework knitters who tried to keep up their income by asking Parliament to act against manufacturers of inferior goods. Indeed, the structure of inherited legislation that had once helped to protect laboring men was being demolished. In 1813–1814, the wage regulation and apprenticeship clauses of the Elizabethan Statute of Artificers (1563) were repealed. The wage arbitration clauses in the Combination Acts had remained a dead letter. And with the repeal in 1824 of the Spitalfields Act of 1773, which had provided agreed wage rates in the uneconomic silk industry, legislative interference with wages vanished until 1909.

The working classes fared badly in postwar legislation because they lacked political power; realizing it contributed to their growing interest in the suffrage. But even more important in explaining the country's failure to help the poor by legislation were pervasive attitudes among the upper and middle classes towards the question of what we would call social welfare. To some, effective regulation seemed impossible in a rapidly changing economy; to others, no human intervention could alter a divinely ordained social order of which the poor were an inevitable and necessary part. Still others—a small minority—were convinced of the futility of intervention by the political economists' doctrines of laissez-faire, or by concern about

---

*A measure of how despised the tax was is the provision, in the act abolishing it, that the records be destroyed. Copies were kept, however, and the machinery was re-erected when the tax was reintroduced in 1842.
†In English usage, corn means grain. All the Corn Laws provided similar controls for other grains, but as wheat was the most important, its prices were always quoted. The act permitted free importation for warehousing, but wheat could be released to the market only when the price was above 80s. Below that level a prohibitive duty was payable.

costs in the face of foreign competition. The widely held belief that it is wrong for individuals to rely on any exertions but their own might in some of its advocates have masked a repellent callousness, but it could also reflect a genuine and noble idealism. Whatever the rationale, there is little doubt that the gulf of heedlessness that had appeared since the late seventeenth century between the well-to-do or middling classes and the working classes or the poor was carried over into the new industrial economy. It was relieved only partially and often unintelligently by remnants of old state regulations, such as the poor law, or by the widening efforts of the humanitarians.

Peel, Brougham, and Owen = *outsiders*

A few new departures were tried to improve the lot of the poor, but they came to little. In 1802 the wealthy textile manufacturer Sir Robert Peel (father of the future prime minister) introduced and carried a bill to limit the hours and humanize the treatment of the parish apprentices sent to work in cotton mills, but because the act relied on the traditional mode of enforcement by justices of the peace, it did not accomplish much. In 1819, urged on from inside by Peel and from outside by Robert Owen, Parliament extended the twelve-hour daily limit to other working children, though the regulation was again confined to cotton factories and the age limit below which work was not permitted was set at a mere nine years. Again deficient in provisions for inspection and enforcement, the act was largely ignored.

In education, considerable advances had been made in setting up schools to teach the rudiments of reading and writing to poor children, the work largely of voluntary bodies—the National Society for Promoting the Education of the Poor in the Principles of the Established Church, founded in 1811, and the British and Foreign School Society, which emerged in 1814 from earlier efforts of supporters (largely Dissenters) of the educational reformer Joseph Lancaster. Schools of both societies used the monitorial system, in which a teacher taught older children who in turn taught the younger, a plan that got round the shortage of teachers and had the attractions of cheapness; but it was not very effective educationally, especially in view of the brief, casual attendance that was all that could be expected from working-class children. In 1816, Henry Brougham, who was becoming the spokesman of the more radical Whigs, procured the appointment of a royal commission to investigate educational charities; but in 1820 he failed to carry a bill proposing a national system of education, thanks in part to residual distrust of educating the poor but mostly to the mutual suspicion of Anglicans and Dissenters, which was to hamper educational reform for the rest of the century.

The one wholesale plan for solving Britain's problems sprang from the fertile, if somewhat narrow, mind of Robert Owen. A Welshman, Owen in 1800 took over David Dale's cotton mill at New Lanark near Glasgow, a firm in which Jeremy Bentham and other philanthropists later became partners. Owen made a fortune at New Lanark and there had the chance to put into effect social theories derived (like Bentham's) from Helvétius. Convinced that man was a creature of circumstances and rejecting the notion of personal responsibility, Owen was certain that human nature could be regenerated by establishing a proper environment. In the village of New Lanark, some three thousand people lived in what then seemed ideal conditions: there were well-constructed, sanitary houses; a shop sold goods at low prices; children were not allowed to work before the age of ten, were limited to ten hours a day, and were educated in carefully supervised schools. The life of the working people and their families outside the factory was a matter of paternal concern, and music, dancing, and games were provided. The village lost some people who could not abide the regimentation, but the experiment was an important contribution to the civilizing and disciplining aspects of industrialization. It was prophetic too of some persistent concerns in modern community planning.

Owen was not the only man who ran an enlightened and socially responsible enterprise—though the manufacturers who could afford such luxuries were necessarily that minority whose economic position was secure and whose religious or philosophical positions enforced such obligations. But Owen differed from other paternalistic factory owners by moving on from the conception of New Lanark to what he called in the title of one of his books "a new view of society." He proposed the establishment of cooperative villages whose inhabitants would till their common ground, own their own factory, and live in "parallelograms" built around a central square, with common kitchens, recreational areas, and so on. With his curious blend of forward- and backward-looking elements—he urged spade cultivation, for example, to create more work and more intensive yields— Owen stands at the beginning of socialism in England and is a major representative of the school of socialist thought scornfully dismissed by Marx and Engels as utopian. Despite the radical nature of his proposals, Owen aroused much interest among benevolent and philanthropically inclined men, among them Robert Southey, the Lake poet who had become poet laureate, the prime minister Lord Liverpool, and enlightened despots on the Continent. But in 1819 he sacrificed most of his potential support from the upper ranges of society by an outright attack on religion, and from that time on found his following almost exclusively among the working classes.

The Role of the Government ✓ = foreign policy

The three men—Brougham, Peel, and Owen—who initiated these abortive efforts at educational, factory, and social reforms were an opposition politician and two factory owners; the fact is revealing. Such proposals were to be looked for only from men outside the government, for the government's responsibility was still as narrowly defined as it had been seventy years before. Ministers had to carry on the king's business, defend the country, handle its external relations, raise the money for these functions, and make it possible for the magistrates and their sketchy and inefficient local establishments to keep the peace. The problem of internal peace has loomed large in histories of the postwar period, for it was in the manifestations of discontent and the responses to them that we see so clearly issues that were to affect British life for generations. But we must always remember that other preoccupations seemed more important in the daily business of worried and overworked ministers.

The cooperative effort of the great powers to impose order on a reconstructed Europe fully occupied the genius of Lord Castlereagh, the Foreign Secretary, and took much of the cabinet's time as well. The financial picture was black. The national debt, some £900 million, had nearly quadrupled its prewar figure; the interest and charges on the debt were £32 million, about a third of the total annual government expenditure in 1815, two thirds in 1818—compared to something under 9 per cent in Britain today. The Army and the Navy had to be maintained on a larger footing than before the war, and other expenses—not least those incurred by the Prince Regent—had risen sharply. At the same time the country and Parliament had deprived the government of its most valuable single resource, the income tax. The result was a series of annual deficits that had to be made up more and more by borrowing.

The ministers themselves were not men from whom one could expect miracles of imagination or ingenuity.* Inheriting a proud tradition of service to the state, Liverpool was sensible, not illiberal, and a good if not dominating chairman of the cabinet; in the immediate postwar years he tended to be influenced and certainly over-

---

*The one government-sponsored effort to deal with fundamental social problems was the appropriation of a million pounds in 1819 and a further half-million in 1824 to build new churches. Such a measure was thoroughly justified in the context of the then ruling view of the proper relationship between Church and society, and in view of the increase in town population for which no Anglican provision had been made. But given the competition of Dissent and apathy, the results of the act are more important for the history of architecture than for social history.

shadowed by other ministers. Castlereagh was steering a remarkably skillful course in Europe,* but most of his contemporaries admired or despised him simply as the man who was keeping Europe from revolution, while his detractors quite unjustly linked him closely with the Tsar's hare-brained scheme for a holy alliance to guarantee peace and legitimacy throughout Europe and its dependencies. Lord Sidmouth, the Home Secretary, was as bureaucratic and safe as he had been when (as Addington) he was prime minister in 1801–1804, but now he was more harassed than ever. The Lord Chancellor was John Scott, Lord Eldon. The son of a Newcastle coal merchant, Scott became Solicitor-General in 1788, Attorney-General in the early 1790's, Lord Chief Justice of the Common Pleas and a peer in 1799; in 1801 he was named Lord Chancellor, to remain in that exalted post, with one brief intermission, until 1827. Enormously learned, infinitely cautious, reluctant to commit himself, utterly averse to change, a fanatical defender of the privileges he had so recently earned, Eldon had an almost symbolic role in his period.

The governmental machinery with which these men had to work was at best rudimentary, at worst obstructive or useless. They and their tiny staffs were overworked. For knowledge of what was going on outside their immediate range, they had to rely on reports from magistrates and other local officials who were often narrow, suspicious, and as frightened as most respectable people were by the dark doings of revolutionaries at home and abroad. They also used spies, possibly more given to manufacturing evidence than to reporting it. And as guides to making sense of what they learned, the ministers had only good intentions and a lot of irrelevant experience. They had served under William Pitt and were still dominated by his ghost; they had fought and won a great war; but both of these distinctions were in fact disqualifications for dealing effectively with the challenges of the peace. Their attitudes had been formed in the eighteenth century, and they were unprepared for a time when the world they knew was rapidly crumbling away.† Limited and well-meaning, caught in a terrible situation with few resources, Liverpool's ministry in the immediate postwar years has had little sympathy from contemporaries or historians.‡

*See below, pp. 169–170.

†R. J. White , in *Waterloo to Peterloo* (1957), points up the transitional character of the period by noting that one member of Liverpool's cabinet was robbed of his watch by a highwayman in 1786, and another was killed by a railway train in 1830.

‡The poet Shelley snarled "I met Murder on the way—He wore a mask like Castlereagh." His views in *The Masque of Anarchy* and Byron's in *The Age of Bronze* were seconded by a host of radical writers and cartoonists.

Postwar Radicalism *takes clearer direction*

want to agitate for representation

The social problem of the postwar period was closely related to economic distress. British industry, which had expanded rapidly between 1793 and 1803, fared less well down to 1815 as capital was diverted into agriculture, port facilities, and other necessities of war. Still manufacturers had done well enough in supplying the armies of the coalitions and, after 1809, of Spain, Portugal, and their colonies. With the peace, these demands simply dried up. A stopgap solution was sought in dumping English products in Europe, but in the long run that helped neither the state of the markets nor the price level. *no big picture* Faced with the rebirth of foreign competition after so long a period of war-enforced protection, and not yet entirely aware of the clear margin Britain had gained over the economies of the Continent, British manufacturers tried to keep costs down by cutting wages, now protected by neither trade unions nor legislation; in doing so, they reduced the advantage the working class might otherwise have gained from lower prices. Some manufacturers, caught by long-range economic developments such as obsolescent techniques and styles or the changing industrial geography of the country, were forced to run their mills only part time, when they could get orders to fill. Such threats to the incomes of lower-class families were coupled with bad harvests, a succession of commercial crises, and the chronic problem of technological underemployment or unemployment, made worse by the demobilization of hundreds of thousands of soldiers and sailors. Distress always produced disturbances, and the postwar years, with their resurgence of Luddism, were no exception.

At the same time the diffused working-class radicalism of the preceding twenty years was beginning to take a clearer direction. Luddism and old-style violence were to continue for some years, but they were no longer a major instrument of social protest. Effective trade unionism and socialism were still some distance in the future. But a distinctive shape was given to agitation in these years by the growing belief in parliamentary reform and universal suffrage as the remedies for all ills. The propaganda that Major Cartwright's Hampden Clubs had disseminated somewhat futilely since 1812 took hold throughout the country after the war and was strongly reinforced by other voices. The loudest of these was that of Henry Hunt, the most successful demagogue of the time and the darling of the crowds. Hunt did much to popularize the goal of political reform, but the quarrels he provoked with other claimants to working-class leadership were a serious disservice to the cause.

More significant in the long run was the press. Here again William Cobbett took the lead. Newspapers at this time had to bear a stamp on each sheet; they were usually limited to a single sheet (four pages) crammed with advertisements, announcements, parliamentary debates, police reports, and other news. The tax had been successively raised through the eighteenth century so that by 1815 a daily newspaper such as *The Times* cost sevenpence, the equivalent of perhaps a dollar in American money today. Newspapers passed from hand to hand (the readership of a single copy in London has been estimated as high as thirty), men clubbed together to buy them, they were taken in at taverns and coffee shops to be read by customers or, sometimes, read aloud for the illiterate.

In 1816, Cobbett, whose weekly *Political Register* reached only a small circle of readers at the price of a shilling, decided to try an experiment. He began to publish his paper as a pamphlet, thereby escaping the high newspaper tax on each copy and making himself liable only to a small pamphlet duty on the entire edition. He at once slashed his price to twopence, and his readership shot up. A host of imitators flourished, the most notable of them T. J. Wooler and Richard Carlile. Wooler, publisher of the popular *Black Dwarf*, was an associate of Place and published Bentham's *Plan of Parliamentary Reform* in a cheap popular edition. Carlile, who along with a series of newspapers published reprints of Paine and many other radical works, was under almost continual attack for sedition and blasphemy and did much of his editing from jail, a true martyr to the cause of a free press. These cheap papers circulated throughout the country to a degree never before known and were a force of the first importance in the political indoctrination of the mass of British workmen.

The new excitement about reform was also reflected in the formation of clubs and societies. Some of them were offsprings of the Hampden Clubs; others borrowed their organization from the class system of the Methodists. Often important means of self-education, these clubs were also training grounds for working-class leaders and, like the still clandestine trade unions, imparted a sense of solidarity and determination. Sometimes they held military drill, to ensure the discipline needed when tens of thousands of people marched in small groups from town to a piece of open land to hear speakers like Hunt and to adopt petitions asking Parliament for reform. But clubs and military drill carried quite different connotations for most people in the upper and middle classes, who were still terrified by anything reminiscent of the French Revolution, and there was just enough republican and revolutionary rhetoric, just enough blasphemy, just enough disrespect for superiors, to be very alarming.

Despite the efforts of many of the leaders of working-class radicalism to prevent machine-breaking and violence and to promote peaceful pressure for political reform, there were a number of threatening incidents, usually arising from the mysterious workings of crowd psychology or panic or from the blind pressures of hunger and misery. In December, 1816, a mass meeting at Spa Fields in London, supposed to be addressed by Hunt, ended in a riot, thanks to the machinations of a little group of self-conscious revolutionaries who called themselves the Society of Spencean Philanthropists. In January, 1817, the Regent's life was endangered, as George III's had been in 1795, by bullets fired (were they only pebbles thrown?) at his coach. In March, a procession of unemployed weavers started from Manchester for London; they were called the Blanketeers, because each man carried a blanket and a petition to the Regent, on trade subjects this time, not reform. In June a little group of Derbyshire men staged the only true rising of the period, a pathetic rebellion led by Jeremiah Brandreth, possibly a Luddite, certainly no new-style parliamentary reformer. To get justice for the poor man, Brandreth set out first to overthrow the government, a simple plan that brought him and his lieutenants to the gallows.

These incidents, the meetings up and down the country, the delegates journeying back and forth, seemed frightening portents. The government watched and waited. Sidmouth tried to keep in touch through his spies and to force dangerous men into criminal or seditious actions by *agents provocateurs,* the most famous of whom was the notorious "Oliver." In 1817, Parliament appointed two secret committees to look into rumors of a plot against the safety of the country; their alarmist reports led to the passing of four bills to suspend habeas corpus and to tighten the antiradical laws of the nineties. But the worst panic was felt by magistrates and parsons, sober, God-fearing townsmen, and residents in lonely country houses.

A good harvest in 1817 brought a relaxation of tension; and, though in 1818 the state of trade provoked some serious strikes, political agitation and mass meetings disappeared almost completely. But because the harvest of 1818 was bad, 1819 became the climactic year. Clubs were refounded, mass meetings began again. The most famous of these meetings took place in St. Peter's Fields in Manchester on August 16. Perhaps fifty thousand people came, and the meeting was orderly enough until Henry Hunt began to speak. The magistrates decided to arrest him; bypassing the mounted troops stationed nearby out of sight, they ordered the local yeomanry to take him. Mostly small tradesmen set on horses, the yeomanry were amateurs with no knowledge of how to control crowds. When they became trapped amid the milling, jeering people, the regular troops were ordered to force their way through to rescue them. Wounds were inevitably inflicted, panic ensued, and when the crowd dispersed, eleven were dead and hundreds injured. This was the battle christened "Peterloo," in derisive reference to a nobler victory four years before. The government did not help matters or its reputation by automatically congratulating the magistrates. The outcry from reformist, liberal, and humane people alike was enormous, and although the government easily survived the attacks, the impact of Peterloo still lives in Shelley's searing sonnet *England in 1819:*

> An old, mad, blind, despised, and dying king,—
> Princes, the dregs of their dull race, who flow
> Through public scorn,—mud from a muddy spring,—
> Rulers who neither see, nor feel, nor know,
> But leechlike to their fainting country cling,
> Till they drop, blind in blood, without a blow,—
> A people starved and stabbed in the untilled field,—
> An army, which liberticide and prey
> Makes as a two-edged sword to all who wield,—
> Golden and sanguine laws which tempt and slay;
> Religion Christless, Godless, a book sealed;
> A Senate,—Time's worst statute unrepealed,—
> Are graves from which a glorious Phantom may
> Burst, to illumine our tempestuous day.

Politically victorious but morally damaged, the government secured passage of the so-called "Six Acts," which, as a symbol of tyranny, have acquired a collective fame they do not quite deserve. Dealing with symptoms rather than causes, the acts fitted neatly into the old framework of assumptions about the purpose and limits of parliamentary legislation. By imposing restrictions or by setting up clearer definitions and heavier penalties, they were intended to reduce disturbances and to achieve uniformity and simplicity of enforcement. Two of the acts dealt with the press, closing up loopholes in the tax laws which permitted the cheap press to flourish, and clarifying the law of libel. Other acts prohibited military drilling by civilians, set out a comprehensive code governing public meetings, and temporarily restricted the right to bear arms. The sixth act had an excellent result: aimed at ending the exploitation of the complexities of English judicial procedure by journalists under prosecution, it helped to speed up trials.

Opposition in Parliament and in the country tended to run to harmless generalities, such as the threat to ancient English liberties (e.g., the right to bear arms) or the sufficiency of statutes already in existence. The latter was the line taken by the parliamentary Whigs who were anxious to defend their libertarian heritage—and did so by attaching some substantial amendments to the Six Acts—but who at the same time were careful not to offend politically important and frightened opinion by too wholehearted a defense of the radicals.

Though radical publishers were curbed and mass meetings fell off, the chief factor in reducing tension was the improvement in economic conditions. The year 1820, however, saw two grotesque postscripts to the bleak years since Waterloo. Early in the year, Arthur Thistlewood, a survivor of the Spencean Philanthropists who had provoked the Spa Fields riot in 1816, and a group of fellow conspirators were discovered (thanks to spies) in a Cato Street loft, about to go out to murder the members of the cabinet as they dined at Lord Harrowby's house. The assassins then planned to parade through the streets with the ministerial heads on pikes to proclaim a republic of which Thistlewood would be president with—a connection made only in his twisted brain—Burdett and Cartwright as his collaborators. But the "Cato Street Conspiracy" was as irrelevant to the future course of working-class politics as Brandreth's resort to the tradition of brute agrarianism.

Meanwhile, George III had died, almost forgotten, and the Regent became King George IV. Gross in appearance and manner, his elegance going rapidly to seed, the new king was petulant and presumptuous without the determination and devotion that had made his father respected. Not entirely without redeeming qualities, George IV was held in contempt by many of his subjects, including the cartoonists, who treated him with the utmost savagery.* The country's hope that, after George IV, it would be delivered from the loathsome progeny of George III had been dashed in 1817 by the death of Princess Charlotte, the daughter of the Regent and his consort Caroline. When George succeeded to the throne, Caroline came back to England, adopting the somewhat inappropriate posture of the injured woman, to claim her prerogatives and to be greeted by cheering crowds all along her route. With public opinion in such a state, it was a profound embarrassment to the ministers that the King insisted on obtaining a divorce. The government introduced a bill of pains and penalties into the House of Lords, depriving Caroline of her title and privileges. Brougham and Denman, leading Whig lawyers and politicians, served as counsel to the Queen. Revelations of sordid goings-on to which the country was treated daily did nothing to shake popular devotion to the Queen, expressed in one monster demonstration after another. The divorce bill passed the Lords by

*The late eighteenth century and the early decades of the nineteenth were a great age of political cartoons and social satire; among the leading artists were Rowlandson, Gillray, and Cruickshank. There are many collections, but the best study is M. Dorothy George, *English Political Caricatures* (1959).

only nine votes, a margin that promised a rout in the Commons, so, to George's great disgust, the government withdrew the bill, and a joyous London was illuminated for three days.

By 1821 the bitterness of five years was melting away. Trade swiftly revived. The Queen, after being refused entrance to the Abbey for the coronation, died suddenly; London paid tribute to her memory in some street riots. The King was well received on visits to Ireland and Scotland. Napoleon died on St. Helena. Sidmouth retired from the Home Office, and in 1822 Castlereagh, who had succeeded his father as Marquess of Londonderry, worn out by work and responsibility and suffering deeply from the attacks made on him, put an end to an era by cutting his throat with a penknife.

NEW DIRECTIONS, 1820–1830

Foreign Policy

The biggest problem in the reconstruction of Lord Liverpool's government was Canning. His political behavior after his resignation in 1809, following the duel with Castlereagh, had endeared him to no one. In 1812, he was offered the Foreign Secretaryship, but he refused to serve under Castlereagh, who was to be leader of the House of Commons, a post Canning demanded for himself. Ignored for a time, then shunted off to the embassy in Portugal, he re-entered the cabinet only in 1816 and then in the relatively minor post of President of the Board of Control, with responsibility, that is, for India. He resigned early in 1821 because of differences with the ministry about the Queen's trial. Liverpool wanted him back; the King would not have him at all. When Sidmouth retired, the Home Office went to Robert Peel, the eldest son of the manufacturer, a young man who in 1812 had become Chief Secretary for Ireland—the principal administrative office in that country—at the age of twenty-four. Canning could hardly object; Peel's abilities, his interests, and his remarkable performance in Dublin* fully qualified him for a post with duties not much in Canning's line. It was finally decided to send Canning to an honorable, useful, and distant exile as governor-general of India. While he was waiting to leave, Castlereagh committed suicide, and, the King's objections overborne, Canning succeeded as Foreign Secretary.

Stress has been laid on Canning's appointment, partly because of its intrinsic political interest, but more because of its symbolic importance. From 1822, the country sensed a change of tone in Liver-

*See below, pp. 190–191.

pool's administration, and because its most obvious manifestations were in the realm of foreign policy, Canning was credited with major responsibility for the change. Actually, he was following the main outlines of policy as Castlereagh had laid them down, and he was strongly and sensibly supported by Liverpool.

Castlereagh, as we have seen, had given a new direction to peacemaking at Paris and Vienna by insisting on a broad European settlement controlled and supervised by the Quadruple Alliance. But while committing himself to collective action to prevent a recurrence of French aggression, he had carefully kept free of the supplementary proposal of the Tsar that the monarchs of Europe unite in a holy alliance, recognizing the overlordship of Christ and making the precepts of Christianity their guide in policy. Castlereagh could hardly object to the sentiment, but he refused on constitutional grounds to let the Regent sign. This tactical move became a major strategic victory: the Alliance, emanating as it did from the despotic rulers of Russia, Prussia, and Austria, quickly became a bugaboo to all liberal-minded men, and when in the twenties the Alliance moved away from pious platitudes to antirevolutionary intervention, it became even clearer that Britain was well out of it. Castlereagh could never purge himself completely from the taint of despotism because he neither understood nationalism nor felt any sympathy for liberal movements, and because the radicals found it easy and rewarding to accuse him of complicity with tyrants. But he held Britain scrupulously to a policy of nonintervention in European squabbles.

In 1820 a liberal explosion occurred in Europe. The Spanish army and then the nation rose against Ferdinand VII, forcing him to adopt the liberal and highly impractical constitution that had been drawn up in 1812, at the time of the expulsion of Joseph Bonaparte. Within a few months, Portugal followed Spain's example, and the Kingdom of the Two Sicilies rose against another wretched Ferdinand. The great monarchs who had proclaimed their belief in legitimacy were appealed to by the weak ones who could not maintain it. The Tsar now found that Christian principles demanded support of divine-right rulers everywhere, and at the Congress of Troppau in October, 1820, the English observer was presented with a declaration of the right of the powers to intervene in any case where internal change had come about by means other than the unconstrained grace of the king.

Castlereagh protested strongly. To accept the monarchs' interpretation, he said, would force the British king to abdicate, and, in any event, Stuart principles would come ill from the mouth of a Hanoverian ruler. Despite the Whigs' desire to strike a great blow against the Holy Alliance (of course without the risk of war), Castlereagh stuck to his neutrality. Metternich put down the Neapolitan revolt and another in Piedmont, strengthening Austria's grip on Italy. At Verona in 1822 the allies were ready to support French intervention in Spain, as a more practical and safer alternative to the Tsar's pet project of marching his troops across Europe to do the job. By that time Castlereagh was dead, and Wellington, the British representative at Verona, spoke for Canning, from Castlereagh's instructions. Finding it impossible to accept the allies' position, he walked out.

So long as the French confined their intervention to restoring the perfidious Ferdinand in Madrid — an enterprise from which no one emerged with credit — Canning was willing to maintain a disapproving inactivity, applying somewhat more openly Castlereagh's policy of disengagement. Only in Portugal did Canning intervene. There, King John VI, who as regent had fled to Brazil in 1807, was persuaded to return and to proclaim his allegiance to a liberal constitution. Confronted by a nagging cabal of his wife, the sister of Ferdinand of Spain, and his absolutist-minded younger son, Dom Miguel, the King was forced by a coup in 1824 to take refuge with the British fleet; with its backing he was able to regain the initiative and exile his son. Meanwhile, Dom Pedro, the heir to the throne, had been proclaimed emperor of the Portuguese colony of Brazil, which had declared its independence in 1822. By a treaty in 1825 mediated by the British, separation of the two countries was agreed upon. In 1826 John VI died; Dom Pedro succeeded him, but chose to remain in Brazil and to pass the Portuguese title to his seven-year-old daughter Maria, whom he also considered marrying off to her reactionary uncle, Dom Miguel. Before his abdication Dom Pedro had proclaimed a liberal charter that continued to be an annoyance to Metternich and his colleagues and a challenge to the dowager queen of Portugal, whose encouragement of military action led to Canning's sending troops. The ground of such intervention was the old alliance with Portugal, and Britain was strong enough to make her primacy respected by the Continental monarchs.

In more important and more distant areas, nonintervention brought spectacular results. Canning made it clear, when the French expedition to Spain was being planned, that Britain would not tolerate extending intervention (as the Holy Alliance wanted) to the Spanish colonies in South America, by that time also in revolt. Recognizing the commercial possibilities in a South America detached from Europe, Canning first proposed joint action with the United States; the latter preferred, however, to go it alone, and in late 1823, the Monroe Doctrine declared that the Western Hemisphere was no longer a field for European (or British) colonization.

Somewhat annoyed by the apparent desire of the Americans to

keep all the gains for themselves, Canning recognized the independence of Buenos Aires, Colombia, and Mexico, to the horror of the
legitimist powers and over the more relevant opposition of George
IV, Eldon, and Wellington. As Britain had the fleet and the willingness to use it, her intentions rather than Monroe's abstractions
made the deeper impression both on Europe and on South America.
In a famous speech in December, 1826, Canning reminded the House
that the world was not what it had been at the time of William III and
Anne, that the balance of power now had wider scope. "Contemplating Spain, such as our ancestors had known her, I resolved that, if
France had Spain, it should not be Spain 'with the Indies.' I called the
New World into existence to redress the balance of the Old." No critics then, and not even historians since, have denied the essential
truth of that claim, and for a century the large part played by Britain
in the Latin American economy underlined it.

The issue was somewhat less clear-cut in Greece, where a
rebellion against Turkish rule had begun in 1821. British sympathies
were overwhelmingly on the side of the rebels; classically educated
men who helped to make opinion, seeing (incorrectly) the resurgence
of a great civilization, supported the revolt with their money, their
military services, and their lives. Canning, taking a much dimmer
view of the Greeks, had rather to consider a basic fact in nineteenth-
century British diplomacy, that Turkey was an important counterpoise to the threat of Russia, where Tsar Alexander, impelled by national interest and his confused residual liberalism, had taken the
Greeks under his patronage. The trouble was that Turkey, as so often
was the case, refused to be helped. Unwilling to accept intervention,
or make concessions, unable to put down the rebellion, given to
senseless cruelty in her efforts at suppression, Turkey outraged British opinion and infuriated Canning. In March, 1823, he recognized
the "belligerency" of the Greeks, implying their right to wage war as
an independent state, but he still refused to cooperate with Russia.

In 1825, Tsar Alexander died and was succeeded in most confus-
ing circumstances (involving the abortive Decembrist revolt) by
Nicholas I. Nicholas was thoroughly reactionary, but he hated Metternich and, moreover, as an Orthodox Christian ruler he was conscious of his special relationship to people of that faith, among whom
were the Greeks. Playing on these circumstances and forced on by
Turkish intransigence, Canning made a joint declaration with Russia
in 1826 — negotiated by Wellington, who went somewhat further
than Canning had originally intended — which, while not recognizing Greek independence outright, at least proposed Greek autonomy
under nominal Turkish rule. This Protocol of St. Petersburg at last
impelled the Sultan to action. He withdrew his troops from the

Rumanian principalities and Serbia, and at the same time took a characteristically violent step towards modernizing his country by setting up a regular army and massacring the mutinous corps of Janissaries, who had served as Turkey's military arm but were now a major stumbling block to effective action. So, by the end of Liverpool's administration in 1827, the Greek question was on its way to a settlement. Even better, the Protocol had split the Holy Alliance wide apart, a seemingly final blow to the illiberal spirit of postwar Europe.

By his policy of disengagement from the Continent and by his skillful actions in Portugal, Latin America, and Greece, Canning had become a hero to all Englishmen of liberal inclinations. He should have been more puzzling to them than he was. He had little sympathy with revolutionary movements, unless supporting them might forward British interests, and except for Catholic Emancipation, he remained a bitter opponent of all reform at home. Why was it, then, that English liberals were willing to overlook so obvious an inconsistency? In part, they had convinced themselves that a liberal foreign policy was a first step in Canning's reeducation, that the rest would follow in time—probably a vain hope, had Canning lived, and certainly an inaccurate appraisal of the consistency of British policy since 1815. But more, perhaps, the liberals were indulgent because Canning had turned his victories in foreign policy to such good effect. He played skillfully on public opinion; he cultivated the press; his speeches in the House were intended to have their chief effect outside. In all this he was employing a changed style and a novel technique in politics—calling yet another new world into existence to redress the balance (and prolong the existence) of the old. It is not surprising that Canning should have been the model for the hero of *Vivian Grey*, the first novel by an ambitious and imaginative young man named Benjamin Disraeli.

Towards Free Trade

Though Canning seemed to most contemporaries the pivotal figure in the liberal trend of British policy, a more consistent, though no less controversial, liberalism was being applied in domestic policy. By 1820 the state of trade was improving, and the teachings of the political economists were being taken seriously. Government expenditures were systematically reduced in the early twenties, and there was a parallel reduction in assessed taxes. In 1821, the Bank of England implemented "Peel's Act" of 1819, the result of the work of a committee whose report had been written by the younger Robert Peel, then returned from his Irish post. The act provided for a gradual return to convertibility of paper currency into gold, undoing the sus-

post-war depression eases in 1820

pension of specie payments that had been in effect since 1797. The possible deflationary effects of tying currency to gold alarmed many agriculturalists, who were troubled by persistently low prices. Some country bankers and manufacturers were also concerned; their lives had been eased and their business promoted by the ready availability of fully acceptable and expandable paper money. But Parliament agreed unanimously to the report, and the state of the gold reserves was so good that the Bank could dispense with some of the delays permitted in the act and make the transition completely in 1821. There seems to have been no significant contraction of the supply of money, and after some initial shocks, not all due to resumption, the general prosperity and increasing productivity of the country managed to cushion the long-term decline in price levels. By 1823, even the farmers thought they were getting decent prices.

In accepting the recommendations of the 1819 committee, the government was putting itself in full agreement with the best economic opinion, expressed chiefly by David Ricardo, a stockbroker who entered Parliament in that year. In 1820 a petition from the merchants of London asked for a national policy of buying in the cheapest market and selling in the dearest, though this avant-garde sentiment was forced by a doctrinaire minority—with encouragement from the government—on a resistant majority of merchants who, concerned about their differing and often contradictory vested interests, still tended to favor protection. In 1821, Frederick Robinson, at the Board of Trade, reduced the stiff preferential tariff on timber that had tended to replace imports from the Baltic by imports from Canada, to the considerable profit of shipowners. The following year, the complicated structure of the Navigation Laws was simplified and liberalized. Many antiquated statutes were repealed. All European nations were put on an equal footing so far as British trade was concerned. Goods entering from a European port could originate anywhere, provided they were finally carried to Britain in a ship of that port. The reciprocity concluded in 1816 with the United States was extended by opening British colonial ports to American ships, as they were also opened to ships from Latin American countries. And the colonies were permitted to export all their produce directly to Africa or Europe, provided it was carried in British ships.

The protective wall around British industry was then further breached. Robinson, on moving from the Board of Trade to the Exchequer, virtually abolished the duty on imported wool and silk and went on to a complete overhaul of the tariff system, lowering duties generally from 50 to 20 per cent on manufactured goods, and from 20 to 10 on raw materials. Some cuts—on cotton and woolen goods, linen, glass, earthenware, and iron—were even more drastic.

protectionist tariffs repealed

Internal trade, in coal for example, was freed from regulations that had benefited one part of the industry at the cost of another, and at the same time, William Huskisson, a follower of Canning who succeeded Robinson as President of the Board of Trade, negotiated a series of reciprocal treaties with European nations. Other legislation simplified and speeded up the ordinary day-to-day processes of economic life—a freer bonding system, the abolition of fees paid by English ships to English customs and consular offices abroad, and a reform of weights and measures. It is important, however, not to ascribe too much foresightedness to the ministers. Informed though they were about the teachings of the political economists, they were chiefly concerned about rational administration and about encouraging industrial exports to pay for the importation of food, which they had finally come to accept as inevitable. They were pleased by the growth and prosperity of English industry, but they were closer to the mercantilists than to the mid-century believers in progress in their general view of Britain's economic potential.

Still another step towards economic freedom was secured in 1824 by liberal forces outside the government. For years, Francis Place had been mounting an attack on the Combination Laws. He knew that they were ineffective, and he thought that in fact they perpetuated combinations, which somehow seemed more desirable when they were proscribed. He was sure they would ultimately disappear in the enlightened individualism of a truly free economy. The parliamentary spokesman for this attack was Joseph Hume, a constant pleader for government economy and retrenchment and a parliamentary advocate of nearly every liberal cause for close to forty years.

In 1824, Hume secured the appointment of a select committee of the House of Commons to look into three categories of restrictive laws: the Combination Laws and those acts forbidding the emigration of artisans and the export of machinery—holdovers from the days when British industry was trying to keep its secrets from foreign competitors. A succession of expert witnesses, expertly coached by Place, was produced, and out of the committee came legislation permitting free emigration and drastically revising the laws governing trade unions. Not only were trade unions given the right to exist and to bargain collectively, but the common-law doctrine of conspiracy in restraint of trade was repealed so far as trade unions were concerned. The act passed with little debate and with almost no notice outside Parliament, and the prime minister confessed later that he himself had not been clear about what the act contained. It is another excellent example of the casual way in which legislation that today would be a major concern of a government could be passed a century and a half ago, provided it was not central to the government's immediate administrative purposes.

in 1824 Combination Laws repealed — trade unions may exist

Trade unionists at once took advantage of their new freedom to
organize strikes, break contracts, intimidate other workingmen, and,
incidentally, to outrage employers and alarm much respectable opinion. The result of the outcry was a new committee—where Place's
stage-managing became even more crucial—and new legislation
which, however, fell far short of the employers' demands. Unions retained the right to organize and to bargain collectively for wages and
hours; but they were limited in their use of contract-breaking or intimidation, and were again subjected to the common law of conspiracy. Though it was a partial victory for the repealers, the act of 1825
seriously limited direct industrial action by the unions, particularly
in view of the steady hostility of the law courts. The measure of
freedom the unions got was in advance of anything in Europe, but it
would be many years before their ability to fight an industrial battle
as they wanted or needed to was substantially recognized.

Banking Policy

The prosperity of the early twenties, which had done so much to
make the liberalization of trade tolerable, and the machinery by
which the economy was administered were put to a severe test at the
end of 1825. The banking system was unstable and only loosely
unified. At the head of the system stood the Bank of England, the
only bank in the country that was publicly owned by stockholders.
Other banks—some sixty in London and almost eight hundred outside—were private banks, organized as partnerships and hence limited in their capital resources. By this time London bankers no longer
issued notes, preferring to rely on the Bank of England's notes and on
their own checks. But the country banks issued notes in profusion;
indeed, in some parts of the country there was a deep distrust of
Bank of England notes. During the long period of suspension of
specie payments, bankers had got out of the habit of thinking much
about reserves. Having secured the right—against the better judgment of most economists—to issue notes smaller than £5 at least until
1833,* they had relied simply on the confidence of local people in
their paper, a reliance that lasted until a panic made men want hard
cash instead of promises to pay. In rural districts, banks served
mainly as places of deposit; the surpluses thus accumulated were in-
vested through London correspondent banks in those parts of the
country that needed capital. Drawing on these resources, the banks
in the industrial districts found their main business in making loans
and discounts, and they frequently were imprudent or indulgent in

*One reason for persistent official distrust of one-pound notes was the temp-
tation they offered to forgers.

taking risks to accommodate friends or local capitalists. Bank failures were fairly common, and it was always advisable for a country banker to have a correspondent bank in London to tide him over in difficult times. The London bankers, in turn, relied on the Bank of England.

The Scottish system was very different. There, banks could organize on the joint-stock principle and operate branches. Checks were practically unknown, and small bills circulated freely. The freedom and sobriety of Scottish banking attracted men south of the Border, and they looked primarily to Scotland when the time came to reform the English system. That tendency was strengthened by the fact that Scotland came out of the panic of 1825 much better than England.

The crisis of 1825 came from several directions. The prosperity of the early twenties led to the projection or flotation of several hundred new enterprises which had a remarkably low survival value. There was, nevertheless, a stock-market boom, involving the kind of headiness we have now come to reckon as a danger signal and a call to tighten controls, but which then seemed simply a good way to make money. This domestic boom coincided with a burst of enthusiasm for the economic possibilities of the South American colonies, which Canning's policy had opened to British exploitation. Manufacturers sent shiploads of their products across the South Atlantic, promoters of mining enterprises conjured up visions of fabulous returns, and the new republics found as many eager buyers for their bonds as they wanted. But Latin America was not yet prepared for such a headlong plunge into the modern world. The manufactures remained unsold, the mines did not produce, the republics could not pay; and, at home, companies and individual investors—including Lord Eldon, who developed an incurable distrust of joint-stock organization—saw stock prices plummet, their savings vanish, and their ideals tarnish though not disappear.

At the same time, the Bank of England was drained of gold for shipment abroad. This was not abnormal when there were large shipments of grain to be paid for or large flotations of foreign loans. But in 1825 the foreign drain coincided with a panic demand for gold at home from holders of notes on threatened banks. The gold reserves of the Bank of England shrank alarmingly and indeed might have forced the Bank to suspend payment again, had not its directors been able to buy gold for silver at the crucial moment from a benevolently inclined Bank of France. But though the Bank of England survived, in one week in December three London banks and sixty-three country banks failed.

One way of preventing such a crisis in future was for the Bank of England to take appropriate action to check a boom. It had actually increased its issue of notes against gold in 1824 and again, this time without additional gold reserves, in early 1825. Such steps could have been guarded against, and indeed future legislation for the Bank was to enforce such caution. Similarly, the Bank had been highly accommodating about making loans to London and (indirectly) country bankers, by "discounting their paper" — lending them money on the basis of obligations owed to those banks by their creditors. Whereas today, in a dangerous boom, central banks raise their rates, to make credit more expensive, in 1823 the Bank of England lowered its rate and fed the boom. It is only fair to note that the usury laws forbade the Bank to raise its rate above 5 per cent — a serious handicap — but there is no evidence that the directors of the Bank would have taken so bold a step had they been able to.

The solution tried in 1826 was to reorganize the banking structure of the country. Outside a sixty-five-mile radius of London, banks were to be permitted to organize as joint-stock companies, thus providing them, it was hoped, with larger capital resources. The right of banks to issue notes of less than five pounds in face value was revoked, an action that made the gold sovereign (a coin worth a pound) the standard medium of exchange for day-to-day transactions and created, as Clapham has so well put it, a "metallic reserve in the pockets of the public."* As a check on and spur to country banking the Bank of England was given the right to establish branches in the country. The presence of branches was resented by some of the larger country banks, which disliked the competition and the doubt the proposal cast on their management. But the branches survived as active commercial concerns into the 1930's, and in their early years they helped to make Bank of England notes more readily acceptable throughout the country.

Law Reform

At the Home Office, Peel was engaged in carrying a remarkable series of reforms in the law. The tangle of Navigation Laws with which Robinson and Huskisson were dealing was clarity itself compared to the legacy of the law. In the civil courts, cases were subject to enormous delays because of insufficient judges (in certain courts), accumulations of undecided cases, obsolete procedures, and general inefficiency. Even worse, there were two competing and often contradictory systems of law — the common law administered in the

---

*Scottish banks managed to get an exception made for their long-established one-pound notes, on the understanding that they would not circulate outside Scotland.

three courts of King's Bench, Common Pleas, and Exchequer; and equity, administered in the Court of Chancery by a much harassed Lord Chancellor and his too small staff. The criminal law was one of the harshest systems in Europe on paper, but one of the most lenient in practice. The death penalty was prescribed for hundreds of crimes, ranging down to the most petty, but was administered with relative infrequency because juries were so appalled by the lack of proportion between crime and punishment that they would acquit a prisoner in preference to convicting him, even when they knew he was guilty — hardly a means of gaining respect for law or adequate enforcement of it. There was no regular police force in England, except for an insufficient and unprofessional body in London and (after 1792) Middlesex. Indeed, the word police, just then entering the language, was likely to mean the whole range of social control, not merely a professional body of law-enforcement officers.

From the late eighteenth century criticism of this legal chaos grew rapidly. Humanitarians protested against the law's savagery and the wretched state of the prisons, the most notable critics being John Howard and Sir Frederick Eden. Continental ideas on penal reform, particularly those of Beccaria, were imported by a number of English writers, far and away the most important of whom was Jeremy Bentham, whose work aiming at a fundamental reconstruction of the law on first principles was becoming more widely known. The campaign against the inefficiencies and inhumanities of the criminal law was undertaken in Parliament by Sir Samuel Romilly, one of the leading Whigs, and after his suicide in 1818 by the Whig philosopher and M.P. Sir James Mackintosh. Their particular target was the wide sweep of capital punishment; mitigation on this score, they were sure, would result in more certain penalties, more reliable enforcement, and so better observance.

When Peel came to the Home Office he lost no time in gracefully taking the initiative away from Mackintosh and showing himself a reformer to a degree that surprised and impressed observers. Moreover, his reforming was not a grandstand play such as many of Canning's efforts must be called; rather it was dictated by a powerful administrative mind working in the same comprehensive way that it had worked in Ireland. Peel undercut resistance from the House of Lords and the judges, especially Eldon, by sedulously referring all his proposals to the judges for their opinion and by treating the opposition generously. He also went beyond the dramatic question of capital punishment to reform what were called secondary punishments — the means that would have to be resorted to when the death penalty was removed, such as jails and transportation to the colonies.

Peel made some inroads on the administration of the law by an act in 1825 consolidating all the statutes relating to juries (common, of course, to both the criminal and civil law) and by reorganizing in the same year the system of paying judges: he raised salaries and did away with perquisites and fees, by which judges had added to their income at the cost of delaying, often disgracefully, the cases before them. In the civil law, he arranged for investigations into such complex problems as the Court of Chancery and the House of Lords, in its judicial capacity as the highest court of appeal, though the proposals made did not reach the statute books.

paid judges

More was done on the criminal side. An act of 1823 thoroughly reformed the prison system of the country, providing for the regular establishment of local prisons, paid for from taxes and subject to visitation by the magistrates. Reports to the Home Office were required, a uniform system of discipline was imposed, and, short of setting up a central prison inspectorate which was not instituted until 1835, Peel brought at least the larger prisons from the medieval into the modern world, though it is only fair to note that local reformers had already taken some effective steps in that direction. In the early twenties Peel repealed a number of acts imposing the death penalty for crimes such as larceny of sums or goods valued up to forty shillings, stealing from ships in navigable waterways, breaking riverbanks, cutting hopvines, and breaking machinery. Judges were given the power to withhold the death penalty for any crime save murder, thereby cutting down the kindly and chaotic discretion of juries. Peel did away with the medieval relic of benefit of clergy, whereby certain persons had been able to claim unfair exemptions in procedure and punishment. In 1827, when Peel was briefly out of office, a bill he had drafted was carried to consolidate the entire law relating to theft—abolishing the distinction between grand and petty larceny, raising the limit to five pounds beyond which the crime of stealing from houses became capital, and making the maximum punishment transportation for seven years for a first offense, for life for a second. This much done—the proposals made by reformers without Peel's support got nowhere—he was ready to move to his great work of 1829 in reforming the police. It was a record that even so thoroughgoing and iconoclastic a reformer as Bentham came grudgingly to admire.

new prisons

The radical writer Harriet Martineau, rigorously opposed to any compromising of principles, criticized the ministers of the twenties for being "bit-by-bit" reformers; she quoted Huskisson, somewhat disapprovingly, as saying that he had opened the fingers of his hand one at a time. Certainly no more sweeping reforms could have been got through, no assertion of principle could have failed to enrage the opponents of reform—who, however, found it hard to fight concrete measures when a good case had been made. In accomplishing as

Critics of slowness of reform

much as they did, these ministers were preparing the way for more far-reaching reforms by accustoming Parliament and public to the possibility of effective state action against inherited evils.

The Whigs *without coherent policy*

The record must have been both galling and mystifying to the Whigs. After Fox's death in 1806, the Whigs had been all but leaderless: only the specialized work of someone like Romilly, in his campaign for law reform, redeemed them from futility. In the postwar period, the leadership problem remained unsolved. The ineffective George Ponsonby remained nominally in command until his death in 1817. At about the same time the Whigs lost their other main spokesmen: Samuel Whitbread killed himself in 1815; Francis Horner died in 1817, Romilly in 1818. The one dazzling star that had appeared in the Whig firmament, Henry Brougham, was a man of virtuosity, humanity, ambition, and boldness, but he lacked both steadiness and the family connections needed for leadership in so aristocratic a faction. In policy, the Whigs did little but limp after the government, insisting that repressive laws were unnecessary and deploring the sedition and violence that they thought should be handled by established procedures.

When prosperity and the queen's affair made the radicals temporarily irrelevant, the Whigs—purged still further by the defection of the small group around Lord Grenville—turned up new leaders just in time to benefit from the unpopularity of the government. Lord Grey, Fox's lieutenant in the nineties and the sponsor of a measure for parliamentary reform in the dark days of 1797, was able sufficiently to overcome his preference for life on his north-country estates to take more initiative in the political arena. His son-in-law, John George Lambton, the possessor of a great fortune founded on coal mines, began to show marked liberal tendencies. Brougham went his mercurial, intermittently effective way. And the third son of the Duke of Bedford, Lord John Russell, took over the day-to-day tasks of keeping the Whigs together, determining tactics, and speaking for them. They formed an impressive phalanx.

Their trouble was policy. Catholic Emancipation, one of their old rallying cries, was equally the political property of Canning. On law reform, the thunder of the Whig spokesmen was stolen by Peel. They were divided on free trade, for Grey and Russell, among the greatest of landed aristocrats, could hardly look with enthusiasm on a doctrine that endangered agricultural protection. On parliamentary reform, at least by 1819, they could agree, and although the issue was not very lively in the twenties, their steadfastness was to serve them well at the end of the decade when it at last became important. With a degree of cohesiveness and a new measure of popular support and respect, the Whigs of the twenties were gradually making the transition from the eighteenth-century connection to the nineteenth-century party, carrying Burke's ideas on party closer to their logical conclusion.

This is not to say that the Whigs or the Tories had the machinery that we have come to associate with modern parties, particularly parties as they operate in the country at large to attract and mobilize voters. But both groups were taking on more and more of the characteristics of definite parliamentary combinations, wedded to particular sets of measures or special political positions, characteristics more modern and less oligarchical than the largely personal loyalties that had dominated eighteenth-century politics. This transition was to be a long time in the working-out. By no means all of the members of Parliament bore a party label in the twenties, though the pressure to do so was increasing; it was still possible, and even easy, for politicians to move back and forth from one side to the other. But the trend was set in the twenties, and something of a milestone was reached when, in 1826, John Cam Hobhouse, a minor Whig leader, referred to his party as "His Majesty's Opposition." The horror that Newcastle and Hardwicke had felt seventy years before for a "form'd opposition" was giving way to the view that regular opposition was an essential part of His Majesty's government.

[margin handwritten notes: "party politics not like today"; "Whigs become official opposition party"]

Intellectual Influences

The pragmatic, administrative character of reforms in the 1820's should not be taken to mean that the ministers were working independently of, much less against, the currents in opinion that were creating the assumptions, priorities, and structure of thought of early Victorian Britain. Indeed, they were remarkably responsive to them. Peel corresponded with Bentham. Liverpool took seriously the ideas of Robert Owen and the recommendations sent to him by Coleridge; more practically, he, like Huskisson, was informed about and respectful of the opinions of the political economists.

The political economists, indeed, were steadily extending their sway, not only with ministers but with the public. Issues like the Corn Laws and specie payment gave real urgency to their teachings. David Ricardo, in his four years of parliamentary life, put forward a somewhat more optimistic set of deductions and recommendations that were to be found in his *Principles of Political Economy and Taxation* of 1817, but the abstractions of that book were to dominate economic thought for more than forty years, despite the many criticisms that other economists brought against it, especially in the thirties. Malthus, less successful than Ricardo in getting across his "heretical" views on production, rent, and the Corn Laws, remained an authority on any subject connected with population (e.g., emigration) and dominated much social thinking. A host of textbooks of the new economic science were published, such as James Mill's *Elements of Political Economy* (1821) and J. R. McCulloch's *Principles of Political Economy* (1825). The English universities set up professorships of political economy and so caught up with the Scottish universities where political economy had long been a province of the professors of moral philosophy. Popularizations soon appeared to teach simplified economic orthodoxy to children and the working classes, the most famous example being Harriet Martineau's twenty-seven tales, *Illustrations of Political Economy*, published serially in 1832–1834.

The great French historian of nineteenth-century Britain, Élie Halévy, found a fruitful line of interpretation in the interplay of influences stemming on the one hand from the classical economists, with their emphasis on the self-regulating nature of society, and on the other hand from Bentham and his disciples, with their emphasis on the positive role that the legislator and the state must play in reconciling conflicting interests. Halévy concluded that in the mid-century amalgam of the two views, the free-trade philosophy of Manchester triumphed over the interventionist philosophy of Westminster, a conclusion that historians recently have been at pains to modify by pointing to the continuing role of Benthamite influences, especially in creating new state machinery.*

Another construction of the major intellectual influences of the time can be drawn from two stimulating essays by John Stuart Mill on Bentham and Coleridge. Mill, the son of Bentham's closest friend and disciple, James Mill, was raised by his father to be the perfect Benthamite, receiving an education—brilliantly recounted in his autobiography—so rigorous and yet so limited that at twenty the young man suffered a hardly surprising nervous breakdown. Then he discovered the joys and insights of poetry—always suspect to Bentham—and he read Coleridge, who, a renegade from a Unitarian, radical past, had become the leading philosopher of English conservatism. Coleridge's Burkean respect for the intricate legacy of the past and his belief in an organic society were combined, not always to his advantage among ordinary readers, with an advocacy of German metaphysics and some distinctly radical and pregnant suggestions, such as his proposal for a publicly supported intellectual class (the clerisy), to combine the functions of a national church and of education and

*See below, pp. 243–249, 260–261, 263–267.

the advancement of knowledge. Bentham, Mill said, proceeded ana-
lytically and historically, asking of every institution the simple question "Does it work?" Coleridge, attuned rather to history and intu-
ition, tried to explain how institutions survived and how their inner
significance could guide present wisdom. So far, the distinction is
neat and true. But when Mill asserted that it was "not too much to
say" that everyone in England learned to think from these two men,
he was clearly overstating his case.

It is misleading to see any age as divided between two or three
major influences. Great thinkers and seminal minds can and should
be singled out for study, yet it is important not to ascribe more to
them in their own time than they deserve. As their ideas filter down
to lesser men, they simplify, blur, and intermingle with other ideas,
similarly vague. Disciples usually come to the great figures as mature
men attracted by something in the thinker's approach or program
that strikes a responsive chord; they are separately formed and cooperative intellects, working with him rather than sitting at his feet.
Problems of intellectual obligation and influence cannot be solved by
mere association or by simply pointing to common interests, programs, and rhetoric. Fame by association can be as damaging, historically, as guilt.

It is easy to point to the many sources of the intellectual currents
of the twenties and thirties. The Scottish universities, drawing on
their own eighteenth-century enlightenment and a distinct philosophical school, sent south many of their products (both Scotsmen
and Englishmen); scientists and doctors brought distinctive, increasingly professional training to bear on wider social problems; the
products of provincial intellectual circles transmitted a peculiar
amalgam of enlightened thought and localism, readily distinguishable in metropolitan mixtures; businessmen argued from
sometimes idealistic positions to often corrosive conclusions; and in
a society where religion was a major force and where religions
tended to segregate and educate their own kind, every sect offered its
own peculiar style in thought as well as in devotion. Men often arrived by different paths at common ideas and formulations, so cooperation was often possible if by no means consistent: to take one obvious example, the emphasis on utility was something Bentham
shared with many very different men, but agreement on its importance as a critical tool or cooperation in applying it did not necessarily make its advocates intellectually identical. The fact that historians
have found it difficult to define "the utilitarians" as a school and are
unable to agree on who really belongs to it or in what degree,
suggests not merely that the problem is complex, but perhaps that it
has been put in the wrong way. The treacherous morass of early

Future work mapping early 19th cent. intellectual life

nineteenth-century intellectual life offers one of the greatest challenges to historians of Britain today.

Whatever the picture will one day be, there is no doubt about the ferment of ideas that swirled through postwar Britain, stating problems, offering solutions, and claiming allegiances that were sometimes temporary, sometimes permanent. The press was the main instrument for their dissemination. Newspapers, rapidly emancipating themselves from servility to the politicians who had subsidized them, thrived on a growing readership and the revenue of advertising to become a true fourth estate of the realm, jealous of their independence and proud of their influence. One can easily discern distinctive styles and inclinations: the *Courier* in the twenties was progovernment, the *Standard* was ultra-Tory, the *Globe* and the *Morning Chronicle* were liberal. *The Times* followed an independent line, and a shift in that line could be a serious blow to a politician. *The Times* was entering the period, dominated by two great editors, Thomas Barnes and J. T. Delane, when it far outdistanced its rivals and earned its nickname "The Thunderer." Moreover, the provincial press was coming into existence; still weekly rather than daily, these newspapers often came to an end or changed their politics when a proprietor died or retired; but a few examples of continuity had begun to appear, the most famous being two liberal papers, the *Manchester Guardian* and the *Leeds Mercury*.

Perhaps even more influential in expounding the views and nostrums of competing schools of thought was the periodical press. Here, pride of place went to the Whig *Edinburgh Review*, founded in 1802, and the Tory *Quarterly Review*, founded in 1809, to which the radical (but not consistently Benthamite) *Westminster Review* was added in 1824. Published quarterly, these serious and demanding journals examined major problems in politics, literature, and thought by means of anonymous reviews of current books and pamphlets. The early *Edinburgh* was the work of Francis Jeffrey, Francis Horner, Sydney Smith, Henry Brougham and their friends; the *Quarterly* not only drew on brilliant writers like William Gifford and J. W. Croker, but could claim Robert Southey from the literary world as the *Edinburgh* from the late twenties could claim Macaulay. The history of the *Westminster* was spottier; less successful financially and torn by personal jealousies, it lurched from one editor and proprietor to another, and did not always reflect the same portion of the radical spectrum. From the late twenties, the weekly *Spectator* expounded a pure and consistent radicalism; *Blackwood's Magazine* spoke monthly for the high Tories; and after 1832 the monthly *Fraser's Magazine* offered its highly idiosyncratic and heterodox brand of Toryism. The religious periodicals circulated among the sects to which they belonged, and within those relatively narrow confines were influences that can be underestimated only at the historian's peril.

An important center for disseminating new currents of thought was the University of London, founded in 1828 as a nonsectarian college by a group of London Dissenters and radicals, including Bentham and Brougham. With a distinguished faculty headed by Leonard Horner, a Scottish geologist whose ultimate career was to lie in the civil service, and a curriculum offering a new emphasis on modern studies, the college attracted many young men, excluded by their religion from Oxford and Cambridge, who otherwise would have had to seek higher education in Scotland or in the few liberal Dissenting academies. The appearance of "the godless institution in Gower Street" led to the founding in London in 1831 of the Anglican King's College. In 1836, the original university, renamed University College, and King's were united in a new University of London, an examining and degree-granting institution to which many other colleges and schools have since been attached.

Many of the ideas advanced in these years were propelled far outside the circle of readers of expensive newspapers and magazines. In 1825, Brougham published a pamphlet urging that the technical possibilities of cheap publication should be exploited to bring new knowledge and awareness, particularly in science, to the working classes. It was work that badly needed doing, to supplement the wretched educational provision for the poor, which there seemed little chance of improving by a national system of schools. Institutions with this aim, called Mechanics' Institutions, were founded with great enthusiasm from the mid-twenties, though few of them fulfilled the hopes of their founders. They became involved in disputes between working-class students and middle-class patrons, and too often workingmen were insufficiently prepared or too tired to study after a long day's work. Brougham's plan for self-education seemed somewhat more promising. The organization he founded, the Society for the Diffusion of Useful Knowledge, was, however, too inefficient and timid to be really effective; too many of its patrons took alarm at proposals to leave the safe ground of science or the benumbing diversion of "entertaining knowledge" to branch out into politics and political economy. It should be added that most workingmen would probably have rejected any systematic course of indoctrination by the Society; they rejected its occasional publications condemning machine-breaking and trade unions as narrow and unfair. Still, the Society's cheap six-penny books and its *Penny Magazine* pointed the way for other, more successful popular publishers, though "improving literature" never acquired the audience that was held by newspapers, cheap fiction, and often dubious street literature. Small cooperative or socialist classes were more useful in spreading views acceptable to workingmen and in creating a sense of solidarity among them.

An emerging public opinion, gaining in definition and growing in maturity at all levels of society, provided the background for the constitutional revolution that took place between 1828 and 1832.

THE CONSTITUTIONAL REVOLUTION, 1828–1832

The Wellington Ministry

In February, 1827, Lord Liverpool suffered a stroke; at the end of March he resigned, removing the one force that had kept an ill-assorted ministry together. When the King, after much hesitation, finally called on Canning, there was a rash of resignations from the government. The most important losses were Peel, who was so committed against Catholic Emancipation that he could hardly serve under its main champion, and Wellington, who added to that disagreement a dislike of Canning's foreign policy and a strong personal distrust. Catholic Emancipation, having broken up the old ministry, became the basis for the new, a coalition of Canning's followers and some leading Whigs. But Canning was already ill, and in early August he was dead. *Canning dies*

More patching followed. Frederick Robinson, the former Chancellor of the Exchequer, now Viscount Goderich, became probably the weakest premier in English history, and his ministry came to an end in January with no accomplishment to its credit. The one striking event of the period happily came to nothing. Following up an alliance embodied in a supposedly secret treaty concluded at London in July, 1827, the fleets of Britain, France, and Russia tried to force a settlement of the Greek question by blockading the Egyptians, then somewhat uncertainly fighting on the Sultan's side in Greece. On October 20, 1827, an incident turned into a battle and the allies wiped out the Egyptian and Turkish fleets. The Battle of Navarino pushed ahead the cause of the Greeks, but it left a tangled European situation as a legacy to the new government.

The King sent for the Duke of Wellington. Peel returned to office, the Whigs departed, and the Canningite faction under Huskisson came into the government for a time but left four months later amid a flurry of misunderstandings. Wellington's government was not strong, as governments go, because of the political uncertainties that underlay it, but it bore clearly the impress of the remarkable man at its head. Wellington was a complete aristocrat—distant, upright, grand—and a thorough Tory. Some Whigs talked foolishly about the threat of military dictatorship, but few great soldiers have been so responsive to the differing demands and priorities of politics. Not that the Duke was a great politician—he was too lacking in tact and subtlety for that—and although he was capable in civilian life of the kind of application to business that had brought him to the top of his profession, his intelligence was not rapid and was sometimes clouded.* As a matter of fact, his military qualities probably served him best. He could assess a situation and act, if not to win, at least to retreat in orderly fashion; he knew when he was beaten. But, lacking political temperament, he made his changes of front bluntly, without trying to preserve a veneer of consistency. Though he had distrusted Canning, he helped to bring George IV around to accepting him in 1822, and this selfless, toughly pragmatic attitude was one of the constant and most valuable factors in English political crises for more than thirty years.

Again at the Home Office, Peel made the most significant contributions of the Wellington ministry. He returned to the work of law reform, coming into closer contact with both Bentham and Brougham, who in an impressive speech on law reform turned the Whig efforts into the broader channels of the civil law. The early Whig proposals in the field of criminal law had had, however, a stronger humanitarian tone than Peel's somewhat chilly administrative reforms, and by 1830 Peel's cautious decision to retain the death penalty for certain offenses, such as forgery, was clearly being outmoded by rapid developments in public and parliamentary opinion, leading to further wholesale restriction of capital punishment in the next decade. But the administrative approach itself was by no means exhausted; Peel consolidated the law relating to all offenses against persons and to the crimes of forgery and counterfeiting.†

In 1829 Peel created a modern, professional police force for London—a measure that still could arouse the libertarian instincts of many Englishmen, most of all the working-class radicals who viewed the police as Continental, inquisitorial, and inconvenient. In place of a few hundred scattered and incompetent patrolmen, constables, and watchmen who were supposed to maintain order in an urban complex of more than a million persons, Peel put a force of a thousand trained and disciplined police, recruited from former Army NCO's and men of equivalent talents and qualifications. The force was ad-

---

*One famous remark about him was that he had "a social contempt for his intellectual equals, and an intellectual contempt for his social equals."

†Between 1825 and 1828, 278 acts had been repealed and their revised provisions summarized in eight acts. Peel said in 1830 that nine-tenths of the cases coming before the courts would now come under reforms introduced since 1825.

ministered by two commissioners chosen for their ability; the pay was modest but it was possible to rise in the ranks, as the force was not organized on a class or caste basis. After some initial difficulties, the London police became noted for morale and pride; their efficiency was quickly demonstrated to those segments of the London mob who set out to see how far they could go. Copied in the independent police forces of other large towns, generalized on a permissive basis for the counties in 1839 and made compulsory in 1856, the institution of professional police was one of the most important steps in civilizing the English and instilling in them the decent, lawabiding behavior that remains one of their most admired qualities. The attitude of affectionate respect felt by much of the public for the police—so unlike other countries—was early caught in nicknames that have stuck: "peelers" and "bobbies" still recall the country's obligation to their creator and patron.

The Wellington administration produced another statute of great political importance, the Corn Law of 1828. The simple arrangements of 1815, whereby foreign wheat was excluded when the price fell below 80s. and admitted when the price was above, had been virtually nonoperative, for prices since 1818 had come nowhere near that level. By a modification of 1822, absolute prohibition gave way to a simple sliding scale: when the price of wheat rose above 70s., there would be a duty of 12s., above 80s., a duty of 5s., and above 85s., there was a nominal one-shilling duty. The act was a sop to the agricultural interests insofar as it raised the level of free entry from 80s. to 85s., but its principle—the sliding scale—was an important concession to free traders. Unfortunately for the protectionists, the act was not to come into operation until the price of wheat again reached 80s., and it too remained a dead letter. Canning tried unsuccessfully to implement this concession in 1827; the Wellington ministry succeeded in 1828. Wheat was now to carry the prohibitive duty of 20s. per quarter when the domestic price was 54s. As the price rose above that level, each shilling's increase brought a shilling's decrease in duty, until the price of 66s. was reached; reductions then became larger, until at 73s. wheat would be admitted for only a nominal duty. Aimed partly at easing fluctuations in price—the less gradual changes of the old scale tempted speculators to hoard grain in the hope of higher prices—the act was a still greater concession to free trade while retaining the principle of protection. This Corn Law was to become the most important political issue of the thirties and forties.

Abroad, Wellington's government was not nearly so successful. Disliking both the methods and the implications of Canning's policy, the Duke and his foreign minister Lord Aberdeen weakly followed their antiliberal and pro-Turkish prejudices. In Portugal in 1828, Dom Miguel staged a coup, driving his young queen into exile in England, and set about a ruthless suppression of all vestiges of liberalism. Against the opinion of their fellow countrymen, Wellington and Aberdeen stood neutral, assuming that authoritarian rule was what Portugal wanted (or needed?) and that keeping hands off would best serve the interests of British trade. In the eastern Mediterranean, where Russia had launched a rapid and successful war against Turkey ending in the Treaty of Adrianople in 1829, the British government lost the initiative and the balance of prestige to the Russians, whom it was trying to seal off in that region. When Greek independence was finally arranged by the so-called London Protocol of 1830, Britain was the least important of the western signatories. In explanation of such diplomatic weakness, however, it must be said that the ministry was caught up in a domestic constitutional crisis of immense proportions and could hardly bring to foreign affairs more than routine policies based on traditional high Tory attitudes.

The Test and Corporation Acts

The constitutional revolution began quietly enough with a motion by Lord John Russell on February 26, 1828, to repeal the Test and Corporation acts and so to relieve Dissenters from the statutory prohibition against their serving in municipal corporations or in Crown offices without first taking communion according to the Anglican prayerbook. The Corporation Act of 1661 had been directed primarily against Dissenters; the first Test Act of 1673 was concerned chiefly with Roman Catholics but because it required Anglican communion (Dissenters had no scruples against the oaths involved) caught Dissenters as well. Although the practice of occasional conformity, the indemnity acts after 1727, and sheer inertia or ignoring of the acts allowed Dissenters to hold office in practice,* they came to regard the principle of their exclusion and the possibility of capricious enforcement as major grievances. Early in the reign of George III they had tried to get these disabilities removed and had almost succeeded, but the fear of change growing out of the threat of revolution had destroyed their chances of obtaining repeal after 1790.

In supporting Russell's motion, the Whigs were of course being loyal to a long libertarian tradition and to an important political obligation. On balance, the Tories were against the proposal, as Canning had been, to the mystification of the Dissenters who had supported him as a liberal. But by 1828 few Tories were willing to take a

*See above, pp. 36–37.

[handwritten top margin: Conservative: strict reading of laws, rules, etc. Liberals: Loose reading: spirit, not the letter]

firm stand—the Duke, a minister or two, some of the bishops. Even at Oxford, the stronghold of Anglican sentiment, feeling was not very strong, and Peel grounded his opposition not on principle but on his wish not to disturb a good relationship that he thought had grown up between the Church and the Dissenters it graciously tolerated. The motion was carried against him, and the government agreed to a plan that had been worked out by the bishops. The two acts were repealed insofar as they required taking communion; thus the declaration in the Test Act against transubstantiation remained as a bar to Roman Catholics. In place of the sacrament, an oath was required from all municipal officers that "upon the true faith of a Christian" they would not use their office to weaken or hurt the Established Church or to disturb any of its rights and privileges.

[handwritten margin: Caveats]

Liberal sentiments, the growth of religious indifference, and political obligation all contributed to promoting the quiet passage of this act, hardly a revolutionary development on the surface. The act made little change in actual practice and left in force many more real discriminations against Dissenters—the obligation to pay church rates to the Anglican Church, the inability to be married by anyone but an Anglican minister, burial difficulties, exclusion from Oxford and Cambridge, and so on. But the concession of principle made in 1828 was of the first importance. Now only entrenched political power, not constitutional principles, could preserve the remaining disabilities of the Dissenters. The concession of 1828, then, opened a new chapter in Dissenting history.

[handwritten margin: other hindrances]

Catholic Emancipation

Possibly, in the expansive atmosphere of the time, Catholic Emancipation could have been granted almost as easily, had it not been an Irish rather than a religious question. As it was, Catholic Emancipation was the major political issue of the twenties. The campaign for it had gone on in Ireland since the failure of Pitt's plan to implement the Union by granting Emancipation in 1801.* Matters took a new turn in 1811 when the Catholic Board was founded. Prior to this time, the Irish Whigs under Grattan and the Irish aristocracy had been willing to work for Emancipation with provision for "securities," the most frequently discussed of which was a veto by the English government over the appointment of Roman Catholic bishops. But this the Roman Catholic Church would not have, and popular opinion in overwhelmingly Catholic and not very enlightened Ireland was violently opposed to such controls. This position was taken up by the

*See above, pp. 141–143.

Catholic Board, whose agitation for unrestricted Emancipation became so troublesome to Dublin Castle by 1814 that Peel, then Chief Secretary, decided to suppress the Board.

By doing so, Peel put a temporary end to organized Emancipationist activity in Ireland, but he by no means settled the problem of public order in that wild and unhappy country; indeed, the last years of the war saw a new extensiveness and savagery in Irish rural violence. Characteristically linking repressive and forward-looking measures, Peel renewed the Insurrection Act for three years, which made it easier to put down disturbances; at the same time, under the Peace Preservation Act, he set up a professional police force to serve as a more effective continuous control than the Army. Less successful at first than Peel had hoped, the police were further reformed in 1822 and again in 1836, at last proving highly successful in reducing disorder; Peel's experience in Ireland underlay his initiative in London in 1829.

The Whig opposition at home continued to talk Emancipation. In 1817, a motion was defeated, thanks to a speech by Peel, who was consequently elected M.P. for Oxford University when a bye-election occurred at that fervently Anglican institution. But when in 1821 a motion passed the House of Commons and was defeated in the Lords, it was probably apparent to Peel, especially with the coming to power of the Emancipationist Canning, that it was only a matter of time until the concession would have to be made.

In 1823, the Irish Emancipationist agitation began again with the founding of the Catholic Association. Its leading spirit was Daniel O'Connell, a Dublin Roman Catholic lawyer of great ability and charm. Personally ambitious, unscrupulous, and a powerful demagogue, O'Connell formed an extraparliamentary pressure group with which he consolidated his control of Irish opinion and which, once Emancipation was achieved, he used to make himself the absolute dictator of Irish politics and a main pivot of English politics.

The technique of agitation was impressive. The Association was a middle-class club; early in 1824 it began to collect "Catholic Rent" contributed by poor people in parishes throughout the country, creating a campaign chest which by 1825 was bringing in £2,000 a week, not counting income from investments worth more than £13,000. Priests were admitted ex officio, serving as both recruiters and collectors. In 1825 Parliament responded with an act to suppress any association organized to agitate for changes in Church or state that met for longer than fourteen days or that collected money. The Association obediently dissolved and promptly reappeared as the New Catholic Association, operating by devious legal maneuvers within the limits of the act. In the general election of 1826, Ascendancy candidates were defeated wholesale by Emancipationists, even in places where the Ascendancy members held estates and possessed the usual electoral influence. Association agitators and priests literally marched Catholic forty-shilling freeholders to the polls to vote for the Association's candidates.

Faced with repeated Emancipationist motions in Parliament, Liverpool's government could only play for time, and the political confusion following his stroke and resignation made still further delay inevitable. But when Wellington's ministry came into office, it was clear that action could not be put off much longer—a decision not to renew the 1825 act against the Association was an important symptom—and in June, 1828, the government's hand was forced. In the reconstruction of the government after Huskisson's withdrawal, an Emancipationist named Vesey Fitzgerald, member for County Clare in Ireland, was given a ministerial post; constitutional practice required that he stand for reelection. O'Connell himself decided to oppose Fitzgerald, thus throwing down the ultimate challenge, for as a Roman Catholic he was ineligible to take the seat if elected. He won overwhelmingly, showing clearly that Ireland preferred her own representative over even a sympathetic Protestant landlord. Fortunately for the government, Parliament was not in session, so a decision could be postponed.

Wellington knew as soon as the election was over that further resistance was hopeless, and he said so to the King. Peel knew it too, though he saw no course for himself but resignation. After months of negotiation and uncertainty, the King was dragooned into consenting to Emancipation, and Peel's insistence on resigning was overborne. Political necessity triumphed over logic: in March the House was treated to the remarkable spectacle of the main spokesman for the opposition to Emancipation moving a bill to grant it. Other than keeping Catholics out of a few named offices, the act contained only one, possibly rather flimsy guarantee: the requirement that Catholic members take an oath upholding the royal power, rejecting the temporal power of the papacy, and agreeing to maintain the property settlement in the realm and to support the Protestant religion—in short, they were to promise not to undo the Reformation.

A separate act was passed to ensure that Emancipation would not be politically exploited; most of the Roman Catholic Irish to whom Pitt had given the vote in 1793 were disfranchised, by setting the Irish county franchise at £10 instead of 40s. But, whatever injustices resulted, England felt safer for knowing that there was no longer a large army of docile voters to be marched about at every election as had been done in County Clare. The Catholic middle and upper classes were willing enough to see the poorer voters go, as the necessary price of their own entry into Parliament.

Peel made one concession to consistency: he resigned his seat for Oxford, was defeated in the bye-election, and, just before introducing the bill, was returned somewhat embarrassingly under the patronage of a wealthy Jewish boroughmonger with a reputation for corruption. His resignation was not enough to save him from a savage attack by the "high and dry" Tories who felt that he and Wellington had betrayed them.

The Whigs in Power

In late June, 1830, George IV died, lamented by almost no one. He was succeeded by his brother, the Duke of Clarence, as William IV. A bluff, unintelligent man, and no model of morality for the nascent Victorian age, William IV was nonetheless popular, partly because he was a professional sailor and partly because he had somehow acquired a little reputation as a liberal. George's death automatically dissolved Parliament. The Wellington administration, despite the sniping of infuriated Tory extremists, seemed in a good position for the general election that had to follow. Little had disturbed the country in the year since the passage of Catholic Emancipation: Britain's reduced role in Europe called out no expressions of injured pride; and the government's policy of economy seemed to fit in with general desires. Even Whigs were speaking well of the prime minister, to be sure, with some hopes of promoting a coalition.

But two new elements had entered the picture. One was the revival of the issue of parliamentary reform. Overshadowed throughout the twenties by Catholic Emancipation, reform could now be brought forward as the great unsolved constitutional problem. Cobbett traveled about the country lecturing on reform. The question was regularly discussed in the Rotunda, a theater on the south side of the Thames that had become a gathering place for the metropolitan radicals. In January, 1830, Thomas Attwood, a Birmingham banker, organized the Birmingham Political Union to work for reform. Yet, in spite of these signs, the movement for reform grew slowly and unevenly. The working-class radicals remained isolated from politically potent opinion among the upper and middle classes, and even at the Rotunda, reform had to compete with other prescriptions for curing working-class ills — trade unionism, Owenite socialism, or the atheism preached by the Reverend Robert Taylor, "the Devil's Chaplain." Attwood's conversion to reform was the result of his frustration at being unable to bring the country around to his scheme for undoing the resumption of specie payments; flying in the face of economic orthodoxy, Attwood saw in paper money and inflation the solution for the country's economic problems, a plan that branded him as mad throughout most of the century, though recent generations have found some sympathy for him. Although Attwood's Political Union drew considerable support from Birmingham, it was discouraged at first by Joseph Parkes, the political manager of Birmingham radicalism, and supported by some ultra-Tories who were actually talking reform as a means of preventing further "treachery" from an irresponsible government. In February, 1830, the Marquess of Blandford, an ultra-Tory, and Lord John Russell each moved unsuccessfully a bill for moderate reform; in May, O'Connell introduced a bill for universal suffrage, which fared even less well. But by July, when Brougham, standing for a county seat in Yorkshire, made reform a main item of his program, it had become the dominant political question.

The second new element was the situation in France. The ultraconservative government of the Prince de Polignac responded to liberal victories in the July Elections by dissolving the Chamber of Deputies before it met; the upshot was a revolution that sent Charles X into exile in England and put Louis Philippe on the throne. There was widespread interest in these developments in Britain, much like the reaction to French events in 1789; the liberal upsurge and the revolution were matters for congratulation and complacent reflection. Very few, even among ardent reformers, thought the revolution an injunction to go and do likewise; and, although the news from Paris arrived in Britain while the elections were taking place, it had little electoral effect. After all, only a quarter of the seats were contested; half of them had been decided when the news came; and a sampling of the others shows that, as one would expect, elections still conformed to the eighteenth-century pattern of determination by local and personal forces. Where reform was an issue, as in Yorkshire, the decision to raise it had been made long before, and the French were only to be congratulated.

The government was afraid, nevertheless, that British radicals might take a cue from France; certainly excitement about reform grew rapidly in the months following the election. But at least until the new Parliament met in November, the Wellington administration seemed reasonably secure. To speak of "winning an election" remains anachronistic for 1830; the stability of a ministry still rested on the confidence of the king and on its ability to govern, one element in which was a general sense of confidence in the House of Commons; that in turn rested on the government's ability to combine personal loyalty and material obligation to produce majorities. Actually, political control had been seriously undermined by administrative and economical reforms, which had drastically cut down the numbers of places and sinecures available for political lubrication. Lacking the means or the idea of modern party discipline, politicians directly concerned with manipulating the patronage in the twenties were worried about how government could be carried on, given all the cleaning up that had been done. But Wellington and his ministers worried neither about that nor about the hysterical antics of his enemies on the right; they thought their greatest weakness was a shortage of talent in ministerial speakers, not in numbers. Overtures were made to the Canningites, and there was a general expectation, helped on by the events of 1829, that Wellington and Peel between them would produce a moderate measure of parliamentary reform. But when Parliament met, it quickly became clear that the government had lost the ability to maneuver and that it could be reinforced only at the price of concessions it was unwilling to make. Indeed, Wellington outraged the country by an incautious and extreme panegyric on the perfection of the representative system as it stood. Defeated on a relatively unimportant motion on the Civil List, Wellington resigned on November 16.

The King sent for Lord Grey, whose ministry was a compound mostly of Whigs and Canningite Tories. Huskisson was dead, killed by a railway engine in September at the opening of the Liverpool and Manchester Railway. But from Huskisson's followers Grey drew Lord Palmerston as Foreign Secretary, Lord Melbourne as Home Secretary, Lord Goderich (the former prime minister) as War and Colonial Secretary, and Charles Grant at the Board of Control. Of the Whigs, Lord Grey put his own connections into office, the most important being his son-in-law, Lambton, now raised to the peerage as Lord Durham. The elder statesmen of the group, Lords Lansdowne and Holland, having declined the Foreign Office, received cabinet posts with great dignity but few duties; Lord Althorp, heir to the earldom of Spencer, was Chancellor of the Exchequer; within a few months, Lord John Russell entered the cabinet as Paymaster General. Sir James Graham and Lord Stanley, who went to the Admiralty and to the Chief Secretaryship for Ireland, represented a small independent faction around the Marquess of Stafford. The Duke of Richmond, a Tory, became Postmaster General. The government was overwhelmingly aristocratic, more so than any government since the eighteenth century; only four of the fourteen members of the cabinet sat in the Commons, all but one were great landlords, and the one—Poulett Thomson, a free trader named vice-president of the Board of Trade—was left in no doubt by the sneering reception he got in the House as to what it meant to be a mere merchant. There was one more problem:

Brougham was an embarrassment in the Commons. The only way the Whigs could get rid of him was to raise him to the peerage as Baron Brougham and make him Lord Chancellor.

The Reform Acts

The new government did not act much like an administration speeding on the historians' "age of reform." It undertook rigorous enforcement of the laws against the unstamped press, which in the growing excitement was gaining a new lease on life. It also moved firmly — there was no choice — to suppress a series of violent outbreaks in the southern agricultural districts. The riots, which Mr. and Mrs. Hammond called "the last labourers' revolt," were an expression of an ancient but usually suppressed hostility. Changes in the mode and standard of life that the new agricultural order had brought about had been made more difficult to bear by intolerably low wages, kept that way by the Speenhamland plan of wage subsidies and by degrading practices in the administration of the poor law. Serving "Captain Swing" as industrial workers had served "General Ludd," the rioters burned hayricks, smashed threshing machines (just then being introduced), and managed to get some raises in pay. But there was no general or concerted plan, no (or very little) impact of ideas, though many worried people put the blame on everything from foreign agents to beershops, from unstamped papers to Cobbett's lecture tours. Government action against press and rioters quickly destroyed any admiration working-class radicals had had for the Whigs, a word that now became a term of abuse in their vocabulary.

In early 1831 the country was in an uproar. Reform, which six months before had been advocated spasmodically by an ill-assorted collection of radicals and ultra-Tories, was now being talked about everywhere. The Birmingham Political Union quickly played down its connection with currency reform, and other political unions were organized by self-conscious middle-class elements in provincial towns. When Lord Stanley was made Chief Secretary for Ireland and had to stand for re-election to his seat at Preston, he was opposed by Henry Hunt, the old demagogue of the postwar years, and Hunt won — not too surprising considering the excitement and the fact that Preston had a very wide suffrage. There were some serious strikes among the miners and the Lancashire cotton spinners, and in Ireland O'Connell chose to launch a new agitation for repeal of the Union.

Against this background, Parliament reassembled in February, and on March 1, Lord John Russell redeemed the commitment of the Whigs to parliamentary reform. The comprehensiveness of his bill stunned the House, which had expected no more than a moderate tinkering with the constitution. The bill had been drafted by a committee composed of Russell, Lord Durham, Sir James Graham, and J. W. Ponsonby, a team whose orientation fell between moderate and radical. Durham's radical proposal of the secret ballot was rejected by the prime minister and the cabinet, who as landowners were not anxious to see their influence over their tenants destroyed at a blow. But beyond that, and in spite of the fact that the ultimate results of reform were not greatly to increase the number of voters, the bill proposed a drastic reorientation of the constitution.

The old constitution displayed wide diversity in its franchises. Illogical, complicated, picturesque, and defensible on no rational scheme, the variety was nevertheless eloquently defended, and not without some justification. Nomination boroughs, where there might be no or few residents, or residents entirely under the influence of one or two men or families, could be defended as devices for getting unknown young men into Parliament early, or for seating spokesmen for unpopular opinions, or as safe havens for ministers who could not undertake the labor and expense of fighting elections. On the other hand, the large scot-and-lot and freemen boroughs allowed otherwise unrepresented groups to have a parliamentary voice—Burdett sat for Westminster, and Hunt for Preston. Landed property was justly represented by nominees of landowners and by the independent members chosen under the wide and reputedly responsible county franchise; other forms of property were spoken for by wealthy businessmen and bankers who, for whatever reason, secured control of parliamentary boroughs, and by members elected by municipal corporations. The Church, the universities, and the government were guaranteed spokesmen for their interests. Out of this variety and tension of interests emerged the sense of the nation —effectively enough, it should be said, that the old system could be swept away by an unreformed Parliament when the country demanded it. The bill proposed to introduce order into this electoral variety. The new scheme was complicated, but it was intellectually defensible; at the same time, it took a long step towards substituting individuals for interests as the basis of representation.

The government proposed to retain the distinction between the county and borough franchises. The English county franchise was to remain basically the forty-shilling freehold, but to it were added copyholders and leaseholders whose tenure was long enough or whose property was valuable enough to guarantee their respectability. The terms of this franchise offered a good chance for negotiation, and there was much discussion and considerable revision in the precise terms. As finally passed, the act enfranchised, in addition to the old forty-shilling freeholders (subject to certain minor limitations), copyholders whose land had a "clear yearly value" of £10;* leaseholders whose leases were drawn for terms of at least sixty years and whose land had a clear yearly value of £10; leaseholders whose terms ran from twenty to sixty years, where the clear yearly value was £50; and, finally, persons actually occupying land rented on a yearly basis for not less than £50. This last qualification, usually referred to as the Chandos Clause, was proposed by the Tory Marquess of Chandos; the government opposed it, on the grounds that such "tenants at will," lacking the security of a long lease, would be subject to overwhelming landlord (and largely Tory) influence, but they had to give in to the combined pressure of landlords who wanted to increase their influence and radicals who wanted to enfranchise as many people as possible. In the counties, then, the franchise became more complicated than it had been under the old arrangements, and it unquestionably strengthened the political power of landlords.

In the boroughs, however, the franchise was drastically simplified. Those who had the vote before 1832, the so-called "ancient right" voters, could continue to vote as long as they were resident and did not move; there was, then, no serious disenfranchisement, though the possibility of it was much complained about by working-class radicals. But the basic borough voter was to be the ten-pound occupier—the man who either as owner or tenant actually occupied premises of a clear yearly value of £10, provided he had been resident for a year, was liable for the payment of poor rates, had paid all taxes and rates due from him when he came to register, and had not himself received poor relief for the preceding year. Although the franchise was uniform, the results of it were not. In London and certain other towns where rentals were high, most householders qualified under the act; in Cornwall, very few townsmen would qualify, and they would be well up on the social scale. In Leeds, few workingmen voted after 1832; in Manchester, a considerable number did. Certainly, one cannot say that the Reform Act enfranchised the middle classes and kept out the working classes: the provisions and the results were too complicated to allow so simple a summary.

Russell's bill also provided for a thorough reworking of the electoral map. The most drastic changes in the act as finally passed involved the complete disenfranchisement of fifty-six boroughs and the reduction of the representation of thirty others from two members to one; the Whigs showed a much less tender attitude towards property than Pitt had shown in his proposal in 1785 to abol-

*The "clear yearly value" was the amount which the property might reasonably be expected to let for, over and above taxes and incidental charges. This sum was roughly equivalent to the rent paid by a tenant.

ish nomination boroughs only with consent and compensation. The "curable" boroughs, as Lord Durham called them, were to have further therapy at the hands of commissioners authorized to redraw their boundaries, in the hope that enlargement would make corrupting them less easy. At the other end of the scale, twenty-two towns were given two representatives for the first time, including large urban centers like Leeds, Manchester, and Birmingham, and twenty new boroughs were created with single members. Nevertheless, large towns were still underrepresented: nearly half of the 187 English boroughs had registered electorates of between 300 and 1,000, and thirty-one had fewer than 300 registered electors; only sixty-four had over a thousand voters.

Eighteenth-century efforts at reform had stressed the county members as the guarantors of the independence of the Commons; consequently, the act as passed raised the representation for Yorkshire from four to six, two for each riding;* Lincoln and twenty-five other counties were divided, each part returning two members; the Isle of Wight was made a separate county with a single member; and seven counties each received a third member — a total increase in the English county representation of sixty-two. But this increase went only a little way towards redressing the gross overrepresentation of boroughs: 62 per cent of the English seats were still for boroughs, 38 per cent for the counties, though the counties contained over half the electorate. The smaller boroughs were often under rural influence, and certainly the new House was not antagonistic to the landed interest; but the disproportion indicates that the map makers did not think in terms of land versus commerce and industry. They were trying rather to balance the desire for a degree of independence and freedom from flagrant corruption with the necessities of political manipulation.

Other provisions set up a registration requirement for voters and a complex scheme for administering it,† rules for determining where votes should be cast in case of dual qualification, and limits on certain electoral expenses. There were also two further acts dealing with Scotland and Ireland. That for Scotland did little in the way of redistribution, except to add eight members for the towns (burghs). The franchise arrangements were similar to those in England — a £10 occupier franchise in the burghs, and a combination of ownership and leasehold qualifications in the counties — but their effects were revolutionary; an electorate that had numbered less than 5,000 in a

---

*Prior to 1974, the three divisions of Yorkshire were called "ridings," from the Anglo-Saxon word for "third."
†See below, pp. 211–212.

population of over two million now rose to something over 65,000. Scotland ceased to be primarily an electoral tool of a few large families and entered true parliamentary life for the first time since the Union. The Irish bill had less to do, as the reduction of the Irish parliamentary representation from 300 to 100 at the time of the Union had forced the disenfranchisement of the rotten boroughs; in consequence, the only change made in constituencies was the addition of five members, four for towns and one for Dublin University. The franchise in Irish boroughs was set at the usual £10 level, which gave the vote to a very small number, thanks to the poverty of the country and its low rentals. In the counties, the disenfranchisement of 1829 — a condition of Emancipation had been the substitution of a £10 freehold in the counties for the old forty-shilling freehold — was allowed to stand; the most the government was able to do (or wanted to do) was to extend the vote to leaseholders. At first they proposed enfranchising fifty-pound leaseholders for twenty-one years, an extremely high qualification reduced in later versions to ten-pound leaseholders for twenty years, still a very restricted franchise in a poor country. The Irish settlement was much less generous than the Scottish; probably no English government could have been expected to do more, considering the political situation and the automatic distrust of the Irish. But Irish members and spokesmen expected more, and the grudge they bore at what seemed to them a real injustice was an important ingredient in Anglo-Irish politics for decades.

The Scottish and Irish bills were introduced shortly after the English bill, and their fate followed the course of the centrally important debates on England. The final provisions of the act varied little in detail (the Chandos Clause was the most important change) and not at all in principle from the provisions of the bill as introduced. But the time elapsed was over a year, a year probably unmatched in English history for the sweep and intensity of its excitement.

After considerable debate, the first bill was passed in the Commons on March 22 by a majority of one vote: in mid-April, when Lord John reintroduced the bill with minor changes, the Tories protested against the reduction in English representation and carried a motion against it. The government had announced that they would consider acceptance of this motion a rejection of the bill; they now persuaded a reluctant king to dissolve Parliament to enable them to carry the specific issue of reform to the country in a general election. Demanding "the bill, the whole bill, and nothing but the bill," the government and their supporters in the country won a clear victory, and the new bill, introduced in June, was carried on the second reading by a majority of 136. The discussion of detailed provisions occupied the House until September, and changes were proposed, adopted, and withdrawn as the delicate political balance in the House and the pressure of public opinion dictated. The bill was taken to the Lords on September 21; there, two weeks later, it was defeated on the second reading by a majority of forty-one.

The outcry in the country was directed against the peers and especially against the bishops. Twenty-one bishops had voted against the bill; only two had voted for it, and seven had abstained; had the episcopal noes been ayes, the bill would have carried. There were riots in Derby; at Nottingham, the castle, which belonged to the Duke of Newcastle, was burned down; at the end of October, in Bristol, the mob, like that at Derby, broke open the jails, and went on to burn the town hall and the bishop's palace. The political unions were active everywhere, and in London the Rotunda group organized, to Place's disgust, a class-conscious socialist body grandiloquently called the National Union of the Working Classes; its agitation was to culminate in a mass meeting in early November. The government, in full cry after the unstamped press and the self-conscious revolutionaries, issued a proclamation calling for suppression of every disorder, mobilized troops under Wellington, and persuaded the National Union to postpone its meeting. The middle-class political unions also began to take a more cautious line. In December, Lord John introduced a third bill; it passed the Commons shortly with a second reading majority of 162. Details again occupied the House until March; in April, the bill passed a second reading in the Lords by nine votes, only to be defeated on a minor amendment which the government refused to accept. The King refused Grey's request to create new peers to swamp the opposition, and on May 8 the ministers again resigned. The King sent for Wellington, and the initiative returned to the country.

The continued political crisis during 1831 had had a seriously adverse effect on the economy. The stagnation in turn increased the pressure on popular opinion and was certainly a major ingredient in the short-lived violence of late October. In spite of the continued recession, there were no more serious disturbances, a fact that speaks well for the discipline the political unions were able to impose and for the nonrevolutionary nature of a country sufficiently conscious of its liberty to believe that reform would come in spite of setbacks. But the national temper underwent a new trial early in 1832 when Asiatic cholera arrived from the Continent in epidemic proportions; the religious elements in the country, reading a divine judgment into the plague, proposed a national fast day which the government, to the derisive parodies of the ultraradicals, proclaimed for March 21. Against this background was set Wellington's attempt to form a ministry. Rumors flew about; great meetings were held; church bells were rung nightly; taxes were stopped; there were ugly demonstrations; and on the morning of May 13, London and some provincial towns were placarded with signs reading "To stop the Duke, go for gold": Francis Place and his friends had organized a run on the Bank of England. The demonstration probably had little effect on Wellington, who was rumored to be planning a measure of moderate reform; but on May 14, a number of prominent Tories spoke sharply about the immorality of such a proceeding, especially from ministers who had already appeared as turncoats on Catholic Emancipation. The next day Wellington gave up, and the King recalled Lord Grey.

Wellington confidentially told the King that he would not oppose the bill but would abstain and use his influence to persuade other opponents to do likewise—a characteristic act which Grey nevertheless chose to reinforce by exacting a promise from the King to create peers if necessary. This promise forced Wellington to make his position public, and, on June 4, the bill passed by 106 votes to 22. The royal assent was given on June 7.

The Reform Acts completed the revolution in Church and state which had begun in 1828. Of the three changes, Catholic Emancipation had the largest immediate effect, in opening politics to Catholics and particularly to Irish nationalists. The actual position of Dissenters changed little, and the reformed Parliament, as we shall see, was not unlike the unreformed Parliament. Yet 1828 and 1829, taken together, marked a theoretical departure of great constitutional importance. Though the implications were a long time in working out, one can properly date from those years the breakdown of the theory of a single politico-religious society and the devaluation of the idea of an Establishment. So too with reform. The Tories foresaw (from their standpoint) the worst: that the balance of the constitution would be upset, that the king could no longer choose his ministers, that the Lords would be unable to stand against a determined House of Commons, nor the House of Commons against a determined public. They predicted the destruction of old institutions, the ruin of deference and legitimate influence, the subjection of land and agriculture by commerce and industry or, worse, by shopkeepers. They were sure, moreover, once a single concession was made, once the illogic of the old system was swept away by rational devices, however complicated, that in due time more concessions would be demanded and granted, more reform would come, and the old world they wanted to hold on to would slip more rapidly into history.

To such laments the Whigs replied that the reform was in fact moderate, that land received notable, indeed increased, guarantees, that influence and deference were built into the political structure, especially as there was no secret ballot. In fact, they said, in its practical results their measure was no more than a slight opening of the oligarchy to interests and individuals who had proved by their wealth, intelligence, and responsibility that they deserved to be included. But these arguments did not touch the theoretical farsightedness of the Tories; it was certainly no answer to say that a comprehensive but moderate reform such as the Whigs carried would obviate the necessity of further reform. To talk, as Grey and Russell did, of a final settlement was political fantasy. The only conclusive argument the reformers offered was that they had no choice: there was enough unrest, enough violence, enough organization, and enough remembering to make men think first of the possibility of revolution and how to avoid it by reform—a reform whose revolutionary quality only later generations could discover.

Through fifteen months of debate there was much talk of fundamental principles, distilling long experience and revealing wisdom on both sides. The debates are worth reading because they are still applicable and always will be, while men retain political choice. But Professor Gash has summed up the debates by observing simply: "What the tories said was true; but what the whigs did was necessary."* The competing positions were at bottom irreconcilable, and both sides lost: the Tories the world they wanted to preserve, the Whigs the security they hoped to create. But for many years—and in spite of the exceptions, injustices, and timidities with which the new arrangements were riddled—the reformed constitution worked.

Selected Readings

With 1815, the *Oxford History of England* moves on to E. L. Woodward, *The Age of Reform, 1815–1870* (1938, 2nd. ed. 1962). The still commanding analysis of the first volume of Elie Halévy's *History of the English People, England in 1815* (1913, trans. 1924) is indispensable, and the series turns to narrative with *The Liberal Awakening, 1815–1830* (1923, trans. 1926). Asa Briggs's *Age of Improvement*, already cited, remains the best single volume that puts the period in context.

The troubled years of 1815–1822 have received much attention. The famous indictment of the government in J. L. and Barbara Hammond, *The Town Labourer, 1760–1832* (1917) is echoed in E. P. Thompson's *Making of the English Working Class*, already cited, but sympathetic views of the government's dilemma and response are advanced in R. J. White, *Waterloo to Peterloo* (1957) and J. E. Cookson, *Lord Liverpool's Administration: The Crucial Years, 1815–1822* (1975). Books cited in the previous chapter for Luddism remain relevant, and as Major Cartwright returns to the lists, John W. Osborne's life, cited in Chapter 2, returns to the list. Thompson and White give

*Norman Gash, *Politics in the Age of Peel* (1953), p. 11.

interestingly contrasted interpretations of the Pentrich rising of 1817, and some of the disturbances of the preceding year are treated in A. J. Peacock, *Bread or Blood: A Study of the Agrarian Riots in East Anglia in 1816* (1965). Robert F. Wearmouth, *Methodism and the Working-Class Movements of England, 1800–1850* (1937) is also valuable. The most traumatic event of the period is dealt with in Donald Read, *Peterloo: The "Massacre" and Its Background* (1958) and R. Walmsley, *Peterloo: The Case Reopened* (1969). See also Malcolm I. Thomis and Peter Holt, *Threats of Revolution of Britain, 1789–1840* (1977). A persuasive revisionist study of crucial economic and legislative decisions of the period, the Corn Law of 1815 and the return to specie payments, is Boyd Hilton, *Corn, Cash, Commerce: The Economic Policies of the Tory Government, 1815–1830* (1977).

Hilton's work also qualifies the interpretation of the liberalizing years after 1822 given in W. R. Brock's influential *Lord Liverpool and Liberal Toryism, 1820 to 1827* (2nd ed., 1967). Some of the principal ministers involved in the perceived but partial shift in policy and tone have received authoritative biographical studies: Peter Dixon, *Canning, Politician and Statesman* (1976); the balanced essays in P. J. V. Rolo, *George Canning: Three Biographical Studies* (1965); Wilbur Devereux Jones, *"Prosperity" Robinson: The Life of Viscount Goderich, 1782–1859* (1967); Norman Gash, *Mr. Secretary Peel: The Life of Sir Robert Peel to 1830* (1961); and (on the other side) Elizabeth Longford, *Wellington: Pillar of State* (1972); but two central ministers (also opposed), Huskisson and Eldon, remain biographical blanks.

On the continuities that underlay the apparent shift in foreign policy between the two periods of the Liverpool ministry, C. K. Webster, *The Foreign Policy of Castlereagh, 1815–1822* (1925) and H. W. V. Temperley, *The Foreign Policy of Canning, 1822–1827* (1925). Greece was the most appealing cause of the Liberals but one of the more ambiguous areas of government policy; on that question, C. W. Crawley, *The Question of Greek Independence: A Study of British Policy in the Near East, 1821–1833* (1930, 1973); C. M. Woodhouse, *The Philhellenes* (1971); and W. C. St. Clair, *That Greece May Still Be Free: The Philhellenes in the War of Independence* (1972).

On aspects of economic policy, besides Hilton, there are many valuable studies: R. L. Schuyler, *The Fall of the Old Colonial System* (1945); F. W. Fetter, *The Development of British Monetary Orthodoxy, 1797–1875* (1965); L. S. Pressnell, *Country Banking in the Industrial Revolution* (1956); and S. G. Checkland, *Scottish Banking, a History, 1695–1973* (1975). On political economy, coming into its own in these years, D. P. O'Brien, *The Classical Economists* (1975), an excellent introduction, and J. R. McCulloch, *A Study in Classical Economy* (1970); Marian Bowley, *Nassau Senior and Classical Economics* (1937); Lionel Robbins, *Robert Torrens and the Evolution of Classical Economics* (1958) and *The Theory of Economic Policy in English Classical Political Economy* (1961); Mark Blaug, *Ricardian Economics* (1958), a study of controversy among the economists in these years; and Barry Gordon, *Political Economy in Parliament, 1819–1823* (1977).

On law reform, in addition to Gash's life of Peel, see Leon Radzinowicz, *A History of the English Criminal Law and Its Administration from 1750* (4 vols.,

1948–1968) and J. J. Tobias, *Crime and Industrial Society in the 19th Century* (1967).

On the press, which moves in these years to its maturity, A. Aspinall, *Politics and the Press, c. 1780–1850* (1949); Donald Read, *Press and People, 1790–1850* (1961); the multi-volumed, anonymous *History of the Times* (1935–1952); and David Ayerst, *Guardian: Biography of a Newspaper* (1971). The periodical press is best approached through John Clive, *Scotch Reviewers* (1957), on the *Edinburgh Review;* G. L. Nesbitt, *Benthamite Reviewing* (1934), on the *Westminster Review;* and Francis E. Mineka, *The Dissidence of Dissent* (1944) on the outstanding Unitarian periodical *The Monthly Repository* (1806–1838), with an introductory chapter on religious periodicals. On the early phase of the radical "unstamped" press, W. H. Wickwar, *The Struggle for the Freedom of the Press, 1819–1832* (1928), and R. K. Webb, *The British Working Class-Reader, 1790–1848: Literacy and Social Tension* (1955), which deals primarily with middle-class efforts to counter the effects of radical publishing, notably the S.D.U.K. On cheap literature generally, Richard D. Altick, *The English Common Reader* (1957). Adult education, a new, promising, and sanitizing movement in these years, J. F. C. Harrison, *Learning and Living, 1790–1860* (1962) and Mabel Tylecote, *The Mechanics' Institutes of Lancashire and Yorkshire before 1851* (1957). There are some perceptive remarks on the contributions of the press and self-education to working-class consciousness in E. P. Thompson, *The Making of the English Working Class,* Chapter 16.

John Stuart Mill's essays on Bentham and Coleridge (1838 and 1840) appear in his *Dissertations and Discussions* (4 vols., 1859–1875) but have often been reprinted elsewhere and are easily available. On Coleridge's seminal conception of "clerisy," Ben Knights, *The Idea of the Clerisy in the Nineteenth Century* (1978). The most striking new initiative in higher education is treated in detail in H. Hale Bellot, *University College, London, 1826–1926* (1929).

Years in the political wilderness brought important changes to the Whigs and to their constitutional role: Austin Mitchell, *The Whigs in Opposition, 1815–1830* (1967); C. W. New, *The Life of Henry Brougham to 1830* (1961); Archibald S. Foord, *His Majesty's Opposition, 1714–1830* (1964); and Caroline Robbins, "'Discordant Parties': A Study of the Acceptance of Party by Englishmen," *Political Science Quarterly,* vol. 73, pp. 505–529 (December, 1958). The unity of the constitutional reforms of 1828–1832 is argued in G. F. A. Best, "The Constitutional Revolution, 1828–1832," *Theology,* vol. 62, pp. 226–234 (June, 1959).

Richard W. Davis, *Dissent in Politics, 1780–1830: The Political Life of William Smith, M.P.* (1971) deals with the principal parliamentary spokesman for Dissent, whose career culminated in the repeal of the Test and Corporation Acts; see also Ursula Henriques, *Religious Toleration in England, 1787–1833* (1961). The Irish background of Catholic Emancipation can be traced in R. B. McDowell, *The Irish Administration, 1801–1914* (1964); T. Desmond Williams, ed., *Secret Societies in Ireland* (1973), dealing among other groups earlier and later with the Orange order, which is the subject of Hereward Senior, *Orangeism in Ireland and Britain, 1795–1836* (1966). Galen Broeker,

Rural Disorder and Police Reform in Ireland, 1812–36 (1970) is important not only for Irish disturbances but for the precedent established for police reform in Britain. There is, alas, no satisfactory biography of Daniel O'Connell. G. I. T. Machin, *The Catholic Question in English Politics, 1820–1830* (1964) is indispensable for the other side of St. George's Channel.

Michael Brock, *The Great Reform Act* (1973) is now the standard account of the passage of reform, and the opening chapters of Norman Gash's *Politics in the Age of Peel* (1953) form a valuable summary of the acts' provisions and of debate over them. The extensive rural disturbances that were part of the context of reform are dealt with in an overwrought way in the famous book by J. L. and Barbara Hammond, *The Village Labourer, 1760–1832* (1911), which has been supplanted for most purposes by a not less sympathetic study, E. J. Hobsbawm and George Rudé, *Captain Swing: A Social History of the Great English Agricultural Uprising of 1830* (1968). S. G. Checkland, "The Birmingham Economists, 1815–1830," *Economic History Review*, 2nd ser., vol. 1, pp. 1–19 (1948), explains the economic circumstances and heterodox thinking that helped to bring Attwood and the Birmingham Political Union into the fray. Norman Gash, "English Reform and French Revolution in the General Election of 1830," in R. Pares and A. J. P. Taylor, eds., *Essays Presented to Sir Lewis Namier* (1956), discounts the influence of the contemporary upheaval on the Continent. Joseph Hamburger, *James Mill and the Art of Revolution* (1963) is a suggestive interpretation of the radical agitation for the bill, and M. I. Thomis and P. Holt, *Threats of Revolution*, cited earlier, is also relevant. A controversial interpretation of motivations behind the bill appears in articles by D. C. Moore, whose book, *The Politics of Deference: A Study of the Mid-Nineteenth Century English Political System* (1976), incorporates the argument and gives the citations.

Part II
THE EXPANDED OLIGARCHY: EARLY VICTORIAN ENGLAND

1832–1867

Chapter 5
The Impact of Reform

1832–1848

For forty years the Reverend Sydney Smith made educated Englishmen laugh. He was a founder of the *Edinburgh Review*, a canon of St. Paul's, and a perfect Whig; complacent, rational, a little old-fashioned, and a little skeptical, he was perhaps the finest and certainly the best-known wit of his time. When the House of Lords rejected the Reform bill, he made a speech at Taunton comparing their Lordships to a Mrs. Partington who during a great storm vainly tried to keep the Atlantic away from the door of her cottage. He exactly caught the national mood, and may well have been more symptomatic than, say, the National Union of the Working Classes: no revolution was needed to defeat an institution people had come to think of as an old woman, singularly defective in a sense of proportion, trying to fight back an ocean with a mop.

Sydney Smith made still another incisive remark about the reform excitement which can serve as the text for this chapter:

> All young ladies will imagine (as soon as this bill is carried) that they
> will be instantly married. Schoolboys believe that gerunds and supines
> will be abolished, and that currant tarts must ultimately come down in

price; the corporal and sergeant are sure of double pay; bad poets will expect a demand for their epics; fools will be disappointed, as they always are. . . .*

In prospect, the Reform bills seemed to promise more than the theoretical and symbolic values historians now attach to them. Much of the country had really come to believe that reforming Parliament would mean great changes, for good or bad. But the changes directly ascribable to the Reform Acts were difficult to interpret, not always easy to account for, and sometimes astonishing.

POLITICS AND THE CONSTITUTION

Party Politics

The techniques and tone of politics changed very little from pre-Reform days. To be sure, some places now represented for the first time acquired a political life they had not had before, but they did little more than take over practices hardly questioned by most people and untouched by legislation. In some small boroughs whose boundaries had been enlarged, the balance of interests changed and new patrons and viewpoints had to be accommodated, but these were shifts of people, not methods. The already high cost of elections went up: election officials still had to be paid their fees; as contested elections increased in number, paid agents became more necessary and canvassing more extensive; there were more electors to be treated or bribed. Riot and violence remained ever-present possibilities, and as long as the candidates had to make public appearances on the hustings—the platforms from which they spoke on nomination day—they could expect the traditional pelting with stones, dead cats, rotten eggs, or anything nasty that was throwable. The practice lasted until the hustings were abolished in the Ballot Act of 1872, and as late as 1868 the very rich and very serious Dissenting M.P. Samuel Morley had to address his constituents in Bristol from behind an open umbrella.†

More important than the survival of these irrational and colorful customs was the perpetuation of influence. There were still pocket or

---

Works (Philadelphia, 1844), III, 114–115.
†E. Hodder, *The Life of Samuel Morley* (1887), pp. 272–274. Two contemporary fictional accounts of elections deserve mention: the prereform election for the borough of Onevote, near the large town of Novote, in Thomas Love Peacock's *Melincourt* (1817)—in which one of the candidates was an orangutan—and the famous Eatanswill election in Charles Dicken's *Pickwick Papers* (1836).

proprietary boroughs, where the electorate was so small and the influence of one man so great that he could in effect name the member. William Ewart Gladstone, the future prime minister, entered Parliament in 1832 for the borough of Newark, which "belonged to" the Duke of Newcastle; when Gladstone committed himself to free trade in 1845, his protectionist patron refused to accept him as a candidate for re-election. But even in larger constituencies, the influence of a large landowner with voting tenants, a dominant manufacturer, a university, or the government could be decisive. In the rural districts, influence was least disturbed. Though their numbers were decreasing, many constituencies still managed to escape political contests; in such places elections continued to be mere formalities to register decisions reached in quiet meetings of the leading political families. When a contest occurred, it was likely to reflect a struggle for power between rival families; it was not to give the voters a choice.

Although the survival of influence depended on open voting, it would be wrong to think that most voters were coerced into voting against their wishes. To be sure, vengeance could be threatened and in cases carried out against hardy souls who dared to disagree with the announced choice of a patron or landlord, but, given a free choice, voters and tenants in rural districts would probably have agreed with their superiors on almost everything. Except among politically vocal townsmen, there was little open questioning of the wisdom or the power of the men who owned the land, handed down justice from the bench, and sat proudly in Parliament as the natural representatives of their localities. Despite some stirrings, early Victorian England remained what Walter Bagehot, in mid-century, called a deferential society.

By and large, then, the electorate behaved in traditional ways and was appealed to or controlled locally by traditional methods. But more and more candidates bore party labels. Even though the name of Whig or Conservative might mask political positions that were essentially local or personal — much like party labels in the United States today — the trend forecast the doom of the independent members, the "country party," who had counted for so much in the political calculations of the preceding century. Moreover, the reduction of offices and sinecures and the waning of "the influence of the Crown" had seriously reduced the government's ability to control the House of Commons by eighteenth-century methods, and consequently "winning" elections became more important. Modern political parties were still a generation or two in the future, but their foundations were necessarily laid in the thirties and forties.

The Reform Acts provided one new means of mobilizing the electorate by requiring the registration of voters. Strictly speaking, the many complex qualifications for the franchise set down in the Reform Acts were qualifications for entry in the register of voters, a list compiled by local officers and kept up to date by barristers appointed by the judges of assize to hold annual revising courts. Challenging unqualified and inimical voters and encouraging qualified but apathetic men to register were important jobs for local party enthusiasts. In some instances it was even possible to create qualifications. Thus, a landlord out to increase his political power might subdivide a large parcel of land into forty-shilling freeholds and sell them to those among his tenants whose leaseholds were insufficient to qualify them as voters. He might lease the land back from them, if he wished, so that the operation of the estate would remain unchanged, but the new freeholders would have the vote and would undoubtedly use it in his interest. In the forties, the Anti-Corn-Law League resorted to such creation of "faggot" voters; so did party managers.

In the localities, keeping an eye on the register and cultivating voters were responsibilities of local agents who in turn formed associations to help in the work. But these local bodies were often isolated from each other, and, given the growing importance of elections and the political needs of government, a central clearinghouse was necessary. In the eighteenth century, the day-to-day work in London — the planning of strategy and tactics, the interviewing, the endless letter writing — had been done by men like the Duke of Newcastle or George Rose; they were members of Parliament, ministers, or civil servants as well. By the early Victorian period, political agents were becoming professionals or near-professionals. Francis Place had been highly effective as a free-lance radical manager maneuvering for his own causes; the evolution of the breed reached a new stage in the thirties and forties with F. R. Bonham, Peel's chief political adviser, and Joseph Parkes, the lawyer from Birmingham who ran the machine for the Radicals and Whigs.

These men had no party headquarters in the modern sense and not much staff; though political managing was no longer a part-time job, the task was still small and informal enough to be handled personally or through one or two lieutenants. But it was useful to have bases to operate from, and they were found in the London political clubs. There M.P.'s from the country could stay and dine, local agents could report on sentiment at home, constituencies could be found for unattached candidates, and strategy could be plotted. The Whig clubs, Brooks's and White's, were politicized descendants of eighteenth-century gambling clubs, but the Carlton, founded by the Tories in 1832, was more serious; it quickly became their political center, its position assured by imposing a strict test of party regularity for membership. In 1836, a few Radicals, Parkes among them, organized the Reform Club. They were certain that if only they could get the Whigs in a good mood and talk to them—they had no doubt of their own persuasiveness—they could win them over; so they hired the fashionable architect Charles Barry to design the building and Alexis Soyer, one of the great chefs in Europe, to run the kitchens, only to find that real Whigs were harder to convert, even when well fed, than they had thought.*

The House of Commons

Politics in the country remained much the same, then, after 1832. So did politics at Westminster; and much that seemed new was rooted in the pre-Reform past. Many observers thought that the House of Commons elected in 1832 was noisier and less gentlemanly, but if there was such a change in tone, it must have been owing rather to the political excitement of that time, to the feverish temper of the country, and possibly to the livelier conversational style becoming common in society in those years. Except perhaps for the Irish, it could not be blamed on the influx of "new men." Indeed, the composition of the House of Commons in 1833 was little different from what it was in 1831, nor did it change significantly before the last quarter of the century. In 1838, the property qualification for membership—£300 in yearly value—was modified to include movable property as well as land; in 1858, it was abolished; but members were still unpaid and the cost of serving was likely to be high. When elections took place, they were expensive; ordinary political costs rose; and being in Parliament was becoming time-consuming enough that earning a living on the side was increasingly difficult. The country expected its representatives to be independently wealthy, and most of them were. The House remained overwhelmingly the preserve of the landed classes. There were no more businessmen in the first reformed Parliament than had been there before 1832; there was a mere handful of Dissenters. The numbers of both businessmen and Dissenters increased in subsequent elections; but they remained very much in a minority, and, while Dissenters grew more and more vocal in advancing their principles, not many businessmen showed

*Norman Gash, *Politics in the Age of Peel* (1953) contains a fascinating chapter on "Club Government." Soyer was impressive. The modern kitchens of the Reform Club were a sight shown to all distinguished visitors to London. A pioneer of modern quantity cookery, Soyer set up soup kitchens during the Irish famine and field kitchens to feed the troops in the Crimean War. See Helen Morris, *Portrait of a Chef* (1938).

their "newness" aggressively.* Though there were only 150 or so Tories in the House of Commons elected in 1832, most of the huge Whig majority fundamentally agreed with them and gracefully acknowledged it by electing a Tory as speaker.

There was one new element in the post-Reform House—the little group of self-styled Radicals. Twenty or so of them formed "O'Connell's tail," an Irish nationalist group serving their own purposes by alliances of convenience and obstruction. But only among the English Radicals could be found what one worried Tory, in the debates on the Reform bill, had called "the active, pushing, intelligent people" who he feared would come from the manufacturing districts to overwhelm the simpler squires.† The Radicals are not easily reducible to obvious patterns. Henry Hunt had been defeated for Preston, but William Cobbett, now M.P. for the textile town of Oldham in Lancashire, was there to speak, in his idiosyncratic way, for the working classes. John Fielden, though a wealthy factory owner, was another defender of the working classes and an ardent champion of factory regulation. Burdett, still classed as a Radical, was rapidly turning his back on his old associates; Attwood, on the other hand, had forsaken his earlier inclinations to Toryism and as member for Birmingham was to speak for moderate reform and, as always, his currency scheme. George Grote, a London banker, came from the inner circle around Jeremy Bentham, whose death had occurred just after passage of the Reform bill; the novelist Edward Bulwer Lytton was for a time associated with the utilitarians, as were a number of other young men. Some of these M.P.'s were radicals by experience, others were radical intellectuals. Few of them agreed, and they certainly could not be welded into a disciplined party. They did not, then, represent any simple version of "middle-class interests." The essence of their radicalism probably lay in nothing more than the fact that they wanted action. But, at least for the time being, they thought of themselves as standing apart from the older combinations.

The role played by the Radicals illustrates two vital characteristics of parliamentary history in the early Victorian period. First, although the idea of a division between government and opposition had quickly become normal,‡ and although most members bore

---

*Businessmen may have been seduced by the aristocratic style, but at the same time the aristocrats took warmly to the financial opportunities increasingly offered to them in business—as investors and as impressive and decorative names on boards of directors. See W. O. Aydelotte, "The Business Interests of the Gentry in the Parliament of 1841–47," an appendix to G. Kitson Clark, *The Making of Victorian England* (1962).

†Alexander Baring, quoted in Gash, *Politics in the Age of Peel* (1953), p. 6.

‡See above, pp. 180–181.

party labels, there was nothing like the party discipline that governs the parliamentary parties in the Commons today. Individual members consequently had much more power then than they have now; personal enthusiasms could be translated into bills, promoted, and carried — with or without government support. In such a situation, the advantage lay with men like the Radicals who knew what they wanted, whose intellect, training, and experience had taught them what was needed and, usually, the one sure way of getting it.

Secondly, the Radicals were spokesmen for segments of public opinion outside Parliament, a public opinion that continued in a state of high excitement and expectation after the passage of the Reform bill. The political unions did not at once disband, but flooded the Commons with petitions; so did other interested groups — there was so much petitioning that the House had to revise its rules to avoid wasting time by hearing them all read. To be effective, of course, public opinion had to be brought to bear upon enough members to win divisions in the House, and the parliamentary history of the next few decades makes it clear that the House was more a barrier to popular desires than it was a channel for them. The organs of opinion, the machinery of party, the cultivation of voters were still too rudimentary to depreciate seriously the independence and initiative of Parliament. But if the Reform Acts left the Commons much the same as before and acting in much the same way, despite the hopes of the more radical reformers, the very passing of the acts had shown that a really concerted expression of national opinion could not long be trifled with.

The Balance of the Constitution

Opponents of reform had predicted drastic effects on the balance of the constitution, as it had existed between king, Lords, and Commons. That they were proved only partly right may be another indication that a clear and unmistakable groundswell of opinion alone could force a fundamental alteration in the constitution; it was not going to fall easily to public whim or the tactics of pressure groups.

The intense unpopularity of the House of Lords after its rejection of the Reform bill in 1831 led to widespread expectations that the Lords would be drastically reformed or even abolished; it came as something of a surprise that the upper house survived intact for eighty years. Not that the Lords were ciphers: they were a constant stumbling block for Whig measures, and measures that got through were often badly mangled in the process. Yet the subjects on which the Lords dug in their heels were, for the most part, those on which a substantial part of the political country agreed with them — Ireland

and the Church. On the question of greatest urgency between 1832 and 1867, repeal of the Corn Laws, the Lords gave in, even though the measure seemed to threaten dire results for the economic interests of many of them. There was a certain amount of statesmanship shown in deciding the course taken by the upper house (Wellington is an excellent example), but the magnitude and inevitability of the aristocratic defeat in 1832 had shown even the less perceptive peers that they could not stand against a determined government relying upon a determined Commons: they had learned enough prudence to know what they dared and dared not do. Not until a new generation of peers faced more serious challenges to the security of their order, did the House of Lords again raise the question of whether or not their political power should continue.*

The king's power, on the other hand, was seriously curtailed shortly after 1832 because William IV tried to exercise it against the manifest will of the country. The crisis was complicated. Lord Grey's government was a coalition, as most governments had been, and coalitions could survive only when, as in the eighteenth century, no serious issues arose on which the collaborators disagreed. But a sweeping program of legislation, undertaken by the Grey government at the insistence of Radicals and its own radically inclined members, Durham, Russell, and Brougham, was certain to create alarm among more conservative ministers. As had been the case in the twenties, Ireland and the Church were the most controversial questions. Proposals for drastic reform of the Irish Church, including some reduction of its endowment,† brought the resignations of Stanley, Graham, Lord Ripon (formerly Goderich), and the Duke of Richmond—all Tories or former Tories—late in May, 1834. They were replaced by weak and colorless Whigs, to avoid tipping the balance of the cabinet towards the Radicals. The Radical faction meanwhile had been working out a collaboration with O'Connell—not the safest course, though one that continued to be a necessity of Radical politics—and when Lord Grey outraged O'Connell by insisting on renewing the Coercion Act to keep down Irish violence, Althorp, who had been in on the negotiations with O'Connell, resigned rather than support the renewal. Old, tired, and anxious to go back to his estates in Northumberland, Grey felt he could not continue without Althorp; early in July, he resigned.

The King wanted a coalition of Whigs and Tories, now an utter impossibility; he settled for Lord Melbourne, the Home Secretary and a former Canningite, as premier. Melbourne was a decorative

*See below, pp. 319, 427, 431, 461–466.
†See below, pp. 230–232.

survival: a consummate aristocrat, responsible but casual, hard-working while affecting indolence, liberal in the eighteenth-century sense, intensely conservative in nineteenth-century terms.* He persuaded Althorp to come back into the government only to lose him in November, when Althorp succeeded his father as Earl Spencer and went to the House of Lords. Melbourne then had little choice but to reinforce his weak ministry from the more radical wing of the party, specifically by promoting Lord John Russell to Althorp's post as Chancellor of the Exchequer. Neither Melbourne nor the King liked to do it, and the prime minister gave the King every chance and encouragement to turn his government out, which the King did promptly.

Wellington was sent for, standing in for Peel, who hurried back from an Italian holiday to form a ministry.† Peel characteristically inaugurated a series of reforms, carrying further his accomplishments of the twenties and threatening as before to steal the thunder of the Whigs and Radicals. But he was in a serious minority, even though the liberal majority was reduced in the general election of January, 1835. He resigned early in April after being defeated in the House of Commons on the Irish Church. Melbourne then returned to office under the most difficult circumstances: the Whig majority was down, Radical representation had doubled, and O'Connell was riding high. Melbourne's new government, though, was much as before: Brougham, who had made himself intolerable to the Whigs by his intrigue and injudicious language, was not reappointed, but Russell became Home Secretary, and the work of moderate reform went on.

This complicated cabinet crisis was a severe blow to the monarchy. To the public, the dismissal of Melbourne in 1834 looked like a royal *coup d'état*, and the results of the election of 1835 proved that the royal prerogative was no more insulated from a clear expression of opinion in the country than was the House of Lords. But the larger implications of this royal defeat were not easy to grasp. When Queen Victoria came to the throne in 1837, at the age of eighteen,‡ she

*The political diarist Greville reported that when Melbourne was offered the premiership, he said to his secretary that "he thought it a damned bore, and he was in many minds, what he should do—be a minister or no." His secretary replied that it was a post such as no Greek or Roman had ever held, and that even if the government lasted only two months, it would be worthwhile to have been prime minister of England. "By God, that's true," said Melbourne. "I'll go."
†On the eve of the "railway age," it took Peel as long to make the journey as it had taken Roman couriers 1,600 years earlier.
‡She was the daughter of the Duke of Kent, the third son of George III, who had died in 1820; as her two uncles had no legitimate surviving children, she was heiress presumptive from the accession of William IV.

depended entirely on her beloved Lord Melbourne who was, so to speak, father, tutor, and confessor rolled into one. In 1839, he was defeated on a vote in the Commons, and Victoria had to send for Peel. The Queen was so headstrong a Whig that Peel insisted that she show her confidence in him by allowing him to name a group of Conservative ladies of the bedchamber to replace the Whig ladies who attended her. Victoria refused, and Peel (with some relief) declined to take office. The "Bedchamber Crisis" confirmed the Queen in some unwarranted notions about her own power. Peel could have fought it through, had he really wanted to, for the lesson of 1835 was certainly that ministers were responsible to the House of Commons, not to the monarch. The balance of the constitution, as it had existed when George III came to the throne in 1760, had been destroyed. Talk about mixed government went on for years, however. It was in the mid-sixties that Walter Bagehot, in a famous essay on the English constitution, made the change obvious by lumping the monarchy and the peerage together as the "dignified" elements of the constitution, in contrast to the "efficient" elements—the House of Commons and the government responsible to it.

Responsible Government in the Colonies

This fundamental rearrangement of the British constitution had been going on for more than sixty years, at least from the time of North's resignation in 1782; it took nearly a century to get to Bagehot's intellectual ratification of the change. When the central shift occurred in the thirties, the issue of responsibility was presented, oddly enough, much more starkly in the colonies than at home, both in fact and in theory. India, being despotically ruled, and the West Indies, in the throes of ending slavery, were largely irrelevant to this issue,* but it became immediately pressing for Canada and was raised urgently in connection with the opening up of the convict colony in Australia.

In 1827 a young man about town, Edward Gibbon Wakefield, and some of his friends concocted a wild scheme for his abducting and marrying an heiress. The girl they fixed on was Ellen Turner, then a sixteen-year-old schoolgirl; though Wakefield had never met her, he invented a pretext for getting her away from school and persuaded her that being married to him was precisely what she wanted. The wedding took place at Gretna Green, a famous spot for quick marriages just over the Scottish Border, and the pair were finally seized in France by the authorities and the girl's indignant parents. An annulment followed, and Wakefield spent three years in

---

*On the West Indies, see below, pp. 320–321; and on India, see pp. 311–316.

Newgate prison. Before this escapade, Wakefield had been in touch with the London Radicals, including Place, and had published a couple of pamphlets, including one on transportation of convicts to the colonies. During his enforced retirement from the world, Wakefield devoted himself closely to the study of colonial problems; in 1829, while still in jail, he published *A Letter from Sydney*, under the name of a young colonist, Robert Gouger. The pamphlet was a remarkable performance; not only did Wakefield's skill at description make it difficult to believe that he had never been to the colonies, but he advanced a plan that was to dominate colonial debate for twenty years.

At the heart of Wakefield's proposals was a scheme for the systematic disposal of land. If land in the colonies were sold at a high price, emigrants would be forced to work for a time until they could accumulate enough money to buy land; in this way shortage of labor in the colonies would be eased, the dispersal of population would be slowed, and a fund could be raised for sending from England the kind of emigrants the colonies needed — artisans, professional men, and respectable women, not the convicts, paupers, and prostitutes most advocates of emigration seemed to be anxious to get rid of. Wakefield's proposals were more or less put into effect in the Australian colonies, notably in South Australia after its founding in 1834. That his land plan did not work well, he blamed on an obstructive and unimaginative Colonial Office.* In 1840, discouraged by what seemed to be government apathy, Wakefield and his friends privately launched the settlement of New Zealand. But meanwhile, he had acquired a following in Parliament and the press, most notably in *Spectator*, the Radical weekly paper.

Another of Wakefield's suggestions was of the first constitutional importance. To attract the kind of settlers he wanted, he proposed to offer them an active and not merely a formal role in government, either through representation at Westminster or by making colonial governments responsible to their legislatures rather than to the governor, who was subject to the Colonial Office. The same pro-

---

*There was some lack of imagination in colonial administration. A philanthropic advocate of "shoveling out paupers," Sir Robert Wilmot Horton, the principal spokesman for emigration in the late twenties, was at least partly guilty; the politicians at the head of the Colonial Office may be blamed too, though they came and went in such quick succession in these years that one's scorn should properly be blunted. But the charge cannot lie against the permanent head of the Colonial Office, Sir James Stephen, and his remarkable staff; yet it was against Stephen in particular that the Colonial Reformers directed their gibes; he was "Mr. Oversecretary Stephen" or "Mr. Mother-country."

posal had been worked out independently in Canada in the late twenties by W. W. Baldwin and his son Robert, local insurgent politicians whose reputations as constitutional innovators are not seriously damaged by the undoubted fact that they, like leaders of emerging ex-colonial nations in the past twenty years, wanted autonomy to get power and patronage for themselves.

Discontent was manifest throughout Canada. In Upper Canada, now Ontario, which had been settled largely by American loyalist refugees, protests were growing against the monopolizing of power by a few leading families, the so-called Family Compact; the critics were also unhappy about the privileges of the Anglican Church, which had been handsomely endowed with land (the "Clergy Reserves") under the Act of 1791. In Lower Canada, now Quebec, the issue was nationalism; the French Canadians, a huge reactionary majority, resented the power of a minority of Englishmen and were annoyed, moreover, by government tampering with arrangements the French thought had been guaranteed under the Quebec Act. Increasing exasperation at the flat refusal of governors and the Colonial Office to make concessions led to rebellions in Upper and Lower Canada in 1837. Both were minor affairs that were easily and harshly put down, but the situation was alarmingly reminiscent of 1776. The government responded by suspending the Canadian constitution and sending out a new governor-general to investigate and make recommendations.

The government's choice was Lord Durham. Durham, like his archenemy Brougham, had been a problem to the Whigs. One of the most promising young men in the twenties, he had helped to draft the Reform bill and was the leading spokesman for the radical wing of his party. But he was excitable, vain, and difficult; the cabinet was relieved when he resigned in 1833, and he was kept out in the reconstructions in 1834–1835.* In 1837 Durham was showing some signs of putting himself at the head of English Radicalism, and when "Radical Jack" was sent off to Canada in April, 1838, Charles Buller, the chief parliamentary spokesman of the colonial reformers, went along as his secretary, while Wakefield (who could hardly be given a formal appointment) was there too as an unofficial adviser. Seeing himself as equivalent to a lord-lieutenant of Ireland or a viceroy of India, Durham moved into Canada with a magnificence and imperiousness as inappropriate as they were characteristic. His actions too were highhanded; indeed, his staff called him "The Dictator." He quickly

---

*Durham brought upon himself a lot of unfavorable publicity in the twenties by an only half-jocular remark that a man ought to be able to "jog along on £40,000 a year."

restored order, cultivated the right people, and made friendly gestures to the United States, but he made a serious error in exempting rebel leaders from amnesty and banishing them to Bermuda, a territory outside his jurisdiction. When the government disallowed his action, and quickly curbed Durham's powers, he resigned in a huff and returned to London. By that time, the Radical cause whose leadership he returned to take up was weakening, and in 1840 he was dead.

In the five months Durham was in Canada he and his Radical colleagues surveyed the situation with the quick grasp of doctrinaires and early in 1839 produced a report of the first importance in the history of not only Canada but of the whole Empire. While the Durham Report made many recommendations, including some about Wakefield's special interest, land, there were two main points. In the first place, Durham decided that so resolutely backward and divisive an element as the French needed drastic treatment. He proposed joining Upper and Lower Canada into a single colony, hoping that by swamping the French he could force them to become modern and English, a notion revealing an innocence of the force of nationalism common to most English Radicals of the period. The solution was accepted in the Canada Union Act of 1840. More important and portentous was Durham's uncompromising insistence on the granting of "responsible government" by making the governor choose his executive council from political groups acceptable to a majority of the elected house of the legislature. Although he reserved powers over foreign and commercial relations and land to the British government, he was calling for full self-government inside Canada. He was, in effect, saying that, within their borders, the colonies should receive the kind of government Britain had just attained at home.

This recommendation was very difficult for less radical English politicians to understand. For one thing, as we have seen, Englishmen had not quite realized the degree to which responsibility in England had shifted from the monarch to the Commons; again, the proposal seemed to run counter to everything that was taught about the indivisibility of sovereignty by the dominant theorists of the time, led by one of Bentham's disciples, John Austin. On a more practical level, did not such recommendations really mean giving independence to the colonies? How could a governor take orders from his ministers, responsible to the local legislature, and from the Colonial Secretary as well?

For the next few years, the newly united colony of Canada proved the impossibility of the old arrangements. As governor from 1839 to 1841, Poulett Thomson, now Lord Sydenham, tried to rule much as William III had done, by choosing men from all parties. His successors also found it necessary to serve, in effect, as their own prime ministers. But the situation grew more difficult as the men to whom Durham had proposed to give power began to demand it on their own terms. During the governorship of Lord Elgin, at the end of the forties, responsible government was attained, thanks to the imagination of the Colonial Secretary, Lord Grey (the son of the prime minister), and to the gradual education of Lord John Russell, prime minister after 1846. Lord Elgin chose his ministers from the majority party in Canada and gave them free rein, even though it meant accepting a bill granting compensation to the rebels of 1837 — anathema to Canadian loyalists and to many people in Britain — for losses they had suffered in the rebellion. Even worse, Canada and the Australian colonies, which received responsible government in the fifties, began to impose tariffs on British goods. Free traders at home were appalled; conservatives said it was only what one might expect from ungrateful colonists who were given their head. But the good sense shown by the Colonial Office in accepting these actions helped to retain a degree of loyalty and affection for Britain that a more restrictive policy would surely have alienated.

THE DEMANDS OF THE MIDDLE CLASSES

Slavery and Monopolies

The most striking political consequence of reform was, as we have seen, the destruction of the classical balance of king, Lords, and Commons in the constitution; on the level of practical politics or in the composition of the House, there was little change. It cannot be said with any confidence or pretension to accuracy that the Act of 1832 brought "new forces" or the middle classes into power. But might it be true that the reformed Parliament was more responsive than the unreformed Parliament to demands from those classes, that a still aristocratic government, reminded of its responsibility and expanding the limits of its proper functions, would adopt a program dictated by the dynamic elements of commercial and industrial Britain? Here again the answer is very confused. The Radicals in the House spoke only for themselves or for special points of view, however much they may have believed that their ideas and their remedies were or should be those favored in the country at large. The means for mobilizing and expressing a general public opinion were, it is true, still in their formative stages. But it is equally true that there was no clearly defined and enforceable public opinion, at least at the national level. There was no middle class; rather, there were the middle classes — growing, eager, confident, but divided by economic differences, geographical isolation, religion, and a host of competing enthusiasms. As a look at some of the reforming statutes of the early thirties will show, the government had to work pragmatically; its good intentions were blunted by lack of precedent, insufficient knowledge, and emotional and political crosscurrents both in the country and in Parliament, the only place where intentions could be transformed into policy.

One of the major reforms of the early thirties was the statute in 1833 that ended slavery in the British colonies. Far from being a response to an upsurge of agitation by a newly enfranchised and reformist middle class, the act was the culmination of a long campaign, led by Radicals, Evangelicals, and Dissenters. This moral crusade epitomized a flowering of conscience and humanity at all levels of society, and only the overriding issues of Catholic Emancipation and reform had prevented earlier action.

At the same time, antislavery produced some powerful enemies, particularly among those landed and commercial interests closely tied to the West Indies. To some extent the West India proprietors were placated by the payment of twenty million pounds in compensation to slaveowners and the creation of an apprenticeship system to ease the transition from slavery to free labor. All Negro children under six were to be unconditionally free after the passage of the act, but those over six were to be held in apprenticeship, with limited hours of labor and guaranteed wages. If all their wages were kept by their "employers," the apprentices could earn their freedom in seven years. Thus the West Indies were unwillingly launched on a perilous experiment. Some Englishmen at home, including the Radical Joseph Hume, urged caution, and the merchants in the sugar and cotton trade did everything they could to prevent passage of the bill.* Even on slavery, there was no single middle-class point of view.

In the same year the East India Company, which had lost its monopoly of Indian trade in 1813, lost its monopoly of the China trade and became a purely governing body without any commercial functions, while the Bank of England lost its monopoly of joint-stock banking in London. But these two attacks on monopolies came in the year following reform, not because there was a surge of middle-class sentiment against monopoly, but because the charters of the two

---

*Young William Gladstone, who had just begun a parliamentary career that was to make him four times Liberal prime minister, voted against emancipation; his father was a Liverpool merchant, and Liverpool had been the center of anti-emancipationist sentiment in England. On the abolition of the slave trade, see above, p. 145; and on the abolition of slavery and its consequences in the West Indies; see below, pp. 320–321.

companies were about to expire: the East India Company's new charter evoked almost no interest in the House, and the change in the Bank's position was decided on after a secret hearing of expert witnesses and with a large measure of agreement of all concerned.

Finance

The best illustration of the difficulty of pinpointing middle-class interests lies in the area of government finance. Responding to administrative necessity and the teachings of the economists, Conservative ministers in the twenties had gone a considerable distance in liberalizing the structure of British trade and in revising tariffs downward; their actions were piecemeal, as we have seen, not doctrinaire. Whig finance in the thirties, despite the presence in the cabinet of the free-trading merchant Poulett Thomson, was still more timid. Balanced budgets were assured by cutting the expenses of the armed forces, easy enough to do in time of peace; retrenchment of government expenditures was always popular. But on the revenue side, Lord Althorp and his successors at the Exchequer were content merely to tinker. The Whig expert, Sir Henry Parnell, and a number of powerful politicians, including Peel, favored drastic cuts in the confusion of indirect taxes and the substitution of an income tax. But the ministers could not agree on so bold a step, and, moreover, were still divided on the question of protection of agriculture. Nor were they given any clear mandate by economic interests in the country. Petitions came in regularly for repeal of the Corn Laws, and in 1838 Charles Villiers, a radical Whig M.P., offered the first of his annual motions on the subject, motions the divisions on which were to serve as a barometer of parliamentary opinion. Yet the agricultural interests, which were strong enough to prevent the Corn Law issue from becoming serious, were not strong enough to get their other goal, the repeal of the tax on malt. The shipping interest and the silk industry were dead set against any further reduction of their protection, and when in 1831 Althorp tried to make up for the reduction of certain indirect taxes by imposing new taxes on the import of cotton and on the transfer of landed and funded property, the outcry from the affected interests forced him to abandon the changes.

It is difficult not to feel some sympathy for the ministers. When the agriculturalists or Thomas Attwood (the Birmingham political reformer) and his inflationary friends urged their own pet remedies for distress in the country, ministers could not reply decisively because they lacked the information to make their replies more than counterassertions; it was some time before the new statistical department in the Board of Trade could function effectively to provide hard facts.

Moreover, since most of the proposals made were absolutely new in the world and would have to be implemented in an unprecedented situation, how could ministers be confident of the outcome? For example, in 1840 the government adopted the penny postage scheme of the postal reformer Rowland Hill, a plan strongly backed by many economic interests. It was the one bold financial step the Whigs took —yet postal revenue dropped by more than two-thirds in the first year, a loss no government could view with equanimity and an experience hardly encouraging for similarly untried schemes.* Then, too, ministers faced an uncertain political situation. Without stringent modern party discipline, with members committed to the economic interests of their own localities, with overriding issues like reform, the Irish Church, and the poor law stirring complicated political currents, it could well seem dangerous to add another explosive issue by making major innovations in finance. The ministers could rely on no clearly formed economic opinion in the country, so they temporized.

Municipal Reform

Whatever differences about economic theory, commercial policy, humanitarianism, or religion may have cut across England's middle classes in the thirties, there was one reform on which the town dwellers among them were almost as fully agreed as they had been on Parliamentary Reform—the need to reform the municipal corporations. Most town governments in the British Isles were closed corporations, small, self-elected bodies of men whose functions were not at all like those of a modern municipal government. Rather, these corporations, in a pale extension of the old administrative concept of the role of the central government, saw their role largely as the supervision of the properties and income of their towns. Being responsible to no one, the corporations were often corrupt; they were likely to be extremely cautious except when it came to periodic feasting; and, with few exceptions, they were totally lacking in imagination. Rapidly growing towns in the eighteenth and early nineteenth centuries had to find other means than their governments to deal with pressing

---

*Down to 1840, postage was paid by the receiver, not the sender; it varied with distance and the number of sheets in the letter and was very expensive. Hill's plan for prepaid postage (facilitated by the invention of the adhesive stamp) at a uniform rate per ounce, no matter what the distance traveled, was predicated on the assumption that the lower rates would produce a vast increase in the use of the mails and so in time an increase in revenue. That he was ultimately right could not reduce the dismay at the figures in 1840, though of course ministers could properly plead other benefits of cheap postage.

problems; concerned citizens banded together to get, by private act of Parliament, a board of improvement commissioners, say, or other ad hoc bodies to supervise paving, lighting, police, and drainage. Even where corporations did not have the additional drawback of being the sole electors of their boroughs' representatives in Parliament, the dislike of them grew; they were wasteful, useless, inert, and a bar to the political activity and influence of the growing body of respectable and wealthy inhabitants.

In 1831, an act had made it possible to reform the organization of vestries, the parish assemblies, by providing for election to these bodies, where the inhabitants so desired, by vote of all the ratepayers, male or female; the secret ballot was provided for, and so were annual elections, as a third of the vestry were to retire each year. This installment of local representative government, being permissive, not compulsory, was not widely adopted, but the Whigs systematically applied its spirit to municipal corporations. In 1833, the corporations in Scotland were reformed. The local franchise for voters in electing a municipal council was set at ten pounds, the same as the parliamentary franchise; the act applied to all but nine of the smallest royal burghs, and thirteen other towns were raised to municipal status. Irish corporation reform, coming much later, in 1840, also imposed a ten-pound qualification; like the Irish Reform Act of 1832, this provision enfranchised many fewer people in that poor country than in Scotland. Moreover, only ten elective councils were set up, while forty-eight corrupt and useless corporations were suppressed. It is hardly surprising that the act should have been so conservative: it was drawn for Ireland, and the Whigs, in a weak position, had to placate both Tories and Protestants.

The important statute, however, was that for England and Wales, passed in 1835, following the report of a royal commission, whose secretary was Joseph Parkes, the Radicals' political agent and an associate of Place and Bentham. By its terms, 184 corporations were suppressed, to be replaced by elected councils, chosen by all ratepaying householders who had been in residence for three years; each council in turn chose a mayor, who held office for a year, and aldermen. The aldermen were to make up a third of the corporation, and to hold office for six years, half of them retiring every three years. Ordinary councilmen held office for three years, a third of them retiring every year; they were required to hold a certain amount of property to be eligible—a provision which, like the insistence on aldermen, was not in the royal commission's recommendations, but which was added to pacify Conservatives who were alarmed by this seemingly dangerous dose of democracy. In contrast to the Scottish act, no new corporations were created, but within a few years, the act was extended to towns that had not had corporations before; thus Manchester and Birmingham received their first municipal governments in 1838. London, omitted from the act of 1835, remained so complex a problem that, except for the stopgap Metropolitan Board of Works (1855), little was done for its better government until 1888.

The powers given to these new, elective corporations were limited. They took over the corporate property and were empowered to levy a rate if town income was insufficient to meet their needs. They assumed the task of lighting and safeguarding the streets, though they lost the power the old corporations had had of administering religious trusts. They could make certain kinds of bylaws. They had to make reports to the Home Office. Their greatest power was potential: a responsible and publicly accountable unit had been created on which new functions could be conferred by act of Parliament; and in the next decades towns were authorized to provide museums, public libraries, baths and wash-houses, asylums, and many other services we now automatically associate with municipal governments. By mid-century, the councils themselves were requesting private acts of Parliament granting very broad powers, for, among other things, housing, slum clearance, and the operation of gas and water works.

Another accomplishment of municipal reform was the separation of justice from administration: town officials were no longer automatically magistrates. Pressure in the Lords forced the government to retain the appointment of the justices of the peace in its own hands instead of giving the power to the councils, as had been recommended and provided for in the original bill; but Lord John Russell promised to follow the councils' recommendations. It also became possible for larger towns, with a considerable volume of judicial business, to request the appointment of salaried justices— "stipendiary magistrates"—and to pay them out of the rates.

The alarming implications of the act of 1835 were not lost on the gentry and aristocracy. While their power in towns had never approached their stranglehold on country districts, fear of the implications of municipal reform for their own future led to stiff opposition in the House of Lords. In such a situation, the government can hardly be blamed for not attempting to reform the government of the counties. Although the Radicals urged such action, Joseph Hume especially, and although some degree of rationalization and democratic responsibility had been realized in the administration of the poor law,* county government was left firmly in the hands of the justices of the peace, who were also given supervision of the police forces that were authorized in the counties after 1839. The only breach in

*See below, pp. 245–249.

aristocratic control of the countryside was made when Lord John Russell ignored the advice of the lords lieutenant and began to appoint Whigs and even Dissenters as justices to redress the Tory preponderance, an action that hardly increased his popularity with his own class.

The significance of municipal reform would be difficult to overstate. The town franchise, although not fully operative until the fifties, was far more nearly democratic than the parliamentary franchise, while the yearly retirement of a third of the councilors went at least some distance towards satisfying the old radical demand for annual elections. Through this installment of popular responsibility, a new and potentially vital engine of administration was created. Although the role of the central government in social policy was expanding rapidly in these years, it did not yet seem the normal channel; indeed it was profoundly distrusted by many men, for convincing reasons and not merely out of self-interest.* In a decentralized country only just getting a railway network, it was easier to think in terms of local action, the more so as the organs that had now been provided were so responsive to local pressures and so penetrable by local talent. If one is looking in England of the thirties for a striking expansion of the political power of the middle classes, one must look not to the reformed Parliament but to the towns.

RELIGION

The Dissenters

Reform was expected to have sweeping results for the churches, but the profound transformation that took place in the thirties and forties on the religious scene emerged from pressures and impulses largely independent of the legislated changes of 1828–1832. The character of the transformation was, moreover, quite different from what had been hoped or feared while the constitutional revolution was in progress.

The renovation of town governments, bringing them into congruence with the culture that had grown up in so many provincial towns since 1760, gave new prominence to Dissent. Although they had been a political factor of some importance both nationally and locally before 1832, and although the repeal of the Test and Corporation acts in 1828 had merely ratified a largely accomplished fact, the Dissenters in the thirties experienced a new elation at their wholesale entry into power in the towns, and their appetite for change

*See below, pp. 293–295.

grew by what it fed on. They wanted not only to even old scores but to create a new, more moral and less exclusive society. But their most pressing goals could be attained only by parliamentary action.

Repeal in 1828 had made the fundamental theoretical concession that no one should suffer in his civil capacity by the mere act of dissenting from the Established Church, yet in fact Dissenters remained second-class citizens, suffering discrimination in matters often more galling than the office-holding that had been the primary issue in 1828. Church rates — for the upkeep of church buildings, churchyards, and burial grounds — could be imposed by the churchwardens and vestry on all the inhabitants of a parish, Anglicans and Dissenters alike. Dissenters still could not be married in their own chapels, or buried by their own ministers in the churchyards for whose maintenance they paid. They were excluded from Oxford; they could enter but not take degrees at Cambridge; and the other institutions in which they could obtain higher education — the academies and London University — could not grant degrees. To redress these grievances, the Dissenters brought mounting pressure to bear on the government and Parliament, where, though only a handful of members were actually Dissenters, they should at least have been able to count on their ancient political allies, the Whigs.

The Whigs tried honestly to move on all fronts. In 1834, the government attempted to substitute a grant to the Church of £250,000 from the land tax in lieu of church rates; but Churchmen would have none of it, and the Dissenters were unhappy about the mere disguising and shifting of the incidence of a payment they opposed on principle. Russell was forced to withdraw the bill. Although Dissenters could prevent the legal enforcement of church rates if they could stop the vestry from voting them, the grievance remained where their local political power was insufficient to control the vestry. In some parishes, there were open revolts against church rates — courting martyrdom was not at all unattractive to the Nonconformist mind — but no final solution to the problem was arrived at·until Gladstone abolished compulsory church rates in 1868.

Lord John Russell introduced a marriage bill in 1834 that would have allowed Dissenters to be married outside the Church, but banns were still to be published in the parish church, i.e., due notice of the impending marriage had to be given in the traditional way. Facing another matter of principle and conscience, Lord John was again forced by Nonconformist clamor to withdraw the bill. In 1836 he tried once more, taking over a scheme hit on by Sir Robert Peel in his brief ministry in 1835; this time Russell carried it, permitting those not married in church to be married in properly licensed places (such as Dissenting chapels) or by civil ceremony before the local registrar of births, deaths, and marriages. By setting up a civil registry of vital statistics at the same time, he superseded the old parish registers kept (often inefficiently) by the local parson, and circumvented the need to publish banns, which had been the stumbling block two years before.

Again, in 1834, an attempt was made to deal with the university question. The government chose to bypass the obvious course of giving London University a charter and authority to grant degrees, and, instead, tried a frontal assault with a bill allowing Dissenters to take degrees at Oxford and Cambridge. The bill passed the Commons but was thrown out in the Lords. In 1837 a charter was finally granted to London University, though this university was only an examining and degree-granting corporation; teaching was to be done in constituent colleges, the original Radical "University of London" now becoming University College. Not until the middle fifties were Dissenters permitted to take degrees at Oxford and Cambridge, and not until 1871 could they hold fellowships and university or college offices.

Even with the ear of a sympathetic government, then, the Dissenters accomplished little in the reformed Parliament to improve their civil position; their political power did not amount to much. But they took these defeats as a signal to move towards an even more radical goal—the disestablishment of the Church of England. Joined in this extreme position by only a few free-thinking Radicals, the Dissenters could still count many partial allies who were interested in drastic reforms of the Church. Some Radicals and many Whigs wanted to maintain the power of the state over the Church to force a modernization and even secularization of its teachings and its role in society. Evangelicals wanted to see a revivified Church regain its missionary spirit in a secularizing society; they too were unwilling to see old views of doctrine and organization stand in the way of a higher religious mission. But changes in the Church of England strengthened what the Dissenters wanted to destroy and produced a new religious movement which ran exactly counter to the aims of the Evangelicals, the latitudinarians, and the secularists.

Church Reform

The most pressing ecclesiastical problem and the most glaring abuses lay in Ireland. There the United Church of England and Ireland ministered indifferently to some eight hundred thousand communicants through a hierarchy of four archbishops, eighteen bishops (compared with two and twenty-four, respectively, in England), and nearly 1,400 parish clergy. Ridden by absenteeism, pluralism,

and sinecures, the Irish Church was primarily an engine of ecclesiastical patronage. Notwithstanding its vast landed wealth, it imposed
tithes and church cess (the equivalent of church rates in England),
which in the south were paid mostly by Roman Catholics—80 per
cent of the population as opposed to the 10 per cent belonging to the
Church of Ireland—and in the north by Presbyterians. The tithe
stood as a particular grievance to the Irish, as it did to many English
farmers. Originating in the Middle Ages as a voluntary gift, tithe had
become a tax for the support of the parish clergy, although in many
cases since the Reformation, the ownership of tithes had passed into
the hands of laymen and had developed a nearly unfathomable
complexity. Usually levied in kind, its collection was often the occasion for bitter disputes between farmers and tithe owners or their
agents, and the more so in Ireland, where the smallness of agricultural holdings meant that ludicrously disproportionate power was
brought to bear to collect mere pittances. In the early thirties, the
Irish peasants put the country into a state of virtual insurrection by
mass refusals to pay the tithe, and the government proposed to deal
with this challenge to public order by the usual coupling of repressive and liberal legislation—a Coercion Act and a plan to reform the
Irish Church.

Introduced in 1833, the Irish Church bill proposed to replace
church cess by a graduated tax on the stipends of the clergy. Where
absenteeism or lack of parishioners had made services unavailable
for three years, it was provided that a commission could suspend the
appointment of clergy, though the bill did not go as far as Lord John
Russell wanted in giving authority to the commission to suppress
parishes and to use the income for popular education. But the major
quarrel arose over the plan to rationalize the bishoprics: two arch-
bishoprics and eight bishoprics were to be suppressed and united
with other dioceses, and the organization of the estates from which
episcopal income came was to be revised to provide a guaranteed
yield, while making it possible to divert the surplus revenue to other
purposes. The Radicals were enthusiastic; but the Conservatives and
most Churchmen reacted so violently that Lord John Russell had to
withdraw the appropriation clause. In its amended form the bill
passed, but at a high political price. Conservatives and Churchmen
remained suspicious and hostile; the Radicals and O'Connell were
annoyed by the abandonment of appropriation; and Russell's concession had only covered over serious divisions in the cabinet.

The matter of Irish tithe proved even more difficult to remedy. In
1833 the state took over its collection, advancing money to the clergy
to make up for the refusal of the peasants to pay. The government
then proposed to commute the tithe into a land tax, an obligation that

could be redeemed (i.e., escaped from permanently) by a heavy lump-sum payment; the administration of the tithe was to be in the hands of a commission. The proposal side-stepped the question of whether the commissioners might use a surplus for other purposes than paying the clergy, and when the Radicals pressed this new version of appropriation, the rift in the cabinet became irreparable. Stanley, Graham, Ripon, and the Duke of Richmond resigned, setting off the train of events that ended in the cabinet crisis of 1834–1835.* Not until 1838 was an Irish tithe commutation measure finally passed, although two years earlier the compulsory conversion of tithe into a regular charge added to rent, according to a complicated formula tied to the price of grain, was accomplished for England.

The chief political beneficiary of the Whigs' Irish Church policy was Peel. Not only did Graham and Stanley become his lieutenants, but Peel was increasingly looked to for leadership by those, both inside and out of Parliament, who had been willing to go along with moderate reform but who were frightened by the apparent inclination of Russell and some other Whigs to give in to the Radicals. Yet Peel's serious churchmanship, allied with his powerful administrative impulses, dictated action, not inaction, on Church questions, and he found a remarkable collaborator in Charles James Blomfield, the Bishop of London, who had long believed that reform had to come if the Church was to function effectively and to prevent later and possibly more successful Radical attacks. Between them, Peel and Blomfield concerted the measures which, taken over by Melbourne, brought about a moderate reform of the Church in Ireland and England and kept the demand for disestablishment from ever becoming a serious threat.

In 1836 the Ecclesiastical Commission was created, with power to redistribute the incomes of the English bishops and to remedy the gross disparities that had made translation from one diocese to another so important a factor in ecclesiastical politics. Further statutes reformed cathedral chapters and dealt with abuses such as a clergyman's holding appointments in places so far apart that he could never exercise more than one, if that. As rationalization of the English Church proceeded, the bishops' powers grew: they dominated the Ecclesiastical Commission; they acquired the appointing power of cathedral chapters, which, until then had elected their own members; their disciplinary control over the clergy was strengthened. There were protests, particularly from those whose autonomy was reduced, but, with the new religious seriousness in these years, cen-

*See above, p. 216.

tralization of a rationalized establishment brought the nineteenth-century Church at least some distance into a modern world in which its role was steadily becoming more ambiguous.

The Oxford Movement

While the imperatives of politics and administration were nullifying the sometimes extravagant intentions of Radicals and Dissenters towards the Church, a religious reaction was profoundly altering the whole tone of English religious life. On July 14, 1833, at Oxford, the Reverend John Keble preached a sermon on "National Apostasy"; his target was the government's plan to suppress the Irish bishoprics, an act that Keble and his friends saw as sacrilege, since the property had been set apart for the use of the Church, and as intolerable interference by a liberal, secular state. More significant, perhaps, than that sermon in summoning many Englishmen to a new religious battle was the decision taken by a group of Oxford men, deeply worried about the developments Keble had denounced, to undertake the publication of a series of pamphlets called *Tracts for the Times,* from which was derived the name, Tractarians, frequently used for the protestors.

Though Radical and Whig intentions towards the church provided the pretext for the Oxford Movement, the basic impulses were not political, but profoundly religious, and had been growing for some time. The High Church tradition of the seventeenth century had in the eighteenth century been overshadowed by latitudinarian views and held in check by the dominance of the liberal Whig bishops.* Still, in spite of its eclipse, the High Church party remained loyal to its distinguishing emphases — the continuity of the Catholic tradition of the Anglican Church; the importance of the visible Church; the role of the Church as interpreter of the Bible; the value of prayer, ordered and stimulated by liturgy, decoration, music, and other aspects of what Archbishop Laud two hundred years earlier had called the beauty of holiness; and the greater relative importance of good works as against the predestination of the Calvinists or the simple justification by faith of the Lutherans. These deeply devotional views found their principal adherents not among the advanced intellects of the times but among the country clergy who had tried vainly to protest against the rationalistic, modernist views of their bishops.

In the early nineteenth century High Churchmanship began to

*See above, pp. 37–38.

regain prominence and impetus, partly because of an intellectual reaction against eighteenth-century modes of thought and feeling, partly through the reassertion of an old Anglican tradition against the emotional but doctrinally suspect appeal of Methodists and Evangelicals. High Churchmen looked naturally to the past, indeed far beyond the Reformation (which they played down) to the earliest centuries of the Church and the writings of the pre-Augustinian Fathers; consequently, they fitted well into a period that was showing a new historical interest and sophistication. At the same time, High Churchmen clung the more desperately to institutions and views of life that were being undermined by industrialism and by those writers and politicians who were trying to deal boldly with its consequences.

The men of the Oxford Movement were not content to sit and lament, nor were they satisfied with mere intellectual demonstrations of their position; they tried instead to reassert the applicability of the old High Church teachings to their time. Being concerned not only with technical problems in theology (e.g., baptism or grace) but also with the visible Church, devotion, and worship, they were able to appeal to many people, increasingly hungry for beauty, awesomeness, and mystery, who were dissatisfied by the range of intellectual, economic, and political explanations they were being offered — the religious manifestations of romanticism.

The men of the Movement were of no single type. Keble had given up his Oxford post for a country parsonage. In 1827 he had published *The Christian Year*, a volume of devotional poetry which had an enormous success, a straw in the wind showing how much men wanted such guidance. Edward Pusey, Regius Professor of Hebrew at Oxford, was a mystic, and like Keble a cautious man who always retained his loyalty to his Church. Hurrell Froude, a brilliant young man who died in 1836, and the journalist W. G. Ward were stronger stuff — egoistic, passionate controversialists, anxious to strike telling blows and perfectly willing to shock. The greatest of them all was John Henry Newman, a banker's son raised in an Evangelical household, who found in his passionate assertion of the High Church position a cause for which he was willing to mount barricades. He was enormously learned, sophisticated in his handling of his materials, and a literary genius. But he was no mere intellectual; he was deeply imbued with the devotional ideals of the Movement.

The *Tracts* aroused increasing interest. Before long, some younger and bolder writers were saying harsh things about the sixteenth-century reformers, and cooler heads at Oxford grew worried about the direction the Movement might ultimately take. Then in

1841, Newman, in *Tract XC*, offered an interpretation of the Thirty-nine Articles — already very flexible — that seemed to most readers to lower all the barriers between the Anglican and Roman Catholic Churches. Newman was certainly not at that time contemplating re-union with Rome; he was trying, rather, to find a universally valid interpretation of the Articles, to appeal to the sense of the undivided, pre-Reformation, Catholic Church, but his fellow subjects, worried immediately about Ireland and since Elizabeth's time about Rome, made no such careful distinctions. *Tract XC*, the last of the series, was condemned by the heads of the Oxford colleges, and disapproved, though not censured, by the bishops; the outcry in the country was frantic. Turned out of Oxford, Newman spent the next few years writing his imposing *Essay on Development*, and in late 1845, goaded by the university's action in depriving Ward of his degree for having said (as an *enfant terrible* might) that when he had subscribed the Ar-ticles he had not given up a single Roman doctrine, Newman himself joined the Roman Catholic Church.

Newman's conversion marks the end of Tractarianism as a movement. But conversions to Rome continued and left many En-glishmen alarmed about the safety of the Church and the country. Some of these conversions were undoubtedly examples of fashion-able rebellion; some were neurotic; others were the result of sincere study and self-examination. Still others were forced on the converts by circumstances. To the heated minds of many High Churchmen, the government must have seemed calculatingly contemptuous of what they saw as the true nature of the Anglican Church. In 1836 the Whigs appointed a liberal divine, R. D. Hampden, as Regius profes-sor of divinity at Oxford, the premier theological post in the country; in 1847, Hampden was made a bishop. In 1841, responding to pres-sure from Lord Shaftesbury, the Evangelical reformer, and from Prus-sia, the government agreed to establish a bishopric in Jerusalem, to be filled in alternate terms by an Anglican and a Prussian bishop — a missionary device of doubtful value that contravened the central belief of High Churchmen in the apostolic succession, for Prussian bishops were outside that tradition. In the late forties, the High Church Bishop of Exeter, Dr. Henry Phillpotts, had brought a clergy-man named Gorham to trial for heresy, because of his views on bap-tism; in March, 1850, the Judicial Committee of the Privy Council, the court to which final appeal lay from the ecclesiastical courts, upheld Gorham's right to maintain what opinions he wished despite the au-thority or traditional doctrines of the Church, an attack on the dog-matic basis of the Church by the secular power that drove Dr. Henry Manning out of the Anglican Church, to become in time a cardinal and the head of England's Catholics. Nor was this the last time that the Judicial Committee would so act.*

Though the Oxford Movement made no headway in public policy, and though it seriously frightened most Englishmen, the ultimate religious results of the Movement were very great. Coalescing with the current Gothic revival in architecture, High Churchmanship revolutionized religious practice. A new solemnity and ceremony quickly pervaded all levels of religious practice, within the Church and even among some groups of Dissenters. Devotion to the Church and its ancient traditions permanently changed the lives of many people, leading them into religious and social service, with a sense of mission likely to evaporate among less firmly rooted sects in an increasingly secular world. Conversions to Rome have remained common, and there have been individual excesses in the High Church movement that have at times been frankly comical, but there is no gainsaying that in a world where religion was declining into a specialism, the most impressive seriousness was likely to be found among the heirs of the Tractarians. The Radicals and the Dissenters had triggered an Anglican revival.

THE CONDITION OF THE WORKING CLASSES

Living Standards

For a final exploration of the impact of reform, we must turn to the working classes. But to understand what lay behind their demands,

---

*On the cases involving *Essays and Reviews* and Bishop Colenso, see below, pp. 406–407. This dispute about the supremacy of the state over the Church is analogous to late nineteenth-century struggles in France and Germany. Still more germane was the contemporary schism in Scotland. There, in the twenties and thirties, under the leadership of the Reverend Thomas Chalmers, an Evangelical movement had begun within the Established (Presbyterian) Church of Scotland. The Evangelicals blamed the latitudinarian views of the majority of ministers on the appointment of ministers by lay patrons of churches, and they urged that it should be possible for a patron's appointment to be vetoed by heads of families in the parish, a proposal upheld by the General Assembly of the Church. Such a veto in the parish of Auchterarder in 1835 was appealed to the civil courts, and the House of Lords finally held that the veto was illegal. After some years of confusion, and when it was realized that the change of government in 1841 would not change the relationship between state and Church, Chalmers and his followers withdrew to set up the Free Church of Scotland. That the Evangelicals and their successors, the Free Church, built up an entire system of churches in a few years, without any benefit from the endowments of the Established Church, is testimony to the strength of religious feeling at the time. The two branches were reunited in 1928.

we must first look into the vexed question of the conditions under which they lived at a time when modern industry was firmly established and moving into its maturity.

The classic and most influential view is that of Marx and Engels, who saw capitalism as it was organized in England as a terrible misfortune for the working classes. They believed that the standard of living had declined, and that belief rested on more than a theory of social conflict. They could back up their assertions that the rich were growing richer while the poor grew poorer by citing private and public investigations of the circumstances of the poor, and in 1845 Engels summarized the gloomy findings in his important tract, *The Condition of the Working Class in England in 1844*. In one form or another, this pessimistic interpretation of the standard of life in the early nineteenth century pervaded historical writing and popular understanding at least until the 1920's.

The revisionists have not denied the extent of poverty and suffering that many among the working classes had to endure. Agricultural workers were paid contemptibly small wages and in addition were wretchedly housed and badly abused by the poor law. The immigrant Irish, coming to England in increasing numbers from a backward country, took the most menial jobs, and crowded into the noisome cellars of Liverpool and other towns in conditions utterly unfit for decent human life. More tragic were those families in declining trades who faced the competition of machines and the obsolescence of skills and of a way of life; untrained for other lines of work, with neither knowledge nor advice, and clinging to hope of a miracle, they watched their standard of living sink until, perhaps, they ended their days in a workhouse. These casualties of a fundamental transition in the organization of economic life were perhaps less numerous than those who benefited from the change, and the worst situations gradually corrected themselves. The Irish acquired civilized standards from their more prosperous (and not very friendly) English neighbors; the numbers of handloom weavers shrank; and workers engaged in agriculture dropped steadily from about 35 per cent of the working population in 1801 to 21 per cent fifty years later.

Estimates of the proportion of the population employed in manufacturing and other forms of industry are highly speculative, but it seems likely that around 40 per cent of the working population was so employed in 1841 and that the figure edged slowly upward to the present day without ever reaching 50 per cent. But until the late nineteenth century, the proportion of *factory* labor was small, compared to the numbers employed in workshops and handicrafts.

As these smaller units of manufacture were also increasing their efficiency, the men who worked in them shared the benefits of the factory workers. By contemporary standards, manufacturing wages were good; they tended to rise and, once the war was over, they rose in a period of falling prices and lowered taxes. For some workers—highly skilled factory workers and artisans or the laborers who built the railways—wages were high. When wives and children worked, family income might be quite decent, and while hours of labor were long and child labor was appalling to later generations, it is certain that these features of the economy were no worse, indeed, may well have been better, than they had been in the eighteenth century. But no firm conclusions to support either an optimistic or a pessimistic view of the workers' condition can be based merely on the ambiguous efforts of historians to determine the complex course of real wages, and similar difficulties abound when it comes to assessing the qualitative changes in working-class life. Government regulation and autonomous developments in industry, as some manufacturers became better established and more imaginative in industrial management, helped to improve the conditions of factory life for some, yet wretched conditions continued to exist alongside. Improved organization of marketing and distribution should have made more food—and different kinds of food, such as fish—available to working-class tables; yet those developments were offset by the growing practice of adulteration of staple foods, such as bread and milk, and we can only guess at how much bad cooking and housekeeping or rigid prejudices about what foods were and were not acceptable interfered with improved nutrition for much of the population. By the forties, it seems clear, life expectancy was rising, and by mid-century some steps were being taken to provide decent housing, recreation, and open spaces; yet most towns were dismal and depressing and contributed to a widespread sense that conditions were growing worse, not better.

Workers in industry were periodically victims of a downturn in the business cycle, and unemployment could be desperately serious in industrial occupations in areas where there was no alternative employment. The well-meant advice of self-appointed friends of the working classes that they should "become capitalists," that they should save against hard times and take themselves out of the labor market when jobs were scarce, was likely to be received with derision by those whom the advice was supposed to help. But a significant number of workingmen, if not able to follow that advice to the letter, were in a position to improve their social standing, for as industry grew in extent and efficiency, the demand for new skills conferred both better income and enhanced prestige. Capitalism was far from creating the race of automata Marx and Engels had predicted.

Socialism and Trade Unions

The immediate demands of the workers in the thirties sprang from resistance to the painful readjustments imposed by economic developments. At any time men are likely to be more impressed by individual examples of suffering and injustice than they are by the gradual leveling-up of standards, which is harder to see; as Lord Keynes, the twentieth-century economist, put it in a famous epigram: "In the long run, we are all dead." Some workers and their families went on doggedly trying to improve themselves and to maintain steadily rising standards; others remained sunk in apathy or escaped into the national vice of drunkenness. But a minority of self-conscious, sensitive, and ambitious workingmen were determined to improve not only their own lot but that of their fellows as well. For all their limitations, these working-class leaders were cast in a truly heroic mold; they fought with courage and self-sacrifice in the face of misunderstanding and resentment from above and apathy and sometimes ingratitude from those they tried to serve.

Determination to bring about a new society had underlain working-class support for reform. Convinced by the arguments for the suffrage as a weapon, one element among the workingmen remained primarily loyal to the political approach; the National Union of the Working Classes was its best expression. The limited concessions of the Reform bills had led some working-class radicals to reject Whig reform as a hollow pretense, but the majority had followed leaders who promised that 1832 would be a first installment. When the Whigs made it clear after 1832 that they regarded the settlement as final, the disillusion was crushing. All Lord John's political maneuvering and all his liberal tendencies could not prevent his appearing contemptible to working-class radicals; he was "Finality Jack," in pointed contrast to Durham, who briefly acquired the nickname of "Radical Jack." This disillusion was a major ingredient in the working-class agitations of the thirties and forties.

The political solution did not, however, exhaust working-class resources. Another major current was Owenite socialism. Owen's vision of supplanting the present form of society by cooperative communities had appealed to some important men in the upper classes, but, as we have seen, his attack on religion had alienated any possible support from that quarter. Many workingmen, however, had come to share Owen's antireligious views, either because of the rationalist arguments of Paine and other radical writers or because of the obvious alliance that the Church and much of Dissent maintained with rulers and employers. They were therefore even more easily convinced by Owen's ideal of a new moral world in which competition would vanish and common ownership would share out the proceeds of labor equally. From early in the twenties small socialist societies, classes, and papers sprang up throughout England to apply the principles of Owenism to a criticism of society as it then was.

Some enthusiasts actually set up communities; all of them failed. Others tried to establish cooperative workshops — a plan that reached something of a peak in the early thirties when, under Owen's sponsorship, the Equitable Labour Exchange was organized in London to exchange cooperatively produced goods by means of "labor notes" representing units of labor value inherent in the articles. However hopeless or foolish such projects were, the devotion and idealism they embodied — resilient enough to survive defeat after defeat at the hands of the real world — are important historical facts. Owen found himself, almost accidentally, at the head of a movement he never understood. The men were democrats, he was not; concentrating increasingly on his own schemes, he was unable to appreciate other points of view and was quite insensitive to practical considerations of politics or organization. Fortunately, his followers lacked his singlemindedness; they were active as well in the more realistic business of political reform and trade unionism. But the Owenite vision made their self-sacrifice in more mundane campaigns worthwhile.

The real alternative to the political solution lay, not with an ambiguous and distant socialism, but with the trade unions, now freed to some extent to operate openly. But they remained weak, and at this distance in time it is immensely difficult and in some ways impossible to reconstruct their early history. Trades were fragmented, organizations were local and short-lived, the leaders were quarrelsome. Little unions worried out their brief lives supported by penny and shilling dues and often by the efforts of a single organizer and secretary whose devotion was sometimes tempered by self-interest in keeping a job, and even occasionally spoiled by temptation. One of the saddest features of early trade union history is the number of times unions were ruined by officers who decamped with the funds; not until 1855, when unions were allowed to register as friendly societies, did they have any measure of legal protection. It is sad, too, to read how often a union fought through a just and hopeless strike to accomplish nothing but its own extinction.

Difficulties like these were inevitable, but the impulse to organize was unconquerable, and a consciousness of solidarity was growing. For those with a sense of mission and a burning grievance, it was sometimes hard to put up with opposition or apathy and impossible to tolerate action undercutting union policy, whether it was the treachery of blacklegs (strikebreakers) or of men who wanted to be left alone to support their families on what they could get. There was violence, sometimes against masters, sometimes against other workmen; the unions themselves were not necessarily responsible for it. But any hint of violence grew by hearsay into something horrible, and the enemies of the unionists and many people with the best interests of the workers at heart mixed up genuine abuses with rumor and saw terrible, dark rites in the initiation ceremonies the union branches used in a pathetic effort to enforce solidarity and to bring a little color into drab lives.

The most urgent and immediate trade-union efforts went into improving the conditions of labor. For one thing, the men wanted the equalization of wages, understandable and necessary when rates differed from employer to employer in the same trade within a single town. Pressure for rises in wages was frequent and symptomatic of a general improvement. Such trade concerns had almost invariably to be enforced by strikes, for the unions had no other bargaining power to speak of. Still another trade object was the regulation of machinery — preventing its introduction to speed the extinction of an already declining trade, such as wool combing or shearing. This aim was not very likely to be attained, and a strike against machinery only hastened its adoption. At this point trade unionism most often came into contact with socialism, for cooperative ownership seemed a way to make machinery work for the workers instead of against them.

In the late twenties the Lancashire spinners had organized the National Association for the Protection of Labour. In Yorkshire a confederation of small combinations grew into a large union. By 1833, the Builders' Union, centered in Lancashire and Birmingham, was spreading rapidly. Because of their socialist enthusiasm, many union leaders were also attracted to Owenite organizations like the Society for National Regeneration. Behind this activity lay the notion that if all the workingmen in the country could be brought into a single union, their aims could be quickly accomplished by calling a general strike. In 1834 these efforts suddenly culminated in the formation of the Grand National Consolidated Trades Union (GNCTU) under the presidency of Owen. In March, 1834, with the country in a state of high alarm, the government prosecuted and transported six agricultural laborers from Dorsetshire for organizing a union; they were tried under an act of 1797 forbidding the taking of illegal oaths. In the Dorchester laborers the trade union movement acquired its first true martyrs, but martyrs were useful only later. Their immediate importance was as an example: the government's determination to crush the unions was so clear that they could not survive; giving up their oaths was not enough. Chasing Owenite fantasies of a cooperative revolution, the Grand National collapsed in June. The Builders, who had held aloof from the GNCTU, did not survive much longer. General union fell because of government repression and from its own weight.

The Factory Movement

Increasingly, the unions were drawn into the movement for factory reform. The factory acts of 1802 and 1819* had been narrowly limited in their application—the first to parish apprentices, the second to all children in the cotton trade—and deficient in enforcement machinery. The early efforts at factory regulation were mostly the province of philanthropists of one stripe or another; in the thirties it became a mass movement. In 1830, Richard Oastler, a Methodist and the steward of a Yorkshire landowner, visited his friend John Wood, a woolen manufacturer in Bradford. In the course of talk about the antislavery movement, Wood remarked that some children in Yorkshire worked as hard as Negro slaves. Oastler was astonished—his ignorance of industrial conditions was not at all unusual—and the briefest inquiry shocked him into action. He launched his career as an agitator by writing a series of letters published in the *Leeds Mercury*, one of the two leading provincial newspapers, under the title "Yorkshire Slavery."

In the mass movement of the thirties, factory reform was neither an expression of disinterested humanity nor a clean-cut issue between manufacturers and workers. In Lancashire, the center of the cotton trade, Short Time Committees of workingmen had been organized in the late twenties, to be revived when Oastler's agitation stirred up Yorkshire workingmen to similar action. These committees provided the impressive numbers who gathered in mass meetings to demonstrate and petition for factory regulation. But the working-class agitators were not merely concerned with protecting children; they knew that if the hours of children were limited to, say, ten a day, the hours of adult laborers would be similarly limited, for the simple reason that so many children were employed that factories could not be run without them. At the same time, it is perfectly true, as was alleged by opponents of the agitation, that many of the children were in actuality employed and maltreated by workingmen themselves; master spinners, for example, chose and controlled their own assistants. There were many workers, too, who resented limits on child labor, as they inevitably cut total family income.

*See above, p. 159.

On the other hand, a significant number of manufacturers supported the proposals for reform. Oastler's friend Wood and a number of Bradford woolen manufacturers backed his campaign at the outset; so did John Marshall, the Leeds flax-manufacturer who had recently reduced hours in his works. The wealthy Lancashire spinner and Radical M.P., John Fielden, instituted a ten-hour day in his factory for a time and was a principal spokesman for the cause. These philanthropic manufacturers were, of course, those who were most securely set economically; it is easier to be generous when one is rich. But Wood, Marshall, and their friends did not speak for all Yorkshire manufacturers, and the strongest protests against reform came from Scotland, where the woolen industry was weaker than in Yorkshire. The weightiest support for the movement came from certain Anglican clergymen and from country gentlemen who, however, badly off their own agricultural laborers may have been, enjoyed the chance to embarrass manufacturers whose pretensions and philosophy they disliked. More surprising was the support that came from the political economists: although as believers in free labor they rejected regulation of adult labor, McCulloch and other economists of greater or lesser degrees of orthodoxy firmly upheld the right of the state to limit the hours worked by children and to regulate the conditions of their employment.*

The parliamentary leadership of the factory agitation was taken by Michael Sadler, an Evangelical Leeds banker who had written a fervent answer to Malthus. Sadler got the Commons to appoint a select committee to investigate the question, and in 1832 he introduced a bill, covering all manufactures whatsoever, which prohibited night work below the age of eighteen and any employment below the age of nine; between the ages of nine and eighteen, workers were to be limited to ten hours a day. The justices of the peace were to remain the enforcement agents, but on a second conviction they could sentence the violator to two months' imprisonment, a sterner remedy than the modest fines imposed by earlier acts.

When Sadler was defeated in the general election in 1832, the leadership in Parliament passed to Lord Ashley, another Evangelical

---

*Nassau Senior, a professor of political economy at Oxford, argued in 1834 and 1837 against a general limitation of the working day on the ground that the profit of a firm was made in the last hour of operation, a remark that has earned Senior an unenviable reputation. But he supported intervention to deal with child labor and was willing to see increasing limitations in the forties and after. Given the still backward nature of much British industry at the time, there was perhaps something to be said for his caution.

and heir to the earldom of Shaftesbury. Ashley offered Sadler's bill, slightly modified, to the reformed Parliament, where it was side-tracked for a further investigation by a royal commission. The working-class leaders were furious. As the factory question had been investigated once by Sadler's committee, the commission appeared to them merely a way of delaying matters, and they decided to boycott the commissioners as they traveled about the country seeking evidence. But the commission was not an evasion. It was dominated by two men, Edwin Chadwick and Southwood Smith, who had been close associates of Jeremy Bentham; the former was a barrister and journalist who had come to Bentham's attention through articles he had written on preventive police; the latter was a Unitarian theologian and physician who had made an important medical reputation at the London Fever Hospital, and, who, like a number of Unitarians, had gravitated to Bentham early in the 1820's. They were admirable examples of the kind of radical who was beginning to transform British administration — men with a quick grasp of a situation, a clear sense of what needed doing, and the energy and imagination to work out solutions and to apply them consistently. The factory bill seemed at first sight less sweeping and less attractive morally than Ashley's, but for all its limitations, the commissioners' bill was sounder both medically and administratively. Though the act applied only to textile mills, not to all manufactures, and though it made exceptions for the faltering silk industry, it extended regulation to areas of industry untouched by earlier legislation, most notably the woolen and worsted industries which dominated the Yorkshire industrial scene. Like Ashley's bill, the act of 1833 prohibited all work by children below the age of nine. From thirteen to eighteen years of age, "young persons" were considered able to work up to a limit of twelve hours in a day and sixty-nine hours in a week. But between nine and thirteen, the labor of children was limited to eight hours a day and forty-eight hours a week. Moreover, they were required to attend school for two hours every day, a provision that attracted much support to the bill, though as yet no effective state-supervised schools were available — it was left to the masters to provide them. The most important innovation in the act was the creation of a staff of four inspectors, working under the Home Office and armed with the powers of justices of the peace. Unlike earlier acts, this act was genuinely enforceable. The inspectors could punish offenders and the mere existence of that power gave them a new persuasiveness in convincing reluctant manufacturers to live up to the intentions of the act. The chief factory inspector from 1833 to 1856 was Leonard Horner, a Scottish geologist who had served a stormy term as head of the radical University of London—another of the great early Victorian administrators who knew what he wanted.

In factory reform, then, the working classes did not get exactly what they asked for, nor did they get it in the way they preferred, but they got a first step of enormous importance. But this measure of state action owed little to the reform of Parliament; factory regulation grew out of the linkage between a growing humanitarianism and radical administration.

The New Poor Law

Political agitation, Owenism, trade unions, and even factory reform engaged the steady attention of only a small minority of the working classes. From time to time, during an economic crisis or when the employers of a particular area decided to crack down, these leaders could rally wide support; sometimes the working-class press or the drama of a torch-lit rally could be used to whip up enthusiasm. Most of the time, however, working men and women were sunk in inherited deference or natural apathy. But at the same time that the government was striking down the unions, it was carrying a measure which, more than any other, aroused a persistent, burning sense of injustice among the working classes. The statute was the Poor Law Amendment Act of 1834.

In 1832 the government had appointed a royal commission to investigate the operation of the poor laws. Instead of hearing oral evidence, the commissioners sent out twenty-six assistant commissioners whose reports contained a detailed, if sometimes biased, description of day-to-day relief administration in the parishes. The commission's report was drafted by Edwin Chadwick, Bentham's associate who had been a member of the factory commission, and Nassau Senior, the political economist. Widely circulated, condensed, and popularized, this report confirmed the sense of the middle and upper classes that the poor law was inefficiently and even dangerously administered. The sweeping plan for reform drew on several sources: the experience of the few parishes where successful experiments in poor relief had been tried; the current view, basically Malthusian, of the dangers of overpopulation or of a population uneconomically distributed because of restrictions on its free movement; and the institutional ingenuity of Jeremy Bentham and his friends.

The bill passed easily. In part, this was because most members of Parliament and most peers were intensely aware of the poor-law problem. Poor rates, especially in the agricultural south where the ratio of population to available jobs was very high, had soared and were in some places seriously endangering the payment of rent.* But another reason for easy passage was that the act itself contained only one major innovation—the setting up of a commission to administer poor relief for the entire country. Most of the controversial recommendations of the investigatory commission were simply referred for action to this body of administrators and so were not brought directly before Parliament for discussion. The wisdom of this centralizing proposal could be questioned, especially as the new commission, unlike other government departments, had no spokesman in Parliament; in fact, in the cabinet the Duke of Richmond (remembering the riots of 1830) was very unhappy about the prospect of three irresponsible commissioners in London taking decisions for which his family and his property might suffer. But economic and social urgency triumphed over constitutional doubts.

The subsequent implementation of the new poor law by the Commission has two main aspects, each of far-reaching significance. On the administrative side, the Commission set up a structure remarkably similar to the proposal for an Indigence Relief Ministry in Bentham's *Constitutional Code.* Amateur, casual, local administration gave way to professionalism, centralization, and bureaucracy. For poor-law purposes, parishes were joined into unions—artificial, purely administrative creations, relatively uniform in size and with much greater resources for the work to be done. In each union relief was entrusted to boards of guardians, in place of the old magistrates and overseers. These boards of guardians were elected by the ratepayers and property owners of their unions; larger owners and occupiers received additional votes, according to a prescribed scale. The guardians of each union in turn appointed a salaried overseer to carry out the actual administration of relief, and both overseers and guardians were expected to carry out detailed orders formulated in the Commission's offices in Somerset House in London. Assistant commissioners served as inspectors, transmitting orders and enforcing compliance with them. In 1847 the Commission was converted into the Poor Law Board, whose president would sit in Parliament and the cabinet and assume a constitutional responsibility the earlier Commission could ignore. But the administrative pattern of the new poor law—central determination of policy, local administration, and

---

*It should be remembered that all rates (like tithes) were paid by occupiers, not by landlords. Normally farmers in rural areas and householders and shopkeepers in towns would absorb their costs. When rates rose drastically, however, they could cut dangerously into profits and even rents.

inspection—remained the model for further extension of state activity, most notably in education and public health.

On the policy side, both the investigatory and administrative commissions worked under the pressure of the terrible problem presented to them by the spread of the Speenhamland plan, instituted in 1795 as a local experiment at a time of severe stress.* The plan permitted the payment of outdoor relief, cash allowances in lieu of or supplementary to wages, to bring family income up to a minimum subsistence level. The practice encouraged farmers to pay low wages; administration was often lax; payments rose with the number of children, whether illegitimate or legitimate; and, as a result, the forty years after its inception brought a disastrous decline in the responsibility and morale of the poor. Promiscuity, normal in the rural life of the time, was encouraged as illegitimate children became financial advantages. The able-bodied but shiftless could openly choose not to work, while the worker who wanted to be independent was penalized: he had either to accept artificially low wages or to take the parish pay and the loss of dignity it entailed. Where workhouses were resorted to, there were often appalling abuses. The able-bodied but lazy, the sick, the orphans, and the insane were jumbled together into a single workhouse; brutal overseers had full rein; and sentimental or popularity-seeking magistrates could turn workhouse life in some parishes into subsidized luxury.

In their single-minded concentration on these obvious evils, the commissioners missed other important problems. As their critics have often alleged since, they dealt only with symptoms, though it is hard to know what practical remedies they could have suggested at the time for the more fundamental causes of poverty, the solution to which had to await a further stage in industrial and administrative growth. More to the point is the criticism that they generalized from the rural experience of the agricultural south and failed to understand how different the situation was in the manufacturing districts, where pauperism and resort to the poor law resulted rather from periodic unemployment than from laziness and degradation. And while the investigatory commission and Chadwick were insistent on separating the "able-bodied" from the "impotent" poor—children, the sick, the aged, the insane—the administrative Commission, for economic and administrative reasons, continued to allow the use of the "general mixed workhouse."

The Commission's policy for the able-bodied poor had three main heads. The commissioners wanted to stop all outdoor relief and

*See above, p. 140.

to require all paupers to enter the workhouse, but circumstances necessarily made them cautious. The allowance system was especially useful for the impotent poor and was absolutely necessary in the industrial areas when severe unemployment made resort to the workhouse by thousands of temporary paupers impracticable. Secondly, where outdoor relief was stopped and relief given only in the workhouse, life in the workhouse was to be such that no one would stay there unless one had no choice. Cleanliness and efficiency were insisted upon — most workhouses were probably improvements on the old ones in these respects — but the diet was to be Spartan, discipline harsh, and work hard, tedious, and undignified. The little luxuries of tea, beer, and tobacco that some lenient workhouse masters had permitted under the old law were forbidden; and while entire families were required to come into the workhouse, the sexes were rigorously separated. To this regime the poor-law reformers gave the Benthamite name of "less eligibility," because it was less likely to be elected by the pauper than any independent existence outside. Thirdly, responsibility for bastard children was put on the mother; thus, at the cost of outraging popular sentiment which condemned seducers and forgave erring women, the commissioners avoided the long, costly, and uncertain efforts of authorities under the old law to find fathers. The commissioners were also trying to strike a blow for morality by placing responsibility for chastity on the woman, where they believed, both practically and psychologically, it belonged.

Given its primary purpose, no doubt the new poor law was a success. Poor rates dropped, and wages rose; helped by prosperity in the mid-thirties and by the sudden demand for labor to build railways and in the long run by the shrinkage of the labor force in agriculture, the chronic problem of underemployment in the south of England was largely solved. The act worked less well in the industrial north, when the commissioners moved to introduce it there in 1837, partly because of the inherently different nature of the problems, partly because of a downturn in the business cycle. Certainly the administration of the law was not long on humanity; it was bureaucratic and even harsh; and there were some inevitable scandals.*

---

*The worst of these was the Andover scandal, investigated in 1845, which led to the reorganization of 1847. The case was overlaid with propaganda, personal abuse, and confusion, but there certainly was local maladministration. Public opinion was profoundly shaken by the allegation that touched off the inquiry: one of the nasty tasks some workhouse masters (without Commission approval) used for paupers was breaking up rotting bones for use as manure; paupers at Andover, it was said, were found eating the putrid marrow and gristle because they were insufficiently fed.

Chadwick, who had been made Secretary of the Commission rather than a commissioner, was furious at being given a subordinate post; after years of intriguing against the commissioners, whose policies he strongly disapproved, he finally withdrew (or was excluded) entirely from poor-law business. But, on balance, the reform was popular with the middle and upper classes, who approved not only its efficiency and cheapness but also its underlying moral assumptions.

It was quite otherwise with the poor themselves. They had come to look on relief as a right; indeed, they had been told in the nineties, as a spur to contentment, that the poor law was a clear advantage they had over the French. Now their old expectations were drastically cut away, and they were forced, often through no fault of their own, into a degrading virtual imprisonment. Their anger found upper-class sympathizers; some were traditionalists mourning the passing of old ways, others were sentimentalists; still others had perceptive and rational objections to specific policies proposed. Charles Dickens, whose attack on the new poor law in *Oliver Twist* was muddled and in many ways more applicable to the old law, probably helped the opponents of the reform more than any other writer, unless it was the anonymous author of *Marcus on Populousness*, a parody in the form of a report by a poor-law commissioner urging the drastic reduction of population, if not by contraception, then by infanticide. The tract planted suspicions in the minds of the poor and helped them to believe that workhouse bread was poisoned, or (in South Wales in 1839) that an educational inspector had come to number poor children for extinction, or ten years later, that the opium prescribed for cholera was intended to kill them. The commissioners became the "three kings" or the "three bashaws of Somerset House"; the workhouses were "Bastilles." The already wide gulf between the working classes and their superiors was widened yet further by "the Whig poor law."

Chartism

That growing social and psychological gap, deepened by the emergence of the concept of "class" in English thought and language, became a major concern of leading writers, most notably Thomas Carlyle, in *Chartism* (1840) and *Past and Present* (1843), and Benjamin Disraeli, the future prime minister, who argued in his novel *Sybil* (1845) that England was not one nation, but two—the rich and the poor. But in the thirties, when socially conscious writers and observers were working out their analyses and less sophisticated minds grew worried again about the possibility of revolution, Melbourne's government merely bumbled along, exhausted and timid. Perhaps the one thing that can be said for it — hardly a positive virtue — is that a less liberally inclined and more forceful government might have precipitated a revolution.*

But was there an alternative to the Whigs? Peel was biding his time. In 1834, in his "Tamworth Manifesto," an address to the voters of his constituency, he had committed his party to an acceptance of the reforms of 1832, marking its shift from old Toryism to a new Conservatism, willing to consider timely changes while trying to keep the valuable legacies of the past. Peel was gaining more and more support in the country and in Parliament, but the rehabilitation of a party must mature slowly, and he preferred to let the Whigs flounder awhile. The parliamentary Radicals were no alternative at all. They had thought they were or would be, but in the general election of 1837, made necessary by Victoria's accession, the voters sent one Radical after another down to defeat. Trying to rescue their cause, the Radicals came up with varying prescriptions: the secret ballot, franchise extension, more intensive and effective political education of the country. But the first two remedies had been cut off by Lord John Russell's declaration in the same year against further reform, and the way of education was slow. Only one alternative was offered confidently, indeed urgently. As a welter of discontents coalesced into the phenomenon of Chartism, the working classes asked for sweeping change, perhaps peaceful, perhaps not.

Chartism is one of the most complex and difficult subjects in English history. To speak, as most historians have done, of "the Chartist movement" leads, almost insensibly, to finding a coherent though complicated pressure towards definable social and political goals. Rather, Chartism was a name applied to many widely differing protests, to competing impulses towards a hundred hazy visions of a better world. After the Chartist Convention of 1839, Chartism broke into a miscellaneous cluster of remnants, making obvious its diverse origins. These competing, hostile, and pathetic protests of the forties gave urgency to the social problem, but without even the semblance of unity, they no longer offered the alternative men thought they saw in Chartism of the late thirties. In the fifties Chartism became a memory, save to a few scattered radicals who for a time tried vainly to keep it alive; its cloudy goals and ephemeral organizations were being replaced by tough-minded and practical work for the attain-

---

*The Whigs carried two important reforms in their last years — postal reform in 1840 (see above p. 225) and the creation of an educational department in 1839 (see below, pp. 265–266). But both reforms were forced on the government from outside.

ment of economic and political power. Chartism marked the end of an old world, not the beginning of a new.

There were two main institutional sources of Chartism. One was the London Working Men's Association (LWMA), founded in 1836 by a little band of serious-minded, self-educated London radicals. They had been active in the National Union of the Working Classes and at the Rotunda; they had fought for the reduction of the stamp duty on newspapers, which the Whig government carried in 1836;* they had been Owenites. The moving spirit of the LWMA was William Lovett, a former cabinetmaker and a born and dedicated perpetual secretary; associated with him were three publishers of unstamped papers, John Cleave, Henry Hetherington, and James Watson. The LWMA also had an odd and contradictory assortment of honorary members. One was Bronterre O'Brien, a writer for Hetherington's brilliant paper *The Poor Man's Guardian* (1831–1835) and a radical theorist deeply indebted to French revolutionary thought; others were Francis Place, Joseph Hume, and Daniel O'Connell; and finally there was Feargus O'Connor, formerly an O'Connellite M.P. for County Cork, now a strange and passionate anti-poor-law orator.

In 1838 Lovett, with some advice from Place, drafted a bill for reform which he published as "The People's Charter"; its demands were those of Major Cartwright, a narrowly political platform that could be widely agreed upon and to which everyone could supply his own ultimate aims. The "six points of the Charter" were: (1) universal manhood suffrage, (2) annual elections, (3) the secret ballot, (4) equal electoral districts, (5) abolition of the property qualification for membership in the House of Commons, and (6) payment of members. In appealing to the intelligent and influential workingmen of the country to found organizations like theirs to agitate for the Charter, Lovett and the LWMA were reminiscent of Thomas Hardy and the Corresponding Society in 1792.

The second organizational base of Chartism emerged when Thomas Attwood revived the Birmingham Political Union to press for a further reform of Parliament. Attwood soon agreed to support the Charter and to launch a national petition to bring it to the atten-

---

*The stamp duty of fourpence (see above, p. 163–164) had effectively discouraged newspaper circulation among workingmen, and the Whigs had enthusiastically prosecuted publishers of cheap unstamped papers in the early thirties. The reduction of the duty to a penny in 1836 was a liberal move, though Francis Place insisted that it deprived the poorest readers of their papers. A penny on the price of his paper could mean something to a poor man, but after the reduction of the tax, the economic rewards of publishing without the stamp were not great enough to make risking prosecution worthwhile.

tion of Parliament. The campaign was to culminate in a People's Convention meeting in London as a reminder to Parliament of the practicality of a truer representation of the people; then, if Parliament refused the petition, the Convention would organize a general strike.

The power of Chartism was not, however, to lie with these organizations; it lay in the smoldering discontents of workingmen all over the country, discontents that could be mobilized by leaders far removed from the respectable radicalism of Attwood and Lovett. Long before the Convention assembled, serious rifts had appeared. In 1837, O'Connell, the LWMA's parliamentary spokesman, had made a violent attack on trade unions; thereupon O'Brien and other London proletarians withdrew to form the East London Democratic Association, under the leadership of George Julian Harney, a former shopboy of Hetherington's. Meanwhile, Feargus O'Connor, a colorful, incoherent and exciting orator, began to show himself both a master strategist and a born demagogue. Turning on the LWMA, he took over the Charter as his own and went north to whip up excited crowds by talking about the possibility of using physical force to gain his ends.

O'Connor did more than anyone else, as Professor Briggs says, to "nationalize" discontents. He built up a following that remained loyal to him through defeat after defeat. Besides his energy and his oratory, the main instrument for holding his public was the *Northern Star* at Leeds, his personal mouthpiece but at the same time the national newspaper of Chartism; by detailed reporting of local Chartist activity, it both flattered and set examples. But O'Connor's demagogic success may well be misleading. Incapable of concentrating his activity on a single attainable end, O'Connor appealed to all the diverse currents of working-class discontent, yet, when he was threatened, he could always deny or explain away his cloudy and dangerous rhetoric. He seemed to weld provincial Chartism into a single movement, but what he created was only an emotional unity covering over wide disparities in motive and interest. And hidden below the stir of excited crowds was a deadly expanse of apathy and the certainty that most men would forget when good times returned.

Why did ordinary men become Chartists? After 1836 the business cycle turned down; the years of Chartism were times when trade was bad and work was short. But, in a brilliant essay called *Chartism* (1840), Carlyle looked beyond the "knife-and-fork question" to discern a burning sense of injustice that may have been more impelling. Rural areas, to be sure, were barely touched. On the other hand, the industrial regions of the country responded in a most complex way. Many trade unionists held aloof from Chartism; so did most of the new craftsmen, machine makers and the like. Birmingham, a city of small workshops, displayed a different quality of radicalism from Manchester's, where employers were fewer, richer, and more remote from their workers. But Manchester, Leeds, and Birmingham, with long-standing radical traditions, were quieter and less persistent in their Chartism than the workers in the small, new factory towns around them. Chartism appealed still more effectively to the remnants of an older economy of handicraft and domestic industry. The handloom weavers in Lancashire and Yorkshire, the nail makers in the Black Country north of Birmingham, the framework knitters in the Midlands, the miners of remote Welsh and north-country villages were the enthusiastic Chartists. It was they who had responded so powerfully to the anti-poor-law campaign and who listened enthusiastically to the ejected Methodist preacher Joseph Rayner Stephens when he called for sabotage to bring about factory reform and repeal of the new poor law. These men were victims of industrialism, not its beneficiaries.

The People's Convention began with high hopes early in February, 1839, but it began almost immediately to break up. As the delegates quarreled over credentials or about the role the Convention should play, one after another moderate went home in disgust. Reports and rumors of rioting in the country alarmed the government, which began to arrest Chartist orators and to deploy troops throughout the north. When Attwood received the National Petition in May, he had already withdrawn from the Convention, and when he finally presented it without enthusiasm to the House of Commons in July, the House rejected it by 237 votes to 48. Meanwhile, the "physical force" men had gained control of the Convention and moved it to Birmingham, to be out of the way of the police and nearer to the bases of its popular support. There they bravely proclaimed a general strike, the "sacred month," to start in August. But the Chartist "missionaries" in the country, though they could stir up momentary enthusiasm, especially by talking against the poor law, soon came to realize the bitter truth that there was not enough firm support to make the general strike practicable. They told the Convention so and gave it the final blow. It dissolved in September.

Chartism seemed at an end. Suddenly, on November 5, a small rising took place at Newport on the Welsh border. In April, disturbances in Wales had resulted in the arrest of the Chartist orator Henry Vincent, and for the next six months local men talked often of striking some great stroke, perhaps to release Vincent from jail. The November rising was small and easily put down, but a worried country found it threatening. The leader was John Frost, a Cobbetite radical whom Lord John Russell had made a magistrate, a post to which Frost had some claim as a prosperous Nonconformist draper and local politician. His old-fashioned radicalism led him to support the Charter, and he became a delegate to the Convention, thus causing the government to remove him from the list of justices of the peace. The other leaders of the rising, who like Frost were transported to Australia, were also members of the Convention. To the government and the country, it was clearly a Chartist rising, an identification helped on by rumors that it was to serve as a signal for a general insurrection in the north and by speculation that O'Connor had helped to plan it, though he was away in Ireland at the time and apparently knew nothing about it. But all the rumors and counter-rumors seem to come to little, and the historian of Welsh Chartism has concluded that nothing more was intended than a large demonstration which failed.

The rising had caught up a number of strands. Men like Frost suffered from personal grievances and had got involved in plans and talk from which they could not honorably extricate themselves. The radicalism of Welsh Nonconformity was stirred. The widespread discontent that grew out of the decline of an old rural economy did not exhaust itself at Newport, for the same region in the forties was to witness repeated attacks on tollgates by men in women's clothes who proclaimed themselves, in an old folk tradition, "the daughters of Rebecca." As a postscript to the first and by far most successful stage of Chartism, the Newport rising is a valuable reminder that Chartism was essentially a series of local protests against local wrongs, apparent or real. Charter, petition, and convention were symbols or weapons that every Chartist interpreted in his own way and applied to his own ends.

Selected Readings

Woodward and Briggs continue to be the dependable general works, to which may be added Alexander Llewellyn, *The Decade of Reform: The 1830s* (1972). The volume of the Halévy *History of the English People* is called *The Triumph of Reform, 1830–1841* (1923, trans. 1927).

The structure and principles of government in the post-1832 period are set out in Norman Gash, *Politics in the Age of Peel* (1953) and *Reaction and Reconstruction in English Politics, 1832–1852* (1965). Robert M. Stewart, *The Foundation of the Conservative Party, 1830–1867* (1978) deals with the crucial transition from Toryism. D. C. Moore's *The Politics of Deference*, cited in the previous chapter, continues to flutter the scholarly dovecotes, but a number of local studies tip the scales the other way: R. W. Davis, *Political Change and Continuity, 1760–1885: A Buckinghamshire Study* (1972); R. J. Olney, *Lincolnshire Politics, 1832–1885* (1973); and T. J. Nossiter, *Influence, Opinion and Political Idioms in Reformed England: Case Studies from the North-east, 1832–1874* (1975). The principal political actors are pretty well represented in biographies: Norman Gash, *Sir Robert Peel: The Life of Sir Robert Peel after 1830* (1972); Melbourne twice over in Lord David Cecil's elegant *Melbourne* (1954) and Philip Ziegler's *Melbourne* (1976); Chester New, *Lord Durham* (1929); John Prest, *Lord John Russell* (1972); and, on the throne but still involved in politics, the two royal actors dealt with in Philip Ziegler, *King William IV* (1971), Elizabeth Longford, *Victoria R. I.* [U.S. title, *Queen Victoria: Born to Succeed* (1964)], and Cecil Woodham-Smith, *Queen Victoria, from Her Birth to the Death of the Prince Consort* (1972). The phenomenon of Radicalism, in Parliament and in the country, remains to be dealt with in a satisfactory and consistent way.

On the colonies, in addition to New's biography of Durham, cited above, Helen Taft Manning, *The Revolt of French Canada, 1800–1835* (1962) and J. B. Brebner's *North Atlantic Triangle*, cited in Chapter 1. William A. Green, *British Slave Emancipation: The Sugar Colonies and the Great Experiment, 1830–1865* (1976) may be supplemented by works cited in Chapter 3 on abolition of the slave trade and works cited below in Chapter 7 on the Eyre controversy. Municipal reform and the governance of English towns is covered in Derek Fraser, *Urban Politics in Victorian England: The Structure of Politics in Victorian Cities* (1976) and through the many excellent (though differing) studies of specific towns. Here is a sampler: Arthur Redford, *The History of Local Government in Manchester* (1939–40); B. D. White, *A History of the Corporation of Liverpool, 1835–1914* (1951); Conrad Gill and Asa Briggs, *History of Birmingham* (2 vols., 1952); E. P. Hennock, *Fit and Proper Persons: Ideal and Reality in Nineteenth-Century Urban Government* (1973), which deals with Birmingham and Leeds; A. Temple Patterson, *Radical Leicester* (1954) and *A History of Southampton*, especially vol. 2, *The Beginnings of Modern Southampton, 1836–1867* (1971); and Francis Sheppard, *London, 1808–1870: The Infernal Wen* (1971). On financial policy in the thirties, see the sophisticated summary in Lucy Brown, *The Board of Trade and the Free-Trade Movement, 1830–1842* (1958).

Owen Chadwick, *The Victorian Church*, Part 1, *1829–1859* (1966) is a masterly overview of the subject. On church and state, G. I. T. Machin, *Politics and the Churches in Great Britain, 1832 to 1868* (1977) is a superb study. Particular perspectives on the Established Church are set out in two articles by G. F. A. Best, "The Evangelicals and the Established Church in the Early 19th Century," *Journal of Theological Studies*, n.s., vol. 10, pp. 63–78 (April, 1959), and "The Whigs and the Church Establishment in the Age of Grey and Holland," *History*, vol. 51, pp. 133–148 (June, 1960). Best's *Temporal Pillars: Queen Anne's Bounty, the Ecclesiastical Commissioners and the Church of England* (1964) is a history of the instrumentalities of church reform. Olive Brose, *Church and Parliament* (1959) is an account of the partnership of Peel and Bishop Blomfield as they worked to reform the Church and so to save it. The vexed question of tithe, as difficult for us to understand as it was for the Victorians to solve, is clearly explained and analyzed in Eric J. Evans, *The Contentious Tithe: The Tithe Problem and English Agriculture, 1750–1850* (1976).

On the Oxford Movement, Y. T. Brilioth, *The Anglican Revival* (1925); the admirable introductory essay and documents in Owen Chadwick, *The Mind of the Oxford Movement* (1960); Brian W. Martin, *John Keble: Priest, Professor and Poet* (1977); and Geoffrey Faber, *Oxford Apostles* (1933, rev. ed., 1936), interesting for its psychological speculation. J. H. Newman's autobiographical account, *Apologia Pro Vita Sua* (1864) is magnificent as literature and as self-justification. Newman awaits a definitive study, but mention should be made of William Robbins, *The Newman Brothers: An Essay in Comparative Intellectual History* (1966) because of the fascinating contrast between J. H. Newman and the equally dogmatic (and migratory) religious liberal Francis Newman. Instances of strange religious carrying-on among less exalted figures are the neurotic rebellion of W. E. Gladstone's sister, discussed at length in Sir Philip Magnus, *Gladstone* (1954), and the repeated oscillations between Anglicanism and Roman Catholicism of the Reverend Richard Waldo Sibthorpe chronicled in Christoper Sykes, *Two Studies in Virtue* (1953). Mention should also be made of the account (from both sides) of the standing conflict between squire and parson in a Norfolk parish in Owen Chadwick, *Victorian Miniature* (1960).

Authoritative studies of Dissent remain rare. Two notable works are Robert Currie, *Methodism Divided: A Study of the Sociology of Ecumenicalism* (1968) and Elizabeth Isichei, *Victorian Quakers* (1970); A. D. Gilbert's *Religion and Society in Industrial England*, cited in the introduction, is also relevant. Sweeping more broadly but important for Dissent and above all Methodism is W. R. Ward's uneven and committed *Religion and Society in England, 1790–1850* (1973). On the Scottish church, Andrew L. Drummond and James Bulloch, *The Scottish Church, 1688–1843: The Age of the Moderates* (1973) and *The Church in Victorian Scotland, 1843–1874* (1975). The lack of a modern study of the Reverend Thomas Chalmers, whose influence ran in so many directions, is a severe handicap, but the excellent sketch in L. J. Saunders, *Scottish Democracy, 1815–1840* (1950) is a help.

Friedrich Engels's *The Condition of the Working Class in England in 1844* (1845), based on his own observations of Manchester where he was in business and on the findings of many official and unofficial investigations, was reprinted in 1958 with a critical introduction by W. O. Henderson and W. H. Chaloner. In *Engels, Manchester, and the Working Class* (1974), Steven Marcus discusses Engels's sources and models and offers a strained literary analysis of the book's contents.

For the historiography of the debate about whether the standard of living rose or fell in the first half of the nineteenth century—the principal controversialists are E. J. Hobsbawm for the "pessimists" and R. M. Hartwell for the "optimists"—see Arthur J. Taylor, *The Standard of Living in Britain During the Industrial Revolution* (1975). The matter is also discussed in Sidney Pollard, "Labour in Great Britain," in Peter Mathias and M. M. Postan, eds., *Cambridge Economic History of Europe*, vol. 7, part 1, pp. 28–96 (1978). Duncan Bythell, *The Handloom Weavers* (1969), cited in Chapter 2, is particularly relevant, as is the discussion of the growth and significance of family income in Neil McKendrick, "Home Demand and Economic Growth: A New View of Women and Children in the Industrial Revolution," in Neil McKendrick, ed., *Historical Perspectives: Studies in English Thought and Society in Honour of J. H. Plumb* (1974), pp. 177–210. Utopian solutions are discussed in two books by J. F. C. Harrison: *Quest for the New Moral World: Robert Owen and the Owenites* in *Britain and America* (1969) and *The Second Coming: Popular Millenarianism, 1780–1850* (1979).

G. D. H. Cole's article of 1939, somewhat expanded as *Attempts at General Union . . ., 1818–1834* (1953), gives the background of the Grand National Consolidated Trades Union. For a biography of a prominent early trade union leader, R. G. Kirby and A. E. Musson, *The Voice of the People: John Doherty, 1798–1854, Trade Unionist, Radical and Factory Reformer* (1976). For a detailed account of the campaign for factory legislation, see J. T. Ward, *The Factory Movement, 1830–1855* (1962), and for the laws, Maurice W. Thomas, *The Early Factory Legislation* (1948). Cecil Driver, *Tory Radical* (1946) is an admirable life of Richard Oastler. L. R. Sorenson, "Some Classical Economists, Laissez Faire, and the Factory Acts," *Journal of Economic History*, vol. 12, pp. 247–262 (Summer, 1952) discusses the ambiguous attitude towards intervention on this particular front.

The classic work on the poor law — Sidney and Beatrice Webb, *English Poor Law History*, part 2: *The Last Hundred Years*, vol. 1 (1929) — continues their account of the old poor law, cited in the Introduction. It should be supplemented by the essays in Derek Fraser, ed., *The New Poor Law in the Nineteenth Century* (1976). On the background of the act, J. R. Poynter, *Society and Pauperism: English Ideas on Poor Relief, 1795–1834* (1969) and the revisionist interpretation, more favorable to the Speenhamland system than is usual with historians, in Mark Blaug, "The Myth of the Old Poor Law and the Making of the New," *Journal of Economic History*, vol. 23, pp. 151–184 (June, 1963). Nicholas C. Edsall, *The Anti-Poor Law Movement, 1834–44* (1971) documents one of the great agitations of the century.

On the class-consciousness that grew rapidly among working people in these decades, see Asa Briggs, "The Language of 'Class' in Early Nineteenth-Century England," in Asa Briggs and John Saville, eds., *Essays in Labour History* (1960) and E. P. Thompson, *The Making of the English Working Class* (1963), which points to the intellectual and institutional sources of the awareness. Among those institutions was the radical press, which reached a pinnacle in the thirties: in addition to books by Altick, Webb, and Wickwar, cited in Chapter 4, see Patricia Hollis, *The Pauper Press: A Study in Working-Class Radicalism of the 1830's* (1970), and Joel H. Wiener, *The War of the Unstamped: The Movement to Repeal the British Newspaper Tax, 1830–1836* (1969). John Foster, *Class Struggle and the Industrial Revolution: Early English Capitalism in Three English Towns* (1974) is a provocative, difficult, and aggressively Marxist interpretation based principally on the case of the cotton-manufacturing town of Oldham. The book is important enough to warrant noting two extensive review articles: Gareth Stedman Jones, "Class Struggle and the Industrial Revolution," *New Left Review*, no. 90, pp. 35–69 (March–April, 1975), and A. E. Musson, "Class Struggle and the Labour Aristocracy, 1830–60," *Social History*, vol. 1, pp. 335–356 (October, 1976), this last with a comment by Foster, pp. 357–366.

The old standard history of Chartism, Mark Hovell's *The Chartist Movement* (1918), has now been supplanted for narrative purposes by J. T. Ward, *Chartism* (1973). Valuable for the regional and personal complexities are G. D. H. Cole's *Chartist Portraits* (1941) and Asa Briggs, ed., *Chartist Studies* (1959).

More detailed biographies are A. R. Schoyen, *The Chartist Challenge* (1958), on G. J. Harney, and Alfred Plummer, *Bronterre: A Political Biography of Bronterre O'Brien, 1804–1864* (1971). Less satisfactory is the brief sketch by Donald Read and Eric Glasgow, *Feargus O'Connor: Irishman and Chartist* (1961). There are also two famous Chartist autobiographies: William Lovett, *The Life and Struggles of William Lovett . . .* (1876) and Thomas Cooper, *The Life of Thomas Cooper, Written by Himself* (1872). Some important observations on political rhetoric in the thirties, suggesting that much of its apparent violence reflects the influence of cheap, popular romanticism, appear in G. Kitson Clark, "The Romantic Element, 1830–1850," in J. H. Plumb, ed., *Studies in Social History* (1955), pp. 209–239. F. C. Mather, *Public Order in the Age of the Chartists* (1967) explains the means and limitations of police and military action. David Williams contributed a summary essay on Welsh Chartism to Asa Briggs, ed., *Chartist Studies* (1959), but more important are his *Life of John Frost* (1939) and *The Rebecca Riots* (1955).

Chapter 6
Peel's Decade

1841–1850

SOCIAL REFORM

The Resources for Governing

The Chartist alternative had failed, and the Melbourne government limped along to an ignominious death in June, 1841. Lord John Russell thought he had found a way out: he proposed a reform of the Corn Laws and a revision of the protective structure of the British economy. The Tory protectionists responded by appealing to an anti-slavery sentiment and defeated Russell in May on his proposal to admit foreign sugar free of duty, sugar that, unlike British sugar, was grown by slaves. Then, as the ministers still clung to office in the hope of forcing a vote on the Corn Laws, Peel decided that his time had come. He moved and carried a vote of no confidence, and the government chose to dissolve Parliament. In the ensuing general election Peel was swept into office with a clear majority of seventy-six votes.

A striking change in tone marked Peel's accession to power.

Where the Whigs, certainly after 1835 and to some extent before, seemed tentative, compromising, and forced, the Conservative government after 1841 was confident and masterful. In part, the change was accounted for by personality. In contrast to Melbourne, Peel was broadly competent and thoroughly professional. He had held high executive posts almost continually from 1812 to 1830 and had revamped much of the administrative and legal structure of England and Ireland; in a series of reform proposals during his brief tenure as prime minister in 1834–1835, he had shown that his proclamation of a new, more liberal conservatism was not idle rhetoric. His lieutenants too were remarkably able. Stanley, his Colonial Secretary, had been a Whig minister in the early thirties; as Lord Derby he was to be three times prime minister in mid-century. At the Home Office, Sir James Graham, another dissident Whig, displayed the same kind of administrative grasp as his chief. At the Board of Trade, first as vice-president and after 1843 as president, was the young William Ewart Gladstone, then famous mostly as a High Church defender. But he was also the son of a Liverpool merchant, and his apprenticeship to Peel developed the financial and administrative talents that underlay his claim to decades of Liberal leadership later in the century.

Peel was determined, as Melbourne could not be, to weld his cabinet into a single political and administrative instrument. He also saw the necessity of keeping a firm control over Parliament. While the initiative of the individual member was not seriously interfered with, Peel's superiority was ensured by his own surpassing abilities and by careful political calculation: F. R. Bonham, the political agent, was one of his chief advisers; Parkes had never been so close to the Whigs. Moreover, nearly every member of Parliament now bore a party label, a fact that Peel could to some extent presume upon.

Peel was also the beneficiary of some long-term institutional developments. Many of the uncertainties and fears of the thirties had settled, and the new machinery of government had gone successfully through its testing period. The House of Commons had reorganized its clerical staff and was beginning to find ways around the time-consuming business of private bills for companies, railways, towns, or individuals: such bills might be referred to committees, or Parliament could pass general acts authorizing the provisions most frequently asked for in private bills; future applicants then could simply refer by number to the clauses they wanted without having to draw up special bills needing close parliamentary scrutiny. There was a marked improvement in the standards of legislative drafting. Ways of providing information to Parliament and government alike were expanding and becoming normal. Select committees of either House of Parliament were one investigatory device, royal commissions another; their reports and those of other investigators sent out to examine particular problems were the "bluebooks'" whose facts and conclusions dominated social policy debates in these decades, in Parliament and out. Asking for information from the government and the government's willing provision of facts and figures for Parliament and the country were becoming regular practices: the Statistical Department of the Board of Trade, the new office of Registrar-General, individual departments, and private statistical societies were increasingly providing the basis for decision and legislation.

Parallel to these inventions, which our modern political world takes for granted, was the increasing reliance on expert, professional administration. The administrative principles enshrined in the Poor Law Commission were taking root on all sides. Some historians see the main stimulus to this development in the permeation of government by the disciples of Jeremy Bentham, others in the nature of the administrative process itself. Whatever the answer to the question of origins, it is important to remember that this administrative revolution, though well on its way, was still in its early stages, and that the great civil servants of the early Victorian period were a far cry from the modern British civil service. Today the civil service takes young men and women from the universities and trains them up, not only to their specialties but to a long-standing, all-pervading tradition that is both apolitical and anonymous. But Chadwick, Horner, Hill, Kay-Shuttleworth, and a host of other administrators who really transformed Victorian England came into government service from private life as mature men, with their schemes and methods full-blown; they used every political trick to get their way; and they were as famous in their time as the politicians, and sometimes more hated.

The Chartist Revivals

Peel did not take office at a quiet time. The economy had not recovered from the slump of the late thirties; after six years of cooperation with the Whigs, O'Connell began a new agitation for repeal of the Union; and the Chartist leaders had come out of jail. But the Chartism of which the nation was aware in 1842 was far more fragmented than the Chartism of three or four years before. O'Connor was moving towards a kind of reactionary radicalism, a rejection of all the works and ways of the industrial world. In 1841, he ordered Chartists to support Conservative candidates by a show of hands on nomination day, and in some instances where the franchise extended to workingmen, his followers managed to turn elections. Increasingly he devoted his energies to an ill-conceived "land plan," under which workingmen contributed small sums to finance the settlement of increasing numbers of their fellows (chosen by lot) on small allotments. Some Chartist leaders took up the project to have something to offer, since attaining the Charter was now remote; but that so harebrained a scheme could retain such loyalty from the rank and file says much about their old-fashioned ambitions.

Not all of O'Connor's lieutenants approved of his new course. Bronterre O'Brien criticized O'Connor's abandonment of political radicalism and was excommunicated by the great demagogue in 1842. O'Connor's most valuable recruit of the early forties, a Leicester shoemaker and poet named Thomas Cooper, turned to moral force after spending two years in prison; after 1846 he turned his back on Chartism to become a lecturer on free thought and still later, following a sudden conversion, on religious evidences. Harney remained loyal longer, ultimately pursuing his own brand of left-wing socialism to an alliance with Marx and Engels. The old moral-force men supported Lovett, who came out of prison in 1840 with a new educational scheme, the National Association, by which he hoped to make workingmen increasingly aware and responsible; he was backed by a number of distinguished middle-class patrons. The leaders chased after their private enthusiasms, each insisting he had the one true way to attain the Charter and the new world. But O'Connor kept what mass support there was.

In 1842 a serious attempt was made to reconcile the Chartists and middle-class radicals. The latter, now increasingly committed to free trade as the answer to England's social problems, were anxious to cultivate working-class allies; moreover, many of them, especially among the Dissenters, were firm believers in a further measure of reform. A wealthy Birmingham corn merchant, Joseph Sturge, took the lead in summoning a Complete Suffrage convention. He and his middle-class friends were willing to accept all the points of the Charter as the basis for a new united radical movement like that which had helped to bring reform in 1831–1832; all they asked was that the name of the Charter be given up, because it was so frightening to the middle classes. The condition was rejected, curiously and a little pathetically, by William Lovett; proud, dedicated, and class-conscious, he could not bring himself to surrender the name for which he and his fellows had fought and suffered. O'Connor, who had attended the meeting to wreck it, seconded his old enemy, and the Complete Suffrage movement collapsed. Despite O'Connor, and as O'Brien saw, middle-class cooperation was necessary to gain the political enfranchisement (and subsequent power) of the working classes, but the workingmen had to discover that truth in their own time. Sturge and his friends were forcing the pace.

The troubles of 1842, which have rightly given a terrible aspect to the early forties, were not simple. Staffordshire miners were protesting against wage reductions in a situation already alarming because the government was about to cut family income by excluding children from the mines. Crowds of men, women, and children marched slowly through northern mill towns protesting in a traditional way against economic forces and half-blind political calculation they could neither understand nor control. Local leadership of strikes and demonstrations was often Chartist, at least by descent, and some national leaders tried to turn them to advantage. O'Connor, however, urged his followers to keep clear of strikes that he insisted were precipitated by middle-class agitators. To some extent he was right. The wage cuts that caused the strikes in the northern districts were in good part politically intended, to spark demonstrations and riots to force repeal of the Corn Laws.

The disturbances of the early forties mark an important transitional stage in the history of industrial discontent. Although they affected the entire cotton industry and much of the mining industry, there was little violence, in contrast to the Luddite riots a generation earlier. Observers commented on how little damage was done to machinery, when so much could have been done. The main act of sabotage was the cheap, effective one of knocking the plugs from the boilers in the cotton factories, to make it impossible to work the factories with black-leg labor. The real affinities of the "Plug Plot," to give the strikes their local name, were less to Luddism and Chartism than to the trade union demonstrations and strikes of the 1880's. Industrial protest was coming of age.

An improvement in business, a sharp drop in food prices, and watchful waiting on the government's part produced a marked change by the end of 1842; the unrest quieted down without much action ever taken against it. The government, meanwhile, was pursuing long-range aims ultimately better adapted than suppression to the solution of the social problem.

Mines, Public Health, and Education

In 1840, the Whig government had appointed a royal commission to examine the question of child labor. Their first report, on mines, appeared in 1842, illustrated with woodcuts, and the graphic evidence of the terrible conditions in which women and children worked underground horrified a largely unsuspecting public. Miners at the coal face worked naked in the heat; small children were confined for hours in total darkness, expected to work the trapdoors controlling the ventilation of the mines—and not to go to sleep; women and children served as draft animals, pulling coal carts through tunnels not more than three feet high by means of chains about their necks and passing between their legs. The villains on whom public opinion fixed were the coal owners, not middle-class businessmen but aristocratic landowners, identical, at least in the eyes of the increasingly aggressive free traders, with the men who kept food prices artificially high by means of the Corn Laws. Lord Ashley, the Evangelical factory reformer, introduced and easily carried an act forbidding the employment underground of children under ten and—a significant innovation—all women. H. S. Tremenheere, another of the new breed of civil servants, was named inspector of the mining areas, to see that the law was obeyed. He was not, curiously, expected to visit the mines themselves, only the mining areas; but he was instrumental in bringing mine owners and their agents around to a greater degree of social responsibility and also in obtaining in 1850, with the support of the better and more prosperous mine owners, an act requiring underground inspection.

At about the same time, another far-reaching and influential investigation of a social evil was undertaken. Edwin Chadwick, in violent disagreement with the Poor Law Commission, found or was making his position as secretary increasingly nominal; after 1841 he turned his attention fully to what he had come to see as the basic cause of the poverty the Commission was trying to cure by palliatives. He ascribed the terrible human wastage of his time primarily to conditions of public health and to the state of the rapidly growing and wretchedly unsanitary towns. In his investigation he had the full cooperation of some remarkable doctors, including his old colleague from Bentham's circle and the factory commission, Southwood Smith. In a series of reports in 1842–1844, Chadwick and his colleagues built up an indictment of local inaction and individual irresponsibility that demanded legislation.

Medical knowledge was defective. The science of sanitary engineering was in its infancy, and the experts disagreed sharply about the best technical solutions to a given problem. Such uncertainties gave at least a color of plausibility to the objections of traditionalists and vested interests. But recommendations for massive state intervention in public health attracted the support of many concerned men and women and as well of many free traders whom one would normally expect to stand up for laissez-faire. Full-scale legislation had to wait until 1848, just in time to encounter a reaction against intervention and centralization,* but meanwhile the sanitary reformers' advocacy of cleanliness, good drainage, light, fresh air, and pure

*See below, pp. 280, 294–295.

water went a long way towards saving lives and making them decent.

In education, a social need of extreme urgency, the Peel government suffered a severe defeat. For a multiplicity of reasons, as we have seen, worried men and women had done much to provide education for the poor: Conservatives were trying to preserve social order by inculcating obedience, discipline, and right ideas; Churchmen and Dissenters, while sharing such political and social concerns, were more interested in teaching children to read the Bible and to be good Christians of the right kind; radicals of nearly every stripe had a broader vision of education as the instrument for constructing a better and possibly perfect society. Brougham's effort in 1820 to introduce a national system of education based on the Established Church had fallen foul of Dissenting objections; J. A. Roebuck, a Radical M.P., failed even more dismally in 1834. So education remained the preserve of private enterprise and voluntary organizations, and in the confusion and permissiveness, children's exposure to teaching was sporadic and ineffective. While it is incorrect to think of the mass of English working people as illiterate, very few of them were educated.

In 1833, following a precedent Peel had set in Ireland, Parliament began to make small annual grants to the two large private educational societies, the Anglicans' National Society and the largely Nonconformist British and Foreign School Society, to help them to build schools. Six years later, in 1839, an increase in state grants came with an important string attached — the acceptance of inspection. Inspectors for the schools of each society reported to a new government agency, the Committee of Council on Education, in form a committee of the Privy Council, whose head, the Lord President, became the parliamentary spokesman on educational matters. The important figure, though, was the secretary of the Committee of Council, Dr. James Phillips Kay (later Sir James Kay-Shuttleworth), a physician who had made a nationwide reputation for his work among the poor in Manchester. As an assistant poor-law commissioner, he grew more and more interested in education; from his new position after 1839 and by his writings after his retirement in 1849, he did more than any other man to move a protesting, pigheaded nation towards a system of national education.

The inspectors had no coercive powers, and even unfavorable reports — their indirect means of bringing pressure — had to be used with the utmost caution, because of the jealousy of the competing religious sects. The bishops insisted on having a veto of inspectors appointed for the schools of the National Society, while the Dissenters, furious at a mildly critical report, forced the transfer of one of the first inspectors, H. S. Tremenheere, who then became inspector of the mining areas. In 1843 the government set out to placate this hypersensitive sectarianism.

In that year, the royal commission on children's labor issued a report on factories. At the same time Sir James Graham, the Home Secretary, introduced a new factory bill, reducing the hours of labor of children between the ages of eight and thirteen from eight to six and a half per day, and requiring attendance at school. To provide the schools, Graham proposed that in those factory districts where there was no satisfactory educational provision, schools should be set up in connection with the workhouses, each under the supervision of a board of trustees composed of the parish clergyman, two churchwardens, and four others, including (if possible) two factory owners. The Scriptures were to be taught daily, Anglican children were to be instructed in the Catechism and Liturgy by the clergyman, and Dissenting children whose parents wished would be given special instruction by local Dissenting ministers.

The measure was quite clearly the best that could be got through Parliament. It made basic concessions to the Dissenters' fears, and it was strongly supported by many of the most respected and influential M.P.'s, who saw how essential a national program was. But the Dissenters exploded. Frustrated by their failures in the thirties and infuriated by the Anglican revival, they were moving towards an increasingly visionary demand for disestablishment of the Church and were becoming more and more shrill in their insistence on uncompromised principles of sectarian purity. They expected the worst from Anglican domination of the trustees; they saw a Puseyite in every priest; they feared the conversion of Dissenting children whose parents were not strict enough to insist on separate instruction. Incapable of appreciating the political imperatives imposed by an overwhelming Anglican majority in Parliament and the country, they demanded their own schools for their own members and preferred that others get no education, lest they get dangerous education. Petitions poured in from huge public meetings. Graham's efforts at still further, and really rather astonishing, concessions were rejected out of hand. He had to withdraw his bill, and to reintroduce it the next year as an ordinary factory bill without the educational clauses.

For another twenty-seven years education in England was left to private enterprise — the two great societies and a few similar educational bodies which the Committee of Council recognized by giving them grants. Whatever advance was made came through administrative supervision, enforced by the lure of grants-in-aid. The most important innovation was set out in the Committee of Council's Minute of 1846. Moving away from the old, inefficient monitorial system, in which older children taught the younger, the Committee began to subsidize teachers' salaries. By setting up a system of apprenticeship, training colleges, and retirement pensions, they gave to teachers, who had until then been looked on as menials or incompetents, an assured, if modest, economic position, a new social status, and professional pride.

THE ECONOMY

Banking

As we have seen,* the banking structure of the country was reorganized in 1826 and 1833. But though in the latter year the Bank of England had been to some extent freed to set its interest rate — the "bank rate" — at a level above that permitted by the usury laws, no one at the time could foresee how potent a weapon the bank rate would become a century later. The Bank was not yet a central bank, in the twentieth-century meaning of the term. Its directors saw themselves as owing their first obligation to their stockholders, not to the nation; and Peel told them plainly to behave like any other bank. They actively participated in the discount market, lending money to whoever wanted it at competitive rates. Not until 1878 did the Bank voluntarily give up its ordinary discount business and confine itself to accommodating only its regular customers (mostly, increasingly, but not entirely banks) at rates above the level of ordinary commercial interest. In succeeding decades the Bank moved slowly towards the modern doctrine of central banking, in which one bank serves as the "lender of last resort" for other banks. Once that position was reached, the bank rate could determine the interest rate charged by the commercial banks that were the Bank's customers, and so the Bank was enabled to control the supply of credit in the country. But such sophistication was far beyond the grasp of early or mid-Victorian bankers. Throughout most of the nineteenth century, the Bank, by heeding the demands of business, tended to feed unhealthy booms by making credit easy; and what controls there were were sought not by managing credit, but by managing the currency through the maintenance of cash reserves.

The panic of 1825 led the Bank to attempt to control the amount of money in circulation by varying its issue of notes as its gold reserves fluctuated, but the plan was not carried out consistently and indeed proved unworkable when a severe drain on the gold reserves

*See above, pp. 175–177, 223–224.

took place following the panic of 1837. The widespread failures of business firms in those bad years were generally ascribed to the instability of prices, and as always the Bank was the main target of criticism. The dominant school of thought, whose chief spokesman was a provincial banker named Samuel Jones Loyd (later Lord Overstone), believed it necessary to go even further than the Bank had done in controlling the circulation of money, but Loyd failed, like everyone else, to see that controlling currency without controlling credit could be only a partial remedy.

Peel was convinced, and in 1844 the Bank Charter Act divided the Bank into two strictly separated parts. The banking department took care of the ordinary commercial business of the Bank; the issue department was solely concerned with the supply of banknotes: £14 million in notes were issued against securities, and the rest of the supply was to vary pound for pound with the gold reserves. The most forward-looking provision of the act was a first step towards creating a Bank monopoly of note issue: no new banks were to be allowed to issue notes, old banks of issue were limited to the amount they issued just before the act, and if any bank ceased to issue notes, it could not begin again. But the strict limitation on note issue was a dangerous straitjacket in times of great shortages of money. In 1847 the Bank's reserves again fell dangerously, because the disastrous harvest made it necessary to buy large amounts of food abroad; the note issue was therefore restricted at exactly the time when railway companies and tottering country banks needed vast amounts of cash. The Bank had to be authorized by the government to issue notes in excess of the legal limit under the act of 1844; similar authority was needed again in the panics of 1857 and 1866. Yet we must not be too scornful of either Bank or government: they were taking the best advice there was. The trouble was that economic knowledge was simply insufficient, and men had to grope towards the best solutions they could find.

Railways

Peel's government also moved to deal with the severe problems presented by the railways. The railway age may properly be said to have begun in 1830, when the Liverpool and Manchester Railway opened.* Railways had existed before 1830; indeed the wooden or

---

*During the opening ceremonies the great liberal Tory minister William Huskisson was killed. When the train on which they were traveling stopped to take on water, he and other distinguished passengers behaved as they were accustomed to do when a coach changed horses—they idly walked about. He was struck down by an engine on a parallel track. It was not only the workers who needed to be broken to the discipline of modern life.

iron "railed ways" of the colliery districts determined the odd distance between rails — four feet, eight and one-half inches — that is now standard in the United States and Great Britain. But these early railways had used horses or, later, stationary engines as motive power. The Stockton and Darlington, a coal line opened in 1825, used a combination of stationary and locomotive engines and also allowed customers to put their own carriages on the line. The Liverpool and Manchester can be called the first modern railway because it used locomotive power for the entire distance, and the engines and rolling stock were all the property of the company.

The victory of railways was by no means certain at the outset. There were formidable technical problems to be solved; the expense of building and equipping a line was enormous; and the opposition of canal companies and coaching interests was intense. Moreover, many ordinary people were highly suspicious of these fiery, noisy engines, which frightened horses and might (they thought) kill cows and sheep grazing beside the line. The speed was too great, accidents were too awful. Morals might suffer — momentarily in tunnels, permanently in bringing, according to the worried headmaster of Eton, his boys within easy reach of the fleshpots of London. But doubts were rapidly resolved in the thirties, and within five years of the opening of the Liverpool and Manchester it was clear that the railway age had begun.

The railway was a triumph of industrial organization, an as yet unexampled blending of technological and engineering feats with managerial and financial skill. An entirely new kind of mobilization of labor was needed — from the gangs of navvies to build the lines to the skilled and responsible men who drove the engines and operated the signals: never before had so many lives depended on the judgment and skill of individual workingmen. These magnificent enterprises had a striking impact on the economy, the ways of life, and the sensibilities of the entire country. Railway construction employed huge numbers of workmen, and the vast expenditures — capital outlay on railways by 1865 equaled half the amount of the national debt — created booms in those industries, notably iron and engineering, that supplied the materials. Goods were transported more rapidly and so less capital was tied up in transit; canals and coaching lines declined; new industries flourished, from catering to hotels to newsstands. Ordinary people could visit distant places and faraway relatives, especially when in the forties excursion trains became a regular feature of British life. Holidays were transformed, and by mid-century the seaside and the mountainous areas were swarming with tourists from all classes. A new unity was given to the country — mails moved rapidly; the provinces were tied more closely to, and increasingly subordinated to, London; the easy transport of bulky building materials meant that one kind of brick might appear anywhere, replacing cheaply the old local building materials that had lent variety to the landscape. Perhaps most impressive of all was the effect on men's consciousness: cuts, embankments, bridges, and tunnels changed the landscape everywhere; the stations were built self-consciously as monuments by entrepreneurs who knew they were building for posterity; the speed, steam, color, excitement, and dirt became part of men's lives. One rightly speaks of the railway revolution.

This revolution posed tough problems of public policy. There was a considerable railway boom in 1835–1837; then, after the crisis of the latter year, though some 1,500 miles were opened, relatively few new lines were authorized. In 1844 the enthusiasm returned, and by 1845 the boom had become the "Railway Mania," ending in another crash in 1846. But, despite the slump, the 2,000 miles of 1843 had grown to 5,000 in 1848. It is hardly right to dignify the nation's railways with the word *system*. They had grown haphazardly, as local enterprise, pride, vision, or delusion had dictated. Political pressure was inevitably involved in getting the private act of Parliament needed to set up the company and to procure a right of way, and capital had somehow to be found; most of the money seems to have been raised locally, or from provincial merchants. But lines launched in this casual way were not necessarily paying propositions: there was often little basis for realistic estimates of potential traffic; the competition was sometimes intense and foolish; some companies were badly managed; and the necessity of cutting costs to pay the essential dividends or to defeat competition helped, with other causes, to produce a succession of disastrous accidents.

There were two possible directions for policy in a country that had willy-nilly decided to build its railways without plan or foresight. One was amalgamation, the consolidation of companies into long continuous lines, the creation, in other words, of a monopoly of traffic in one part of the country — by diplomacy where possible, by war if necessary. The most spectacular and notorious of the amalgamators was George Hudson, a linen draper and Tory politician from York. With the vision of a true railway imperialist, Hudson made himself the richest man in the country in 1845–1846; but the ways of financial manipulation were both new and difficult, and circumstances, ignorance, and greed led Hudson into the chicanery that brought his fall in 1848. Once the most courted, he became the most hated man in England — the scapegoat for a country that had momentarily gone mad.

The other recourse was state intervention. In 1840, a Railway Department was set up in the Board of Trade, to oversee, through its inspectors, the building and operation of lines, especially so far as safety was concerned. In 1844, Gladstone, at the Board of Trade, introduced a bill that would have conferred real powers on his department. He asked for authority to buy any railway after fifteen years from its date of charter or, alternatively, to revise its rates if it had made over 10 per cent in profits for three years. Although the act was to apply only to new lines built after 1844, the railway lobby went furiously to work, with at least tacit approval from Peel. By the time it had finished little was left. There remained a remote possibility (never realized) that the state, if Parliament approved in each specific case, might purchase new lines after twenty-one years. Beyond that there was only the famous provision that every passenger-carrying line must run a train every day in each direction and stopping at every station — the famous "parliamentary train." Some companies had entirely ignored, and most had mistreated, third-class passengers; now they had to be carried in closed carriages at a speed of at least twelve miles an hour for a fare of a penny a mile. In exchange for this requirement, which was usually carried out in as niggardly a way as possible, the companies were freed from a tax on passengers and given extremely favorable terms for carrying the mails — at twenty-seven miles an hour. The Railway Department and its successors, the Commissioners of Railways, retained only advisory powers; not until 1871 did their inspectors have compulsory powers. The Railway Act of 1844 was one of the few clear victories of laissez-faire in the early Victorian period.

The early nineteenth century is still firmly fixed in most people's minds as the time when laissez-faire triumphed. To be sure, old mercantilistic controls had been removed, many of them for the obvious reason that they had long ceased to be effective; their removal merely recognized the fact that a free economy existed in eighteenth-century England. But as soon as the human, social, and material consequences of industrialization became obvious, the state began to move in, and from the thirties state intervention grew rapidly. One can hardly count as victories for laissez-faire those limitations imposed by vested interests or the government's need to economize when, after all, the vital principle of intervention had been conceded and was seen to be infinitely expansible.

Company Organization

A third major piece of economic legislation in 1844 might be characterized as a law through which Parliament intervened to expand freedom by ensuring its responsible use. For well over a century,

English opinion had been intensely distrustful of joint-stock organization, which seemed to be a certain invitation to manipulation and fraud. Happily, for most of the period, capital requirements were not of a magnitude requiring the wide sweep of joint-stock organization. As late as 1875, the fixed capital investment in plant and equipment of all industry was less than the capital of the railways. Individual enterprises came nowhere near the scale of the railway companies, and so partnerships sufficed, where single families did not themselves have enough capital. Such private firms continued to dominate the English economy until the late nineteenth century.

From the repeal of the Bubble Act in 1825, however, the question of company organization and finance grew more pressing. Joint-stock organization now became possible without parliamentary approval, but the grant of incorporation, which alone could make large-scale combines feasible, was still jealously guarded. This legal conservatism was compromised by private acts allowing large partnerships to sue or to be sued through their secretaries; and in 1837 companies were enabled to secure incorporation by letters-patent issued by the executive government, a somewhat more flexible and cheaper procedure than a Crown charter or a private act of Parliament. In 1844 procedure was further simplified: all companies except banks were permitted to incorporate simply by registering with the Board of Trade, a method that drastically cut the expense of company organization and so contributed greatly to the flexibility of the economy. But, while the act increased the degree of freedom available to British businessmen, the very act of registration brought their prospectuses under the supervision of a government department and secured a measure of publicity and public accountability which was some guarantee of the reliability of the system.

Partners or investors in companies still remained liable for the debts of their companies to the entire amount of their personal wealth; they could not limit their liability to the amount of their investment. Certainly this risk kept much private capital out of the stock market and in government funds, but it was generally believed that unlimited liability was an essential spur to honesty and good management. The railway booms helped to accustom men to the idea of investment, and even those companies that failed or were poorly conceived or managed proved to investors that, while a bad investment might mean suspended dividends or some loss of capital, it need not mean selling houses or lands to pay the creditors of the company. So while limited liability was denied in 1844, it was only a matter of time. In 1856 limited liability was permitted for all companies, except banks, provided they proclaimed their intention by putting the abbreviation "Ltd." after their names; banks obtained the privilege in 1858; and in 1862 a great consolidating statute summed up the innovations of twenty-five years in company law.

Free Trade

The overriding importance of fiscal policy in Peel's administration was made clear by the Prime Minister's first actions. Within a week of the opening of Parliament in 1842, he introduced a bill revising the sliding scale of 1828.* The new maximum tariff for wheat was set at twenty shillings per quarter, to come into effect when the price stood at fifty shillings. Above fifty shillings, the duty dropped a shilling for every shilling's rise, with pauses between fifty-two and fifty-five and sixty-six and sixty-nine shillings; at the old level of seventy-three shillings, a nominal duty of a shilling would apply. New methods of calculating average prices were provided to stop corn merchants from forcing up the price to get larger profits. Lord John Russell's proposed reform of a fixed duty of eight shillings was bolder, but Peel was caught between the free traders Graham and Gladstone and the protectionist majority of his cabinet and party and could do no more.

His first budget, however, was a triumph of boldness. In effect, he adopted the program that the Whig financial reformer Sir Henry Parnell had proposed for his unheeding party in 1830. Tariffs were drastically cut on some 700 of 1,200 dutiable commodities; no import was to be forbidden; raw materials were to carry no more than 5 per cent, partly manufactured goods no more than 12 per cent, fully manufactured goods no more than 20 per cent. The drop in revenue — not as large as one might expect, for nearly all the customs revenue came from a few items — would be made up in time by increased volume of foreign trade. But meanwhile the deficit was to be met by the reintroduction of the income tax, which Parliament had abolished so gleefully in 1816. Peel got the revised tax through Parliament because the rates were low — sevenpence, about 3 per cent per pound of income of all kinds over £150 — and because he called it (and seriously thought it) temporary, though of course it has never disappeared. By 1844, Peel's policy had been justified, and he moved to a further measure of tariff reduction in the next year.

Peel was not, however, allowed to rest on his laurels; the Anti-Corn-Law League saw to that. The League had been formed in 1839, a transmutation of an Anti-Corn-Law Association founded the year before by a group of Manchester radicals. In 1840 the League contested a bye-election in Walsall, and although their candidate lost

*See above, p. 188.

and helped to put in a Tory over a protectionist Whig, the election gave them both experience and a national reputation. In 1841, their support went generally to the Whigs, thanks to Lord John Russell's stand on the Corn Laws. But by 1842 the League's situation had become complex and ticklish.

Free trade was clearly attractive to radicals whose hopes of further measures of political reform had been dashed by 1837: it might actually accomplish more immediate practical good than, say, the ballot; it carried the authority of scientific truth, at least to the converted; and it appealed to increasing numbers of merchants and manufacturers. The strength of this appeal was at once seen by the Chartists, who tried to break up League meetings and to blacken its members as tools of employers who wanted only to lower wages; Feargus O'Connor's support of the Conservatives in 1841 reflected this hostility. At the end of 1841, the Complete Suffrage movement of Joseph Sturge and his friends, though they saw it as complementary to the fight for free trade, seemed divisive to the Leaguers. Finally, Peel threatened to steal a march on them by his sweeping budgetary reforms. The League responded to these challenges in various ways. They organized squads of fighting Irishmen to take care of Chartist disrupters; at the same time, they appealed for working-class support by stressing the improvement in the standard of living that would come with free trade and especially with cheap corn. They accused Peel of offering tariff advantages to manufacturers while withholding them from the poor, and poured a steady stream of vilification on him, quite unjustly, as the prisoner of the Tory landlords. At one point veiled threats of assassination were made, and early in 1843 Peel's private secretary was killed by a murderer whose real target was the Prime Minister. Peel accused the League of fomenting disorder; Richard Cobden, the most prominent leader, replied by repeatedly blaming Peel, directly and personally, for the country's misery. The two men did not speak for more than three years, and the protectionists were delighted.

Peel's charge against the League had more than a shadow of truth to it. There were Leaguers, including the Rochdale manufacturer John Bright, on his way to becoming one of the great radical spokesmen of the century, who in 1841–1842 toyed with the possibility of inciting revolt among the working classes by closing their factories. Calmer heads prevailed, but wage reductions and inflammatory propaganda created the same result. The abortive strikes of 1842 discredited the Chartist leaders who tried to take advantage of them, and as Sturge's Complete Suffrage movement had been killed by Lovett's and O'Connor's unexpected alliance, the League was left as the main focus of radical sentiment in the country.

Rarely has an opportunity been so effectively used. Huge campaign funds were collected. A newspaper, *The League*, began to appear in 1843 and was supplemented by an enormous output of
propagandistic tracts, circulars, handbills, almanacs, and so on, from
League headquarters in Manchester, which remained the publishing
center (and in many ways the emotional center) even after the
League's administrative headquarters were moved to London. Paid
missionaries and orators stumped the country, whipping up great
meetings into a frenzy of excitement: the Covent Garden and Drury
Lane theatres were the sites of London meetings; in Manchester the
League erected Free-Trade Hall, today rebuilt after its destruction in
the Second World War as Manchester's main public auditorium.
Ministers denounced protection as sin and gave the League's campaign its special quality of a crusade, dominated by the uncontrolled
emotionalism that goes with revivalist meetings at any time and that
characterized nearly all mass movements in mid-nineteenth-century
England.

Men who were not Leaguers worried about this unprecedented
extra-parliamentary pressure, about the violence and the revolutionary overtones. But the League did not convert Peel or Parliament;
protection was struck down through the votes of men persuaded by
events and economic logic.

For three years, from 1842 to 1844, England had had good harvests; besides easing social tension, they helped Peel to a further installment of tariff reduction, and exasperated the League. Then, in
the summer of 1845, it rained almost without stopping. England had
had bad harvests before and would not have suffered severely,
though the League looked forward to a sharp rise in prices that
would serve their advantage. The trouble came in Ireland. The grain
harvest in that unhappy country was satisfactory, but Irish grain
went to England. The Irish lived on potatoes, and the potato crop was
a complete failure, due to a fungus infection made worse by the wet
weather. There had been potato famines before, but none like this.
The government swiftly organized a system of public works, and
private charity moved in, but more drastic measures were called for,
and Peel stood ready to provide them, if he could. He was now
prepared to repeal the Corn Laws.

Gladstone had withdrawn from the cabinet early in 1845, disa-
greeing with Peel's increased subsidy to the Roman Catholic training
college at Maynooth in Ireland; so the free-trade group in the cabinet
consisted only of Graham, Sidney Herbert, and Lord Aberdeen. Unable to convince his protectionist colleagues, Peel resigned on December 6. Two days before, in Edinburgh, Lord John Russell had announced his conversion to the League's program of complete and

immediate repeal. Now, with a chance to form a government, he faltered. Not without reason: his own party contained many landlords and protectionists; moreover, he would have been in a minority of over a hundred. His position was not unlike that of Peel in 1839; since Peel was certain to fall, if he did away with the Corn Laws, it would be better for him to do it, allowing the Whigs to come in without embarrassment and with a new election in prospect. Providentially, a Whig quarrel arose: Lord Grey, the son of the former prime minister, refused to serve as Colonial Secretary if Palmerston was at the Foreign Office, and Palmerston would take nothing else; so Russell declined the invitation to form a government, and Peel returned. Lord Stanley, the Colonial Secretary, resigned on principle; Gladstone, who had gone out earlier on principle, came back in on (apparently) a higher principle to replace him; Stanley's protectionist colleagues forgot principle and stayed in office. Cobden announced that a straightforward course from Peel would have the League's support.

Peel's proposals, made early in February, 1846, were masterly. He offered a further comprehensive installment of tariff reform. To prevent the protectionists from pointing to high tariffs remaining on manufactured goods, he abolished duties on shoes, hats, leather goods, soap, carriages, and coarse cloth; other duties were cut sharply. Duties were to be reduced on butter, cheese, hops, preserved fish, and seed; all other foods except corn and livestock were to enter free. Maize, American corn, was to come in free at once; the other grains would be subject to a reduced sliding scale for three years; in 1849 they would be allowed to enter freely, subject only to a nominal shilling duty. To compensate farmers and landlords for the loss of protection, Peel revised the law of settlement so that paupers from the manufacturing districts would not have to be returned to the parish of their birth; the state took over a part of the cost of medical relief under the poor law and of workhouse schools; it took over all the cost of bringing criminals to justice and all the cost of the new police. His concessions, of considerable importance to the level of local rates, were also steps towards further centralization.

The Corn and Customs bills passed the Commons in May; Wellington, who disapproved of repeal, nevertheless piloted the bills through the dangers of the Lords. On the day the Corn bill passed, Peel fell, defeated in the Commons on a coercion bill, introduced to deal with the new outburst of rural violence from starving Irishmen who took vengeance wherever they could. The Irish members voted against the bill, of course; the Whigs voted against it to bring Peel down; so did a couple of hundred protectionist Conservatives. Peel had split his party as he had done in 1829. But in a country indoctrinated by the League, Peel's popularity was immense. An administrator first, he had always put necessity above party. But another great, though still obscure man, Benjamin Disraeli, was turning the crisis to his own advantage. Excluded from the government in 1841 (though he was considered), he had to compass Peel's defeat to assure his own rise. The leading spokesman for the protectionists in Commons was Lord George Bentinck, a genial, horse-racing younger son of the Duke of Portland; he had little political sense or interest, but in a situation where the talent in the party was on Peel's side, he served well enough. Bentinck was sincerely indignant at what he considered Peel's treachery; but he was animated by a subtle intelligence in the background, by the man who was to be his biographer and the new leader of the Conservatives. Disraeli was the chief beneficiary of Peel's fall.*

THE TURNING POINTS

The Irish Famine

In the absence of disaster, the Whigs might have done well in Ireland. Melbourne's government had had its one clear success there: a new poor law and a new constabulary act combined with a determination to trust Catholics and an expectation of responsibility from landlords had worked wonders. Moreover, O'Connell was their ally. But in 1846 the Whigs could no longer count on Thomas Drummond, the scientist turned administrator, who as undersecretary in Ireland from 1836 to his death in 1840 had helped to provide the clear-sighted, firm, and just drive to good government. Moreover, O'Connell was not what he had been. In the early forties, distrusting Peel and the Tories, he began a new agitation for repeal, which suggested a repetition of the twenties. But in 1843 a turning point was reached in Irish politics. Peel managed to resist Anglo-Protestant demands for a stern Irish policy, but when a scheduled mass meeting seemed to threaten the peace, the government forbade it. A week later, O'Connell was arrested, although he had responded to the government's ban by revoking his order for the meeting. He was released from prison on an appeal to the House of Lords, but having seemed to knuckle under to the English government, he was unable to regain his power; he died on a pilgrimage to Rome in 1847. His place was

---

*Another beneficiary was Lord Stanley, who resigned from Peel's government over repeal; he was to become the formal leader of the Protectionists and ultimately Prime Minister and is only recently emerging from the historical preoccupation with Disraeli to appear as a statesman in his own right.

taken by men he had raised up to be his successors, but they were of a very different stripe: intellectuals, free-thinkers, and true nationalists in the modern sense. Grand rhetoric and clever maneuvering at Westminster were not for them; they were principled advocates of independence and revolution.

The Whigs inherited a crisis in Ireland that grew steadily worse; in human terms, probably no catastrophe in nineteenth-century Europe was more terrible than the Irish famine. The potato blight of 1845 could have been survived, as other crop failures had been survived; there were reserves, and public works and importation of food helped. But the summer of 1846 was worse. Not only were food reserves wiped out, but the total loss of the crop meant a lack of seed potatoes for the next year. The government simply could not meet the challenge. There was a confusion of facts and assertions, a welter of conflicting advice, no relevant experience to draw on, and as good as no machinery for administration.

Peel's public works program was modified. The Irish, fearing unemployment on the land and wanting the money, had flocked to the public works, even though the pay was less than farm wages. Deluged, Russell's administrators imposed a means test, centralized the administration with consequent delays in approving projects, and dogmatically insisted on "unproductive" works, such as road building, leaving plans for remunerative long-range efforts like drainage and railway building to private enterprise, which accomplished little. The import of food was bedevilled by troubles. Wheat continued to be shipped to England throughout the famine, not in the vast amounts alleged, but enough to be infuriating to the Irish. The maize from America came slowly, and the Irish neither liked it nor knew how to cook it. The reasons for the inefficiency were two: concern about the English food supply in a time of a severe European shortage, and a dogmatic determination that the trade in food should be left to normal commercial channels. By 1847 the situation was so bad that the government had to set up a soup-kitchen plan, based on the successful experience of the Quaker relief programs. Deficiencies in government policy and administration were so severe that major credit for what saving of life was done is due rather to private charitable enterprise.

The longer-range government solutions were three: a revised Irish poor law which recognized a right to relief, as the 1838 law had not done, in the workhouse normally, but out-of-doors if necessary; legislation to encourage or even force landlords to improve their land and to open wasteland to agriculture; and the Encumbered Estates Act of 1849, to make it possible for new capital to come into Ireland to buy debt-ridden estates with a clear title—an act that followed the recommendations of a royal commission on Irish land appointed by Peel in 1844. These steps were clearly based on English assumptions: Irish problems were to be solved by substituting large consolidated farms for the fragmented small holdings of the Irish peasants, and by applying capital in large doses to modernize Irish agriculture.

The situation was beyond legislation or English dogmatics; the solutions came more drastically from other directions. Throughout the famine years and immediately after, old- and new-style landlords were consolidating their estates; because they held key positions on boards of guardians, they were in a position to enforce a clause in the poor law denying relief to anyone who held over a quarter-acre of land. To get relief, then, many peasants had to sell their land; many more were evicted for nonpayment of rent. In ten years, the nearly 600,000 holdings of more than an acre fell to half that number, with most of the reduction accounted for by the sale of holdings of one to five acres. The dispossessed and the discontented who were able to do so emigrated—to England, Australia, Canada, and the United States. The population of Ireland, which had grown by three million in the sixty years before 1841, dropped in the famine decade from eight million to something over six. A million Irish emigrated, the rest died; mortality arising from the famine has been estimated most recently at around half a million, from outright starvation or from disease, during the famine at home, or on ships or in the inhospitable ports abroad. In October, 1846, Sir Charles Trevelyan, the civil servant most directly involved in the administration of famine relief, wrote that the Irish problem was beyond the power of men: "The cure had been applied by the direct stroke of an all-wise Providence in a manner as unexpected and as unthought of as it is likely to be effectual."*

1848

Beset in Ireland, the government had to face economic difficulties at home; they began late in 1846 and by 1847 had become serious. It was an odd crisis, arising partly from the harvest failures and partly from the Continental depression, but it was primarily a commercial and banking crisis related to serious overspeculation, especially in railways. A rash of bank failures in the summer of 1847 threatened the stability of the Bank of England itself, at a time when the Bank of France was also tottering. The Russians saved the situation by selling

*Quoted in T. P. O'Neill, "The Organization and Administration of Relief, 1845–52," in R. D. Edwards and T. D. Williams, eds., *The Great Famine* (1957), p. 257.

their grain to the Western powers for gold, and reinvesting that gold and much of the output of their new mines in Western bonds. The Bank's reserves nevertheless dropped to dangerous levels, and the government had to authorize the directors, as we have seen, to break the act of 1844.*

Beyond these two problems of famine and depression, the work of the Whig administration was that of consolidation and fulfillment. In 1847, a ten-hours bill was passed into law over the protests of the manufacturing interests by the combined votes of humanitarians and embittered protectionists out for revenge against the millowners who had beaten them on the Corn Laws the year before. By limiting the hours of children, the factory reformers hoped to limit the hours of adults, but Russell had consented to a provision that made it possible to employ children in relays, an abuse not stopped until an amending act was passed in 1849. In 1848, a public health act was passed, following up the pioneer work of Chadwick and the Royal Commission on the Health of Towns; the act set up a central board of health and made it possible for local communities that wanted action to establish local boards to undertake sanitary improvement. In 1849, the Navigation Laws were repealed, destroying the last important vestige of protective legislation at precisely the time when the transition to steam and iron in shipping was giving the British a new guarantee of mercantile supremacy on the seas.

It is a remarkable testimony to the liberal and responsible impulses of the forties that, in spite of the slump of 1847, the year 1848, which saw one after another European government fall to revolution, passed quietly in England. The European excitement of the preceding two years had begun to have an effect on some English working-class leaders, among them Harney and Ernest Jones, the son of a well-placed army officer, something of a poet, and a new recruit to Chartist leadership. Harney and Jones were in close touch with Marx and Engels, and in 1851 Harney's paper, the *Red Republican*, first published the *Communist Manifesto* in English. English working-class leaders were beginning to develop an interest in international working-class movements, which grew as refugees from the suppression of the Continental revolutions sought asylum in England and brought their heady, novel brands of radicalism and socialism with them.† But in England what some worried souls thought would at

---

*See above, pp. 267–268.
†The liberal sympathies of English workingmen reached a climax of sorts in 1851, when the Austrian General Haynau, who had put down the abortive Hungarian revolt, came to visit London. Like all distinguished visitors, he was taken on a tour of Barclay's brewery; Haynau was mobbed by the workingmen and barely escaped with his life.

last prove to be the revolution turned out, instead, to be a complete fiasco.

Early in March a serious riot took place in Glasgow, followed by rioting in other cities. The unrest was traceable to rising unemployment, but it also owed something to excitement provoked by the European revolutions. The surviving Chartist leaders, however, were much too divided to take advantage of what was no more than froth on a sea of apathy. O'Brien, Harney, and Jones were headed in more or less the same direction, though O'Brien would have nothing to do with plans for another convention. The convention met on April 4 to petition again for the Charter and to follow the inevitable refusal by some vague ulterior measures. On April 10, a great rally was scheduled for Kennington Common in south London; from there, a procession was to carry the petition to Westminster for presentation. The government moved efficiently and quietly. Wellington stationed troops throughout the metropolis, keeping them hidden; the regular police were supplemented by a host of merchants, tradesmen, peers, and members of Parliament enrolled for the occasion as special constables. On the morning of April 10, an orderly, good-natured, and colorful crowd, claimed by the Chartists to number 150,000, by others to be around 25,000, marched from central London across the river to Kennington; there were nearly 200,000 special constables. After a conference with the police, O'Connor told the crowd that the procession to Westminster had been forbidden and that they could not cross the river again in a body; he urged them to obey. They did. O'Connor and a few friends carried the petition to the House in hansom cabs. Chartism had made its last gesture. London was the wrong place for it.

In Ireland, the nationalists too had been stirred by Continental events; some of them talked violently and were arrested and prosecuted. When one leader, John Mitchell, was sentenced to transportation, the news touched off a riot in Manchester, a minor convulsion of a dying Chartism. The other Irish leaders escaped for a time, only to suffer the same fate after a pathetic attempt at rebellion in July.

In 1849, the Queen and her husband visited Ireland; the crisis there had passed. Indeed, for more than fifteen years, many Englishmen thought that the Irish problem had been solved, however dreadful the remedies that Providence had chosen to apply. English problems seemed solved too. The bogey of Chartism could still be raised feebly in the early fifties, but it had no substance. Feargus O'Connor patched up his differences with Harney and Jones in 1851; they summoned another convention for April 10, which called on a heedless world to turn to socialism. In 1852 O'Connor went finally mad, to die peacefully three years later. Old Chartists at home and abroad—many of them emigrated to America—went on fighting for democracy and social justice, goals that, almost as if to spite them, were gradually being attained in other ways.

But a greater force than O'Connor or Chartism passed from the scene in 1850. Peel was thrown from his horse and died on July 2. It was an irreparable loss. After 1846 as before, he had been the one tower of strength in English politics. Russell survived on Peel's sufferance, and to a remarkable degree on Peel's ideas, ineptly carried out. Occupying the middle ground between uninspired Whiggery and a demoralized and not yet Disraelian Conservatism, Peel had gathered about him the best political talent in the country. With him—he was only sixty-two when he died—the political history of the next decade might have been very different; without him, it was sterile. But there are times when a nation can afford political sterility, and the 1850's were such a time for England.

Selected Readings

The relevant volume of Halévy's History was published posthumously: The Age of Peel and Cobden, 1841–1852 (1947).

Of especial value for developments in parliamentary organization and procedure are two books by O. Cyprian Williams: The Historical Development of Private Bill Procedure and Standing Orders in the House of Commons (2 vols., 1948–1949) and The Clerical Organization of the House of Commons, 1661–1850 (1954). M. J. Cullen, The Statistical Movement in Early Victorian Britain: The Foundations of Empirical Social Research (1975) deals with both government statistics and the widespread statistical societies. The argument in Oliver McDonagh's case study of the regulation of the emigrant passenger traffic, A Pattern of Government Growth, 1800–1860 (1961), is extended to other areas of intervention in his Early Victorian Government, 1830–1870 (1977). The important debate over the nature of intervention and of the influence of Bentham's ideas on it, which was carried on in the late fifties and early sixties by Mc-Donagh and Henry Parris, is critically placed in an authoritative review of the whole controversy by Roy M. McLeod, "Statesmen Undisguised," American Historical Review, vol. 78, pp. 1386–1405 (December, 1973). Of histories of individual ministries, particular mention should be made of Henry Roseveare, The Treasury: The Evolution of a British Institution (1969) and Howard Robinson, The British Post Office, A History (1948).

On the troubled situation of the early forties, G. Kitson Clark, "Hunger and Politics in 1842," Journal of Modern History, vol. 25, pp. 355–374 (December, 1953) and the article by F. C. Mather on the Plug Plot in Roland Quinault and John Stevenson, eds., Popular Protest and Public Order: Six Studies in British History, 1790–1920 (1975). Two philanthropists of particular importance in this decade, one outside government and one inside, are dealt with in brief compass in G. F. A. Best, Shaftesbury (1964) and R. K. Webb's study of H. S.

Tremenheere in "A Whig Inspector," *Journal of Modern History*, vol. 27, pp. 352–364 (December, 1955). The greatest of the interventionist civil servants is the subject of two books, S. E. Finer, *The Life and Times of Sir Edwin Chadwick* (1952) and R. A. Lewis, *Edwin Chadwick and the Public Health Movement, 1832–1854* (1952). On the efforts to cope with a killing disease, Norman Longmate, *King Cholera, the Biography of a Disease* (1966).

The tricky and unsatisfactory statistics on literacy are interpreted in R. K. Webb, "Working-Class Readers in Early Victorian England," *English Historical Review*, vol. 65, pp. 333–351 (July, 1950) and "Literacy Among the Working Classes in Nineteenth Century Scotland," *Scottish Historical Review*, vol. 33, pp. 100–114 (December, 1955). For a broader, differently based evaluation, Lawrence Stone, "Literacy and Education in England, 1640–1900," *Past and Present*, no. 42, pp. 69–139 (February, 1969). The conflicting currents of educational history are the subject of John Hurt, *Education in Evolution: Church, State, Society and Popular Education, 1800–1870* (1971); and, despite its dogmatic intentions, the argument in E. G. West, *Education and the Industrial Revolution* (1975) must be taken seriously. Donald H. Akenson, *The Irish Education Experiment: The National System of Education in the Nineteenth Century* (1970) is an account of yet another reform that served in part as a model for England. The abortive effort to maintain the nonsectarian town schools in Liverpool is discussed in James Murphy, *The Religious Problem in English Education: The Crucial Experiment* (1959). Pamela and Harold Silver trace the story of a single school in south London in *The Education of the Poor: The History of a National School, 1824–1974* (1974). But not all children went to weekday schools: Thomas Walter Laqueur, *Religion and Respectability: Sunday Schools and Working Class Culture, 1780–1850* (1976) argues convincingly for their importance.

Railways dominate the economic life of this decade and after. Jack Simmons, *The Railways of Britain: An Historical Introduction* (1961) is a good book to start with. Robert E. Carlson, *The Liverpool and Manchester Railway Project, 1821–1831* (1969) gets the first true railway founded and operating. On aspects of the railway economy, G. R. Hawke, *Railways and Economic Growth in England and Wales, 1840–1870* (1970); M. C. Reed, *Investment in Railways in Britain, 1820–1844: A Study in the Development of the Capital Market* (1975); and F. C. Mather, *After the Canal Duke: A Study of the Industrial Estates administered by the Trustees of the Third Duke of Bridgewater in the Age of Railway Building, 1825–1872* (1970), a fascinating account of the clash and accommodation of canal and railway interests, reliably criticized in some respects by Eric Richards, *The Leviathan of Wealth: The Sutherland Fortune in the Industrial Revolution* (1973). John R. Kellett traces *The Impact of Railways on Victorian Cities* (1969); and in *The Railway Navvies* (1965), a study of the laborers who built the railways, T. Coleman traces a different kind of impact. Biographies of great figures in railway history include two by L. T. C. Rolt, *Isambard Kingdom Brunel* (1958) and *George and Robert Stephenson: The Railway Revolution* (1960), while R. S. Lambert, *The Railway King, 1800–1871* (1934) follows the rise and fall of George Hudson, the amalgamator. Henry Parris unravels the complex interrelationships of *Government and the Railways in Nineteenth-Century Britain*. Jeremy Warburg, *The Industrial Muse* (1958) is an anthology containing a large selection of poems illustrating the effect of railways on early Victorian sensibilities.

The conventional economic wisdom that ruled in Britain for nearly a century takes great strides in the 1840's. Aspects of the tension between control and freedom are set out in F. W. Fetter, *The Development of British Monetary Orthodoxy, 1819–1875* (1965) and B. C. Hunt, *The Development of the Business Corporation in England, 1800–1867* (1936). The agitation for free trade is traced in Norman McCord, *The Anti-Corn Law League* (1958), and the League is put in a wider context of political agitation in Patricia Hollis, ed., *Pressure from Without in Early Victorian England* (1974) and D. A. Hamer, *The Politics of Electoral Pressure: A Study in the History of Victorian Reform Agitations* (1977). Keith Robbins, *John Bright* (1979) is a short balanced biography of a leader in free trade movement who towered over his times, but who now seems less notable than he should be. But it was Ireland that triggered the change, not agitation. For the perpetual challenge of Irish reality to English theory, R. D. Collison Black, *Economic Thought and the Irish Question, 1815–1870* (1960). The Irish political background is accessible in Angus Macintyre, *The Liberator: Daniel O'Connell and the Irish Party, 1830–1847* (1965) and Kevin B. Nowlan, *The Politics of Repeal: A Study in the Relations Between Great Britain and Ireland, 1841–50* (1965). The demographic background of the tragedy of the Irish famine is set out in Kenneth H. Connell, *The Population of Ireland, 1750– 1845* (1950). On the tragedy itself, the essays in R. D. Edwards and T. D. Williams, eds., *The Great Famine* (1957) are of the first importance; the fullest narrative account is Cecil Woodham-Smith's passionate *The Great Hunger* (1962). But free trade has its opposite: on that subject one may consult Travis L. Crosby, *English Farmers and the Politics of Protection, 1815–1852* (1977) and Robert M. Stewart, *The Politics of Protection: Lord Derby and the Protectionist Party, 1841–1852* (1971).

Chapter 7
Consensus

1850–1867

THE LIBERAL TRIUMPH

The Great Exhibition

The keynote was struck by the Great Exhibition of 1851. This first "world's fair" was the pet project of two remarkable men. One was a prominent civil servant, Henry Cole, for whom the first Christmas card had been designed, and who was especially concerned about the challenge of Continental superiority in industrial design. The other was the Prince Consort, Albert of Saxe-Coburg-Gotha, whom the Queen had married in 1840. He was a cousin with whom she was deeply in love and to whose judgment she constantly deferred. Victoria and Albert were no mere figureheads. They insisted that their ministers keep them fully informed, and the instability of the party structure in the Commons enabled them to dabble effectively. But their interventions were not like those of Victoria's uncles or grandfather. Albert was intelligent, responsible, and progressive. But he was never fully trusted by his wife's subjects: he was foreign, intellectual, reforming, and possibly dangerous—during the Crimean War, some people actually insisted he was a spy.

Scientific curiosity, a faith in progress, and the example of French exhibitions of artistic and industrial productions led the Prince to the idea of the Great Exhibition. Housed in the Crystal Palace, a vast iron and glass structure built in Hyde Park to designs by the Duke of Devonshire's steward and confidant Joseph Paxton, the exhibition showed the best that Britain's and the world's industry could offer. Ingenuity was great, and design was mostly awful; but, at least for the British, the Exhibition was a celebration of their superiority. On Tuesdays, when the admission charge was a guinea, the people of quality were there; on shilling days, hundreds of thousands of ordinary men and women came from all over the country in cheap excursion trains. Even the skeptics returned again and again to be amazed and delighted; not least among the pleasures was the discovery that the working classes were jovial, interested, and on their best behavior. After a decade of turmoil came a decade of good will. Small wonder that G. M. Young, one of the most stimulating of modern historians of the nineteenth century, said that of all decades, one should choose the 1850's to be young in.*

Economic Prosperity

The fifties were a decade of consolidation, punctuated by two sharp intrusions from the world outside Britain: the Crimean War of 1853–1855 and the Indian Mutiny of 1857. But the full effects of these disturbances were felt only in the sixties or after. In the fifties they seemed momentary distractions from the building of a liberal society.

Mid-Victorian liberalism was firmly rooted in economic prosperity. The social tensions of the first half of the century had sprung from fundamental economic causes: unprecedented technological innovation, the dislocations of war and postwar readjustments, the recurrence of crises, the imposition of a hard and unaccustomed discipline. After 1850, thanks to the railways, bad harvests were no longer so threatening and crises were easier to survive; those that did occur, as in 1857 and 1866, were not depressions but crises of confidence in the financial and business community, bringing slack times rather than disaster. People had grown more accustomed to change and were getting used to the discipline of industrial life; and the remnants of older, declining forms of industry were gradually disappearing.

Even in agriculture, the largest single industry in the country, the mid-century decades were prosperous. The reasons for this pros-

*Young's remark is in Victorian England: Portrait of an Age (1977 ed.), p. 87.

perity are easy to find. Despite the predictions of the protectionists, English farmers continued to be protected, not by tariffs, true, but by their proximity to a growing market. Stock farming grew with the well-being of the population, and more and more land was devoted to it. The woolen industry took all that England and Scotland could produce and imported vast quantities from the burgeoning sheep-raising industry in Australia as well. Though a quarter of the country's bread was said to be made from imported wheat, farmers specializing in the production of grain were nearer to their consumers than their competitors on the Continent, and the prairies of America and Canada were not yet Europe's granary.

The removal of protective tariffs nevertheless compelled attention to increasing production and lowering costs. Soil drainage had been extended even to heavy soils, since the invention of a successful tile-making machine in the forties, and knowledge of chemical fertilizers was growing. Mechanization moved rapidly ahead: the threshing machines that had caused riots in 1830 were in general use; reapers were available by the fifties; steam engines drove agricultural machinery; and railways meant quicker access to markets and lower costs. The quarter-century after the repeal of the Corn Laws was the golden age of English "high farming."

Industry, too, profited from the speed, mobility, and unity given to the country by the railways and from the high level of railway investment and construction at home and abroad. As firms settled down to their second and third generations, managers emerged from a period of often perilous experimentation to display a confident mastery of industrial methods. There was continued innovation. The chemical, rubber, and Portland-cement industries were growing. The development of hydraulic machinery improved both working conditions and efficiency, and many man-killing jobs simply disappeared.* Perhaps the most important industrial break-through occurred in the metal trades and in engineering. In some ways, metallurgical knowledge was still backward; castings could fail, and strength often depended on size rather than temper and hardness. Engineers were slow to abandon jealously guarded individual designs for the concept of interchangeable parts. But the invention and improvement of machine tools and a new possibility of precision pointed the way to modern industry. At the Crystal Palace, Joseph Whitworth exhibited gauges which, applied to standardizing screw

---

*In his *Principles of Political Economy*, first published in 1848, John Stuart Mill speculated that all the invention of the preceding century had not significantly lightened human labor. He was probably right, but the next few decades quickly falsified his statement in many trades.

threads, speeded the unification of not only British but world industry by the 1880's. Above all, the Bessemer process, patented in
1851, and the open-hearth process, perfected in the sixties, made
possible the cheap quantity production of steel and so began a fundamental transition from an age of iron.

In these years a new assault was made on those industries still
organized on the putting-out system. Hosiery moved into factory
production in the middle decades of the century, and the number of
hand nail-makers in the Midlands dropped steadily as nail-making
machinery spread. Except for cutlery in Sheffield, and the tailoring
and dressmaking trades everywhere, no major industries based on
domestic production survived at the end of the century.

The British made what the world wanted and needed. Inferior to
the French in designing and manufacturing luxury goods, they concentrated on cheap, durable textiles and on coal, hardware, machinery, and railway iron. In time, the export of British capital goods
would boomerang, for it speeded the industrialization of the rest of
the world; but in the mid-nineteenth century Britain had no important competitors, seemed likely to have none on the same scale, and
so, ironically, erected her dogma of free trade on the basis of a secure
monopoly. Indeed, it has been ingeniously argued that the supposed
anti-imperialism of these years really reflected an "imperialism of
free trade": through a combination of economic superiority and
pragmatic politics, Britain made much of the world (South America,
for example) into something very like colonies without the necessity
of formal political domination.

Throughout the first half of the century, however, and increasingly thereafter, Britain imported more goods than she exported —
raw materials, most notably cotton, and a growing proportion of her
food. To overcome the imbalance, Britain had an essential advantage
in her "invisible exports," — the shipping with which she covered
the seas, the international banking and insurance services concentrated in London, the engineering and managerial skills of her contractors. Services like these brought millions of pounds in income
into British hands and subsidized the imports that an increasingly
industrial and affluent society needed to survive.

By mid-century, too, Britain could rely significantly on the interest from her investments overseas. In the first half of the century,
most of the country's savings went into building up transport facilities and industry at home, though some capital was going abroad
even then, typically to buy the bonds of foreign governments. At
times the investing public fell into a mania for foreign investment, an
enthusiasm usually quickly dashed, as it was by the collapse of the
South American mining shares in 1825 or the repudiation of bonds

by some American states in 1837. But bad memories quickly faded, the attractions of high yields beckoned, and by mid-century the trickle abroad had become a sizable stream. The flow was beginning to shift from the Continent to the colonies (India in particular in this period), South America, and, above all, the United States. Mines, railways, and docks were being opened around the world, many of them with British capital, and British money was going into other forms of commercial enterprise, such as land companies, banking, and shipping lines. It has been estimated that by 1875 Britain's foreign investment amounted to at least £1,200,000,000, and, while that sum seems paltry compared to the scale of British foreign investment on the eve of the First World War, it was large enough to have a real effect on the rest of the world and to provide a secure foundation for British prosperity. Britain's dependence on the world outside was potentially dangerous, but the danger was largely unrealized.

Self-help, Cooperation, and New-Model Unionism

Above this growing and reasonably secure prosperity developed something like a consensus. Historians once talked about a "Victorian Compromise," whereby the expanded, middle-class oligarchy maintained their hold on political power by conferring social benefits on the working classes, amid general agreement throughout society on the fundamentals of economics and morality. The phrase is misleading. The social legislation of the years following 1832 grew from moral, political, or administrative necessity; it was not a concession to "buy off" an insurgent working class, and, as a matter of fact, the fifties saw no great expansion of social legislation. Unskilled workers and their families still lived perilously close to the borders of subsistence; they suffered from occasional unemployment and from endemic drunkenness and irresponsibility, and depended to an alarming degree on chance, private charity, and the poor law. They benefited from the general rise in wages and the general fall in prices; and as their lot grew easier, most of them remained as apathetic as they had always been. The explosive elements in the declining trades were, as we have seen, falling in numbers and potency. But the more prosperous skilled laborers, who had provided the leadership for so much of the protest in the preceding decades, were by no means complacent; in the fifties they were regrouping after their earlier defeats and working out more practical and permanent methods and organizations. They still had ulterior goals in mind, and the more sweeping working-class demands of the last quarter of the century were possible because firm foundations had been laid in the fifties and sixties. Insofar as respectable workingmen came to share many of the economic and moral views of their social superiors, they were responding to ideals and standards that seemed to have worked. It is wrong to think that the virtues of respectability, sobriety, thrift, and hard work reflected nothing but cringing subservience on the one hand or Machiavellian deceit on the other.

At least from the eighteenth century, workingmen had combined to protect themselves from calamity. Friendly societies—clubs to help with the costs of illness or burial—had grown steadily under benevolent upper-class patronage and from the thirties under the supervision of the state. Often local, but increasingly regional or national in scope, these valuable institutions were strengthened in the forties and fifties by better actuarial knowledge, which made it possible to put their financing on a firmer basis. The development of savings banks and, somewhat later, of building societies helped not only to tide men over difficult times but to instill prudence and responsibility, reinforcing the pride and status that came with new skills and growing opportunities. But these sensible, matter-of-fact institutions could never evoke the emotional attachment of two more narrowly working-class movements that came to maturity in mid-century—cooperation and trade unionism.

The cooperative efforts of the twenties and thirties had been manifest failures, victims of visionary schemes for founding communities and of hurried or unintelligent planning. But the collapse of the Grand National and the failures of Chartism did not kill the cooperative impulse. In the early fifties it even received important middle-class support. The most celebrated sponsors of cooperatives were the Christian Socialists, notably Charles Kingsley, a liberal Anglican minister and novelist, Thomas Hughes, the author of *Tom Brown's Schooldays,* and J. M. Ludlow, who became Registrar of Friendly Societies. Inspired by the great Anglican theologian, Frederick Denison Maurice, and alarmed by the rejection of Christianity evident among the more intelligent workingmen, they encouraged groups of workingmen to seek both pride and economic advantage in cooperative production. The workshops failed, and, as a movement, Christian Socialism came to an end by the mid-fifties, but the Christian Socialists did not lose their sense of mission. They continued to encourage intelligent working-class organization and to justify it to resistant middle-class opinion.

Real success came to another form of cooperation which began independently of the Christian Socialists, though they welcomed it. The modern consumers' cooperative movement is generally dated from the setting up of a shop in 1844 by a small band of Owenites in the Lancashire textile town of Rochdale. The capital of the Rochdale shop, and of others soon founded on the same principle, was subscribed by the people who used the shop or by benefactors, and interest was paid on it; at the same time, profits from the sale of goods at the market price were returned to the customers in proportion to their purchases, thereby offering an inducement to regular and increasing use of the cooperative store. So successful were such enterprises — not least because they gave value for money — that by the sixties cooperatives were moving into the wholesale trade; in the eighties cooperative factories and warehouses were supplying the country's "co-ops." Thus, on a large scale and rather more practically, some of the less sweeping ideals of the early Owenites were realized.

Still more important was "new-model" trade unionism. The debacle of 1834 had wiped out the colossal and unrealistic Grand National and some less grandiose national unions as well, such as the Builders and the Spinners, but a number of large unions, like the Stonemasons and the Carpenters, survived along with many smaller societies. These survivals were often rudimentary, and none of them was very active, especially as so much working-class energy was absorbed by Chartism, but by the early forties the trade unions were again on the move, notwithstanding a succession of severe defeats in the strikes of that decade.

The successful unions were those of the skilled trades in progressive segments of the economy. Some, like the Typographers, Compositors, Boilermakers, and Engineers, were craft-based and restrictive, relying on apprenticeship to keep up standards and to keep down competition for jobs; in other trades, like cotton spinning, where apprenticeship was not enforceable and where piecework rather than time on the job was the basis of payment, the unions directed their efforts rather to securing favorable wage rates and factory conditions, and to limiting the hours of labor. But, however much unionism varied from trade to trade, certain features were common to the New Model unions. One was a tendency to amalgamation, first successfully demonstrated by the Amalgamated Society of Engineers (ASE), founded in 1851 and well run by its efficient and cautious secretary, William Allan. The funds of such unions were administered locally, but the levels of dues and benefit payments were fixed nationally, and the national union would permit no strikes without its authorization. The ASE's example was followed by other unions, notably the Builders. The Spinners, organized in 1852, and the Weavers, organized in 1858, were less highly centralized, but even these unions — of "operatives" rather than craftsmen — took on much of the same coloration.

A second characteristic of new-model unionism was the combination of trade union and friendly society. The Engineers' dues were a shilling a week, a scale that excluded poorer workers, but that could mean substantial benefits to members caught by misfortune or to everyone, when strike pay became necessary. A corollary of this double role of the unions was the necessity for careful and efficient management, a feature that contributed not only to making trade unions respectable in middle-class eyes but to making statesmen out of their leaders.

These qualities underlay a third characteristic, a cautious and conservative trade policy. When the ASE mounted a nationwide strike in 1852, the employers replied with a three-month lockout; the men returned to work on the employers' terms, as the Spinners had to do when they went out on strike the following year. But, in general, strikes were uncommon and were resorted to only for strategically well-conceived ends. Again, a cautious policy impressed the politically powerful middle classes, while it allowed the unions to build up their resources to a point where long strikes could be supported, if they became necessary.

Finally, and most important, these unions lasted. The 1852 strike left the Engineers stronger than before, even though the men had to sign "the document" — an agreement renouncing union membership — as a price of returning to work; the promise was simply ignored, and the display of sympathy at home and abroad was heartening. So too with the Spinners and the other national unions newly organized in the fifties or expanded from older, simpler organizations. Forgetting the impractical schemes of the thirties and forties, concentrating on the attainable, keeping an eye both to sensible administration and to the public interest, mid-Victorian union leaders were soon in a position to advance far-reaching political claims. Meanwhile, pursuing their pragmatic course and apparently impervious to the influence of Continental socialists, they and their followers shared increasingly in the assumptions and prejudices that made mid-Victorian England liberal.

The Liberal Assumptions

In the years immediately following 1832, there was, as we have seen, no single clear opinion in the country; ministers had rather to pick their way among the nostrums offered by vocal politicians and insistent radicals and the objections of vested interests and sincere opponents of change. It was far different in the fifties; insofar as Englishmen thought about policy, there was general agreement as to what was needed and what was not. First among liberal dogmas was the belief in free trade. Historians now agree that the Anti-Corn-Law League had made little direct parliamentary contribution to the repeal of the Corn Laws, but in the country at large, the League was highly successful in creating and focusing public opinion, which for eighty years kept Britain a free-trading country in a protectionist world.

Certain that the world would follow their example, the English believed that great moral results were inevitable. Trade meant peace, and many enthusiasts looked forward to the end of empire, unjust exploitation, and war, a faith that survived even the disillusions of the Crimean War and the Indian Mutiny. Colonial controls were successively abandoned,* and in 1861 a treaty with France, appropriately called the Cobden Treaty, more or less completed the demolition of the protective walls around Britain. The only manufacturers who remained secure from foreign competition were those whose products were more attractive to the public and the revenue officers than to moralists—alcoholic drinks, tobacco, and playing cards. Even there, the Cobden Treaty cut down the duties on French wines, and in 1867 dice were allowed to come in without the duty of a guinea a pair.

By mid-century, almost all Victorians were believers in progress. They had every reason to be so. A hundred years before, fundamental change had been inconceivable; now it seemed not only certain but beneficial, and men of good will were eager to help it on. Along with many manifestations of public and private conscience, this faith gives the lie to the charge so often made that the Victorians were complacent. To be sure, any prosperous and comfortable society generates smugness and self-satisfaction, but certainty should not be confused with complacency. The Victorians believed with their ancestors of George II's time that the world would go on forever in the course in which it was set, and that England would always be at its center. At the same time, they tried to make the world better.

Most Victorian liberals were convinced individualists. Again, there was good warrant for their being so. Whatever qualifications historians of administration must make, the early nineteenth century was changed to an astonishing degree by the efforts of individuals following their own interests or their own demons.† It is hardly surprising that they believed in individual moral virtues. In the fifties, Herbert Spencer began to develop a deductive, evolutionary philosophy centered on the clear-eyed, self-reliant individual who had survived the competitive struggle for existence without aid from his fellows or the state. But *Social Statics* (1850) and *The Man Versus*

---

*See below, p. 356.
†The story goes that Queen Victoria once asked Melbourne for a definition of "bureaucracy," a strange word she had just heard for the first time. "That, Madam," he replied, "is something they have in France."

the State (1884) were tracts masquerading as scientific treatises; they are less significant for an understanding of mid-century, as they were less popular, than the works of Dr. Samuel Smiles, a Leeds radical who recounted the *Lives of the Engineers* (1861–1862) for an admiring generation and whose best-selling books, *Self-Help* (1859) and *Thrift* (1875), were injunctions operating through example.

This prejudice for individualism reinforced the distrust of the state, a complicated feeling that arose from several sources. In part that distrust was carried over from the assumptions of the early Victorian liberals who set out to destroy the old forms of state control. Mercantilistic intervention had been inefficient, distorting, and corrupt; and, once local government was reformed, the idea of self-government could easily imply that, where collective efforts were necessary, they should be local, not national. Localism also came naturally to the Dissenters: preference for congregational rather than joint action was a long-standing tradition with most of them, and they had usually found the state hostile to granting their full civil rights; why then should they trust it with the ordering of their lives? For some, a vigorous local community represented the oldest and truest English tradition, as opposed to Continental centralization. Localism also asserted provincial pride against London pretension. All these arguments could easily conceal the desires of vested interests, which could control or neutralize local government when they could not sway more distant bureaucrats in London. But for many believers in decentralization, the fight was a fight for principle, not for selfish advantage. They believed, honestly if idealistically, that the free play of enlightened self-interest in an aware citizenry would bring the millennium.

The major victory of localism in the fifties was the rejection of Edwin Chadwick's efforts to do something about public health. The investigations in the forties had disclosed appalling situations. Dirt, smells, and disease made it evident enough that stringent steps had to be taken. Except for areas with unusually high mortality, the Public Health Act of 1848 was not compulsory, nor was it widely adopted; by 1854 the outcry against even that much intervention was strong enough to force Chadwick out of office. The most famous civil servant of his time, and the least adaptable politically, he was perfectly prepared to be authoritarian, if necessary, to produce a clean, healthy, tidy nation. "Unable to bend," his biographer remarks, "he was made to be broken."[*] And while Chadwick often testified before committees and royal commissions and produced a stream of ingenious plans and programs until his death in 1890, he never held another government post. He came up against the root insistence of the

---

[*]S. E. Finer, *The Life and Times of Sir Edwin Chadwick* (1952), p. 6.

English that they were a free people. "We prefer to take our chance of cholera and the rest," rumbled *The Times*, "than be bullied into health."

Meanwhile, in quiet, subterranean ways much good work was done by less well-known officials, and some local initiatives had positive results: all the really large towns made it a point of pride to meet their sanitary needs by local acts, tailored to suit their individual situations. But not until the seventies was central initiative openly resumed.

Public Schools and Universities

Middle-class demands for free trade, individual enterprise, and local initiative were soon to be shaken by a new generation of theorists and by the hard facts of the modern world;* by the end of the century, they were merely articles of faith, not guides to action. But other developments of mid-century provided the solid foundations for middle-class attitudes, confidence, and power that have survived with increasing strength down to the present.

Middle-class children were indifferently educated by charity foundations, town schools, or private schools run by Dissenting ministers, Anglican clergymen, or private individuals of widely varying abilities. Down to 1840, when the courts got the power to change the terms of their charters, most of the old foundations operated under such severe restrictions and with such tiny incomes that they could do little to improve their teaching, had they wished to do so. The sons of the wealthy had private tutors or went to one of the so-called "public schools," certain old foundations which, by taking boarding pupils, had ceased to be local. But education in the early nineteenth-century public schools was of doubtful value. It consisted almost entirely of reading, writing, and memorizing Greek and Latin; living conditions were dreadful; and discipline was brutal or nonexistent. We are assured now that the Duke of Wellington never said that the battle of Waterloo was won on the playing fields of Eton, but had he said it, he would have paid tribute less to the discipline and sense of honor instilled in team sports than to the toughness developed in combat. On one occasion the militia had to be called out to put down a rebellion of boys at Winchester.†

The most famous reformer of the public schools was Dr. Thomas Arnold, headmaster of Rugby from 1828 to 1842. Building on prece-

*See below, pp. 381–383, 410–412, 460–461.
†In the early nineteenth century, the public schools were nine in number: Eton, Harrow, Rugby, Shrewsbury, Winchester, Westminster, and Charterhouse were the boarding schools, and two London day schools — St. Paul's and Merchant Taylors' also ranked as public schools.

dents set by other less famous masters, at Rugby and elsewhere, Arnold introduced French, modern history, and mathematics as subjects. He examined the boys on the contents of the classics they read as well as on language. He encouraged organized games. He transformed a prefectorial system in which older boys disciplined the younger from a license for brutality and oppression into a way of teaching (at its best) the responsible exercise of power. Above all, by the strength of his personality, he enforced on his boys his image of a Christian gentleman. As the Arnoldine reforms spread, the sons of the upper classes were prepared, through a Spartan life of "clean living and high thinking," for responsibilities that the Christian gentlemen of England were expected to shoulder in a world increasingly tributary to them: it was not primarily intellectual, but moral and social education. Whatever its disadvantages in separation from the poor or the perpetuation of social prejudices, the public school was one of the major cultural facts of the Victorian era. From the fifties, many new boarding schools were founded on that pattern, and though the government did little to regulate the older grammar schools or private schools, middle-class expectations and snobbery forced them to keep pace.

The early nineteenth century had seen reform in the universities as well. At the turn of the century both Oxford and Cambridge introduced serious examinations and honors degrees to encourage able students; but the reforms were spotty, and both universities remained Anglican monopolies. In the fifties the pressure of public opinion forced the appointment of a royal commission for each university, boycotted by most senior university officials, but aided by a minority of reformers inside. In 1854 and 1856, Parliament removed the religious tests for entrance and taking degrees; the final bastion, restriction of fellowships and offices to Anglicans, fell in 1871.

Meanwhile, the younger tutors and some older allies were modernizing the curriculum, making the colleges more effective institutions for teaching, and encouraging newer and more relevant research and learning. The best of them were as concerned as Dr. Arnold had been to enforce Christian ideals, an emphasis that made the universities acceptable to lay opinion to a degree that no exclusively intellectual training could have attained. In time, the reforms helped to maintain the primacy of Oxford and Cambridge over the very different universities of Scotland and the new universities that were beginning to appear in England. The University of Durham had been founded in 1832; Owens College in Manchester was opened in 1851; specialized schools, especially for medical education, at Birmingham and Sheffield were shortly to point the way for the founding of other so-called "red-brick" universities.

The Professions

The reform of the schools and universities was paralleled by the rise in status of old professions and the emergence of new. The only members of the medical profession with high social standing in the early nineteenth century were the rather small number of fellows of the Royal Colleges of Physicians and Surgeons; most people were doctored by apothecaries or operated on by surgeons who still bore the stigma of their having been barbers as well in the seventeenth century. Medical education in England was so indifferent that serious students usually went to one of the Scottish universities. But in the eighteenth and early nineteenth centuries, medical knowledge was put more firmly on a scientific basis through the work of such men as William and John Hunter and Sir Charles Bell; surgery was advanced by new techniques and the improved study of anatomy in the early decades of the nineteenth century and by the discovery and quick spread of anesthesia and antisepsis in mid-century. In the 1820's, the development of medical schools in the University of London and in the provinces and the rapid improvement of medical teaching in the hospitals made possible the Medical Act of 1858, which set down the procedures by which a physician or surgeon had to qualify and gave the several professional bodies those powers of admission and discipline on which the technical definition of a profession depends.*

Barristers had always qualified as a profession in this narrow definition because of their connection with the Inns of Court. But solicitors, or attorneys, however great their local importance as agents and advisers, were considered much inferior and only began to rise to professional prominence and real respectability as the demands for their services grew with the increasing complexity of late eighteenth-century England. The needs of business and industry in the nineteenth century created the new professions of accountancy and engineering. Ordinary clergymen found their position improved by the reforms of the Church and the better distribution of stipends, though they remained generally, as they are today, dreadfully under-

---

*A crisis in medical education occurred in the late 1820's. The operators of anatomy schools could not look too scrupulously into the sources of scarce cadavers, which as often as not came from grave robbing. Popular prejudice was inflamed by the infamous Burke and Hare murders in Edinburgh in 1828, when it was discovered that the two criminals were murdering for sale. In 1824, Southwood Smith wrote an important article in the *Westminster Review* called "The Use of the Dead to the Living," which helped to create a climate of opinion that made possible the passage of an act providing that unclaimed bodies in the workhouses be turned over to science.

paid. The lowlier Dissenting ministers rose in status as the congregations to which they ministered grew richer and as exclusive prejudices against Dissent broke down. Teaching, as we have seen, was set on its way to becoming a respectable profession rather than a refuge for incompetents by the Committee of Council's Minute of 1846. Nursing, throughout the early part of the century a haven for slovenly and disreputable women, was raised suddenly to distinction by the heroic work of Florence Nightingale and her assistants in the Crimean War and by Miss Nightingale's incessant, authoritarian efforts at professionalization after the war and throughout her long life. In one salient after another, then, of the rapidly expanding middle classes, there was a steady pressure upward by trained specialists whose professional competence was publicly certified. Set off from the steadily growing numbers of "white-collar" or "black-coated" workers — supervisors, draftsmen, and clerks — the expanding professions gave a new tone to mid-Victorian society, rapidly undercut received notions about the structure of society, and provided a new plateau from which the higher professions and the public service could be recruited.

Civil Service Reform

One of the most far-reaching of the professional reforms begun in the fifties took place in the civil service. We have already seen how the recruitment of able clerks and administrators in certain departments and the provision of decent salaries and pensions had started to professionalize government service as early as the period of the French Revolution. But civil servants kept a popular reputation of doing little work and doing that badly, and too often the facts bore out the allegations. The growing demands upon administration made such relaxed conditions intolerable. Pressure inside and outside government led to an investigation of the structure and recruitment of the government service.

In the early fifties, Sir Charles Trevelyan was Assistant Secretary to the Treasury; Sir Stafford Northcote was a Conservative member of Parliament. Commissioned by Gladstone, then Chancellor of the Exchequer, they produced in 1854 a report that is the point of departure for the modern history of the civil service. Their main recommendations were four: (1) There should be a single civil service under the supervision of a civil service commission; members of the service could be sent to work in any department. (2) There should be a strict classification of the service, with the administrative civil servants recruited on different criteria from the clerical grade; thus young men could be brought into the service at the policymaking level without having to serve a long apprenticeship in copying letters and other routine work. (3) There should be an age limit for recruitment, so that men would enter the service at an age when they could be properly trained. (4) Both recruitment and promotion should depend on competitive examinations, based not on specialized knowledge but on the liberal arts education given in the universities.

The report caused a sensation. Queen Victoria and many others feared that open recruitment by ability alone would lead to the swamping of the service by middle-class or even lower-class men; veteran civil servants, many of them highly competent, resented the slur that the report seemed to cast on them and on the process by which they had been chosen. Some ministers were afraid that the limits set on patronage would make political life intolerable. But predominant opinion was deeply impressed, and gradually the recommendations were put into effect. In 1855 the Civil Service Commission was set up; under the Superannuation Act of 1859, a certificate from the Civil Service Commission was required for a civil servant to qualify for a pension. Finally, in 1870, an order in council made recruitment by competitive examination mandatory throughout the government, except for the Foreign Office; there, social standing was still considered a prime necessity, and open competition came only in 1919.*

The Intellectual Aristocracy

The reform of the universities and the emergence of the professions provided the institutional framework for the creation and expansion of a new intellectual aristocracy. Drawing on an old, cloistered academic and clerical tradition, and reinforced from newly wealthy business families, this powerful class began to penetrate every area of English life where learning, ability, and responsibility were needed; its members became scientists, teachers, writers, philanthropists, civil servants, pro-consuls, members of Parliament, and

*In the early days of examinations there were ways around them. One civil servant recalled that in the fifties Sir William Hayter, Secretary of the Treasury, in making up the list of three candidates required for an examination, repeatedly put up a special couple known as the "Treasury Idiots," who could be counted on never to pass anything; he could then be certain of appointing the man he wanted because his candidate would inevitably win. (Sir Algernon West, *Recollections, 1832 to 1886* [1900], p. 45.) An amusing novel about civil service reform is Anthony Trollope's *The Three Clerks* (1858); Trollope was Inspector of Posts in Ireland and a critic of the Trevelyan-Northcote recommendations. The spirit of the proposals was anticipated in a remarkable little book, *The Statesman* (1836), by Sir Henry Taylor of the Colonial Office.

statesmen. Because they were usually well-to-do and well connected and because they were unquestionably gentlemen, they were acceptable to the older ruling groups. Because they were flexible and imaginative, and because their ranks were penetrable by talent, they were acceptable to those whose ability and ambition outranked their social standing. Moreover, this intellectual aristocracy was self-perpetuating; just as the names of noble families occur in generation after generation of English history down to the nineteenth century, so the names of these intellectual dynasties have appeared in generation after generation of England's cultural and political life with undiminished distinction from the early nineteenth century right down to the present. Because they were, as their historian has said, "secure, established and, like the rest of English society, accustomed to responsible and judicious utterance and sceptical of iconoclastic speculation," they explain "a paradox which has puzzled European and American observers of English life: the paradox of an intelligentsia which appears to conform to rather than rebel against the rest of society."*

John Stuart Mill

The mid-Victorian liberal consensus was most clearly distilled in the life and works of John Stuart Mill. Educated by his father to be a perfect Benthamite, Mill became the leading philosopher, though a somewhat atypical member, of that potent but not always clearly definable philosophical school, the Utilitarians. Yet Mill was more than a mere transmitter of the Benthamite tradition. He never abandoned Bentham's rigorous analytical methods or the criterion of utility, but he expanded and humanized them, transforming a typical eighteenth-century philosophy into a broad view of men and affairs acceptable to the nineteenth century. From his reading of Wordsworth and the romantic poets he evolved a conception of pleasure broader and more emotional than Bentham's more mechanistic sense of it; through the study of Coleridge and the French positivist Auguste Comte, he reinforced a profound historical sensibility. For a time he and Carlyle were friends, sharing an intense moral concern about what seemed to be the dominant characteristics of the thirties — shortsighted selfishness, formulistic explanations, and class cleavage. Because Mill was always a critic, his observations of his own society cannot be taken as clinically exact, as they too often are; but his criticisms and his remedies grew out of political, moral, and psychological assumptions thoroughly characteristic of his time.

*On the seminal idea of a "clerisy," or intellectual class, see above, p. 182–183.

Except for religion, no major aspect of English life was left untouched by his remarkable intelligence. His *System of Logic* (1843) was a guide to modes of scientific thought for a generation caught up in an intellectual revolution. His *Principles of Political Economy* (1848) was the classic restatement of Ricardian doctrine, though in the famous third chapter, "On the Probable Futurity of the Labouring Classes," he looked forward to changes in the patterns of distribution in a way that led him in later years towards a quasi-socialist position. In *Representative Government* (1861), the mid-Victorian polity was brilliantly justified, though his advocacy of further parliamentary reform was modified by a concern, derived from reading Tocqueville's *Democracy in America* (1835), about the effects of leveling on the claims of quality and intellect; he was, consequently, impelled to search out safeguards for unpopular but valuable minorities. *On Liberty* (1859) is the finest defense ever written of individual freedom, a defense grounded not in religion or abstract rights, but in the purely utilitarian argument that the clash of opinions is necessary to the attainment of truth. Nor was Mill content with writing. Like his father, he served in the London headquarters of the East India Company, and he was closely connected with the men who worked the new apparatus of government, a major source of the new intellectual aristocracy. In 1865 he contested a bye-election for Westminster and was returned to the House of Commons as a Radical; there he served as a major spokesman for the labor movement centered on the new-model unions.

For the next two generations, Victorian intellectuals looked to Mill as the most important English philosopher, if not always as an inspiration, then as a challenge; he has been the major intellectual force behind Anglo-American liberalism ever since. But for all the clarity with which he reflected and transmitted the best assumptions and ideals of his age, he was not its most representative man: intellect is not life. No one has ever talked or ever will talk about "the age of Mill." Mid-century was the age of Palmerston.

PALMERSTON

Foreign Policy, 1830–1852

While Peel towered over domestic politics, Lord Palmerston dominated foreign policy. Except for a few months in 1834–1835, he was Foreign Secretary from 1830 to 1841 and again from 1846 to 1851. He returned, after a cabinet crisis that put him briefly out of office, to serve as Home Secretary from 1852 to 1855 and then as Prime Minister, again with intervals of only a few months, from 1856 to 1865. Extraordinarily able in the technicalities of diplomacy, he appeared to increasingly exasperated Continental observers to embody Britain for more than thirty years. His hold on public opinion at home was quite as remarkable. A Regency survival hardly in keeping with the dominant moral tone of mid-century, he grew increasingly hostile to liberalism at home; he had a host of enemies, from the Queen and Prince Albert through nearly every prominent politician to the spokesmen for liberal opinion, with Cobden and Bright at their head. But a colorful reputation was no disadvantage, at least in a peer, among many not so respectable Englishmen; reform was at a discount in the quiet of the fifties; some men loved him for his enemies and others in spite of them. As an Irish peer he was eligible to sit in the House of Commons; using that forum and the press, he played on popular sympathies and prejudices even more effectively than Canning had done. He fought for liberal causes abroad, and he insisted, with supreme confidence, that Britain in his hands was arbiter of the world she dominated. What his critics thought conceit, bluster, and levity struck a responsive chord in the nation. The ordinary Englishman was liberal, to be sure, but he was also John Bull.

When Palmerston first went to the Foreign Office in 1830, he inherited three European problems and soon saw two of them solved. Dom Pedro, chased off the Brazilian throne by a revolution in 1831, returned to Portugal to support his daughter Maria against her absolutist uncle Dom Miguel; with the help of the British commander of his navy, he sent Miguel into exile and in 1836 saw Maria married safely to a prince of the little German house (from which Prince Albert came) of Saxe-Coburg-Gotha. In Spain, where Ferdinand VII had died in 1833, an army of British volunteers was sent to fight for the constitutionalist cause of the Queen Regent Christina, an unwilling ally of the liberals in the interests of her infant daughter Isabella. A civil war between the liberal forces of Christina and Isabella and the reactionary, church-supported backers of Don Carlos dragged on until 1839, when the Carlists at last collapsed from utter incompetence. The third inherited problem, the Ottoman Empire, was not so easily settled. Against the tortuous policy of Russia, Palmerston simply reiterated the old though ultimately futile British policy of supporting the Sultan, hoping to keep Turkey intact, if not to get it reformed.

More immediately critical were two new problems that had burst on Europe just before the change of government in 1830. The July Revolution had put Louis Philippe on the throne in France, and the Belgians had revolted against the Dutch to whom they had been joined in the settlement of 1815. For the British, the strong sympathy that existed between Belgians and French raised the traditional question of the Channel ports, a problem which Palmerston and Talleyrand, who had been sent as ambassador to London, settled between them. But there still remained the resentment of the Dutch, who were unwilling to see their enlarged kingdom dismembered. Had the Dutch been able to claim support from the absolutist powers, Russia, Prussia, and Austria, serious trouble might have resulted. But those powers, conveniently occupied with troubles of their own, consented reluctantly to a settlement in November, 1831, which recognized a separate kingdom of Belgium under King Leopold, also of the house of Saxe-Coburg-Gotha. The Eastern powers held back again a year later when an Anglo-French blockade was launched to coerce the Dutch into accepting the settlement. The Dutch were forcibly persuaded into a temporary settlement in 1833, and the final solution was arrived at in 1839 when the Concert of Europe agreed to a final boundary settlement and to that fateful guarantee — of such importance in 1914 — of the neutrality of Belgium.

Britain's complex relationship with the France of Louis Philippe turned on no single incident and could not be so handily solved. In the eyes of absolutist Europe, the two constitutional monarchies were equally suspect, but the French king, ambitious for his family and deeply conservative, and his governments moved steadily to the right and into conflict with Britain. Palmerston and Talleyrand had worked out a fairly fruitful understanding on Belgium; in 1834, Palmerston engineered an alliance of the two nations with Portugal and constitutionalist Spain, as at least a temporary liberal front against the Miguelist and Carlist sympathies of the Eastern Powers. But by the end of the thirties France and Britain were completely split apart by conflicting policies in the Near East. In 1831, Mehemet Ali, the pasha of Egypt, smarting from what he felt was insufficient recognition of his services against the rebellious Greeks, declared war on the Sultan and sent his son Ibrahim to occupy Palestine and later Syria, a challenge to which the Sultan replied by concluding a treaty with Russia in 1833. There matters stood until 1839, when the Turkish-Egyptian war again broke out. The French favored the victorious pasha; the British, worried about a possible alliance between Mehemet Ali and Russia or by the danger of French or Russian domination of the route to India, backed the Sultan. In 1840, Palmerston and the three Eastern powers concluded an agreement supporting the Sultan; France, left out in the cold, was not only isolated but, worse, lost her protégé when Mehemet Ali backed down because of trouble at home. By 1841, Palmerston's daring had settled matters , but at the cost of a serious rift between the two Western powers.

Under Lord Aberdeen, the foreign policy of Peel's government of 1841–1846 was aimed at calming the resentment caused by Palmerston's brilliant but rambunctious pragmatism. Good relations were maintained with France, whose conservative minister Guizot was a historian of England, and a similar willingness to reach accommodation promoted settlement of two bitter boundary disputes with the United States: the common banking interests of the negotiators, Daniel Webster and Lord Ashburton (a member of the Baring family), facilitated an agreement in 1842 on the question of the Maine-New Brunswick frontier; and in 1846 the Oregon dispute was ended by an agreed extension to the Pacific of the boundary at the 49th parallel, with the concession to Britain of Vancouver Island.

Good relations with France could not, however, withstand Palmerston's return, following Peel's defeat in 1846. Aberdeen's conciliatory attitude had managed only to damp down, not to settle, the question of whom Queen Isabella of Spain would marry; the four candidates discussed in the early forties were two worthless Spanish cousins, still another Coburg prince—that house was now connected with the British royal family by the Queen's marriage with Prince Albert—and the son of Louis Philippe. The informal agreement of the two countries to support one of the cousins was threatened by a scheme of the French ambassador at Madrid to marry Isabella's sister to Louis Philippe's son, on the assumption that Isabella's Spanish husband would prove impotent; thus, the throne would ultimately go to the French prince. Louis Philippe demurred, but when Palmerston came back to favor the claim of the other cousin and indirectly to revive the Coburg claim, Louis Philippe had had enough and announced that the ambassador's plan would be carried through. The celebration of the two marriages in October, 1846, wrecked whatever cordiality had been built up since 1841. England had to accept the *fait accompli*, but the French victory had no sequel. In 1848 the revolution sent Louis Philippe and Guizot into exile in England—where they were cordially welcomed by Palmerston.

The revolutions of 1848 had complex effects in Britain. While the British could again congratulate themselves on their stability, a good many serious-minded men set to thinking about guaranteeing that stability by putting both political and social affairs in better order. To Chartists and a number of radicals the revolutions were a heady inspiration; and most men were happy enough to see the Poles, Hungarians, and Italians in revolt, Metternich in exile, and a constitutional convention meeting in Berlin. Englishmen, however, failed to understand the force of nationalism that lay behind the Central and Eastern European revolutions; insofar as some of them did respond to the nationalist enthusiasm it was likely to be to the more idealistic and less practical kind preached to English working-class radicals by Continental exiles like Mazzini.

In this excited atmosphere Palmerston's liberal foreign policy endeared him to the general public. Dangerously confident, Palmerston increased his reputation by a series of actions that got him into serious trouble. He blithely disregarded his cabinet colleagues; he infuriated the Queen and Prince Albert, both pro-Austrian and strongly convinced of the monarchy's rightful involvement in foreign affairs. His most dramatic gesture was an ultimatum to Greece in 1850 demanding full restitution after an Athens mob had destroyed property belong to one "Don Pacifico," a Portuguese Jewish usurer who claimed to be a British subject because he had once lived in Gibraltar. The claim was dubious, but Palmerston backed up his ultimatum with a naval squadron, and finally, after an unsuccessful French mediation, the Greeks gave in. Palmerston's bullying outraged Europe and brought down on him an impressive coalition of parliamentary enemies, to no avail. In June, he triumphantly defended himself in the House of Commons, reviewing all his successes since 1830, and rising to a famous peroration. "As the Roman in days of old," he declared, "held himself free from indignity when he could say *civis Romanus sum* [I am a Roman citizen], so also a British subject, in whatever land he may be, shall feel confident that the watchful eye and the strong arm of England will protect him against injustice and wrong." Canning had called the new world into existence to redress the balance of the old; Palmerston put the whole world, old and new, on notice.

There was no gainsaying the extent of his victory in Parliament and the country. But the next year he made the Queen even more angry by his lack of sympathy when General Haynau, the brutal Austrian commander in Hungary, was mobbed during a visit to London. Only reluctantly did he agree not to receive Louis Kossuth, the Hungarian rebel chief, passing through London on his way to America, and his statements made his admiration for the exiled leader clear. But when in December, 1851, he expressed his approval of Louis Napoleon's making himself emperor of the French, his presumption had finally carried him too far. The cabinet and the Queen had good reason to be cautious about the *coup d'état*, and finding themselves undercut by an overconfident minister, they summarily dismissed him. A little later, still riding high, Palmerston, with protectionist help, brought down the government from which he had just been ejected, giving his old colleague Russell, as he said, "tit for tat." The fifties were his decade.

Political Instability

No one was sorry to see the Russell government go. It had accomplished some secondary reforms in the late forties, but in 1850–1851 Russell could rise to nothing better than an anti-Catholic campaign.

In 1850, to cope with the growing number of Catholics in England — partly converts, but mostly immigrant Irish — the papacy decided to restore the normal administrative structure of bishops and dioceses which the English Roman Catholic Church had not had since the Reformation. All the old suspicion of Rome welled up in fervent Protestant imaginations, and this Catholic plan — sensible and moderate, despite the unfortunate extravagance of language with which it was advanced by the papal curia and received by English Catholics — was turned into "papal aggression." Russell tried to capitalize on the excitement by his Ecclesiastical Titles Bill, imposing a fine on any bishop of a church, other than the Anglican Church, who took a territorial title. Reduced in debate to a fire-eating preamble and an enforcement clause, the bill was passed by huge majorities; its paltry provisions were never applied, and in 1871 Gladstone repealed it.

The badly divided Conservatives scarcely seemed an alternative. When Palmerston brought Russell down in February, 1852, the Conservatives, still without the Peelites, tried to govern as a minority. Stanley, now Earl of Derby, was Prime Minister; Disraeli was Chancellor of the Exchequer; the rest of the ministry were nonentities so obscure that the aged Duke of Wellington had to ask that their names be repeated and explained to him as they were read out in the Lords, an incident that tagged the ministers as the "Who? Who? cabinet." In the general election that summer, despite Disraeli's insistence that protection must be abandoned as a principle, the Conservatives were still left in a minority. When the government met Parliament in November, Disraeli's budget proposed to compensate the interests most aggrieved by free trade — land, shipping, and sugar — by tax relief and other concessions financed from an increased income tax and house tax. The opposition would have none of it, and the government fell.

The new ministry was a coalition of Peelites and Whigs under Lord Aberdeen; the Peelite strength in the Commons was not large, but the muster of talent at the top allowed them to command half the seats in the cabinet. Gladstone, at the Exchequer, began the series of budgets for which he was once so celebrated, carrying further the reduction of customs duties and promising the end of the income tax in 1859. Russell took the Foreign Office but gave it up within a few months to the Earl of Clarendon, while Palmerston was at the Home Office. The country and possibly Europe would have been better off had his talents been available in his old post. Having so often come to and escaped from the brink of war, perhaps he could have done it again. As it was, out of a morass of confusion and cross-purposes came the Crimean War.

The Crimean War

The immediate cause of the war was insignificant. A dispute had grown up in the Turkish province of Palestine over the custody of the "Holy Places," several churches and shrines at the presumed sites of Christ's birth, crucifixion, and burial. In recent years Greek Orthodox monks had looked after them; Roman Catholics wanted to regain the share in them they had once had; and both sides in the contest found powerful support. Napoleon III, seeking popular endorsement for his unpopular regime, set himself up as the patron and protector of Roman Christianity, and Tsar Nicholas I saw in the reaffirmation of his centuries-old role as protector of the Orthodox faithful a new opportunity for profitable dabbling in the alluring though protracted demise of the Ottoman Empire.

The fundamental causes of the war lay much further back, in the ambitions of Russia toward Turkey and in British suspicion of Russian designs on Constantinople or on the route to India. Moreover, Russia had become increasingly loathsome to liberal-minded Englishmen, and by the thirties and forties Russophobia was beginning to take on a hysterical tone, encouraged by the propaganda of a fanatical former diplomat and M.P., David Urquhart. In consequence, British policy invariably came down on the side of the Turks, and one of the greatest of British ambassadors devoted himself to the thankless task of keeping the Turks in line. Stratford Canning, a cousin of George Canning, had served at Constantinople from 1808 to 1814, from 1824 to 1829, and from 1841 to 1852. He had tried to bring some order into Turkish administration and to impose a sense of responsibility on her rulers, but when he returned home in 1852, becoming Lord Stratford de Redcliffe, he did not expect Turkey to survive for long.

Nicholas, trying as always to separate France and Britain, proposed that he and the British partition the Ottoman Empire, a notion which Aberdeen and Russell received with sympathy and no intention of action. Meanwhile, the Tsar sent an envoy to Constantinople with a series of demands, including the right to protect all Orthodox Christians in Turkey; the Sultan, counting on British sympathy, rejected them. Stratford, back again at his old post, tried vainly to arrange an accommodation. The Russians sent troops into the Turkish Rumanian provinces, and the British and French sent a naval force to the Dardanelles to prevent any aggression against Constantinople. With Turkish-Russian negotiations in a stalemate, the Sultan declared war early in October, 1853, and at the end of November, Russia wiped out a Turkish naval force at Sinope on the Black Sea. Now public opinion forced the British government on. British and French fleets were sent to the Black Sea in January, 1854, ambassadors were withdrawn in February, and war was declared in March. The only way in which the incompetence of the pre-Crimea diplomacy (excepting Stratford) can appear less than abysmal is in comparison to the incredible inefficiency of the conduct of the war itself.

The aim of the military operation was restricted; under Austrian threats the Russians had already withdrawn from the Rumanian provinces, so the allies wished merely to seize the Black Sea naval base of Sebastopol to immobilize the Russian fleet and to protect Constantinople. As the port was heavily fortified to seaward, the attack had to come from the landward side. Landings were made in September, but it became quickly apparent that the siege would be a long one. In late October the Russians unsuccessfully attacked the British base at Balaclava, a battle in which the cavalry displayed fantastic courage in a tactical blunder famous in military history and poetry as "the Charge of the Light Brigade." A second attack at Inkerman early in November was repulsed with huge Russian losses. The troops then settled down to a terrible winter.

The first French commander was both timid and dying, the second was decent and able but indecisive. The British commander in chief was Lord Raglan, who had lost an arm at Waterloo; he had seen no action for forty years and could not break himself of a habit, engendered in fighting Napoleon, of calling the enemy "the French," even when they were Russians. Refusals to take bold action that might have broken Russian resistance early are easy to criticize in retrospect, and some of the allied timidity was related to understandable fears that there were not enough troops or supplies. But the failure to secure a protected position for encampment of the army or to undertake early the necessary steps to provide roads and access to supplies can be laid squarely at the commanders' feet, though still greater blame rests with the authorities at home for the niggardliness and chaos of the recruitment and supply of the armies. The lack of food, medicine, fuel, shelter, and equipment was scandalous; and losses from disease far outnumbered losses from battle. The heroic work of Florence Nightingale and other ladies who went out as nurses to Scutari, fine as it was, could not undo all the damage.

The British public had welcomed the war. Except for a few vocal internationalists and pacifists, like Cobden and Bright, most of the Queen's subjects were eager to see the Tsar beaten, and a significant number of otherwise sensible persons also welcomed the war as a chance to prove that England had not been ruined by the luxury and effeminacy of peace. But the emotional indulgence in celebration of war quickly turned to disillusion and vindictiveness when the actuality of war was brought home. This was the first war covered by newspaper correspondents, who now could send their dispatches by telegraph. Victories at Inkerman and Balaclava and the heroics of the Light Brigade could cheer Englishmen at their breakfast tables the day after they happened; equally, the grim facts of that Crimean winter were drummed daily into their heads. Demanding both action and retribution, the country got a little of each.

In January, 1855, when Parliament reassembled, a Radical member, J. A. Roebuck, called for an inquiry; when the motion was carried over government objections, the pacific but indecisive Aberdeen resigned. But neither Derby nor Russell proved capable of forming ministries, so the Queen had to send for Palmerston to head a reshuffled cabinet. By spring, the worst was over. Gradually though not efficiently, the allied forces wore down the Russians; Sebastopol fell to them early in September. The chief points at the Treaty of Paris, signed in March, 1856, were the autonomy of the Danubian principalities, soon to become Rumania; a guarantee of Turkish independence; and neutralization of the Black Sea. Russia abandoned her claim to be protector of Christians in the Ottoman Empire and by her poor military showing forfeited her dominant position in Europe for half a century. The British had won another reprieve for Turkey and so protected what seemed vital interests; they had unwittingly promoted nationalist causes in Rumania and Italy (Piedmont had come into the war as an ally of convenience); and by reducing Russia's power they may have helped to set the stage for a unified Germany. They had also made a gesture on behalf of international law and the balance of power. But the case for the treaty is not self-evident and must be argued.

Even at home the war's impact was unclear. In offering his motion, Roebuck was questioning the whole conception and structure of aristocratic rule, in the state as well as in the army; the demand for civil service reform was reinforced by a wide, war-induced awareness of the ineptitude built into the traditional system. But sweeping change was beyond the grasp of the fifties. Palmerston could be a forceful administrator, using the machinery he had; he was no reformer. The army that had won in the Peninsula and at Waterloo had stood intact for forty years, protected by its reputation and by Wellington's inability to imagine that it might be improved. In 1852, the Duke died, and three years later his army won another war. That they won it badly was less noticed than it should have been. A few changes were made at the top. The secretaryship for war and colonies was split in two; the two departments, already separate, thus acquired different heads. The division of civilian responsibility was partially repaired by absorbing the primarily financial office of the secretary-at-war into the office of secretary of state for war. Partly because of Florence Nightingale's hectoring, partly because of the devoted administration of Sidney Herbert at the War Office in the early sixties, some steps were taken to improve the lot of the ordinary soldier, who down until this time was recruited for long terms, wretchedly paid, housed, and looked after, and on occasion cruelly punished. But the officer corps remained a preserve of aristocratic gallantry and incompetence; though merit carried some weight in the artillery and the engineers, in the infantry and cavalry commissions were still purchased. Not until 1870 was there a strong enough administrative hand to do what needed doing.

China

In 1857, Palmerston's triumph was threatened by a war with China. The Far East stands outside the usual generalizations about the dominant anti-imperialist sentiments of early nineteenth-century British policy. Thus, between 1815 and 1831, economic and strategic imperatives led to the conquest of the barbaric kingdom of Kandy in central Ceylon, the wealthy island captured from the Dutch in 1796. Deprived of Java, also taken from the Dutch, by the treaty of 1815, the British, under the urging of the great imperial adventurer Sir Stamford Raffles, moved into Malaya, where in 1819 Singapore was founded as a free port and naval base; the new colony was recognized by the Dutch in a treaty of 1824 in which the two nations sorted out their competing claims in the East Indies.

A somewhat desultory war with China between 1839 and 1842 originated in the clash of two irreconcilable policies: the Chinese were determined to reassert their isolation from the rest of the world, and the British were as determined to break it down. The immediate issue between the two countries concerned the opium trade from India to China. Opium was an export that helped to balance Britain's trading account with China at a time when Britain took large quantities of tea and silk from China and sold relatively little to her. But the opium habit was a national vice in early nineteenth-century China, so much so that after 1817 China was having to export silver to pay for it. For this reason, and to put down what was becoming a serious moral problem, the Chinese government set out in 1839 to put a complete stop to the trade. The British merchants, who had increasingly infringed the monopoly of the trade once held by the East India Company, hardly took the order seriously, for, technically, the whole trade was carried on in violation of earlier orders, made possible by inefficient and corrupt local administration. Although the British officials most concerned were not unsympathetic to the Chinese efforts, the methods the Chinese used were so drastic that the British felt compelled to reply with force. In 1842, the Treaty of Nanking ceded Hong Kong to the British and opened Shanghai, Canton, and other "treaty ports," while a year later the British got the valuable concession of extraterritoriality—the right to try their own subjects for offenses in China.

The Treaty of Nanking was indifferently observed by China, close as she was to anarchy, and British officials and traders in the Far East were faced with repeated challenges and threats. Finally in 1856, the *Arrow*, a small ship of doubtfully British registry, was seized by the Chinese authorities at Canton for piracy. The chief British official in the area was Sir John Bowring, once Bentham's associate and a Radical M.P., who was now Governor of Hong Kong and Plenipotentiary and Chief Superintendent of Trade in the Far East. Bowring, an enthusiastic free trader, used the pretext of the *Arrow* to assert British rights forcibly, and when his opponent, Commissioner Yeh, refused to back down, Canton was bombarded and war broke out. The war was brought to an end in 1858—after Bowring had been succeeded as Plenipotentiary by the more diplomatic Lord Elgin—in the Treaty of Tientsin, which gained many of the privileges that Bowring had demanded. This successful piece of principled rascality, while it commended itself naturally to Palmerston, brought all of his enemies together in the House of Commons. He was defeated on a motion condemning the war, and rather than resign he appealed to the country. In the general election in March, 1857, his fame and his policy won resoundingly. Bright was defeated at Manchester, as Cobden was in the Yorkshire textile town of Huddersfield, an ironic rejection in the home of free-trading principles of the most effective spokesmen for the internationalist implications of those principles. Dislike of their pacifism was the main cause of their defeat, but in retrospect the election of 1857 can also be seen as the first indication that the sentiments of businessmen were swinging away from radicalism. That fateful trend was not yet general, however; though Cobden did not return to the House for two years, the more widely diffused, populistic radicalism of Birmingham returned Bright a few days after he was beaten in Manchester.

The Indian Mutiny

It was in India, however, that the most dramatic questions of policy were posed and resolved. The vast subcontinent was ruled throughout the first half of the century by officers of the East India Company, under the supervision of a government department called the Board of Control.* The Company lost its commercial monopoly in India in

*For the circumstances out of which this peculiar double administration grew, see above, pp. 99–100, 102.

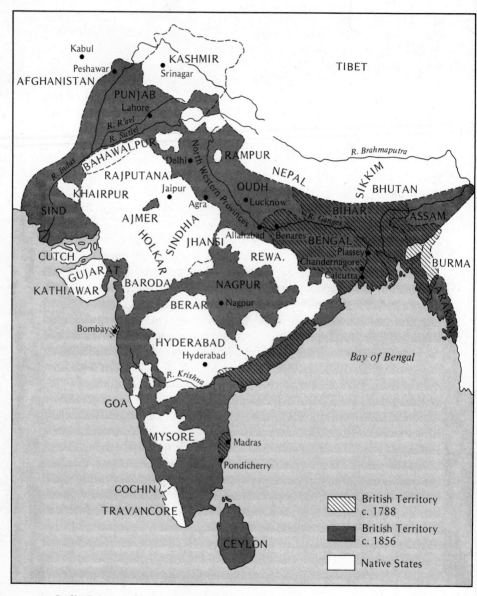

Map legend:

- British Territory c. 1788
- British Territory c. 1856
- Native States

India Prior to the Mutiny (c. 1856)

1813 and in China in 1833; down until the latter year its main commercial concern was the tea trade, but increasingly from 1784 and entirely after 1833 the Company's function was not trade but government. The administration of India was divided into the three presidencies of Madras, Bombay, and Bengal, each with its separate army. Over all was the viceroy, appointed by the government; his headquarters were at Calcutta in Bengal. The office of viceroy was held by a succession of aristocrats of varying abilities and policies, a circumstance that gives a somewhat fitful and contradictory character to the history of Indian policy. In the most practical way the viceroy made policy: he was under instruction from home, true, but the distance was great and communication slow; his judgment not only determined the degree and effectiveness of carrying out orders but could commit the Company and the Board of Control to adventures from which they could not extricate themselves. And, as in all administration, the solution of one problem was likely to lead to the discovery of further problems; once initiated, a policy tended to go forward by a kind of inertia of motion, forcing a wider grasp and more drastic action than was originally foreseen. The history of empire is no simple story of a few clear intentions consistently applied by men who later seem evident saints or manifest villains. It is rather the complex interaction of half-realized assumptions, good intentions, and practical necessities. Its administrators were perhaps rather more often prisoners in a complex situation than masters of it.

We can disentangle three main lines of Indian policy in the years between Waterloo and the Mutiny; each of them contributed to the alienation out of which the Mutiny came. The first was a policy of economic and social reform. The interest or even absorption in Indian life and culture, so evident in Englishmen in India in the eighteenth century, was giving way in the nineteenth to confident Victorian self-righteousness. Convinced that their civilization was the most advanced in the world, Englishmen tried increasingly to impose their values and procedures on the old, often decadent, utterly alien cultures of India. The Evangelical impulse reached out to India early in the century through the influence of Charles Grant and Bishop Reginald Heber. In the twenties and thirties, particularly during the viceroyalty of Lord William Bentinck (1828–1835), a full-scale assault was made on aspects of Indian life and religion repellent to the British: the *thugs,* a secret religious society that seized and murdered victims as sacrifices to the goddess Kali, were largely suppressed, and *suttee,* the practice of burning widows (often mere children) on the funeral pyres of their dead husbands, was gradually abolished. In the thirties, T. B. Macaulay, a Whig politician already famous as a writer and about to start his history of England, went out to India to devise plans for reforming the legal and educational systems. Central to his purpose was the imposition of English as the language of government and education, an ultimately wise if hardly generous decision by men who believed with Macaulay that a single shelf in any European library was worth all the native literature of India and Arabia. Because of conviction or ambition, some Indians were willing to help on this process of Anglicization, but interference with traditional religion and customs created much subterranean discontent. This sense of insecurity and disturbance was increased by the large-scale economic reforms begun under Lord Dalhousie in the fifties; railways, canals, and telegraphs were further assaults on the ingrained ways of a backward society.

A second line of policy concerned expansion. The first Burmese war of 1823–1826 was a response to an invasion of the northeastern frontier; in 1852 a second Burmese war, growing out of mistreatment of British merchants, led to the annexation of Rangoon and other ports. More important, however, was the northwest frontier; there, beyond the perpetually squabbling rulers of ill-organized and hostile territories, lay the threat of Russia, pressing southeastward as well as towards Constantinople. Lord Auckland, viceroy from 1836 to 1842, inaugurated a forward policy beyond the territory of the Sikhs in the Punjab; an invasion of Afghanistan resulted in the disastrous defeat of a British force in 1842. The new viceroy, Lord Ellenborough, sent a punitive expedition back to Afghanistan; then, having procured the release of prisoners, the British withdrew to leave that wild country undisturbed for nearly forty years. At the same time, however, the commander of the army of Bombay, Sir Charles Napier, the radically inclined general who had commanded the troops in the north of England during the Chartist troubles in the thirties, undertook a frankly aggressive war against the Amirs of Sind, whose territory lay along the lower Indus, south and west of the Punjab. He annexed Sind in 1843, calling his action "a very advantageous, humane piece of rascality. . . ."* Two years later the Sikhs, alarmed at British annexations on their flanks, invaded British territory, to be defeated with difficulty in the following year. But the Treaty of Lahore, which reduced their frontiers and forced a British resident on their ruler, was only a temporary truce; in 1848–1849, a second Sikh war ended with the annexation of the Punjab. Easily pacified, the Sikhs became the most stoutly loyal of native troops, a fact of great importance during the Mutiny.

*There is an old, alas untrue story that Napier notified the authorities of his victory in a one-word message: *"Peccavi"* (I have sinned). He was probably the most colorful British officer to serve in India.

The third line of policy concerned the native states, whose rulers were tied to the British in client relationships of varying degrees of closeness. Misgovernment, by British standards, was frequent in these states, and the obvious cure was annexation. Lord Dalhousie, viceroy from 1848 to 1856, proclaimed the so-called "doctrine of lapse," applicable to those states subject to princes whom the British had conquered or whom the British had themselves set up. If a ruler in one of these states had no natural heir, Dalhousie refused to allow him the usual Indian practice of adoption; consequently, on the death of the incumbent prince, the state would come under direct British control. Four states were annexed in this way between 1848 and 1854. Then, in 1856, Dalhousie went further in deposing the corrupt Nawab of Oudh, to whom (because he had heirs) the doctrine of lapse did not apply; his action seemed to undercut the security of all native princes.

The implementation of all these policies produced unrest on almost every level of Indian life. The spark was struck in the Bengal army. In a tense situation, already complicated by racial hostilities and poor discipline, a rumor spread among the troops that cartridges for a new rifle were greased with animal fat. Since the cartridges had to be bitten before insertion into the rifle, Hindu soldiers would be defiled if the fat came from cattle, Muslim soldiers, if it came from pigs. The cartridges were withdrawn, but the disturbances that had begun among the troops started a train that burst into violence at Meerut, near Simla, in May, 1857.

The Mutiny was confined largely to the Ganges Valley in the north; the main action was the siege of Delhi, where the aged King of Delhi still lived on British sufferance as successor to the Great Mogul, whose empire the rebels thought they could restore by driving the British out. Militarily, the rebels turned in a poor performance, and the outnumbered British troops, reinforced by the loyal Sikhs, were able to restore peace to India early in 1858. To the savagery of the rebels the British replied in kind, most notably in reprisal for the massacre of two hundred British women and children at Cawnpore. This bitterness was not shared by the new governor-general, Lord Canning, the son of the prime minister. The outraged military derisively called him "Clemency Canning"; he adopted the nickname proudly, and within a decade his reasonableness had paid dividends.

Yet India after the Mutiny was never the same, nor was Britain. In an act carried by the Derby government in 1858 the East India Company was abolished; India was now to be ruled directly under a new secretary of state. The estrangement of British and Indians, growing for fifty years, became irreparable. Many Indians, reacting against British progress as well as against the certainty that the British now would stay, retreated to an orthodox Hinduism. The British were more careful about flouting native prejudices, but they had also lost respect for, and generosity towards, a people whom they no longer believed amenable to civilization or to ultimate self-government, which earlier British rulers had quite confidently looked forward to. A great experiment had failed; and since leaving was impossible, the only alternative was firmness.

NEW DIRECTIONS, 1859–1867

In January, 1858, an Italian refugee named Orsini tried and failed to assassinate Napoleon III; the plot had been hatched in London, throughout the century the mecca of European political exiles. Palmerston, sensibly responding to French indignation, tried to institute controls over manifest abuses of the privilege of political asylum. But the opposition, trumpeting English freedom, for once out-Palmerstoned Palmerston and drove him from office. A short-lived Conservative government under Derby lasted until March, 1859, when it was defeated on an opposition amendment to a reform bill.* Clearly, a House that had turned out two governments in such quick succession needed surgery; Derby called a general election, only to find himself in a worse minority. Palmerston again became Prime Minister; Russell went to the Foreign Office; and Gladstone took the Exchequer, emerging from the Peelite wilderness to join (after some hesitation) what was coming to be called the Liberal party. The increasingly confident and vocal liberalism of mid-century, moral and religious at its base and widely spread in the middle ranks of society, permeated the new party as it could never have done with the aristocratic Whigs, and a new generation of political leaders were drawn to the Liberal party as spokesmen for the cause. Thus, the last years of the 1850's, despite their barrenness in domestic policy, mark a new political orientation. Its consequences were, however, some time in the working out, and other years might compete with 1859 as the turning point. But no one could dispute the crucial importance of that date in the intellectual life of England.

The year 1859 was, in a way, miraculous. Perhaps never have publishers' lists pointed quite so revealingly to the central issues of an age; the answers returned were nicely poised between an old world and a new. Mill's *On Liberty* and Samuel Smiles's *Self-Help* epitomized pivotal social assumptions of the mid-century consensus,

---

*On reform bills in the fifties, see below, pp. 324–326.

yet by the latter third of the century invoking those assumptions was likely to be rhetorical rather than real. Darwin's *Origin of Species* summed up a half-century's work in science, and (to borrow one title from 1860) *Essays and Reviews* did the same for Biblical scholarship; amid the agonizing debates they fed, these books pointed the way to scientific and religious dispensations that few men in mid-century were ready to recognize or welcome. Tennyson's *Idylls of the King* and Dickens's *A Tale of Two Cities* were firmly rooted in early Victorian literary tradition; but George Eliot's *Adam Bede* injected a new, rigorous objectivity into a heritage of moral intensity, and George Meredith's *The Ordeal of Richard Feverel* pressed even further towards a radical pagan sensibility. Finally, Edward Fitzgerald's *Rubáiyát of Omar Khayyám*, though almost unnoticed on publication, now seems to herald a highly un-Victorian flight, soon to become frequent, to skepticism, hedonism, and resignation.

These books were harbingers, and fuller consideration of the religious and cultural revolutions they helped to initiate must wait until we come to the time when their results were more widely diffused.* But the year 1859 can stand, both symbolically and actually, as a point of departure in other areas of English life as well. The world in which Britain had grown accustomed to effortless domination was suddenly transformed by political events abroad that the English hardly understood. At home, there was a clear polarization, or toughening, of opinion on social change that threatened the harmonizing of class interests that had gone on, in one way or another, even during the harsh years of the hungry forties. There was a resurgence of activity by organized workingmen, both within their own institutional framework and in challenging the dominance of the widened oligarchy that still ruled England. Understanding these three developments is essential to a proper assessment of the political events of the sixties and seventies.

Italy, America, and Germany

In 1859, war broke out in Italy, a fight led by Piedmont against Austria to gain Italian independence and unification. In spite of their distrust of Piedmont's patron, Napoleon III, the English could give full rein to their sympathies and prejudices: Italy was the country of Rome, on whose exploits generations of schoolboys had been raised; England was full of second-rate Italian painting (along with some masterpieces) avidly admired by connoisseurs; Piedmont had kept her liberal constitution when the rest of Italy collapsed in 1848. And

*See below, pp. 405–415.

who kept the Italians divided and suppressed? Austria, Palmerston's old adversary; Ferdinand of Naples, the meanest of European despots; and, above all, the Pope. But the implications of the game of power played by Cavour in Piedmont and Napoleon in France were quite lost on the British. Their naive enthusiasm, especially aroused by the colorful exploits of Garibaldi, was almost as irrelevant to the final outcome of the war as the pro-Italian Whiggery of Palmerston and Russell, the pro-Austrian inclinations of the Court and some Conservatives, or the overriding fear of France.

The American Civil War put the British in an even more peculiar position. For fifty years antislavery had been one of the main concerns of British foreign policy, yet most Englishmen in a position to affect opinion could not see the war solely in that light. A dislike of Yankees, a prejudice in favor of the more aristocratic South, commercial connections, a belief in self-determination, a desire to see a rival immobilized or destroyed, and a nascent racism entered into the complex amalgam of British opinion. Government policy was neutrality, but the outcry in England, when a Northern naval vessel stopped the British sloop *Trent* in 1861 to remove two Confederate agents, was as pathological as the anti-English exultation in America. Men talked of war, and the Prince Consort, just before his death, helped to soften the working of a stern government note that might have worsened a tense situation. Official ineptitude later allowed the escape of Confederate sea raiders, built in British yards; they did great damage to Northern shipping and plagued Anglo-American relations in the postwar years. The Emancipation Proclamation helped to clarify British opinion, and by his death Lincoln had come to be something of a hero in Britain. But, except for slavery, the issues of the war were incomprehensible to the British: they understood liberalism, in a constricted sort of way, but they never really grasped nationalism. Perhaps their own nationalism had been around so long that they could not recognize its analogues elsewhere.

On Italy they saw partially; on America they were myopic; on Germany they were blind. In the early sixties the British saw their most serious threat in the France of Louis Napoleon. The Orsini incident in 1858 and the Italian war of 1859 produced a war scare in England that set ordinary Englishmen to comic drilling in the volunteer militia. The fright lingered for five years, strongly enough to make English statesmen suspect the most devious intentions in Napoleon's proposals to refer the Schleswig-Holstein dispute, over which Prussia was about to fight Denmark, to European mediation and settlement. When Bismarck, whom Palmerston thought a fool, engineered a war with Denmark in 1864 and then with Austria in 1866, the British merely stood by in utter incomprehension.

Polarization of Opinion

The changing context abroad had parallels at home. The political balance among the upper classes was shifting, more rapidly as a further installment of reform was talked about; moreover the House of Lords began to stir. In 1857, the Lords, in what has come to be known as the Wensleydale Case, had rejected a proposal to create a distinguished judge a baron for life only. The move might have been intended — and certainly appeared to many — as a first step at reconstructing the House of Lords, through an infusion of proved ability. Then, in 1860–1861, a more serious storm blew up. Gladstone proposed as part of his program for tax reduction the abolition of the tax on paper. Rebuffed by the Lords, Gladstone countered the next year by combining all his financial proposals, including repeal of the paper duties, into a single finance bill, thus giving the Lords the choice of accepting the entire financial program of the government or rejecting it all. Noble protest was loud and vehement, but the peers had not quite got their courage or their hostility up to the sticking point.* The grounds of this sharp dispute on a seemingly innocuous measure were as much social as constitutional. The paper duties were the last of the so-called "taxes on knowledge," and the repeal of the last penny of the newspaper tax in 1854 and of the advertising tax in 1855 had led to a vast expansion of the popular press. With the *Daily Telegraph* selling 150,000 copies at a penny, a serious threat was posed to the traditional lines of influence of a deferential society. The peers saw the drift and drew back.

These two incidents in the Lords were signs of a gradual polarization of opinion, making still more real the class division that had played so vital a part in English thought and society over the past thirty or so years. As the proportion of real power held by land decreased, business families, especially those in the second and third generation, increasingly gravitated into an identification with upper-class, conservative interests. The religious, humanitarian, and moral impulses that had driven so many early Victorians in the upper and middle classes into action contrary to simply conceived class interests were beginning to lose their power, as the bankrupt voluntary principle gave way to state intervention and to the institutionalization of charity.

In all this there is a strangely reminiscent ring. In the 1760's events following on the accession of George III precipitated a new awareness of the direction in which political institutions had drifted

---

*When they did, fifty years later, they found their stand a costly one. See below, pp. 464–466.

during the preceding half-century; revitalized politics led to the agitation for reform. A century later, it became suddenly apparent that the reforming policies of the preceding thirty years were creating a kind of society that could not be contained in traditional forms. Those who favored radical change found new encouragement and methods and garnered new support; many others, even some old reformers, began to realize that they did not like what was happening. Because social issues are more complex than political issues, and because the numbers of interests involved had multiplied, the question was not posed so clearly as the political question had been posed a century before. The shift in the 1860's showed less in revitalized politics than in a gradually deepening bitterness, defensiveness, and a profound concern about the threat of democracy. From time to time an incident might precipitate reactions whose significance went far beyond the immediate question at hand, like the Lords' balking at the paper duties, or the widespread anti-Northern sentiment during the Civil War. Perhaps the most striking of all these reactions was the case of Governor Eyre.

The Eyre Controversy

Edward Eyre had served with distinction in Australia and New Zealand, where he had gained a reputation (and some notoriety) for his ability in handling the aborigines and the Maori, in whom he was deeply interested. In 1864 he became Governor of Jamaica. The West Indies, which Eyre knew from long experience in the fifties on the island of St. Vincent, were a persistent colonial problem throughout the nineteenth century. Their economy, largely tied to the single crop of sugar, had been hit hard by the emancipation of slaves in 1833 and again by free trade after 1846. The planters' methods were inefficient, labor was unproductive and in short supply, and the general state of the islands was one of steady decay. In Jamaica, the largest of the islands, this decline had been reflected in continual political difficulty. In 1839 the constitution was suspended. A new constitution in 1854 brought no real improvement in the island's ineffective and corrupt political life. Early in the 1860's an agitation for reform was undertaken by one George William Gordon, the son of a Scottish planter and a slave-woman. His fervent criticisms of the government and the governor were caught up in a wave of religious revivalism, and at Morant Bay in October, 1865, a skirmish led by one of Gordon's followers developed into a riot, whose victims included a couple of dozen white residents. Eyre's troops from Kingston, forty miles away, sealed off the infected parish and prevented the spread of the rebellion, but in the suppression nearly a hundred Negroes were shot without trial and 354 were executed by court-martial. Gordon, who had taken no part in the riot, was tried and hanged.

In England, an investigation of the incident resulted in a mildly critical report stressing technical objections rather than the excessively vigorous suppression. The outcry in the country, far from being satisfied, grew. Protests from newspapers and humanitarian and missionary organizations were given focus by the Jamaica Committee, which included such important figures as John Stuart Mill, Frederic Harrison, Thomas Hughes, Herbert Spencer, and T. H. Huxley. For five years the Committee and its supporters tried unsuccessfully to bring Eyre, who had been retired as governor, to trial for murder. The anti-Eyre campaign, as the names of the Committee show, was a magnet for radical, progressive, and humanitarian sentiment. But there was a pro-Eyre campaign as well, organized around a committee whose members included Thomas Carlyle, Alfred Tennyson, John Ruskin, and Charles Kingsley. The pro-Eyre forces were no mere cluster of reactionaries, although Kingsley had long shown his distaste for blacks, and Carlyle was by this time far gone in an unattractive, racist hatred of the world he had been unable to hector into his own image. In public opinion at large, Governor Eyre attracted as defenders many men who disliked what was happening around them; they were neither evil nor inhumane, but they believed sincerely that men of whatever breed should be kept in their places and ruled firmly — through natural deference where possible, by force if necessary.

Labor's Insurgency

While this polarization was taking place in the upper levels of society, a forward movement was beginning among the working classes. In 1859–1860, the builders had gone on strike for a nine-hour day, but that issue was submerged by the contractors' demand that the men sign "the document," renouncing all union membership before returning to work. The struggle went on for months, drawing strong support from other unions; when it ended, the employers were defeated on their demand for the document, though they won on the nine-hour day, which the men did not gain until the end of the sixties. The bitterness, length, and partial success of the strike alarmed many in the upper classes; at the same time it helped to stimulate further, more effective union organization. Even more important, the interunion cooperation shown in the strike led to the founding in 1860 of the London Trades Council. It was not the first organization for coordinating trade union activity in a locality; from time to time throughout the early nineteenth century, there had been similar organizations in large provincial towns. But the London Trades Council was based on strong national unions whose leaders were strategically placed in London, and the men who composed it, later called the "Junta" by Sidney and Beatrice Webb, immediately leaped to a controlling position in union matters and in politics.*

Increasingly well set organizationally, the trade unions were winning middle-class allies, thanks in part to the apparent results of better education and improved conditions among the upper levels of workingmen. One manifestation of seriousness and responsibility that especially impressed middle-class radicals was the behavior of the masses of unemployed in Lancashire during the "cotton famine" resulting from the American Civil War. In 1860, 80 per cent of raw cotton for the mills came from the American South; the Confederacy had hoped that the Union blockade of Southern ports, by creating unemployment and unrest among the English working classes, would force British recognition of the South. But, despite the suffering, no significant disturbances took place, and pressure for recognition from that quarter did not materialize. Insofar as it was not mere apathy, this restraint can be explained by the success of a public works program and an international relief drive, and still more by the discipline and determination of those politically conscious workers who (unlike their social superiors) saw the war clearly as a struggle against slavery.† This sense of English working-class involvement in larger issues in the world was further shown in the impressive enthusiasm during Garibaldi's visit to England in 1864 and in the close ties established in these years between the English union leaders and the international workers' movement represented in the International Working Men's Association, the "First International," founded in London in 1864, a connection that remained close until the revolutionary days of the Paris Commune in 1871.

Opposition to trade unionism was strong among employers and many members of the upper and middle classes. The profound distrust of union motives and methods engendered by the Builders' Strike was turned into hysteria by the "Sheffield Outrages" in 1865–

---

*George Howell was the first secretary, succeeded in 1862 by George Odger; other members were William Allan of the Engineers, Robert Applegarth of the Carpenters, Daniel Guile of the Iron-founders, and Edwin Coulson of the Bricklayers. George Potter, who had led the Builders' Strike, was an independent force, a sort of gadfly to the Junta. They were all men of uncommon ability and personal attractiveness.

†The "famine," by forcing reorganization of the industry and some attention to alternative sources of supply, left the Lancashire cotton trade in better condition after the war than it was before.

1866. The cutlery industry in Sheffield, with its tiny workshops and unsavory conditions, had had a long tradition of violence, which condoned the "rattening" of nonunion employees, a revenge that might run from stealing tools or damaging machines to personal violence. In the mid-sixties there was a particularly serious outbreak, dramatized by an incident in which a can of gunpowder was thrown down the chimney of an offending black-leg. Antiunion sentiment in the country insisted on steps to curb all unions, and the upshot was the appointment of a royal commission in 1867 to investigate trade unionism.

In the same year the Court of Queen's Bench handed down a decision in the case of *Hornby* v. *Close*. Trade unions had been allowed to register under the Friendly Societies Act of 1855, thereby permitting appeals to the courts to deal with the old and persistent problem of local officials who decamped with union funds. The decision held that, while trade unions were not engaged in specifically illegal activity since the act of 1825, they were, in their nature, in restraint of trade, and so, under the common law, were ineligible for the protection of the courts. Legislation in 1868 and 1869 gave the unions some temporary protection against embezzlers, but it was up to the royal commission to provide the basis for permanent legislation. The presentation of the workers' case before the commission was firmly in the hands of the Junta. They had managed to get the investigation broadened to take in the whole trade union movement and not just the Sheffield outrages, hoping thus to direct attention from clearly criminal to clearly admirable actions. Then they got two middle-class sympathizers appointed to the commission—Thomas Hughes, the Christian Socialist, and Frederic Harrison, a leading Positivist; while Robert Applegarth of the Carpenters was permitted to be present at the hearings. In collaboration with Hughes and Harrison, Applegarth conducted the case much as Place had stage-managed the trade union hearings in 1824. The majority report in 1869, reflecting the skill with which the union argument had been presented, recommended the legalization of unions and protection for their funds, provided that union rules were not restrictive; the minority report of Harrison and Hughes came out against all legal discrimination against workingmen or unions, urging that no action by a workingman be considered against the law unless it was illegal for others as well, and that no act of a combination be illegal unless it was illegal for a single person.*

Meanwhile, the unions had made progress on another front by securing legislation in 1867, after several years of pressure, to revise

---

*For trade union legislation in the seventies, see below, pp. 346, 351–352.

the master and servant laws. Under the old laws, breach of contract by a master was a civil offense punishable by a fine; breach of contract by a workman was criminal and punishable by imprisonment. A workman charged with such an offense could be summarily arrested, tried secretly, and imprisoned by a single justice of the peace, who might possibly be an employer; he could, moreover, give no evidence on his own behalf in disputes with his employer. The act of 1867 did not remove all the inequalities, but it made summary arrest and secret trial impossible and allowed workmen to testify for themselves. In that year, too, though the trade unions were not primarily responsible for them, the Factory and Workshop Acts brought all industrial establishments, however small, under government supervision. For years Parliament had been adding dangerous or unhealthy trades to the textile factories that had been regulated earlier; now state intervention was generalized, though really effective administration was not attained until 1878. It is striking testimony to the wide spread of concern for humanity and decency that these acts in the sixties were passed with little debate — in contrast to the principled obstruction of thirty years before — and without damage from the contemporary distrust of trade unions.

The unions were not, however, exclusively concerned with trade matters. In their growing interest in, and demand for, further political reform they were linked yet more closely to middle-class radicals.

The Second Reform Act

There had been frequent expressions of interest during the fifties in a further installment of Parliamentary Reform. In 1837, Lord John Russell had emphasized the "finality" of the Reform Act, but by 1848 he had retreated from his position; in 1852 and 1854 he introduced bills calling for the reduction of the borough franchise from £10 to £6 and the creation of a simple £10 occupier franchise in the counties. But the reformers in Parliament remained a tiny minority of old-line radicals, free traders, and Dissenters who at least from 1837 had come to see in an extension of the franchise the only sure method of arriving at their various goals in Church and state. Most members of Parliament were hostile or indifferent and were not at all impressed by Russell's attempt in 1854 to counteract the dangerous dose of democracy in the lower rental qualification by adding "fancy franchises" — £10 income in dividends, forty shillings a year in direct taxes, savings bank deposits maintained for three years, or a university degree — under which highly respectable and solid men could presumably qualify.

The fifties were no time for reforming Parliament. The country was generally prosperous; politically conscious workingmen were only beginning to emerge from their distrust of middle-class allies who they felt had betrayed them in 1832 and were in any event more likely to be concerned just then with their own trade unions. Most important of all, there were distractions—the Crimean War, the Mutiny, and Palmerston himself, whose liberal posturings abroad drew the lightning of the reform he was increasingly determined to resist at home. There were, however, two new reform bills at the end of the decade. In 1859 Disraeli introduced a bill that kept the old qualifications, but added a series of fancy franchises, including holders of £60 savings accounts and lodgers (especially numerous in London and other large cities) if they paid £20 a year in rent, as almost none of them did. The county franchise was to be reduced to the same ten-pound occupancy that was the rule in the boroughs; at the same time, the boundaries of boroughs were to be again extended to reinsulate the expanded rural electorate from the spreading infection of urban radicalism. Defeated in debate on the bill, the government resigned, and the ensuing general election swept the Liberals under Palmerston and Russell into office. But when Russell introduced his own bill in 1860, based on the old six-pound proposal for boroughs, he was caught in a complicated tangle of irrelevant preoccupations. The Italian war, the fear of France, and the Volunteer movement made reform seem ill-timed to many;* the Builders' Strike made it seem dangerous to others; and the paltry provisions of the bill aroused no enthusiasm among the unenfranchised. Russell withdrew the bill in June.

Serious commitment to reform was difficult to find in the early sixties too. The Junta were deeply interested in it, as were many workingmen, but their organizational work necessarily remained subterranean for a time and was overlaid by more evident trade union and international issues. But one man continued to hammer home the need for reform in a series of tours and speeches employing a technique that had helped to awaken the country to the earlier

*In *The Times* for May 9, 1859, Tennyson, the poet laureate, published a poem in praise of the Volunteers. The third stanza of what may be his worst effort takes up precisely this point:

> Let your reforms for a moment go!
> Look to your butts and take good aims!
> Better a rotten borough or so
> Than a rotten fleet or a city in flames!
> Storm, Storm, Riflemen form!
> Ready, be ready against the storm!
> Riflemen, Riflemen, Riflemen form!

quasi-revolutionary imperative of repealing the Corn Laws. When John Bright was defeated in Manchester in 1857, he became a member for Birmingham, a city with a democratic radical tradition that served as a powerful stimulus to his radicalism. By his Quaker inheritance he was the enemy of the Established Church; as one of the two leading spokesmen of the "Manchester School" of free traders he was the enemy of the landed classes who still monopolized the Commons. Self-conscious and self-righteous, he tried to stir up the country, and he did—ultimately with some benefit to the cause of reform, immediately by frightening many respectable conservatives. That fright was not lessened by the plain fact that Bright's household suffrage proposals, when it came to formulating a bill, were much less threatening than the democracy and leveling he had preached from platforms.

Given the impossibility of revolution in mid-Victorian England, agitation in the country, whether by a single demagogue or by mass insistence, could have little effect unless it could be brought to bear at the right time in support of the right man rightly placed. The reformers had fixed on W. E. Gladstone, who, as Chancellor of the Exchequer in the new government, was now firmly committed to Liberalism, midway in his long pilgrimage from the High Church Conservatism he had espoused on his entry into Parliament in 1832. Increasingly impressed by evidence of working-class seriousness and responsibility, Gladstone was led in 1864 to insist, in a debate on a motion for reform, that "every man who is not presumably incapacitated by some consideration of personal unfitness or of political danger, is morally entitled to come within the pale of the constitution." He went on to say, with characteristic haziness, that reform should be reasonable and should come at proper times and among "selected portions of the people," but qualifications were lost on the country. His constituents at Oxford recognized him as the apostle of reform by throwing him out at the general election in 1865; the radical voters of South Lancashire returned him overwhelmingly. As Bright had found a new footing and a new freedom in Birmingham, so Gladstone was transformed by being transplanted to the north.

In October, 1865, after the general election, Lord Palmerston died; everyone recognized that the old man's disappearance from the scene would mean changes. Russell (who in 1861 had been raised to the peerage in his own right as the first Earl Russell) became head of the government, and in March, 1866, as leader of the House, Gladstone introduced a reform bill. Its provisions—£7 householders and £10 lodgers in boroughs, and £14 occupiers in counties—were less generous than any of Russell's earlier bills and greatly disappointed reformers. But the parliamentary course of the bill helps to explain its conservatism. Bright saw — and indiscreetly proclaimed — that it was only a "lever" for further reform; at the same time, a significant segment of the Liberal party showed that even this concession (especially with Bright talking as he did) was too much for them. This Liberal opposition was brilliantly led by Robert Lowe, whose fear of democracy had been reinforced by a long residence in the rough frontier society in Australia; in June, on a crucial amendment that would have ruined the bill, he carried some thirty followers — Bright quickly tagged them as the "Cave of Adullam"* — into the lobby against the government, joined by the Conservatives. Russell's government gave way to Lord Derby's third administration.

Now the time had come for agitation in the country. In 1864 a predominantly middle-class Reform Union had been organized, highly reminiscent of the Anti-Corn-Law League, to work for reform on a household suffrage basis; the next year, the Reform League was founded on a manhood suffrage platform. Primarily working-class and trade-unionist in composition — the Junta were much in evidence — the League garnered support from two important quarters: Ernest Jones, the last of Feargus O'Connor's lieutenants, and long a foe of any middle-class cooperation, came into the League as a vice-president, thus cementing a bond with the remnants of Chartism; there were also some valuable middle-class allies. Bright, though he was willing to settle for the terms of the 1860 bill, was indispensable to the League and they to him. John Stuart Mill, now Radical member for Westminster, and Thomas Hughes were sympathetic and in close touch, and the President of the League was a barrister named Edmond Beales. The agitation of these two bodies, and particularly of the League, was given greater urgency by the economic collapse that followed the failure in May, 1866, of the famous (though by this time overrated) London billbroking firm at Overend, Gurney. As in the thirties, economic distress and unemployment fed the fires of reform.

The Union and the League accepted Gladstone's bill, though not happily; when it was defeated, they managed to sink their differences for a time and to agree on a measure of household suffrage as the one possibility of gaining wide support. Then in July, 1866, the League summoned a mass meeting in Hyde Park in London. The government ordered the gates of the park closed, but the press of the crowds made the railings give way, and the people surged into the park. Troops were called out to assist the police, but no action was taken, and thousands of people simply milled about in the park for

*I Samuel, 21–22: "David therefore departed thence, and escaped to the cave [of] Adullam . . . And every one that was in distress . . . and every one that was discontented, gathered themselves unto him. . . ."

three days. Finally, through the mediation of Mill, the government agreed to call off the troops and the League promised to control the crowds. The crisis of the "Hyde Park Riots" had passed without real trouble. When the League made another attempt to test the right of public meeting in the park in May, 1867, the government—despite some stern talk and the demands of the far right—did not interfere. It had no intention of provoking the reformers into becoming revolutionaries.

When his bill was defeated in 1866, Gladstone warned his opponents that they could not fight the future, that time and the great social forces were on the side of reform, by which he meant the Liberal side. That a radical reform bill would be carried by the Conservatives, and that the great social forces—insofar as they were represented by the agitation in the streets—would have little or no direct effect on the outcome, would have been predicted by no one.

The Conservative government had to introduce some sort of reform bill, to forestall another Liberal attempt and to respond to a growing sentiment that the vexed question should be settled. But the Tory leaders felt no sense of urgency and, indeed, were uncertain what the basis of a bill should be. It was Derby who proposed that the bill should grant household suffrage—"of all possible hares to start I do not know a better," he wrote to Disraeli—provided it was counterbalanced by giving a plurality of votes to respectable, safe voters. Resolutions to that effect were introduced early in February, 1867, Derby having intended that a royal commission would be appointed to study the matter, with legislation to follow the next year. But Disraeli, to everyone's surprise, promised a bill at once. Feverish calculations then followed, to determine the probable effects of differing detailed provisions, though the statistical reliability of any conclusion was doubtful. Uneasiness in the cabinet crystallized when Lord Cranborne made his own estimates. He had already gone into print to deplore the official stance of the party and to call for a less opportunistic, purer conservatism,* and when he and two other colleagues announced that household suffrage would mean their resignations, the cabinet hurriedly changed front and ten minutes before a party meeting at which Derby was to explain the bill agreed on a measure placing a fixed lower limit of six pounds on the urban suffrage. When Disraeli introduced this "Ten Minutes Bill" in mid-

---

*Cranborne wrote regularly in the Quarterly Review, for money as well as to put across his principled views. A younger son of the Marquess of Salisbury, who disapproved of his marriage, Lord Robert Cecil became Lord Cranborne on the death of his elder brother in 1865 and three years later succeeded to the title. On his later career, see below, pp. 428–433.

February, his manner made clear his lack of enthusiasm, which the House of Commons appeared to share: household suffrage, suitably hedged about, seemed a better principle for a definitive settlement.

Disraeli withdrew the Ten Minutes Bill early in March, and by the middle of the month a bill granting household suffrage was agreed to in the cabinet, from which Cranborne and his two allies resigned, isolated and unable to form their own cave of Adullam. The bill set the proposed county franchise at £15; the vote in boroughs was to go to householders who had been resident for two years and who paid their rates (i.e., local taxes) personally. Those who paid £20 a year in direct taxes could also vote, and if they were householders as well could vote a second time in that capacity. There were other fancy franchises, to make assurance doubly sure. What then, from an antiradical viewpoint, went wrong?

Gladstone, fearing what was called the "residuum"—the poorest and presumably most unreliable potential voters—preferred a minimum qualification set at a low level, say £5, but his attempts to revise the bill in that direction were beaten back by an alliance of Disraeli and most of his followers on one side and the radicals on the Liberal benches on the other. Determined that reform would come through a Conservative bill and not in response to Gladstone's moves, Disraeli also saw the opportunity to widen the gulf between the Liberal leader and the radicals; so devastating was Gladstone's defeat that he seriously considered giving up the leadership and retiring to the back benches. And, having held the initiative, sensing the possibility of a real settlement and sure of his own followers, Disraeli then proceeded, when the details of the bill were being debated in May, to accept one after another radical amendment, either because they remedied some difficulty in the original drafting or because they offered some political advantage. The period of residence was reduced to a year; lodgers were given the vote; and on May 17, in a sparsely attended House, Disraeli agreed to an amendment that did away with the limitation on compounders. Disraeli had insisted on personal payment of rates as a qualification, thus denying the vote to those who compounded for their rates, that is, paid them through their landlords, as part of the rent; the radical Hodgkinson, cleverly accepting Disraeli's argument, in effect forbade compounding by requiring personal payment of all rates.* Once that was conceded, there was no point to retaining the other fancy franchises, which

---

*The arrangement created chaos in local government and in landlord-tenant relationships; compounding was restored, but with the vote, in 1869 and 1878.

disappeared, and the county franchise was lowered to £12. The only radical proposal that was rejected was John Stuart Mill's effort to give the vote to women, to which Disraeli did not object in principle but which he knew was premature.

Assured of radical support and with most Conservatives delighted over the prospect of such a famous victory, Disraeli easily weathered the abuse heaped on him for his treachery, and the third reading of the bill passed without a division. Derby, dominating the House of Lords, prevented any serious damage to the bill by assuring his colleagues that it would guarantee Tory predominance. The only amendment of significance in the Lords affected the parallel redistribution bill: there Disraeli had proposed a third seat for each of four large towns — Liverpool, Manchester, Birmingham, and Leeds — and the upper house, hoping to assure representation for a Conservative minority in what was assumed to be solidly Liberal territory, limited voters to casting their ballots for only two of the three seats.* A bill that, in its original form, promised to enfranchise at most a quarter of a million new voters doubled the electorate in the end and gave a majority in urban Britain to the working classes. Disraeli and his followers provided some retrospective justification by arguing that all along he had seen his mission as educating his party so as to capture workingmen for Conservatism. But there is little evidence for this vision of Tory democracy in Disraeli's role as it has now been recreated: assuming that the towns were lost to Liberalism and that his chief task was to secure the loyal countryside, he started with a sharply limited goal, like that of reform bills that had gone before; then, seeing the chance for a succession of tactical victories, he took what Derby conceded to the House of Lords was "a leap in the dark," and committed Britain to democracy.

For nearly a decade a good many Englishmen had worried about democracy. To worry did not necessarily mean to lament; indeed, as Asa Briggs has observed, the true division was not between Liberals and Conservatives, but between optimists and pessimists. But for the ten years or so after 1867 the pessimists had an intellectual field day. Now that the urban working classes had the vote, it was easy to predict the worst; and much of what the critics of democracy forecast was borne out in time. But in these years no one really knew what lay on the other side of the divide; men knew only that the new world would not be easy. Carlyle, not surprisingly, put the uncertainty better than anyone else. His bitter, despairing pamphlet was called *Shooting Niagara*.

*For the consequences of this provision, see below, p. 424.

Selected Readings

This chapter covers the last phase for which Woodward and Briggs serve as general guides, and four remarkable interpretative books come into their own. G. M. Young published his *Victorian England: Portrait of an Age* in 1936. A highly personal essay, it has stimulated and delighted historians ever since, but it has also frustrated or even outraged professionals and students alike by the absence of footnotes and the highly allusive writing, with its casual references to the harvest of Young's voracious, eclectic, and affectionate reading in the period. The book was reissued in 1977 with an indispensable introduction and extensive annotation by G. Kitson Clark, who with the help of others tracked down the sources of Young's allusions (though inevitably not all of them). Kitson Clark himself published his Ford Lectures, *The Making of Victorian England* (1962), which take their departure from the mid-Victorian decades, looking back and forward and serving an especially useful purpose in the emphasis on religion. Closer to Young in learning, provocativeness, and idiosyncrasy is W. L. Burn's interpretation of mid-Victorian England, *The Age of Equipoise* (1964), emphasizing the elements of stability rather than change—landed society, the law and its enforcement, the institutions and unrealized assumptions that made the individualist social philosophy of the time tolerable. Finally, there is Geoffrey Best's delightful *Mid-Victorian Britain, 1851–1875* (1971), four essays on the environment, making a living, leisure, and the social order.

A stimulating and controversial interpretation of Britain's position in the world at mid-century was put forward by John Gallagher and Ronald Robinson in "The Imperialism of Free Trade," *Economic History Review,* 2nd ser., vol. 6, pp. 1–15 (August, 1953). This should be supplemented by Bernard Semmel, *The Rise of Free-Trade Imperialism: Classical Political Economy, the Empire of Free Trade, and Imperialism, 1750–1850* (1970) and by Donald Winch, *Classical Political Economy and the Colonies* (1965). Oliver McDonagh has reminded us of "The Anti-Imperialism of Free Trade," *Economic History Review,* 2nd ser., vol. 14, pp. 489–501 (April, 1962), but the principal dissentient from the Robinson-Gallagher view has been D. C. M. Platt, notably in *Finance, Trade and Politics in British Foreign Policy, 1815–1914* (1968), though the wounds inflicted have been by no means fatal. Platt's views are amplified in a work on the consular service, *The Cinderella Service: British Consuls Since 1825* (1971). On the debate, Wm. Roger Louis, ed., *Imperialism: The Robinson and Gallagher Controversy* (1976). Economic relations with the rest of the world are approached from different perspectives in L. H. Jenks's delightful survey of a formidable subject, *The Migration of British Capital to 1875* (1927) and, especially important for balance of payments, in A. H. Imlah, *Economic Elements in the Pax Britannica* (1958). For a description of the financial machinery by which these vital enterprises were handled, see Walter Bagehot, *Lombard Street* (1873).

Four crises in the period involved colonies or quasi-colonies. The Chinese entanglement is surveyed in W. C. Costin, *Great Britain and China, 1833–1860* (1937), and the nefarious trade that brought about conflict is dealt

with in David Owen, *British Opium Policy in China and India* (1934), a problem
not resolved until the present century. On the second Chinese war, Douglas
Hurd, *The Arrow War* (1967). Many Englishmen made efforts to appreciate
Indian culture, but the attempts at modernization and westernization in
India had fateful consequences. These ambiguous involvements have been
much studied: S. N. Mukherjee, *Sir William Jones: A Study in Eighteenth-Cen-
tury British Attitudes to India* (1968); David Kopf, *British Orientalism and the
Bengal Renaissance: The Dynamics of Indian Modernization, 1773–1835* (1969);
A. T. Embree, *Charles Grant and British Rule in India* (1962); John Rosselli, *Lord
William Bentinck: The Making of a Liberal Imperialist, 1774–1839* (1974); and rel-
evant parts of John Clive, *Macaulay: The Making of the Historian* (1974). John
Pemble, *The Raj, the Indian Mutiny, and the Kingdom of Oudh, 1801–1859*
(1971) traces the growing conflict, and Christopher Hibbert, *The Great Mu-
tiny: India, 1857* (1978) provides a gripping narrative. The troubles in Jamaica
in the sixties and the English aftermath are recounted in Bernard Semmel,
The Governor Eyre Controversy (1962). On the Jamaican background, W. A.
Green, *British Slave Emancipation*, cited in Chapter 5, and Philip D. Curtin,
Two Jamaicas (1955); on the wider context of ideas and prejudices, Christine
Bolt, *Victorian Attitudes to Race* (1971) and A. P. Thornton, *The Habit of Au-
thority: Paternalism in British History* (1966).

Palmerston is central to the diplomatic history of the period. There is a
biography, *Lord Palmerston* (1970) by Jasper Ridley, but more useful is
Donald Southgate, *"The Most English Minister . . .": The Policies and Politics of
Palmerston* (1966). C. K. Webster, *The Foreign Policy of Palmerston, 1830–1841*
(1951) is a masterly survey of the earlier phase of his diplomatic career. On
relations with countries where conflict seemed likely, W. D. Jones, *The American Problem in British Diplomacy, 1841–1861* (1974); E. D. Adams, *Great Britain
and the American Civil War* (1925); and Derek Beales, *England and Italy, 1859–
60* (1961). On the conflict that did come about, J. H. Gleason, *The Genesis of
Russophobia in Great Britain* (1950); Cecil Woodham-Smith's account of the
Charge of the Light Brigade and what lay behind it, *The Reason Why* (1953);
and Olive Anderson, *A Liberal State at War* (1967). Yet another perspective on
foreign affairs is given in Henry Weisser, *British Working-Class Movements
and Europe, 1815–48* (1975).

There are many facets to the social consensus that emerged in mid-century. The increasingly shared assumptions of middle and working classes
can be seen in P. H. J. H. Gosden, *The Friendly Societies in England, 1815–1875*
(1961) and, more generally, in his *Self-Help: Voluntary Associations in 19th-
Century Britain* (1974); Torben Christensen, *Origins and History of Christian
Socialism, 1848–54* (1962); G. D. H. Cole, *A Century of Co-operation* (1945), still
the best of the histories of the cooperative movement, which tends to engen-
der enthusiam rather than criticism; and, for representatives of contrasting
views on the solution of social problems, J. D. Y. Peel, *Herbert Spencer: The
Evolution of a Sociologist* (1971) and Jo Manton, *Mary Carpenter and the
Children of the Streets* (1978). David Owen's *English Philanthropy, 1660–1960*
(1964) demonstrates the shift from voluntary activity to institutionalized
charity in these years.

The important debate about the impact and accomplishment of what the

Marxists call "the labor aristocracy" is concisely summarized in E. J. Hobsbawm, "The Labour Aristocracy in Nineteenth-Century Britain" (1954) reprinted in his *Labouring Men* (1964), pp. 272–315, and in Henry Pelling's reply, "The Concept of the Labour Aristocracy," reprinted in his *Popular Politics and Society in Late Victorian Britain* (1968), pp. 37–61. More generally, see Trygve R. Tholfsen, *Working-Class Radicalism in Mid-Victorian England* (1977). An excellent biography of an exemplar of this fusion of attitudes is F. M. Leventhal, *Respectable Radical: George Howell and Victorian Working-Class Politics* (1971). Trade-union history for this period must on the whole be extracted from general histories of the labor movement, but two special studies may be singled out: W. O. Henderson, *The Lancashire Cotton Famine, 1861–1865* (1934) and Sidney Pollard, *A History of Labour in Sheffield* (1959), important for the background of the Sheffield Outrages. Henry Mayhew, *London Labour and the London Poor* (4 vols., 1851–1862) is a celebrated journalistic and sociological effort to capture city life. On Mayhew, E. P. Thompson, "The Political Education of Henry Mayhew," *Victorian Studies*, vol. 11, pp. 41–62 (September, 1967) and the introductions written with Eileen Yeo to *The Unknown Mayhew* (1971).

The machinery for educating the upper and middle classes has been much written about: T. W. Bamford, *The Rise of the Public Schools* (1967); J. R. de S. Honey, *Tom Brown's Universe: The Development of the Victorian Public School* (1977); David Newsome, *Godliness and Good Learning: Four Studies on a Victorian Ideal* (1961), and *A History of Wellington College* (1959), one of the new public schools founded in mid-century; and Brian Heeney, *Mission to the Middle Classes: The Woodard Schools, 1848–1891* (1969). There is now even more on universities: Sheldon Rothblatt, *The Revolution of the Dons: Cambridge and Society in Victorian England* (1968), and *Tradition and Change in English Liberal Education: An Essay in History and Culture* (1976), which sees a discontinuity between the educational ideals of the two centuries; W. R. Ward, *Victorian Oxford* (1965); E. G. W. Bill and J. F. A. Mason, *Christ Church and Reform, 1850–1867* (1970); on two of the reformers, Geoffrey Faber, *Jowett* (1957) and V. H. H. Green, *Oxford Common Room: A Study of Lincoln College and Mark Pattison* (1957). Michael Sanderson, *The Universities in the Nineteenth Century* (1975) is a collection of documents with commentary. On the Scottish universities, G. E. Davie, *The Democratic Intellect* (1961).

W. J. Reader, *Professional Men* (1966) is a valuable history of professional development in the nineteenth century. On doctors, Sir George Clark, *History of the Royal College of Physicians of London*, vols. 1–2 (1964–1966), down to 1858, and vol. 3 (1971) by A. M. Cooke thereafter; M. Jeanne Peterson, *The Medical Profession in Mid-Victorian London* (1978); and F. B. Smith, *The People's Health, 1830–1910* (1979). There is nothing on barristers. In *The Attorney in Eighteenth-Century England* (1959) Robert Robson traces the rise in status of that branch of the legal profession, soon to be called solicitors, but nineteenth-century developments remain to be studied. There are revealing chapters on engineering in A. E. Musson and Eric Robinson, *Science and Technology in the Industrial Revolution* (1969). On teaching, A. Tropp, *The School Teachers* (1957); on nursing, Cecil Woodham-Smith, *Florence Nightingale, 1820–1910* (1951) and Brian Abel-Smith, *A History of the Nursing Profes-*

sion (1960). Two approaches to the study of ministers in the Established Church are Diana McClatchey, *Oxfordshire Clergy, 1777–1869* (1960) and Brian Heeney, *A Different Kind of Gentleman: Parish Clergy as Professional Men in Early and Mid-Victorian England* (1976). Studies concerning the civil service are cited in Chapter 6, but they should be supplemented by Henry Parris, *Constitutional Bureaucracy: The Development of British Central Administration since the Eighteenth Century.* The seminal idea of a "clerisy" was discussed in Chapter 4. Ben Knights, *The Idea of the Clerisy in the Nineteenth Century* (1978), being chiefly concerned with post-Coleridgean writers, is even more appropriately cited here. The key study is Noel Annan, "The Intellectual Aristocracy," in J. H. Plumb, ed., *Studies in Social History* (1955), pp. 243–287, an expansion of an argument first advanced in Annan's biography, *Leslie Stephen* (1951). The most important and symptomatic Victorian intellectual was, of course, John Stuart Mill, who is the focus of a virtual industry; two outstanding studies are Alan Ryan, *John Stuart Mill* (1970) and John M. Robson, *The Improvement of Mankind: The Social and Political Thought of John Stuart Mill* (1968). Mill's autobiography is an essential intellectual document of the century. It should be read in conjunction with Jack Stillinger, ed., *The Early Draft of John Stuart Mill's Autobiography* (1961) and F. A. Hayek's *John Stuart Mill and Harriet Taylor: Their Friendship and Subsequent Marriage* (1951).

Prest's biography of Russell is cited in Chapter 5 and Stewart's study of Derby's involvement with protectionism in Chapter 6, while biographies of Gladstone and Disraeli are noted in the following chapter. Of several excellent books on Prince Albert, the most recent is Daphne Bennett, *King Without a Crown: Albert, Prince Consort of England, 1819–1861* (1977). The social and psychological sources of the "papal aggression" scare of the early fifties are explored in G. F. A. Best, "Popular Protestantism in Victorian Britain," in Robert Robson, ed., *Ideas and Institutions of Victorian Britain* (1967), pp. 115–142. The political history of the fifties is peculiarly the province of J. B. Conacher, whose two books—*The Peelites and the Party System, 1846–52* (1972) and *The Aberdeen Coalition, 1852–1855: A Study in Mid-Nineteenth-Century Politics* (1968)—are indispensable.

The emergence of the Liberal party from Whigs and Peelites in the late fifties is the subject of John Vincent's *The Formation of the Liberal Party, 1857–1868;* there is also much information to be found about voting patterns in his *Pollbooks: How Victorians Voted* (1967). R. W. Davis, *Political Change and Continuity, 1760–1885: A Buckinghamshire Study* (1972) is a good local illustration of midcentury liberalism in action. James Winter, *Robert Lowe* (1976) is a biography of a Liberal opponent of reform, while the principal Conservative opponent, Lord Robert Cecil, later Lord Salisbury, can best be seen in this period in the convenient reprinting of his hard-hitting articles, Paul Smith, ed., *Lord Salisbury on Politics: A Selection from His Articles in the Quarterly Review, 1860–1883* (1972). The clearest narrative of the parliamentary course of reform is F. B. Smith, *The Making of the Second Reform Bill* (1966). The most influential argument for a narrowly political, tactical interpretation of the events is Maurice Cowling, *1867: Disraeli, Gladstone, and Revolution* (1967), which stops short with the crucial concession of Hodgkinson's amendment.

Cowling is at pains to reject the argument that popular pressure was important, a view best set out in Royden Harrison, *Before the Socialists: Studies in Labour and Politics, 1861–1881* (1965). See also the interpretation by Gertrude Himmelfarb, "Politics and Ideology: The Reform Act of 1867," in her *Victorian Minds* (1968), pp. 333–392. Robert M. Stewart, *The Foundation of the Conservative Party, 1830–1867* (1978) continues to be essential for the whole period covered in this chapter.

For Victorians confronting the consequences of the commitment to democracy, on both sides of the divide, Benjamin Lippincott, *Victorian Critics of Democracy* (1938); Christopher Harvie, *The Lights of Liberalism: University Liberals and the Challenge of Democracy* (1977); and Christopher Kent, *Brains and Numbers: Elitism, Comtism, and Democracy in Mid-Victorian England* (1978).

The French historian Hippolyte Taine recorded his impressions of England during successive visits between 1859 and 1871. Translated by Edward Hyams as *Taine's Notes on England* (1957), they are both perceptive and entertaining.

Part III
THE CLAIMS OF
DEMOCRACY

1867–1918

Chapter 8
The Great Rivalry

1868–1886

THE WORKING-OUT OF REFORM

Gladstone and Disraeli

In February, 1868, following Derby's retirement because of illness, Disraeli became prime minister. He hoped to win the general election in the following November and thus vindicate his extraordinary performance on the Reform bill. While some workingmen did in fact vote Conservative (in Lancashire especially, where Derby's influence was paramount), his hopes were dashed, at least for the immediate future. Party labels had become sufficiently meaningful by this time to make the Liberal majority of 112 seats painfully clear, so Disraeli resigned at once, without waiting, as prime ministers had always done, to test his strength in a division in the House of Commons.

The Queen sent for Gladstone. The extremes in the new administration balanced unobtrusively: Robert Lowe's hatred of democracy did not prevent his taking the Exchequer, and the appointment of John Bright as President of the Board of Trade was not so much of a concession as it seemed, for his radicalism was that of an earlier era. Much of the working strength of the government came from men like Lowe, Edward Cardwell, and G. J. Goschen, who had made their way from middle-class backgrounds to political eminence by sheer ability; they now reached the front bench for the first time. But the Foreign Office, the Colonial Office, and the India Office all went to peers (Clarendon, Granville, and Argyll, respectively), and there were still other representatives of the old Whig families in the cabinet to remind us that the nature of English politics had not been suddenly transformed by the mere extension of the electorate. Gladstone never controlled this highly capable cabinet as his master Peel had done in the forties, yet in the eyes of most men he towered over his colleagues.

For nearly twenty years, from the mid-sixties, British political consciousness was dominated by the rivalry between Gladstone and Disraeli. The striking contrast of their styles and characters was rooted firmly in the circumstances of their youth. To understand those roots explains more, however, than the mere fact of their rivalry. Because they projected attitudes and concerns characteristic of the early part of the century into the politics of the late Victorian era, they found themselves in difficulties when a later generation supplanted the men they had known before they rose to the highest office, and when events demanded solutions to which their preparation was not always equal.

Gladstone, the son of a Liverpool merchant, had entered Parliament in 1832 as member for the Duke of Newcastle's borough at Newark. Politically, however, his main obligation was to Peel. Peel recognized Gladstone's administrative grasp, and it was Peel's commitment to free trade and efficient government that Gladstone carried through in his great budgets of the fifties and sixties. Intellectually, Gladstone was formed in late Georgian Oxford; that strain was evident throughout his life in his passionate, if eccentric, scholarly devotion to the classics (Homer, especially) and theology. Indeed, his early theological interest led to his first reputation as a spokesman for the High Church party, a position that won him the seat for Oxford University in 1845.

But Gladstone's historic role as the great exemplar of Victorian liberalism owes more to a trait of character than to training: his response to moral imperatives. The disgusting inefficiencies and barbarities he saw in the Kingdom of the Two Sicilies during the early fifties helped him to cast his lot with the Liberals rather than the Conservatives, when both were courting him in 1859. In the seventies, Turkish atrocities in Bulgaria brought him out of retirement into a new, more radical phase of his career.* Gladstone was, in

*See below, pp. 353–354.

a way, Cromwellian. Few Victorian intellectuals could have admitted the "hand of God" as it touched the great Puritan general; but they could recognize the high demands of morality. Men who thought or felt that way understood Gladstone, in spite of the often tortuous language in which he defended his course. Those who did not, or whose seriousness took them in other directions, found him unfathomable, contradictory, or even dangerous.

Disraeli, the son of a writer who had left the Jewish faith, was famous first as a novelist and a dandy. Like Gladstone an outsider, he came to rest, after a Radical flirtation, with the Tories, who were more receptive to sheer talent than the more aristocratic Whigs. He had no mentor, but made his way by his own ambition and genius. While Gladstone progressed from triumph to triumph, Disraeli, down to his premiership, looked oddly unsuccessful: his maiden speech was a failure; he was passed over (though considered) for a ministerial post by Peel; when he rose to the leadership by cutting Peel down,* his party was left an obscure and nearly talentless remnant; he was a minister only in three brief minority governments; he was a poor administrator; his gamble on reform in 1867 was paid off only with leisure to write another novel. Yet modern Conservatism looks back to him (if not with full historical warrant) as its principal founder.

Five years older than his rival, Disraeli bore the stamp of Byronic romanticism, a flamboyant quality easier to grasp than Gladstone's moral seriousness. Yet Disraeli was serious too — in his ambition and in his dedication to politics. Intuitive rather than scholarly, he brought an artistry to politics that our more objective or sophisticated age has learned to appreciate rather than distrust. And unlike Gladstone's undoubted political skill and percipience, it comes to us unclouded by a moral rhetoric for which we have lost our taste.

To see how these differing styles affected the works of the two men and their governments, we shall survey their domestic, foreign, and colonial policy. Then we can turn to examine the forces working to create a society vastly different from that from which they had sprung. They gave their names jointly to an age that was slipping away from them.

Ireland

The preoccupation of the first year of Gladstone's ministry was Ireland, and the Irish question was to dominate English politics for the next forty years. The Famine and the pathetic uprising of 1848 did

*See above, pp. 276–277.

not solve but changed the direction of the Irish problem. The traditional English remedies were as irrelevant to the new intensified nationalism as they had been to the older forms of the problem. But English statesmen and administrators still thought consistently in terms of making the Irish English by applying English capitalistic methods, by extinguishing the wasteful system of highly fragmented landholdings that made modern agricultural techniques inapplicable, and by firmness to give their cures a chance to work. On several occasions in the post-Famine period, legislation was passed to make eviction easier, with a view to consolidating farms. This threat to their land drove many peasants abroad, where they nourished a bitter grievance against the English, nowhere more vehemently than in the United States. Irishmen who remained behind were bitter too, and showed it from time to time in agrarian violence. But the knowledge that there was no longer a concerted political movement, like O'Connell's, and the fact that the poor Irish had not yet recovered from the blows of the late forties led a good many Englishmen to believe that, with patience, Ireland would soon be pacified and civilized; some even thought it would become Protestant.

In the fifties and early sixties Gladstone was busy at the Exchequer, and, as Ireland did not obtrude, he showed no interest in it. Suddenly, in 1865, English confidence was shattered by the Irish Republican Brotherhood, the Fenians, a secret society devoted to Irish independence which was founded in the United States in 1858 and which had an underground counterpart in Ireland. The Irish Fenian leaders were arrested in September, 1865, but James Stephens, the chief and most able of the leaders, escaped from prison and fled to America, where he raised the banner of liberation. In May, 1866, a raid on Canada was attempted. Incidents took place in both Ireland and England, and in December, 1867, part of the wall of a London jail in which some Fenians were imprisoned was blown up, causing twelve deaths and many other casualties. With that violence, the movement had shot its bolt; an avowedly revolutionary effort, it attracted neither the security-seeking peasantry nor the Roman Catholic Church. Many of the later nationalist leaders could claim a Fenian apprenticeship, but the movement's main contribution was in awakening some Englishmen, and particularly Gladstone, to the need for action.

When Gladstone received the Queen's commission to form a government in December, 1868, he was engaged in his favorite recreation of chopping down a tree on his North Wales estate; he turned to his companion and said, "My mission is to pacify Ireland." His first step was extraordinary for a man of his religious views: he proposed to disestablish and disendow the Church of Ireland, to break, that is, its connection with the state and to leave it merely one among competing churches, of which, of course, far and away the strongest was the Roman Catholic Church. In March, 1868, while still in opposition, he had carried resolutions to this effect in the House of Commons, a victory that forced Disraeli to announce a general election for November. As soon as the new government was settled in office in 1869, Gladstone introduced a bill for disestablishment which easily passed the Commons and had no difficulty in the Lords, since the peers were reluctant at this point to provoke the newly expanded and apparently Liberal electorate. The defenders of the Church of Ireland were moderate too, a tactic that resulted in the Church's keeping a somewhat larger share of its total endowment than had been originally proposed; the portion that was taken away went to public works, education, and other worthy purposes.

Gladstone then turned to the much more difficult question of land. Most of the Irish peasants held their tiny parcels of land at the will of the landlord, but with the competition for land among a superabundant population, the notion of free contract had clearly become a fiction, though one in defense of which much parliamentary oratory was expended. The peasants paid rents that absorbed nearly all the income produced by their land and so had to live on the yield of their tiny potato patches. One way out of the problem, in fact, was to sweep away the landlords by state loans on easy terms that would enable tenants to purchase their holdings. This solution was proposed by John Stuart Mill in the sixties and was to be a part of the Land League's program in the eighties; in Gladstone's government its chief advocate was John Bright. But Gladstone and most other ministers saw numerous objections to purchase as the immediate solution, however sympathetic they were to it as an ultimate answer. For one thing, the commitment of government funds would be enormous; for another, given the political state of Ireland, local authorities were unequal to the administration of such a scheme, and so the risk of default by the peasantry seemed too great. Though each of the Liberal land acts contained some modest encouragement to land purchase, the main line of attack was to introduce a measure of decency and justice into the landlord-tenant relationship by revising the conditions of tenancy and reducing rents to a reasonable level.

The Irish Land Act of 1870 confirmed and, in a roundabout way, generalized a custom that had existed throughout the northern province of Ulster and to some extent elsewhere: a tenant who had made improvements to the land he occupied could be compensated for them when he left (or was forced out of) his tenancy, whereas in some parts of Ireland such improvements automatically reverted to the landlord without compensation. Tenants evicted for any cause other than nonpayment of rent would be compensated for their eviction according to a scale set down in the act. Gladstone had difficulty with his cabinet, and in Parliament he had to fight the Conservatives and the Lords, for he was seriously qualifying what was assumed to be a landlord's rightful prerogative; in theory, at least, the act made mere occupancy a kind of property by giving the tenant an interest in it that the courts could protect.

In the event, the act of 1870 accomplished little. It did little to promote the security of tenure that the Irish peasants really wanted; it only provided for compensation after they were turned off their land. A radical provision in the act that the courts might order compensation even when tenants were evicted for nonpayment of rent, if the rent was judged too high, came to nothing because the Lords had limited such interference to "exorbitant" instead of "excessive" rent, as had been provided in the original bill. But Gladstone was not aware that his act had failed until long after he had left office. Then an agricultural depression and intensified misery and violence in Ireland drove the lesson home.*

Education

In England, the government's mandate for action was clearer to more people. Problems that had remained suspended during the fifties and sixties were suddenly precipitated by an unambiguous majority, the advent of a new generation of political leaders, and the challenge of a drastically widened electorate. Moreover, by the seventies many of the nostrums or makeshifts to which the nation had clung in the hope of keeping the state out of men's lives had been shown too weak to bear the weight. Under Gladstone and Disraeli, solutions were found to problems that had vexed the nation for forty years.

Perhaps the most pressing of these problems was national education. In 1861, a royal commission had reminded the country that the children of the working classes, most of whom by that time got some experience in school, received no systematic training, learned little, and often forgot what they did learn, even elementary skills. The commission recommended setting up local school boards with the power to levy rates and to examine schools as to their qualifications for receiving grants. Afraid of sectarian objections, Palmerston's government did nothing to set up the boards, but Robert Lowe, the minister in charge, tied the examining proposal to the system of national inspection already in existence. After 1862, in order to

*For the developments in Ireland after 1870, see below, pp. 365–372.

be eligible for state grants, schools had to turn out a certain number of pupils able to pass examinations on the rudiments. The "Revised Code" can be seen (as Lowe saw it) as a normal stage in the development of a workable bureaucratic administration: inspection was simplified and made more consistent than it had been before. Moreover, an economy-minded government and nation could be more certain than they had been that they were getting value for money; while those who looked on schools mainly as engines for producing literate and moral workmen and housemaids were reassured that working-class children would get no ideas "above their station." It is probably true that the improvement of many bad schools by enforced attention to elementary skills was what the nation needed most at that time; but Kay-Shuttleworth and other supporters of the freer and more optimistic efforts of 1839 and 1846 disliked the Revised Code, and the teachers, whose profession had only just been born, found it hard to be reduced to mere drillmasters.

In 1869, the National Education League was founded in Birmingham by the rising radical politician Joseph Chamberlain. That Chamberlain and other founders were Dissenters indicated a clear departure from the uncompromising Nonconformist attitude in 1843; a significant number of spokesmen for that touchy interest had decided that both voluntary activity and sectarian education were irrelevant to a new democratic age. But the supporters of religious education were very strong, and the act carried by W. E. Forster in 1870 was a compromise that destroyed his reputation with both the Dissenters from whom he came and the radicals. The existing voluntary schools were left untouched and still, when the inspectors so certified, eligible for government grants; but in those areas of the country where the churches and other voluntary organizations had not provided enough schools, locally elected school boards were empowered to establish schools and to levy a rate to pay for them. Religious instruction was given in most state schools, but under the Cowper-Temple clause, no sectarian formulations could have a place in it. In spite of its legacy of political discontent, Forster's act was a giant step towards creating a common level of education beneath which no child was allowed to sink. Elementary education was made compulsory in 1880; but, though school boards could exempt poor children from paying fees, it was not until 1891 that elementary education became entirely free.*

---

*Little was done for state-inspired improvement of secondary education except the creation of a commission to revise statutes of old grammar-school foundations.

Trade Unions and Local Government

The Trade Union Act of 1871 passed into law the recommendations of the royal commission on trade unions* by legalizing unions and giving them the protection of the courts. But the original bill also contained stringent penal clauses against picketing and any other action deemed obstructive or intimidating. The steady agitation of the Junta and others finally got those provisions put into a separate act, their hope being to isolate the obnoxious limitations so that they could later be repealed. But while it was on the books, the Criminal Law Amendment Act, as it was called, was a nearly complete brake on any effective trade union efforts to gain perfectly legal ends. Neither Parliament nor the Liberals were yet ready to concede the reality of power to the unions.

The principal administrative reform of Gladstone's government was similar tentative and constricting. G. J. Goschen, president of the Poor Law Board, had proposed to carry through the reforms begun in towns in 1835 by setting up a comprehensive scheme of representative government for parishes and counties. But he could get no more than the creation of the Local Government Board, combining the three offices in Westminster most concerned with local government—the Poor Law Board, the Local Government section of the Home Office, and the medical department of the Privy Council, then under the direction of a brilliant physician and administrator, Sir John Simon. At this point Goschen moved to the Admiralty, and James Stansfeld, a Dissenting brewer, became president of the new board, with a seat in the cabinet. The trouble with the new arrangement was that the poor-law activities of the department, being by far its largest concern, were allowed to dominate its entire outlook; hence a department that might have served to stimulate effective sanitary and welfare activity by local governments was imprisoned in a mentality geared to deterrence, the final bureaucratic form of the drastic attack on excessive relief in the 1830's, a defect made worse by the dedication of both Liberals and Radicals to retrenchment of government expenditures. Sir John Simon's medical department was broken up in 1876, its functions simply turned over to the poor-law authorities.

Army and Law Reform

The mandate of 1868 was a powerful stimulus to institutional reform. In 1872, the secret ballot was attained after half a century of radical agitation. The creation of the modern civil service was completed by

*See above, p. 323.

an order in council in 1870 opening all government posts (except the Foreign Office) to competitive examination.* Next, the government carried its attack on aristocratic casualness into its last stronghold in the Army, which the terrible experience of the Crimean War had only slightly shaken. Edward Cardwell, at the War Office, brought the three offices of commander in chief, surveyor general of the ordnance, and financial secretary firmly under the superintendence of the Secretary of State for War, a subordination symbolized and promoted by their being moved into the same building.† The commander in chief was given vastly increased powers over forces at home and abroad, though even the spectacular demonstration of Germany's military superiority in the Franco-Prussian War did not stimulate the creation of a British general staff, a reform that had to wait until the twentieth century.

Cardwell also improved the lot of the ordinary soldier. In 1868, flogging in peacetime was abolished, over strong objections from officers; in 1870, the paying of bounties for recruits—a practice that often lured desperate or drunken men into the service—was abolished; and the term of service was shortened. Instead of the twelve years that had been mandatory since 1847, men were now to enlist for six years on active service and six years in the reserve. Cardwell also brought about a complete reorganization of the regimental structure. The chaotic competition of regiments for scarce recruits was done away with by a strict territorialization of infantry regiments, with each regiment assigned one of sixty-nine districts to serve as its home base and recruiting territory. These new regiments absorbed the old units, taking over their battle colors and their traditions. They included the local militia and volunteer infantry, but at the center of each regiment were two professional linked battalions, one serving at home while the other was abroad, thus guaranteeing that morale and numbers would be effectively maintained by periods of home service, and that troops sent overseas would be properly trained.

But none of these reforms would have been successful without some change in the provision of officers. In 1871, with the backing of a few able young officers. Cardwell introduced a bill abolishing the purchase of commissions; it passed the Commons with difficulty and was defeated in the Lords on the ground, stoutly and even violently

---

*See above, pp. 298–299. On the provisions and results of the Ballot Act see below, pp. 421–423.

†The commander in chief was Victoria's cousin, the Duke of Cambridge. Opposed to every aspect of Cardwell's reforms, he resisted as long as he could being moved from his traditional headquarters at the Horse Guards in Whitehall to the War Office, then in Pall Mall. Even after he was moved, until he was forced out of office in 1895, the Duke continued to give his address on his letters as Horse Guards.

maintained, that the old system kept commissions in the hands of gentlemen and saved the country from the disgrace and potential danger of a professional officer corps. Two days later, purchase was abolished by royal warrant, an action denounced by the defenders of purchase and by some radicals as an unjustified abuse of royal prerogative; Cardwell could get the central feature of his reforms, in other words, only by circumventing Parliament. Although the change did little to lessen the aristocratic monopoly of commissions in the "better" regiments, it was a large step towards professionalization, essential to the creation of an effective fighting machine. Cardwell's reforms did much to strengthen Britain's hand for the vexed and complex responsibilities she was about to undertake in foreign and colonial policy.

In 1873, the Gladstone government accomplished a sweeping reform of the legal system, capping sixty or seventy years of criticism, inquiry, and piecemeal change. The three unequally employed common law courts of Queen's Bench, Common Pleas, and Exchequer and the parallel and competing system of Chancery were replaced by the single Supreme Court of Judicature. The lower level of that court was the High Court of Justice, which sat in three divisions — Queen's Bench; Chancery; and Probate, Divorce, and Admiralty.* Judges from the single panel attached to the Supreme Court were assigned to the various divisions; cases went usually to the division dictated by the nature of the question at issue. These courts also heard cases on appeal from the magistrate's courts or the county courts. Appeals from divisions of the High Court were to go to the second level of the Supreme Court of Judicature, the Court of Appeal, composed of three judges. The original act proposed to end appeal there — in other words, to abolish the judicial function to the House of Lords. But there were both sentimental and practical objections to allowing only one appeal, and in 1876 the authority of the House of Lords was restored in civil cases; as a court, it is only nominally the House of Lords, its judicial functions being vested in and limited to a group of life peers called "Lords of Appeal in Ordinary," and other peers who have held high judicial office. All these courts administered both common law and equity, and in cases where the rules of the two systems of law conflicted, it was provided that equity should prevail.† These reforms created the basic structure of the English courts for the next century.

---

*The latter linkage is explained by the obligation of these three branches of law to Roman law — the first two embodying jurisdictions that once belonged to the Church, the last the business of the old High Court of Admiralty.
†Criminal cases continued to be tried at the assizes, which were staffed by judges of the High Court on circuit. See Appendix 4.

The End of Gladstone's Government

In a debate in 1872, Disraeli referred to the ministers on the government front bench as "a range of exhausted volcanoes"; after a series of such far-reaching and hotly contested reforms, one could hardly expect them to be anything else. But the government's popularity in the country was declining well before Disraeli made his stinging attack. In 1871, Robert Lowe, the Chancellor of the Exchequer, having to find new sources of revenue to cover increased expenditures on the Army, proposed a tax on matches. The manufacturers of this new invention insisted that the tax would ruin them — though similar taxes had not hurt manufacturers abroad — and the poor match-women of London marched on the House of Commons to protest. Though dispersed by the police, the women captured public sentiment, and Lowe lost not only his tax but any popularity he had as well. In the same year H. A. Bruce, the Home Secretary, introduced a licensing bill to control the liquor trade, a step strongly supported by the religious public, for whom temperance was becoming increasingly important. The brewers and distillers managed to get the bill defeated but could not prevent a somewhat milder act in the following year. Recent scholarship has disposed of the theory that the election of 1874 was determined by the defection of the distilling and brewing interests, which had been predominantly Liberal, to the Conservatives; but Gladstone and the temperance advocates thought that the Liberal cause was swept away "on a torrent of gin and beer."

Defeated on a bill to set up a Roman Catholic university in Ireland, Gladstone resigned early in 1873, but Disraeli wisely refused to take office without a general election, so Gladstone returned to office and held on for a year in which the court reforms were the only significant piece of legislation. Early in 1874, the Prime Minister announced a dissolution of Parliament; the February election returned the Conservatives with a solid majority of eighty-three. Gladstone told his colleagues he would retire not only from the premiership but from the leadership of the party. Kept secret for nearly a year, his decision was put into effect early in 1875. After some uncertainty, Lord Hartington, heir to the dukedom of Devonshire, became the Liberal leader.

A Conservative Majority

Disraeli was getting old when he formed his second administration. In 1876, unable any longer to give the constant attention necessary in the Commons, he accepted a peerage, and as Earl of Beaconsfield directed the government from the upper house. The leadership of the Commons was in the hands of his capable but not brilliant Chancellor of the Exchequer Sir Stafford Northcote, one of the authors of the 1854 report on civil service reform. Fortunately, Disraeli, who had little head for administration, had a highly effective cabinet. The Marquess of Salisbury, his old enemy, became Secretary of State for India; no more than Robert Lowe did he let his distaste for reform keep him from office, once reform was an accomplished fact. The Earl of Carnarvon, one of Salisbury's allies in 1867, became Colonial Secretary, and Lord Derby (son of the former prime minister) took the Foreign Office. The most interesting appointment, however, was R. A. Cross, a barrister and banker from a business background, who represented the middle-class interests that were being increasingly drawn into the Conservative camp. A dedicated social reformer, Cross had never held a ministerial post, but went directly to the Home Office, a key position in which to secure his reputation—and the government's—in the field of social reform.

The aging Prime Minister had not lost his touch. He quickly gained himself a powerful ally in the Queen, whom he assiduously flattered, using language in his letters nearly as extravagant as that used about Queen Elizabeth I by her courtiers. This rather comic courtship had important results. Since the death of her husband in 1861, Victoria had lived in almost complete retirement, either at Balmoral in Scotland or at Osborne in the Isle of Wight. She refused to open Parliament in person or to take part in public ceremonies or even to receive distinguished visitors. The invisibility of the Queen, the manifest irresponsibility of the Prince of Wales, the expense of maintaining a large and growing royal family all helped to produce widespread criticism of the monarchy by the late sixties. Among some more advanced radical Liberals, like Joseph Chamberlain, who became Lord Mayor of Birmingham in 1873, or Sir Charles Dilke, a rising young Liberal M.P., the criticism fell into avowed republicanism. Disraeli brought the Queen out of her retirement, flatteringly though with little real significance declared her Empress of India in 1876, and confirmed the monarchy's place as chief among the "dignified" elements of the constitution. Disraeli also left the Queen a violent Tory partisan. She had begun her reign as an enthusiastic Whig, devoted to her dear Lord Melbourne and barely tolerating Peel. She had been helpful to Gladstone (most notably over the Irish Church) in his first administration, but from the seventies on the Liberals could do no good in her eyes, and at every change of government she tried to avoid sending for Gladstone. His attitude to the Queen was correct and polite, but she complained that he did not consult her and that when he did, he addressed her as though she were a public meeting.*

---

*Small wonder: she kept him standing throughout their interviews.

It is less easy to define the magic Disraeli worked on the country at large. In April and June, 1872, he had made two celebrated speeches to party gatherings, one in Manchester, one at the Crystal Palace in London. Primarily attacks on the Liberals, portrayed as weakening the inherited institutions of the country and as captives of their left wing, the speeches also appealed to patriotism and pride in empire and to the need for social rather than political reform: indeed, much of the history of modern Conservatism has been seen as descending from these speeches and their invocation, however brief and vague, of grand themes that were to resound so often in Tory rhetoric. So far as social reform goes, it is difficult to credit much of his administration's undoubted accomplishment to Disraeli himself. He had shown a deep awareness of the two nations and of the claims of the poor in his novels of the 1840's and in his involvement with Young England; the Second Reform Act quickened in him an interest in the working classes that had not been much in evidence in the interval. But Disraeli had no taste for administration and detail, which are inescapable in legislating and carrying through social reform, and not many in his party were willing to take up the social cause: "Disraelian Conservatism in office was found to mean much the same as other Conservatism: empiricism tempered by prejudice."* But Cross did win a reputation for the social measures he piloted through, and a few other, less elevated ministers made contributions as well.

That a minister's inclinations and skills were vital is proved by the worst failure of the government, in the confused wavering in 1875–1876 over proposals to intervene, either directly or by revising the marine insurance system, in the matter of unseaworthy ships and the protection of seamen against dangerous practices like the deck loading of timber. Caught between a powerful agitation waged by the "seamen's friend," Samuel Plimsoll, M.P., and the resistance of the shipowners, the minister C. B. Adderley escaped to the arguments of his permanent civil servants at the Board of Trade and to those ideas of economic freedom that he and his colleagues shared fully with the Liberals; the resulting legislation was a mere gesture to reform. The entire record is impressive, however: a food and drug act, a public health act, an act to encourage the building of working-class housing, a further installment of factory legislation — all to some extent flowing readily from piecemeal legislation in earlier years, testimony to the widening grasp of a new administrative state.

The boldest departures had to do with labor. In addition to the factory act of 1874, which further reduced the hours of women and children, the Master and Servant Act was replaced by an Employers and Workmen Act in 1875, which made breach of contract punish-

---

*Paul Smith, *Disraelian Conservatism and Social Reform* (1967), p. 200.

able not as a criminal offense but by civil damages, and ordinary actions of trade unions were exempted from the law of conspiracy. Cross was reluctant to do away with the Criminal Law Amendment Act, passed in 1871* and a standing threat to peaceful picketing; but under pressure from Robert Lowe on the opposition benches, Cross and his colleagues gave way and repealed the act. Aside from the interventionist factory act, then, these measures were perfectly consistent with the laws that were presumed to govern a free economy; on a far more nearly equal footing with employers and secure in their legal position, the trade unions could move on to a generation of growth.

The year 1876 can be seen as the end of a long phase of social reform that had begun in the 1820's. The main work had been done, and Britain stood between two attitudes. Early- and mid-Victorian philanthropy had defined areas where action was needed and had evolved the principles, attitudes, and machinery to deal with them. Within this framework, the organs of central and local government defined new problems and tried to solve them by appointing more and more officials and by asking Parliament for further powers to tackle details that had come to their attention. But older principles and attitudes were being replaced by new views and aspirations, and time was needed before they could be brought to bear on social policy. The eighties and nineties were not entirely quiescent, especially among the Liberals: Chamberlain's "unauthorized program" of 1885 and the Newcastle Program of 1891 pointed the way to the future, as did a flurry of legislative activity in 1886. But not until 1906 was there to be another era of social reform comparable to that in the early Victorian period.

BRITAIN OVERSEAS, 1870–1886

Gladstone's Attitude Towards Foreign Policy

Gladstone was increasingly responsive to the cause of liberty and the claims of nationality. But in extending the liberal side of the Palmerstonian tradition, he rejected its bluster and bravado. In part his caution grew out of devotion to economical government, a matter about which he had repeatedly quarreled with Palmerston; in part it grew from the plain fact that, though the British Navy doubled in strength in the late sixties, the Army, just being reformed by Cardwell, was small and doubtfully effective for any engagement beyond the wide

*See above, p. 346.

colonial burdens it had to bear. But, at base, Gladstone's pacific policy grew from his Christian commitment to peace and law.

The most severe external challenge presented to his first administration was the Franco-Prussian War of 1870–1871, a war sought by both belligerents for their own domestic ends; the possible succession of a Prussian Hohenzollern prince to the Spanish throne from which Queen Isabella had been driven was merely a pretext. British attempts at mediation had proved fruitless, and the country simply stood by in unbelieving (and profitable) neutrality to watch the emergence of Bismarck's German Empire from the destruction of France. In the new European situation, with a France that appeared weaker than she actually was and a subtle and aggressive Germany, the British were isolated and robbed of much of the influence they had been accustomed to exercise. Lacking military strength, Gladstone could do little more than appeal to peace and international law.

He had salvaged those noble principles for Europe in 1870 when Russia, taking advantage of the war in the West, announced that she would no longer be bound by the clauses of the Treaty of Paris of 1856, neutralizing the Black Sea. Britain demanded and got an international conference, which, though it recognized Russia's *fait accompli*, at least maintained the importance of agreed as against unilateral action. Similarly, in 1871–1872, Gladstone demonstrated his devotion to the idea of arbitration in the case of claims (much exaggerated) by the United States against Great Britain for damage allegedly done by Confederate raiders built in British shipyards. Here Gladstone flew in the face of strong popular sentiment by agreeing to arbitration in the first place and then by accepting the award, which was against Britain for fifteen million dollars.

Gladstone's seeming weakness, unforgivable to a nation raised on Palmerston, helped to provide Disraeli with his majority in 1874. Disraeli, lacking Gladstone's intellectual commitments but with full confidence in his own pragmatic flair, moved in the last years of his ministry onto the world stage in a way that brought him up sharply against Gladstone's moral rigor.

The Eastern Question

Turkey's misrule in her Balkan provinces produced a revolt among the Serbs in 1875 and the Bulgars in 1876; the three Eastern powers, Germany, Austria-Hungary, and Russia, reviving their old collaboration, attempted to impose a settlement on the Turks, which Britain refused to consider. Britain's attitude encouraged Turkish nationalist reformers, and the Sultan and his successor were quickly deposed. The ruler who came out on top, Abdul Hamid II, proceeded to defeat the Serbs. He also put down the Bulgarian revolt — his armed irregulars murdered some twelve thousand Christians with the most dreadful barbarity.

The news of the massacre touched off a storm of protest in Britain. Led by a strange alliance of High Churchmen and Dissenters, and superbly organized, the agitation kept the country in a turmoil throughout the summer of 1876 and produced a division in the political and intellectual world similar to and more far-reaching than the Eyre controversy of ten years before. Caught off-guard by the re-emergence of the Eastern Question to which he was not attuned, and embarrassed both by his former membership in a government that had fought the Crimean War and by his abdication of the Liberal leadership in 1875, Gladstone was slow to respond; but in time the intensity of the moral protest in the country touched a vital chord in his nature. Early in September he published a pamphlet, *The Bulgarian Horrors and the Question of the East*, with results of the greatest magnitude. Not only could the agitation coalesce around a major political figure, but Gladstone's return to the leadership of the Liberal party was made inevitable; less certainly, perhaps, but more portentously, the agitation influenced the stance he ultimately took on the not dissimilar Irish question. Disraeli was furious, for he rightly saw behind the Eastern powers' efforts the ambitions of the Austrians to get Bosnia and Herzegovina, adjoining Serbia, for themselves and a Russian design to take over the Balkans from Britain's long-standing ally. The injection of Gladstone's moral indignation seemed to justify Russian intervention to protect Christians.

In April, 1877, war broke out between Russia and Turkey. At first Russia was victorious, but the Turks recovered and under some able generals threw the Russians back. This surprising counteroffensive, by awakening all the old Russophobia in England, did much to neutralize the effect of Gladstone's agitation. English opinion became more hysterical when the Russians finally starved out the Turkish forces at Plevna and concluded an armistice early in 1878. Disraeli, concerned about British interests in the Eastern Mediterranean and the route to India, sent the fleet to Constantinople, and a famous music hall song added the word *jingoism* to the language.* In March, the Treaty of San Stefano was forced on the Turks; its terms served Russian interests so transparently that Austria-Hungary, whose own Balkan drive conflicted with Russian ambitions, proposed a European conference to revise the treaty. Disraeli agreed at

---

*We don't want to fight;
   But by Jingo, if we do,
We've got the men, we've got the ships,
   We've got the money too.

once, and as a bargaining counter called up reserves and sent Indian troops to the Eastern Mediterranean, a move which Derby could not agree to; he resigned as Foreign Minister, to be succeeded by Lord Salisbury.

At the Congress of Berlin, the treaty was indeed revised, largely on the basis of secret agreements concluded beforehand. The new Balkan arrangements were doubtful improvements on San Stefano. Nothing was done to satisfy the ambitions of the Rumanians or Greeks, and the "Big Bulgaria," which the Russians had originally created, certain that it would be a grateful client state, was broken up with an utter disregard of nationality — an indication of how insensitive statesmen then were to the truly powerful forces in Europe. Meanwhile, Austria was given the administration of Bosnia and Herzegovina, splitting apart the Serbs in Serbia and the Serbs in Montenegro, and the Conference recognized the British occupation of Cyprus, to which the Turks had earlier agreed in order to give the British fleet a base in the Eastern Mediterranean. France, angry about the Cyprus occupation, had to be compensated by secret British consent to her occupation of Tunis, undertaken with Bismarck's encouragement in 1881. And while Germany got no territory, the setting of the Conference and Bismarck's role as "honest broker" confirmed the pre-eminence of Germany on a restructured continent.

Disraeli brought back "peace with honor" — and some profit. But Gladstone was not resigned to the Disraelian style in foreign policy or in colonial affairs; an aggressive line had been taken all over the world. Early in 1879 Gladstone was selected as the Liberal candidate for Midlothian, the county in which Edinburgh is located. In November he launched the famous Midlothian campaign. Starting with a speech in Liverpool, he spoke all along the way to Edinburgh and, after a week of oratory there, he returned making another series of speeches. Such an appeal to the country by a politician, a natural corollary to an expanded electorate, was unprecedented; outside the House, politicians had always spoken primarily to their constituents. The Queen was profoundly shocked, but the effect on the country and on the Liberal party was electric; when Disraeli dissolved Parliament in March 1880, Gladstone undertook a second Midlothian campaign. In April, 1880, the Liberals were returned with a majority of 137 over the Conservatives; there was also an ominous Irish nationalist party of over 60 members. The country had responded to Gladstone's fervent moral rhetoric, but his new government was to demonstrate how inapplicable high-sounding words were to real events. To understand what happened, since foreign policy and the empire became inextricably entwined, we must return to compare the two styles in imperial matters.

The Question of Empire

Insofar as Gladstone thought seriously about colonial problems, he saw them as an early sympathizer of the Colonial Reformers, a free trader, and an advocate of economy. Strengthened by his devotion to liberalism and its institutions, he was prepared to see the formal ties of empire abandoned where the trend to self-government was set, and, except for the most pressing reasons, he opposed extensions of British control. At least in the English-speaking parts of the Empire, that sense of things seemed justified. Responsible government had been granted to Canada in the late forties, to New Zealand in 1853, and to the separate Australian provinces during the fifties, except for the convict colony of Swan River (Western Australia), which had to wait until 1890, nearly twenty-five years after transportation ceased to be a penalty in English law. In 1867, after long and difficult negotiations, the provinces of Canada came together in a confederation, completed by the addition of Prince Edward Island in 1871 and given economic viability by the construction of a transcontinental railway. As an obvious corollary of self-government was self-defense, the first Gladstone ministry speeded up the withdrawal of British troops from the colonies. Yet it will not do to consider Gladstone and those who thought like him as dogmatic "little Englanders," however much they may have seemed so to colonists who felt that their claims on sympathy and support from home were repeatedly ignored. Ministers simply did not want to take on more than they had to, and they counted on enlightened rule where they had to exercise it and the attraction of their reputation, economy, and ideas to support their influence throughout the world.

By the sixties some people were questioning these assumptions. The Indian Mutiny had shaken any easy hopes in the steady conversion of non-English peoples to English civilization, and, as we have seen, there was even questioning of the basic tenets of liberalism. While this was happening at home, some colonists were beginning to affirm their loyalty to the mother country against the separatism of colonial nationalists; their views found a focus in the Royal Colonial Institute (later the Royal Empire Society), founded in London in 1868 to promote the exchange of information about the colonies and to serve as a gathering place for colonials in London. In his celebrated speech at the Crystal Palace in 1872, Disraeli added pride in the British Empire to the maintenance of institutions and the promotion of social welfare as a rallying cry for his brand of Conservatism. This new emphasis was at once branded by his Liberal opponents as "imperialism," a word they hoped would imply an analogy to the discredited imperialism of Napoleonic France. The word was soon extended to the policies of Disraeli's government in the Empire and from that has passed into its current meaning.

Yet Disraeli was no more a dogmatic imperialist than Gladstone was an anti-imperialist. In the years before 1872 Disraeli had expressed both exasperated impatience with colonies—"a millstone round our necks," in his most famous phrase—and a deep awareness of the importance of the Empire to British well-being. In office, the ambivalence remained: uninterested in many parts of the Empire, he was still attracted by the dominant role that Britain might play in the East. As always, he was bored by detail and was inclined to leave subordinates alone and to respond to events as they occurred. Piecemeal responses to threatening circumstances abroad and a few imaginatively bold improvisations on his own part allowed the public then and historians since to believe that a more consistently aggressive "forward" policy had been inaugurated. For a time that belief helped to shore up Britain's increasingly doubtful force in European diplomacy and to give a false appearance of polarization to English domestic politics.

The Indian Frontier

The key to all British colonial development in the last years of the century lay in India. Sir John Seeley, a Cambridge historian who was one of the publicists for a new sense of empire, once said that though it might be possible someday to leave India to itself, it was necessary for the British to govern it as though they would never leave; that is what they did. The policy of internal economic development begun by Lord Dalhousie in the late forties was beginning to bear fruit in an extensive rail system, irrigation works, and industry, and after the abolition of the East India Company in 1858, there came a period of consolidation and bureaucratic and military administration of remarkably high standards. The resumption of a forward policy on the northwest frontier in 1877–1879, after thirty years of inaction, was not, however, related so much to a desire for imperial extension as it was to the European diplomatic situation, as Disraeli tried to stand firm against Russia, whose aggressiveness was directed not only towards Constantinople but towards Kabul in Afghanistan. Despite the massacre at Kabul in 1879 of the British resident and his staff, the second Afghan war of 1878–1880 was more successful militarily than the Afghan war in the forties, thanks to the leadership of Sir Frederick Roberts, later Lord Roberts. Again, no permanent occupation resulted, but the British were able to secure the establishment of a sympathetic Afghan ruler, though it is arguable whether or not the increased Indian debt and suspicion of British rashness were

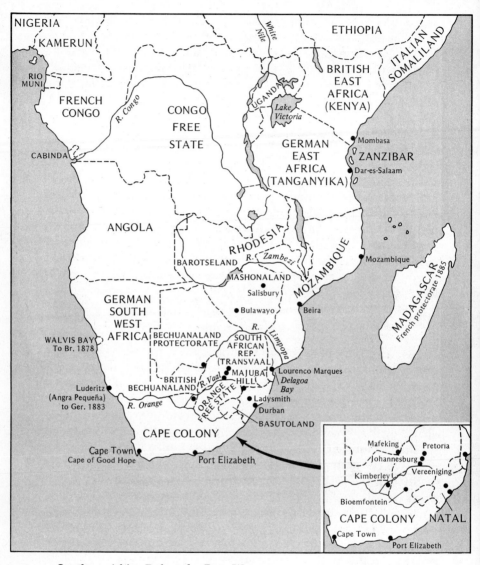

Southern Africa Before the Boer War

358

a price worth paying merely to get an ally. Other Asian expansion, in China, Malaya, and Burma, was in effect a continuation of the tactics employed earlier in the century, to promote legitimate trade where it was resisted and to protect British influence where it was threatened.

South Africa

Equally important in British imagination, official and public, were the routes to India, either through the Mediterranean and across the Isthmus of Suez or around the Cape of Good Hope. Throughout the first two-thirds of the century, the British were content with important way stations: Gibraltar (1704), Malta (1798), Cyprus (1878), and Aden (1839) on the Suez route; the Cape of Good Hope (1795), Mauritius and the Seychelles (1810) on the alternate route. The African coastline was controlled where necessary by influence over native rulers, and the interior was left strictly alone. But in the latter third of the century, the policy of protecting the coasts dragged the British more and more deeply into the interior and soon involved them in the scramble for Africa which dominated so much of the European diplomacy of the period.

The contrasts and similarities of Gladstonian and Disraelian imperial policies are most effectively illustrated in the case of the Cape route. Faced with thousands of miles of African coastline, the British could scarcely hope to do more than maintain a few widely separated bases, supplemented by carefully cultivated influence, most notably with the Sultan of Zanzibar, who controlled an East African port of great importance to the network of Arab trade in the Indian Ocean. This African route, however, had long involved another aspect of British policy, the suppression of the slave trade; naval patrols regularly covered the west coast of Africa to intercept illegal slave ships bound for America. To control slavery by surveillance of the coastal outlets, however, did not get at the heart of the problem, which lay rather in the activity of coastal slave traders who raided tribes in the interior; the government was in consequence under continual pressure from humanitarian elements in Britain to extend its rule inland. The interplay of strategic and humanitarian pressures with the government's desire for economy and freedom from unprofitable and unpredictable entanglements goes far to explain the erratic course of events in South Africa. Only belatedly did pressure from business interests enter the picture and then with ambiguous effect.

When the British took the Cape of Good Hope from the Dutch in 1795 and were confirmed in its possession in 1815, they got with their valuable strategic prize a nationality problem that has plagued them ever since. The Dutch settlers of the Cape, called Boers, were a pastoral people whose culture was long cut off from progressive currents in the European homeland. They spoke, and still speak, a Dutch dialect, now called Afrikaans; they held, and still hold, to a fundamentalist version of the Calvinist faith of the Dutch Reformed Church; they were and are patriarchal, proud, and resentful of any outside interference with their traditional way of life. In 1834, with the abolition of slavery, there was drastic interference, for the Boer economy was founded on the use of slaves. Already disgruntled by the replacement of Dutch by English as the official language and by the influx of British settlers, many of whom took a protective attitude towards the native population, the Dutch decided to escape.

The Great Trek of 1837–1844 was a complicated series of starts and stops, as land, the disposition of natives, and tentative British efforts at pursuit dictated. There were, however, two main lines of movement. One thrust was eastward into what is now Natal. There the Dutch encountered a small English settlement on the coast at Durban, but more importantly they encountered the resistance of the fierce Zulus under Dingaan, who treacherously murdered the Boer leader and many of his followers. A new leader, Andreas Pretorius, returned to the attack, broke Dingaan's power, and set up the Natal Republic. When the British intervened in the native interest, the Boers trekked northward, leaving Natal to become a British colony in 1843. The other, more important, movement was northward, across the Orange River and later, to escape British meddling, across the Vaal.

Continuing humanitarian pressure and the expansive imagination of Sir Harry Smith, an able soldier who became governor of the Cape colony, led to the annexation of the Orange River colony in 1848. A forward policy, involving a succession of native wars and much expense, was not, however, agreeable to dominant opinion at home, in the government or in the country. In the Sand River Convention, in 1852, the British agreed to abandon any claims to sovereignty over the area beyond the Vaal, where the Boers were consolidating the Transvaal Republic. In the Bloemfontein Convention two years later, control was similarly abandoned over the Orange Free State, an action less clearly demanded by the inhabitants (now including a number of British) but one that obviously reflected the disinclination of Whitehall to be unnecessarily troubled by involvement in the coastal hinterlands.

The two Boer republics led a shabby existence; their pastoral economies were poor, and the British were determined that they should not prosper, lest they threaten the coastal supremacy essential to British strategic security. Every Boer attempt to gain independent access to the sea was thwarted and when in the late sixties a fabulous diamond field was discovered in Griqualand, north of the Cape colony and west of Orange River Free State, the British promptly annexed it to the Cape to prevent its wealth from aiding the Boer republics. As soon as the discovery of diamonds turned the unprofitable Cape colony into a going concern, the British began to think seriously of getting rid of the expense of maintaining it, as they had recently done by shifting defense burdens to the other self-governing colonies. But the grant of self-government, made to the Cape in 1872, could logically be carried a step further by annexing the Boer republics and joining them to the Cape in a federation, so solving the wider strategic and diplomatic problem.

Gladstone's government, which had taken over Griqualand and (for military reasons) Basutoland, broached the scheme, but Disraeli's government carried it out, boldly annexing the almost bankrupt Transvaal in 1877 and undertaking at the same time to break the military power of the Zulus. The removal of the native threat, however, smashed the one advantage the Transvaal Boers could have seen in an annexation that otherwise outraged their nationalism. A Boer rebellion in 1880 found Gladstone again in office, swept in by the wave of revulsion in the country against the forward policy of the Conservatives. But the Liberals in power were dangerously divided, and the Boer rebellion forced them to choose between force and conciliation. The Whigs and humanitarians won out at first—Gladstone, it will be remembered, did not regularly impose his will on his cabinet—but when, early in 1881, the Boers resoundingly defeated the British at Majuba Hill, patriotic opinion rallied briefly in a determination to put them down. The radicals and Gladstone managed to assert themselves, however, and negotiated the Pretoria Convention, which abandoned the attempt to hold the Transvaal, save for the vaguest assertion of suzerainty.

The South African policy of both parties and both leaders, then, was much of a piece, aimed at strategic security, humanitarian protection of native populations, and economy. In none of these difficult decisions, which inevitably became political issues, was there more than a stylistic difference or a legitimate, usually narrowly based, disagreement about priorities between the two parties. Only by dangerous oversimplification can one see a conflict of "little-Englandism" and "imperialism"; there was as yet no broad national enthusiasm for a doctrine of imperial expansion.

Egypt

In northern Africa, along the shorter and more heavily traveled Suez route, the essential identity of the policies of successive governments and the limitations on them are made even clearer. Palmerstonian

**Egypt and Its Surrounding Areas
in the Late Nineteenth Century**

policy, as we have seen,* was geared to protecting the Mediterranean-Suez route from pressure or disruption by Russia, through Constantinople, or by France in Egypt and the Levant. Britain's counterweight against both threats was the moribund Turkish Empire, the Sultan being resolutely supported by London not only against the Tsar but against his rebellious Francophile client-ruler Mehemet Ali. After Mehemet Ali's death in 1849 and a brief period of internal chaos, Egypt resumed the march to modernization. A French engineer and entrepreneur, Ferdinand de Lesseps, gained a concession, in spite of all Palmerston's intrigues against him, to construct a canal through the Isthmus of Suez—a project made practicable by the increasing use of steam, more reliable and easier to steer than sailing ships. The canal was opened in 1869. Meanwhile, in 1863, Ismail, the first Khedive of Egypt, had come to power. He was a man with grandiose visions of a modern, prosperous Egypt, but he lacked the good administrative sense to bring it off. He borrowed money from willing European financiers at grossly inflated interest rates, which rose with his debts. Although bankers of all the leading European nations were involved in the Egyptian boom—sparked not only by canal construction but by railway building and the closing of American cotton ports by the Civil War—the French predominated. By 1875, Ismail's finances were in such a bad way that he tried to mortgage his share of the Suez Canal Company. Learning of Ismail's efforts, Disraeli offered to buy Ismail's shares outright for a little over four million pounds. The deal was promptly closed and ratified by Parliament, and the British government thus became the owner of nearly half of the stock of the Company. Disraeli's boldly imaginative move struck the public fancy as a clear proof of a new imperialist direction, though in truth it is best seen as a step to protect the route to India.

More significant was the acceptance by the bankrupt Ismail in the next year of control of his finances, in the interests of his European creditors, by two administrators, one French, one English. In 1878, the British followed the French in imposing political reforms on Ismail, and in 1879, when Ismail rebelled against his tutelage, the two powers got the Sultan to depose his nominal and inconvenient vassal and to set up a puppet in his place. So gradually the British edged towards direct involvement in the internal administration of Egypt, a burden with which no British statesman wanted to be saddled. But to have left such unwanted tasks to the French would have given that nation, still thought to be potentially hostile, a stranglehold on Suez, where British traffic was overwhelmingly dominant.

The imposition of European control and the weakening of the

*See above, p. 303.

power of the Khedive produced in 1881 a revolt led by Colonel Arabi Pasha, one of the first truly nationalist uprisings among an Oriental people against Western domination. This result, so mystifying to contemporaries, so obvious today, caught Gladstone in a position where a resolute policy was impossible. His cabinet was split between the Whigs, led by Lord Hartington, and the radicals (chiefly Bright and Chamberlain); this split was driven deeper by disagreements on Irish policy and by the Transvaal revolt and the defeat at Majuba Hill. More clearly than the situation in South Africa, the Egyptian troubles involved British prestige, both in India and in Europe. Gladstone, caught up by the Midlothian spirit, had turned his back on Turkey. He himself, moreover, was able to appreciate the justice in the Arabist revolt, a prodigy of liberal imagination of which his colleagues were incapable. But, overborne by the needs of security and political unity, Gladstone had to sacrifice his scruples and consent to a show of strength. Sending a naval force to Alexandria as a threat only made the Arabists more determined and touched off a massacre of Europeans. When the bombardment of Alexandria followed, the redoubled anti-European violence began to look like lawlessness and inhumanity that had to be put down, if any stability was to be achieved; even Gladstone argued that premise in justification of the Egyptian policy into which his government was drifting. Wanting to protect not only law and order but the canal; unable to call on the Turks as Disraeli would surely have done; and suddenly deprived, by a French cabinet crisis, of help from that quarter, the British landed troops and broke Arabi's power in August and September, 1882.

The occupation, which the earlier bluffs were meant to avoid, was intended to be temporary, but it soon became apparent that this easy assumption was wrong. If administrative stability and financial solvency were prerequisites, then evacuation would not come in a few months or a few years. Reluctantly recognizing the inevitable, the British government recalled Sir Evelyn Baring from India, where he had gone as a financial officer after serving for two years as joint administrator of Ismail's affairs; installed in Cairo as consul general in 1883, he governed Egypt until his retirement in 1907 — by then he was Earl of Cromer — when he passed on to his successors a country efficiently ruled in the manner of an Indian province. But British involvement soon went far beyond Egypt to a deep entanglement in the interior of Africa.

The Sudan, drained by the upper Nile, had long been under Egyptian rule, or misrule, and the collapse of khedivial authority in Cairo let loose a Sudanese revolt, under the leadership of the Mahdi, a former slave trader turned religious fanatic. A nationalist Egypt could not tolerate this affront to its dubious authority, so the Khedive sent a huge army under Hicks Pasha, a British officer in his service, to wipe out the rebels. The Egyptian army was destroyed instead. The British government decided to try to rescue the Egyptian garrisons cut off by the rebels. To do the job they sent General Charles George Gordon, a fearless Evangelical who had gained wide popularity in England not only by his military exploits but by his suppression of the Sudanese slave trade when he was serving Ismail. Gordon's impulsiveness soon got his forces bottled up in Khartum, necessitating still another relief expedition. London was slow in authorizing the new move, in part because of the distractions of the third Reform bill,* and there were serious delays in the progress of the column up the Nile. When it reached Khartum on January 28, 1885, the city had fallen; Gordon and his men had been killed two days before. The outcry in England was violent. Gladstone's indecisiveness was blamed for the hero's death, and that hostility guaranteed Conservative inroads in the general election of November, 1885. Yet the Liberal majority was still sufficiently Gladstonian to support abandonment of the fruitless attempt to conquer the Sudan; when the Conservatives came into office in 1886, they were wise enough to forget their denunciations and to maintain the policy.

Ireland

By the mid-eighties, the Liberals were on the verge of dissolution. The divisions in the cabinet, which hampered action in both South Africa and Egypt, emerged from intraparty developments that in retrospect can be seen stretching back to mid-century. The rising force of radicalism strengthened the resistance of the aristocratic Whigs who had traditionally dominated the liberal side of English politics. At the same time, the radicals alarmed more and more businessmen who, having gained their political ends, were rapidly assimilating the traditional ways and outlook of the landed classes, while some of the radicals themselves — W. E. Forster, for example, or John Bright — had drifted to the right in their old age. But Gladstone inclined more and more towards the radical pole, and when he faltered, Joseph Chamberlain, at the Board of Trade, was there to urge him on.

The fate of the Liberals turned on Ireland. There, Gladstone's impressive but insufficient concessions of 1869–1870 had suddenly become irrelevant. Disraeli, once deeply concerned about Irish questions, did nothing constructive during his time in office; but Glad-

*See below, pp. 426–428.

stone, determined to see justice done in Ireland, found powerful segments of opinion in his own party as firmly pledged to the land and the Empire as the Tories. In an atmosphere poisoned by the bitter hatred and contempt felt by the Irish and English for each other, he had to fight his way almost alone.

The agricultural depression, which set in after 1873,* brought catastrophe to Ireland. Prices and incomes fell so far that rents could no longer be paid. Landlords, many both greedy and inefficient, were thoroughly alarmed and increasingly insisted that someone should pay, while efficient landlords were forced to take steps their tenants were bound to resent. By the late seventies, a new burst of evictions had begun, and evictions in turn offered occasion, among a peasantry still on the edge of famine, for renewed violence. In 1879, this agrarian misery and bitterness found a new channel for agitation in the Land League, founded by an ex-Fenian, Michael Davitt, who had been released from prison two years before. Looking immediately to relief for rack-rented tenants, the League had as its ultimate program the elimination of landlords through the remedy of peasant proprietorship or even land nationalization.

The second cause of the new Irish crisis was political. The Irish Republican Brotherhood—the Fenians—had been smashed in the sixties; its program had made little progress among the peasantry and was hateful to the Roman Catholic hierarchy, whose support was essential to any successful political movement. Many Fenian leaders, like Davitt, switched to different kinds of agitation; others kept alive an underground organization, able to draw on considerable American sympathy, but isolated from Irish developments by its devotion to a conspiratorial approach and to the ideal of revolution. A new turn was taken in 1870 by Isaac Butt, a conservative Protestant lawyer who had defended the Fenian leaders in the sixties; Butt and his friends began to argue for a milder version of O'Connell's old goal of repeal, in the form of a separate Irish legislature to deal with Irish affairs. In 1874, fifty-six Irish members were returned to Parliament committed in one way or another to Home Rule. This thoroughly respectable, constitutional agitation made no progress at all in Parliament; and soon stronger spirits than Butt's were turning to parliamentary obstruction: if the Commons persisted in doing nothing for Ireland, Ireland would let the Commons do nothing about anything else.

In 1877, Butt was succeeded in the leadership of a rather uncertain Irish party by Charles Stewart Parnell, a Protestant landowner who had entered Parliament as a home ruler in a bye-election in 1875

*On the depression, see below, pp. 375–377.

and who, after nearly a year of anonymity, emerged as one of the chief obstructionists. In 1880, the Irish voters returned 61 Home Rule members. More than half of the 34 large landowners who had sat for Ireland in the 1874 Parliament were not returned; in their places were new, less respectable men whose appearance on the scene shocked many contemporaries. When Parnell forced a clarification of the position of the members of the Irish party, many of whom were Home Rulers only for electoral convenience, a mere 24 members proved to be his devoted followers; 19 of them had been elected for the first time in 1880. But in 1885, the newly expanded electorate returned 86 members, all firmly pledged to the Parnellite program. The Irish had come to realize that the ballot, granted in 1872, was truly secret.

At base, Parnell's program was moderate. To his left stood the Fenians, contemptuous of any open or parliamentary movement, the agrarian bloc centered in the Land League, and the American sympathizers. To his right were some friendly landlords, the small Irish middle class, most of the Irish M.P.'s, and, most important of all, the bishops and clergy of the Roman Catholic Church. Parnell's genius kept the revolutionary energies channeled toward constitutional and parliamentary forms — however wild his rhetoric sounded to Englishmen — and gained the all-important support of the priests and hierarchy. Skillfully exploiting this unstable combination, Parnell dominated British politics for ten years.

When Gladstone's government took office in May, 1880, it faced the old linking of necessities: strengthened law enforcement to reduce Irish anarchy to order, and a measure of reform. In mid-June, under pressure from Parnell, the government introduced a bill to compensate certain evicted tenants; the bill passed the Commons easily and was thrown out in August by a huge majority in the Lords. Ireland responded with a new burst of violence, and while in Parliament Parnell was reasonable, during the recess that started in September, he began to speak in a much more radical vein to the Irish in Ireland — to restrain the pressure from the antiparliamentary left. He had already been elected President of the Land League; now he launched a new technique of agrarian agitation: anyone who took a farm from which the previous tenant had been evicted was to be treated "as if he were a leper of old." The punishment was first used against a Captain Boycott, whose crops had to be harvested by Protestant laborers brought in from Ulster under military guard, a measure that only served to publicize the success of the tactic, which came to be called by the name of its first victim. Significantly, there was a sharp drop in the number of evictions.

Parnell's new turn, incomprehensible to nearly all Englishmen, helped to determine the government's order of priorities. As soon as the new session opened in January, 1881, W. E. Forster, the radical politician who had carried the Education Act in 1870 and who was now Chief Secretary for Ireland, introduced a coercion bill, a sign of the desperation to which he had been brought by events he did not understand. As the bill provided for suspension of habeas corpus and so for unlimited use of arbitrary arrest and preventive detention, the Irish party responded with a vigorous and expanded campaign of parliamentary obstruction. The House of Commons had been unwilling in the late seventies to counter obstruction by limiting its precious freedom of debate; now, after a sitting of forty-one hours, the Speaker took the initiative and closed the debate, so securing a first reading for the bill. Shortly after, a mild but novel resolution was introduced to permit closure of debate, but even with its use, it was a month before the coercion bill could be passed.

Gladstone, who almost alone had opposed coercion in the cabinet, now introduced his second land bill, and by late summer got it through with only minor modifications. Hurried and complex, political rather than economic in purpose, the main provisions of the act were summed up in the catch phrase "the three F's." The right of free sale was a further step in recognizing the legal interest of a tenant at will in his tenancy by allowing him, subject to certain protections for the landlord, to sell his tenancy to another party. Fair rents and fixity of tenure were secured by allowing the county courts or the Irish Land Commission to fix rents on application by either tenant or landlord; once rents were fixed, eviction was forbidden, except for failure to pay the fixed rent or for violation of certain specified conditions. While this extremely radical measure shocked property-minded Englishmen, it did not go far enough to satisfy the Irish. Leaseholders—the better class of Irish tenants who were also suffering severely from the depression—were not included, nor were some 130,000 tenants already in arrears with their rents when the act was passed. Parnell knew that these loopholes should and could be filled, but he also knew that no more sweeping basic measure could be got through Parliament at that time, so he urged that it be tested by an orderly submission of cases to the courts. But again, with an eye to the left, he and some of his colleagues voted against the bill and in the parliamentary recess returned to violent speechmaking. Parnell was arrested under the Coercion Act and thrown into Kilmainham Jail. He and his associates issued a "no-rent" manifesto, and there was a sharp rise in the number of disturbances.

Prison was a convenience to Parnell, for it masked his essentially moderate attitude with martyrdom, but he could not stay long without risking his leadership. At the same time, the government was embarrassed by having used coercion—intended for perpetrators of agrarian outrages – to silence a prominent M.P. On both sides there was need for accommodation, and in April, through intermediaries, the "Kilmainham Treaty" was arranged, an understanding that Parnell would abandon the land war and damp down revolutionary agitation, while the government would tacitly abandon coercion and remedy defects in the land act. Parnell had re-emphasized his loyalty to the parliamentary approach.

Unfortunately, his essential moderation was lost on most Englishmen when, within a few days of his release from prison, a terrible crime was committed by a terrorist group with which he had no connection at all. Forster, committed to coercion, had resigned rather than agree to the Kilmainham understanding; his place as chief secretary was taken, not by Chamberlain, who was the expected choice, but by Lord Frederick Cavendish, a close friend of Gladstone and the brother of Lord Hartington, the Whig leader in the cabinet. Just after arriving in Dublin, Lord Frederick Cavendish and his chief civil servant were walking near the viceregal lodge in Phoenix Park, where they were set upon and stabbed to death. The murders, a terrible personal blow to Gladstone, caused a deep revulsion against Irish terrorism. Had the English been capable of restraint, the moderate Irish cause might have been greatly strengthened. But they were not, and another measure of coercion was introduced and carried, in spite of the efforts of Parnell and his party against it.

Gladstone upheld his end of the Kilmainham bargain by introducing a measure to amend the land act. The bill provided that if any tenant paid one year's arrears and could satisfy the Land Commissioners that he could not pay the rest, the state would cancel half the remainder and pay the landlord the other half from the surplus appropriated at the disestablishment of the Church in 1869. After fighting the bill through the Commons, Gladstone got it through the Lords by threatening a dissolution of Parliament, and, though many tenants were unable to pay even one year's arrears, nearly all of more than 130,000 applications for the benefits of the act were accepted.

For the next two years the Irish question remained in the background. Gladstone carried some useful measures aiding Irish fisheries and tramways and giving assistance to the building of laborers' cottages, but he refused to amend the land acts further and failed to get through Chamberlain's scheme for a new system of Irish local government. Gladstone was not only weary but immobilized by the irreparable cleavage in his cabinet and party, and in 1884 he was preoccupied with franchise reform and Egypt. In spite of the success of the new Reform Bill,* his ministry's reputation was destroyed by

*See below, pp. 426–428.

the death of Gordon, and in June, 1885, Gladstone resigned, after a defeat on an amendment to the budget.

Disraeli had died in 1881. He had been succeeded as leader by his old opponent Lord Salisbury, who now took office with a minority government. Salisbury had, however, the tacit support of Parnell, who was anxious to emphasize his power by setting the parties to bidding for his favor; launched on a determined effort to get Home Rule, he had some reason to favor the Tories. Salisbury, after the bitterest denunciations of Gladstone's policies, was making agreeable noises; Lord Randolph Churchill, the rising young Tory radical, had promised Parnell that his party would abandon coercion; a number of Conservatives had been genuinely converted to land purchase as the solution most acceptable to the Irish peasants and a way of rescuing the landlords; and the new Tory viceroy, Lord Carnarvon, had been converted to Home Rule, which the Conservative party might well be able to get through the Lords, as the Liberals probably could not. But little could be done before the general election that Salisbury called in November. Parnell ordered the Irish throughout the country to vote Tory.

Meanwhile, Gladstone had himself become convinced of the necessity of Home Rule. Like Parnell, he preferred to see the Conservatives carry it, because they would have less trouble with the House of Lords; he too was hopeful that Carnarvon's influence in that direction would help. But because of the hostility he knew his views would arouse in his own party, he kept his decision to himself, even at the risk of losing Parnell's support to the Tories. When the election produced a Liberal majority of eighty-six, almost exactly balanced by the Irish party, Gladstone was in no hurry to take office again. But increasingly he saw in Home Rule an issue on which the divided and quarrelsome Liberal party might appeal successfully to the country, while some of his lieutenants and supporters saw it as a weapon that could firmly establish Gladstone's leadership against any challenge that the increasingly vocal radical Joseph Chamberlain might mount against it. In December 1885, Gladstone's son Herbert, always solicitous of his father's reputation and authority, gave interviews to a number of like-minded journalists, revealing the new direction of the elder Gladstone's thinking. Though the published reports went somewhat further than Herbert Gladstone intended, the political ends were accomplished by what has come to be known (from the name of Gladstone's Welsh estate) as the Hawarden Kite. Ireland returned to the center of the stage, and Chamberlain was shoved unceremoniously off it; the Conservatives were freed to return to their much more congenial role of pampering English prejudices in favor of union; there was a rash of Tory resignations, including Carnarvon's; and Parnell shifted his support at once. Gladstone, having thought Home Rule might allow him to unite his party, found that it was a new source of division.

Early in January, 1886, Salisbury's government was defeated in the Commons on an amendment for agrarian reform and resigned. Gladstone came back into office, without Hartington and Goschen, with only lukewarm support from Chamberlain, and deprived of the help of Sir Charles Dilke, the fastest-rising radical star in the Liberal heavens, because Dilke had just been named corespondent in an unsavory divorce suit. When the Home Rule bill was put before the cabinet, Chamberlain resigned. The bill, introduced in April, proposed a separate Irish legislature and executive, with power over all Irish affairs, save certain imperial matters—the Crown; defense; foreign affairs; trade, customs, and navigation; the post office; and coinage. No Irish members were to sit in Westminster, though Gladstone later expressed his willingness to modify that provision, since the one-fifteenth of the imperial budget that was to be met from Irish revenue would amount to something like 40 per cent of the Irish tax yield; to exclude the Irish from participation at Westminster would be "taxation without representation." The new Irish parliament was to consist of two "orders" in a single house, each with a veto over the other, the upper order to consist at first of twenty-eight life peers, presumably there to protect the interests of the Protestant minority in Ulster.

The crucial role in the outcome of the bill was played by Chamberlain. A Birmingham manufacturer and a prominent Dissenter, he had risen meteorically in his native town as master of its new political machine,* as Lord Mayor and advocate of "gas-and-water socialism," and finally after 1876 as its spokesman in Parliament. Alarming to the numerically predominant Whigs in the party hierarchy for his radicalism as well as for his political power, in the early eighties he was Gladstone's most prominent lieutenant and in some ways his inspirer in Irish matters. He and Gladstone had stood almost alone against coercion in the cabinet; he had been deeply involved in the Kilmainham negotiations; he was nearly universally expected to become Chief Secretary for Ireland in 1882; and he had advanced a far-reaching though abortive scheme to create local boards on which many governmental functions could be devolved from the old centralized but inefficient administration in Dublin Castle. But Chamberlain had got on increasingly badly with Parnell. The estrangement was partly due to the influence of Captain William O'Shea, who was Chamberlain's chief emissary to Parnell. O'Shea, an opportunist who

*See below, p. 424.

had attached himself loosely to Parnell's party, was a double-dealing incompetent; he was also the husband of the woman who since 1880 had been Parnell's mistress—with O'Shea's almost certain knowledge. Chamberlain was further shaken by Parnell's Tory alliance in 1885 and even more by the hostility with which the nationalist leaders, for sound tactical reasons, treated an Irish tour which Chamberlain and Dilke had consequently to abandon. To some extent Chamberlain, who was still a free trader, may have been worried about a protectionist Ireland, though trade and navigation were explicitly reserved subjects in Gladstone's bill; but basically, in spite of his interest in a reformed, active, and responsible local government in Ireland, he could not accept breaking up the Union. Backed by Bright and in unaccustomed alliance with Hartington, Chamberlain led 93 Liberals into the lobby against Gladstone's bill, which was beaten by a vote of 343 to 313. In the general election in July, 1886, the country returned 316 Conservatives and 78 Liberal Unionists (to give them their new name) against only 191 Liberals and 85 Irish nationalists.

Between 1870 and 1886, Britain had seen her accustomed superiority in Europe shrink in the shadow of a unified and forceful Germany. In the colonies, the traditional interest in strategic security and economic nonintervention had confusingly but ineluctably dragged an unwilling government into ventures in Afghanistan, South Africa, and Egypt that entailed endless expense and trouble and, worse, humiliating defeats. In Ireland, the severest of challenges, the rapidly moving situation outstripped the imagination of the thoughtful minority and only confirmed the majority in their prejudices. The result was a marked shift in the two-party system and the temporary paralysis of English government. The succeeding twenty years showed little advance and more confusion, as politicians and ordinary citizens continued to apply old categories to the new problems they faced. But beneath their futilities was being created what we may call the modern context: the economic, political, and cultural framework within which Britain still lives, and within which it has continued a slow decline from its mid-Victorian pinnacle.

Selected Readings

R. C. K. Ensor's *England, 1870–1914* (1936), which is one volume in the *Oxford History of England,* is an admirable narrative. The official life of Gladstone is in three volumes by his lieutenant, John Morley (1903). Sir Philip Magnus's single-volume life, *Gladstone* (1954), is an excellent recreation of a personality in many ways alien to our age. E. J. Feuchtwanger, *Gladstone* (1976) is a good brief sketch, chiefly political in emphasis. S. G. Checkland, *The Gladstones: A Family Biography, 1764–1851* (1971) is indispensable for the Liverpool background. Gladstone's diaries are being published: vols. 1–2, 1825–1839, ed. M. R. D. Foot (1968); vols. 3–4, 1840–1854, ed. M. R. D. Foot and H. C. G. Matthew (1974); vols. 5–6, 1855–1868, ed. H. C. G. Matthew (1978). Disraeli's official life is the six volumes by W. F. Monypenny and G. E. Buckle, *The Life of Benjamin Disraeli, Earl of Beaconsfield* (1910–1920). For all but quarrying purposes, it has now been replaced by Robert Blake, *Disraeli* (1966).

The Irish problem and attempts to deal with it are covered in many good recent studies. The context and consequences of disestablishment are set out in Desmond Bowen, *The Protestant Crusade in Ireland, 1800–70: A Study of Protestant-Catholic Relations Between the Act of Union and Disestablishment* (1978); Donald Harman Akenson, *The Church of Ireland: Ecclesiastical Reform and Revolution, 1800–1885* (1971); and R. B. McDowell, *The Church of Ireland, 1869–1969* (1975). On the secret, revolutionary political movement of the period, Leon ó Broin, *Fenian Fever: An Anglo-Irish Dilemma* (1971). The central question of land is explored in E. D. Steele, *Irish Land and British Politics: Tenant-Right and Nationality, 1865–1870* (1974); Barbara Lewis Solow, *The Land Question and the Irish Economy, 1870–1903* (1971); and J. S. Donnelly, *The Land and the People of Nineteenth-Century Cork: The Rural Economy and the Land Question* (1975). The English national characteristic of hatred of the Irish is demonstrated in two books by L. P. Curtis, Jr., *Anglo-Saxons and Celts: A Study of Anti-Irish Prejudice in Victorian England* (1968) and *Apes and Angels: The Irishman in Victorian Caricature* (1971).

The Revised Code, which governed education after 1862, is set out in detail in W. F. Connell, *The Educational Thought and Influence of Matthew Arnold* (1950); a poet and social critic, Arnold was also an inspector of schools who opposed the new departure, the professional importance of which is central to A. Tropp's book, cited in the previous chapter, on the schoolteachers. But the bad historical press that the Revised Code has received is subjected to some healthy revisionism in D. W. Sylvester, *Robert Lowe and Education* (1973). The course of educational change after the Forster act is the subject of Gillian Sutherland, *Policy Making in Elementary Education, 1870–1895* (1973). The most convenient access to public health issues of the period is through R. J. Lambert's biography, *Sir John Simon, 1816–1904, and English Social Administration* (1963). On the Army, Gwyn Harries-Jenkins, *The Army in Victorian Society* (1977), and Alan Ramsay Skelly, *The Victorian Army at Home: The Recruitment and Terms and Conditions of the British Regular, 1859–1899* (1977).

Theo Aronson, *Victoria and Disraeli: The Making of a Romantic Partnership* (1977) is a good popular account. Paul Smith, *Disraelian Conservatism and Social Reform* (1967) is a persuasive and skeptical scholarly interpretation to which the analysis in the text is much indebted. The politically explosive forward policy of Disraeli's government abroad and in the colonies and reactions to it can be traced in the following: C. C. Eldridge, *England's Mission: The Imperial Idea in the Age of Gladstone and Disraeli, 1868–1880* (1973), a nicely balanced discussion; Richard Koebner and H. D. Schmidt, *Imperialism: The Story and Significance of a Political Word, 1840–1960* (1964); and R. T. Shannon, *Gladstone and the Bulgarian Agitation, 1876* (1963, 1975). The political consequences of the agitation and the subsequent Midlothian campaign can be seen in Trevor Lloyd, *The General Election of 1880* (1968). On the background of African involvement, Philip D. Curtin, *The Image of Africa: British Ideas and Action, 1780–1850* (1964); Howard Temperley, *British Antislavery, 1833–1870* (1972); and, on the creation of the South African colonies and other entities, John S. Galbraith, *Reluctant Empire: British Policy on the South African Frontier, 1834–1854* (1963), and Eric A. Walker, *The Great Trek* (1934). Gladstone's southern African problems of the eighties are dealt with in D. M. Schreuder, *Gladstone and Kruger: Liberal Government and Colonial "Home Rule," 1880–1885* (1969). The most influential recent interpretation of British involvement in Africa, north and south, is that of Ronald Robinson and John Gallagher, *Africa and the Victorians* (1961), to which must be added D. K. Fieldhouse's essay, *The Theory of Capitalist Imperialism* (1967) and the historiographical summary, *Imperialism,* edited by William Roger Louis and cited in Chapter 7.

The Irish problem in the eighties begins with land, on which the Solow book, mentioned above, is valuable, but becomes a political problem issuing ultimately in Gladstone's conversion to home rule. F. S. L. Lyons, *Charles Stewart Parnell* (1977) is an authoritative biography of the chief actor in the drama, while R. F. Foster, *Charles Stewart Parnell: The Man and His Family* (1976) shows him in a non-political perspective, particularly as an Irish landowner. Conor Cruise O'Brien, *Parnell and His Party, 1880–90* (1957) is an ingenious and valuable analysis of political maneuvering that puzzled and outraged the English. On the formation of the clerical-nationalist alliance, Emmet Larkin, *The Roman Catholic Church and the Creation of the Modern Irish State* (1975). The events of the crucial turn in Gladstone's career and in English politics is reconstructed and idiosyncratically analyzed in meticulous detail in A. B. Cooke and John Vincent, *The Governing Passion: Cabinet Government and Party Politics in Britain, 1885–1886* (1974). See also Dudley W. R. Bahlmann, ed., *The Diaries of Sir Edward Walter Hamilton, 1880–1885* (2 vols., 1972), Gladstone's private secretary; and D. A. Hamer, *Liberal Politics in the Age of Gladstone and Rosebery* (1972).

Chapter 9
The Erosion of the Liberal Consensus

c. 1873–1900

THE GREAT DEPRESSION, 1873–1896

Agriculture

During a boom of remarkable proportions in the early seventies, Great Britain reached a peak of optimism that had grown pretty steadily since the fifties. In the mid-seventies a change occurred in the economic climate, and by the early eighties men were talking of depression. A somber tone lasted until nearly the end of the century. What caused this change of mood, and how far was it justified?

In agriculture, no doubt, there was good reason for it. In five bad years in the fifties and early sixties—when grain prices would naturally be high—wheat brought a little over 61 shillings per quarter. In the late seventies, when even lower yields should have forced prices higher, wheat was selling for an average price of a little under 50 shillings. In 1886, the price was 31 shillings; in the preceding ten years it had dropped more than a third, and other grains did not do much better. Given farmers' shrinking incomes, landlords had to agree to some reduction in their income or face vacant farms. On an average, rents dropped by one-fourth between the late seventies and the first years of the new century.

The agricultural depression was directly related to an influx of foreign grain, at last justifying the pessimistic predictions made by the protectionists when Peel got rid of the Corn Laws. During the thirty years after 1846, English agriculture remained protected by distance and by a series of historical accidents. The American and European wars of the fifties and sixties slowed the internal development of the great continental areas and disrupted world markets, generally to the advantage of the British farmers. By the seventies these political disturbances had settled, and the technological barriers began rapidly to crumble. The rich virgin plains of the United States, Canada, and Russia were opened by railways, and the cost of ocean carriage dropped steadily as better ship design and new, more efficient engines made possible shortened voyages and a larger volume of cargo space.* Imported wheat rose from 50 per cent of British consumption in the seventies to nearly 80 per cent in the nineties.

At least since the eighteenth century, the production of grain had been central to the fluctuating prosperity of British farming, and historians have not been immune to the temptation to generalize about the comparative health of agriculture from the fever chart of wheat prices. But the agricultural depression in the late nineteenth century was largely confined to that part of the country, in the eastern and southern regions, that specialized in arable farming; it was worst of all in those areas with heavy soils that had been improved, with vast expense and relatively little profitability, in the so-called "golden age" after 1846. The government helped out by cutting rates and shifting to the landlords the tithe charge that tenants had paid since 1836 as part of their rent. On the farms themselves, even in hard times, it was possible to improve efficiency by using new fertilizers, rotations, and machinery; and a marked southward migration of Scottish farmers and dairymen helped to transform some backward English counties by their more advanced methods. But generally, at least on its arable side, English agriculture remained conservative; and while it survived, it did so under constant threat, and the road to the ultimate solution of state subsidy was open.

---

*It should be remembered, however, that sailing ships accounted for a large, though shrinking, proportion of the merchant fleet down to the First World War and that well into the late-Victorian period they carried most of the goods in British overseas trade. They were particularly important for bulky commodities like grain. See G. S. Graham, "The Ascendancy of the Sailing Ship, 1850–1885," *Economic History Review*, 2nd ser., IX, 74–88 (August, 1956).

In parts of the country where grain was not king, the situation was not nearly so bad, and in some instances it even improved. Farms immediately dependent on large towns remained reasonably prosperous, even with little increase in efficiency. Market gardens, greenhouses, and fruit orchards expanded to take advantage of better transportation and changing tastes that resulted from a rising standard of living. The factory manufacture of cider and jam, and canning and other large-scale food processing stimulated the expansion of this segment of the industry still further. Dairying prospered most of all. The rising standard of living pulled up demand, and while Britain was increasingly dependent on imported milk products, milk prices remained stable.

The good fortune of dairying points to a distinction of fundamental importance in understanding the course of English agriculture in the last decades of the nineteenth century. While arable farmers could legitimately talk of depression, graziers were much better off. To be sure, sheep farming was hard hit in the late seventies by the collapse of the wool market: the unnaturally high prices reached during the boom of the early seventies dropped by more than half within a few years. But, in general, stock farmers prospered. The rising standard of living increased the importance of meat in the English diet — the corresponding decline in the importance of bread was another blow to wheat — and the fall in the price of grain meant cheaper feed for cattle and higher productivity. The appearance of refrigerator ships after the mid-eighties made possible the importation of meat from Australia, New Zealand, the United States, and, later, Argentina; but good English or Scottish meat commanded the premium market, and the drop in meat prices in the latter half of the so-called depression period may have been due as much to lower costs of production as to the competition that had been so ruinous to the grain farmers. Although the situation of arable farming stabilized after 1890 and improved sharply during the war years of 1914–1918, a major long-term result of the so-called depression of the seventies and eighties was to stimulate further the steady shift from arable to pasture land that had gone on throughout modern English history.

The Decline of Landed Society

In 1874–1876 returns were published from a government survey of landownership, the first such survey since the Domesday Book was completed, following the Norman Conquest, in 1086. The "New Domesday Book," as it was tagged, showed that there were about a million landowners in Britain and Ireland but that fewer than seven thousand of them owned 80 per cent of the land, a degree of concentration that strongly reinforced the demand for land reform. In due course, some legislation followed — notably the Settled Land Act of 1882 — but the more dramatic results were owing, not to legislation, but to the agricultural depression. By striking at the economic foundations of landed fortunes, the depression changed what had been a relative decline, as against the commercial and industrial segments of the nation, into an absolute decline; the seventies and eighties made evident changes that for years had been effectively, even magnificently, masked.

Peers and gentry in the eighteen century had, as we have seen,* stood at the center of English life, as much because of the extent of their economic influence as their near-monopoly of political power at the national and local levels. From the economic and political positions they established then, landed gentlemen moved into the nineteenth century with a confidence in bearing, taste, and assumption that made them marvels, not only at home but abroad. To be sure, the numbers of peers increased markedly from the time of William Pitt's new creations at the end of the eighteenth century, but the new creations were for the most part drawn from the same landed class and were able to sustain their political and social claims by the incomes necessary to an enhanced station. The early nineteenth century, indeed, saw a marked rise in social competitiveness, a heightened awareness of gradations in rank that encouraged and made acceptable the state's increasing resort to honors that were justified by political expediency and even in many instances by merit.

Within the ranks of peers and gentry, most families became richer. Those who were wealthier to begin with — particularly those who had the luck or canniness to profit from mineral rights, urban property, or even commercial and industrial investment — became richer than the relatively less fortunate families whose incomes depended only on their rent-rolls; to this extent the nineteenth century saw a growing differentiation in landed society. But, at the same time, physical mobility and more complex social and political responsibilities brought about a somewhat freer and easier association between gentry and peers than seems to have been the case earlier. Families in the gentry declined and disappeared, as they had always done, but their places were taken, with a new ease of adaptation and acceptability, by recruits from commerce and industry, who had not only the wealth to acquire landed estates but, thanks to the reformed and expanding public schools, ready access to the means of planing away the rough edges of an obscure origin. It took two or three generations to accomplish the full transition from commerce and in-

*See above, pp. 7–13, 51–54, 58–61.

dustry to a status supported primarily by landed income; but even while old ties to the trade remained, assimilation into county society —indicated, for example, by becoming a justice of the peace—might be accomplished in relatively few years.

The consolidation of the position of landed society in the first three-quarters of the nineteenth century was brought about in many ways, but we may usefully isolate two of them to illustrate the point. No doubt of most interest to the economic historian is the marked improvement in the management of landed estates. Although the landlord's approval was required for any major economic decisions, relatively few landlords involved themselves in the day-to-day management of their property. There was no fixed way of organizing the hierarchy of an estate, and landlords might reshuffle that hierarchy or, more frequently, bring in new men to guarantee the honest and efficient administration with which they were increasingly concerned. But normally the key figure was the steward or agent, and in the nineteenth century his calling was elevated to the status of a profession. The high farming and the expensive schemes of improvement undertaken in mid-century grew not only from economic necessity, following the loss of protection, but as well from new, or rather newly diffused, ways of assessing the imperatives and opportunities of an essentially capitalistic enterprise. It is no criticism of reformed estate management that returns on the vast capital outlay in mid-century agriculture were small, compared to the profits that could be made in commerce and industry; few men at the time would have questioned the superior social and political advantages that attached to landed income. But had the transition to professional management not taken place—as the fate of less progressive estates showed—the shift from a relative to an absolute decline in landed fortunes might have set in without an agricultural depression.

Important as improved estate management was, most landed gentlemen in Victorian times were probably more directly interested in developments in sport, which has a unique symbolic value for historians. Racing was a distinctively aristocratic pastime, but one in which participation was vicarious, as owner, patron, or spectator. The active sports in which gentlemen themselves engaged were hunting and shooting—the mounted pursuit of the fox and the stalking of wild game, game birds in particular. In the eighteenth century, the aristocratic monopoly of these sports was asserted in a series of game laws, which provided for increasingly severe penalties against the poachers who took game illegally. Sentences of death and transportation and barbarous protective devices (still to be seen in local museums), like the mantrap and the spring gun, fell to the tide of humanitarian concern in the nineteenth century; but they were also made less necessary by the better organization of game preserving. More and more land was devoted to private "parks," in which game was carefully nurtured by professional gamekeepers.

A true enthusiast devoted a large part of his income to keep up the apparatus of sport, and even less enthusiastic sportsmen felt it socially (or politically) necessary to contribute handsomely to the upkeep of the hounds belonging to the local hunt. Maintaining a stable was so expensive that only gentlemen could afford it, and it needed a very rich man to support an entire hunt alone. By the early nineteenth century, the country had been divided up into the territories of particular hunts, which more and more came to be financed by subscription. This practice allowed a certain democratization of the sport, and hunting became a means for binding together nearly everyone in rural society above the rank of laborers; even some city dwellers were able to take part. Shooting, on the other hand, because it required parks and gamekeepers, was more likely to be confined to gentlemen and their guests. With them, shooting—involving the slaughter of thousands of birds, rabbits, and hares, often in a single week or weekend—at times seemed to border on a mania. To farmers worried about their crops or their animals, a game-preserving landlord or an enthusiastic huntsman could be a severe trial; but, despite the efforts of the Anti-Corn-Law League to use the issue as a wedge to separate farmers from landlords on protection, it was not until 1881 that farmers got the legal right to destroy rabbits or birds on their land without permission from the landlord. To the rural laborer, however, game preservation provided its peculiar satisfactions in the challenge offered by the gamekeeper to a casual or even quasi-professional commitment to the art of poaching.*

Gentlemen could be found at any time, perhaps increasingly from the forties, who grumbled about the high cost of living and being caught in what we would call an inflationary pinch. By the end of the century, the reality of that pinch was not in question. The costs of servants and of the newly important process of educating children at public schools were perhaps the most significant items of expenditure that made the decline in landed income so painful. The depression pushed further the need for diversification and the quest for additional and restorative sources of income, whether company directorships or American brides. Even so, the parlous state of agriculture, declining land prices, death duties, and reform in national

---

*Fox-hunting was essentially a creation of the late eighteenth century, as were the many myths associated with it; the organization and prosperity of hunting were profoundly affected by the coming of the railway and, later, by the agricultural depression.

and local government helped, for all but the most fortunate, to make landed estates into liabilities in the twentieth century. Between 1909 and 1921 more than a quarter of English land was sold, a transfer of a size, as one historian has remarked, not seen since the dissolution of the monasteries in the sixteenth century; much of the land thus passed from the great landlords to their tenants. The holders of fortunes made in commerce and industry have continued to draw their income from those much more profitable sources and have looked on their country houses — with or without large acreage — merely as a way of escaping from town. In recent decades few have found it profitable or even satisfying to invest in a great estate in the sense in which the early nineteenth century would have understood such an investment, as a source of income and political power.

The agricultural depression and subsequent economic and political developments did not destroy the aristocracy. The proportion of the House of Commons drawn from landed families shrank from at least three-quarters in the 1840's, to two-thirds in 1868, to half in 1886, and then drastically to about a tenth in the years just before 1914. But at the very center of politics, in the Cabinet, the aristocracy remained disproportionately important right down to the First World War, and they still retain enormous social prestige. In more recent years, aristocrats who have attained importance have done so, not because of pedigree, but because they have brought personal qualities and training to their task that English society rightly or wrongly has thought relevant to its broader needs: they are no longer automatically the governors of England. The old aristocracy, central to an understanding of the nineteenth century, have since 1901, certainly since 1914, been as tangential to English society as the snobbish magazines (in which they still figure largely) are to modern English culture.

Trade and Industry

However much their relative social position may have improved, and despite the general rise in both comfort and display, many late-Victorian businessmen found the economic outlook less than encouraging. The "great depression in trade and industry," conventionally dated between 1873 and 1896, presented problems as fascinating and as ambiguous to contemporaries as they are to modern economic historians. We know now, and the wisest economists knew it then, that there was no depression in the sense of a general contraction of the economy like that of the 1930's. The late-Victorian economy had its cyclical ups and downs, and some of the troughs were severe indeed; but over the long term, British industry increased both its production and its efficiency. What was especially disturbing was the general downward movement of prices and profits. These two facts nearly involve us in a pun: the Great Depression was a crisis of confidence, a spreading sense of unease, a depression in the morale of the business community.

Contemporary efforts to account for these price movements dealt at length with the banking and monetary systems, the latter explanation receiving some color of authenticity when the upturn in the economy after 1896 coincided with the sudden increase in the gold supply from South Africa and North America. But what impressed most people was the invasion of the home market by foreign competition. The rapidly increasing British dependence on imported manufactures was brought home to the man in the street by an act of 1887 requiring that the country of origin be indicated on all imported goods; suddenly Britain seemed deluged, and in 1896 an alarmist book called *Made in Germany* became a best seller. It was easy to answer these fears by pointing out that a prosperous country inevitably increases its imports, but such an argument could not gloss over the more profound effects of competition from other countries for the export markets by which Britain lived.

For most of a century, Britain had been the major exporter of manufactured goods to a world clamoring for them; characteristically and profitably, her manufactures were the simple basic needs of backward, agricultural or incipiently industrial countries: cloth, iron, hardware, steam engines and railway equipment; by all odds the largest volume was in cotton textiles. Britain was committed to a large and even dangerous degree to those staple manufactures that other countries could make as well or better once they industrialized. At the same time, by exporting machinery, men, and capital, Britain was helping other countries to undertake this very transition to industrialism. But while the new industrial countries, barricaded behind tariffs, improved their basic industries and branched out into newer forms of manufacture, Britain fell far behind in the rate at which her output and efficiency increased, both in the older staples and even in some of the newer industries. While the Great Depression saw the consolidation of the British electrical and chemical industries, in the older manufactures Britain's competitors were able to exploit more effectively than Britain could the growing link between science and industry; they often had the advantage of greater adaptability, superior design, and better technological education.

France and Belgium were serious competitors for railway contracts almost from the beginning, and American machine makers were early giving the British a run for other countries' money. In the last two decades of the century, American industrial production far outstripped Britain's; by 1896, British steel output was less than that of either the United States or Germany. It was not that the British economy did not grow, but that other economies grew faster; hence Britain suffered a relative decline. Much American and German production was absorbed at home, but increasingly these countries broke into export markets that the British had once had virtually to themselves.

Tougher competition in the export trade was one indication that Britain was losing the monopoly she had held temporarily by the simple reason of her priority as an industrial country. Falling prices and profits in the home market likewise have a natural explanation. Successful pioneers, when the foundations of an industrial economy are being laid, often make abnormally high profits; the extreme example is surely the return of 100 per cent every two months on the original investment in Henry Bessemer's steelmaking enterprise in the sixties. By the seventies, however, the basic equipment of British industry was complete. The railway network, save for one unprofitable stretch of main line, was finished, and by the mid-eighties the railways had made the transition from iron to steel, the last important innovation in the industry before the start of electrification in the twentieth century. The opening of the big steel complexes around Cleveland on the northeast coast and Barrow on the northwest coast was the last large geographical displacement of industry to the north in search of raw materials. Thereafter, ease of transport allowed industry to look southward to pleasanter surroundings and proximity to the metropolitan market. Increasing efficiency, the elaboration of products, the growth of competition, the saturation of markets all led to lower prices and profits. In short, the late-Victorian economy had entered its maturity and required from its masters a revised level of expectation.

In this changed context, British industry began to take on its modern appearance. In the first half of the century, most industry — cotton being the notable exception — was still organized on a small scale, usually too small for the meaningful application of our understanding of the word *factory*. In the later nineteenth century, the size of industrial and commercial enterprises grew rapidly, in numbers of workers and amounts of capital. Eventually, such firms turned to procedures made available earlier in the century but largely ignored: easy incorporation under the act of 1844 and the grant of limited liability in 1856. The family firm had once been as jealously guarded by its proprietors as a landlord, by strict settlement, protected his estate for his heirs. Family control was workable even for quite large operations, and in 1885 no more than 10 per cent of large firms — mostly in cotton, iron and steel, and shipping — had taken advantage of limited liability. But in time the resources of a family, a partnership, or even a locality were outgrown. Experience with the railways had accustomed the public to the idea of investing in industry, and in the last years of the old century and the early years of the new, one after another company "went public."

At the same time, important factors were working against as complete a modernization of industry as the country's situation, in retrospect at least, seemed to demand. Temporary brief recoveries before 1896 and the general economic upswing thereafter seemed to hold out the possibility of salvation without much sacrifice. When the United States and Germany invaded old markets, Britain, because of her extensive capital investment, could still find new ones, in her growing Empire or outside it; thus export of capital to Australia and (in the nineties) to Argentina helped to renew demand for the old staples. In some cases, thanks to superior quality or simply to the magnitude of importers' needs, Britain could even break into tariff-protected markets. Perhaps British industrialists too easily accepted the victory of their competitors and the inevitability of falling prices and profits: not at all eager to meet the challenge head-on, many of them agitated for the abandonment of free trade.

It has been widely accepted that the persistence of family management and the marked tendency of successful British businessmen to raise their sons to traditional aristrocratic expectations in leisure, culture, and public service eroded the aggressiveness that had helped Britain to sweep the world during the Industrial Revolution. Historians have also pointed to the long-lamented backwardness of British industrial design and the deficiency of British technological education, to the lack of opportunity that led many skilled workers and technicians to emigrate, and to the challenges abroad that attracted some of the most famous British entrepreneurs, like Cecil Rhodes or Barney Barnato, who dominated the economy of South Africa. It is easy to discover examples of firms in which later generations failed to maintain the momentum of the founders or to find evidence for the slow improvement in Britain's performance compared to other industrial nations. A still-growing population provided a ready supply of labor; it was often cheaper, when demand rose, to increase output by using more workers than it was to invest in expensive though ultimately rewarding labor-saving machinery. Moreover, the British labor movement, organized earlier than elsewhere, could better resist mechanization and new methods, often compounding the failings of indolent or conservative management.

It now seems increasingly doubtful that these depressing conclusions are as widely applicable to the late-Victorian economy as has been thought. Even in the traditional heavy industries, we seem to have overestimated the performance of earlier generations, by concentrating on atypical examples, and to have overlooked the extent to which late-Victorian entrepreneurs (who lacked our hindsight) responded rationally and imaginatively to controlling circumstances. Just as late nineteenth-century agriculture, seen broadly, appears more prosperous than when one's perspective is confined to grain growing, so what was happening in many sectors outside the older industries helps further to modify the notion that some vast inheritance of entrepreneurial skill had been frittered away. One new set of industries catered to demands engendered by a rising standard of living: food processing, home products, soap, boots and shoes, patent medicines, newspapers and magazines. Another set of industries was developing the modern forms of retailing; it is in this period that department stores and the multiple stores, or chain stores, in the clothing, food, and drug trades make their first appearance. Small shopkeepers have survived in modern Britain far more successfully than have their analogues in the United States; from the late-Victorian period, however, they no longer monopolized the distribution of goods but were facing instead the growing efficiency and ultimately lethal competition of the giant retail firms. Professor Wilson has estimated that, leaving aside textiles, engineering, and the capital goods industries, these growing sectors in the economy accounted in the early twentieth century for a third of the gross output of British manufacturing and employed a quarter of the labor force. They were also able to call on the best available managerial talent to carry through an economic revolution based not on striking technological innovation, but on steadily improving organization and efficiency.*

One more point needs to be made, because it explains how a relatively declining economy could support itself in increasing splendor, and because it helps one to understand the economic problems of the twentieth century. As we have seen, British capital went readily abroad; profits from that capital, together with the income from other services like shipping and insurance (the so-called "invisible exports") helped to pay for British imports, the costs of which were never entirely covered by the mere export of goods. In the last quarter of the century and the first years of the new, the investment of capital abroad rose to extraordinary heights: it has been estimated that to equal the British rate of overseas investment in 1913, American overseas investment in the early 1950's would have had to be

*Charles Wilson, "Economy and Society in Late Victorian Britain," *Economic History Review*, 2nd ser., XVIII, 183–198 (August, 1965), reprinted in Wilson's *Economic History and the Historian: Collected Essays* (1969), pp. 178–200.

thirty times as large as it actually was—equivalent to carrying out the Marshall Plan twice each year.* The widening gap between exports and imports in the late nineteenth century was even more effectively filled than had been the case earlier in the century by the yield from investment. It helped too that so much of Britain's foreign investment was in fixed-interest securities, which brought steady returns when (until the very end of the century) prices and profits were generally declining.

Britain's most important resource was the East. Taking visible and invisible exports together, it has been estimated that by 1910 nearly half of the British deficits in international trade were paid for by receipts from India alone, a feat which India managed to sustain by selling food and raw materials to other countries. The importance of invisibles in the accounting is indicated by the estimate that in 1864–1873 about 12 per cent of Britain's foreign trade consisted of imports paid for by invisible exports, while the percentage rose to nearly 24 per cent by the turn of the century; then, as exports and export prices rose in the early twentieth-century boom, the percentage dropped back to 15 per cent for 1904–1913. Clearly, in a situation like this, British prosperity depended heavily on a complaisant Empire and on a peaceful world in which trade and capital flowed easily and whose center remained in that delicate complex of brokers, banks, merchant houses, and insurance and shipping companies in the City of London.

THE LABOR MOVEMENT

Conditions of Life

The years of the Great Depression, in which the modern British economy began to emerge, also witnessed the creation of the main characteristics of the labor movement which has done so much to shape twentieth-century Britain. Owenite and Chartist forms and ideals were now little more than a traditional memory; the point of departure was, rather, the New Model Unionism that had struck such firm roots in the prosperous decades of mid-century.† The fortunes of the late-Victorian economy provided a set of circumstances that allowed British labor to develop quickly, in both institutions and tactics.

The population of Great Britain rose from about 26 million in

---

*A. K. Cairncross, *Home and Foreign Investment, 1870–1913* (1953), p. 3. On the export of capital earlier in the century, see above, pp. 288–289.
†See above, pp. 290–292.

1871 to some 37 million thirty years later; only in the twentieth century did the rate of increase from census to census drop significantly below nineteenth-century percentages. But the Malthusian fears of the early part of the century were little in evidence. In the long view, the late-Victorian economy was capable of supporting most of that growing population in steadily improving conditions. Two generations of effort, in central and local government and among private individuals, had vindicated the "sanitary idea" of Chadwick and Southwood Smith. There were still many bad, unsanitary towns, where local authorities did the minimum required by law or less, and where local conditions or the nature of industry presented sanitary problems beyond the ingenuity or willingness of government; while even in improved towns there were bound to be districts that pulled down the general level. But the degree of success was reflected in the steady drop of the death rate from a level of between 20 and 25 per 1,000 in mid-century to about 15 in the early years of the twentieth century, a decline that would have been still more striking had not the rate of infant mortality stubbornly resisted medical and sanitary efforts at least until 1900. Even London conformed quite closely to the national average; it was less of a killer than it had once been or than other great cities in the world still were, owing partly to metropolitan improvements and partly to the decentralization of the city. In contrast to the Continent, the English preferred single-family row houses to vertical blocks of flats. London sprawled in all directions, and by the end of the century cheap public transportation made it possible even for relatively poor workers to live at a distance from their workplaces.

The provision of housing varied through the country. Many too small and noisome houses survived because slums made of stone and brick were more durable than the wooden warrens of American cities. But again there was improvement, distinctly measurable by the standards of fifty years before, however inadequate it may seem when we see such "improved" housing today in the grimy, depressing back streets of a provincial factory town, where the bombings of 1941 and after could seem a blessing.*

The state was educating all working-class children, without fees for anyone after 1891, at least in the rudiments, and a vast industry of

---

*Fifty years of experimentation and research went into this sanitary success. In other areas, knowledge was less advanced. The working-class diet, for example, seems to have deteriorated in some respects. Regulation was protecting people from the worst forms of adulteration so common in mid-century, but roller-ground flour, which had superseded stone-ground flour, and cheap tinned milk compounded the evil of distrust felt by poorer people for vegetables and fruits. The importance of vitamins and minerals in the diet was simply not known.

cheap and, on the whole, innocent papers and publications had come
into existence to cater to the new habit of reading. The old and often
brutal traditional pastimes had pretty much disappeared by the middle of the century. Racing, for which workingmen shared a taste with
the aristocracy, had been reformed and cleaned up, and railways
made the racecourses easily and cheaply accessible. Professional
football (soccer), which grew rapidly after the sixties, was a new enthusiasm. Music halls, workingmen's clubs, and libraries offered
ways to escape from cramped houses or monotonous factories; and
the national vice of drunkenness, though still evident enough, was
declining under the combined pressures of raised standards, the
temperance movement, and successive licensing acts. From the fifties, there had also been a concerted effort to prevent open spaces
and common land from being built over and to promote the building
of new parks.*

The long-range improvement in health, housing, and amenities
was paralleled by the movement of wages. The pattern of money
wages necessarily varied from one industry or one area to another.
They rose and fell with the short-term fluctuations of the economy,
and incomes were certainly adversely affected by sharp, temporary
rises in unemployment in 1879, 1886, and 1893. But the over-all record of money wages in these years was one of remarkable stability;
together with the fairly steady fall in prices, that meant a rise in real
wages, that is, in wages seen not as a quantity of money but as the
amount of goods that could be bought with them. Clapham estimated that a man in 1900 would be making 50 per cent more, in real
terms, than a man in a similar job in 1850, and suggested further that
the improvement might run to 75 per cent, if one takes into account
the undoubted fact that the younger generation frequently went into
better paying lines of work than their fathers.

Working-class women had less need to work, yet the opportunities for women in industry, except perhaps in the brief periods of
depressed trade and high unemployment, were more numerous, easier, and pleasanter, with the expansion and diversification of light
industry, such as hardware, clothing, and food processing. Heavy
work for women had all but disappeared, even in agriculture, where
gang labor, so dependent on women and children, had faded away
after exposure of its abuses in the sixties. Domestic service, of course,
remained the largest occupation for women, but the comparative lack

---

*The growth of the cheap press has been the cause of much lamentation
among those who see literacy primarily as an engine for culture improvement rather than a means of entertainment. Certainly the popular papers
were characterized by sentimentalism, prejudice, and sensationalism.

of freedom it entailed was reducing the number of young women who went into it early in the new century. This shift away from domestic service was encouraged by the gradual opening up of a whole new level of occupations, in offices and the retail trades, for women as well as men. While clerks and shop assistants before the First World War came largely from the lower middle classes, perhaps the sons and daughters of men who were clerks already, it was not long before they began to come from working-class families inching up the social scale.

The New Unionism

It might seem at first sight as though a growing and diffusing prosperity would weaken the impulse underlying working-class movements: why make a concerted effort to better oneself, when things were getting better without it? There are several convincing explanations of this apparent paradox. In the first place, workers responded not to improvements taking place over a generation but to such questions as the size of their pay packets, the hours they had to work, where they had to spend them, who told them what to do and how; and their conclusions about these matters were deeply affected by local and personal considerations, such as a threatened custom or a harsh employer. Short-term fluctuations in the economy were felt at once and long-term improvements are easier for us to see than they were for contemporaries who too often knew poverty and insecurity at first hand. If the management of a firm sought to meet a decline in orders or the steady drop in prices by the perfectly intelligible remedies of cutting wages or lengthening hours, it was likely to meet resistance from workers who had attained what seemed to them a rightful level and who suspected the motives for tampering with it.

Secondly, the nature of work was changing. In the earlier stages of industrialization, factory work as often as not required of workers skills and flexibility that made them difficult to replace and gave them a sense of pride. The growth of factory organization, the division of labor, the continuing spread of mechanization, though as always it called new skills into existence, depreciated some of the older skills, making the threat of dilution (and strikebreaking) easier. At the same time, the increasing size of firms submerged the old, relatively easygoing workshop in the large factory: what had once characterized cotton almost exclusively came to apply to more and more kinds of industry. With this growing impersonality came the techniques of American scientific management, which interfered or threatened to interfere with traditional ways of doing things. New grievances were added, then, to those old complaints that had been lessened but by no means eliminated: insecurity, the danger of accident, the lack of decency and amenities.*

Thirdly, long-term improvement raised standards of expectation and strengthened the desire to share in a prosperity whose benefits seemed to go largely to capitalists and employers. This pressure of prosperity functioned the more effectively in those trades where there were unions with the resources and experience to fight, if necessary. Working hours provide a good illustration. The state had intervened increasingly from the 1830's to limit the hours of children and women in certain industries; such intervention indirectly limited the hours of work of adult men, whom early Victorian theorists persisted in regarding as free agents able to contract rationally for themselves and on an equal footing with employers. By the seventies, most important and organized trades had secured a working week of about 55 hours; some factories outside the textile trades ran it up to 60 hours; and a few very well-placed or favored trades got down to 50 or less. In general, workers managed to maintain these gains throughout the late-Victorian period, in spite of pressure from managements whose profit margins were shrinking. By the eighties the eight-hour day was becoming a standard trade-union goal, and some trades actually got it; it was not until 1908 that the Liberal government gave it to the miners, and only in the twenties did it become general. A similar illustration of the impact of strong unions could be drawn from the history of wage negotiations; one need only consider the disadvantages suffered by the poorly organized woolen workers compared to the well-organized cotton workers.

Fourthly, prosperity could lead to the desire not merely to increase one's own share, but to share it with others less fortunate. Here public sympathy was more likely to be enlisted than for more narrowly trade union aims that could easily seem grasping or presumptuous to men who still believed that servants had their place.

The possibility of public and administrative sympathy was increased in these years by some striking revelations of the extent of poverty and degradation. In 1886 a wealthy Liverpool shipowner, Charles Booth, organized an elaborate survey of the East End of London, where the working population of the metropolis mainly lived. Booth's seventeen volumes, the last of which appeared in 1903, demonstrated conclusively that, even by a minimal criterion, some 30 per cent of London's population was living in a state that could rightly be

---

*Enlightened employers were doing much in these years to provide pleasant factories and model towns and to promote in other ways the welfare of their employees; but these moves for "industrial betterment" were more exceptional than they have become today.

called poverty. These poor people were not trade unionists and skilled laborers, but the unorganized men and women in sweated industries, casual workers, and the unemployed or unemployable. Booth's depressing conclusions were paralleled by an extensive survey conducted early in the new century by the son of a great family of chocolate manufacturers, B. Seebohm Rowntree, in his native city of York. Rowntree found 28 per cent of York's population receiving an income insufficient to satisfy the barest physical needs, a proportion that rose to 43 per cent of the working population alone. These inquiries, of the first importance in the history of empirical social investigation, were confirmed by other investigators in other places and shook British consciences deeply. That they did so may suggest that philanthropists and administrators, as well as visionaries, were questioning an old assumption. Poverty had once been accepted as a decree of nature; now an expanding economy and better techniques of social control raised the expectation that poverty could and must be eliminated.

It is against this background of new problems, raised expectations, stirred consciences, and continuing misery that we must place trade union developments in the late-Victorian era. Confined, for the most part, to craftsmen in the highly skilled trades, the older New Model unions relied heavily on friendly-society benefits to maintain their existence. Strikes were rare, and the caution and eminent soundness of union leaders did much to weaken the prejudices of middle- and upper-class politicians on whose good will the legislative security of British trade unionism had to rest.

The slump of the mid-sixties and the gradual recovery into the boom of the early seventies stimulated a new interest in unionism. Among the engineers, whose amalgamated union had been the prototype of the New Model, a local strike in the northeast gained the nine-hour day, an example followed by other local engineering groups and by a revived and successful agitation among the builders who had been so thoroughly defeated when they sought that goal in 1859. The revival also struck root in those parts of industry whose workers had been unable to bring quite such firm organizations out of defeats earlier in the century, as the "aristocrats" of the New Model unions had done. These workers Professor Phelps Brown distinguishes as "operatives"—miners, textile workers, railwaymen, and others whose jobs involved some skills, but not of the order required in the apprentice-based crafts of engineers, builders, and printers. These operative efforts were not uniformly successful. In the woolen industry, almost completely unorganized since the thirties, the General Union of Textile Workers appeared in the seventies, but, hurt by a chronic excess of labor, unionism made almost no headway in the

woolen districts before the First World War. The railway workers
kept their unions alive, but the companies steadily refused to recognize them. On the other hand, the miners brought their regional associations together into the Miners' Federation in 1888, which had
over 200,000 members in the early nineties; the remarkable progress
of the miners was symbolized early by their sending two of their
number into Parliament in 1874. The gas stokers were perhaps the
most dramatically successful of all the operatives, for from a defeat
and savage prosecutions in 1870 they rose as the Gasworkers and
General Laborers' Union in 1889 to win the eight-hour day from most
employers without a strike.

The operatives, then, led the revolution known as the "new
unionism" of the eighties, but the newness that most impressed the
general public was the further extension of agitation to the unskilled
workers. In the early seventies there were some temporarily successful unions of agricultural laborers under the leadership of Joseph
Arch, but for the most part unskilled "general" laborers seemed too
poor or ill-educated or apathetic to make a union work. In the
eighties that situation changed, with the help of men from other already established unions or from the middle classes. In 1888, a few
hundred London matchgirls came out in a brief strike against the terrible conditions in which they had to work; they were inspired by an
article written by a colorful radical, at that time in the Fabian Society,
Mrs. Annie Besant, who also helped to raise money for them. In the
next year the gasworkers' victory stimulated a strike in the London
Docks. There the stevedores, trained and well-organized operatives,
came to the aid of the miserably poor dockers, who, because they
depended on casual employment, formed an uncomfortably large
proportion of Charles Booth's statistics. The leadership was taken by
Ben Tillett, a docker who had organized the Tea Operatives' and
General Laborers' Union two years earlier, and by two socialist engineers, Tom Mann and John Burns. The dockers enlisted wide public
sympathy and built up a strike fund of £50,000, heavily aided by contributions from Australian laboring men. Cardinal Manning, the
head of England's Roman Catholics, was one of the mediators in negotiations that ended in an almost complete victory for the men; their
demands were for a minimum wage of sixpence an hour ("the
dockers' tanner"), minimum casual employment of at least four
hours, and overtime pay.

In these years, then, were born the "general unions," drawing
on the unskilled or less skilled workers whom earlier union efforts
had missed or excluded; by the nineties unions were beginning to
spread even among lower-middle-class clerks and shop assistants.
But these general unions accounted for only a small part of organized

labor at the end of the century; numbers and force lay with the unions of operatives, who were making important inroads in the nineties on the leadership and policy of the Trades Union Congress, the labor parliament founded in 1868 at the height of the Junta's influence. By 1900, in spite of many vicissitudes, the trade unions could claim around two million members, perhaps a quarter of the adult male manual workers in the country.

British unionists preferred occupational divisions to industry-wide organization and remained generally loyal to the practice of collective bargaining. In the last half of the century there was considerable experimentation with other industrial machinery. Joint boards of conciliation and arbitration became popular, and in the iron and coal industries a novel and imaginative "sliding scale" became standard; a means of tying wages to prices of the final product, the sliding scale was welcome to employers in a period of falling prices, a circumstance the workers had not foreseen when they proposed it. But the experiments were wrecked by trade depression and a new militancy, and the British system of industrial relations returned to the old forms in which it still largely operates.

The new trade-union leadership looked beyond immediate trade objectives to the collectivization of industry and land. This was a new turn, for the Junta and the older leaders had pretty much accepted the assumptions of classical political economy — just at the time when the economists themselves were beginning to reject them. The stimuli to these new working-class socialists were, as they had been for the Owenites, moral and emotional: a demand for social justice, for a good life, and for the elimination of the tyranny of competition and profits. Undogmatic and very English, these men were the objects of considerable attention from little bands of socialist intellectuals, who provided the forms into which these moral ambitions were poured and much of the rhetoric as well. The main origins of the modern socialist movement must be sought, then, in the middle classes.

Socialism

The first prominent socialist was an unlikely one. H. M. Hyndman was a Cambridge graduate, the son of a family whose fortunes came from West Indian estates; he supported himself and his agitation by some highly speculative and moderately profitable mining and stock-jobbing enterprises. Throughout his life he remained a nationalist and an imperialist; he began his writing career as a radical Tory. His conversion was brought about by two experiences: study of the place of India in the British economy, which turned him into a life-long foe of British exploitation there, and a reading of Karl Marx's *Das Kapital* (in a French translation) during a business trip to America. In 1881, he organized the Democratic Federation to work for a general radical reform; as the self-appointed apostle of Marx, he distributed to the delegates at the first meeting copies of his book *England for All*, which gave the first extended English account of Marxian economic theories.

Late in the same year, Henry George, the American advocate of the single tax, went to Ireland to lecture. His system rested on an old Ricardian observation: that good land, through the bounty of nature, produced at a cost well below the market price, which was determined by poorer land. George went on to argue that the "unearned increment," unjustly taken by landlords as rent, should be subjected to a confiscatory tax, which would not only redress injustice but make other taxation unnecessary. A doctrine of land reform could be logically, but not safely, preached in Ireland in 1881, and when the government banned George under the Coercion Act, he carried his message to England; he made a triumphal second visit in 1884. His large audiences were composed of men seeking a simple explanation of England's social and economic predicaments. Marx's theory of surplus value, of course, went far beyond George by taking into its sweep the entire industrial system, perhaps the more persuasively since the agricultural depression was rapidly undermining the economic position of the landed classes. Hyndman was in close touch with George and debated publicly with him.

The appeal of such nostrums attracted a number of young men, rather like Hyndman, into the Democratic Federation; by 1884, the weekly *Justice* had begun to appear, and the organization, now the Social Democratic Federation (SDF), became openly Marxist. In 1885 it nearly came to an end in universal scorn, when Hyndman allowed two SDF candidates in the general election to be helped to fight the hopelessly middle-class constituencies of Hampstead and Kennington by "Tory gold," pumped in modestly and quietly by a Conservative agent to split the Liberal vote. The sharp recession of 1886 rescued the SDF. On February 8, 1886 — "Black Monday" — they were confident enough to organize a counterdemonstration of the unemployed in Trafalgar Square, where neo-Protectionists were holding a rally for "fair trade"; after adopting some resolutions, a motley crowd straggled west to Hyde Park, with John Burns in the lead, carrying a small red flag. It was a rather paltry riot: windows in some Pall Mall clubs were broken and some of the rowdy hangers-on took to looting shops, but the marchers quietly broke up their procession at Hyde Park when the police asked them to, though troubles continued, more seriously, over the two days following. Hyndman, Burns, and two other leaders were arrested, tried for sedition, and acquitted. More demonstrations followed, climaxed in November, 1887, by a huge rally, drawing on much more than the meager resources of the SDF, held to protest a police ban on Trafalgar Square meetings; it ended in violence and with the jailing of Burns and R. B. Cunninghame Graham, a radical M.P. who had lately turned socialist.

The Trafalgar Square demonstrations were the high point of SDF influence. The middle-class and working-class radicals in the original body had long since left, unable to stomach the increasing doses of Marxism and Hyndman's dictatorial nature. On the other hand, Marx and Engels looked on Hyndman with contempt or worse, partly because he struck them as merely an ambitious and inept Tory renegade, partly, perhaps mainly, because in *England for All* Hyndman, while praising "a great thinker and original writer," had failed to mention Marx by name. After Marx's death in 1883, Marx's daughter and her husband carried on the vendetta, working for a time through members of the SDF sympathetic to them and later, when their allies withdrew, by continual denigration and intrigue.

More serious was the defection in 1885 of a small group whose chief luminary was the poet and artist William Morris, who had turned to socialism under the influence of the powerful denunciations of the economic system and political economy in the social writings of the art critic John Ruskin.* Morris and his friends formed the Socialist League, which soon fell under the influence of Continental anarchists living in London and quickly — and appropriately– disintegrated. After Black Monday, Hyndman's growing interest in violence, a course the police had shown to be futile, alienated an ex-army officer, H. H. Champion, who had been Hyndman's chief lieutenant, and as well two workingmen, John Burns and Tom Mann; after the break became final in 1888, the three defectors were primarily responsible for carrying socialist influence into the Dockers' Strike in 1889. Some new recruits came into the SDF from the New Unionism, and Hyndman remained active to the end of his life, but after the eighties the SDF was no more than a small sect on the left wing of the labor movement.†

The most important of the socialist groups of the eighties was the Fabian Society, founded in 1884. A colorful and imposing band of men and women, the early Fabians reflected an extraordinary diversity of views, with little more in common than a growing dissatisfaction with the various strands of the Radical tradition, to which

*Ruskin's main works of social criticism were *Unto This Last* (1862) and *Fors Clavigera* (1871–1884).
†The SDF survived until the Second World War.

they were all deeply indebted. Some, fired by moral and mystical preoccupations, found their way into Fabianism from an earlier group called the Fellowship of the New Life. Bernard Shaw, a young, poor, failed Irish writer and an instant convert to the doctrines of Henry George, came to the Fabians after dabbling in several varieties of socialism and anarchism, which appealed to his rebellious individualism. Sidney Webb, a promising civil servant of lower-middle-class origins, had moved from his family's radical liberalism to positivism, that skeptical "religion of humanity" adopted by the English disciples of Auguste Comte. He married a fellow-Fabian, Beatrice Potter, a devout Anglican, the daughter of a wealthy, radical manufacturing family in Lancashire, who had worked as one of Charles Booth's assistants in his survey of London poverty; as a team the Webbs produced a remarkable series of historical and theoretical works that undergirded Fabian doctrine, from the influential *History of Trade Unionism* of 1894 to the multi-volumed history of local government in the 1920's and 1930's. By 1889, when the *Fabian Essays* appeared, this disparate group of enthusiasts had come together in a new faith in collectivism, which was to be the Fabians' principal theoretical legacy to the Socialist and Labour movements in Britain.

The feature that most strikingly set the Fabians apart from the Marxians and most other socialists was their firm belief in gradualism: the new society had to be created not through cataclysm or revolution but step by step through careful planning and ingenious tactics.* The Fabians' method was perfectly suited to British prejudices, however unpalatable their belief in the ultimate victory of public ownership and state control seemed to most of their contemporaries. The keynote of their strategy was permeation—working in local government (as Sidney Webb did, among others), serving on royal commissions, buttonholing and convincing politicians and civil servants. Though they accomplished much in generating and encouraging opinion in important places, the Fabians' political judgment was often askew; and the central streak of authoritarianism in the Webbs' outlook drove out some of the Society's early adherents—among them, the political scientist Graham Wallas and the writer H. G. Wells. For nearly a couple of decades now, historians have been painstakingly re-evaluating the Fabians, in an attempt to see them as they were and not as they persuaded a couple of generations they were. Yet, however imperfect their actual accomplishment, however

---

*The name "Fabian" is explained in a motto on the title page of the first *Fabian Tract:* "For the right moment you must wait, as Fabius [a Roman general] did, most patiently, when warring against Hannibal, though many censured his delays; but when the time comes you must strike hard, as Fabius did, or your waiting will be in vain, and fruitless."

much credit must be shared with others, no single group of thinkers and writers did more to create the climate of opinion in which the forms of twentieth-century British collectivism developed.*

Labor Politics

While the Fabians' pragmatism appealed to one persistent English prejudice, their coolness to the formation of a separate socialist or labor party ran counter to another prejudice that was particularly strong in the ranks of labor. Their aloofness, more evident in practice than in theory, was in part a question of timing — whether working-men were yet ready for concerted political action — and it also allowed them to permeate Liberals and Conservatives as well. Ultimately, the Fabians not only accepted the necessity of a labor party but virtually took over its policymaking. They were not, however, a major practical force in its early history.

English labor movements, as we have seen, have always gravitated towards parliamentary action, because it was sometimes necessary to accomplish specific trade-union or other working-class goals and because Parliament loomed so large in English life. Cobbett, O'Connor, and others had spoken for the working classes at Westminster, but no real workingman had sat in the reformed Parliament. It was not for want of trying. William Newton of the Amalgamated Society of Engineers stood for Tower Hamlets in 1852, and there were other candidacies of equal unsuccess. The Junta tried to do something about it, through the new London Working Men's Association and then through the Labor Representation League (LRL) in the late sixties. The first workingmen to enter the Commons were two miners, Thomas Burt and Alexander MacDonald, the only successful candidates of thirteen labor aspirants in the general election of 1874. In 1880 they were joined by Henry Broadhurst, the secretary of the LRL.

It is important to note that at this time there was little intention to create a third, labor party; what the union leaders were trying to do was to get workingmen and trade unionists into the House to speak for their particular interests. Since the sentiment of working-class electors was overwhelmingly Liberal, it is not surprising that working-class candidates usually stood as Liberals. For thirty years, then, the "Lib-Labs" represented labor, and the importance of the al-

---

*G. K. Chesterton (in *The Victorian Age in Literature* [1913], p. 58) said that Beatrice Webb ordered the citizens of the state about as she might order her servants about the kitchen.

liance was recognized—there were eleven Lib-Labs (six of them miners) in 1885 and nine in 1886—by Broadhurst's being made undersecretary at the Home Office in the brief Gladstone government in 1886.

Lib-Labism was not, however, to the taste of the new union leaders of the eighties and nineties. Some of the socialists were frankly anti-parliamentary, and while this attitude did not affect many workingmen, the Liberal alliance did not seem the way to get what they wanted, the more so as most of the older generation of trade-union leaders, Liberals in more than name, were obstacles to a socialist program. This generational clash was made painfully clear in an assault on Broadhurst, who was also secretary of the parliamentary committee of the Trades Union Congress (TUC), at the annual meeting in 1887. The attack misfired, but two years later Broadhurst retired as secretary, and socialist influence began to grow rapidly in the TUC.

Broadhurst's attacker was James Keir Hardie, a Scot who as a boy had gone to work in the mines and who had early determined to do something to the system that had made his early life so miserable. He trained himself in oratory on temperance platforms and in evangelical preaching. Drawn into mining trade unions and influenced by Ruskin and Henry George, he failed to join the SDF only because he disliked clubs and the oratory he heard at SDF meetings. When he stood for a Scottish constituency in a bye-election in 1888, he refused all Liberal support; but the intervention of the London socialists, Champion and Mann in particular, did Hardie no good with the Scottish voters, and he got nowhere. Then, with Cunninghame Graham, he set about organizing a Scottish labor party. In the general election of 1892, still refusing official Liberal help but appealing to Liberal voters, Hardie was elected for the London constituency of West Ham, South, one of three independents to be returned; one of the others was John Burns.

Hardie made his first appearance at Westminster wearing tweeds and a worker's cloth cap instead of the customary formal dress; his enthusiastic supporters sent him to the House in a wagon with a trumpeter. But the shock that this innocent exhibitionism caused to the respectable was nothing compared to the alarm that arose from Hardie's self-conscious role as spokesman for his class; he refused to bow to the powerful traditions of the House, which had overawed other workingmen M.P.'s. The climax was reached in late June, 1894. On the day that the future King Edward VIII (and later Duke of Windsor) was born to the Duke and Duchess of York, 260 miners were killed in an explosion in South Wales; the next day, the President of France was assassinated. When the House received a motion to congratulate the Queen on the birth of her great-grandson and another to convey condolences to the French people, Hardie asked for a resolution of sympathy with the miners' families. The leader of the house, Sir William Harcourt, refused, casually expressing regret over the accident in a way that Hardie considered insulting; Hardie then spoke against the congratulatory motion to the Queen, causing an uproar in the House and denunciation in the papers, making it clear that such solemn proprieties were matters of class, for which he had scant respect. Passionate, powerful, proletarian in loyalty, and evangelical in style, he made a deeper impression on newly politically-conscious workingmen than could ever have been made by Champion, still very much the officer, or Hyndman, the elegantly dressed stockjobber, or the wittily intellectual Shaw, or the many former workingmen who, then or later, "went over" to respectability and the beguiling forms of English public behavior.

In 1893, at Bradford, the Independent Labour Party (ILP) was launched, despite a boycott by the SDF and the skepticism of the Fabians. Its program was frankly socialist: tax reform to redistribute the income of the rich; free education through the university; welfare provision for the unemployed, the disabled, and those unable to care for themselves; and collective ownership of all land, industry, and means of distribution and exchange. Though the ILP fared badly at the election of 1895, when even Hardie lost his seat, the conversion of the labor movement to socialism proceeded steadily, partly through the agency of the new unions, partly through the brilliant propaganda of publications like Robert Blatchford's influential *Clarion*. Perhaps most important of all the stimuli were the forces we have seen at work throughout the late-Victorian period—a growing and heightened awareness of how much needed to be done, and now could be done, in the realm of social justice, and a burning impatience with things as they were. In the event the ILP was not to be the main instrument of the labor cause, but it cried loudly and well in the wilderness.

A CHANGING MIDDLE-CLASS CULTURE

The Expansion of the Middle Class

The middle classes were the main beneficiaries of the changes in the last half of the nineteenth century. As we have seen, the Reform Act of 1832, which has so long stood in the textbooks as the crucial victory of that class, in actuality only whetted an appetite for a transfer of political power that was accomplished slowly between the municipal reforms of 1835 and the local government reforms of 1888. At the same time, reforms in schools and universities and the growth of professionalism allowed the middle classes in mid-century both to entrench themselves in the working parts of society from which the final assaults on the bastions of privilege could be safely and confidently made and, at the same time, to absorb so much from aristocratic culture that the victory was almost painless.*

Untouched by the agricultural depression, the middle classes came through the alleged depression in trade reasonably well. Some among the business community felt what Sir John Clapham has called "the chill and heavy air of Lombard Street," but its damage was more likely psychological than financial. While the matured economy no longer returned such high profits, by the same token it was no longer so obviously necessary to plow profits back; certainly there was more profit-taking in the late nineteenth century — however unfortunate that decision may have been to long-term British interests — and greater comfort and luxury. Beatrice Webb recalled that her parents, members of this very upper-middle class in mid-century, were rich but not given to display; she found the distinguishing characteristic of her class in their being accustomed to command and to be obeyed, a characteristic they shared with the aristocracy.† But display increased, and one can justly speak of "plutocracy" in the late nineteenth century.

But the middle classes extended far beyond the rich. They took in the intellectual aristocracy in the universities, professions, and arts; small merchants and manufacturers; the purveyors of the rapidly multiplying services in a ramifying prosperity; the new professions of engineers, nurses, accountants, and teachers; technicians like the draftsmen and bookkeepers; and the enormous range of clerkdom.‡ These less wealthy members of the middle classes also shared in improved housing, in new comforts and luxuries, in greater ease of travel — the Continent was becoming as familiar to the English middle classes as the seaside — and in wider opportunities to rise on the social scale. But the tone of this middle-class society was very different from that of its predecessors in early and mid-Victorian England. It was partly that they had arrived, and no longer had or needed the myths of a determined but excluded class; it was partly the breakdown of isolation, bringing with it an increased depen-

---

*For earlier stages in the growth of middle-class power in the nineteenth century, see above, pp. 222–228, 292–300.
†*My Apprenticeship* (1926), p. 37.
‡One pretentious and absurd but comfortable fictional representative of clerkdom is depicted in the comic classic *The Diary of a Nobody* (1892) by George and Weedon Grossmith.

dence of the provinces on London and a blurring of lines that had once kept even small provincial societies in quite distinct social and religious compartments. At the same time, the greater freedom of movement among the middle classes was accompanied by increasing isolation from the working classes, as those who could afford it moved farther out from the towns to the new dormitory suburbs.* Their sense of social responsibility correspondingly declined, helped downward by the knowledge that the state and corporate charity could look after those unfortunates whose lot their parents and grandparents had, however ineptly, tried to improve. But none of these complex and gradual changes had the impact of developments that were undermining the two main pillars of Victorian responsibility—the family and religion.

The Family

The sanctity of the family was the most fundamental belief of the early-Victorian middle classes. Stretching back into mysteries which social historians are only beginning to unravel, the ideal of the Victorian family in these years came remarkably close to reality. A middleclass family at the beginning of Victoria's reign was large; six to nine children were not at all uncommon, even allowing for almost inevitable infant deaths, and to that number were likely to be added grandparents, spinster aunts, orphaned cousins, and other dependents, including of course the servants. The family was still to a remarkable degree self-sufficient; clothes for women and children, for example, were usually made at home, within the family or by seamstresses. The family was also highly self-contained. Although well-to-do families even early in the century would travel great distances to visit (at length) other branches of the family, the minor comings and goings of a modern family were less frequent. In the early nineteenth century, families as a rule lived close to the father's business or shop, and the other main external focus of family life, the church or chapel, was never far away.

The inevitable centrifugal pressures of an increasingly popular industrial society slowly changed these characteristics. Victorian children in prosperous households were always held at a distance from their parents by that superior and genteel domestic, the govern-

---

*This flight to the suburbs, which still goes on, was facilitated by improved transportation by railway, bus, and, in London, the Underground. The first Underground railway was opened in the sixties, a circle line connecting the main-line railway stations. But in 1890 the first electric "tube" trains appeared, running outward.

ess, and always by the patriarchal aura surrounding the father. To some extent the father withdrew further. As families moved to the suburbs, the main meal was shifted from midday to early evening, and by the end of the century, in imitation of fashionable society, still later;* the rapid spread of men's clubs was a further distraction from the claims of the family. The falling away of Puritan distrust of the theater, better transportation, the multiplication of entertainment and games, wider opportunities of respectable employment for unmarried girls, all helped to break down the cohesiveness of the family circle, just as the growing manufacture of clothes, the factory processing of food, and the retail trade helped to undermine its former self-sufficiency.

Two developments in the family were more basic than these changes in manners and household economy. One was a marked decrease in family size, brought about by rational planning. Malthusian theory early in the century had quickly convinced most educated persons that England was overpopulated, but they saw the problem primarily as one of persuading the working classes to limit their numbers by emigration or postponement of marriage. Late marriage did, however, become a characteristic of the Victorian middle class; in mid-century the average age of marriage in the upper and professional classes was around thirty. While Malthusian conviction may have helped to rationalize postponement, the main explanation seems to have lain in the insistence—enforced by stern social pressure—that a man refrain from marriage until he could properly support a family; this soon became not merely a matter of decent support, but of support at the level which the couple's parents had already attained. In mid-century, then, there was a steady rise in expected standards of life, and at the same time a rise in their cost. Even in the period of falling prices and rising real incomes after 1875, some expenses for important outward signs of status went up, schooling and servants in particular.

Restraint from marriage to assure a sufficient income in early and mid-century did not mean small families, once marriage took place; given the hazards of life for the young, large families were essential to be sure of a reasonable number of survivors. But with steadily rising costs and, after about 1880, apparently stationary or slightly declining incomes among many middle-class families, the notion of family limitation began to take hold. A knowledge of birth-

---

*The north of England lagged behind in this development; there, the main meal still often comes at midday, with high tea taken early in the evening. The custom of afternoon tea is a late-Victorian innovation. Fascinating information on these customs can be found in Arnold Palmer, *Movable Feasts* (1952).

control methods was spread widely after 1877, in part because of the publicity that accompanied the trial for obscene libel of the inveterate radicals Charles Bradlaugh and Annie Besant, who were convicted of selling Dr. Knowlton's booklet on contraception, *The Fruits of Philosophy*. The way was prepared too by the marked decline in the effect of religion on men's private lives and by a rising concern about the apparent moral cost of delayed marriage and the rigidity of the Victorian moral code.

Vice and prostitution, which had flourished openly in the eighteenth century, were driven underground by the spread of Evangelical morality in the nineteenth, but not so far underground as to be invisible or unimportant. The Victorian underworld, with its swarms of prostitutes and its increasing supply of pornography, was brought to the attention of the reading public by the last volume of Henry Mayhew's account of the life of the London poor at mid-century, by the discussion of prostitution by the surgeon William Acton, by a long controversy in the sixties over proposals to license prostitution, and by the sensational trial of the journalist W. T. Stead in 1885 for purchasing a twelve-year-old girl in order to expose the ease with which depravity could be catered to. Victorian morality was a powerful weapon of civilization, and its taboos and restrictions in many ways made it possible for middle- and upper-class girls to live less confined lives than was possible for their counterparts on the Continent. But its dictates were breaking down, and it was being asked whether the psychic and social costs might not have become too great.

The second basic change in the late-Victorian family involved the role of women. In mid-century the traditional subjection of wife to husband was still emphasized by the complete vesting of any property she might have had before marriage in her husband, by the impossibility of divorce except through a prohibitively expensive private act of Parliament, and by a legally enforced double standard of morality, which made adultery a worse offense in a woman than in a man. Legal subjection was reinforced by the expectations of the moral code, which buttressed the institution of the family by an astonishing idealization of woman. Any expression of interest by a woman in things beyond marriage and the home or in efforts to improve women's lot or to promote their equality were usually scorned as unfeminine.

The legal situation was gradually improved. In 1857 the setting up of the Divorce Court made divorce generally available on proof of certain matrimonial offenses, the most important being adultery by the wife or adultery aggravated by cruelty or desertion by the husband; the expense, however, still limited recourse to the middle and upper classes. Married Women's Property Acts in 1870, 1882, and 1893 gave a wife the same property rights as an unmarried woman. But the moral barriers were less easy to overcome. Some remarkable women made their careers in letters and journalism early in the century; indeed the novel had for a long time been peculiarly the province of women. But while working-class women were often the financial mainstays of their families, middle-class women, when they had to support themselves, were virtually limited to being governesses.

Florence Nightingale reformed the profession of nursing and made it available to respectable women. A long, bitter, and frustrating fight against professional prejudice and exclusiveness was waged in mid-century, particularly by Elizabeth Garrett Anderson and Sophia Jex-Blake, to get women admitted to medical schools. By the end of the century, teaching and the civil service were providing outlets for the abilities and needs of many middle-class women, and at a somewhat lower level women were beginning to go into shops and offices. These steps towards "emancipation" were further aided by a new concern after mid-century with improving the wretched quality of most female education and, of course, by the new freedom that came to women by the spread of family limitation, which drastically shortened the years in which a wife was fully occupied with bearing and raising children.

Although pride of place must go to Mary Wollstonecraft's *Vindication of the Rights of Woman* (1792), a woman's movement developed later in England than in the United States. In the sixties, feminism received a considerable impetus from the professional insurgence and from the long campaign against the Contagious Diseases Acts. These acts tried to deal with the persistence of venereal disease in garrison and dockyard towns by licensing and inspection of brothels. Proposals to extend the acts led to a concerted demand that even the original acts be repealed as insulting to women (because they maintained a double standard) and encouraging to vice. Led by Mrs. Josephine Butler and James Stansfeld, the campaign was finally successful in 1886; in the course of it many women not only became well known as champions of their sex, but found a new commitment to the cause. John Stuart Mill, whose book *The Subjection of Women* (1869) is a major landmark in the history of the women's movement, had failed two years earlier to carry an amendment to the Reform Bill that would grant women's suffrage; the agitation went on quietly and effectively—with small victories such as winning the vote in local government elections—preparing the way for the dramatic confrontations of the early twentieth century.

Religion

Changes in the institution of the family and in the status of women were paralleled by another profound alteration in the assumptions and practices of the English middle classes: a rapid decline in the importance of religion. Of course, it is easy to overstress the extent of religious observance earlier in the century. The religious census taken in 1851 had shocked the pious by its revelation of empty pews throughout the country, and there was mounting concern over the failure of organized religion to appeal to more than a minority of the working classes. But in outward conformity and, for many, through inner conviction, middle-class England made religion a central element in the character of the early Victorian age and in determining its political and social course.

Nonconformity, one of the most distinctive features in the religious landscape, became increasingly blurred after mid-century. Sects multiplied, and Methodism — by far the largest of the Nonconformist denominations — was weakened by internal division. Statistics, to be sure, showed a continuing growth of membership in Dissenting congregations, and there were far larger numbers of Dissenters in Parliament than had been possible in the thirties and forties. But the health of the Free Churches (as they were beginning to be called) was more apparent than real. Much Dissenting energy went into demands for disestablishment of the Church of England, the ultimate, unattainable goal of the Liberation Society, which was, however, far more successful in its work as an electoral pressure group in the service of the Liberal Party. In the same way, the National Education League came into existence to agitate for changes in Forster's education act, which outraged much though by no means all Nonconformist opinion, but had its principal impact as a political base for the ambitions of the rising Birmingham politician Joseph Chamberlain. The political strength of Dissent was in fact diffused and blunted, except as it served other nonreligious ends, and in the twentieth century the decline in that strength was swift and decisive.

The upward movement of middle-class families often carried second and third generations out of Dissent into the socially advantageous Church of England, or sometimes into freethinking or indifference. Greater ease of association between Dissenters and Anglicans helped to speed the decay of the sense of special identity that had kept Dissenters loyal to their creeds and chapels. The social zeal that some more radical Dissenters had brought to those sects where the tendency to exclusiveness was clearest lost its strength and sting in many congregations; and in those chapels that had catered so powerfully to the lower middle class and to a minority of working people in the late eighteenth and early nineteenth centuries, outward observance was often substituted for inner regeneration. Dr. Kitson Clark has pointed out that total abstinence was often taken for the mark of a religious man, not the sense that he had been saved or behavior in any way distinctively Christian.*

In the Church of England, the older traditions of relatively non-doctrinal, civic religion had been peculiarly vulnerable to aggressive minorities with fervently held dogmas, and so, by the middle of Victoria's reign, the Established Church was dominated by two groups that earlier in the century had been minorities — the Tractarians and their Anglo-Catholic descendants, and the Evangelicals. Both groups found the enemy in religious liberalism, but beyond that there was no possibility of agreement. The Evangelicals' hatred of Rome and their view of the Church as an invisible community of converted individuals stood in stark opposition to the Tractarian emphasis on the visible Church of Catholic tradition.

In the late Victorian period, these fundamental conflicts found expression chiefly in a bitter dispute over the forms of worship. While increasing numbers of Anglican clergy were moving towards a more elaborate ritual and a higher conception of the priesthood, in many places the laymen agreed with the Evangelicals in preferring simpler, more "Protestant" forms of worship, a gap in taste and communication that even produced rebellion in some parishes. In 1874, Disraeli, with Shaftesbury's support, carried the Public Worship Act to curb Anglo-Catholic practices. Clergymen were prosecuted under it, and in 1889 a group of Protestant enthusiasts brought the new Anglo-Catholic Bishop of Lincoln, Dr. King, to trial before a special ecclesiastical tribunal, which decided in the Bishop's favor.

The liberals within the Church saw danger both in the attempt to maintain doctrines clearly in conflict with modern thought and in the futile quarrels of the irreconcilable advocates of orthodoxy. The liberals, usually referred to as the Broad Church Movement, aimed at not only modernizing the Church's teaching but embracing diverse

---

*G. Kitson Clark, *The Making of Victorian England* (1962), p. 128. The best illustrations of political concern for the maintenance of the forms of piety and religion are the wrecking of the political careers of Dilke and Parnell because of their involvement in divorce scandals, and the persistent refusal of the House of Commons to seat the radical Charles Bradlaugh, who on his first election in 1880 refused to take the oath because he was an unbeliever. He was re-elected four times, but even though he was willing to take the oath subsequently, he was expelled each time by a House unwilling to seat an atheist. He was finally allowed to take his seat in 1886.

opinions.* To the embattled conservatives, however, such liberal efforts only betrayed the existence of enemies within the gates. In 1860, a group of liberal Churchmen, including the headmaster of Rugby and three famous Oxford teachers, published *Essays and Reviews,* a mildly modernist criticism of old-fashioned and dogmatic interpretations of the Bible and the Thirty-Nine Articles. The book was condemned by Convocation, and two of the authors were tried for and convicted of heresy, a judgment reversed by the Judicial Committee of the Privy Council. The Judicial Committee intervened again in 1865 to quash the deposition and excommunication of the Bishop of Natal, J. W. Colenso, a Cambridge mathematician for whom missionary work among the Zulus had raised simple but devastating questions about the truth of Biblical narrative. Colenso's curiously literal-minded attack on the authenticity of the Mosaic books of the Bible now seems hardly worth the trouble, but in the hectic atmosphere of the sixties, he appeared to carry the critical rot into the hierarchy itself.

The Reverend Frederick Denison Maurice is usually thought of as the most profound of Broad Churchmen; he was a main source of inspiration to the Christian Socialists† and for a number of years taught regularly at the Working Men's College, set up in London in the fifties. But Maurice's concern with individual redemption and his institutional conservatism set him apart from socialists of whatever stripe, as his passionate and uniquely personal religious views kept him from identification with any religious group; sectarianism and partisanship were anathema to him.

Raised as a Unitarian and deeply influenced by Coleridge, Maurice was especially well qualified by education and temperament to recognize the virtues of all religious positions and so to work for the old Anglican ideal of unity, which he saw rapidly becoming lost among the sectarian battles of High and Low. He played down such ancient questions as sin or God's sovereignty, about which so many bitter quarrels had raged, and emphasized incarnation and the indwelling of Christ, the means of mediation between God and man; his appeal was not to the authority of a closed system but to the God who had shown Himself in men's historical quest for Him and to the

---

*The liberal Bishop of St. David's, Connop Thirlwall, said that Broad Churchmen were opposed not so much to High or Low as to Narrow. "I understand it as signifying a certain stamp of individual character, which I would describe as a disposition to recognize and appreciate that which is true and good under all varieties of forms, and in persons separated from one another by the most conflicting opinions."
†See above, pp. 290–291.

individual need for religious reconciliation. Strikingly parallel in style and concern to his Danish contemporary, Søren Kierkegaard, and intensely relevant to much twentieth-century religious awareness, Maurice was incomprehensible to most of his contemporaries. Indeed, in 1853, under attack from all sides, he was removed from his professorship at the Anglican King's College, London — the bishop of London had said he would accept no ordination candidates while Maurice continued in the theological chair — an action that in the end brought Maurice new respect and, towards the end of a life of controversy, a professorship of theology and moral philosophy at Cambridge.

The ultimate recognition that came to Maurice, like the intervention of the Judicial Committee in the cases involving *Essays and Reviews* and Bishop Colenso, seems to suggest that victory in the doctrinal struggles of mid-century lay with the liberals and the rebels: whatever their disagreements among themselves, they were confident in their assumptions and methods, while their orthodox opponents were uncertain and worried, taking action more from panic than from strength. Biblical criticism and the hypotheses of the scientists were easily absorbed by subsequent generations of theologians. Even the vexed question of Church and state solved itself largely by disappearing. Penalties were never exacted for heterodoxy; lay judges, never happy about having to pronounce on vague and uncertain matters of doctrine as if they were questions of civil law, invariably came down at last on the side of the widest liberty of interpretation. At the same time, when it suited them, Churchmen could simply ignore the presumably authoritative pronouncements of courts or Parliament. Although Bishop Colenso was restored to his post by the decision of the Judicial Committee, the bishops in England and most Anglicans in South Africa recognized another bishop who had been sent out as exercising true ecclesiastical authority. Again, after 1928, when Parliament rejected a revised prayerbook proposed by the Church, clergymen who preferred the revised service simply proceeded to use it, as they still do, without penalty. But the solution to these problems in such very English compromises also suggests that the problems themselves had come to mean little to most Englishmen: religion remained of intense concern only to those with a vocation for it.

In a period of general religious decay, the Roman Catholic Church prospered. Its authoritarianism provided the security its communicants craved, whether they were the growing number of poor Irish immigrants after mid-century or intellectuals, who in small but potent numbers continued to "go over to Rome" long after the ripples of Newman's conversion had died away. But the Roman

Catholics suffered a somewhat similar fragmentation of attitude. The liberal party in the Church owed a large debt to John Henry Newman and counted as one of its most distinguished intellects the historian Lord Acton, who had brought the teachings of German liberal Catholics into England. But the liberals made little headway in the first generation of their existence against the conservatism of Cardinal Wiseman, the first English archbishop. After 1870–1871, the liberals were struck down by the victory of the papalist ultramontanes in the Vatican Council, at which papal infallibility was proclaimed for a Church whose central leadership was reactionary in the extreme. Wiseman's successor, Cardinal Manning, a convert from Anglicanism in the fifties, managed, however, to keep the English Church on an even keel and also to show himself aware, as Rome was not, of the social imperatives of his time.

INTELLECTUAL LIFE

The Triumph of Science

So far as the great majority of Englishmen were concerned, the increasing irrelevance of religion in the late Victorian period can be explained by indifference, competing attractions, and the diffused secularism that filtered down from the intellectual challenges of mid-century. The number of men and women directly and profoundly confused and shaken by scientific discoveries was fairly small, but they were people whose opinions counted for much. The crisis of mid-century was, however, long in preparing. The "higher criticism," both English and Continental, had shaken simple faith in the Bible as the literal word of God, and earlier scientific discoveries, especially in geology, had made a literal interpretation of the story of creation untenable. Charles Darwin's *Origin of Species,* published in 1859, was the last of a series of shocks, not the first; but for many it gave the final push into agnosticism: no longer could it be maintained that man was the result of an act of special creation.

As scientific explanation spread rapidly in all fields of human knowledge, the complexity and esoteric qualities of the new learning increasingly limited true understanding to specialists. Despite the advances of science, the ill-educated and anxious sought order and certainty through reaffirming the simplicities of the Bible or in prophecy and emotional religion: indeed, the sixties witnessed a widespread, frankly anti-intellectual Evangelical revival. Apocalyptic preachers like the Reverend Charles Spurgeon preached regularly to thousands at the Metropolitan Tabernacle in London until his death in 1892. The rigidly fundamentalist Plymouth Brethren, founded in the early part of the century, grew by leaps and bounds. In the seventies, William Booth founded the Salvation Army; its most important contribution was probably social service among the poor, but its military organization and its simple, emotional religion were intended to make inroads on the indifference so common among the lowest classes.

The sensitive and educated were denied resources like these, when they found themselves both dissatisfied with traditional religion and unable to discover the all-embracing explanations they wanted in the rapidly fragmenting disciplines of science. Enthusiasm for one or another intellectual cult provided at least temporary answers for some. The "religion of humanity" was preached by the little band of apostles of Auguste Comte, the French positivist; among his followers were men whose lives were dedicated to social improvement, such as Frederic Harrison. Interest in psychical research and spiritualism in the last third of the century or the eugenic enthusiasm of those who sought to bring the millennium by promoting racial purity also had something of this quality of fumbling for a faith to replace the security that religious belief had once provided. But for many educated laymen the ultimate answer was found in resignation: explanations of man and the universe either were taken on authority or became matters of indifference.

For the scientist and scholar, on the other hand, the late nineteenth century was heady and fruitful. When the most powerful advocates of the all-embracing claims of scientific method — T. H. Huxley, Karl Pearson, and W. K. Clifford — struck with true evangelical fervor at religion, their confidence did not seem misplaced. Darwin's stunning hypothesis was soon followed by an important advance in physics, in the mathematical statement of electromagnetic theory by James Clerk-Maxwell, a breakthrough in conceptualization of which Michael Faraday, the early Victorian pioneer in electrical studies, admitted himself incapable. In nearly every field, science went from strength to strength.

The social sciences followed the physicists and biologists; in adapting scientific method to their studies, they speeded their separation as scholarly and academic disciplines from their old allegiance to the ill-defined field of moral philosophy. Although the aggressive claims of the scientists offered the most compelling challenge to the social sciences, they were stimulated as well by the teaching of Comte, who reserved the highest place in the hierarchy of the sciences — ranked in order of their emergence from the theological through the metaphysical to the positive state — for the emerging discipline of sociology. Herbert Spencer, like Comte an evolutionary thinker and a system-maker of vast ambition, had a wide influence on social thought in the next generation, though most readers today are repelled by his naive deductiveness and by the individualistic prejudices he stated as conclusions.

Within the emerging social disciplines, the natural sciences had their greatest impact in statistics and anthropology. In the eighties, Francis Galton and Karl Pearson, both interested in the application of quantitative methods to biology, laid the foundations of modern mathematical statistics. While making possible a much higher degree of sophistication in natural and social science, that development also brought a speedy end to the amateur investigation of society that had been so fruitful in the early-Victorian period, even though it was as often wildly inadequate from a technical point of view: the statistical societies, in short, became professionalized. Anthropology, on the physical side, owes much to Galton's interest in heredity and inherited mental characteristics (though not to his subsequent eugenic deductions). On the cultural side, in *Primitive Culture* (1871), E. B. Tylor of Oxford launched the scientific, comparative study of backward races, creating a discipline from what had been merely a kind of curiosity shared by travel literature and moral philosophy; at the end of the century, Sir James Frazer's seminal book *The Golden Bough* helped to bridge the gulf between the new science of human culture and popular interest, and to make a wide public aware of the common mythical basis of much in the world's religions.

In the seventies, the field of economics was in ferment. Its separation from moral philosophy was finally institutionalized by the creation of a new curriculum and examination in economics at Cambridge in 1903 and by the foundation in 1895 by the Webbs and their allies of the enormously influential London School of Economics and Political Science. The key figure in the economic revisionism of the seventies was W. S. Jevons, whose theory of marginal utility challenged the labor theory of value that underlay the classical Smithian and Ricardian school, ironically at the very time of the centenary of the publication of *The Wealth of Nations*. The newly expanded role of the state, changing population patterns, and the altered positions of landlords and laborers in the late-Victorian period all helped to bring into question the validity of the Malthusian theory, the wages fund, and the doctrine of rent. In 1890, Alfred Marshall's *Principles*, though still within the broad framework of classical models, displayed a great advance in sophistication and technique over Mill's authoritative summary of 1848 and signalled a new determination to put social science at the service of social reform.

The central role of Parliament and the stability of English politics kept the historians operating almost entirely within the assumptions of Whig liberalism. But as history became primarily an academic rather than a literary discipline, it found new ideals of objectivity and empiricism in the work of the scientists and in the German historical school stemming from Leopold von Ranke. Meticulous documentary work was done, most notably by the medievalists William Stubbs and J. H. Round, and the important government-sponsored collections of documents began with the calendars of government records and private collections put out by the Historical Manuscripts Commission. By the end of the century, F. W. Maitland, the medieval legal historian, was pointing the way to revolutionary reconstructions of the past which twentieth-century scholars were to carry through.

In field after field, then, rationalism and its chief instrument, scientific method, seemed sovereign by 1900, applicable, apparently, to all fields of knowledge.

The Arts

The development of late-Victorian architecture suggests themes relevant to the other arts as well, as they also had to adjust to a rapidly changing social and intellectual context. The wide-ranging eclecticism of the architects implies a less certain sense of direction than had been the case a generation before. The monuments of early- and mid-Victorian architecture, despite increasing preoccupation with Gothic as the "national style," were vigorous and powerful. Moreover, its individualistic impulse was turned to a social purpose: the country is dotted with town halls, railway stations, hotels, and government buildings that testify to its strength. Railway architecture, though sometimes decorated in traditional or fanciful ways, brought architecture and engineering together to serve a technological revolution, and in Paxton's Crystal Palace, the early-Victorian period produced a prefabricated and mass-produced iron and glass building in which twentieth-century functionalists have discovered strong ties to themselves. But the public building of the late-Victorian period became largely a matter of form-filling—Norman Shaw's Scotland Yard is a notable exception—and the architects whose names we remember from the last years of the century and the first years of the new are men more famous for their domestic architecture than their public buildings: Norman Shaw, Philip Webb, who designed the Red House for William Morris, and Sir Edwin Lutyens, in whose hands the modern country house received its ultimate definition. It is as though, faced with the breakup of a consensus of style and purpose, the architects diverted their most creative efforts to the private sphere and turned inward.

Painting in late nineteenth-century England, apart from the

work of the American expatriate James Whistler and the influential design of William Morris, remained insular and decorous, either didactic or (increasingly) sentimental. Victorian music never rose above the level of second-rate and is remembered today mostly for the brilliant facility of Sir Arthur Sullivan, whose serious works are nonetheless forgotten. But when Sullivan's musical ingenuity was wedded to the satirical wit of the playwright W. S. Gilbert, the result was a succession of operettas which gaily dissected one after another aspect of the late-Victorian world. The cleverness and fun have assured their immortality, and, with detailed acquaintance, the operettas become invaluable companions to the history of the period.

No clear lead was given to intellectual life by the philosophers. To the older traditions of English empiricism and Scottish intuitionism was now added the widespread and convincing enthusiasm for the seemingly sovereign scientific method and for the special but potent application of it in the social and moral implications of Darwinism; other thinkers chose to follow the lines laid down by the German idealists, a school virtually ignored in England until the sixties. Oxford was the main center of English idealism, and three great teachers in the latter part of the century — T. H. Green, F. H. Bradley, and Bernard Bosanquet — sent out a generation of converts. Earlier in the century, the clues to understanding man and nature could be found in one of two or three clearly definable and all-embracing systems; now, facing radically new complexities, men sought their answers where they could. In doing so, they shattered the fundamental unity that had characterized intellectual enterprise down to mid-century. In 1869, a group of famous men in Victorian science, literature, and theology came together in the Metaphysical Society to discuss the acute philosophical, scientific, and religious problems of their time. The Society was, in its way, the high-water mark of the century's intellectual life; the very idea of it would have been impossible later, for in the two decades of its existence, the disciplines represented by its members were rapidly losing their shared concerns and their common language.

A similar diversity of interests and language grew among the novelists and poets. Early-Victorian writers shared a common stock of knowledge and attitudes: they were deeply serious, distrustful of the cultivation of beauty as an end in itself, socially concerned, morally certain, and more or less convinced that with enough application society could one day emerge realized and reconciled. By the middle decades of the century, the intellectual and religious crisis had challenged some of those shared assumptions; yet most writers were able to draw strength from other assumptions that remained secure. Alfred Tennyson, made poet laureate after Wordsworth's death in

1850, shared to a remarkable degree the material pride and liberal consciousness of the upper classes; some of his most significant poems are concerned with the impact of science. *In Memoriam,* published in 1850, demonstrated his awareness of the metaphysical and moral revolution that was under way and began his uncertain quest for assurance of some larger force behind the assertions and silences of the scientists. George Eliot, though she had moved swiftly from orthodoxy into agnosticism in the forties, remained deeply committed to a humanitarian morality divorced from the religious sanctions that had once underlain it. George Meredith, whose first successful novel was published in 1859, looked less to morality than to a beneficent Nature, as the central characters in his novels escaped from the conventionalities of society.

By the sixties, the social criticism of Carlyle's brilliant, corrosive essays had degenerated into petulance and bitterness, but Carlyle was succeeded by two powerful critics whose influence has remained and even grown. In his poetry, Matthew Arnold explored the ambiguity and emptiness of a world in which religious faith was dying or dead, and in his essays he contributed a searching diagnosis of a society immune to ideas and spiritual values; he tried to capture for literature the moral and intellectual leadership that had once come from religion and sought in a heightened common culture a source of social purpose and unity. The art critic, John Ruskin, began as a defender of J. M. W. Turner, whose paintings mystified a generation raised on historical and genre painting. After *Modern Painters,* which began to appear in 1843, Ruskin's interest shifted back to the early Renaissance and then, increasingly, to Gothic; from there the passage was easy to social criticism that attacked the dominant individualism of his time and envisioned a world regenerated through organic social arrangements and the diffusion of beauty.*

These men and women dominated the literary scene in the eighties, carrying the high seriousness and essentially social concerns of their youth into the changed and changing world of their maturity, a fusion that could not outlast a transitional generation. Eliot and Meredith had written in a realistic vein shocking to many early Victorians; in the eighties, George Moore and George Gissing pursued realism as an end in itself, under the influence of French writers, especially Flaubert and Zola. Thomas Hardy, writing about ordinary men in a rural setting, argued a gloomy fatalism which he tried to raise to a broad philosophical plane in his historical poem *The Dynasts.* The emphasis on duty and strenuousness in the work of W. E. Henley and Rudyard Kipling at the end of the century was ex-

*On Ruskin's influence on the labor movement, see above, p. 395.

ternalized and physical, a world away from the pervasive morality of mid-century but neatly suited to a decade when imperialism at last made its full impact on the British public.

An even more striking departure from the norms of mid-century was aestheticism. Among Ruskin's first disciples were a little band of poets and painters who in 1848 had organized themselves as the Pre-Raphaelite Brotherhood. The most important of the group was Dante Gabriel Rossetti, both poet and painter and a man whose life and work testified to the unique, self-justifying, and unchallengeable role of the artist — a word, by the way, that was just beginning to be used in its modern generalized sense. By the seventies, Rossetti's close friend William Morris was beginning his pursuit of the ideal of an organic society suffused with beauty and pride of craftsmanship, an ideal that made him a passionate socialist; yet the main influence descending through Morris was not socialist but aesthetic, in the powerful stimulus he and his friends gave to the revival of handicraft, a flight from "modernity" led by Morris with his designs of furniture, wallpaper, and books. The essayist Walter Pater and the decadents at the end of the century — Oscar Wilde and Aubrey Beardsley are the most famous — carried the pursuit of art to its English extreme. For them, art was no longer a means to transform society; rather, it was to be cultivated for its own sake or became a way to escape from a world whose materialism and ugliness seemed repellent and whose many creative aspects they could not appreciate. In the early- and mid-Victorian period the arts had been servants of morality, both social and individual; by the end of the century, in many hands, they were becoming as irrelevant to the main pursuits of society as theology.

We have examined four areas in which the late-Victorian period saw striking new departures: the economy, the labor movement and socialism, the quality of middle-class life, and the art and intellect of the nation. By 1886, all these changes were evident to intelligent observers and were vaguely but uncomfortably sensed by nearly everyone. By 1900, the changes were manifest and explicit, and by 1914, with the old Victorian culture smashed beyond recognition, the nation was in the throes of crisis. Perhaps the crisis stemmed from the fact that, throughout most of the period when these new departures were confirmed, the stuff of politics (as opposed to its structure) remained very much what it had been.

Selected Readings

The essential study of rural England is F. M. L. Thompson, *English Landed Society in the Nineteenth Century* (1963); to which should be added David Spring, *The English Landed Estate in the Nineteenth Century: Its Administration*

(1963). Thompson's essay on Britain in David Spring, ed., *European Landed Elites in the Nineteenth Century* (1977) clearly balances the decline and persistence of landed influence and is informative on the extent of insurgence of newer forms of wealth into the peerage and on the multiplication of honors. A contemporary record of what the author called the "acre-ocracy" is John Bateman, *The Great Landowners of Great Britain and Ireland* (1876, 4th ed., 1883, reprinted 1971). Mark Girouard, *The Victorian Country House* (1971), for the setting of aristocratic life. The best statement of the revisionist view of the agricultural depression is T. W. Fletcher, "The Great Depression of English Agriculture, 1873–1896," *Economic History Review*, 2nd ser., vol. 13, pp. 417–432 (April, 1961). The vast extent of semi-popular literature on rural life can be represented by G. E. Mingay, *Rural Life in Victorian England* (1977) and two books by Pamela Horn, *The Victorian Country Child* (1975) and *Labouring Life in the Victorian Countryside* (1976). J. P. D. Dunbabin, *Rural Discontent in Nineteenth-Century Britain* (1974) concentrates on the latter part of the century. M. K. Ashby, *Joseph Ashby of Tysoe, 1859–1919* (1961) is a biography of a rural radical, while striking glimpses into another form of protest are to be found in G. Christian, ed., *A Victorian Poacher: James Hawker's Journal* (1961).

On fox-hunting — essentially a creation of the late eighteenth century and quickly elevated to a myth that survives the profound effects of the railway and depression — David C. Itzkowitz, *Peculiar Privilege: A Social History of English Foxhunting, 1753–1885* (1977) and Raymond Carr, *English Fox Hunting: A History* (1976). The sporting writer R. S. Surtees created a very popular series of tales about a London Cockney grocer, Mr. Jorrocks, with a passion for hunting; we may read them not only for the stories but for the insights into rural sociology. The most readily available collection is *Jorrocks's Jaunts and Jollities*, of which there have been many subsequent editions. On another aristocratic sport, Wray Vamplew, *The Turf: A Social and Economic History of Horse Racing* (1976).

Modern discussion of the late-Victorian business cycle takes its rise from H. L. Beales's celebrated article, "The 'Great Depression' in Industry and Trade" (1934), reprinted in E. M. Carus-Wilson, *Essays in Economic History*, vol. 1 (1962), pp. 406–415. S. B. Saul, *The Myth of the Great Depression* (1969) is a conclusive general discussion. Received wisdom has it that Britain's decline relative to the newer economic powers, especially Germany and the United States, is related in some way to the quality of British entrepreneurship. One aspect of the problem was aired in H. J. Habakkuk's influential book, *American and British Technology in the Nineteenth Century* (1962), which puts particular stress on the scarcity and abundance of labor in the two countries; and for a general comparative account, see Philip S. Bagwell and G. E. Mingay, *Britain and America, 1850–1939: A Study of Economic Change* (1970). On the managerial side, thinking has been much affected by W. G. Rimmer, *Marshalls of Leeds, Flax-Spinners, 1788–1886* (1960), the history of a firm that made the first John Marshall a very rich man and that then declined under the management of his sons and grandsons until its liquidation in 1886. Similar views emerge in other studies, notably A. J. Taylor, "Labour Productivity and Technological Innovation in the British Coal Industry, 1850–1914," *Economic History Review*, 2nd ser., vol. 14, pp. 48–70 (August, 1961). S. B. Saul, ed., *Technological Change: The United States and Britain in the Nineteenth Century* (1970) partly counters Habakkuk by detailed examination of differences between the two countries, notably in the engineering industries, noting some British successes and seeking explanation in differing market conditions. Donald N. McCloskey, *Economic Maturity and Entrepreneurial Decline: British Iron and Steel, 1870–1913* (1973) argues that in that industry neither productivity nor entrepreneurial skills lagged behind the American performance. See also the essays in a volume edited by McCloskey, *Essays on a Mature Economy: Britain After 1840* (1971). Two versions of a historiographical and interpretative account, favorable to British managers, are P. L. Payne's *British Entrepreneurship in the Nineteenth Century* (1974) and his chapter "Industrial Entrepreneurship and Management in Great Britain," in Peter Mathias and M. M. Postan, eds., *Cambridge Economic History of Europe*, vol. 7, part 1 (1978), pp. 180–230. C. H. Feinstein's chapter in the same work, "Capital Formation in Great Britain," pp. 28–96 is also helpful, as are Francis E. Hyde, *Far Eastern Trade, 1860–1914* (1973) and A. K. Cairncross, *Home and Foreign Investment, 1870–1913* (1953). Charles Wilson's summary article, "Economy and Society in Late Victorian Britain," *Economic History Review*, 2nd ser., vol. 18, pp. 183–198 (August, 1965), refers to many business histories and also emphasizes the importance of developments in retailing, a subject explored in the history of a grocery combine in Peter Mathias, *Retailing Revolution: A History of Multiple Retailing in the Food Trades.* (1967). Charlotte Erickson studies the origins of businessmen in two contrasting industries in *British Industrialists: Steel and Hosiery, 1850–1950* (1959).

Two contemporary surveys of great importance can serve as a starting point for the study of working-class life in the late nineteenth century: Charles Booth, *Life and Labour of the People in London* (17 vols., 1889–1903) and B. Seebohm Rowntree, *Poverty: A Study of Town Life* (1901). There are excellent biographies of both men, Booth's by T. S. and M. Simey, *Charles Booth, Social Scientist* (1960), and Rowntree's by Asa Briggs, *Social Thought and Social Action* (1961). A sensitive recent study is Gareth Stedman Jones, *Outcast London: A Study in the Relationship Between Classes in Victorian Society* (1971). The continuing forms of private philanthropy are dealt with in C. L. Mowat, *The Charity Organization Society* (1961), Margaret Simey, *Charitable Effort in Liverpool* (1951), and David Owen, *English Philanthropy, 1660–1960* (1964). On experiments in industrial relations, E. H. Phelps Brown, *The Growth of British Industrial Relations* (1959), and W. H. G. Armytage, *A. J. Mundella, 1825–1897* (1951), the biography of a textile magnate and Liberal politician who was the main force in popularizing conciliation procedures. An enormous amount of detailed information is to be found in H. A. Clegg, Alan Fox, and A. F. Thompson, *A History of British Trade Unions since 1889*, vol. 1: *1889–1910* (1964). See also the highly pertinent article, "British Gas-Workers, 1873–1914," in E. J. Hobsbawm, *Labouring Men* (1964), pp. 158–178, which also contains other relevant chapters.

For a modern reformer's indictment of Victorian working-class housing, see Enid Gauldie, *Cruel Habitations: A History of Working-Class Housing, 1780–1918* (1974); for a historian's perspective, Anthony Wohl, *The Eternal Slum: Housing and Social Policy in Victorian London* (1977). The concern about urban and rural amenities is documented in William Ashworth, *The Genesis of Modern British Town Planning* (1954). On the disappearance of traditional amusements, Robert W. Malcolmson, *Popular Recreations in English Society, 1700–1850* (1973) and Peter Bailey, *Leisure and Class in Victorian England: Rational Recreation and the Contest for Control, 1830–1855* (1978). A case study for a later period is Helen Meller, *Leisure and the Changing City, 1870–1914* (1976). See also Richard D. Altick, *The Shows of London* (1978). Reading was a rational recreation; in addition to citations given in Chapter 6, see R. K. Webb, "The Reading Public," in Boris Ford, ed., *Pelican Guide to English Literature*, vol. 6: *Dickens to Hardy* (1958), pp. 205–226. On temperance, Brian Harrison's magisterial *Drink and the Victorians: The Temperance Question in England, 1815–1872* (1971); and the political agitation for prohibition mounted by the United Kingdom Alliance is discussed in D. A. Hamer, *The Politics of Electoral Pressure: A Study in the History of Victorian Reform Agitations* (1977).

On the varieties of socialism: E. P. Thompson, *William Morris: Romantic to Revolutionary* (1955, 1978); Ian Bradley, *William Morris and His World* (1978); Chushichi Tsuzuki, *H. M. Hyndman and British Socialism* (1961); Kenneth O. Morgan, *Keir Hardie: Radical and Socialist* (1975). For a group portrait, Norman and Jeanne MacKenzie, *The First Fabians* (1977). The emergence of Fabian ideas from radicalism is traced in Willard Wolfe, *From Radicalism to Socialism: Men and Ideas in the Formation of Fabian Socialist Doctrines, 1881–1889* (1975). The most careful assessments of Fabian tactics and accomplishment are to be found in A. M. McBriar, *Fabian Socialism and English Politics, 1884–1918* (1962) and Paul Thompson, *Socialists, Liberals, and Labour: The Struggle for London, 1885–1914* (1967). The first assault on the Fabian myth, admittedly highly partisan, was by E. J. Hobsbawm in "The Fabians Reconsidered," reprinted in his *Labouring Men*, pp. 250–271. For an authoritative account of political developments, Henry Pelling, *The Origins of the Labour Party, 1800–1900* (1954). The two volumes of Beatrice Webb's autobiography, *My Apprenticeship* (1926) and *Our Partnership* (1948), make unforgettable reading and are historically valuable in all directions.

The middle classes have been so far less studied, but there are signs that the lapse is being remedied. Geoffrey Crossick, ed., *The Lower Middle Class in Britain, 1870–1914* (1977) is a useful but uneven set of essays, with a most suggestive introduction. See also M. A. Simpson and T. H. Lloyd, eds., *Middle-Class Housing in Britain* (1977). Two contrasting contemporary views are B. G. Orchard's sober investigation, *The Clerks of Liverpool* (1871) and George and Weedon Grossmith's comic novel, *The Diary of a Nobody* (1892). Gregory Anderson's *Victorian Clerks* (1976) is brief but excellent within its range. On growing London, H. J. Dyos, *Victorian Suburb: A Study of the Growth of Camberwell* (1961), F. M. L. Thompson, *Hampstead: Building a Borough, 1650–1964* (1974), and T. C. Barker and Michael Robbins, *A History of London Transport*, I: *The Nineteenth Century* (1963). For a superb study of the expanding metropolis, Donald J. Olsen, *The Growth of Victorian London* (1976); relevant here, as to many other parts of this book, are chapters in the imposing two volumes edited by H. J. Dyos and Michael Woolf, *The Victorian City: Images and Realities* (1973); and Asa Briggs's series of urban portraits, *Victorian Cities* (1968).

On the family, Arnold Palmer, *Movable Feasts* (1952) is a fascinating history of mealtimes, which shift through the century and accommodate the introduction of afternoon tea, like many presumably traditional English habits a late invention. J. A. Banks, *Prosperity and Parenthood* (1954) and J. A. and Olive Banks, *Feminism and Family Planning in Victorian England* (1964) are important contributions to an understanding of middle-class mores. O. R. McGregor's *Divorce in England* (1957) is invaluable, particularly the third chapter on the myths and actuality of the Victorian family. Michael Anderson, *Family Structure in Nineteenth-Century Lancashire* (1971) is a pioneering work. On sexual attitudes and realities much poor material has been published. Eric Trudgill's *Madonnas and Magdalens: The Origins and Development of Victorian Sexual Attitudes* (1976) is an exception. Steven Marcus's celebrated study of nineteenth-century pornography, *The Other Victorians* (1966) is open to criticism, some of which is effectively delivered by F. B. Smith, "Sexuality in Britain, 1800–1900: Some Suggested Revisions," in Martha Vicinus, ed., *A Widening Sphere: Changing Roles of Victorian Women* (1977), pp. 182–198. W. E. Gladstone made the rescue of prostitutes his principal personal charity; on the complexity of his sexual concerns, see vols. 3–4 of *The Gladstone Diaries* (1974) and particularly the astute introduction by one of the editors, H. C. G. Matthew.

On Victorian women, the volume edited by Martha Vicinus, noted above, was preceded by another useful collection with the same editor, *Suffer and Be Still: Women in the Victorian Age* (1972). Each volume contains an admirable bibliographical chapter by Barbara Kanner. See also Lee Holcombe, *Victorian Ladies at Work: Middle-Class Working Women in England and Wales, 1850–1914* (1973). Cecil Woodham-Smith, *Florence Nightingale, 1820–1910* (1951) and R. K. Webb, *Harriet Martineau, a Radical Victorian* (1960) show what "strong-minded women" could accomplish against overwhelming odds. On the origins of the political women's movement, F. B. Smith, "Ethics and Disease in the Later Nineteenth Century: The Contagious Diseases Acts," *Historical Studies*, vol. 15, pp. 118–135 (October, 1971).

There is much information and insight on the entire mid-Victorian religious scene in G. Kitson Clark, *The Making of Victorian England* (1962), Chapter 6. Owen Chadwick continues his comprehensive coverage in *The Victorian Church, part 2: 1859–1901* (1970), and Alan D. Gilbert, *Religion and Society in Industrial England*, cited earlier, remains useful. For a political *cause célèbre*, one of many in which the Victorian religious mentality proved troublesome or worse for politicians, Walter Arnstein, *The Bradlaugh Case* (1964); an even more crucial instance is dealt with in F. S. L. Lyons, *The Fall of Parnell, 1890–91* (1960). The declining political fortunes of Dissent are traced in Stephen Koss, *Nonconformity in Modern British Politics* (1975). For doctrinal and pastoral developments, A. O. J. Cockshut, *Anglican Attitudes: A Study of Victorian Religious Controversies* (1959); Horton Davies, *Worship and Theology in England*, vols. 3–4 (1961–1962); L. E. Elliott-Binns, *English Thought, 1860–1900: The Theological Aspects* (1956); Standish Meacham, *Lord Bishop: The Life of Samuel Wilberforce, 1805–1873* (1970); P. T. Marsh, *The Victorian Church in Decline: Archbishop Tait and the Church of England, 1868–1882* (1969); and Olive Brose, *Frederick Denison Maurice: Rebellious Conformist, 1805–1872* (1971). On Roman Catholicism, J. L. Altholz, *The Liberal Catholic Movement in England* (1962), and V. A. McClelland, *Cardinal Manning* (1962). On freethinkers, Basil Willey, *More Nineteenth-Century Studies: A Group of Honest Doubters* (1956) and Edward Royle, *Victorian Infidels: The Origins of the British Secularist Movement, 1791–1866* (1974). Much has been written on the social outlook of the clergy: R. A. Soloway, *Prelates and People: Ecclesiastical Social Thought in England, 1783–1852* (1969); G. Kitson Clark, *Churchmen and the Condition of England, 1832–1885* (1973); E. R. Norman, *Church and Society in England, 1770–1970* (1976); and P. T. Phillips, ed., *The View from the Pulpit: English Ministers and Society* (1978), the last dealing with a number of Dissenters as well as churchmen.

On the "crisis of faith," two literary classics deserve mention: Sir Edmund Gosse's *Father and Son* (1907) tells of the trials of his father, at once a fundamentalist Protestant and a natural scientist of some repute; and Mrs. Humphry Ward (Matthew Arnold's niece) wrote an account of loss of faith in *Robert Elsmere* (1888). Anthony Symondson, ed., *The Victorian Crisis of Faith* (1970) is a series of brief, pointed lectures. On the earlier challenge of science, Charles Gillispie, *Genesis and Geology* (1951). By all odds the best study of an intellectual freethinker is Noel Annan's *Leslie Stephen* (1951), and for efforts to find a third alternative, Frank Miller Turner, *Between Science and Religion: The Reaction to Scientific Naturalism in Late Victorian England* (1974). James Obelkevich, in *Religion and Rural Society: South Lindsey, 1825–1875* (1976), tells the complex story of the rise and decline of religious enthusiasm in one relatively isolated area and also underlines the persistence of superstition. On working-class indifference and efforts to combat it, K. S. Inglis, *Churches and the Working Classes in Victorian England* (1963).

For a general discussion of Victorian intellectual life, W. E. Houghton, *The Victorian Frame of Mind, 1830–1870* (1957). Two interpretations of more narrowly literary attitudes are J. H. Buckley, *The Victorian Temper* (1951) and Graham Hough, *The Last Romantics* (1949). See also John Gross, *The Rise and Fall of the Man of Letters: Aspects of English Literary Life Since 1800* (1969). For philosophical developments, Melvin Richter's study of T. H. Green, *The Politics of Conscience* (1964) and A. W. Brown, *The Metaphysical Society: Victorian Minds in Crisis, 1869–1880* (1947). J. W. Burrow, *Evolution and Society: A Study in Victorian Social Thought* (1960) deals with a vital new influence, and T. W. Hutchison, *A Review of Economic Doctrines, 1870–1929* (1953, 2nd ed., 1962) traces the decline of an old orthodoxy and the rise of a new. On architecture, Henry-Russell Hitchcock, *Early Victorian Architecture in Britain* (2 vols., 1954); Stefan Muthesius, *The High Victorian Movement in Architecture, 1850–1870* (1972); and, for a brief sketch covering the entire period, Roger Dixon and Stefan Muthesius, *Victorian Architecture* (1978).

Chapter 10
Politics and Empire

1886–1911

THE NEW FORMS OF POLITICS

The Attack on Corruption

The Reform Act of 1867 had left much of the political system—in the country and the smaller towns—untouched, but adding a million working-class voters in the boroughs meant a challenging prospect in the larger towns, where the new voters were in an overwhelming majority. Workingmen themselves, as we have seen, were groping towards their own political solutions, but meanwhile the middle and upper classes, and the politicians in particular, responded to the challenge of the new electorate with some measures intended to protect the body politic from the consequences of democracy and others to turn democracy to advantage.

The large numbers of new voters drawn from the poorer and possibly more irresponsible classes—so the reasoning ran—raised acutely the matter of electoral corruption, a persistent feature of British politics so complex as to defy correction. For one thing, corruption was not easy to disentangle from what in those days was called "legitimate influence." The right of a landlord to influence the vote of his tenant was rarely questioned; on the other hand, similar practices were universally denounced when used by candidates or their agents — at least on the opposing side. Again, there were so many forms of corruption. Some were violent — abducting, intoxicating, or intimidating potential voters; gentler means were treating voters with beer or food, giving them jobs, entertaining them, or buying their votes outright. Because all these devices were used regularly, a close or upsetting election was almost certain to be challenged.

Down until 1770 contested elections had been referred to the whole House of Commons, as judge of its own membership; in that year George Grenville, against government opposition, carried a bill confiding the decision to a select committee, invariably constructed on partisan lines. In 1852, after some years of trying to persuade the Lords, the government secured a further reform, whereby the Election Committee of the House, when it suspected corruption, could initiate a royal commission to investigate the constituency; such a commission was much more likely to be nonpartisan, but creating it was difficult because the two Houses of Parliament might not accept the proposal. Where flagrant corruption was proved by either the old or the new procedure, members could be unseated, and the borough itself might be disfranchised, as happened at Sudbury in 1844 and St. Albans in 1852.

In 1854, Parliament tried another tack by carefully defining the main electoral offenses: bribery, treating, and undue influence and intimidation. Guilty candidates could be fined for bribery and, if elected, expelled from the House; a scale of fines was provided for both candidates and voters guilty of the other offenses. An auditing requirement to deal with the central problem of election expenses simply failed to work — it was either ignored or became a mere formality — and was done away with in 1863; but the other provisions seem to have had a good effect.

During 1867 and 1868, while occupied with the Reform bill, Disraeli's government was also trying to provide new machinery for dealing with contested elections, which reached a new height in the general election of 1865. Under an act of 1868, each of the three Common Law courts was to choose one of its members each autumn to try election petitions. In the next few years, the judges began to build up a body of election law, which had not existed until then. They had many opportunities to do so, because the bitterly contested election of 1868 produced thirty-four petitions; it was also marked by an unusual amount of rowdiness and violence.

The secret ballot can also be seen as insurance against democracy, although many of its advocates hoped that voters, freed from intimidation and influence, would vote for their particular side. When the question of secret voting was canvassed in 1832, majority opinion held that the vote should be exercised openly as a privilege and public trust; behind the noble justification, of course, lay a nagging concern that secrecy would undermine legitimate influence. The latter point was the main reason for opposition to the ballot in 1870–1872, especially in the upper house. Evidence of corruption, however, persuaded many M.P.'s to support the ballot, and in 1872 Gladstone was finally able to force the bill through a protesting House of Lords. The Ballot Act was to expire in 1880, and was renewed annually thereafter until 1918, when the ballot was made permanent.

Secret voting did not seriously reduce corruption or allegations of corruption: twenty-two petitions were tried after the general election in 1874, twenty-eight after the election of 1880. Moreover, expenses in the latter election had risen sharply thanks in part to an act (agreed to in record time in the Lords) permitting free conveyance of voters to the polls. The revelations of 1880 led to the Corrupt and Illegal Practices Act of 1883. Corruption — defined as bribery, treating, undue influence, assault or abduction, impersonation, or perjury — was made punishable by severe fines, while less severe but still deterrent penalties were provided for "illegal practices," including paying for conveyances, employing voters, wearing party favors, or overspending. The statutory limits on electoral expenses were highly confining: £350 in a borough with under 2,000 voters, £380 for boroughs with over 2,000 voters and £30 for each additional thousand; in the counties, £650 and £710 for the two categories, with the addition of £60 for each additional thousand; in Ireland the limits were lower. Quite cleanly, the act put an end to any significant electoral corruption. Since then, British elections have been quiet, dull affairs compared to the circuses across the Atlantic, but they have at least been kept sensibly to candidates and issues.

Political Parties

Gladstone's Midlothian campaigns of 1879 and 1880 were portents: a wide electorate need not merely be checked; it could also be cultivated. Gladstone fought all his campaigns on single issues, a practice especially well adapted to convincing a heterogeneous electorate, and highly congenial to Gladstone's moral intensity. But a number of cynics pointed out that bribery and treating by money and beer had only given way to the more expensive blandishments of promised acts of Parliament and legislated raids on the Exchequer for the benefit of particular classes or groups of voters. Thus, in 1885, the radical Joseph Chamberlain, finding it hard to make headway against the conservative Whigs whom he was so ironically to join the next year over Ireland, stumped the country advocating his "unauthorized program." He called for disestablishment of the Church, land and local government reform, abolition of plural voting, better housing and social services, free education, and "three acres and a cow" for agricultural workers. He proposed to finance the program by increased taxation of the well-to-do, asking brutally, "What ransom will property pay for the security which it enjoys?"

But programs require more than oratory to be translated into reality. The mobilization of voters was the job of party organizations, which received a powerful new impetus after 1867. In the paltry redistribution provisions in the Reform Act of 1867, there was one striking experiment. Four large towns — Birmingham, Manchester, Liverpool, and Leeds — were given three members each, but each voter could vote for only two candidates; the intention was to secure one Tory, or at any rate minority, seat from the expected radical dominance. The next year Chamberlain and his radical friends in Birmingham organized a careful canvass to determine where their allies lived, and strict voting instructions were issued to spread radical votes in the most effective way. The result was a clean radical sweep of the three seats. From this victory Chamberlain went on to build up a complex and powerful local machine, which gave the appearance of democracy, while actually confining decisions to a small committee at the top dominated by Chamberlain and his chief manager, Francis Schnadhorst. This organization was denounced by Disraeli as a copy (which it was not) of the unsavory American caucus; as so often happens with abuse, the name stuck.

The size of the Liberal victory in 1868, however, led most Liberals to neglect systematic development of their rudimentary machinery of registration associations and local Liberal clubs. The Conservatives, on the other hand, were forced by defeat to rebuild through better organization — their chief manager was John Gorst, who took office as party agent in 1870 with Disraeli's full support — which helped materially to bring victory in 1874. Then roles were reversed: the Tories relaxed, and the Liberals organized. The focal point was Birmingham, whose caucus was copied or paralleled in many large towns; and in 1877 Chamberlain took the lead in organizing the National Liberal Federation. The Federation's control of national Liberal politics was spotty. With its headquarters in Birmingham, it looked like a provincial assault on London, but England's regions were not necessarily compatible, and Manchester Liberals, for instance, carried on a running fight with Chamberlain's group. The Whigs distrusted a popular organization clearly dedicated to radicalism, and a number of men, including some radicals, were deeply worried over the implications of a central party organization that presumed to dictate how men should vote. Strong local organizations could also stimulate rebellions by outsiders; it is worth noting that much of the working-class radicalism that found its way into the ILP was in revolt against local party oligarchies who could unquestionably deliver votes, but who looked down on workingmen with political ambitions.

After the Liberal organization was split in 1886, the Conservatives had the better of it. The National Union of Conservative and Constitutionalist Associations dated from the late sixties, although it did not become either well organized or important until the eighties, when, following the shock of 1880, Gorst and Lord Randolph Churchill, the rising *enfant terrible* of the Tories, tried and to a degree carried off its conversion into a Conservative caucus. In 1883, the Primrose League was founded, ostensibly in memory of Disraeli: it was a "Tory militia," organized like a lodge, with local chapters, regional and national gatherings, officers with high-flown titles, orders, decorations, a strong appeal to women, and an endless succession of tea parties.

By 1886, then, both parties had advanced their organization far beyond anything imagined in the sixties. The roles once played by the Carlton and Reform clubs and agents like Bonham and Parkes were now taken over by central party offices and batteries of officials; liaison with the parliamentary parties was maintained through the chief whips. The party in office could subsidize its organizational activities by using the old secret-service fund, of so much value to the Duke of Newcastle in the reign of George III, but in 1886 its use for politics was forbidden. Thereafter both parties had to appeal primarily to wealthy supporters to build up party funds; luckily there were many of them. The volunteer workers at the constituency level were held together by political devotion and local pride, and tied with varying degrees of success to the center; their national sounding board was the yearly party conference.

Parliamentary Discipline

Mass party machinery was directed chiefly at winning elections and at keeping local enthusiasm in good repair. In the intervals between elections, the political initiative passed to the parliamentary parties and their leaders. As legislators, they made policy and presented the national party officials with platforms they had little choice but to support; looking back, we can see how unjustified was the common worry that irresponsible party officials would dictate to Parliament. On the other hand, parliamentary leaders had to carry through their promises, and to that extent it became necessary to limit increasingly the independence and initiative of ordinary members of Parliament. It took another sixty years to evolve the present arrangements of rigorous timetables and stern party discipline, with only limited chances for private members to introduce bills. But there were already complaints in the eighties about the amount of time Gladstone's government required from the House to debate and pass the many bills for which it demanded priority.

In the eighties, the House took its first step to limit debate. Both Tories and Radicals had practiced obstruction before the Irish made it their specialty, but the Parnellites forced the issue. The Speaker's intervention to stop debate and put the question in February, 1881, was exceptional, and it was only with difficulty that Gladstone, by making it a question of confidence (i.e., one on which he would resign if defeated), carried a resolution permitting closure on a motion by a minister. To take effect, the motion had to be carried by a proportion of three to one in a house of over 300, but the rules later became more stringent; in 1887, closure was permitted on the motion of an ordinary member, and in 1909 the Speaker was given authority to choose what clauses would be discussed in the report stage, the so-called "kangaroo." By such means the House was gradually brought under firm cabinet control. Eighteenth-century influence had been resurrected as twentieth-century party discipline, a more certain and less troublesome means of assuring a majority. The classic, individualist phase of the constitution, when votes in the House could make and unmake governments and when private members could change the face and life of the country, was retreating from actuality into the pages of textbooks on comparative government.

The Third Reform Act

By the end of the eighties, then, Parliament had done its best to protect the public from its own greed and passions by requiring a secret ballot and by placing stringent limitations on electoral abuses. At the same time, politicians had found more positive ways of regarding the enlarged electorate; they increasingly appealed to the voters for support of particular legislative programs and armed themselves with sterner parliamentary discipline to carry them through. But the eighties also saw legislation that broke with some central assumptions of English politics. The first Reform Act had asserted the possibility of change and opened the way to future alteration; but, except for the king's role in the constitution, it left the balance of political power largely undisturbed and the practice of politics much as it had been. The second Reform Act made a clear commitment to a democracy in which the unpropertied and ill-educated would one day predominate and so forced the reconsiderations we have just examined. Still much of English political life remained unchanged. The third Reform Act of 1884 and the accompanying Redistribution Act of 1885 carried further that commitment to democracy, not only by giving the vote to workingmen in the countryside but by institutional changes that undermined the political power of the landed aristocracy.

Ever since the Reform Act of 1867 had given household suffrage in the boroughs while retaining a property qualification in the counties, there had been agitation for the assimilation of the rural to the town franchise. In the eighties, Chamberlain took the lead in forcing the Liberal government to take up a further measure of reform, against the considered judgment and the legitimate fears of the Whigs. The bill passed the Commons quickly in early 1884, but in the Lords there was violent resistance, particularly from Lord Salisbury, whose anti-democratic instincts had mellowed not at all since 1867. But Gladstone refused to be drawn by the Lords' insistence on taking up a redistribution bill first, and during the summer, Chamberlain and John Morley led the radicals in full cry against the peers who, if they rejected the bill, might (following Morley's famous slogan) have to be mended or ended. The threat was enough to bring the peers to reason; and (perhaps more to the point) after Gladstone and Salisbury reached an agreement on the terms of the acts, the Reform bill passed late in the year and the measure for redistribution early in 1885.

Household suffrage became the rule throughout the country, although recent estimates have put those adult males excluded by the relatively high lodger franchise and stringent registration requirements at two out of five; plural voting, too, increased the electoral weight of the middle and upper classes. Still, by admitting a good proportion of agricultural laborers to the vote with the protection of the ballot, the Liberals struck a blow at the deferential structure of county politics. Until that time, for the most part, politics in the many counties and small towns had remained the monopoly of great families, qualified only by the intrusion of new patrons—manufacturers or railway companies, say, which exercised their political influence in much the same fashion as their predecessors. Now the newer forms of politics extended to the countryside. Gentry and sons of peers still continued to sit in the Commons, but only because they had fought elections and won. Perhaps, in districts where they had estates, they might benefit from sentiment, but they were no longer in Parliament as a matter of right, or of power disguised as right.*

---

*Although householding was the main qualification, the act characteristically retained the old tenure qualifications and the "ancient right" voters. These and other anomalies were not done away with until 1918. See below, pp. 496–497.

The Redistribution Act of 1885 was passed, at Conservative insistence, before a general election could bring in what was generally expected to be a House dominated by radicals. Political patterns were altered nonetheless. Any borough with fewer than 15,000 inhabitants lost its member or members and was merged into its county. Boroughs of 50,000 got one member, and larger boroughs more. But with certain exceptions, all the counties and larger boroughs were cut up into divisions, each returning only one member. This change was of great practical and theoretical significance. Roughly approximating the old Chartist ideal of equal electoral districts, the act broke up the historical constituencies, extinguishing the peculiar prestige that had always attached to county members, and making a member not so much the representative of the whole constituency as the delegate of the majority who returned him. Two-member constituencies had often linked a Whig and a Tory, or a Whig and a Radical, a practice not only politically convenient but reflecting the old medieval sense of community. The constituency now became an arbitrary electoral convenience, and the way of minorities or independents was made harder.

The reforms of 1884–1885 made changes in local government inevitable, and Lord Salisbury's government took the step in 1888. Judicial business remained in the hands of magistrates appointed by the Crown, but the administration of the shires, or of separate divisions of large counties, was turned over to elected county councils. Boroughs of over 50,000 inhabitants were exempted from county council control and made "county boroughs" under their own municipal governments, while a new county of London was carved from the counties in which its various boroughs were located and given a council of its own, the famous London County Council. The LCC was to be the locus of much imaginative experiment in education and local government, but it was only the most obvious and celebrated of the councils, which in rural areas added a new dimension to political life that had once been the unquestioned domain of lord and squire.

THE TORY HEGEMONY, 1886–1905

The Problem of Leadership

For nearly twenty years, from 1886 to 1905, the Conservative party dominated British politics; even during the Liberal governments from 1892 to 1895 the Tories held the whip hand. Yet when Salisbury formed his second administration in August, 1886, that long tenure of power was not entirely predictable. With 316 seats the Conservatives could easily outvote the Gladstonian opposition, but it was still possible that the Liberal Unionists might on occasion vote with Gladstone and put Salisbury in a minority. Salisbury recognized the pivotal position of the Liberal defectors by urging Lord Hartington, the leader of the renegade Whigs, to take office as premier, advice that was at once refused. But for at least a year it remained possible that some of the Unionists would return to the Gladstonian fold. Early in 1887, following a series of conferences aimed at reconciliation, a few defectors did return, chief among them Sir George Trevelyan, who had been Chief Secretary for Ireland in 1882–1884, but Chamberlain, the main waverer, resisted the temptation. The Unionists kept their separate existence as a parliamentary party until 1912; but in 1891, Chamberlain, who had just succeeded to the Unionist leadership in the Commons when Hartington went to the upper house as Duke of Devonshire, rejected any future possibility of rejoining the Liberals. With this unlikely recruit firmly in place, Salisbury's coalition was secure.

In domestic legislation, the period of the Tory dominance is nearly devoid of interest. There were a number of valuable measures: a factory act, a tithe act, and the provision of free education in 1891, a small-holdings act in 1892, a workmen's compensation act in 1897, and a secondary-education act in 1902. But, except for the workmen's compensation act — which applied to all accidents suffered by workmen in the course of their employment, whether due to negligence or not* — none of these acts marked a departure in principle from what had gone before; they and a number of lesser measures were, in effect, rounding off responsibilities which the state had already taken on and for which machinery was already provided. So too the one Conservative statute of constitutional importance, the Local Government Act of 1888, was, as we have seen, no more than an inevitable sequel to the Reform Act of 1884.

To some extent, this relative torpor in domestic legislation reflected the real desires of the country. In the mid-twentieth century, given our own political preoccupations, we are likely to overstate the desire for social reform in the nineteenth. Even among the working classes, where the benefits would presumably have been greatest, there was no consistent or focussed demand for legislated social change; the energy of the trade unions was largely absorbed in their own growth and in occasional, limited confrontations with employers. In the middle and upper classes advocates of radical change

---

*Compensation was paid by employers, who of course protected themselves by insurance. Agricultural laborers and seamen were not protected until 1900 and 1906, respectively, and other exceptions remained until 1925.

and sweeping plans for social reconstruction were few and by no means in agreement. But this relative stagnation also reflects the state of political leadership.

For a time contemporaries saw a source of new vigor and political imagination in Lord Randolph Churchill, the third son of the Duke of Marlborough. Like Chamberlain earlier, Churchill established his political base in mass party organization, the National Union of Conservative Associations and its auxiliary, the Primrose League, which he helped to found. In the early eighties, Churchill, John Gorst (Disraeli's old political manager), Sir Henry Drummond Wolff, and Arthur Balfour made up a small clique in the House of Commons, nicknamed the "Fourth party"; their purpose was to force a more aggressive Conservative line in the Commons than could be expected from Sir Stafford Northcote, the leader of the House, who at that time shared the party leadership with Lord Salisbury. By 1883, Churchill was strong enough to put in a claim to leadership of the House, though he was too young or too unpopular to assert it successfully; in 1884, following a quarrel with the party leadership, he ostentatiously resigned as chairman of the National Union and got himself triumphantly re-elected. When Salisbury formed his second ministry in 1886, Lord Randolph's position in the country gave him a very strong claim on office; he chose the Exchequer, a strategic post for launching a substantial legislative program. But his proposal for a wholesale and potentially popular overhaul of the tax structure could be accomplished only if there were sweeping retrenchment, particularly in the Army and Navy. When W. H. Smith, the war minister, refused to cut his estimates, Churchill tried to force the issue by resigning—an effort to repeat his successful tactics with the party chairmanship in 1884. It was a bad miscalculation. Men outside the government, ignorant of the budget proposals, were only puzzled by what seemed a piece of inexplicable petulance, and Lord Salisbury was glad enough to be rid of what he called "a boil on his neck." Lord Randolph spent the last few years of his life (he died in 1895) trying to return from a political wilderness that almost completely engulfed him.

A more obvious place to look for new departures was the Liberal party. Hampered for years by Whig footdragging, the radicals had been finally freed by the split in 1886. Although Chamberlain was gone, new leaders appeared in John Morley, Sir Henry Campbell-Bannerman, and H. H. Asquith; they gained the cooperation of Sir William Harcourt, Gladstone's veteran lieutenant in the Commons, and even in some respects of Gladstone himself. In 1891, the Liberals presented the country with their "Newcastle Program," a platform calling for triennial parliaments, abolition of plural voting, local government reform, land allotments, employer's liability, local option on the sale of alcoholic drinks, disestablishment of the Church in Wales and Scotland, Irish Home Rule, and some other, vaguer suggestions. What they offered was radical but scarcely new; it was also miscellaneous, reflecting the hodgepodge of interests and groups to whom the radicals appealed: the Lib-Labs, the Dissenters, the Irish, the Welsh, and the Scots. They were facing that old Liberal necessity of making a majority out of minorities. Their proposals were anathema to most middle- and upper-class Englishmen; and many older Liberals left the meeting at Newcastle troubled by the very idea of a program: "Some of us," said one of them wistfully, "look back to the good old time when we took up one great burning question and fought it."* The Liberals opened the way for that promissory device of modern elections, the manifesto, but when they were briefly in office from 1892 to 1895 they lacked the will, the agreement, and the political force to carry through; most of their bills came to grief in the House of Lords.

The only important radical accomplishment emerged from Harcourt's 1894 budget. One source of government revenue had long been a complicated cluster of taxes levied on estates when their owners died. In 1886, Lord Randolph Churchill had proposed a simplification and reform of this inefficient system but fell from power before he could carry through his plans. In 1889, the Liberal Unionist G. J. Goschen introduced an additional death duty of 1 per cent on estates worth more than £10,000, and in 1894 Harcourt went back to the Churchill scheme, removing the distinction between landed and personal property and introducing graduation, from 1 per cent on estates of £100 to 8 per cent on estates worth over a million pounds. The yield—like Goschen, Harcourt had to finance rapidly increasing naval expenditure—was nearly double what the old death duties had brought ten years before, but the greater importance of the innovation was prospective. Later Chancellors of the Exchequer not only increased the death duties to finance steadily growing government expenditure but, consciously or incidentally, used them as a means of redistributing wealth.

Weak in the country as a whole, and relatively ineffective in Parliament, the radicals had to contend with the two men who headed the Liberal party in the nineties. Despite some surprisingly radical inclinations, Gladstone—eighty-three when he took office for the last time—was failing physically, shielded by family and friends from regular political involvement, and unwilling or unable to confront

*Quoted in H. V. Emy, *Liberals, Radicals, and Social Politics, 1892–1914* (1973), p. 10.

the problem of a successor. Moreover, he was singlemindedly concerned with getting Home Rule and held on for only six months after
his second bill was defeated in September, 1893. In his retirement as
in office, he refused to desert his early financial principles; he
disapproved the temptation to increased expenditure in Harcourt's
death duties. Gladstone's successor was Lord Rosebery, a very
wealthy peer who had been Foreign Secretary in both the third and
fourth Gladstone governments. His two avocations were writing history and racing; his horses won the Derby in both years of his
premiership, a turn of fortune that fulfilled one of his life's ambitions
but probably did him little good with the Dissenters in the Liberal
ranks. Rosebery disapproved of much of the legislation called for by
the clamorous sections of the Liberal party and opposed Harcourt's
death duties in the cabinet. Like Gladstone, he believed in seeking a
single issue on which to unite the party and thought he had found a
way to transcend the petty struggles of party in a commitment to a
modern, liberal imperialism. It is not clear that imperial enthusiasm,
even with the promise that it could serve as a basis for social reform
at home, commanded the attention of much of the country, and it certainly alienated important segments of Liberal opinion. When Rosebery gave way to Salisbury's third administration in June, 1895, and
an election followed a month later, he was happy enough to contemplate a period in opposition, to allow the necessary regrouping.
But the magnitude of the Conservative victory, with an absolute majority of 152, the defeat of Harcourt and Morley, and the rout of
working-class candidates — were the last pieces of evidence, if any
were needed, to prove that the Conservatives answered the mood, if
not the needs, of the nation.

Now, once again, it seemed that Joseph Chamberlain's hour
might have come. Increasingly isolated in the Liberal party in the
early eighties and left high and dry by Gladstone's conversion to
Home Rule, Chamberlain gradually came to rest, but not to office, in
alliance with the Conservative party. His stature and his grasp for
power gave him a strong claim on office in 1895. To general surprise,
he chose the Colonial Office, a post rarely held by a front-rank politician but a choice of great symbolic as well as practical significance. Chamberlain had the abilities and the social and intellectual
background to mediate between new social forces and the old political world; but he found little occasion or impulse to do so among the
Conservatives, a generalization not seriously qualified by his sponsorship of some remedial legislation, including the Workmen's Compensation Act of 1897. The energy he had once spent on social reform
and near-socialism in Birmingham and in the cabinet was now transferred to the Empire and in time to the advocacy of protective tariffs

—as though some recessive characteristic in the industrial Nonconformist tradition had suddenly become dominant.

Salisbury was left the most important political figure at the end
of the century. Preoccupied with foreign affairs and, in his last years
in office, ill and in semi-retirement, he had little interest or confidence
in the domestic course of a spreading democracy he despised. But
Englishmen, as the quip goes, dearly love a lord, and Lord Salisbury
—wealthy, intellectual, clever, and remote—was peculiarly qualified
to be admired by the prosperous and comfortable late-Victorian middle classes, whose upward ambitions were being so fully satisfied.

He was succeeded in 1902, not by a social upstart like Chamberlain, but by his nephew Arthur Balfour, who, after a brief dalliance with Churchill's Fourth party, had made (or rescued) his reputation by his toughness as Chief Secretary for Ireland from 1887 to
1891. Balfour was a reformer of sorts, but his personal qualities both
narrowed his sympathies and blunted his political effectiveness. He
shared with his uncle an unfortunate taste for cutting and sometimes
brutal language; moreover, his aristocratic, Anglican traditionalism
was compromised by a philosophical skepticism which, like his language, not infrequently alienated his supporters as well as his
enemies. But his worst political fault was a natural indolence that
kept him from the necessary engagement in serious political business. As a result, when he was finally driven from the leadership in
1911, his party was abandoned to nerve, opportunism, and invective
in the unreliable hands of men trying to use Balfour's techniques
without his ballast. For nearly a generation, the party that represented a majority of Englishmen needed vision and imagination and
got style instead.

Ireland

The results of the general election of 1886 had proved the hostility of
most Englishmen to Home Rule. In a speech that same year Salisbury
made evident his belief that the Irish were incapable of governing
themselves, and explaining away his harsh reference to the Irish as
"Hottentots" affected neither his conviction nor the country's sympathy with it. Churchill, his mind set on strengthening the party's
position in the constituencies, struck at a weak point in the Home
Rulers' arguments by "playing the Orange card"—summoning up
fears among Protestant bigots in England and Ulster of the prospective tyranny of the Roman Catholics. More than once the government
summarily refused further concessions to distressed Irish tenants,
only to grant them in 1887 by bringing leaseholders under the protection of the land acts. The Tories were forced to take that step by the

urgings of a commission of their own appointment; their loathing of Parnell was too great for them to believe or follow his moderate insistence on the same point throughout the preceding year.

Sir Michael Hicks Beach, the Chief Secretary, found the Irish landlords immune to his advice. The Irish peasants turned to a more effective weapon than advice, the "Plan of Campaign," launched late in 1886. Under the plan, the tenants of a particular estate were to bargain as a unit with their landlord; if he refused the rents they offered, they were to pay their rents instead into a general fund to be used for fighting him and for supporting tenants who might be evicted. Eighty-four estates were subjected to the plan; on sixty the landlords came to terms. Of the twenty-four holdouts, the most stubborn was Lord Clanricarde, whose rents were some 25 to 30 per cent above judicial rents fixed for neighboring estates; he steadily refused to reinstate evicted tenants, and in 1892 his former tenants were still being supported by public subscription. The land act of 1887 had to be wrung from a government and Parliament favorable to the landlords, but the coercion act that accompanied it was eagerly accepted, even at the price of still further limitation of debate to prevent Irish obstruction. Balfour, Chief Secretary from 1887, faced with a virtual state of insurrection in Ireland, enforced the law with great effectiveness.

On the day of the second reading of the coercion bill, *The Times* published a letter, purportedly written by Parnell, which implicated him personally in the planning of the Phoenix Park murders five years before. Like most members of Parliament, the government at once concluded that Parnell was guilty, despite his denials. At a trial for libel, brought by one of Parnell's supporters, more such letters were produced by the newspaper's counsel. Parnell then demanded that a select committee of the House inquire into their authenticity. Instead, the government set up a special commission of three judges, and at the hearing it was found, under brilliant cross-examination, that the journalist who had supplied the letters, one Richard Piggott, had forged them. Nevertheless, it was clear from Salisbury's language that he believed Parnell was capable of writing them.

The dramatic outcome of the hearing helped Parnell's cause even in English public opinion; so did the fact that the Plan of Campaign was sufficiently like trade-union action to seem natural and justifiable to many working-class radicals, and in the last years of the eighties, it seemed possible that Gladstone's campaign for Home Rule was set fair for victory. Then, on the day before Christmas, 1889, Captain O'Shea sued his wife for divorce and named Parnell as corespondent. It is morally certain that O'Shea was lying when he maintained in court that he was not a consenting party to the liaison; but the case was undefended, so O'Shea's statements could not be subjected to what would almost certainly have been devastating cross-examination. If he did know of the relationship, O'Shea had consented to it as a means of furthering his political ambitions — Parnell had risked a serious intraparty quarrel by supporting O'Shea's candidacy for Parliament in 1886 — and because his wife stood to inherit a large sum of money from an aunt who had to be kept ignorant of her domestic irregularities. By 1889, however, the aunt was dead, and the will was in dispute, and O'Shea decided to move. It has often been said that O'Shea decided to move in collaboration with *The Times* and certain politicians, but the most recent evaluation of this extremely complicated story concludes that O'Shea's personal reasons were sufficient to provoke the suit in 1889, and the fact that some members of the government had certain knowledge of Kitty O'Shea's liaison with Parnell — Chamberlain in particular — does not permit us to go so far as to conclude connivance. The case was, however, a great stroke of luck for the Unionist cause, succeeding where the deliberate plot of the Piggott forgeries had failed.

Parnell wanted to make Mrs. O'Shea his wife. Out of respect for her wishes and financial interest, he could not urge that she sue for a divorce until after her aunt's death. But even when O'Shea took the initiative, Parnell remained confident, apparently, that O'Shea's connivance would somehow be shown or that he could be bought off and would withdraw. None of these things happened; had the suit been defended successfully, the divorce would have been denied and marriage between Parnell and Mrs. O'Shea made impossible. The decision in November, 1890, gave O'Shea not only the divorce but the custody of children who were certainly not his. Beaten and humiliated, Parnell tried to stave off political defeat, first by denying the relevance of his personal affairs to his leadership, then by trying to raise popular sentiment in Ireland against enemies who were now able to emerge in the Irish parliamentary party. Gladstone had already had to make the unhappy decision that his party, and particularly its Nonconformist elements, would never accept an alliance with a proved adulterer, and a series of dramatic meetings of the Irish party culminated in December, 1890, in the withdrawal of forty-five members of the party, leaving Parnell with only twenty-eight supporters. The next year was occupied with fruitless negotiations. As Parnell's political strength declined, so did his health; he died early in October, 1891.

The breakup of the Irish party, the time required for regrouping, and the incalculable damage done to English opinion made Home Rule again a political impossibility. The second bill, introduced in February, 1893, was the pitting of Gladstone's determination against public apathy and hostility. The bill was much like that of 1886, except that it would have allowed Irish members to sit in Westminster to vote on those Irish and imperial measures that were to remain outside the competence of the Irish parliament. Despite the able opposition of Chamberlain, the bill passed the Commons easily, for the Liberals (now purged of their dissidents) and the Irish had a majority. But the Lords struck the bill down by the overwhelming vote of 419 to 41. Besides killing Home Rule, the vote showed how completely the Liberals had lost their aristocratic supporters—a hard blow to their finances as well as their political strength—and made it still more certain that a later Liberal government would be faced with the problem, largely dormant since 1831, of doing something about the Lords' veto.

Meanwhile, the Conservatives had begun to pursue an entirely different course. Balfour, though his secretaryship from 1887 to 1891 was necessarily concerned primarily with law enforcement, was lacking in neither reforming instincts nor a sense of tactical advantage. His device to solve the Irish problem was land purchase. Gladstone's land acts had contained purchase provisions whereby the state could through loans help individual tenants to buy their holdings, and by the early eighties, such arrangements had come to be looked on favorably by many reformers in both parties. In 1885, Salisbury's first government carried an act—called Ashbourne's Act—to implement land purchase; it was partly a gesture to the temporary Tory alliance with Parnell, but it was made possible by sincere conviction among some Conservatives and by the collapse of the land market in the agricultural depression. Because the act was experimental, the financial resources made available were not large, but the act required no down payment from the tenant and set repayment and interest at a level that did not exceed the rent.

In 1886, Gladstone had introduced a land purchase bill to parallel the Home Rule bill; to some extent, the proposal was an encouragement to landlords not to block the more important provision for self-government. In the long run, however, the bill was intended to replace the old Irish land system by a peasant economy, the solution John Stuart Mill had urged in the sixties. On theoretical or economic grounds, some men believed that a large-scale puchase scheme was doomed to disaster; but the chief opposition came from the Liberal Unionists who found in it a pretext for undermining Home Rule—this notwithstanding Chamberlain's earlier commitment to land purchase. The Unionists addressed their argument to the British taxpayer who, they insisted, would be paying out money to benefit an unstable and ungrateful Ireland.

Purchase, then, was not a new approach to the Irish land problem; the novelties in the acts of 1888 and 1891 lay rather in their scale, their terms, and the skill with which Balfour stole the initiative for the unresponsive Conservative party at a time when the Home Rule cause was crashing in ruins. The principle of the acts was largely that of Ashbourne's Act, though the terms of payment were readjusted in the tenants' favor. The five million pounds made available experimentally in 1885 was doubled in 1888. The act of 1891 raised the sum by an additional £33 million; that fund was to be the limit of advances, but once it was reached, money returned to the fund could be reallocated. Finally, in 1903, the land question was settled all but finally by Wyndham's Act, carried by a Balfour protégé who had taken over as Chief Secretary in 1900. The provisions of the act were made particularly favorable to landlords, who were offered a bonus of 12 per cent on the sale price negotiated between tenants of an estate and the landlord; the tenants received still more favorable terms than in 1891, and the outside limit of state loans was raised from £43,000,000 in the 1891 acts to £150,000,000. English opposition did not materialize, and in Ireland, where Michael Davitt — the founder of the Land League and a socialist who wanted land nationalization — and a few others were violently opposed, the new leader of the Irish parliamentary party, John Redmond, swung opinion and votes behind the plan. The debate was concerned largely with amendments in detail.

Although changes proved necessary in 1909, Wyndham's Act was a complete success. Those who had argued that ownership would make the Irish peasantry sober and responsible were right: by 1922, although state loans amounted to £120,000,000, only £12,000 had gone into unrecoverable debts. A land problem more than a century old had been solved, though it had taken more than thirty years of educating Parliament and landlords to do it. The scheme was intended to "kill Home Rule by kindness"; that did not happen: the moral and emotional nationalism that fired the demands for self-government and even independence was a cause for which many Irishmen were still willing to die. But few could have imagined that in the relative peace of the first decade of the twentieth century.

Foreign Affairs

Salisbury was one of the best diplomatic technicians England has produced, and the diplomatic world was one in which his aristocratic manner and confidence were still valuable assets. Yet what he did was a far cry from the work of Castlereagh, Canning, or Palmerston.

It was rather a holding operation for a country whose decline he probably at heart thought inevitable.* As in all holding operations, the initiative lay in other hands. By the end of the nineties, the reins were seized by the impulsive Chamberlain, now able to do what some people had predicted he intended to do from the day he took office — run foreign affairs from the Colonial Office. But more important was the passing of initiative in Europe from British hands to others eager and now able to take it. One by one, Salisbury's inherited assumptions were flouted or falsified, and when he retired in 1902 Britain was being forced into an entirely new orientation in world politics.

Throughout the nineteenth century, Britain's Continental policy of isolation had conferred enormous power on her: economic indispensability, the Navy, and overwhelming prestige were guarantees of that. This situation was changed by the unification of Italy and Germany and by the emergence of a still unstable but ambitious and vengeful Third Republic in France. It was changed too by the growth of democracy in Britain. In the simpler world of mid-century Palmerston could control or ignore the public as he chose. Late-Victorian politicians were unsure of themselves when faced with a public opinion that fluctuated unpredictably in its enthusiasms and hostilities. Instinctively, most politicians remained mid-Victorian, but they also remembered what had happened in the Midlothian campaigns.

On balance, down to the nineties, Russia still seemed to pose the major threat, while France was the persistent nuisance in the foreground, squabbling, demanding compensation, and repeatedly changing front with changes of ministries. But the real center of European power lay in Berlin. There, from the creation of Germany in 1871 to his dismissal in 1890, Bismarck played a secretive, complicated, and masterly diplomatic game, the key to which was the frustration of a Franco-Russian alliance that might force him to fight on two fronts. In the eighties he erected an elaborate series of secret agreements with Austria-Hungary and Italy — to become famous as the Triple Alliance — and at the same time with Russia, though the other alliances were directed specifically against her. To absorb energies that might otherwise upset his carefully achieved balance, he encouraged both Italy and France in overseas ventures. But in all these conflicting policies in Europe, there was a common undercurrent: everyone was perfectly willing to see Britain suffer for her past sins. While there was little explicit anti-British intention in any of the

*Salisbury is said to have enjoyed and often repeated a remark of a Chinese diplomat that they conversed on equal terms as representatives of two decadent empires.

agreements, the effect of them was to enforce Britain's isolation and to make it a result of Continental intent rather than of British convenience.

North Africa

Most of Britain's diplomatic involvement with Continental nations in the last two decades of the century grew out of conflicts originating in competition for overseas empire. Here, too, Britain responded rather than initiated. Her older possessions were of little account in this new kind of conflict, so alien to the Palmerstonian universe. Canada, Australia, and New Zealand had been largely satisfied by the grant of responsible government, and its extension to the Cape colony in 1872 had worked as well as could be expected, given some lingering sympathies among the Cape Dutch for their trekking kinsmen in the republics to the north. India, the greatest of British possessions, was ruled without apparent difficulty; the firmness that the Mutiny had dictated was applied efficiently and profitably, without harassment by a barely discernible nationalist movement. For the rest of the world, Britain's policy remained based on its three traditional aims: the maintenance of strategic security, by influence if possible, by control if necessary; the encouragement of trade; and the steady avoidance of involvement and expense.

It has already been shown how respect for the third principle and to some extent for the first led the Gladstone government in the early eighties to abandon the compulsory federation of South Africa and to confer on the Boer republics a slightly qualified and miserable independence. We have seen how the first principle led the same government to a wholesale violation of the third in Egypt.* Robinson and Gallagher have argued that the scramble for Africa in the last decades of the century can be traced to the upsetting of the European balance of power by the British occupation of Egypt. Once the British were unwillingly settled in Cairo, they found early evacuation impossible: the nationalism that had forced their intervention would not simply fade away, and Conservatives were even more easily convinced than Liberals that at least twenty years of firm discipline were needed to salvage the country. Once this conclusion was drawn, it was a logical further step for the British to shift the base of their policy in the eastern Mediterranean from a steadily weakening Turkey to a Cairo they could not let go. The security of the route to India had forced the occupation in the first place; now Egypt became a strategic end in itself.

*See above, pp. 361–365.

British Egyptian policy ran in two main diplomatic channels: seeking tacit approval of the occupation by other powers, and safeguarding the River Nile on which the Egyptian economy depended. The former concern, we may say, dominated the North African diplomacy of the eighties, the latter of the nineties. These two concerns led the British into deeper and deeper involvements in the largely unknown interior of the continent, which had challenged explorers, missionaries, and a few businessmen, but which the British public had viewed apathetically and the ministers saw only as a source of entanglement and expense.

From the seventies, Africa became of increasing interest to traders from countries on the Continent who made their claims seem more and more compelling to their governments. The French were the most aggressive, laying claim to a huge empire in Saharan and equatorial Africa, the hinterland of their Algerian and Tunisian colonies. Bismarck, never himself much interested in colonial enterprise, was prodded into support of his merchants' interests in the eighties. The Portuguese belatedly awoke to possibilities in their vague, centuries-old claims on the two coasts and expanded them into a dream of a Portuguese belt across Africa. The Italians struck inland from Eritrea and Somaliland on the east coast; and a grasping private combine, in which King Leopold II of the Belgians (in his private capacity) was the prime mover, began to assert itself in the vast basin of the Congo. Most British ministers were immune to such enthusiasm and thought of no more than maintaining their accustomed influence and welcoming trade where private enterprise showed itself able to prosper.

Given such an unambitious attitude, it was easy enough for British governments, whether Liberal or Conservative, to bargain away potential interests in many parts of Africa for security in the few places that held real meaning for them. In the early eighties, they recognized the claims of Britain's "oldest ally," Portugal, a bilateral solution that provoked an immediate European reaction. Britain thereupon went quite willingly to the Berlin Conference in 1885* to give up its Portuguese agreement and to recognize, as she had not yet done, the existence of the Congo Free State. Similarly, Britain freely abandoned most of equatorial Africa to the French, whose indignation over Britain's unilateral action in Egypt was especially strong. That Britain managed to rescue for herself the great delta of the Niger and its interior was due not so much to governmental

---

*This, it should be noted, is the Berlin *Conference,* as opposed to the Berlin *Congress,* called to deal with the results of the Russo-Turkish War in 1878. See above, pp. 354–355.

foresight as to the imagination of Sir George Goldie, at the head of what later became the Royal Niger Company. Goldie hurriedly concluded the necessary treaties with native chiefs, bought out two French companies, and agreed (to the ministers' great delight) to take over the expenses of administering the region; such individualist success had always had the blessing of a grateful, relieved, but not very interested government.

The most striking partition was the agreement with Germany in 1890; it established German claims in eastern and southern Africa, British paramountcy in the territories that are now Kenya and Uganda, where the headwaters of the Nile lay, and a protectorate over Britain's traditional ally, the Sultanate of Zanzibar on the east coast. William II was eager to grant what the British wanted so that in return he might get from the British the small island of Heligoland, off the German coast, a base of great potential value for his naval ambitions.

In the nineties, the British moved to consolidate. In 1894, in Uganda, a British sphere of influence since the Anglo-German agreement, Rosebery created a formal protectorate because the British East African Company had disappointed ministerial expectations by coming to the edge of bankruptcy. In the west, where the French threat was still expanding, Chamberlain boldly asserted direct government control of an area that had been left to Goldie's company; and a conference on the Niger in 1897–1898 arrived at a careful delimitation of territories subject to the two countries.

In the east, Britain had deliberately encouraged Italian ambitions in Ethiopia to keep out the French and to gratify a useful Mediterranean ally, but that scheme was nullified in 1896 by the defeat of the Italians at the hands of the Ethiopians and their allies, the Dervishes, who had killed Gordon and forced evacuation of the Sudan ten years before. The native threat gave new force to the notion of reconquering the Sudan. With far from unanimous support in Egypt or at home, General Kitchener (later Lord Kitchener) accomplished it by a careful, slow progress up the Nile, climaxed by a decisive defeat of the Dervishes at Omdurman in 1898.

This thrust southward encountered a French push from west to east through a gap the British had tried but failed to close in earlier negotiations. The French force was only a little band of reconnaissance troops led by Captain Marchand, who reached the Nile at Fashoda at about the time when Kitchener occupied Khartum. Kitchener hurried south to insist on French withdrawal. The two officers handled themselves with the utmost correctness and civility and threw the problem to the foreign offices. For a time in 1898 war between the two countries seemed a real possibility, but Salisbury's firmness finally forced the French to back down; a convention signed early in 1899 left Britain in firm control of the Nile valley.

South Africa

It will already have been apparent how important private enterprise was in securing parts of Africa that ultimately became British. Explorers and missionaries helped to make the interior of the continent known to white men; the colorful and dramatic exploits of Speke, Burton, Stanley, Livingstone, and Mackenzie helped to acquaint the British public with the attractions and opportunities in Africa and to stir enthusiasms that gradually became permanent. But the government remained unsympathetic to missionary claims or to sentimental pressure and responded much more readily to the accomplishments of trading companies where they were sufficiently organized and effective. Humanitarian pressure meant involvement and expense; the trading companies did what was necessary and paid for it themselves.

These companies do not, however, reflect a surge of "economic imperialism" at home. English merchants directly involved in African trading were few in number, and widespread public interest in the possibilities of African sales and investment appeared only in the nineties, after the carving up of Africa was largely accomplished. Even then there was no certainty of success. The Imperial East African Company was slow in gaining government support and failed miserably after getting it. In West Africa, where English interest was almost nonexistent in the formative years, only the extraordinary abilities of George Goldie kept a rather shaky economic venture afloat by a bold policy of expansion.

The most important of the African entrepreneurs was Cecil Rhodes, a clergyman's son, who as a young man had gone out to the Cape to regain his health and to make his fortune. Rhodes believed deeply in empire, a belief that was in part a response to the call to empire sounded by John Ruskin in a famous lecture at Oxford in 1870, when Rhodes had gone back to study. Rhodes was a believer, moreover, in holding the Empire close by the device of federation, and because the devolution of central power was a prerequisite of federation, he sent Parnell ten thousand pounds. In the eighties, Rhodes conceived the grandiose notion of an "all-red" (i.e., all-British) route from Cairo to the Cape, an idea that attracted some highly vocal though scattered support among nascent imperialists at home. Neither Salisbury nor Chamberlain ever trusted Rhodes—the gift to Parnell was enough to ensure that—and in the Anglo-German Convention of 1890, Salisbury made territorial concessions to Germany that ruined the prospect of a Cape-to-Cairo railway. One might expect Chamberlain, himself a businessman, to have been more sympathetic, and certainly the two were necessary collaborators, but a common loyalty to imperialism — an emotion foreign to Salisbury — was not strong enough to overcome the different directions of their ambitions and obligations or the collisions inevitable in the yoking of two immensely masterful men.*

Rhodes made his fortune in the diamond mines, but the controlling element in his career was one from which he made somewhat less money: the discovery of gold on the Rand in the heart of the Transvaal in 1886. Within fifteen years that area was producing a quarter of the world's gold supply. Almost at once the Transvaal was converted from a poverty-stricken state into potentially the richest country in southern Africa. The change not only frustrated hopes of federationists that a bankrupt republic might ultimately have to choose union with the English-dominated colonies to the south, but it even threatened to shift the balance of economic power from Capetown to Johannesburg.

From the time of Majuba Hill and the abandonment of compulsory annexation of the Transvaal in 1881, British policy towards the Boers had been consistent: to force their trade through Capetown and to prevent them from gaining independent access to the sea. When in 1884 the Germans made their first sortie into southwest Africa, the Liberals, needing Bismarck's approval of their Egyptian enterprise, had to concede the breaking of their coastal monopoly; but they at once set up a protectorate in Bechuanaland, until then considered worthless, because it blocked the rail link between the Boers and the ports that the Germans built as soon as they arrived. East of Cape Colony, the British quickly occupied empty coastal areas to forestall further German incursions. The discovery of gold made the isolation of the Boers even more essential, yet the government and Parliament were as averse as ever to spending money to accomplish it. Here Rhodes stood ready with his British South Africa Company, chartered in 1889 to expand Cape interests through a corridor west of the Boer republics to the vast area north of the Transvaal and reaching to the Zambesi, known after 1894 as Rhodesia. Again private enterprise moved in where the imperial impulse was weak.

The Transvaal, growing richer daily, was not likely to be reconciled. Its president, Paul Kruger, who had trekked as a boy, embodied the most aggressive form of Boer nationalism. As the money

---

*Rhodes's vision is also to be found in the setting up in his will of scholarships at Oxford for young men from the colonies, the United States, and Germany, a provision extended to women in 1977.

began to pour in, he bought arms, established informal but important contacts with the Germans, and imported Dutch advisers. He
was determined, moreover, to have the independent outlet to the sea
that the Cape and London intended to deny him. A railway was built
to Lorenço Marques on Delagoa Bay in the Portuguese east-coast
colony of Mozambique, and when it was opened in 1895, Kruger at
once drastically raised rates on the line running from the Rand to the
Cape to divert traffic to his new and shorter route. When the Cape interests replied by setting up a wagon line, Kruger forcibly closed the
fords (or drifts, to give them their local name) along the way. The
Orange Free State and Natal were already gravitating from the Cape
towards the Transvaal.

Rhodes, who in 1890 had become prime minister of the Cape
colony, had built his political power on the retention of Cape supremacy, a policy that brought him support even from the Cape
Dutch, despite their natural sympathies with the Boers. The imminent destruction of that superiority in the mid-nineties made drastic
action necessary; so did Company affairs, because it had now become clear that Rhodesia was not going to duplicate the mineral
windfall of the Transvaal. Rhodes tried repeatedly to buy the Portuguese end of the railway and even the whole colony of Mozambique from Portugal, but Salisbury and Rosebery refused to support
him: the possibility of trouble with Germany was too great. The old
policy of encircling the Boers broke down over the last gap in the
line.

Rhodes and his Cape allies, however, found another card to play.
The gold mines had drawn tens of thousands of non-Boers into the
Transvaal; by the mid-nineties these *uitlanders,* as they were called,
were two or three times as numerous as the Boers and paid nine-
tenths of the taxes. But Kruger was determined that his country
should conform to the old image of a farmers' republic; he was
willing to exploit the rough, vulgar vanguard of progress but not to
yield any political rights. Though the *uitlanders* could still make
money, in spite of Kruger's taxes and monopolies, they increasingly
resented their restriction to what Sir Alfred Milner, the high commissioner after 1898, called the status of helots.

Salisbury and Chamberlain both thought that the growth of a
non-Boer population would ultimately submerge the Boers and bring
about South African union; hence their unwillingness to risk trouble
with Germany to bring the Transvaal to heel economically. Rhodes,
however, was in a hurry and preferred to help evolution on. He had
first to capture the *uitlanders* for his purposes. Many of them were not
English, and English and non-English alike wanted an *uitlander*
republic, not Rhodes's scheme of incorporation in an Empire that

would probably tax and regulate them as heavily as Kruger did; moreover, like nearly all South Africans, they hated the prospect of any philanthropic or government meddling with their control of the essential supply of colored labor. But when *uitlander* petitions to Kruger got nowhere, the reformers began to turn, noisily and clumsily, into revolutionaries. To bring off a coup they needed Rhodes's support and money.

In June, 1895, as all these matters were approaching a climax, Joseph Chamberlain became Colonial Secretary. He was, as we have seen, a convinced imperialist, and, because of his political importance, he was allowed more or less a free hand. But plans were already laid by Rhodes and his friends when Chamberlain took office. Chamberlain's first act was to hand over to the Company a strip of Bechuanaland bordering on the Transvaal, presumably for building a railway to link the Cape and Rhodesia; shortly after, having made arrangements for native preserves to meet the objections of chiefs to Company rule, he turned over the whole protectorate. Chamberlain knew about the possibility of an *uitlander* rising and was prepared to take advantage of it when it came by sending the High Commissioner from Capetown to mediate between Kruger and the insurgents, presumably exacting the political reforms Kruger had consistently refused.* But Rhodes and his close friend, Dr. Leander Starr Jameson, the Company's Rhodesian administrator, had concocted a plan for an invasion from Bechuanaland by a band of mounted Company policemen to coincide with the rebellion in Johannesburg.

Both Chamberlain and the High Commissioner (then Sir Hercules Robinson) refused to be told of Jameson's plan when Rhodes's representatives dropped hints, refusals that were easily and to some extent deliberately construed as support. But while the plan seemed to its inventors an admirable instrument for imperial purposes, its *uitlander* beneficiaries were in a quandary. In December, when plans for a raid and a rising were well advanced, the United States suddenly presented Britain with an ultimatum in a boundary dispute between Venezuela and British Guiana, a politically inspired step that was ultimately resolved by arbitration entirely in Britain's favor. But at the time of the ultimatum, the dispute served only to highlight Britain's diplomatic isolation, and the realization that Britain might be unable to support them damped the enthusiasm of the Johannesburg revolutionaries. The collapse of their movement only height-

*In 1881, the British had kept, without defining, suzerainty; in a subsequent revision of the convention in 1884, at Boer insistence, the word was dropped, though the right to control the Transvaal's foreign relations was specifically reserved. Differences of interpretation of these ill-defined documents were an ingredient in the developing tension.

ened Jameson's impatience, and on December 27, he and a troop of fewer than five hundred men invaded the Transvaal. Jameson's Raid was foolish, ill-timed, and wretchedly organized, but it went on despite the strictest orders from Capetown and London to stop. Kruger, who had been informed of the invaders' progress, simply waited for the best moment to pounce, and, on January 2, Jameson and his men were captured. The *uitlander* leaders, whose names were discovered in a saddlebag, were tried and imprisoned. Jameson and his lieutenants were sent back to London, where, in spite of enthusiastic popular support, they were put in jail for terms of up to eighteen months.

The Raid broke Rhodes's power; his complicity was so clear that he resigned the Cape premiership at once, and Chamberlain forced him off the Board of the Company. But as a symbol Rhodes was as powerful as ever. A parliamentary investigation in 1897 left him censured but unpunished; shortly after, Chamberlain, who had been absolved by the investigation of any complicity, went out of his way to praise him. Face-saving was necessary to advance Chamberlain's personal ambitions and to rescue his imperial program; the country as a whole was satisfied and even a little proud. But abroad, nearly everyone believed with Chamberlain's enemies at home that he had been deeply involved and went on to conclude that the greatest imperial power in the world was willing to stoop to any villainy to extend her grasp over small, defenseless nations. The day after Jameson's capture, the Kaiser telegraphed Kruger congratulating him on putting down the invasion, a deliberate act that made the British public aware of what the government was gradually coming to realize, that Germany, much more than France or Russia, was Britain's main Continental adversary. The Boers, of course, were confirmed in their worst suspicions. Kruger continued to import huge quantities of German arms through Delagoa Bay and after his triumphal election in 1899 set up a virtual dictatorship to prepare for the war he knew was coming. Within a year of the Raid, the Orange Free State, drawing similar conclusions, had elected a nationalist government, which entered into a close alliance with the Transvaal. In 1898, a Dutch ministry came into power at the Cape, headed by a moderate but impelled by extremists. A move meant to strengthen British authority and prestige had ended by bringing them even lower.

The *uitlander* agitation in the Transvaal continued nonetheless. In early 1899 it was reinforced by an explosion of bitterness on the part of British workmen, who had not before taken much part; they were infuriated by a jury's acquittal and commendation of a Boer policeman who had killed an English worker in the course of an arrest. Petitions were sent directly to the Queen, and Chamberlain, after a brief hesitation, decided to accept them and so to champion the *uitlander* cause, a course already marked out by Sir Alfred Milner, the new High Commissioner at the Cape, who had publicly taken a very strong line about Kruger and his republic. In the course of negotiations in the spring and summer of 1899, Kruger made a number of concessions to the *uitlanders'* claims, but Milner and Chamberlain replied by increasing their demands. In October, Kruger was driven to issue an ultimatum, just forestalling a British ultimatum to which the cabinet, at Chamberlain's urging, had reluctantly agreed. There seemed no solution but war.

The Boer War

Chamberlain and Milner were out to reverse what seemed to them a steady decline in British influence in South Africa; their colleagues, less advanced in their views, worried about the naval base and the threat that the Boers, in the republics or in Cape colony, might pose, just as Colonel Arabi had threatened Suez in 1881. Despite the jingoism at the time of the Raid, there was no popular demand for war, and British commercial interests (though not the Cape interests) were getting on quite well enough with things as they were. But conviction in high places led to a war to restore a state of things that had been proved unworkable as far back as the Canadian revolt in 1837.

In the early stages of the war, Boer soldiers far outnumbered British, but the Boers wasted time and strength on sieges of three British strongholds—Kimberley, Ladysmith, and Mafeking. Had they not done so, it is certainly possible that they might have driven the British forces back on Capetown; but, when they did move, the Boers preferred to strike towards Durban in Natal, in quest of their own seaport. These defects in Boer strategy were not immediately evident, however, and in December, 1899, the British suffered a succession of sharp and costly defeats. At this point, Lord Roberts, the hero of the second Afghan war, was put in charge, with Lord Kitchener, fresh from Omdurman, as his second in command. Their extraordinary abilities were soon felt and seen. The sieges of Kimberley and Ladysmith were raised early in the new year; Mafeking was relieved in May, the news touching off an alarming and rather ugly celebratory riot in London. More to the point was the brilliant and resolute crushing of the Boer army, so apparently complete that in October the Transvaal was annexed again.

The victory, however, was delusive, for the Boers excelled in guerrilla warfare, for which the British were completely unprepared. The tactics finally evolved to deal with it were drastic, effective, and alarming. A network of blockhouses was constructed, first along railway lines, then across the countryside, joined ultimately by barbed wire. Each compartmentalized area was then "swept," its farms being systematically emptied, and all noncombatants put into concentration camps, where gross mismanagement brought the deaths of women and children to perhaps a fifth of the total population of the camps — a scandal that became an important political issue at home. Despite occasional victories by small Boer forces against overwhelming odds, their military effort finally ground to a halt; they asked for an armistice in March, 1902. The Peace of Vereeniging, signed in May, promised an amnesty and repatriation for all save certain rebels, provided an oath was taken to the king; English became the official language, with Dutch allowed as an option; civil administration and self-government were promised as soon as possible; and a grant of three million pounds was made by the British towards rebuilding the farms wrecked in the sweeps.

The generous settlement was carried further by the enlightened administration of the High Commissioner Sir Alfred (later Lord) Milner, whose manner and commitments three years before may well have made the war closer to inevitable. While he was no diplomat, he was a superb civil servant and quickly accomplished not only reconstruction but wholesale reforms of the finances, local administration, and public health of the former republics, resolutely steering them towards self-government. He was assisted by a group of young men — nicknamed "Milner's kindergarten" — apostles of empire whose influence in imperial matters remained considerable down to and following the Second World War.

British policy also encouraged the emergence of the moderate Boers, who had been submerged by the extremism of Kruger. General Botha, who had been commander in chief of the Boer armies, became the first prime minister of the Transvaal when self-government was granted by the Liberals in 1906 and later the first prime minister of the Union of South Africa. His closest colleague, General Jan Christiaan Smuts, became one of the leading statesmen of the Empire and Commonwealth. A constitutional convention followed shortly on the grant of responsible government, and in 1910 the Union of South Africa, comprising the Cape, Natal, the Orange River Colony, and the Transvaal, came into existence. The transition from war to self-government and union in less than ten years seemed a remarkable triumph for liberal imperial statesmanship; only some thirty years later did Britain discover that Boer wounds still burned and that the spirit of Kruger was not dead.*

*See below, p. 596.

Escape from Isolation

In Britain, the war had far-reaching results. The military performance showed that the Cardwell reforms, valuable though they were, had not gone far enough. In 1890, a royal commission had urged a reorganization of the top command of the Army, the main proposal being the creation of a general staff, such as all modern Continental armies had, to devote itself entirely to planning and coordination of effort. But the only change made was the removal in 1895 of that venerable obstructionist, the Duke of Cambridge, as commander in chief and his supersession by the brilliant, powerful General Lord Wolseley. But all Wolseley's ability could not make up for poor organization, and the post mortems on the Boer War showed clearly how deficient intelligence and planning were: Roberts and Kitchener had won by improvisation. Even so, it took another five years for a general staff and other army reforms to come under the administration of R. B. (later Lord) Haldane.

The war, as we shall see, had important political effects, particularly in the Liberal party. But perhaps the most stunning impact of the war was its revelation of Britain's isolation from Continental countries. The enmity of Germany was evident, but elsewhere on the Continent opinion was nearly unanimous in condemning Britain's immoral assault on a tiny nation, an assault on which Europe was prepared to put the worst construction, following the egregious blunder of the Jameson Raid.

One reponse to this isolation was to build up the Navy. The technological changes in naval warfare — in ship design, engines, and armament — during the last decades of the nineteenth century seemed to be part of a continuing revolution, for a single change in any aspect of naval technology might make a whole squadron of newly built ships obsolete. A large building program was undertaken in 1888–1889 and another in 1893–1894. Then, in 1898, Germany began to build up her navy. To this new threat from abroad, made worse by her now apparent diplomatic isolation, Britain responded by a third building program, launched in 1904 by the able and controversial first sea lord, Sir John Fisher, a program that created the modern battleship; the *Dreadnought* was the first of them and gave its name to its class. Such naval building plans had not only important diplomatic repercussions but profound effects on government finance and, through that, on politics.

The other response was to seek out new friends in the world. The British had been deeply touched by the loyalty shown during the South African war by the self-governing colonies of Canada, Australia, and New Zealand, each of which sent troops to fight, but more important, in the long run, was the emergence of a new friendship with the United States. Given the diplomatic history of the nineteenth century, no alliance seemed more unlikely. In 1812–1814, the two countries were at war; the British attitude during the Civil War had left strong resentment. The century had been punctuated by a succession of incidents: the Maine boundary, Oregon, the *Trent* affair, the Fenian raid on Canada, the *Alabama* controversy in the early seventies, the Venezuela boundary dispute. The question of an Isthmian canal and disagreements over the Newfoundland fisheries were perennial troublemakers. American expansionists were unable to believe that Canada was not destined one day to join the Union, and they did what they could to promote it. The huge Irish emigration to the United States added another dimension to bad relations between the two countries. In short, no war the United States could have got into would have been more popular at any time in the century than a war against Britain.

Parallel to this tradition of bitter hostility, however, was a tradition of cooperation. Many of the humanitarian and radical movements of the century rested on the joint efforts of dedicated men on both sides of the ocean. Even more to the point was British investment in America; common banking interests had facilitated the settlement of outstanding disputes in 1842, and this factor became even more important as the century wore on, despite American protectionism. By the time the United States began to enter its maturity after the Civil War, many educated, highly placed men were looking to England as a spiritual home, and in the seventies began that steady stream of American brides, daughters of millionaires, who helped to re-establish the shaky fortunes of the British aristocracy. Lord Randolph Churchill and Joseph Chamberlain both had American wives, and the entry of such ladies and their families into the highest circles in England helped to soften English prejudices against Yankees, just as the Anglophiles in the State Department, where they were reasonably safe from the backlash of the twisting of the lion's tail essential to all American politicians, found in British views and manners something more than John Bull-ish condescension or aristocratic effeminacy.

Anglo-American cooperation was quickly established in the Far East, where Britain's economic stake was crucial. The East India Company's monopoly of the China trade had been terminated in 1833, but private merchants had kept and extended a near monopoly for Britain: by the eighteen-nineties, nearly three-quarters of China's trade was with Britain, forming a sixth of Britain's total foreign commerce. But Britain's Continental rivals looked greedily on the huge, moribund Chinese empire and in the last decade of the century were busy carving out spheres of influence clinched by leased ports that could be closed to all but their own traders; talk of partition of the country became increasingly common. The British, anxious to maintain their traditional informal ascendancy, were supported by the Americans, who themselves were eager to break into the China market. The American "open door" notes in 1899 called on all the European powers and Japan to refrain from converting their spheres of influence into exclusive trading preserves; it was a declaration which, though it applied to a British-leased port as well, was welcome to the British, not least because it was widely supported by American opinion.

To some extent the Americans were encouraged to make a gesture to Britain by the support that Britain had given to the United States during the war with Spain in 1898. Much conservative opinion in England was sympathetic to the Spanish cause, but that sympathy was submerged partly by diplomatic calculation, partly by genuine enthusiasm in public opinion for what appeared to be a war of liberation. The seizure of the Philippines had involved the United States, almost providentially, in the Far East, in a way that blunted a heavy-handed show of German interest. In the same way, the United States, alone among the powers, looked benevolently on Britain during the Boer War, despite strong anti-British sentiments among American minority groups; in all consistency, she could hardly do otherwise.

These frankly self-interested informal collaborations were quickly turned to advantage by British diplomats and the strongly Anglophile American Secretary of State, John Hay. Steering through the treacherous shoals that lay in public opinion, sectional interests, Canadian nationalism, and the Senate, the diplomats within a few years had settled most of the outstanding Anglo-American disputes. The question of the Isthmian canal, which had troubled relations between the two countries since the Clayton-Bulwer Treaty of 1850, was resolved by the Hay-Pauncefote Treaty of 1901; Britain's abandonment of the canal to American initiative was part of a general British recognition of American supremacy in the Caribbean. The Alaskan boundary dispute was settled in 1903 by an arbitration in which the British participant, who held the balance between American and Canadian representatives, decided in favor of the American claims, at the sacrifice of intense Canadian feelings. But British willingness to concede American domination of the Western Hemisphere was a small enough price to pay for an alliance, however informal, in a hostile world.

At about the same time, in 1902, Britain concluded a formal alliance with Japan, growing out of a common concern about Russian expansionism in Asia. Determined to keep Korea as her own preserve, Japan wavered between negotiations with Russia and with Britain, but Lord Lansdowne's insistence on her choosing resulted in the treaty which, after the Japanese victory over Russia in 1904–1905, was tightened to include military obligations in case of attacks on Korea or the Indian frontier. Even more remarkable steps were taken from 1903 when negotiations were begun to settle differences with France, the most persistent troublemaker in Britain's diplomatic game. Lubrication by colonial concessions on both sides facilitated an understanding in 1904 by which the British at last gained a free hand in Egypt in exchange for their recognizing the dominance of French influence in Morocco, the coastal kingdom that separated France's north and west African colonies. From 1907 on, secret and informal conversations were taking place between the military commanders of the two nations, and after 1911, the English, aware of the menace of the German fleet, came to rely heavily on the French in the Mediterranean, while the British fleet was concentrated in home waters. This startling reversal of attitude was taken easily enough in Britain, but the ingrained hostility of French opinion might have been a serious obstacle had it not been happily counteracted by popular enthusiasm evoked by successive visits to Paris by the new King, Edward VII, beginning with a triumphal journey in 1903.

The Anglo-French entente had a curious feature. The Russo-Japanese War of 1904–1905 found France allied to Russia, a relationship built on close financial ties established in the eighties, while Britain was allied to Japan. In 1907, British policy made an even more startling reversal in agreeing with Russia to settle the outstanding sources of friction between them. There were three main trouble spots: Tibet, Afghanistan, and Persia, all clearly tied to the question of the safety of India's borders. In all three cases the two powers agreed to respect the sovereignty of the countries concerned, but in the most crucial case of Persia the country was blocked out into two spheres of influence; the Russians in the richer and more populous north were, however, debarred from the outlet they wanted to a warm water port by British domination of the south, thus insulating the Indian frontier. Unlike the agreement with the French, the Russian understanding was far from popular in England, partly because of the traditional hatred of the Tsarist regime, partly because that regime had recently shown itself as despicable as ever by the successful suppression of the liberal revolution of 1905. But diplomatic necessity triumphed, and by 1909, the Triple Entente had been erected as a counterpoise to the Triple Alliance created by Bismarck twenty years before.

The ambiguous factor in this polarization was Germany. In the last years of the nineteenth century, as we have seen, Britain depended on somewhat erratic German acquiescence or good will for her diplomatic security in Egypt. The Kaiser, moreover, was perfectly willing, in his tortuous personal diplomacy, to show himself as a benefactor to Britain when it suited him; for example, in spite of the Kruger telegram, William II claimed credit for discouraging Kruger when he came seeking aid during the war. Both Chamberlain and Lord Rosebery were favorable to a wide understanding with Germany, and Chamberlain tried twice to promote it, without success. The two powers cooperated in an expedition against Venezuela in 1902, a venture which ruffled Anglo-American waters and which the British were only too glad to escape from when the Kaiser agreed reluctantly to accept arbitration of the dispute. In 1905, the Kaiser intervened dramatically in the Moroccan question as a response to the Anglo-French understanding, but got nothing from the Algeciras Conference, called in 1906 at Germany's insistence to settle the problem she had created.

Despite the gigantic German naval building program, the British agreements with France and Russia do not seem to have had any explicit anti-German intention, however much France may have looked on Britain as a valuable ally in a future German war. British diplomacy of the early twentieth century was devoted, rather, to making the best of a bad job—to liquidating the problems that had arisen from incursions on her once unchallenged supremacy and to finding remedies for an isolation that began to look dangerous once it was imposed on her rather than freely chosen. The world of Canning and Palmerston was gone, though it had taken British statesmen more than thirty years to realize it.

The Queen's Death

To many Englishmen, Gladstone's death in 1898 must have seemed to mark the end of an era, but the feeling spread even more widely when, at the age of eighty-one, Queen Victoria died on January 22, 1901. She had reigned for something over sixty-three years. Her unpopularity in the years following Albert's death had long been dissipated, partly by Disraeli's management, partly by the very fact of her longevity, which gave to her symbolic embodiment of the nation a dimension of eternity that fitted well with British hopes, if not with reality. The jubilees on the fiftieth and sixtieth anniversaries of her accession, in 1887 and 1897, had in effect been celebrations of the greatness of the Victorian age, and to the later jubilee was added a full measure of imperial glory. To the disenchanted eye, the Queen herself was a far from perfect symbol. She was dull, increasingly arbitrary, and subject to curious whims, such as the idolization of her crude Scottish servingman John Brown. Some of her personal idio-syncrasies may be excused as the results of the loneliness of an isolated old woman. But she was hard on her ministers, and her in-tense Toryism, amusing as it often is in her remarkable letters, becomes alarming when one thinks how far it was shared by the upper classes who led in her near-deification. It must be said in her favor, however, that she took her responsibilities seriously, worked hard, and was not lacking in ability and wisdom.

It would be difficult to imagine a more striking contrast than that between the Queen and her son, who ascended the throne as Edward VII. He was neither very bright nor hard-working; he had been wretchedly educated and trained almost not at all for his responsi-bilities. He was affable; he had lived (to his mother's distress) a gay and even raffish life; he cultivated the society of men whose only claim, in the eyes of many censorious persons, was their wealth; and he had been kept waiting much too long in the wings. Yet his per-sonal qualities served the nation well—symbolically, because the early twentieth century liked gaiety and opulence, and practically, as a representative of his country abroad. The latter role should not be overstressed, but his reign marks the real transition of the English monarchy from a significant political institution to its present pri-marily social function, a part Edward's son King George V and Queen Mary were to carry with a greater degree of sobriety and re-sponsibility. Bagehot had suggested forty years before that, for ordi-nary people, a monarchy was superior to a republic because a monarchy gave them the spectacle of interesting people doing inter-esting things. Edward VII and his successors were doubtfully inter-esting as individuals, but they have managed to do well a useful and attractive job of interesting their nation—and other nations.

THE LIBERAL RESURGENCE, 1900–1911

The Roots of Victory

The Queen's name became an adjective about the middle of the nine-teenth century; it has conveyed many meanings to subsequent gen-erations and has set every historian his own job of definition. The adjective made from her son's name presents similar though simpler problems: to most people it still connotes calm, prosperity, and com-fort, the Indian summer before the great Empire was beset by the de-structive winds of war, depression, and social change. In actuality, the Edwardian period and even more the first years of the reign of George V were troubled and violent, and in them, retrospectively, nearly all the characteristics of the postwar world can be clearly seen.

Domestic political events in the early years of the twentieth century built cumulatively to the Liberal triumph in the general election of 1906; yet in 1900 it would have needed a rash prophet to guess the magnitude of that victory. The "khaki" election in October, 1900, was a clear effort to turn the excitement of an apparently final victory in the Boer War to political advantage. The Tory majority, which had already sunk in bye-elections from 152 to 128, was increased by only three seats; but the margin was more than ample. Their position seemed the more secure because of the state of the Liberals. Rosebery, an outright imperialist, had been driven from the leadership by the Gladstonians in 1896; when Harcourt retired two years later, the leadership passed to Sir Henry Campbell-Bannerman, a wealthy, attractive Scot whose real qualities were not to become apparent until his premiership after 1905. Inclined slightly to the left of center, Campbell-Bannerman finally committed himself during the war to a position that his opponents called pro-Boer; it was essentially the old Gladstonian, humanitarian stance, strengthened by an excellent political issue in the scandal of the concentration camps. Campbell-Bannerman was supported by Morley and John Burns, who had forsaken his socialism for liberalism; more effective than either was a young Nonconformist demagogue from Wales, David Lloyd George. But much of the talent in the party had gone with Rosebery into the liberal-imperialist camp: H. H. Asquith, Sir Edward Grey, and R. B. Haldane, men who dominated much of the history of the prewar years. In taking up that position, they were not merely trying to capitalize on an imperialistic, war-fed sentiment that was finally spreading throughout Britain in the nineties; they held their views seriously, because they had a sense of humanitarian responsibility to backward and decaying countries, a belief that only through responsible, large-scale imperialistic enterprise could social reform and a high standard of living be achieved in England, and an evolutionary faith in the natural superiority of large units, a faith they shared with Joseph Chamberlain and Sidney and Beatrice Webb.

With the Liberal leadership divided, it was even harder to create a majority out of minorities, which was, as we have seen, the political task of the Liberal party. As things turned out, the job was done for them by the Conservatives.* Two acts of Balfour's government—the Education Act of 1902 and the Licensing Act of 1904—consolidated Nonconformist indignation, though quite unjustly, considering the merits of the measures. The Education Act, drawn up by the great civil servant Sir Robert Morant, had been triggered by an agreed test

---

*The Conservative party at the end of the nineteenth century and in the first two decades of the twentieth was often referred to as the Unionist party. The two terms are used interchangeably in the discussion here.

case in 1899 (the Cockerton judgment) in which the courts held, as Morant knew to be true, that the efforts of local school boards to extend their work to secondary education were illegal. The opportunity was seized to overhaul the entire system of state education. In the act of 1902 the school boards created in 1870 were abolished; their responsibilities were turned over to the county councils, or the councils of other local areas such as county boroughs. The new education authorities were empowered to deal with secondary and technical as well as primary education. So far there could be little objection, but as we have seen, the act of 1870 had left England with a dual system of schools: the board schools, supported by the state exclusively and free after 1891; and the old voluntary schools, usually denominational, supported by fees, endowments, and state grants of the kind given since 1833. The voluntary schools were now brought directly under the education authorities; by meeting all their expenses, the state assured a satisfactory leveling-up of teachers' incomes and a more effective supervision of teaching, though the voluntary schools still retained the right to choose their teachers and continued to give denominational instruction.

The state had long been supporting such denominational schools out of taxes, but the Dissenters saw the arrangements of 1902 as giving a new lease on life to Church of England schools, while Roman Catholic schools were subsidized for the first time. Passage of the act was difficult, and the agitation in the country was not unlike that of 1843; but because Dissent was now a more potent political factor in the country than it was then, the act had a severe electoral effect, as Graham's bill did not.

The Licensing bill offended the prejudices of the Dissenters by trying to promote the temperance they advocated. That there were too many public houses nearly everyone agreed, and it had long been debated whether or not there should be compensation for owners of licenses which were not renewed, when local authorities cut the numbers. Balfour proposed compensation not from taxes but from a fund levied on the remaining licensees, whose holdings would become correspondingly more valuable. It was a fair and ingenious plan, but in Nonconformist eyes it only blackened the government by seeming to endow sin.

Irish discontent was to some extent allayed by the land purchase act of 1903,* and it was to be several years before the demand for Home Rule was effectively resurrected. But the Irish parliamentary party had recovered handsomely from the Parnell catastrophe; under the leadership of John Redmond, it was effective in Parliament and

*See above, p. 437.

potentially overwhelming in an Irish election. A newer sectional or, more properly, nationalist group was, in its own way, more prominent. The Welsh, marked off from England by race and tradition, were also reinforced in their sense of national identity by the still living Welsh language. As many of them were fervent Nonconformists, there had grown up in the nineteenth century a powerful demand for the disestablishment of the Church of England in Wales. Accused of being an alien and minority institution, the Church in fact had grown in strength and in its sense of responsibility. But the political demand remained strong and was included in the Liberals' Newcastle Program in 1891, though their disestablishment bill got nowhere. The temperance issue was meaningful to Welsh Methodists, but the Education Act was a particular affront, since in so many parts of Wales the only school was a voluntary Church of England school, whose continued monopoly seemed now to be assured. To Welsh even more than English Nonconformists, the Conservative ministers were the tools of the hated Church; if God would not smite them with lightning — Lloyd George did his best to deputize — they would smite them with the ballot.

The early years of the century also saw a sharp increase in labor agitation. The recovery of the economy and the upturn in prices after 1896 had put an end to the general rise in real wages; industrial unrest became all the sharper by reason of that long-term development. In 1903–1904 there was a short-run downturn and considerable unemployment, and an act of 1905 set up local committees to help to put men into jobs, though financial assistance to the unemployed was limited to the disbursement of voluntary public contributions. But such economic developments fell rather within the province of militant trade unionism; the political side of labor, nearly eclipsed in 1895 and 1900, might have continued to languish. In 1900, the Trades Union Congress had set up the Labour Representation Committee to promote Labour candidacies outside the increasingly discredited auspices of the Lib-Labs, but it met with scant success: only two of the fifteen L.R.C. candidates in 1900 (one of them was Keir Hardie) were returned.

In 1901, a powerful resurgence of working-class political interest was set off by a decision of the House of Lords, in its judicial capacity, that a trade union was financially liable for civil wrongs (torts) committed by its agents. In this particular case the Taff Vale Railway Company, a Welsh line that had been struck by the Amalgamated Society of Railway Servants, sued the union for damages and was awarded £23,000. Since 1871, unions had proceeded on the assumption that they could not be sued; union members or officers might be held personally liable, but union funds were secure. There was, to be

sure, some unfairness in this immunity; on the other hand, the denial of any immunity at all by the Taff Vale judgment made strike action impossible, for it enabled any employer to ruin a striking
union. The way out was clearly to force Parliament to pass remedial
legislation, and the best way to accomplish that was to send to
Parliament a Labour delegation too large to be ignored. The Balfour
government gained no credit in Labour eyes by referring the question to the slow procedures of a royal commission, and in its last
years in office, the government outraged Labour voters and many
others as well by permitting South African mining employers to import Chinese coolie laborers, who were paid wretched wages and
housed in compounds almost like animals. Disguised slavery in
South Africa was easily translatable into the threat of slavery at
home, now that the weapon for destroying unions had been found.

The final blow to Tory prospects was delivered by Chamberlain
in his proposal to abandon free trade for a system of tariffs and imperial preference. His action was rooted in the eighties, at a time when
he was still an orthodox free trader. At that time, in response to the
great depression and the rise of foreign competition, there grew up a
"fair trade" movement, a protectionist campaign in parts of the business community. At about the same time, there appeared in England
and in the colonies a movement for imperial federation, to find some
constitutional scheme to bind the colonies more closely to the mother
country. Neither movement got very far, the first foundering on the
seemingly unalterable conviction of politicians and public that free
trade was God's way, the second on the resistance of colonial politicians and voters who were at bottom nationalists, however sentimental some of them may have grown about the old tie to England.
The main institutional result of the imperial federation movement
was the beginning of a series of regular conferences of the prime
ministers of the colonies — colonial conferences at first, then imperial
conferences: the first was held in 1887, in connection with the golden
jubilee celebration; there were others at the diamond jubilee in 1897
and at the coronation in 1902. In 1907, it was decided to hold them at
four-year intervals; more recently, transmuted into Commonwealth
conferences, they have been held annually, with the British prime
minister, rather than the colonial secretary, in the chair.

Chamberlain, an advocate of closer institutional ties in the Empire, was blind to the hard reality of colonial nationalism, seeing it,
as he had misread it in Ireland and the Transvaal, as a delusion that
proper arrangements would expunge. When his proposals for an imperial council got nowhere with the assembled prime ministers in
1902, he seized on their self-interested suggestion that a system of
imperial preference might be adopted by Britain. Already protec-

tionist, even against British goods, the colonies saw a common imperial tariff and guaranteed access to each other's markets as an important economic gain. Chamberlain saw the proposal as a means to a closer political tie.* On returning from a visit to South Africa in 1903, Chamberlain proclaimed his conversion from free trade, a view that made him the darling of the Unionists, increasingly a party of businessmen; the cabinet, however, was still dominated by free traders. Balfour's response was characteristic. He tried a compromise, rejecting a general tariff but proposing retaliation against discriminatory foreign tariffs. When this plan angered free traders without satisfying the tariff reformers, he reconstructed his cabinet by dismissing the most ardent free traders and accepting Chamberlain's offered resignation, without telling either side that the other was going, a sleight-of-hand trick that did nothing to endear him to his party.

Out of office, Chamberlain moved rapidly to take over the party by a campaign in the country addressed to the now linked enthusiasms for Empire and tariff reform; by 1905 he had captured the National Union, the Conservative analogue of the Liberal party organization he had made his base of operations at the start of his national political career. Balfour, his party disintegrating under him, decided to resign in December, 1905, without dissolving Parliament. He thought the Liberals more divided than they were, because Campbell-Bannerman, chasing his minorities, had recently committed himself to a gradual approach to Irish Home Rule, a step Rosebery at once denounced. But Campbell-Bannerman was able easily to form a government without Rosebery, and in mid-January, 1906, won a sweeping victory at the polls. The Liberals campaigned on many issues, most of them gifts from the Tories, but their most potent argument summoned up the passions bequeathed to posterity by the Anti-Corn-Law League: cheap bread against dear bread. They won not only the disgruntled minorities but a majority sick of Tories and insistent on the cheap breakfast table. The Unionists kept only 157 seats, and at least 109 of their occupants owed their main allegiance to Chamberlain. The Liberals, with 377 seats, had a clear majority of 84 over all other parties combined. But, Unionists apart, the other parties in the Commons could not be laughed off or submerged in a mere majority. Redmond's Irish nationalists numbered 83, and—most portentous of all—the Labour Representation Committee, now transmuted into the Labour party, returned 29 members in addition to the 24 Lib-Labs and miners who still stood by the Liberals.

*Chamberlain's hope was not entirely fanciful: the same expectation underlay the foundation in the 1950's of the European Common Market.

Liberalism Triumphant

Campbell-Bannerman's cabinet was very able. The liberal imperialists got a larger representation in the government than seemed warranted by the nature of the majority in the country, yet they proved their indispensability by their performance in office. Sir Edward Grey, a protégé of Rosebery, took the Foreign Office, but quickly shed his patron's confirmed anti-French attitude and sustained the new military and naval cooperation between the two nations. Haldane, at the War Office, finally set up the general staff Britain had needed for so long and, without superseding Cardwell's system of linked battalions,* organized the Army into the Territorial Force, for home service, and the Expeditionary Force, for service overseas. The Exchequer went to H. H. Asquith, who had come out of a Dissenting background through Oxford and a wealthy and fashionable marriage to a powerful claim on political office which he fulfilled more effectively than his radical former associates were willing to predict when he was in opposition. Morley, at the India Office, was the chief representative of the Gladstonian old guard. The cabinet was much like those of the past forty years, with two exceptions: John Burns, at the Local Government Board, had once been a workingman and a socialist; and the new president of the Board of Trade, David Lloyd George, rightly struck a chill into the hearts of aristocrats and those who thought with them. Chamberlain in the eighties had at least been rich; Lloyd George felt *with* the poor, not *for* them.

In April, 1908, Campbell-Bannerman retired ill, and in two weeks was dead. His place as prime minister was taken by Asquith. Lloyd George's striking performance brought him the wider opportunities of the Exchequer; his replacement as president of the Board of Trade was Winston Churchill, the most brilliant of the undersecretaries. The son of Lord Randolph Churchill, he had served in the Army and as a newspaper correspondent in the Sudan and South Africa. He had begun his political career as a Tory M.P. but followed his family's maverick strain into the Liberal party and an early career of reforming; in 1910, he moved on to the Home Office.

Though the years since 1870 had seen few major initiatives in social legislation, it had been a time of creative social thought. Philanthropists, Fabians, local governments, and civil servants at Westminster had undertaken detailed investigations of the way the English people lived, and many local or voluntary experiments had been undertaken to deal with the consequences of the poverty that had been so starkly revealed. The social services in continental coun-

*See above, p. 347.

tries—especially in Bismarck's Germany—offered sweeping examples for comparison and imitation. Despite the decline of organized religion, a diffused Christian morality continued to dictate, and even to intensify, political and social imperatives. The educated public responded with increased conviction to the teachings of, among others, the Oxford Hegelians T. H. Green and Bernard Bosanquet and the radical London professors and publicists L. T. Hobhouse, J. A. Hobson, and Graham Wallas. And from all parts of the political spectrum came the call for "national efficiency," which meant not only that government should be more responsive and adventurous but that the whole community should be fitter and better organized to face the struggles that lay ahead: the doctrine was not without authoritarian overtones.

Long nurtured in studies, pulpits, and individual consciences, this activist outlook came to political maturity in the Liberal party after 1906. The most prominent ministers of the new generation seemed to have overcome the defects that had plagued the party since the retirement of Gladstone. Asquith himself had been a pupil of Green's at Oxford, while the principal advocates of social legislation in the cabinet embodied complementary strains—the passionate nationalist and Nonconformist sympathies of Lloyd George and the newly powerful myth of Tory democracy in the aristocratic adventurer Winston Churchill. They stood in marked contrast to John Burns, the erstwhile leader of the Dockers' Strike, whose early socialism had evaporated and whose vanity and insecurity made him a prisoner of the unimaginative, poor-law-oriented civil servants at his ministry. Aware that a decade later the Liberal party fell into a rapid decline to be supplanted on the left by a newly militant Labour party, many have questioned the reality of the phenomenon of the "new liberalism." But in the prewar years political labor, its separate organization notwithstanding, showed little tendency to independent activity, and both the electoral situation and the Liberal record argue against trusting too much to the skeptical wisdom of hindsight. The progressivism for which the United States is famous in these same years was paralleled in Britain, and with even more impressive accomplishment.

Social Reform

In 1906, free school meals were made available to poor children; in 1907, a school medical service was set up, and every grant-aided secondary school was required to keep a quarter of its places open, or free, to pupils from the state elementary schools, a step that broke down at a blow the traditional class barrier between primary and secondary education. In 1908, the Children's Act dealt with cruelty and neglect, put an end to imprisonment of children under fourteen, and revised the system of reformatories. In the same year, the eight-hour day was given to miners, and the government set up a system of old-age pensions, payable at the age of seventy. Charged entirely against the state's budget, without the contributory features of many such schemes in other countries, the pensions were far from generous— five shillings a week, or 7s. 6d. for a married couple, provided there was no other income beyond £26 a year—but the concession in principle was a major departure in social policy.

On the day of his resignation in 1905, Balfour had appointed a royal commission on the poor law; it reported in 1909. Both the majority and minority agreed that the old system of 1834 had outlived its usefulness and that administration of the poor law should be transferred to local government, much as the school boards had been absorbed under the Education Act of 1902. The majority recommended that the county and borough councils take over the poor-law machinery intact; the minority, dominated by Beatrice Webb, urged "the break-up of the poor law" by turning over relief, health, and education functions to separate committees of the councils, thereby destroying the dominance of the deterrent mentality. The minority went even further to urge positive state action to remedy the causes of poverty and unemployment.

The old-age pension act of 1908 had already carried one of the Webbs' recommendations into law. John Burns, however, prevented the poor-law recommendations of either majority or minority from being enacted, and the First World War and postwar dislocations prevented poor-law reform from being realized until 1929. But in 1909 Winston Churchill carried an act setting up a system of labor exchanges to inform employers of available labor and workers of available jobs—"organizing the labor market" (to use the Webbs' phrase) to reduce unemployment and increase mobility. Another act of Churchill's dealt with sweated industries, such as tailoring and dressmaking, in which hours were long and wages pitiful because of the persistence of the putting-out system or because the fragmentation of the trades kept them insulated from the factory and workshops acts. Social investigators and Parliament had long been concerned about this evil, but legislative efforts to remedy it had remained ineffective. Sir Charles Dilke, who returned to political life in 1892 after being disgraced by a divorce suit in 1885,* was the leader of the antisweating movement, as of many other causes for industrial reform, but his bill, which finally reached a second reading

*See above, p. 371.

in 1908, ran afoul of the inherited scruples of Herbert Gladstone, the Home Secretary, against the principle of a state-enforced minimum wage. Churchill again seized the initiative and carried the bill in 1909, setting up trade boards for certain named industries. Composed of representatives of employers, labor, and the state, the boards were empowered to set minimum wages for their industries, subject to the approval of the president of the Board of Trade.

In 1911, the National Insurance Act was carried into law. Lloyd George was the sponsoring minister; the civil servants most deeply involved in its preparation were H. Llewellyn Smith, who had organized the labor exchanges, and W. H. Beveridge (later Lord Beveridge), one of the main architects of the later forms of the British welfare state; the chief administrator was Sir Robert Morant, who had reworked the educational system in 1902. Part I of the act provided a system of unemployment compensation for certain industries; Part II set up a system of national health insurance, to provide medical care, maternity benefits, and sick pay. Like the German insurance law of 1889, which was its model, and unlike the Old Age Pensions Act of 1908, the Act of 1911 was a contributory scheme; workers paid their share by buying stamps to be pasted in their insurance books; employers and the state made additional contributions. The existing system of friendly societies was incorporated into the scheme, a concession to the strength of a powerful vested interest. Still, the opposition was intense: some socialists and labor leaders believed the plan should be financed solely from taxation like the old-age pensions; the British Medical Association feared the effects of an act from which its members ultimately benefited greatly; some duchesses and other grand ladies boldly pledged their refusal to stamp the books belonging to their servants. But the government, at the price of a few concessions, carried the bill easily.

The House of Lords

Impressive though these accomplishments in social welfare were, many of the Liberal government's plans and obligations were defeated in the House of Lords. Unwilling to challenge Labour directly, the Lords agreed to a Trades Disputes Act in 1906, which reversed the Taff Vale decision by the simple device of removing the unions' liability for acts committed by their members or agents. But nearly all the other Liberal efforts to fulfill their commitments to their traditional supporters were beaten: an education bill in 1906, a plural voting bill in the same year, a series of land reform bills in 1907, and a new licensing bill in 1908. Needless to say, Welsh Disestablishment or Irish Home Rule would have met a similar fate, had the government dared to attempt them.

The House of Lords was acting in a transparently partisan way. For the twenty years of Conservative rule it had caused no trouble at all; now that the Liberals had an overwhelming majority in the lower house, the peers became the chosen and willing instrument of Conservative leaders who were powerless in the Commons: the House of Lords was no longer the watchdog of the constitution, sneered Lloyd George, it was Mr. Balfour's poodle. But the peers were tramping heavily on thin ice. Their position had been parlous since 1832: an occasional show of statesmanship or prudence had saved them for a time; but the possibility of a clash had been growing since the Wensleydale case and the ruckus over the paper duties in 1861.* In the nineties Gladstone had seriously considered the Lords an issue on which party and country might be united in yet another moral crusade. Now the confrontation came on the question of finance.

In 1909, Lloyd George presented a sweeping, radical budget. He had to find large sums of money to cover the cost of Liberal social reforms, most notably old-age pensions, and the much larger expense of the armed forces, particularly Fisher's growing Navy; newly converted to large-scale social reform, he saw the budget as the base from which he could move to assure Liberal dominance for a generation. Like chancellors before and since, Lloyd George raised the income tax and death duties and put more on those profitable luxuries, alcohol and tobacco. But there were three innovations: first, a small supertax on incomes of over £5,000; second a small duty on the capital value of undeveloped land; and third, a tax of 20 per cent on the unearned increment (or as we might say, capital gains) in land value, paid whenever the land changed hands. The supertax was bad enough, but a direct assault, even a minor one, on land hit the peers where principle was dearest. In November, with no leadership in their House worthy of the name, they rejected the budget, which was not finally carried until the following spring, a year after its introduction.

Lloyd George had not intended the confrontation, but when the deadlock developed, he gleefully carried his case to the country. In a famous and threatening speech at Limehouse, in the East End of London, in July, 1909, he told his audience that no country, no matter how rich, could "permanently afford to have quartered upon its revenue a class which declines to do the duty which it was called upon to perform." At Newcastle, in October, he pointed out that "a fully-equipped duke costs as much to keep up as two Dreadnoughts; and

*See above, p. 319.

dukes are just as great a terror and they last longer." In December Asquith announced that his government would move to limit the Lords' veto, but the general election in January, 1910, made that prospect uncertain. The Liberals fell from the 377 seats of 1906 to 275, while the Unionists rose to 273; the balance, then, was held by 82 Irish nationalists and 40 Labour members. Asquith had failed to extract from King Edward a promise to create enough peers, five hundred perhaps, to swamp opposition in the House of Lords. Within a month of the election King Edward died, to be succeeded by his second son as George V, the eldest son having died as a young man. George was a model of rectitude and sobriety; but coming late into direct succession to the throne and having been trained as a sailor, he lacked political experience and was unprepared for a constitutional crisis. He adopted his father's view that he would create peers only after a second election, and he insisted, moreover, that the House of Lords as then constituted must have a chance to vote on a Parliament bill. There was no Wellington in sight.

After the failure of a round-table conference of representatives of both sides of the dispute, the Parliament bill was accordingly introduced and beaten. In December, 1910, there was a second general election, which produced almost exactly the same results as that in January—272 Liberals, 272 Unionists, 84 Irish, and 42 Labour. In February, 1911, the Parliament bill was reintroduced, passing its third reading in the Commons in May. Meanwhile, the Conservative opposition in the Lords was strengthened by the rebellion of the so-called "diehards," led by a young peer, Lord Willoughby de Broke, to defend the prerogatives of their order. The diehards might have carried the day and forced the creation of peers, had not Lord Curzon persuaded the lethargic Balfour to repudiate them. In August the bill was passed, 131 to 114. It provided that any bill (such as the budget) certified by the Speaker as a money bill would become law without the assent of the Lords, at last converting the Commons' ancient privilege of origination into absolute control. Other bills, which still required the Lord's assent, could at best be delayed, for if a bill passed the Commons and failed in the Lords three times within two years, it became law without the Lords' assent. Finally, the duration of a Parliament, fixed at seven years since 1716, was reduced to five.

In 1911, then, the Liberals destroyed the veto by which the House of Lords could wreck their legislation, and passed the most sweeping welfare measure then imaginable. Yet the years from 1911 to 1914 saw little progressive legislation. Reforming surges do wear themselves out, but more relevant was the diversion of the government's energy into political obligations of great complexity: Irish Home Rule and Welsh Disestablishment were both carried under the

Parliament Act, but the necessity for passing the two bills in identical form two times beyond the first passage gave a sense of marking time that lessened public interest and ministerial vigor. More important still was the atmosphere in which the Liberals had to work. One crisis after another broke over Europe, while at home the government's authority was repeatedly challenged—by labor insurgency, by a newly militant women's movement, and once more in Ireland. Indeed, within Parliament itself, the consensus on which the peculiar strength of the British constitution had rested for nearly two centuries seemed to be crumbling away.

Selected Readings

In addition to Ensor and Shannon, two general studies become relevant at different points in this chapter: R. R. James, *The British Revolution: British Politics, 1880–1939*, vol. 1: *From Gladstone to Asquith, 1880–1914* (1976); and the two volumes of the epilogue of Halévy's *History of the English People: Imperialism and the Rise of Labour, 1895–1905* (1926, trans. 1929), and *The Rule of Democracy, 1905–1915* (1932, trans. 1934).

The basic explication of the nature and structure of politics is H. J. Hanham, *Elections and Party Management: Politics in the Time of Disraeli and Gladstone* (1959, 2nd ed., 1978). On the relationship between mass party organization and democracy, see the classic work of M. Ostrogorski, *Democracy and the Organization of Political Parties* (1902) and the more recent, less pessimistic interpretation, particularly appropriate to the relationship between mass and parliamentary parties in the post-1945 period, R. T. McKenzie, *British Political Parties* (1955, 2nd ed., 1963). On Conservative organization, E. J. Feuchtwanger, *Disraeli, Democracy, and the Tory Party: Conservative Leadership and Organization After the Second Reform Bill* (1968) and Janet Robb, *The Primrose League, 1883–1906* (1942). On the other side, D. A. Hamer, *Liberal Politics in the Age of Gladstone and Rosebery* (1972). Cornelius O'Leary traces the sanitizing of politics in *The Elimination of Corrupt Practices in British Elections, 1868–1911* (1962), a subject seen in a different light in W. B. Gwyn, *Democracy and the Cost of Politics in Britain* (1962). The third reform act and the consequent redistribution of seats involved immensely complex maneuvers, which remain complex in Andrew Jones, *The Politics of Reform, 1884* (1972). On the electorate thereafter, Neal Blewett, "The Franchise in the United Kingdom, 1885–1918," *Past and Present*, no. 32, pp. 27–56 (December, 1965), and Henry Pelling, *The Social Geography of British Elections, 1885–1910* (1967).

Most of the major political leaders have been the subjects of major or minor biographies. Winston Churchill wrote the life of his father, *Lord Randolph Churchill* (1906), understandably partial but a great book all the same; R. R. James, *Lord Randolph Churchill* (1959) is straightforward without being particularly penetrating, as is true also of his *Rosebery* (1963). The massive biography of Joseph Chamberlain by J. L. Garvin was completed by Julian Amery (6 vols., 1932–1968), but there is a good brief life, *Radical Joe* (1977) by

Denis Judd. Salisbury and Balfour were memorialized by family members in official biographies, Lady Gwendolen Cecil on her father, the third Marquis of Salisbury (4 vols., 1921–1932) and Blanche E. C. Dugdale on her uncle, Arthur James Balfour (2 vols., 1937). There are single-volume lives of both: A. L. Kennedy, *Salisbury* (1953) and Kenneth Young, *Arthur James Balfour* (1963). Roy Jenkins has written two biographies of Liberal statesmen, *Sir Charles Dilke: A Victorian Tragedy* (1965), and *Asquith* (1964). For preference, the latter has given way to Stephen Koss, *Asquith* (1976). Among other Liberals whose lives Koss has written about, *Lord Haldane: Scapegoat for Liberalism* (1969) and *Sir John Brunner: Radical Plutocrat, 1842–1919* (1970), the latter the great chemical manufacturer and devoted Liberal. After defeating a succession of biographers, Lloyd George has at last come through in John Grigg, *The Young Lloyd George* (1973) and *Lloyd George: The People's Champion, 1902–1911* (1978). Randolph S. Churchill has brought Winston Churchill's life down to 1914, after which it has been continued by Martin Gilbert; Churchill's own *My Early Life* (1930) is a marvelous account of his pre-parliamentary career.

On Salisbury's premiership, Peter Marsh, *The Discipline of Popular Government: Lord Salisbury's Domestic Statecraft, 1881–1902* (1978), and on attempts to repair the breach of 1886, Michael Hurst, *Joseph Chamberlain and Liberal Reunion: The Round Table Conference of 1887* (1967). On the background of the protectionism that so bedeviled Conservative politics, B. H. Brown, *The Tariff Reform Movement in Great Britain, 1881–1895* (1943). On the reconstruction of liberalism in Gladstone's last years and after, in addition to Hamer's *Liberal Politics*, cited earlier, Michael Barker, *Gladstone and Radicalism: The Reconstruction of Liberal Policy in Great Britain, 1885–1894* (1975); H. V. Emy, *Liberals, Radicals, and Social Politics, 1892–1914* (1973); Peter Stansky, *Ambitions and Strategies* (1964), a study of the struggle for the leadership after Gladstone's retirement; and H. C. G. Matthew, *The Liberal Imperialists: The Ideas and Politics of a Post-Gladstonian Elite* (1973).

On Ireland, in addition to the Solow, Lyons, and O'Brien volumes mentioned in Chapter 8, Peter Gibbon, *The Origin of Ulster Unionism: The Formation of Popular Protestant Politics and Ideology in Nineteenth-Century Ireland* (1975), and L. P. Curtis, Jr., *Coercion and Conciliation in Ireland, 1880–1892* (1963). To the Irish problem was added a Welsh problem, on which see two books by Kenneth O. Morgan, *Wales in British Politics, 1868–1922* (1963, 1970) and *Freedom or Sacrilege? A History of the Campaign for Welsh Disestablishment* (1965). On the African imbroglio, Robinson and Gallagher's *Africa and the Victorians*, cited in Chapter 8, remains central. Alan Moorehead, *The White Nile* (1960) is a fascinating account of exploration, and on missionary enterprise, Owen Chadwick's moving and remarkable book, *Mackenzie's Grave* (1959). Sir Philip Magnus, *Kitchener, Portrait of an Imperialist* (1959) is useful on the military side. The still mysterious and most awkward of the initiatives in the region is the subject of Elizabeth Pakenham, *Jameson's Raid* (1960) and Jeffrey Butler, *The Liberal Party and the Jameson Raid* (1968). On the changing nature of defense and diplomacy in the early twentieth century, Arthur J. Marder, *From the Dreadnought to Scapa Flow: The Royal Navy in the Fisher Era, 1904–1919* (5 vols., 1961–1970); Ruddock F. Mackay, *Fisher of Kilverstone* (1973); Charles S. Campbell, Jr., *Anglo-American Understanding, 1898–1903*

(1957); Bradford Perkins, *The Great Rapprochement: England and the United States, 1895–1914* (1968); Ian H. Nish, *The Anglo-Japanese Alliance: The Diplomacy of Two Island Empires, 1894–1907* (1966); G. W. Monger, *The End of Isolation: British Foreign Policy, 1900-7* (1963); and two books by Zara S. Steiner, *Foreign Office and Foreign Policy, 1898–1914* (1970) and *Britain and the Origins of the First World War* (1977).

The dramatic shift from Conservative hegemony to the last stand of Liberalism is the subject of A. K. Russell, *Liberal Landslide: The General Election of 1906* (1973). On the interplay of ideas, social policy, and politics, Reba N. Soffer, *Ethics and Society in England: The Revolution in the Social Sciences, 1870–1914* (1978); G. R. Searle, *The Quest for National Efficiency: A Study in British Politics and Political Thought, 1899–1914* (1971); P. F. Clarke, *Liberals and Social Democrats* (1978) and *Lancashire and the New Liberalism* (1971); Paul Thompson, *Socialists, Liberals, and Labour: The Struggle for London, 1885–1914* (1967); José Harris, *Unemployment and Politics: A Study in English Social History* (1972); Jeanne L. Brand, *Doctors and the State: The British Medical Profession and Government Action on Public Health, 1870–1912* (1965); and Bentley B. Gilbert, *The Evolution of National Insurance in Great Britain: The Origins of the Welfare State* (1966). The constitutional crisis of 1910–1911 is dealt with in Neal Blewett, *The Peers, the Parties, and the People: The British General Elections of 1910* (1972) and Gregory D. Phillips, *The Diehards: Aristocratic Society and Politics in Edwardian England* (1979).

Chapter 11
The End of Victorian England

1911–1918

THE EDWARDIAN INTELLECT

In the decade or so before the outbreak of the First World War, Western Europe was in ferment. In trying to understand these upheavals now, it is helpful to examine the revolutions under way at the same time in the intellectual world. Some of them had direct impact on political and social action; together, these parallel developments in society and intellect helped to create the modern consciousness. The patron saints of the modern intellect were all European: Max Planck, Albert Einstein, Sigmund Freud, Max Weber; other men, ranking less high in the pantheon, helped to shake their own times and to move much of the world for decades to come: Georges Sorel, Henri Bergson, Émile Durkheim, Benedetto Croce. All were contemporaries of the Edwardians. Perhaps only one Englishman (or, more properly, New Zealander) of the time can rank so high in a world perspective, the physicist Ernest Rutherford (later Lord Rutherford).

Rutherford's main contribution to the scientific revolution of the twentieth century was his research into the disintegration of the atom, significantly rather more an empirical than a theoretical enterprise; he also deserves the fullest credit for stimulating the pursuit of science in England to such a degree that Britain was able to recapture her leadership in the postwar world. Many Edwardian men of science are deservedly famous — English science by no means fell on evil times — but there were no Edwardian theoretical contributions to match those of Lyell, Darwin, or Clerk-Maxwell; and the attitude of English society towards science remained what Professor Ubbelohde has called (in contrasting King Edward to his father) "benevolent impenetrability."

The impact of Freud on England had to wait until after the war. The French intuitionist Henri Bergson had some small influence at several removes through the growing English interest in Continental syndicalism. In *Human Nature in Politics* (1908), Graham Wallas, a lecturer at the London School of Economics and a dissident Fabian, made an important contribution to psychology and political theory by calling attention to the importance of irrationalism in determining political behavior. Primarily interested in strengthening liberal and democratic institutions by finding ways to work them that were psychologically more sound than the usual rationalist prescriptions, Wallas occupies a symbolic place in English social and psychological thought: in the five years after his book appeared, his warnings about the role of unreason became disturbingly apposite. But the main philosophical development in English philosophy in the early twentieth century was the virtual destruction of the dominant late-Victorian idealist school of T. H. Green, F. H. Bradley, and Bernard Bosanquet by two Cambridge philosophers, G. E. Moore and Bertrand Russell. Between them, Moore and Russell reasserted the older rationalist and analytical tradition of English philosophy, while bringing to it a new sophistication — particularly in Russell's contributions to mathematical logic — that are of the first importance for future developments in English philosophy.

The architectural revolutions on the Continent and in the United States were, as we have seen, without important analogues in prewar Britain. To be sure, Edwardian craftsmen and designers made significant contributions to the international movement known as *art nouveau*, and Scotland produced an architect and designer of genius in Charles Rennie Mackintosh; but *art nouveau* was a fascinating byway, and Mackintosh remained a prophet without honor (or many buildings) in his own country. Edwardian music, while undergoing what the English always call a renaissance, scarcely compared with what was going on on the Continent: the decade that saw the meteoric rise of Stravinsky, Ravel, Strauss, and Schönberg found English composition dominated by Edward Elgar. Important work was done in folksong collecting, and younger composers just making their appearance — Ralph Vaughan Williams, Gustav Holst, and Arnold Bax—were much influenced by it, but they never approached the brilliance with which similar materials were exploited on the Continent by Béla Bartók. The flattering elegance of the portraits by the American expatriate John Singer Sargent can perhaps stand as the most appropriate reminders of Edwardian painting, but those painters whose reputations have survived nearly untarnished or grown—Augustus John and W. R. Sickert, for example—broke no new ground. The fifty-year-old techniques of the French impressionists were just becoming domiciled in England, and not many Englishmen were prepared to comprehend the first exhibition of French postimpressionists that took place in London in 1910.

The most impressive artistic accomplishments of the Edwardian age lay in literature. In one literary field, indeed, the early twentieth century saw a break-through where the giants of the Victorian age had failed: the Edwardian theater was bursting with vitality. The late Victorian theater had counted many famous actors; Gilbert and Sullivan aside, the only playwrights who survive on the stage today are Arthur Wing Pinero, a highly competent craftsman, and Oscar Wilde, a witty, scintillating minor genius. But building on the tradition of the great actor-managers and profiting from expert, and even revolutionary, stagecraft, Edwardian writers established themselves partners of, not mere adjuncts to, actors. James Barrie and John Galsworthy flourished in these years, and George Bernard Shaw towered over his contemporaries to assume his place as the finest British playwright since Shakespeare. The enthusiastic Fabian propagandist now subjected one after another aspect of English society to merciless dissection by a clean rationalism and an irreverent wit.

Shaw's destructiveness and more nebulous evolutionary and socialist remedies were paralleled by the work of two novelists. H. G. Wells, like Graham Wallas a dissident Fabian, turned to many of the same themes as Shaw, though with a greater realism, born of his own lower-middle-class background, than Shaw's Irish mockery would allow. Gentler than Shaw, but as deft and corrosive, was E. M. Forster, four of whose five novels appeared between 1905 and 1910. Appealing from conventional emotions and proprieties—and never able in his lifetime to acknowledge publicly the homosexuality that shaped his sensibility—Forster sought a heightened naturalness, epitomized by the challenge of Italy to English ways; and in *Howard's End* (1911) he predicted symbolically the inheritance of England by the unclassed, the alien, and the intellectuals.

For all their brilliance, the Edwardian writers made no break with the literary tradition of the past, which for a time had seemed threatened with inglorious, if not unattractive, extinction by the decadents at the end of the nineteenth century. Though they were deeply critical of the assumptions and actions of their contemporaries, Shaw, Wells, and Forster were not revolutionary; like Russell and Moore, they re-established the claims of rationality and liberal values. Two other Edwardian writers, Hilaire Belloc and G. K. Chesterton, attempted a radical departure from that tradition. Brilliant as storytellers and versifiers, both men turned on the spirit and structure of English society, rejecting not only the materialism and ugliness of industrialism, but the characteristic solutions of social problems by liberal means or by appeals to what Belloc called the servile state. They urged a return to a system based on peasant proprietorship, workshops, and guilds. More penetrating, no doubt, than the aesthetic disciples of Ruskin and Morris, ultimately they were just as evanescent. Belloc was a passionate Catholic, and Chesterton turned Catholic in 1922; perhaps this indicates how far they stood to one side of the mainstream of English intellectual and social life. Only at the very end of the period did a major revolutionary appear. D. H. Lawrence published his first novel in 1911; two years later came *Sons and Lovers*, and in 1915, *The Rainbow*. By then it was clear that he had broken with the rationalistic, liberal strain to celebrate a new morality that was to become an uneasy commonplace in the postwar world.

REVOLT, 1911-1914

The Trade Unions

Insofar as one can find intellectual influences at work in British social and political unrest in the decade before the First World War, they are to be found in the labor movement. Syndicalism spread rapidly to dominate the labor movement in France and Italy and made serious inroads, through the I.W.W., in the United States. Drawing on Georges Sorel's social adaptation of Bergson's vitalist philosophy, some English theorists imported syndicalist thought, while in the guild socialists, among whom G. D. H. Cole was the leading intellect, this strand was united with (and subordinate to) the communal and libertarian inheritance from John Ruskin and William Morris. But English syndicalism was not an intellectual movement: there was perfectly good native warrant for the prevalence of militant tactics, direct action, violence, and contempt for the parliamentary tradition.

The political side of British labor had been notably successful between 1906 and 1910; the mere presence of 29 Labour party members was enough to persuade Parliament to enact much remedial legislation, even though the Liberal party was not dependent on

Labour votes to maintain its majority. But two threats developed. One surfaced in another decision of the House of Lords, in its judicial capacity, in the Osborne case of 1909. A member of the Amalgamated Society of Railway Servants had secured an injunction to prevent the national union from using dues paid by his local branch for political purposes, money that had gone to pay the salaries of sixteen working-class M.P.'s. The decision threatened the financial basis of any Labour political activity whatsoever. Two acts reversed the decision: in 1911, a salary was provided for all members of Parliament, and a statute of 1913 permitted trade unions to use their funds for political purposes, provided that political funds were kept separate from other union funds and that members could choose not to contribute — reservations that in the event had no effect. But the Osborne judgment crippled political Labour at precisely the time when, for others, recourse to direct action was growing in appeal.

The second threat to political Labour was more subtle and pervasive. Parliamentary politics was predicated on certain middle- and upper-class conventions; it was a politics of deference, compromise, and accommodation. Occasionally, as in Keir Hardie's early years in the House, a Labour member would make clear how artificial these conventions were, but the tradition of the House was so strong and entry into power so agreeable that few Labour men could withstand the temptation to conform. But the rapid growth of trade unions had brought into the labor movement large numbers of men who were little susceptible to the attractions of polite society or to that respectability which, since the days of the Junta, had served both as a stimulus to Labour politics and as a guarantee of Labour responsibility. At the same time, in the general prosperity of Edwardian England, wages persistently lagged behind rising prices; following a long period of general improvement, real wages after 1896 began a fairly steady decline until the very eve of the First World War. Driven, as Professor Phelps Brown observes, "before the gale of novel aspirations and resentments," the unions reinforced their new militancy by the self-consciousness of a class no longer satisfied to remain in "its place"; when they set out to bargain for a share of the national wealth, they were no longer willing to have that share gauged by a standard of accepted inferiority. For the first time since the 1830's, British labor, or a significant part of it, showed signs of turning revolutionary. Encouraged by syndicalist successes in France and by the lessons Ben Tillett and Tom Mann had learned from the dynamic labor movement in Australia, British workingmen began to look more aggressively to the weapon of the strike, now secured to them by the Trade Disputes Act of 1906.

Between 1906 and 1914, trade union membership in the country doubled. The number of strikes also shot up; in 1908 more time was lost than in the entire preceding decade. These strikes, alarming to the men who normally arrogated the name of public opinion, involved many industries or regional groupings within industries. But the main industrial history of the period before and after the war revolves around three groups of workers: the dockers, the miners, and the railwaymen. When Tillett and Mann returned to England from Australia, they went back to the dockers who had given them their victory in 1889; in 1910 they created the Transport Workers' Federation. In the early summer of 1911 there was a strike of seamen, which won marked concessions for these poorly paid workers from the notoriously stiff shipping interest. A month later the London dockers came out, with a comparable victory at the end, though they had less success in the northern ports; there was violence at Liverpool, where two men were killed by troops. In 1912, the dockers tried again, but this time, lacking support both in public opinion and in their own ranks, they had overreached themselves. The shipping interests, headed by Lord Devonport, chairman of the Port of London Authority,* demanded full surrender and got it in August. Deprived of any other resource, Ben Tillett prayed at a meeting of strikers for God to strike Lord Devonport dead.

The miners faced more complex problems. Wages and customs had always varied from field to field, partly at least in response to varying conditions in the seams of coal; with great difficulty the Miners' Federation had screwed itself up to national status on the platform of a minimum wage, but it had still not attained a minimum wage when maximum hours were set in 1908, a loophole of which some mine operators took immediate advantage. The miners' demands were not easy to satisfy, however, partly because of regional variations, partly because the mining industry was faced with steadily declining productivity and fairly stationary prices. After long, futile negotiations with owners and government, the miners came out at the beginning of March, 1912. The government's response was an act setting up regional wage boards—the trade boards of 1909 had, of course, been limited to unorganized sweated trades—to determine minimum wages, a compromise between the miners' demands for a legislatively fixed minimum and the reluctance of owners and Parliament to concede the right of the state to intervene at all. Thus pla-

*This public body, which operates all the docks in London formerly operated by separate private companies, and which also exercises jurisdiction over the navigation and maintenance of the tidal portion of the Thames, was created in 1908; but the Liverpool docks had been brought under joint public and private operation as early as 1858.

cated, the men voted by only a bare majority to continue the strike, and the first national miners' strike collapsed, being rather too unwieldy an instrument to work well. The next year, they began to insist on the nationalization of the mines.

The railwaymen were in a weaker position than either the dockers or the miners. With one exception, the companies had persistently refused to bargain with the unions, a hostility explicable partly by the lack of imagination characteristic of private railway managements in most countries, partly by the companies' belief that the quasi-military discipline required for practical and safe operation of the lines was incompatible with unionism. But the main reason was that legislation in 1894 had fixed rates at the end of a period of falling prices and held them unchanged through a period of rising prices. But such explanations, specious or real, carried no weight with the railwaymen, whose wages had been falling steadily behind those in other occupations. Lloyd George had intervened to prevent a railway strike in 1907 by threatening employers with permanent arbitration machinery; he intervened again in 1911, when the first national railway strike took place, by appointing a commission which recommended meeting part of the men's demands. For the first time, real negotiations took place between railway companies and unions.

The government was deeply involved in all the major industrial disputes of these years. State intervention, dating back to Gladstone's naming Rosebery as a conciliator in a strike in 1893, was recognition of the fact that disruption of a major industry could mean disaster in a highly interdependent society. By the time the strikes of the prewar decade came, the Board of Trade had a fully functioning conciliation and mediation service, headed by a remarkable Edwardian civil servant, Sir George Askwith (later Lord Askwith). The Government could bring in legislation where it was necessary and applicable, as in the miners' demand for a minimum wage; it could exercise impressive powers of persuasion; in the last resort it could take a stern line and call out troops. Thus, in 1911, by intimating that war was imminent, Lloyd George brought the railway companies to abandon their all-out resistance. During the dock strike of 1911, Winston Churchill, at the Home Office, rediscovered his military instincts and used troops so freely that it proved wiser to shift his abilities and imagination to the Admiralty, where he could plan for war against a foreign power rather than a domestic enemy.

The unions were not so strong as they seemed. Not only could the government bring them to terms, but rank-and-file support sometimes withered away before a strike realized its full potential. Certainly one union by itself, even on a national scale, was not irresistible. The way out seemed to lie in a new approach to the old ambition of Owenite days: the "one big union" which through a general strike could force the country to submit. That idea was now rediscovered or imported from the syndicalists. Accordingly a scheme for a "triple alliance" of transport workers, miners, and railwaymen was drafted in June, 1914. The plan was hurriedly formed and provided with sanctions that were too few and too weak to assure common action. Yet common action was what the pact promised, and the country gloomily awaited the expiry of the railway agreement in December. But there was no strike. War had come in August, and the formal ratification of the Triple Alliance by the three unions in 1915 was a gesture without meaning.

The Tories

The resort to direct action by British workers was paralleled in more exalted parts of society. In the House of Commons, the temper of the times showed itself in what was called "the new style" — an unaccustomed ferocity of language, a contemptuous disregard for polite forms, a narrow, relentless pursuit of partisan advantage. On July 24, 1911, some Tory opponents of the Parliament Act created such an uproar that the prime minister was prevented from speaking and the Speaker had to adjourn the House in a state of "grave disorder." Asquith met that and later attacks with dignity, and Liberal demagogues like Lloyd George and Churchill, perhaps because they knew they were on the winning side, could avoid the extremes of the new style. It remained a Tory monopoly, led by Lord Hugh Cecil, a younger son of Lord Salisbury, Sir Edward Carson, soon to launch the Ulster rebellion, and F. E. Smith, a brilliant young lawyer making his way from the Lancashire middle class to the Lord Chancellorship (as Lord Birkenhead in the twenties). Balfour watched the new style develop with his usual detachment; he had completely lost touch with the younger members of his party and probably was incapable of seeing some of the roots of the new style in his and his uncle's pursuit of partisan ends or in their own verbal acidity. When the Parliament Act, that sacrifice into which he had himself lured the peers, was passed, his party turned on him with the slogan "B.M.G.": Balfour Must Go. The Duke of Bedford said as much publicly in November, 1911, and Balfour resigned. The succession was in dispute. Joseph Chamberlain had been swept from the political scene in 1906 by a paralytic stroke; his elder son Austen, a mild adherent of the Tory rebels, was one candidate for the leadership in 1911; Walter Long, a worthy but dim squire, was another. In the standoff, a compromise was reached by choosing Andrew Bonar Law, a Glasgow businessman born in Canada, relatively uncultivated, narrow in imagination, and unscrupulous enough to suit the mood of his colleagues. He followed rather than led. In 1911, some Tories were urging the King to undo two hundred years of constitutional development and veto the Parliament Act. In 1913, Bonar Law actually suggested that King George might emulate King William IV and dismiss the ministers for disloyalty.

The Tory revolt was the last important distillation of hatred of what the social and political changes of the past sixty years had done to the power and position of the upper classes. Like all such emotions in extremity, it plumbed alarming depths of irrationality. The movement lacked only the pen of a Rowlandson to make its grotesquerie as permanent a part of our awareness as the vices of the late eighteenth-century rakes he drew so savagely.

Ireland

The issue that precipitated the Tory rebellion was Irish Home Rule. Armed with the powers of the Parliament Act, Asquith introduced a third Home Rule bill in April, 1912. Like the others, it provided for a separate Irish parliament, though this bill looked beyond Ireland to the possibility of a complete federalization of Britain by the future erection of Welsh and Scottish parliaments—"Home Rule All Around," as it was called; the Parliament at Westminster was still to retain a small number of Irish members for imperial purposes. But when Lord Randolph Churchill "played the Orange card" in 1886, he started a cause that grew steadily for the next quarter of a century: the northern province of Ulster was determined that neither its Protestant religion nor its economic prosperity would be subjected to the whims and prejudices of an agrarian, Catholic parliament in Dublin. This intense Ulster nationalism found a leader of genius and daring in Sir Edward Carson, a Dublin-born Protestant barrister and M.P. Under Carson's leadership, the northerners resorted to the old tradition of forming bodies of Volunteers dedicated to enforcing some "alternative" on the day the Home Rule bill was passed.[*]

The Tory leaders in Edwardian England went Randolph Churchill one better. Bonar Law and Walter Long, with Carson and the Anglo-Irish landlord Lord Londonderry, took the salute at a Volunteer review in April, 1912, and in July Bonar Law publicly assured the country that he would follow Ulster to any length in resistance. Two years later, in March, 1914, when the government moved to anticipate an Ulster rising by ordering troop movements, a large number of officers at the Curragh barracks near Dublin chose to resign rather

---

[*]On the eighteenth-century Volunteer movement, see above, p. 91.

than carry out their orders, then or later, without a government pledge that they would not be required to take action to coerce Ulster. The "Mutiny at the Curragh" was covertly approved by Bonar Law and by Sir Henry Wilson, the chief of military operations at the War Office; like so many British officers, Wilson was Anglo-Irish in origin.

The government responded weakly to these successive challenges to its authority. Asquith was always likely to postpone irrevocable commitments, but in this case there were more fundamental considerations. He was reluctant, first, to antagonize Ulster when he was trying to negotiate a settlement. The government's plan for compromise, finally embodied in an amending bill which would come into force at the same time as the Home Rule bill, provided for a six-year delay in Ulster's entry into the Irish parliament. Though their leaders wavered, the rank and file of Ulstermen and Tories would accept no such concession; even a conference summoned by the King at Asquith's request in July, 1914, broke down. It is more difficult to understand the government's inaction in the face of the European threat, which was the second reason for Asquith's temporizing. The concession of the pledge demanded by the officers was disastrous, seen in retrospect. Not only was the weakness noted by the Germans, but some of the generalship of the British Army during the war would seem to indicate that a housecleaning, and particularly the disciplining of Wilson, who got off scot-free, might have been salutary.

Meanwhile, the southern Irish had not been quiet. Redmond and the Irish parliamentary party, in close alliance with the Liberals at Westminster, were out of touch with sentiment in Ireland and with a new generation of leaders. While agrarian discontent had been largely allayed by the working of the land acts, there were still frequent disturbances, to which were added the grievances of a small but growing Irish urban working-class movement, led by a rough and powerful leader, Jim Larkin. Moreover, nationalism had taken a new turn for which Home Rule now seemed an insufficient concession. From the nineties the Gaelic League had been actively working to revive the nearly defunct Irish language, a declaration of cultural independence in the classic pattern of nationalist movements; and during the celebrations of the centenary of the rising of 1798, a new organization calling itself Sinn Fein ("Ourselves Alone") began to agitate for full independence by setting up a *de facto* Irish parliament and by boycotting English courts, Army, and goods.

Following the collapse of the Dublin tramway strike in 1913, Larkin's militant working-class movement came into close alliance with Sinn Fein, and at the end of the year an effort was begun to recruit Irish Volunteers, a southern private army to answer the private army in Ulster. Redmond, disliking the whole development but forced to salvage his leadership, agreed in June, 1914, to head the Volunteer movement. By that time the Ulster Volunteers had already begun to smuggle in arms from Germany through the northern port of Larne; clever planning immobilized the police and coast guards. But when in July the Irish Volunteers followed suit and smuggled arms ashore at Howth, near Dublin, the police and troops were called out. The Volunteers largely managed to elude them, but as the soldiers returned to Dublin, they were attacked by the crowd; they fired, killing three people and injuring thirty-eight. The Bachelor's Walk "massacre" added a new legacy of bitterness to the long-standing resentments of the southern Irish: Protestant gunrunning at Larne was done with dispatch and impunity; Catholics were pursued and murdered.

By the end of July, 1914, Ireland was on the verge of civil war, and if Bonar Law and the army officers were to be believed, there might have been civil war in England too. The Tories' answer to the Parliament Act was to reject the parliamentary process. Threatened more by the Irish situation than by the Triple Alliance of English labor, England had reason to welcome the war with the relief that was evident nearly everywhere. The Tories, having shown themselves scoundrels, bore out Dr. Johnson's famous definition and resorted at the last to patriotism. By general consent—in England—the Home Rule issue was postponed until after the war; the passage of the act for a third time and its coming into force without the Lords' consent, in September, 1914, were, like the official founding of the Triple Alliance, mere formalities.*

The Suffragettes

The war also brought an end to another militant movement, one which had anticipated the others by half a dozen years and which went beyond them in actual violence. The nineteenth-century agitation for women's rights had attained fairly impressive, though admittedly hard-won, success in law, education, and employment.† Even politically, some noteworthy concessions had been made: the

---

*The companion nationalist measure, Welsh Disestablishment, was carried in the same way at the same time; its coming into force was similarly postponed until after the war, when an additional act made the financial settlement considerably more favorable towards the Church of England in Wales. Unlike Home Rule, Welsh Disestablishment attained a fairly full measure of success.
†See above, p. 403.

vote in municipal elections in 1868 and for county councils from their inception in 1888; the vote for and the right to be elected to school boards in 1870; the right to sit on parish and district councils under the act establishing them in 1894; and in 1907 the right to sit as councilors, aldermen, or mayors in county and borough councils. It was clearly only a matter of time until the parliamentary franchise would be granted. What is uncertain is whether the militant campaign for women's suffrage helped or hindered the attainment of that goal.

The women's militancy radiated from an organization called the Women's Social and Political Union (WSPU), founded in 1903 by Mrs. Emmeline Pankhurst, the fragile-seeming widow of a Manchester barrister who had been active in the ILP. "It is not known of Mrs. Pankhurst," George Dangerfield has written, "that she ever proposed to spend her widowhood behind any scene, if there was the slightest chance of getting in front of it"; and it is remarkable testimony to the determination and courage of Mrs. Pankhurst and her two daughters, Sylvia and Christabel, that a movement headed by unknowns of no particular social position and encouraged openly only by labor leaders like Keir Hardie and George Lansbury should for five years have come so close to making British government and public life impossible.

Militant tactics, which brought thousands of impatient and determined women into the cause, were at first pretty much confined to heckling ministers and other politicians at meetings, but in 1909 the agitation turned in two more ominous directions. The suffragettes, as the more militant agitators were called, began to destroy property; when they were imprisoned, they went on hunger strikes, facing the government with the alternatives of releasing them or of forcibly feeding them, a process not too far removed from torture, given an adamant victim. In 1910 a "conciliation bill" was proposed as a step towards enfranchisement by giving the vote to single women with property; in November, Asquith, who was not sympathetic to the women's demands in any event, put it aside to fight through his battle with the Lords and the forthcoming general election. The response to the delay was violence, as it was to the abandonment of two subsequent conciliation bills in 1911 and 1912. In the latter year the government brought in a highly democratic reform bill—for which there had been no obvious demand—for male voters. The possibility of feminist amendments was wrecked by a surprising ruling of the Speaker against amendments to enfranchise classes not foreseen in the original bill; with that, the prewar legislative history of women's suffrage came to nothing.

The militants were not surprised and, it seemed, did not much care. They turned to slashing paintings, destroying letters in letter boxes, bombing, arson, and even martyrdom, when one young woman who had repeatedly tried to kill herself for the cause at last succeeded in May, 1913, by throwing herself under the King's horse in the Derby at Epsom Downs. Irrational violence produced irrational responses: police and mobs treated women demonstrators brutally; the indignities in prisons continued; and in 1913, Parliament passed an extraordinary statute, nicknamed the Cat-and-Mouse Act, allowing the Home Secretary to order the release of hunger strikers when their health was in danger and to rearrest them when they recovered. Mrs. Pankhurst, in London, was in and out of prison, where she staged ten hunger strikes.

Meanwhile the militant movement had undergone a series of splits. One had occurred as early as 1907; in 1912, Mrs. Pethick-Lawrence, one of the original founders of the WSPU, withdrew, unable to accept any longer the autocracy of the Pankhursts. Early in 1914, Sylvia was excommunicated by her mother and sister. Sylvia, a socialist, had carried the battle into the working-class districts of the East End of London; she had also drawn close to the militant trade unionists. Such compromising of the middle-class ideals of the movement was intolerable, especially to Christabel, who had fled to Paris, directing the most violent wing of the movement at a distance from the police. This family quarrel and growing public disgust with both militancy and the authorities' impotent brutality provided a chance for the government to extricate itself. In June, 1914, a deputation of Sylvia's working women was received, and the ministers agreed to support a women's suffrage bill. Sylvia, as a socialist, opposed the war and continued to insist on the suffrage, though it was a futile campaign, at least immediately: there was no opportunity for constitutional change, and she lost both her following and her enemies. Christabel and her disciples had continued violent action right down to the outbreak of war, but in September, 1914, Christabel was back in London, lecturing on the German menace. All sentences were remitted, and the militant women turned their energies and emotions against a foreign foe.

The Victorian age had been an unconscionable time a-dying; the many-faceted revolt of 1909–1914 was its last convulsion.

ARMAGEDDON, 1914–1918

The skeleton of the First World War was provided by two systems of alliances: the Triple Alliance of Germany, Austria-Hungary, and Italy; and the Triple Entente of France, Russia, and Great Britain. Within these alliances the strength of attachment varied, as did motivation, known or concealed, realized or unconscious, from one adherent to the next. Austria-Hungary, a tatterdemalion assortment of nationalities masquerading as an empire, was trying to maintain a crumbling facade of unity by isolating and keeping impotent the Balkan nationalities whose interest in their kinsmen within the imperial boundaries might be dangerous. Russia, seeking as always for an outlet to the Mediterranean (preferably Constantinople), was willing to uphold an ailing Turkey for a time, provided that when death came, she would be residuary legatee. But Russia also had a Pan-Slavist interest in those Balkan nationalities that Austria wanted to neutralize. France, still smarting from her defeat in 1870–1871, had long been prepared for another war in which she could recover her lost provinces of Alsace and Lorraine.

These three powers were pursuing historically definable and comprehensible goals, however dangerous the latent conflict might be. It was otherwise with Germany, once Bismarck was gone. Bismarck's policy had aimed at disengagement in the Balkans and at neutralizing Russia; he knew that another French war was likely, and he did not choose to fight it on the eastern front as well. After his dismissal in 1890, however, the German chancellors lacked his diplomatic mastery and skeptical farsightedness, while the personal diplomacy of the Kaiser kept Europe in a turmoil. Given the tension with France, it did not seem particularly wise to alienate both Russia and Britain, the more so as the two countries were increasingly linked after 1907. But the Kaiser's ambitions ran through the Balkans, where Germany repeatedly deferred to Austrian designs, to the Middle East; the German cultivation of Turkey, particularly her patronage and support of the Turkish army, was a serious affront to Russia. With Britain, to be sure, there were many German attempts at pacification, aimed increasingly at securing British neutrality in case of a war with France. But the British could not accept Germany's insistence on an unconditional refusal to help the French, especially in view of the degree of naval cooperation that had been arrived at and in view of traditional British interest in keeping the ports in the Low Countries out of the hands of potential enemies. Meanwhile, German naval programs forced the British to redoubled efforts to keep ahead, a race that was not only expensive—the Lloyd George budget of 1909 owed more to naval building than to any other consideration—but that made Germany's protestations of friendship seem remarkably hollow. As war drew near, German planners had come to expect British entry, but thought that a short war would prevent the traditional British weapon of blockade from being effective; while for the size and quality of British land forces the German general staff had scant respect—with some reason.

The Origins of the War

The Liberal government's tenure of office was punctuated by a series of diplomatic crises. In 1908, a Turkish revolution gave Austria-Hungary an excuse to annex the two Balkan provinces of Bosnia and Herzegovina, which she had administered since 1878. The Turks, who had little choice, once their German patrons backed their larger ally, were ultimately pacified by the return of a small piece of land. But the Serbs, whose kinsmen formed a majority of the population in the annexed territories, were the more angry because they wanted Bosnia and Herzegovina for themselves. The next incident occurred in 1911, when Germany again intervened in Morocco; this almost adolescent colonial ambition had been rebuffed at the Algeciras Conference in 1906, and another Moroccan dispute with France had been settled by agreement in 1909. Now, when the French and Spanish moved in troops to protect their interests during a revolt against the Sultan, it seemed to Berlin that the French planned to absorb Morocco. According to the code of prewar diplomacy, Germany could not permit such a step without compensation, and a gunboat was sent to Agadir to enforce her claim. At this point Britain intervened decisively with a clear warning that Germany was taking serious risks. The matter was straightened out by the end of the year, but not without provoking a war scare in England.

Meanwhile, Italy had seized Tripoli, on the north coast of Africa, from Turkey, touching off a Balkan war fought by those former client states that saw their way clear to humiliating Turkey still further. The victory of Serbia, Greece, and Bulgaria over Turkey was a blow to Austria-Hungary and a stimulus to Russian influence in the Balkans, for Austro-Russian collaboration in maintaining the status quo in the Balkans had by this time become mere sham. The peace negotiations to end the Balkan War took place in London, where the Foreign Secretary, Sir Edward Grey, tried to show his good will by backing the claims of Germany and Austria-Hungary; he helped rather to inflame Balkan resentment, because Austria was determined that Serbia should have no outlet to the Adriatic. Meanwhile, the Balkan allies fell out, and very soon Serbia, Greece, and later Rumania launched a new Balkan war against Bulgaria, which was badly beaten. The most important result of the war was the emergence of a much larger and more self-confident Serbia, which Austria-Hungary was more determined than ever to stop.

Austria was given the pretext she needed on June 28, 1914, when Archduke Francis Ferdinand, heir to the Austro-Hungarian throne, was assassinated in Sarajevo in Bosnia. Though done by Bosnian Serbs who were subjects of the Empire, the crime was blamed by

Austria on Serbia; assured of German backing, she sent a drastic ultimatum. Serbia gave in almost completely — far beyond what decent national pride could tolerate — but to no avail. Austria's mobilization against Serbia on July 25 brought her face to face with Serbia's patron Russia, where mobilization began on July 30. Germany allowed Austria her head, her general staff having long been prepared for a war to come at about this time. On August 2, after having demanded that Russia stop her mobilization, Germany declared war on Russia and on Russia's ally France the next day.

Sir Edward Grey had been doing his best to play a pacific part, but in the worst circumstances: the country was torn apart internally by labor strife, the Ulster rebellion, and the agitation of the suffragettes; the cabinet was unable to agree on its policy towards the developing war. On August 2, Grey assured the French that the Channel, a British responsibility as the Mediterranean was a French responsibility, would not be open to the passage of German warships. The Germans had hardly expected that it would be; their plan for a rapid victory over France was based on an invasion through Belgium. But that intention raised an even more painful problem for the British, the prospect of the Channel ports in unfriendly hands.

The cabinet could not agree on whether or not to invoke the guarantee of the neutrality of Belgium to which they were committed by the treaty of London of 1839 and further treaties of 1870. Intervention was urged by the old liberal imperialists and by Winston Churchill; the old radicals were against them, and when the interventionists finally carried their policy, John Burns and Lord Morley resigned from the cabinet. Meanwhile, Germany had given the decision urgency by an ultimatum to Belgium demanding passage, which the Belgians refused. On August 4, the German army invaded Belgium; the British time limit on their demand that Germany not violate Belgian territory expired at midnight, and Britain was at war. The immediate issue of Belgium was fortunate; growing out of a traditional interest and involving a powerful moral appeal, it helped to forge British unity. Bonar Law pledged the Tories' support; John Redmond, the Irish leader, at great political risk, approved intervention. Only the pacifists and some radicals, including Ramsay MacDonald, the leader of the Labour party, stood out against war.

The Course of the War

Militarily, the war was both a culmination of nineteenth-century methods and a shattering foretaste of things to come. It was a war, by turns, of movement and position; both techniques grew from the experience of the previous century in ways made possible by the planning of general staffs and by the refinement of material available in advanced industrial economies. To be sure, not all the inventions of the preceding generation were yet fully adaptable to military purposes. Though motor trucks were coming into wide use by the end of the war, transport continued to depend heavily on horses and railways; telephone and radio were still technically uncertain in field conditions. But the cavalry, until then always the most distinguished arm of the service and often the most valuable, was outmoded and nearly useless in this war, and the other basic ground forces could rely on important advances in military technology: improved rifles and machine guns, the latter used in unprecedented numbers, and highly sophisticated artillery, employing impressive new tactics such as the massing of guns and the rolling barrage. In one smallish battle on a three-mile front in 1915, the British fired as much ammunition as they had used in the entire South African war.

Technology and its imaginative use had not, however, acquired the primacy they hold in present-day military thought; the vast deployment of material and improved methods still subserved, far more than they do now, the ingenuity and brute courage of ordinary soldiers and officers. New inventions, made or first exploited during the war, pointed the way, however, to future diversions of manpower and invention into technological warfare and in turn demanded the revolutionizing of old infantry methods, however improved. In 1915, the Germans launched the first gas attack; in 1916, the British introduced the tank, a powerful offensive weapon; both had a devastating psychological effect. Above all, there was the rapid development of the airplane. At the beginning of the war, planes had been used, unarmed, for reconnaissance and photography; by the end of the war, they were combat weapons, fighting each other in the air and bombing or gunning troops and installations on the ground. Ominously, the Germans for a short time exploited their superiority in the air to terrify the civilian population of London and some other British towns with raids by bombers and Zeppelins.

The main theater of war was in Europe. The Germans had planned a holding operation in the east, until a rapid advance through Belgium could knock out the French army; neither intention worked. The Austrian army was badly beaten by the Serbs, and although at Tannenberg in 1914 the Germans and Austrians saved East Prussia from a Russian conquest, the Russians fought well against heavy odds and forced the Germans to detach several divisions from the Western Front to deal with them. In the west, after a rapid advance, the Germans were stopped at the first battle of the Marne, northeast of Paris, in September, 1914, and at Ypres, in Belgium, in November. The war then settled down to a virtually stationary front running through Belgium and northern France, a maze of trenches and fortifications which neither side had the strength to break through and which exacted a terrible toll in casualties on the occasions when one side or the other thought it had enough reserves of men and material to make the attempt: at Ypres in April, 1915; at Verdun and the Somme in February and July, 1916; yet again at Ypres — with the murderous British and Canadian effort to take the ridge at Passchendaele — from July to November, 1917. Such warfare put a terrible strain not only on resources but on patience and determination, both at the front and at home. Much of the hatred and disillusion after the war must be laid to the seeming senselessness of costly advances for insignificant objectives, just as the sorry record of generalship on all sides is attributable to circumstances that might have frustrated even military geniuses, of whom there were none among the commanders of any army.

The ultimate decision was made in the west, but the war was a world war, fought on many fronts. Colonial wars, so central to eighteenth-century European conflicts, were unimportant as the Central Powers had few colonies; yet colonial campaigns, especially in East Africa, dragged on inconclusively for four years. Japan had entered the war on the side of the Allies, her role limited by agreement to naval action against Germany in the Pacific and the Far East, a useful release, to be sure, for the British Navy. Italy, whose alliance with Germany had excused her in case of a conflict with Britain, after some hesitation in neutrality, entered the war in 1915 on the side of the Allies, reassured by secret agreements promising territorial compensation at the expense of Austria; but the Italian front was perhaps as much a liability to the Allied effort as a help in pinning down German and Austrian troops. Rumania also entered on the Allied side in 1916, helping to reopen the theater of war in the Balkans closed for a time by the German defeat of the Serbs. Though hampered by the ambiguous part played by the Greeks, both British and French forces were engaged in a campaign in Macedonia; the main fighting there was done, however, by the revived Serbian army against the Bulgarians.

The event most prolific in secondary campaigns was the entry of Turkey on the side of the Central Powers at the end of 1914. The British, making heavy use of Australian and New Zealand troops, sent an expedition to the Dardanelles in 1915, which got nowhere against the Turks; the trouble lay in the terrain of the Gallipoli Peninsula, in the heat, in defective supply, and in dubious generalship. Frustrated there, the British effort against Turkey was concentrated in fighting in two different sectors. One was the campaign in Mesopotamia, which grew out of a small invasion at the end of 1914 launched from

India, pressing northward from the Persian Gulf. The other, based on Egypt, to which the bulk of the Gallipoli forces were evacuated, thrust across Sinai into Palestine. Both campaigns in time had fairly considerable success and helped to establish British paramountcy among the unstable independent countries which emerged in that region after the war, in succession to the defunct Turkish empire.*

At sea, the main adversaries were the German and British navies. The British had an overwhelming superiority in numbers, though in many respects the Germans outclassed them in design and gunnery. Moreover, Britain's superiority was compromised by a realization that her fleet was essential to her own and Allied survival and that serious loss in battle could mean irretrievable disaster, while the German fleet, less central to the calculations of a land-based power, could be used with greater daring. Important naval action of a traditional kind was pretty much confined to the first half of the war. Initial skirmishes and engagements went badly for the British fleet; they acquitted themselves well, however, in a daring raid on the German base at Heligoland in September, 1914, and in a battle off the Falkland Islands in December, which nearly cleared the high seas of German raiders. But the one great naval battle of the war, off Jutland at the very end of May, 1916, was ambiguous in its outcome.

The main concern at sea was not such traditional engagements but the newer problems of submarine warfare. Aware of Britain's crucial dependence on keeping the sea lanes open, the Germans tried their hand at unrestricted submarine warfare for six months in 1915, and then abandoned it because of neutral (particularly American) protests and the incompleteness of their underwater fleet. But in February, 1917, the policy was implemented again with alarming success. The resumption helped to bring the United States into the war in April, but from the German point of view, the risk was worth taking if neutral shipping could be scared off the Atlantic, and if British and Allied ships could be sunk, as they were at an increasing rate down to April, 1917. The Allies answered by complicated convoy arrangements, which proved far more effective, thanks to the efficient deployment of naval escorts, than many critics had expected them to be.

A clear turning point in the war came in 1917 with the Russian Revolution. In the first stage of the Revolution, the Kerensky regime prosecuted the war with new vigor, but the second, Bolshevik stage of the Revolution in November quickly took Russia out of the war,

---

*The Middle East compaigns benefited from the remarkable mobilization of Arab help by Col. T. E. Lawrence, a mysterious and powerful personality known as "Lawrence of Arabia."

freeing a vast number of German troops for service in the west. In the spring and summer of 1918, a new German offensive broke through in eastern France and advanced to a line less than sixty miles from Paris, where it was stopped, again at the Marne, by Allied troops now strengthened by fresh American reinforcements. It was more than a check; the Allies were able to seize the offensive. As they approached the borders of Germany in November, 1918, the Germans, who had overthrown the Kaiser and established a republic, asked for an armistice, which was concluded on November 11.

At home the swift forging of national unity in 1914 showed itself in the remarkable success of voluntary recruiting, for Britain had no conscription to rely on to build up her pitifully small army. But it soon became clear that a conflict of such magnitude could not be fought while carrying on, in Winston Churchill's phrase, "business as usual." The logic of total war, so obvious a generation later, had painfully to be learned. In January, 1916, conscription was adopted, a hard departure from British libertarian traditions, but conscription could not be allowed to drain the vital munitions factories and mines of irreplaceable skilled labor, nor could a shortage of labor be permitted to right itself by the usual peacetime recruiting devices or by luring workers from one firm to another by higher wages. So step by confused step, the government was forced to intervene in the labor market. The machinery of labor exchanges was there to be used, but the Ministry of Munitions, set up in 1915, and later the Ministry of Labor took primary responsibility. Hiring and wage controls were imposed; regulations governed conditions and amenities in factories; agreements with the trade unions suspended strikes and usual trade union practices and expectations, the most notable invasion being the "dilution" of labor by putting unskilled or partly trained workers, including women, into jobs traditionally reserved for skilled "aristocrats" of labor.

The railways were taken over by the government at the outset, and under a series of acts, the most important being the third Defence of the Realm Act in March, 1915, the government acquired the power to take over factories in industries necessary to the effective conduct of the war. The more common practices were, however, less drastic: requisition of property, price-fixing, cost supervision, limitation of profits, and rationing of raw materials. The administration of these controls was largely in the hands of businessmen brought into government service, and they were imposed not dogmatically or systematically, but as need seemed to dictate. Never so sweeping as the controls over labor, the government's intervention in business was still an impressive demonstration of the power of the state and raised some vital questions for the future. If the state could organize and plan production in time of war, if, moreover, its constant supervision of labor and the rationing of food could guarantee a national minimum which for many workers was more than they had ever known, what was to prevent a similar rationalization of the economy in time of peace?

Domestic Policies and Politics

Two of the great war leaders of the twentieth century were in Asquith's cabinet in 1914, a vantage point from which it would not have been easy to predict what we now know. Winston Churchill fell an early victim to his aggressiveness, his dubious taste for strategy, and the distrust that dogged him from his early days as a Tory radical renegade to his last years as an elder statesman half a century later. After an outsize quarrel that provoked the resignation of the elderly and opinionated admiral Lord Fisher, Churchill was relegated from the Admiralty to a minor cabinet post in May, 1915, and a few months later he retreated to the back benches. He held office again at the end of the war and in the twenties, but prior to his premiership in 1940, it was a career marked more by failure or frustration than by success.

Rising to supreme power after so long and uncertain an apprenticeship lends an epic quality to Churchill's career, a spell not easy to transcend. With Lloyd George the difficulty has been quite the opposite: because he triumphed so completely over Asquith a little over two years after the outbreak of war—and at such cost to the Liberal party—a good many contemporaries, and most historians since, have seen the victory as in some way foreordained and very likely the result of a conquering ambition that spawned disloyalty and plotting. There is some evidence to make the cynicism plausible, and certainly no one can doubt the ambition; but, as with Churchill, the verdict is becoming more ambiguous, and the charge of conspiracy at least seems to be groundless. Indeed, on more than one occasion Lloyd George might have gone into the political wilderness as Churchill did. His decision to remain in the cabinet when the war broke out was an agonizing one, pulled as he was by his old radical pacifist loyalties but ultimately precipitated by the invasion of Belgium. Like most Liberals, he was torn by the crucial dilemma of conscription, that ultimate act of the coercive state. Yet if pragmatism led him to compromise his Liberal inheritance, his record as a war minister was no steady forward march to power. After some impressive early maneuvers in the field of war finance, he puzzled and outraged his Liberal friends by advancing a sweeping scheme in the spring of 1915 for the control and even nationalization of the drink trade, which he saw as endangering the war effort. Defeated almost entirely on that initiative, he performed miracles as minister of munitions after May, 1915; soon after, he succeeded the military hero Lord Kitchener—who was killed when the ship on which he was travelling to Russia struck a mine—as Secretary of State for War, where he had much less freedom of action, in part because of limitations he had himself helped to place on the office to restrain Kitchener. But almost to the end he remained loyal to Asquith—no easy task for a masterful man

Politics as usual was no more acceptable in wartime than was business as usual, though Asquith was slow to realize it. Indolent, excessively dependent on his formidable wife and on his intimate friend Venetia Stanley, Asquith lacked the forcefulness to control events or to respond to disaster. Cabals began early to intrigue against him and his party, among the Tories and among some leading newspaper owners, to whom Lloyd George was close. Yet Asquith continued to dominate the coalition government he was forced to create in May, 1915, by keeping the Conservative leaders in relatively minor posts, along with Arthur Henderson, who had succeeded Ramsay MacDonald as leader of the Labour party. As Asquith's insufficiency and the incompetence of his cabinet became steadily more apparent and as the maneuvers to replace him became intense in November, 1916, it was by no means certain that Lloyd George would be their beneficiary. In the dispute that arose between the two in early December over control of a small war committee, Asquith might well have been the victor. Despite all the analysis of recent years, we shall probably never know exactly what happened or why. But late on December 5, Asquith resigned, and, after Bonar Law declined to serve, the king sent for Lloyd George. The last Liberal government had fallen, the victim of a war that was the negation of its principles, that weakened it in the constituencies as well as in Parliament, and that called for forms of imagination and action unthinkable to Gladstonians and their heirs.

Lloyd George at once replaced Asquith's large cabinet by a five-member war cabinet, including, besides himself, Henderson, Bonar Law, and two brilliant, authoritarian "outsiders"—Lord Milner, whose administration of South Africa after the Boer War had been so effective, and Lord Curzon, a former viceroy of India.* Only Bonar Law, as Chancellor of the Exchequer and leader of the House of Commons, carried direct departmental responsibilities; the other men

---

*A cabinet secretariat was also established and has remained an important step in institutionalizing the cabinet, which had always been technically an informal committee. In 1917, a member from each of the Dominions was added to make the Imperial War Cabinet.

were, in effect, ministers without portfolio to be assigned whatever tasks needed their attention. Henderson counted for less than any of the other members, and Milner counted for more.

Milner's sudden promotion was most surprising. Deeply distrusted by nearly all politicians since his highhanded behavior before and after the South African war, and all but directly censured by the House of Commons for his part in sanctioning "Chinese slavery" on the Rand, Milner had nursed a variety of grudges during his time in the political wilderness. Surrounded by a clique of young intellectuals and with ready access to powerful journalistic channels, Milner came to be the main spokesman for the authoritarian tradition on the English right; placating that awkward and vocal segment of opinion was the political magic that Lloyd George worked by appointing him. But he also gained a brilliant minister. Although Milner had been a bitter critic of both Asquith and Lloyd George and one of the most fervent defenders of the generals against the politicians, once he entered the war cabinet, he rapidly became one of Lloyd George's main supporters, a critic of the generals' policy of exclusive concentration on the Western Front, and certainly the most creative administrator in the war government.

Still, it remained Lloyd George's government. The Prime Minister tended to fill the new ministries with those self-made men, usually businessmen, whom he so admired; and the flexibility of wartime administration gave him a context in which his idiosyncratic talents could flourish. It is easy to find flaws. He despised and could not cooperate with the stubborn and unimaginative commander in chief of the Expeditionary Force, Field Marshal Sir Douglas Haig (later Lord Haig), yet he lacked the political strength to face down the King (who was a personal friend of Haig) or Haig's allies in the Conservative party and to drive him from command. Perhaps worse, at least for the future of the Liberal party, Lloyd George tended to ignore Parliament and to show his contempt for the usual apparatus and procedures of party; he preferred, astutely in a way, to make his appeals directly to the people. It is arguable, too, that the institution of the war cabinet aside, Lloyd George made no fundamental advances on steps taken less showily (and less decisively) under Asquith. But to most of the nation it seemed otherwise. Their hunch that Lloyd George was the man to win the war was confirmed by the fact that he did.

Selected Readings

The second volume of Halévy's Epilogue, cited in the previous chapter, remains the most complete narrative account of the prewar years, to which must be added George Dangerfield's brilliant and still influential book, *The Strange Death of Liberal England* (1936).

Studies of late nineteenth- and early twentieth-century thought related to social policy are cited in the previous chapter; to them can be added Samuel Hynes, *The Edwardian Turn of Mind* (1968); Martin J. Wiener, *Between Two Worlds: The Political Thought of Graham Wallas* (1971); Bertrand Russell's three-volume autobiography (1967–1969) and the one-volume life by Ronald W. Clark (1975); P. N. Furbank, *E. M. Forster, a Life* (2 vols., 1977–1978); and Robert F. Whitman, *Shaw and the Play of Ideas* (1977), admirable on the intellectual debts of that great playwright and lesser politician.

There are two recent portrayals of working-class life: Paul Thompson, *The Edwardians: The Remaking of British Society* (1975), which makes extensive use of oral evidence; and Standish Meacham, *A Life Apart: The English Working Class, 1890–1914* (1977), drawing on some of the same evidence to depict a context of pervasive custom, frustration, and incomprehension. Bob Holton, *British Syndicalism, 1900–1914: Myths and Realities* (1976) is an over-compressed but useful sketch. There is much information on the sources of labor unrest in E. H. Phelps-Brown, *The Growth of British Industrial Relations* (1959), which surveys the subject from the standpoint of 1906–1914. The labor agitation in Ireland is the subject of Emmet Larkin, *James Larkin, Irish Labour Leader, 1876–1947* (1965). The women's movement can be traced in its moderate and militant phases in David Morgan, *Suffragists and Liberals: The Politics of Woman Suffrage in England* (1975) and Andrew Rosen, *Rise Up, Women! The Militant Campaign of the Women's Social and Political Union, 1903–1914* (1974). On the Tory agitation, see the books cited in the previous chapter on the constitutional crisis of 1910–1911 and, in addition, Robert Blake's biography of Bonar Law, *The Unknown Prime Minister* (1955), quite as aptly titled in its American edition as *Unrepentant Tory*. See also the admirable book by A. M. Gollin, *Proconsul in Politics: A Study of Lord Milner in Opposition and in Power* (1964).

Two studies that deal with preparedness for war, military and popular, are Jay Luvaas, *The Education of an Army: British Military Thought, 1815–1940* (1964) and I. F. Clarke, *Voices Prophesying War, 1763–1984* (1966). R. R. James, in *Gallipoli* (1965), recounts the failure of a still controversial strategic gamble; see also Paul Guinn, *British Strategy and Politics, 1914 to 1918* (1965). On the forms and extent of state activity during the war, S. J. Hurwitz, *State Intervention in Great Britain: A Study of Economic Control and Social Response, 1914–1919* (1949). For the social history of the war, Arthur Marwick, *The Deluge* (1965), and Albert Marrin, *The Last Crusade: The Church of England and the First World War* (1974). On the political maneuvering in the Liberal party and outside it, mention should be made of the fascinating but partial account by one of the press lords, Lord Beaverbook, *Politicians and the War* (1928); the latest word on this complex subject is by Cameron Hazlehurst, *Politicians at War, July 1914 to May 1915: A Prologue to the Triumph of Lloyd George* (1971). See also A. J. P. Taylor's incisive *Politics in the First World War* (Raleigh Lecture, 1959), reprinted in his *Politics in Wartime* (1964).

Part IV
THE TRIALS
OF DEMOCRACY

Chapter 12
Between the Wars

1918–1940

RECONSTRUCTION AND REACTION, 1918–1923

Getting Back to 1914

Once it was realized that the war would be long and that business as usual would not do, a good many Englishmen began to think about the shape of the postwar world and what could be done to make it good, at home and abroad. The war had brought a rough social justice to England through conscription, rationing, controls, and some narrowing of the gap in incomes; it had also led to the improvisation of a vast governmental machine that reached into areas of national life where state intervention before 1914 would have been unthinkable. To give some direction to these developments in postwar England and to keep what was best about them, the Reconstruction Committee was set up in 1916 and became the Ministry of Reconstruction in the following year. One after another aspect of English government and English life was studied, and elaborate plans were drawn to deal with immediate problems, such as demobilization, and with long-range problems like the organization of health services and transport, the provision of housing, and the discovery of a new way of promoting cooperation between capital and labor.

The demobilization plans, carefully drawn to prevent mass unemployment, were quickly outstripped by events: demands from the troops themselves and some mutinous incidents led to a rapid demobilization on the principle of "first in, first out." Within a year more than four million men were out of uniform and, thanks to a boom the Ministry had not anticipated, for the most part into jobs. The long-range plans for reconstruction offered a better test of the country's intentions; there the result was nearly total defeat. In 1918 and 1919, the government introduced a great many forward-looking bills that would have extended education at the secondary level, provided large numbers of subsidized houses, and reorganized and coordinated the country's transport and electricity supply; by 1922 most of the program lay in ruins. A new Ministry of Health emerged, to be sure, taking over the functions of the old Local Government Board and the National Health Insurance Commissioner; so did a Ministry of Transport, but without the sweeping powers, extending as far as nationalization, foreseen in the original bill. The plan for collaboration between employers and employees was based on joint industrial councils—called Whitley Councils from the chairman of the subcommittee that proposed them—to set standards in each industry. The plan was launched bravely in 1917. But, for all their seeming early success, Whitley Councils never penetrated those industries that dominated the country's economy; they were little more than one way for poorly organized industries to approach what strong trade unions had long accomplished through collective bargaining. Housing was the most successful of the postwar programs: some 200,000 houses were built by local authorities with the help of government subsidies. But by 1923, that program had been drastically revised and the rate of new construction fell off sharply.

On balance, for all the good will and serious planning, the country (or those who spoke for it) preferred to try to go back to 1914. Lloyd George was caught between these two unequally matched goals. If one looks at the beginning and the end of Lloyd George's career, it is difficult to doubt his radicalism and his interest in social reform, though it was always reform of a liberal rather than a socialist variety. But his sense of the pragmatic, coupled with his ruthlessness, ambition, and impatience with established forms and procedures, had provided the drive that accomplished the miracles of the war. Now, tied to his skill at maneuvering and his determination to stay in office, his pragmatism finally though not intentionally wrecked English Liberalism and threw him into dependence on the Conservatives. The coalition had almost from the first been largely Conservative; after 1918 there was little illusion left.

A month after the Armistice a general election was held. The war

Parliament had been in existence since December, 1910, and the government needed a mandate for its programs at home and abroad. The election was held under the Representation of the People Act of 1918, which finally introduced full manhood suffrage into Great Britain. The vote was given too, without much debate, to women thirty years of age or over, if they or their husbands qualified for voting in local elections by reason of owning or occupying land or premises worth five pounds a year. Except for university graduates, who could still vote for members for their universities, and those in business, who might vote from their business premises as well as their homes, plural voting disappeared. Some two million men voted for the first time in 1918; so did more than six million women.

Lloyd George tried to preserve the coalition. The Labour party, save for a few members whose continued support of Lloyd George cost them their place in their party, refused to cooperate; Asquith remained aloof. Lloyd George and Bonar Law — who had developed a close cooperation during the war — signed letters of endorsement for candidates whom they considered reliable; Asquith derisively called the endorsement a "coupon," and the election has remained the Coupon Election. The coalition, winning over five million votes, emerged with 478 supporters in the House, 335 of them Conservatives; Labour, with nearly two and a half million votes, returned only 63 members; fewer than 30 of the Liberals denied the coupon survived. The election, benefiting primarily the Conservatives, put its stamp on politics for years to come. There were many new men in the House, including a good number of businessmen — "hard-faced men," said someone, possibly Stanley Baldwin, "who look as if they had done very well out of the war." Those M.P.'s who were eager to make a new world had to work in confused and unpromising circumstances and largely failed in their attempts. But the election had not turned on issues. Despite some violent talk about hanging the Kaiser and squeezing Germany "until the pips squeak," it was a quiet election that registered satisfaction in victory and confidence in Lloyd George.

Peace and Its Consequences

The election over, Lloyd George's primary concern was the Peace Conference, which opened in Paris in January, 1919. No previous peace conference had had to deal with such a vast range of problems, and none had had so large a corps of expert advisers drawn from government and academic circles. The main decisions were the work of "the Big Four" — Wilson from the United States, Clemenceau from France, Orlando from Italy, and Lloyd George. Whatever toughness appeared in Lloyd George's election speeches, in Paris he was all suppleness, generally inclined to a conciliatory attitude towards Germany. But his field for maneuver was sharply restricted by prior commitments and by the conflicting aims of the Great Powers themselves. Secret agreements made during the war—notably to bring Italy in on the Allied side and to carve up the Near East—dictated some of the territorial settlements; still other territorial obligations were created by the seizure of German colonies by some of the Allies —the most embarrassing for Britain being the insistence of Australia and South Africa on retaining the prizes they had taken in New Guinea and southwest Africa. At the same time, the Armistice had been signed on the basis of Wilson's Fourteen Points, which carried a quite opposite sense in their insistence on national self-determination, open diplomacy, and the attainment of a new international order. In sharp contrast to the American, or Wilsonian, idealism was the French insistence on compensation for sufferings in the war and on security against Germany in the future.

In the background was Russia, where Bolshevism gave the postwar world a specter analogous to the bogey of Jacobinism that had struck such terror into Tory hearts after 1815. There was little British sympathy, even in the labor movement, for Communism, and in 1919, the British were actually waging war against the Bolsheviks on Russian soil. Lloyd George did not much favor this adventure but could do little to prevent it; Winston Churchill, now Secretary of State for War, found fighting the Bolsheviks a stimulus for his hatred of socialism in all its forms and for the military instinct that, from his earliest days as a soldier, lay close to the surface in his personality. While Lloyd George was in London, Churchill persuaded the ministers in Paris to intervene. The British gave the "White Russians" tanks and other material; British troops, both regulars and volunteers, were engaged at various points around the periphery of Russia and in support of the Poles, who had launched their own war against Russia. By the end of 1920 it was all over: the Whites had been beaten by the Red army, and labor spearheaded resistance in Britain, which reached something of a climax when dockers refused to load a ship, the *Jolly George*, bound for Poland. The Russian imbroglio was one of the distractions that played fitfully in the background of the peace negotiations.

The main concern of President Wilson was to establish the League of Nations, which he believed could prevent future wars. It is ironic that the Senate rejected this commitment (and with it the Versailles Treaty), while Wilson had relatively little difficulty in persuading the European leaders, from whom he had expected resistance, to agree to it. The French looked on the League primarily as an additional guarantee against renewed German aggression; but the idea of a league of nations had been much discussed on broader grounds in Britain during the war, and it was largely on the basis of British projects that the actual structure of the League was based.

But the League was for the future, not the present. The territorial settlement facing the Conference was vast in its complexity. Two empires — the Habsburg and the Ottoman — had disappeared, and "succession states" had to be established, their boundaries drawn, their governments set up and validated. Partition of the Habsburg dominions in Europe followed generally along ethnic and "national" lines, though hostile peoples were uneasily yoked in Czechoslovakia and Yugoslavia and a host of minority problems were created. In the Near East, the settlement was complicated by the interplay of military and political ambitions in an area that knew no natural or national boundaries, and by the wartime commitments of the Allies. The Sykes-Picot Agreement of 1916, intended to delineate French and British spheres of influence, laid out the main lines of the territorial settlement, and British power remained paramount in the Near East until after the Second World War. The exercise of that power was informed by an idealism not always at peace within itself: there was much British admiration for the Arabs and for their attempts to work out national solutions to their destinies; at the same time the Balfour Declaration of 1917 had committed Britain to support a national home for the Jews in Palestine, a territory that, for all its significance in the Judeo-Christian tradition, had been Arab for centuries. But the Near East had more meaning for Britain than sentiment, more even than it had had in the nineteenth century, vital as it was then to the security of India. The twentieth century runs on oil; the Near East was found to be rich in oil. Oil became the most important cargo shipped through the Suez Canal and a major (and increasingly the main) reason for the continued British presence in Egypt, even after that country was recognized as a nominally independent kingdom in 1922.

The main settlement, however, revolved around Germany; to her the Treaty of Versailles was dictated. Alsace-Lorraine was, of course, returned to France; some of Germany's eastern territories were returned to a restored Poland, including a corridor to the Baltic that separated East Prussia from Germany. Germany's former overseas colonies went to their conquerors, usually in the form of mandates. Carried out under technical accountability to the League of Nations, the device of the mandate recognized that colonies were no longer quite so clearly the legitimate acquisitions they had seemed before the war, even though in actual administration many mandates were barely distinguishable from their more honestly named counterparts before 1914.

A clause in the treaty specifically declared Germany guilty of causing the war. Two corollaries followed: Germany should be prevented from committing a similar crime in the future, and she should pay for the crime she had committed. The Rhineland, that prosperous part of Germany facing France, was to be demilitarized and occupied by Allied Forces. The Saar Valley, important to Germany's military potential because of its mines and industry, was detached from Germany and occupied. Occupation was to last for fifteen years, after which a plebiscite was to determine if the Saar would rejoin Germany. The German army was limited to 100,000 men, and German manufacture of armaments was forbidden. All these protective provisions caused resentment in Germany, and the resentment in turn raised the question of their permanence. But a more immediate problem lay in the reparations for war damages. Lloyd George talked a tougher game than he played. He insisted on adding the cost of war pensions to the already gigantic claims for military and civilian damage, but the treaty refrained from setting a sum; that was left to a postwar commission. In 1921, with Germany already in default on initial payments, the commission set the figure at $33,000,000,000, and Germany was forced to agree to it. But, at the end of 1919, long before this fantastic sum was arrived at, the possibility of a Draconian financial settlement was attacked with savage brilliance in a pamphlet called *The Economic Consequences of the Peace*. It was written by J. M. Keynes, the chief representative of the British Treasury at the Peace Conference, who resigned his post to write it. Keynes believed (rightly) that an economically strong Germany was essential and that the peacemakers had knocked out a main prop of a prosperous and viable Europe; his argument and his style helped to create the legend that the peace was vindictive and foolish. Actually, given all the handicaps of prior commitment, internal disagreement, and publicity with which its draftsmen had to work, the treaty was a statesmanlike and forward-looking settlement. But it was born with a bad reputation and from the first was prevented from functioning as an effective foundation for a generation of peace. It was very unlike the settlement arrived at in Vienna in 1815.

Ireland

England had gone into the war with one of her oldest problems temporarily shelved. Irish Home Rule had become law, but the operation of that law was put off until the end of the war, when it was hoped a way would be found to solve the vexing question of the status of the predominantly Protestant counties of Ulster in a self-governing

Ireland. But the Irish—or some of them—would not wait. The strategic threat that Ireland posed in wartime was a main concern of the English. At the beginning of the war, Ireland already had an army of sorts in the Volunteers, and in 1915 Sir Roger Casement, who had resigned as a British consul to devote himself to the Irish national cause, was busy extracting promises of help from the German government for a rising to take place in Dublin on Easter Sunday, 1916. Like the French over a century before, the Germans were too preoccupied with larger strategic problems or too doubtful about the Irish or too unimaginative to take the plans very seriously. Casement landed on Good Friday and was almost immediately arrested. The rising was canceled. But on Easter Monday, a group of nationalists in Dublin proclaimed the republic. The rebellion lasted less than a week. It might not even have been remembered, had the British not executed its leaders, arrested hundreds of other participants, and hanged Casement for high treason: the Easter Rebellion was thus converted from an ill-judged adventure that deserved to fail into a consecration of martyrs.

The new hatred of England thus created (and made worse by the imposition of conscription in Ireland in 1918) went far beyond the old goals of Irish politics. Home Rule, as Gladstone and Asquith had conceived it, was no longer enough; and efforts throughout 1917 and 1918 to reach some sort of accommodation between Great Britain and Ireland invariably foundered. The most important political force in Ireland was no longer the parliamentary party but the radical Sinn Fein ("Ourselves Alone"), the party headed by Arthur Griffith. In the general election of 1918, Sinn Fein swept all but four Irish seats outside Ulster—73 in all as against 25 Unionists and a mere six Home Rulers. Refusing to sit at Westminster, the Sinn Feiners formed themselves into an Irish parliament, the Dáil Éireann, which declared Ireland an independent republic on January 21, 1919; the Volunteers were transformed into the Dáil's nominally dependent military arm, the Irish Republican Army (IRA).

Step by step, the IRA and the Royal Irish Constabulary, the British armed police, found themselves embroiled in a guerrilla war. The ordinary life of the country was disrupted or shattered, not by traditional military operations, but by outrages arising from frustration, irrational hatreds, the desire for revenge, or the arcane rationality of terrorism. There was little to choose between the two sides. Perhaps, though, it can be argued that the Irish tactics were inescapable, given their historic circumstances, while the British forces were further compromising a nation whose claims to leadership of the civilized and enlightened world had always been in danger whenever Ireland was at question. The worst blame has traditionally been laid on the supplementary British forces, the "Black and Tans" and the "Auxis," i.e., the Auxiliaries.

The war dragged on through 1920 into 1921. Meanwhile, the new Government of Ireland Act was passed in December, 1920, to replace the shelved Home Rule Act of 1914. Ireland was to remain in the United Kingdom, but southern Ireland was to have its own "home rule" parliament; so were six counties of the province of Ulster. The partition thus accomplished was not intended (at least by Lloyd George) to be permanent: a Council of Ireland, representing the two parliaments, was to provide for cooperation and ultimately for an increasing degree of unity. Elections were held in May, 1921, as required in the act, and from that time on Northern Ireland, with its own parliament, has existed as an entity within the United Kingdom, increasingly isolated from the larger country to the south. In the south, Sinn Fein again won all the seats (except the four for Trinity College, Dublin) and looked on the election as merely the choice of a new Dáil. The Irish republic took over the functions of government that one by one were abdicated by the British.

The war had become increasingly disliked in England. The case could be made (and was urged by General Sir Henry Wilson, one of the strongest sympathizers with Ulster in 1913–1914 and now chief of the Imperial General Staff) that the government should openly fight and win the war against Ireland in order to impose a settlement. But instead, long, difficult, and largely secret negotiations were undertaken to bring the Irish problem to the conference table. The principal target of these efforts was Eamon De Valera, one of the leaders of the Easter Rebellion who had escaped execution because, having been born in New York, he was technically not a British subject. De Valera had been elected president by the Dáil when the republic was proclaimed in 1919, although he was absent for the next two years on a fund-raising tour of the United States, leaving the effective working out of Irish government to Arthur Griffith and Michael Collins, the military genius of the nationalist movement.

Finally, in July, 1921, a truce was declared; in October, a conference opened in London. De Valera stayed in Ireland: he could be consulted, but he could also dissociate himself from its results, if it seemed wise to do so. The chief Irish delegates were Griffith and Collins, moderates now and subject to attack by the extremists at home. For the British, Lloyd George took the lead, but Churchill played an important mediatory role, and Lord Birkenhead (formerly F. E. Smith) and Austen Chamberlain — two sympathizers of the Tory die-hards and the Ulster rebels before the war — brought their prestige to support a settlement that went against every Tory prejudice. The negotiations were protracted and stubborn; they turned largely on the question of how much substance could be retained while sacrificing some of the appearances in two abstractions — the republic and the Empire. Under the treaty finally signed in December, there was to be an Irish Free State, not a republic; members of the Dáil had to take an oath of allegiance to the Crown. The Free State was to be a dominion in the British Empire, with the same status as Canada — although the full implications of that position were by no means clearly defined at this time. Britain retained the use of certain ports. Northern Ireland was to be given a month in which to decide whether or not to "contract out" of the Free State, and if she did so, a boundary commission would draw the line between the two countries.

The radical nationalists at home disowned the work of the delegates in London; the treaty was nonetheless ratified by the Dáil on January 7, 1922. De Valera, playing a middle game — he wanted a republic in free association with the Commonwealth rather than dominion status — resigned from the presidency of the Dáil and was not re-elected. Griffith succeeded him and became head of the provisional government. But deep disagreements over the treaty gradually grew into civil war. The IRA split into the Regulars, supporting the Dáil, and the Irregulars. A truce was arranged until new elections could take place in June, 1922, when victory went to the treaty forces. Almost at once there was trouble on the border of Northern Ireland; Sir Henry Wilson was assassinated in London; the Irregulars remained in control of the Four Courts, one of the chief government buildings in Dublin, which they had seized in April. Had the British government intervened, the warring Irish would have united. But the temptation was resisted, and the provisional government was forced to assert its authority by suppressing the Irregulars. In the midst of the civil war, Griffith died and Collins was assassinated; the new government under W. T. Cosgrave, another veteran of the Easter Rebellion, pressed forward resolutely against the rebels and gradually vindicated itself. In May, 1923, the Irregulars gave up, except for isolated and pathetic incidents in Eire, Northern Ireland, and England until 1968, when a new phase of the Irish troubles began.

The Empire

The Irish problem stood largely apart from the World War and its aftermath. Not so the rapid evolution in many other parts of the Empire. Canada, South Africa, Australia, and New Zealand — the Dominions, as they were beginning to be called — had made important contributions in men and money to the victory. Their politicians had become imperial statesmen, particularly Jan Christiaan Smuts, a former Boer general who was omnipresent behind the scenes in the last years of the war and in the years immediately after.* In the Peace Conference at Paris, the Dominions were represented separately as well as collectively in the British Empire delegation; they won the right to separate membership in the League of Nations. But all these trappings of nationhood, reflecting the increasing initiative these former colonies had been taking in foreign policy in the early years of the century, seemed to exist in perfect compatibility with a renewed affirmation of the emotional ties that had strengthened the bond to Britain during the war.

The exception to this steady evolution was India. The nineteenth-century history of India had two themes. One was the consolidation of British rule, direct or indirect, carrying with it reforms to bring India into the modern world. The Mutiny in 1857, partly caused by the disturbing thrust of reform, subtly displaced an optimistic view of Indian development by a pessimistic view that saw no alternative to the maintenance of the British raj for the foreseeable future; the gulf between the Indians and their rulers widened. But reforms continued, particularly in the economy: roads and railways were built, the endemic problem of famine was on the way to solution, industry was encouraged, education was extended. These policies were carried through by the Indian Civil Service, a late-Victorian realization of the Platonic ideal of government—by men as wise as the English public schools could make them and imbued with a sense of duty and paternalistic responsibility much admired at home and increasingly resented in India.

The other main current in the history of nineteenth-century India was the effort to round out its frontiers, especially in the northwest to head off the threat—a constant preoccupation of Victorian minds—of an expanding Russia. In these campaigns Rudyard Kipling and a host of imitators found inspiration for their stories, the British public found heroes like Lord Roberts and Lord Kitchener, and much ammunition was manufactured for English politics. The military analogue to the ICS was the Indian army, which fought with great distinction not only in India but in South Africa and in the First World War; the commissioned officers were British to a man.

The viceroyalty of Lord Curzon (1899-1905) saw the culmination of these nineteenth-century developments. Curzon was himself a brilliant administrator—we have already encountered him as one of

---

*Smuts was a principal adviser of Lloyd George at the Peace Conference, an intermediary in the negotiations leading to the Irish treaty, one of the main organizers of the League of Nations, and probably the originator, if anyone has a right to the claim of the phrase "the British Commonwealth of Nations."

the five members of Lloyd George's war cabinet. He brought the Victorian forms of the British raj to their perfection and associated with his government an imperial style that surpassed any of his magnificent predecessors.* He settled the Northwest Frontier and laid out the main lines of the settlement reached in 1907, delimiting Russian and British spheres of influence. His viceroyalty ended as the Russo-Japanese War concluded with the portentous defeat of a European by an Asian nation. The old themes of the history of British India were no more; the substance of Indian history in the first half of the twentieth century was the winning of national independence.

The nationalist campaign began innocuously enough when the government summoned a congress of Indian intellectuals in December, 1885, to find out what Indians themselves were thinking. But successive meetings of the Indian National Congress grew in size and turned to talking about grievances; among them were economic troubles—India needed (and the Indian government knew it) protection for her industry against English free trade and its chief beneficiary, Lancashire cotton—more rapid political reform, and greater participation of Indians in government. As more and more Indians became educated, and as places were gradually opened to Indians in local government and in the courts, the demand grew by what it fed on. Why not the legislative councils? Why not the exclusive senior ranks of the ICS itself? In this charged atmosphere, Curzon's administratively sensible partition of the unwieldy province of Bengal set off a violent reaction among Hindus, who resented the splitting of their "nation." The Hindu opposition revolved around the poles created by the moderate Gokhale and the extremist G. B. Tilak, whose followers resorted to systematic murder as a political weapon. The Muslims, generally the target of Hindu wrath, withdrew from the Congress in 1906 to establish the Muslim League, thereby making evident the communalism that has so deeply troubled the history of the subcontinent in this century.

Against this background, the Asquith government moved to reconstruct the government of India. The Morley-Minto reforms of 1908, so called after Lord Morley (formerly John Morley), Secretary of State for India, and the viceroy, the Earl of Minto—granted the prin-

---

*Curzon's superior manner, much remarked on even in his own time, when men were used to aristocratic airs, has been immortalized in one of the so-called "Balliol Rhymes":

> My name is George Nathaniel Curzon,
> I am a most superior person;
> My cheek is smooth, my hair is sleek,
> I dine at Blenheim twice a week.

Blenheim is the palace of the Dukes of Marlborough near Oxford.

ciple of separate electorates for Muslims, provided for the appointment of Indian members to the Viceroy's Executive Council (and to the Secretary of State's Council in London), and increased the number of elected members on the provincial councils. The reforms were a cautious and insufficient gesture, trying to improve the way India had been governed instead of creating a form of government that might survive in the future. A further installment of political reform could not wait beyond the war, to which the Indian contribution was so great. The Montagu-Chelmsford reforms, drafted in 1917 and enacted in 1919, tried to bring still more Indians into government and for the first time introduced a measure of self-government. It was done cautiously enough, by invoking the principle of dyarchy. Self-government was confided to the provincial councils (not the central government) in certain areas—agriculture, health, education, public works—while more sensitive areas like finance, justice, and police remained subject to the prerogative rule of the provincial governor.

The favorable reception of this act by Indian moderates—because the suggestion of ultimate self-government, implicitly denied by the British for sixty years, was clear—was marred by the suppression of a mob at Amritsar in April, 1919, when Indian army soldiers shot down nearly four hundred persons and wounded more than twelve hundred. The Amritsar Massacre was a response to a wave of lawlessness stemming from a revolutionary agitation begun by a prominent Gujerati lawyer, Mohandas K. Gandhi, in 1919. While working in South Africa, where there was a large suppressed Indian population, Gandhi developed the political technique of non-cooperation; he intended it to be nonviolent as well, but many of his followers, to his great regret, turned to violence. In 1922, after having launched a campaign of civil disobedience, Gandhi was committed to prison. He was certain that his methods could bring *swaraj* (self-government) in a year; it took nearly twenty, and the struggle cost Gandhi his life.

The Fall of the Coalition

For all the resilient cleverness Lloyd George showed in the last two years of the coalition government, events had turned against him. At the end of the World War, Britain was in much the best physical shape of any of the European belligerents: no armies had fought over her soil, and the airplane was not yet a destructive weapon. Some 40 per cent of her merchant ships had been sunk, but they were quickly replaced. The country lost a significant portion of its income from investments overseas, either because the value of those investments had been destroyed through belligerent action or postwar dislocation or because privately held securities had been sold, perhaps some 10 per cent. At worst, these losses only cut the size of the surplus in international payments that had made it possible for Britain regularly to import more goods than she exported. As a highly developed and relatively unharmed industrial country, then, Britain should have been in a peculiarly favorable position to benefit from the civilian demand dammed up during the war. So she did, for a time. But she did not do so intelligently, on the whole: British industrialists, still thinking in pre-1914 categories, expanded the old staple industries and kept them in the areas of the country where they had always been. But even had miracles of foresight occurred, the situation of the postwar world was too chaotic for Britain to prosper healthily and permanently. Old trade patterns had been disrupted; the map of Europe had been redrawn, with broad but ill-understood effects on international trade; exchange rates fluctuated wildly. Above all, there was the uncertainty of reparations — whether Germany would be able to pay, how she would pay, what effect payment would have on the international obligations of the beneficiaries, what degree of salvation for national budgets a considerable installment of reparations might provide. The postwar boom was brief and insubstantially based. By 1920 it had turned into a slump, and by 1921 into a depression.

John Maynard Keynes was then famous only for his attack on the Versailles Treaty; he had not yet taught the world that in a depression governments should spend. The cry was all for economy, and the government responded by appointing a committee in 1921 under Sir Eric Geddes, who had been the coalition's Minister of Transport, to try to revise the estimates. The "Geddes axe" was laid about in all directions, most drastically at the Army and Navy, but it lopped off many social services as well. The economy drive finished the postwar reconstruction plans that had survived parliamentary faint-heartedness and Conservative distaste in 1919. Proposals for nationalizing and electrifying the railways — under government control during the war — were given up, and the railways were returned to private hands in 1921, somewhat rationalized into four big systems. Plans for raising the school-leaving age by a year and for continuing part-time education were scrapped. The imaginative, effective, and expensive housing program administered by Christopher Addison (later Lord Addison) at the Ministry of Health was drastically cut back and in time (and in other hands) transformed out of all recognition. Some inroads were made on the tradition of free trade by continuing at reduced rates the so-called McKenna duties of 1915, levied originally to prevent luxury goods from taking up scarce shipping space; and other protective measures were masked as regulations for safeguarding key industries and regulating the dumping of foreign manufactures. Lloyd George carried a sweeping extension of the unemployment insurance plan he had enacted in 1911 for a few vulnerable industries; but the appalling rise in unemployment in 1920 and 1921 led to a compromise of the insurance principle itself by, in effect, advancing payments against future contributions; thus was born the dole, too often unimaginatively and degradingly administered, and resented by many of its recipients. Even the government's best intentions turned out to have a different look.

Politically, the coalition was shaky. Labour, as we shall see, was reorganized as a party and newly aggressive; what the results might be no one knew, but it was easy for those not in the Labour party to fear the worst. The reunion of the Liberals was an impossibility. Standing aloof from his old colleagues, who distrusted him and resented the tactics of the 1918 election, Lloyd George kept the support of the Conservative leaders — Bonar Law, Birkenhead, Curzon, and Austen Chamberlain. But the rank and file of the Conservatives were restive, and not less so over the turnabout on the Irish treaty.

A brilliant stroke might have pulled it off. But all Lloyd George's attempts failed. He was unable to get a settlement of the reparations question at the Genoa Conference in 1921. He tried to accommodate French and English ambitions in the Near East and, in Europe, to make concessions to the fears France felt for her security. He almost succeeded in negotiations with Premier Briand, who was rather out of the nationalist mold for a French politician, only to see victory snatched away (so the story goes) by the publicity given to a game of golf into which Lloyd George (an expert) had persuaded Briand: made to appear the victim of a frivolous and crafty schemer, Briand was driven from office two days later by a French parliament determined to take a hard line with Germany. Briand was succeeded by the nationalist Poincaré, with whom Lloyd George could get nowhere.

A final piece of bravado almost brought the country to war. In 1920, a treaty with Turkey had been concluded at Sèvres. Having reluctantly agreed to it, the Turks set about an impressive national revival under the leadership of Mustafa Kemal, their commander against the Allies at Gallipoli. The main object of Turkish hatred was the Greeks, who under the terms of the Treaty of Sèvres had retained a foothold at Smyrna on the mainland of Turkey; but they also resented the isolation of Constantinople by a neutral zone along the straits occupied by the Allies. Lloyd George stuck to a pro-Greek policy, even after his favorite, Premier Venizelos, had been turned out of office when the pro-German Greek King Constantine returned in 1920; in this policy Lloyd George was out of tune with the country.

When the Turks drove the Greeks out of Smyrna and threatened the British force occupying Chanak in the neutral zone, Lloyd George and his cabinet made ready for war, and there was at least some chance that a war might make possible another khaki election. The Dominion prime ministers were notified of the impending danger, but because of a blunder they did not receive their messages until after the newspapers had published a cabinet communiqué that seemed to commit them to the war, should it develop. Except for New Zealand, traditionally the most pro-British of the Dominions, the response from abroad was chilly indeed. Discreet delay by the men on the spot in delivering an ultimatum to the Turks provided a needed breathing space, and an accommodation was ultimately reached that made possible a new treaty with Turkey.

Chanak was an important step in British recognition of Dominion autonomy; it was also a successful exercise of diplomatic bluff. But it was a blow to Lloyd George's hopes, for it convinced most Conservatives that the coalition must end. At a meeting of the back-bench Conservatives at the Carlton Club on October 19, 1922, the vote went against continued participation, despite the pleas of Chamberlain. Bonar Law, now restored somewhat in health, reluctantly went along with the rebels, not out of any disloyalty to his old colleague but out of his sense of what his party was thinking. When Lloyd George resigned, the King sent for Bonar Law.

The Advent of Baldwin

Bonar Law had to form a government without being able to call upon the ablest and best-known Conservative leaders: Austen Chamberlain, Birkenhead, and Balfour all remained loyal to Lloyd George. Curzon, who had deserted Lloyd George at the last minute, was the only well-known minister in the cabinet. Many of the obscure men appointed to office were thrust into unexpected (and for some, undeserved) prominence, with powerful claims on office in the future. But for two of the obscure men, more must be said. At the Exchequer was Stanley Baldwin; in the minor office of Postmaster General was Austen Chamberlain's half-brother Neville. Both were to become prime minister; both had qualities that raised them well above the level of their colleagues, however unprepossessing they seemed before taking office.

Bonar Law at once dissolved Parliament and called a general election for November 15. The Conservatives emerged from the quiet campaign with a majority of 88. The Asquithian Liberals got 60 seats, the so-called National Liberals (what was left of the coalition, in fact), 57. But the Labour party nearly doubled its popular vote and returned 142 members. Labour thus became the official opposition party. Bonar Law's government was little more than an interlude, marked by Curzon's settlement of the Turkish question in a treaty, signed at Lausanne in 1923, that returned Constantinople to the Turks, retained the neutral zone, neutralized the Straits, and gained a fabulous oil concession at Mosul for Britain's mandate Iraq. Stanley Baldwin tried to extract a favorable arrangement for payment of the war debt owed to the United States; what he got was not what he wanted, nor was it so favorable as the arrangements the United States later concluded with France and Italy, but it was at least manageable if Germany paid reparations, for Britain had announced her determination long before to pay the United States only what she in turn was paid. Britain was therefore forced, under protest, to accept the French occupation of the Ruhr, Poincaré's device for extracting payment from a defaulting Germany. The result was financial chaos in Europe. The Germans responded to the French initiative by passive resistance; the resulting anarchy made the German inflation unbelievably worse. The inevitable result was civil disorder, one incident of which was an attempted *Putsch* in November, led by General Ludendorff, who was famous, and an agitator named Adolf Hitler, who was not.

Bonar Law had been ill when he took office; his condition worsened — it was discovered to be cancer of the throat — and he resigned in May. His attempts at bridge-building to Austen Chamberlain had failed, so Law would be succeeded either by Curzon, highly unpopular with many Conservatives, or by Baldwin. Law chose to remain neutral. King George V took advice from other Conservative leaders, notably Balfour, and had got the impression, indirectly, that Baldwin was Law's preference. He sent for Baldwin. Curzon, who had got the impression from a letter from Law that he had been recommended, was bitterly disappointed, although he proposed Baldwin's election to the leadership of the party. The constitutional significance of the King's decision was to make it clear, as Balfour had argued, that the prime minister had to be in the Commons.

Stanley Baldwin had said of Lloyd George at the fateful meeting at the Carlton Club in October, 1922, that he was "a great dynamic force," and that a great dynamic force was a terrible thing. Baldwin intended to be, and could be, nothing of the sort. An ironmaster in the family business, he created the impression of a simple, well-meaning ordinary man of common sense, determined that no boats would be rocked. Actually, the facade concealed a clever and ruthless politician, astonishingly resilient when some serious challenge shook him out of his usual indolence; Lloyd George considered him the most formidable antagonist he knew. Much that Baldwin did as a politician remains mysterious to historians. One thing is certain: so far as policy is concerned, the image of the comfortable, pipe-smoking plodder was correct.

Like Bonar Law, Baldwin could not count on the major leaders of his party; he headed a ministry that was little more than an interlude — its only important accomplishment a housing act carried by Neville Chamberlain just before he moved from the Ministry of Health to the Exchequer. In October, 1923, Baldwin drastically altered the shape of politics by reviving the doctrine of protection, last raised effectively by Joseph Chamberlain in 1903 and resoundingly rejected by the country in 1906. Baldwin's explanation at the time was that he could deal with the persistent unemployment only by using the weapon of the protective tariff. What lay behind his decision is still unknown, but at least he reunified the Conservative party. Austen Chamberlain and Birkenhead returned, now that their old party had clearly separated itself on principle from the Liberals; while Asquith and Lloyd George came together to revive the Liberals in defense of their oldest, most hallowed, and only slightly qualified tradition. An election was held on December 6. The Conservatives dropped from 346 to 258 seats; the reunited Liberals returned 158 members. There were 191 Labour members. Baldwin waited to meet Parliament before resigning; on a Labour motion of no confidence, the two opposition parties joined to bring him down. Constitutional precedent dictated that the King should then send for the head of the second largest party. Asquith had declared that he and his followers would support Labour, and the King agreed that Labour should have its fair chance. On January 22, he wrote in his diary: "Today 23 years ago dear Grandmama died. I wonder what she would have thought of a Labour government!"

TOWARDS LABOUR, 1918–1924

The Trade Unions

At the end of the nineteenth century and the beginning of the twentieth, British trade unions had grown impressively in number and experience; after 1906, when falling real wages and sterner attitudes on the part of some employers offered tough challenges, the trade unions responded confidently with a quasi-syndicalist agitation that erupted in some important strikes, forming a major element in the endemic unrest of those unhappy but creative years. The culmination of this development was the founding of the Triple Alliance of the miners, dockers, and railwaymen, which threatened to bring Britain to a standstill with a general strike in the autumn of 1914.

While the war had thwarted that intention, it proved a stimulus to trade-union growth beyond anything that had occurred before. On the one hand, the need to organize production led to official encouragement of unions in industries in which they had been able to secure only a tenuous hold. The trade unions had a little over four million members in 1913; in 1919, that figure had doubled. The leaders of labor, regularly consulted and brought into wartime government as equals (or near-equals), felt new respect and confidence, and most of them grew more moderate in their demands. Although some dilution of skilled labor was made necessary by wartime demands, the general condition of the working classes improved, suggesting the possibility that the forward march might be continued in the postwar world. On the other hand, controls on wages and conditions of labor led to dissatisfaction and a new militancy in the lower levels of some unions. This militancy emerged in the activities of the shop stewards, minor union officials on the factory floor who took on a new stature; articulating the discontents of the rank and file, they challenged the national leaders, whose proletarian purity grew suspect as they came closer to power. The war also altered industrial relations by encouraging a more efficient and extensive organization of employers' associations — as useful to government as strong unions — and in 1916 the Federation of British Industries was founded: it was an employers' counterpart to the Trades Union Congress.

The continued progress that trade unionists hoped for did not materialize, despite efforts to alter the relationship between employers and employees. The Whitley Councils, one of the reconstruction schemes, were intended to provide regular collaboration between employers and employees in regulating the conditions of labor. In 1919, the Industrial Arbitration Act made it possible for the Ministry of Labour (a wartime creation) to resolve disputes by arbitration or conciliation. In February, 1919, was held the first session of the National Industrial Conference, which some hoped would end as a kind of labor parliament. But these efforts came to little, partly perhaps because some of their sponsors (Lloyd George very probably) looked on them as mollifying gestures of no great seriousness, but most of all because they assumed a change in the structure of industrial relations that was acceptable to neither side, least of all to labor. Late nineteenth-century experiments in alternative modes of organizing industrial relations had only confirmed collective bargaining, with some help from government mediation, as the basic method for fixing wages and conditions of labor. Collective bargaining survived the postwar efforts to displace or supplement it by collaborative or judicial methods. Labor resorted to Whitley Councils only in those industries where fragmentation or employer resistance had made strong unions impossible; arbitration remained voluntary, and, with a significant exception that we shall see, largely unused. Labor quit the National Industrial Conference in 1921, convinced that it was a sham.*

Confirmed in their traditional methods and cheated of the world fit for heroes to live in, the trade unions responded with renewed agitation — strikes or threats of strikes, which grew in intensity and importance as the postwar boom gave way to the slump of 1920–1921. Before the war, Lloyd George had proved himself a master of labor negotiations; now, as prime minister, he turned out to be every bit as clever and, from labor's point of view, a good deal less admirable. In September, 1919, there was a national railway strike, the outcome of lengthy and futile negotiations between the railwaymen and the president of the Board of Trade, Sir Auckland Geddes, who was responsible for administering the railways, still under government control. The government asked for and got emergency powers that were to prove useful in the future; but the railwaymen's able and crafty leader, J. H. Thomas, campaigned just as effectively as the government did for public support, and got a settlement that at least kept wages at their wartime levels.

The miners, their militancy little lessened by the war, asked for more and got much less. In 1913, the Miners' Federation had come out officially for nationalization of the mines, a belief confirmed during the war when the government took over the mines and paid the miners according to a national wage scale instead of the regional scales whose variation had been a long-standing grievance. At the end of the war, the government seemed ready to take the miners' demands seriously. A royal commission on the mines was created: three of its members were coal owners; three were industrialists or engineers; three were officials of the miners' union; still another three, selected by the miners, were socialist economists and publicists — Sir Leo Chiozza Money, whose book *Riches and Poverty* had made a great impression before the war; Sidney Webb, the leading theorist of the Fabian Society; and R. H. Tawney, an economic historian and social philosopher. The chairman was a judge, Sir John Sankey. The government accepted an interim report by the chairman in March, 1919, proposing a moderate wage increase and improvement in working and living conditions; the commission then went back to investigate the industry as a whole. Four reports were issued in June. One rejected any basic change in the structure of the industry; in another Sir Arthur Duckham, an engineer, proposed

*On the earlier history of industrial relations, see above, pp. 389–393, 474–476.

regionalization of mines under district coal boards. The six representatives of the miners' side, of course, called for nationalization; so did
the chairman, in a separate report. But the government, having
promised to be bound by the commission's findings, took refuge in
the lack of unanimity and refused to do anything, aside from a few
feeble gestures at setting up machinery for worker consultation.

Balked of their main objective, the miners fell back on wage
demands, which they pursued in no very generous spirit. In a
complex round of negotiations with the government during 1920,
they won some temporary increases, pending a final settlement.
Their success was helped on by a threat of sympathetic strikes — in
effect a general strike — by the railwaymen and dockers: the Triple Alliance had come out of its wartime hibernation. Postponed to 1921,
the problem had to be dealt with after the slump had hit in earnest.
The government responded to the slump, as we have seen, by a final
bonfire of the remaining reconstruction schemes; one of its actions
was to move up to April 1 the date for returning the mines to private
hands. The owners, facing a rapid fall in the prices of coal exports, on
which the industry so heavily depended, and unable to imagine any
course but returning the industry to its old ways, announced reductions in wages and an adherence to district wage scales. The miners
struck on the day that government control ended. The other members
of the Triple Alliance reluctantly agreed to go along with the call for a
general strike.

The reluctance of the miners' partners was understandable. The
railwaymen had won a reasonably satisfactory settlement in 1919.
The dockers, transmuted into the Transport and General Workers
Union by Ernest Bevin, their secretary since 1910, had won a satisfactory settlement the next year in the only important application of the
Arbitration Act of 1919. The union and the employers had agreed to
be bound by the court's decision, and Bevin presented the dockers'
case so skillfully — at one point, he bought food according to what the
employers maintained were normal working-class budgets, brought
it into court, and asked a docker if he thought he could live on what
he saw before him — that he won a favorable settlement from the
court and earned his affectionate nickname of the "Dockers' K.C."*
The railwaymen and the transport workers did not need to strike for
their own ends; their leaders were skillful pragmatists rather than
proletarian doctrinaires; in any event, the pressure they could bring
to bear on the mine owners was at best indirect. They really favored

*K.C., King's Counsel, is a title indicating a superior level of barristers. Bevin
had risen from an agricultural background and an early job as a drayman to
his powerful position.

continued negotiations, but the miners demanded that the strike pledge be honored. As it happened, there was a division of opinion among the miners' officers. Frank Hodges, their secretary, agreed to resume the talks on conditions, among them the future negotiation of a national wage settlement; he was closely outvoted in the miners' executive. On April 15, the railwaymen and the transport workers, annoyed by what seemed to them the miners' obstinacy, called off their strikes: the date has gone down in labor history as "Black Friday." The miners fought on alone until July, when, badly beaten, they went back to work on the employers' terms.

The Labour Opposition

The main beneficiary of the disillusion and anger among working-men was the Labour party. Before the war, when a united Liberal party offered an alternative on the left, the Labour party served primarily as a means of getting labor spokesmen into Parliament and guaranteeing them a hearing; at best it could hope for no more than holding the balance of power in the House of Commons and forcing the Liberals to dance for a time to its tune. Even the party's structure reflected its limited purposes. It was a federation of trade unions, which provided most of the financial support, and a few small social-ist societies—among them the Independent Labour party and the Fabian Society—which provided much of the drive and most of the ideas; one could "join" the Labour party only by joining one of its constituent groups. In its parliamentary guise, the Labour party had no continuing existence; it elected its leader, not always the same man, at the beginning of each session.

As was the case with the trade unions, the war had a marked ef-fect on the fortunes of the Labour party. Some of its members had op-posed the war from socialist and pacifist principles, and Ramsay MacDonald, the party's leader in 1914, resigned his post. But the leaders who supported the war found themselves in a newly en-hanced position, and one of them, the party's secretary Arthur Hen-derson, was for a time a member of the war cabinet. When he resigned from the government in 1917, he devoted himself to reorganizing and enlarging the party. Accordingly, a new constitu-tion was adopted in 1918. To the trade unions and the socialist socie-ties were now added local Labour parties ("constituency parties") which individuals could join without first becoming affiliated with a trade union or a socialist group. But while the Labour party reached out to recruit membership from a wider public, it also cemented more closely its relations with the trade union movement. In 1920, the Trades Union Congress (TUC) created a General Council to serve as its executive; a National Joint Council was set up to coordinate the work of the General Council, the Labour party, and the Parliamentary Labour party. The offices of the TUC and the Labour party remained in the same building — first in Eccleston Square, then in Transport House, the headquarters of the Transport and General Workers Union — until the TUC opened its new building near the British Museum in 1958. The TUC and the party joined in rescuing (from an advertisers' boycott) and then in supporting the *Daily Herald*, founded in 1912, the lone voice of the left (other than the Communist *Daily Worker*) among the daily papers until it fell victim to the lessening commitments of a prosperous society in 1964.

The reorganization of the party proved itself in the general elections that followed in such quick succession in the 1920's: from a mere 63 members in 1918, the party's representation in the Commons increased to 142 in 1922, and 191 in 1923; its popular vote had nearly doubled by 1923, and even when the party lost 40 seats in the general election of 1924, its popular vote rose to nearly 5½ million. The emergence of the Parliamentary party as the official opposition in 1922 forced it in turn to reorganize. The principal step was the election of a leader who would continue from session to session; in a close vote they chose Ramsay MacDonald.

The Labour party owed its increasing prominence to more than improved organization or larger numbers of candidates put into the field. In 1918, the party had taken a marked ideological turn, from defending the generalized interests of labor to advocacy of a program that was definitely, if guardedly, socialist. The program was set out in detail in *Labour and the New Social Order*, a pamphlet written by Sidney Webb which called for a "national minimum" in social services and full employment, sharply raised taxation, a capital levy to reduce the national debt, and "democratic control of industry." The party refrained from spelling out all the implications of this phrase, but its objective was, as the famous Clause IV of the party constitution put it, to secure "for the producers by hand and by brain the full fruits of their industry, and the most equitable distribution thereof that may be possible, upon the basis of the common ownership of the means of production and the best obtainable system of popular administration and control of each industry and service." The wording "common ownership of the means of production" was open to interpretation: it might be taken to mean nationalization of all industry (and land, specifically set down for nationalization in *Labour and the New Social Order*) or merely of the "commanding heights of the economy," as a later phrase had it. Still, this rhetoric remained controlling for the Labour party for more than forty years and has not yet lost its appeal.

For all this cautious bravery, it must be said that Labour was not intellectually equipped to deal other than pragmatically with many of the problems it would have to face as a government. To many of its self-consciously proletarian members, the wartime success of direct controls and the even cruder techniques of the shop stewards' agitation pointed the way to success in peacetime government: if only they willed socialism and were tough enough in doing so, society would be transformed, and socialism would go forward on its own momentum. Another element in the party drew rather more heavily on a long tradition of spiritual and moral commitment; for them good will more than will would carry the day. Of this group the best-known and best-loved spokesman was George Lansbury, the editor of the *Daily Herald*.

The party was not lacking in intellectuals to tell it what to do. A good many members of the Union of Democratic Control, formed during the war to work for open diplomacy and the peaceful resolution of disputes, moved into the Labour party and guided its thinking on foreign affairs. R. H. Tawney provided a powerful justification for socialism in his brilliant indictment of capitalism, *The Acquisitive Society*, published in 1920. But the Fabian Society was not so much in evidence as it had been before and during the war and did not revive as a force in the labor movement until the 1930's. The party had enthusiasts aplenty. In G. D. H. Cole and H. J. Laski, it had promising young theorists. It was well supplied with economic historians to give it historical justification by colorful indictments of the ruling classes in the past and by glorifying those labor heroes whose work seemed to lead straight to the party's imminent success in the twentieth century. But the Labour party did not catch up to advanced economic thought until the Second World War or even after. Apart from the device of a capital levy (itself no monopoly of Labour), the party had little — or certainly little that was distinctive — to offer as concrete answers to the overwhelming economic problems facing Britain in the postwar world. Instead, the party adopted the warmed-over and well-worn remedies of the Liberal past — free trade and a balanced budget. It is an excuse, though a not quite sufficient one, to point out that almost no one else made the necessary break-through, even among professional economists. But it was unfortunate that a party committed to planning should have failed to break new ground in precisely the area most important to its success.

The First Labour Government

After Ramsay MacDonald accepted the King's commission to form a government in January, 1924, he chose a cabinet only two members of which had ever held ministerial office — Haldane, the former Liberal war minister who became Lord Chancellor, and Henderson, whom MacDonald nearly managed to exclude. The lack of experience showed in minor blunders and public embarrassments that occur when outsiders, suddenly thrust into an unaccustomed political position, have to feel their way into its conventions. MacDonald also had to face widespread distrust and even fear in most of the country outside the ranks of the politically conscious in the working classes. Labour's main purpose, therefore, was to prove that it could govern, proof it had to give under almost the worst of circumstances — as a minority government existing on the sufferance of Asquith and his Liberal followers. All things considered, it acquitted itself remarkably well.

Its best domestic accomplishment lay in the field of housing. The coalition government, under the direction of Christopher Addison, had provided housing subsidies to local authorities. But these subsidies — at least once the slump hit — seemed so ruinously expensive (or extravagant) to most people whose political opinion counted that the program was cut back and then abandoned. Neville Chamberlain's program in 1923 committed the Conservative party to state intervention to provide housing, but its provisions were niggardly. It emphasized private developers rather than the local authorities and the construction of houses for sale rather than for rent, while the houses were designed on a demeaning scale. The Minister of Health in the Labour government was John Wheatley — the one representative of the extreme left in the cabinet — who pushed through a new program of council housing, with subsidies both to support building and to keep the rents manageably low. Machinery for slum clearance was missing, but at least the provision of housing moved further down on the social scale than the lower-middle classes and upper levels of the working classes who had been the exclusive beneficiaries of earlier schemes.

In a way Ramsay MacDonald himself was the greatest success of the Labour government. Strikingly handsome and a superb orator, he looked like a ruler; he played his difficult role with dignity; and in the field of foreign affairs — he kept the Foreign Secretaryship for himself — he performed with a flair and accomplishment that bespoke a deep understanding and long interest. The British had repeatedly found France's dogged insistence on security a major obstacle to restoring Europe to some semblance of normality. Here MacDonald was helped by the fall of Poincaré, the French premier who embodied their policy; with Edouard Herriot, the radical who succeeded Poincaré, MacDonald quickly developed a warm relationship. In his last days in office, Curzon had helped set afoot an inquiry into the reparations problem, resulting in April, 1924, in the publication of the so-called Dawes Plan, which called for the stabilization of Germany's ruined currency, a regular schedule of reparations payments tied to specific revenues, and a German loan. The details were worked out in a conference in London in July and August, over which MacDonald presided, and the way was thus paved for a French evacuation of the Ruhr, which had been occupied with such disastrous results in 1923. MacDonald went further to quiet French fears by proposing an agreement, the Geneva Protocol, to move towards disarmament and, even more materially, towards peaceful settlement of disputes and collective security. The Protocol was meant to reinforce procedures set down in the League Covenant and to reconcile conflicting views of the League's functions. That the Labour government fell before it could be ratified was, no doubt, a serious misfortune for Europe, but the drafting of it stands to the credit of MacDonald and his party.

MacDonald also tried his best to regularize relations with Russia. The Russian Revolution had evoked warm enthusiasm among British workingmen, because it overthrew the hated Tsarist tyranny and set up a workers' state. This sympathy, as we have seen, reached something of a peak when British workers refused to allow the *Jolly George* to go on its counterrevolutionary mission to Poland; shortly after, the leaders of labor made it clear to the government that unless intervention ceased, there would be a general strike. But the labor movement, for the most part, remained discriminating in its enthusiasm. Labour generally disliked the dictatorial methods of the Bolsheviks, and the British Communist party, pieced together from a number of smaller and competing groups in 1920, found its proposals for affiliation with the Labour party repeatedly rejected. The British Communists never surpassed the parliamentary peak of two members returned in 1922.

Despite the long and unpleasant wrangling that had gone on between Britain and Russia in the early 1920's, one of MacDonald's first acts on taking office was to accord full diplomatic recognition to the Soviet Union. After arduous negotiations, two treaties were concluded, a commercial treaty and a general treaty foreshadowing further negotiations (that in the event never took place) to determine compensation for British holders of pre-Revolutionary Russian bonds and for British investors in expropriated enterprises in Russia and to arrange for a British loan. The negotiations went on through most of 1924, and the agitation against the government for its "truckling" to Bolshevism increased markedly after the treaties were signed. The agitation was intensified by a ridiculous incident; the government undertook and then dropped a petty prosecution of a Communist journalist, J. R. Campbell, who (like many leftists before his time) had publicly urged British soldiers to refuse to obey orders to shoot their fellow workers at home or abroad — orders that were not at all in prospect. In the anti-Bolshevist atmosphere of late 1924, though, it looked as if political considerations had been allowed to interfere with the course of justice. A motion of censure was introduced in the Commons; the Liberals got it amended to call rather for a committee of inquiry. When they made the vote a question of confidence, MacDonald and the cabinet lost the Liberals' support. Parliament was dissolved, and the third general election in three years was called for October 29.

At the very end of a bitter campaign, in which anti-Bolshevism played an important part, the newspapers published a secret letter ostensibly written by Zinoviev, the head of the Communist International, to British Communists, full of directions for bringing about the revolution in Britain, not least among which was helping to get the Russian treaties ratified. Debate continues about the authenticity of the letter, but if it was a forgery the tactic was probably unnecessary to assure a Conservative sweep: they got 415 seats as against Labour's 152 and the Liberals' 42. By explicitly dropping protection as a Conservative commitment, Baldwin assured his acceptability to the country and made it possible for Winston Churchill, who had not forsaken all of his old liberalism, to stand for Parliament as a Conservative.

TOWARDS A CRISIS, 1925–1931

An Undynamic Force

Baldwin gave the British what most of them wanted — quiet, a sense of stability, "sanity." He did so with a cabinet composed for the most part of mediocrities or of able men radically miscast — Austen Chamberlain, for example, at the Foreign Office, Winston Churchill at the Exchequer. The Geneva Protocol was replaced in the autumn of 1925 by the less sweeping Treaty of Locarno, which brought Germany into the League of Nations and gave British and Italian guarantees to a nonaggression pact between Germany, France, and Belgium. It is easy to dismiss the Locarno treaty as a mere moral commitment, lacking the military provisions for collective security needed to deter an aggressor; but at the time, the moral point seemed important, and throughout the remainder of the decade the "Locarno spirit" spread itself beneficently over the reconciliation of former enemies and a newly emerging sense of Europe. Not that British foreign policy was entirely conciliatory: in 1927, following a trumped-up raid on the London offices of a Russian trading company, the government, pleading subversion, denounced the Russian treaties and withdrew recognition of the Soviet regime — a concession to the Conservative right wing. But for the most part Britain and Europe lived out the twenties in an atmosphere of quiet accommodation. The growing right-wing movements on the Continent could easily be overlooked, and the dictatorship of the former socialist Benito Mussolini in Italy was received sympathetically by men and women from all parts of the British political spectrum: the Fascists' terrorism was either unknown or ignored, and the Italian trains ran on time.

In domestic policy, steady undramatic progress was made towards still greater involvement of the state in men's lives. The Conservatives even took two important steps along the road to nationalization: the British Broadcasting Company, licensed as a monopoly in 1922, was taken over by the government as the British Broadcasting Corporation in 1926, and, in the same year, the wholesale distribution of electric power (but not its generation or retail distribution) was taken over by the Central Electricity Board; the Board expedited the creation of a "national grid" for the efficient transfer of electric power from one area of the country to another as demand dictated. These steps were not taken from a dogmatic belief in nationalization; rather, they seemed the most efficient way of dealing with two relatively new and immensely influential factors in the life of the nation. Housing assistance to local government continued and increased—in 1928, houses built under these auspices made up 40 per cent of the total construction of housing. Enlarged pension schemes were enacted. Finally, in 1929, the structure of local government was transformed, the first major reconstruction since the creation of county councils in 1888 and of urban and rural district councils in 1894. These smaller local government units were reorganized, and provision was made for their future regrouping as population shifted; the powers of the county councils were widely extended; local taxes on much agricultural land and industry were wholly or partially lifted to encourage greater stability, the loss of revenue made up by central government grants out of general taxation. Historically, one of the most interesting provisions of the act was the abolition of the six-hundred-odd poor-law unions, the creations of the Poor Law Amendment Act of 1834; their many functions were given to appropriate local government bodies, and relief was thenceforth given directly through public assistance committees of the local councils. Thus was brought about the "breakup of the poor law" advocated by Beatrice Webb and the minority of the Poor Law Commission in 1909.*

---

*In 1928, in the so-called "flapper franchise," the vote was extended to women between the ages of 21 and 30, and qualification was made the same for both sexes, a three-month period of residence. Remnants of plural voting remained, however.

The minister behind most of these domestic reforms was Neville Chamberlain, back at his old post as Minister of Health. Chamberlain was no socialist; like his father, he had come from a background in business and local government, and the quest for efficiency led him to steps that on more abstract grounds he might well have resisted. There is an interesting parallel between this pragmatic drift towards collectivism in the 1920's and the pragmatic drift (again in the interests of efficiency and administrative good sense) towards liberalism during Liverpool's administration a century before. By a curious coincidence, Chamberlain and Peel shared many personal characteristics: both men were aloof, dull, even cold; both could gain the country's respect, but scarcely its love. Peel was able to follow the dictates of his administrative conscience into what amounted to a political revolution, a turn that Chamberlain could probably never have taken. But the circumstances of their times were different, and Chamberlain was never put to the test in an area where his strengths could tell: he may have been the most unlucky statesman in recent English history. Only now, as his disastrous premiership on the eve of the Second World War recedes, are historians gradually restoring due proportion to his accomplishment.

The Gold Standard and the General Strike

The industrial unrest of the twenties grew out of wartime experience and the postwar alternation of boom and slump. But the business cycle could be influenced by rational decisions of government, and fiscal policy after 1919 was a real cause of social tension.

Most Englishmen in a position to make or affect opinion after the war longed to return to the world they had known before 1914, a world in which Britain was incomparably the greatest power on earth. The most important locus of that power lay in the City of London. British shipping, banking, insurance, and investment touched and often controlled economies throughout the world. The easy meshing of this complex international machinery was made possible by the almost automatic operation of international exchange, based on the free flow of gold from one country to another, in payment of debts incurred in international trade and to adjust and correct imbalances that arose over longer periods between one country and another. By 1875, after three-quarters of a century of debate, the British had firmly tied their currency to gold; in the twentieth century, when some important Continental countries gave up the silver or bimetallic standard, the gold standard became virtually universal. The war had disrupted the operation of this system, but in 1918 a powerful committee of experts urged the earliest possible return to the gold standard and to the relationship between the pound sterling and the dollar (the two most important currencies) that had existed in 1914, when one pound was worth $4.86.

The trouble with this recommendation was that the world after 1918 was not the same as the world before 1914. Britain had lost many of her traditional markets; other nations, relatively untouched by the war, had replaced her in some of them—Japan in the Far East, the United States in Latin America. Her staple manufactures, on which her exports were dangerously dependent, were not doing well. Being old industries, they often found it difficult to compete with newer and more aggressive firms in other countries; the postwar boom held out false hopes and left them overexpanded and unwisely concentrated in their old regions—serious drawbacks in the changed conditions of the slump. The export of coal, which had played an important part in Britain's overseas trading account before the war and in the period immediately after, dropped sharply as mines in other countries, richer than Britain's and more efficiently run, came back into production; and the loss was permanent, for coal—the fuel on which the Industrial Revolution had been made—was being rapidly displaced by oil and electricity. Not until 1950 did British exports (adjusted for changing prices) reach the level they had attained in 1914.

At the same time, the nation was importing more than ever. To some extent the growing gap between the costs of imports and the yield from exports was made less dangerous by a turn in what are called the terms of trade; in the twenties, British prices were relatively higher than prices in many other parts of the world, so that a given value in exports would purchase more imports in the middle of the decade than at its beginning. But the favorable terms of trade only eased the problem; they did not solve it. The gap between imports and exports had, of course, existed through most of the nineteenth century, but it was far more than made up by Britain's invisible exports—shipping, insurance, and banking, and the yield from investments overseas. This cushion was no longer quite so comforting. Britain had recovered her wartime shipping losses by 1921, but during the war other countries had built merchant marines, usually subsidized and protected, and Britain's share of world shipping fell off. So did income from investments. By 1927 the losses of securities sold during the war had been made up; but new overseas investments were less rewarding than such investments had been in the years before 1914. Britain was far from being on her beam-ends in the twenties, but her position in the international economy was weaker, and the confidence of bankers and investors and speculators around the world was impaired. Any persistent pattern in public or private economic policy that threatened to widen the gap between exports and imports could in time mean the devaluation of sterling, decreasing, that is, its worth in relation to the dollar and other currencies. Foreign investors willing to hold sterling in good times, would tend, on any rumor or possibility of devaluation, to sell their holdings of sterling. Because British buyers—normally, in default of others, the Bank of England—would have to pay for these holdings in gold, the gold outflow would be increased, thus widening the gap even further.

A major goal of British postwar fiscal policy, then, was to get Britain back on an even keel, to prevent such a loss of confidence, and to make her industries competitive, problems that have remained at the heart of Britain's difficulties right down to the present. After 1918, the possible areas for action were several: to reduce the national debt or to convert it from a short-term to a long-term basis in order to reduce the huge sum that had to be budgeted for interest and so to free government funds for other uses; to reduce government spending; to prevent an inflationary rise in prices by restricting credit and keeping wages steady; and, if at all possible, to reduce manufacturing costs to bring British prices into line with foreign prices and so to encourage foreign buyers to come to Britain for their needs. These actions were the more necessary, if the pound was to be returned to gold at the old rate, because British prices were relatively high and remained so, particularly compared to the American price level.

Given these priorities, whose correctness few people questioned, the holocaust of the reconstruction plans and the swing of the Geddes axe become more understandable: they were not entirely the doing of political troglodytes or clever prestidigitators. But their results were disastrous. Today it is a commonplace that when depression strikes, the government should increase its spending, say by undertaking public works, to prime the pump; it will lower taxes and interest rates to get industry moving again. Taxes were lowered, of course, from their wartime levels, but throughout the early twenties the interest rate was kept high and credit expensive; the government did its best to restrict its spending—on housing, for example, in 1922–1923. Industrialists, insofar as they tried to reduce costs, were prevented by high interest rates from borrowing to improve their plants; too few found ways of improving management to accomplish the same ends. They therefore fell back on two panaceas that came more naturally to them—protective tariffs and the lowering of wages. Protective tariffs would help to reserve the home market, but they also made exporting more difficult as other countries retaliated or could no longer buy in the British market because they lacked the sterling that would have come from selling in it. Besides, tariffs were politically unacceptable, as the general election of 1923 proved. Lowering wages meant trade-union resistance; but that battle might be won by a straight exercise of power. To a very considerable degree, it was.

For whatever reason, the relative levels of British and American prices drew closer, and on April 28, 1925, Winston Churchill, the new Chancellor of the Exchequer in Baldwin's government, announced that sterling could once more be exchanged for gold (though gold coinage was not restored) and that the pound would be restored to its prewar valuation in terms of dollars. Churchill took the step after receiving conflicting advice from the experts and is hardly to be blamed for coming down on the side of what to most people was orthodoxy. The results are still a matter of debate. According to Keynes's estimates at the time, the return to the prewar standard found British prices about 10 per cent higher than American prices; in other words, he believed that the pound was overvalued in terms of dollars. Overvaluing made exports still harder to sell (though imports were cheaper to buy), and the step simply compounded the long-range difficulties of the British economy: reduction in costs rested more than ever on the reduction of wages.

As coal was the weakest of the major industries of the country — resources dwindling, capital scarce, exports falling, its management stupid — the test case over wages came there. The strike following Black Friday in 1921 was the first act; it ended in a victory for the owners. The second act followed in 1925-1926; it too was won by the owners and the government. But, in the long run, it proved a Pyrrhic victory.

On June 30, 1925, the mine owners announced both a lowering of wages and a lengthening of hours. There ensued nearly a year of negotiations of endless complexity and inevitable frustration. The negotiations were not, however, of concern only to miners and mine owners. The TUC had recently empowered its General Council to intervene in any dispute involving large numbers of workers; in this instance the General Council supported the miners' refusal of the owners' terms. The government also intervened with the first of several official inquiries; although it found largely in favor of the miners, and although concessions were subsequently offered by the owners, the miners refused to go along. When the TUC announced that, once the strike broke out at the end of July, it would impose an embargo on the shipment of all coal, the government promised yet another inquiry, during which wages and hours would stay where they were, and offered a subsidy to the owners. While the royal commission, headed by Sir Herbert Samuel, a prominent Liberal, went about its work, both government and the TUC began to make plans for a general strike. The government's plans were more specific and promised to be more effective: they believed a general strike might really come, and the TUC did not.

The report of the royal commission in March, 1926, gave little comfort to either side. It proposed a drastic reorganization of the industry, with the nationalization of royalties, better worker consultation, and more research — it said, in other words, that the owners had done their job badly. But the commission saw no immediate solution to the industry's problems other than a cut in wages, hedged about with concessions — no increase in hours and a national wage scale. Negotiations were then resumed. The conciliatory Hodges, who had been tempted to give in in 1921, had been replaced by an intransigent former Baptist preacher named A. J. Cook, who was at one with Herbert Smith, the miners' president; the owners were equally stubborn. By the end of April, the TUC had begun once again to threaten a general strike, but everything was obscured in a haze of proposals, counterproposals, and round-the-clock negotiations, in which emotions, exhaustion, and foolish blunders became more and more the determinants of position and decisions. Suddenly, without warning, late on the night of May 2, the government broke off negotiations on the pretext that the typesetters of the *Daily Mail* had refused to set an editorial scheduled for the next morning calling for resistance to the threatened general strike. In a divided cabinet, the party of stern action had won.

The strike began on May 4, when the first-line industries were closed down: railways, transport, docks, the metal trades, building, printing, electricity, and gas. At the local level and at the national level, where Ernest Bevin was the chief organizer, the unions did a remarkable job of improvising strike machinery: local committees arranged for picketing and publicity, dealt with cases of hardship, and issued permits for work or emergency transport, until on May 7 the General Council ordered all permits withdrawn. The government, having planned more effectively in advance, moved swiftly and surely. Large numbers of volunteer workers were called out; the Navy was put to many different tasks; troops were held in reserve. The minister most in evidence was Winston Churchill, all his fighting instincts aroused; as editor of the *British Gazette*, the government's paper (which the TUC answered with the *British Worker*), he saw to it that the public got precisely what he wanted them to get, and he was to be found at the center of any provocative action taken by government forces: it was a role for which labor never forgave him. While much good feeling was in evidence throughout the strike, there were more and more disturbances as the strike wore on—it was not everywhere that strikers and police played football matches, as they did in Plymouth. The government took the position that the strike was revolutionary, directed against the state; and the TUC's denials could not conceal the fact that among many strikers a distinctly revolutionary spirit grew in the last days of the strike.

Peacemakers were much in evidence, but Sir Herbert Samuel proved to be the most effective mediator. On his own initiative, he proposed a reworking of the recommendations of the royal commission he had headed as a means of settling the coal strike. The General Council, most anxious to settle, accepted his memorandum as a basis for negotiations and so as a justification for calling off the general strike. On May 13, the General Council, in spite of the miners' refusal to cooperate, announced the end of the strike: Churchill called it unconditional surrender, which it was not. To many strikers, it seemed another betrayal; many men refused to return to work, especially in those industries where they found they would be victimized. The King and Baldwin intervened, and better terms were worked out in most industries than were originally offered. The railwaymen, the most reluctant to strike, suffered most in the event, except for the miners. The miners refused to go back; their strike did not end until the end of the year, when they straggled back to work longer hours at lower pay.

In May, 1927, the government exacted its final revenge: the Trade Disputes and Trade Union Act was passed. Sympathetic strikes or strikes intended to coerce the government were declared illegal; intimidation was defined and banned; the political levy on trade unionists (the financial mainstay of the Labour party, presumably guaranteed in 1913) was restricted to those members who elected to pay it, whereas before an unwilling contributor had to contract out; and civil servants were forbidden to join trade unions affiliated with the TUC. The strike clauses of this harsh statute were never invoked; the gratuitous penalization of the Labour party cut its income by a quarter and gave it a major grievance to nurse against that day—in 1945—when it had enough power to repeal the act.

The Second Labour Government

After 1927, the popularity of the Baldwin government gradually dissipated, and at the general election held in May, 1929, a few months before the expiry of the statutory life of the Parliament elected in 1924, Labour emerged as the largest party, with 288 seats. But Labour still did not have a majority: the Conservatives won 260 seats, the Liberals, 59. The poor showing of the Liberals did not reflect the brilliance of their campaign, the only source of excitement in an otherwise dull contest. Asquith had gone to the Lords in 1925 and resigned his leadership the next year; in 1928, he died. Lloyd George was once more dominant; he had ambition, an innate radicalism, and a great deal of money—from the "Lloyd George Fund," much of it derived from the open sale of titles and honors during his premiership. All these he welded to fresh ideas that found their way into a series of policy proposals far more imaginative than anything produced in either of the other parties. The Liberals called for the overhauling of agriculture and industry, town planning, national development, and a deficit-financed public works program to get the economy rolling again—the first incursion of Keynesian economics into a political platform. With greater or lesser faithfulness, the Liberal program had been gradually enacted by the major parties. But the Liberals, as a political force, had shot their bolt.

Little was done by Labour, now in office for the second time. If anything, MacDonald chose a cabinet even more moderate than before; he himself had become more remote, jealous, and secretive. The field in which he had performed so well, foreign affairs, he now had to share with the genial Arthur Henderson, who finally claimed the Foreign Secretaryship as a reward for his many services to the party. In 1924, Labour had come into office on a generally rising curve of economic recovery, European peace, and national confidence; success was easy enough to obtain, perhaps, and the fundamental distrust so much of the country felt for Labour was softened. In 1929, it was quite otherwise. MacDonald took office at the beginning of June; in October the New York stock market crashed in ruins, spreading economic destruction throughout the world. Britain's improving but still fragile economic position had been weakened in the preceding year or two by large loans to Germany to help with the reparations payments and, latterly, by a strong outflow of gold to feed the American boom, which was attracting even normally prudent investors. The collapse of raw-material prices after the crash quickly closed down many of Britain's export markets; the loss of confidence everywhere shut off new investment. Britain suffered less than many other countries; but by 1931 her exports stood at little more than half what they were in 1929, and unemployment—persistently high and seemingly insoluble when Labour took office, at a figure of something over a million—rose horrifyingly to two and a half million by the end of 1930.

Against this background, the accomplishments of the Labour government seem meager indeed—a coal-mines act in 1930 that reduced the working day from eight to seven and a half hours and provided for some reorganization of the industry; a housing act; the creation of agricultural marketing boards; a bill for nationalizing London transport that they fell too soon to carry. Labour got nowhere in its attempts to raise the school-leaving age and, most frustrating of all, it failed to undo the Trade Disputes and Trade Union Act of 1927. There was little demonstrably socialist in anything that the government did, unless re-establishing diplomatic relations with the Soviet Union would qualify.

The two men who had to deal most directly with the depression and unemployment were Philip Snowden, at the Exchequer, where he had also been in 1924, and J. H. Thomas, the leader of the railwaymen, who held the nondepartmental office of Lord Privy Seal. Few could have equalled Snowden's devotion to the shibboleths of orthodox finance—the balanced budget, the gold standard, free trade, economy. Thomas and his assistants undertook some public works and launched or proposed some long-range plans; but nothing that was done had a noticeable effect on the rate of unemployment. The efforts of Thomas's lieutenant, Sir Oswald Mosley, a colorful aristocrat who had migrated from Toryism by way of independency to Labour, to persuade government and party to adopt much more radical long-term and short-term measures, led only to Mosley's resignation and to a strange and disturbing later career.

In July, 1931, two reports were published. One, from the Macmillan Committee on Finance and Industry, much influenced by J. M. Keynes, who was one of its members, painted a picture of the basic difficulties of the British economy that raised questions in many people's minds about its viability. The other, from the May Committee on National Expenditure, made public just after Parliament recessed, was a bombshell. It predicted a deficit by the spring of 1932 of £120 million and called for the most stringent measures to set it to rights—a sharp increase in taxation, even sharper economies, especially in the reduction of unemployment benefits, while the unemployment insurance fund was to be forbidden to borrow any further. The cutting of unemployment benefits was the panacea on which most men outside the ranks of labor concentrated. The May report nearly destroyed the confidence of foreign investors and bankers, who demanded a 10 per cent cut in unemployment pay as a condition of loans on which Britain depended to maintain the gold standard, so severe had the drain on her reserves become. Faced with this ultimatum, the cabinet split. MacDonald announced that he was going to see the King and asked for their resignations; the assumption was, of course, that he too would resign. But when MacDonald emerged from his audience, he was again prime minister, commissioned to form a "national government." The resulting coalition government numbered four conservatives, two Liberals, and four members of the former Labour cabinet—MacDonald himself, Lord Sankey, the Lord Chancellor, Thomas, and Snowden.

The feelings engendered in the labor movement by the creation of the national government were so intense and so long-lasting that they have helped to obscure the complex realities of the situation. But certain things now seem clear. MacDonald had found himself increasingly ill at ease in the Labour party and, as he liked power, had certainly had some vague thoughts of a coalition. There is no escaping the fact that his Labour government had dismally failed to do what needed doing, partly because it was in a minority, partly because it was divided, partly because it lacked the will or knowledge even to begin to cope with economic and social problems of such magnitude. The King was himself partial to the idea of a coalition, and when he took advice from other party leaders—as he was constitutionally bound to do once MacDonald had told him that the government's resignation was in prospect—the idea of a coalition was raised. The King's appeal to MacDonald was probably more persuasive than any single element, but many other considerations entered into the decision. The national government sprang from a widely spread predisposition in an unparalleled crisis and is not, when one looks back, particularly surprising. Is not a coalition in the face of national bankruptcy as logical as a coalition in time of war? But the creation of the national government stunned contemporaries.

Cuts were made in unemployment pay and government salaries, taxes were raised, the budget was balanced. But the drain continued, not least because the world was unfavorably impressed by a "strike" of seamen in a few naval ships against reductions in pay. Within a month of taking office, the national government abandoned the gold standard it had come into existence to save. The export of gold was forbidden, and the pound fell to about 70 per cent of its old dollar value. The government, having done the unthinkable, then turned to a general election to legitimate itself and to get what MacDonald called "a doctor's mandate" to deal with the crisis. On October 27, after a bitter campaign in which the principal hard issue was protection, the Conservatives returned 473 members; with various splinter groups, they made up a total of 554 supporters of the coalition. Labour dropped—or was thrust down—from 288 members in 1929 to 52 in 1931, a gross underrepresentation of the more than six and a half million people who voted Labour. A clear majority of 493 (for the opposition also included some tiny splinter groups) gave MacDonald his doctor's mandate and the hospital besides. But MacDonald was a figurehead. The election confirmed in power the men who had exercised it through most of the twenties and gave them a secure following.

THE NATIONAL GOVERNMENT, 1931–1940

Recovery

The way was now clear for returning Britain to protection. There had been a narrow logic to it at least since the 1880's, when Britain's industrial supremacy was first seriously challenged. There was a wider logic against it in Britain's peculiar vulnerability as a nation dependent on exports and international finance; perhaps more to the point, protection was abhorrent to the majority of the nation. The McKenna duties of 1915 were comprehensible wartime measures: fiscal means were well calculated to cut down those nonessential imports that might take up cargo space. They were kept after the war — at reduced rates — for revenue, but governments began to talk about "safeguarding" essential industries, and on this head Churchill had moved forward after 1925. In 1932, the narrow logic triumphed at last: the depression and the terrible problem of unemployment gave it a new urgency. The cabinet itself could not agree. In violation of constitutional practice it announced its agreement to differ, and on February 4, Chamberlain introduced his Import Duties bill, with a tribute to his father's memory. The bill passed easily. It provided for a general duty of 10 per cent, except for goods already dutiable and other goods specifically included in a free list — wheat, meat, and some vital raw materials. The Import Duties Advisory committee was established with power to recommend additional duties to the Treasury, a power it quickly took advantage of to impose an additional tariff on certain manufactures.

Another clause in the act held out the possibility of exemption for imports from the Empire, a promise of imperial preference to be implemented at the Imperial Economic Conference in Ottawa during the summer of 1932. It was a curious position for Britain to be in. In the nineteenth century, the grant of responsible government to a colony brought almost as a first step the imposition of a colonial tariff on British goods. Now the mother country, which had refrained from imposing what it thought its superior wisdom in the nineteenth century, came to a tariff conference, a novice facing men with fifty or seventy-five years of experience in protecting themselves. They did not look kindly on self-sacrifice. They got preference for foodstuffs their countries shipped to Britain, a concession of some value; but the preference they offered to Britain's manufactured goods consisted not in lowering already high duties but in raising duties against other nations. Still, the Ottawa Agreements gave a new appearance of strength to the imperial ideal so recently transmuted into the vision of a commonwealth of nations. The political price was small enough: the government lost some Liberals and Philip (now Lord) Snowden.

The government made efforts to help recovery. The agricultural marketing scheme begun by Labour was expanded to cover certain key products — bacon, potatoes, hops, and, above all, milk. Protected by quotas (but not tariffs) from foreign competition, the British farmer was assured a fair and steady price, either by the appropriate marketing board, operating as a middleman, or by government subsidy. Other devices were tried for other products, for example a processing tax on flour to make up the difference between the market price and the guaranteed price of wheat. Agricultural production and agricultural incomes rose; the subsidies schemes assured that consumer prices would remain low. After decades of agricultural depression, the pattern was set for the later prosperity of farming.

There was much less direct government intervention in industry, although the pragmatic approach to nationalization of the 1920's found expression in the thirties in the completion in 1932 of the Labour government's plan to nationalize London transport and in the nationalization of two disastrously competitive subsidized airlines as the British Overseas Airways Corporation, which came into existence in 1940. Large government subsidies were also poured into the ailing shipbuilding industry to make possible the construction of two giant Atlantic liners, the *Queen Mary* and the *Queen Elizabeth*. But the general policy of the government towards industry was one of benevolent support of industry's own recovery schemes. To some extent British industry sought to reduce its capacity and to amalgamate or kill off weaker firms. The most striking example is to be found in shipbuilding, where the industry itself arranged for the reduction of capacity by a million tons in four years. Both steel and cotton underwent amalgamations and "rationalization," a further step away from economic orthodoxy towards price-setting and cartelization. But new mills were built as well, with healthy effects on the economy generally and on the areas in which they were set down.

Unemployment remained a major social problem, still unsolved when the Second World War came. Much attention was rightly directed to the social and psychological problems created by living on the dole for months and even years. But it would be quite wrong to think of unemployment as endemic throughout the country. It was confined to those regions that were heavily dependent on the old staple industries so drastically contracted in the 1930's. Thus Jarrow, a small shipbuilding town on the River Tyne, near Newcastle, relied almost completely on a firm that was closed down in 1934; in 1935, nearly three-quarters of the insured workers in Jarrow had no jobs. By the end of the thirties, new industry had come in; clever and genuinely sincere publicity had made Jarrow the prime example of national shame, and it got attention accordingly. Not all towns were so lucky. In 1934, an act was passed to deal with distressed areas, a phrase the House of Lords, with an unusual show of squeamishness, changed to "special areas": South Wales, hardest hit of all the coal fields by the drop in exports and hit again by rationalization in steel and iron; the mining and shipbuilding areas of the northeast and northwest of England; the industrial areas in Lowland Scotland. Grants were made, public works and projects were undertaken, but the programs were tentative and restricted. The unemployed in those districts fell between 1935 and 1937 from somewhat more than a third to a little over a fifth, but that fifth was far beyond the tenth of the population unemployed in England as a whole. Government-aided migration from those areas to other areas where there was work helped some; rearmament at the end of the decade helped more.

In general, the thirties were a period of gradual but steady recovery. As Britain had never fallen so far into depression as other industrial countries, her recovery was easier. Leaving aside the grim conditions in the special areas, the decade was marked by a rise in real wages and living standards. Protection got much of the credit, but it is doubtful that protection deserved it, and the various government measures were at best a minor contribution. The economy lifted itself by its own bootstraps — not so far or so intelligently as it might have done with more systematic encouragement and direction. Probably the most important single factor in the expansion of the thirties was the boom in housebuilding, some of it in subsidized council housing, most of it in private building financed by newly aggressive building societies offering highly favorable mortgages. That many, indeed a majority of Englishmen, were living better lives in 1938 than they were in 1929 or certainly in 1931 is one key to understanding their reluctance to face up to the prospect of another war, a war that this time would inevitably mean destruction in Britain.

The Empire

The confident self-assertiveness of the Dominions during the Ottawa negotiations in 1932, though it merely gave new expression to an old nationalist stance, can also be taken as a practical and symbolic reflection of the new legal status they had just attained. Throughout the twentieth century, as we have seen, the predominantly English self-governing colonies had step by step approached full sovereignty. The grant of responsible government had given them a completely free hand in internal affairs, subject to certain restrictions: if a statute passed by a Dominion parliament (and this was true of any colony) was repugnant to an English statute, the Dominion statute was void, and it still remained possible to appeal from Dominion (or colonial) courts to the Judicial Committee of the Privy Council, which among its many other activities served as a kind of supreme court for the Empire—but both of these restrictions largely concerned legal technicalities and had little symbolic or practical meaning. More to the point, foreign policy had been reserved for the mother country. In this area the Dominions made striking progress, first by being associated with negotiations for treaties that affected them—treaties affecting Canadian and American fisheries, for example—then in signing treaties separately; separate representation at the Peace Conference and in the League of Nations moved them still further towards autonomy. The Irish Free State took the initiative in appointing a separate ambassador to Washington in 1924, and Canada followed suit in 1927, although extensive appointment of separate ambassadors did not go very far until the Second World War and after.

In 1926, at an imperial conference, a famous definition of dominion status was arrived at in the so-called Balfour Report: "They are autonomous communities within the British Empire, equal in status, in no way subordinate to one another in any aspect of their domestic or external affairs, though united by a common allegiance to the Crown, and freely associated as members of the British Commonwealth of Nations." By a resolution of the same conference, the governor-general was declared to be merely the personal representative of the king, confined to exercising the constitutional and ceremonial powers of the monarch on the advice only of his dominion ministers; he could no longer take orders from the Colonial Office. After 1931 the Crown usually appointed a citizen of the dominion itself as governor-general, and so, for communications between governments of the Commonwealth, it became necessary to have ambassadors, called high commissioners. Coordination fell to the office of Secretary of State for the Dominions, split in 1925 from the Colonial Office, which from that time on devoted itself solely to the dependent Empire.

In 1931, an act resoundingly called the Statute of Westminster was passed to give constitutional force to this gradually evolved status. The Colonial Laws Validity Act of 1865 was repealed insofar as it concerned the repugnancy of dominion statutes to English law; the dominions were given the right to legislate extraterritorially, i.e., for their nationals and ships abroad; and the British Parliament was to act in future for a dominion only at its request. Concerned with legal technicalities rather than constitutional fundamentals, the Statute made certain significant exceptions. The British North America Act of 1867 was specifically excluded from the operation of the Statute of Westminster; largely because of the tension between the English majority and the French minority, Canada preferred that its constitution, set out in that act, be insulated from the possible whims of a Canadian government; not until 1949 did she request the power to alter the British North America Act. In Australia, where the jealousy of one state for another was considerable, states' rights were specifically protected by the Statute. Newfoundland and New Zealand insisted that the Statute take effect for them only when their legislatures passed it, something New Zealand did only in 1947; while in 1933, Newfoundland, in serious economic trouble, asked to be deprived of dominion status and to revert to the status of a Crown colony.

It was, predictably, the Irish who took fullest advantage of the Statute of Westminster: by abolishing the oath of allegiance; stripping the governor-general of all his powers—even his ceremonial powers—and reducing the office to a joke; outlawing appeals to the Judicial Committee of the Privy Council; and substituting Irish citizenship for British citizenship—a nationalist example followed by the other dominions after the Second World War. The British government, which considered the 1922 treaty with the Irish as paramount law governing the place of the Free State in the Empire, balked at the oaths question and retaliated when President De Valera (who had come into office in 1931) stopped payment on the annuities under the land purchase acts. To recover the cost of the annuities, Britain slapped heavy duties on Irish exports to Britain, and Ireland responded in kind. It was not, however, until 1949—oddly enough, after De Valera had left office—that Ireland took the final step of declaring herself a republic and withdrawing from the Commonwealth, although in 1937 a new constitution had made Ireland a republic in all but name and replaced the historic name of Ireland by the antiquarian name of Eire.

India was quiet through most of the twenties, as the moderates of the Congress party, for a time in control, tried to adjust to the 1919 constitution. The working of that constitution was reviewed at the end of the decade by an all-British commission, which rejected the concept of dyarchy and urged the grant of full responsible government to the provinces and the setting up of a new federal government. The Congress party rejected the proposals out of hand, partly because they wanted the subordination of India's vast minority groups in a unitary state. Nevertheless, two round-table conferences were held in an attempt to hammer out the federal constitution in

1930 and 1931. The first was boycotted by leaders of the Congress party in protest against a new prison sentence for Gandhi, who had started another civil disobedience campaign in 1930; for the second, Gandhi was released from jail and attended as the sole representative of the Congress party, claiming to speak for all of India. Gandhi was regularly consulted by the British, in the hope that a new constitution might be drawn to satisfy him.

The constitution of 1935, the major legislative monument to Stanley Baldwin, carried out proposals of a royal commission in 1930: it gave full responsible government to the provincial governments and proposed a federal government to unite them and the princely states. The Congress party would have nothing to do with the constitution, although it was persuaded to take part in the elections in 1937 from which it gained power in seven of the eleven states. But its intransigence prevented the formation of a federal government, and so full legal powers remained in the hands of the governor-general, who declared war for India on his own authority in 1939.

New Directions in Politics

Although the early thirties confirmed the power of men who had ruled through most of the preceding decade, those same years marked a drastic reorientation within the parties themselves, a reorientation that gave shape to the party politics of the forties and fifties.

The troubles in the Labour party grew from the nearly total failure of the second Labour government and its seemingly treasonable end. A troubling portent of things to come was the turn taken by Sir Oswald Mosley, who had resigned when he was unable to carry his case for a radical attack on unemployment. With a few M.P.'s and some erratic intellectuals, Mosley formed the short-lived New Party. Gradually he drifted into Fascism, forming the British Union of Fascists from the remnants of his own following and some tiny proto-fascist and right-wing groups.

Other disillusioned members of the party turned to the left. The Independent Labour party (ILP), who were characteristically affiliated to the Labour party and dedicated to socialism, was increasingly uncomfortable with the Labour party's moderation. Still, 140 Labour M.P.'s, for tactical, sentimental, or doctrinal reasons, were members of the ILP. When, in 1930, the ILP tried to bind those M.P.'s to its program, it lost 122 of them. Two years later the remnant of the ILP withdrew from the Labour party to pursue its own course and lost still more support. Those members of the ILP who chose to remain within the Labour party were among the founders of the So-

cialist League in the same years. The League's two most prominent
spokesmen were Sir Stafford Cripps, a brilliant barrister and the son
of Lord Parmoor, and Harold Laski, professor of political science at
the London School of Economics. As an organ of the intellectuals in
the party, the Socialist League helped to widen, if not to create, a gulf
between the old-line trade-unionist socialists and the often younger
intellectuals in whom a new intensity and a new dogmatism were
born of the terrible problems at home and the growing threat of Fascism abroad. Perhaps even more striking was the case of John
Strachey, from one of England's most distinguished literary and journalistic families; a member of the little band that had gone with
Mosley into the New Party, he soon withdrew to become in all but
party membership a Communist. Strachey's stirring book *The Coming Struggle for Power* (1932) became a manifesto of a generation of
young people for whom the Marxist categories and prophecies
seemed astonishingly pertinent. A hundred years earlier, young radicals had turned to Smith and Ricardo or to Bentham because their
analyses of society made sense of what was going on around them.
So too the Marxist enthusiasm of the thirties, an enthusiasm impressively illustrated by the publishing success of the decade—the Left
Book Club, founded in 1936; its selections were chosen by Victor
Gollancz, the publisher, Laski, and Strachey. A year before, Sidney
and Beatrice Webb published *Soviet Russia: A New Civilization?*, a
two-volume celebration based on their visit to Russia in 1932; to
them, as to many of their younger contemporaries, Russia seemed
the realization of the planned and managed society into which they
had tried for so many years to convert their own country.

The title of Strachey's book suggests a basic concern of nearly everyone on the left. The second Labour government and the formation
of the national government convinced them that England's ruling
classes were not going to give in to gradualism, enlightenment, and
progress: they were going to have to be fought and beaten. Hence the
enthusiasm for forming a popular front with the Communists; hence
the incessant concern with "emergency powers," the dictatorship
that would have to be assumed (temporarily) by a Labour government once it came to power in order to carry out a true socialist revolution without hindrance from the organized and determined power
of the right. The program of the left transcended the ordinary categories of English politics, understandably so, for the Labour party as
they had known it had been almost annihilated by the general election of 1931.

Ramsay MacDonald, Sankey, Snowden, Thomas, and their little
band of Labour supporters were expelled from the party for their
treachery. The election saw the defeat of every holder of ministerial

office but two, both of whom had been in relatively minor posts. George Lansbury, who had been First Commissioner of Works, popular and greatly respected, survived, and was elected leader of the Parliamentary party; his deputy was the other ministerial survivor, Clement Attlee, a junior minister who had come into the party from a middle-class background and an early career in settlement-house work in the East End of London. Arthur Henderson, who was returned to Parliament in a bye-election, became the chairman of the party until his death in 1935. But increasingly the dominant personality in the labor movement was Ernest Bevin; his primacy among trade unions was assured by his position as head of the Transport and General Workers Union and by his role in organizing the general strike. True to his syndicalist past, he had resisted the temptation that came to so many trade-union officials to become a member of Parliament: Bevin's business was the Union. But the party was the Union's party, and in the thirties he became more and more disturbed at the direction it seemed likely to take. A powerful, shrewd, prejudiced, and dedicated pragmatist, Bevin came increasingly to distrust the party's intellectuals and their pacifism, particularly as he watched the rise of the dictators and the disastrous effect of totalitarianism on Continental trade unions. At the Labour party conference of 1935, the issue of collective security was clearly presented by the imminent Italian invasion of Ethiopia. Cripps, speaking for the Socialist League, rejected the League of Nations as an "International Burglars' Union"; he and his associates looked on any League of Nations action against Italy as a capitalist war in which England should have no part. Lansbury, the leader of the Parliamentary party, gave moving expression to his Christian pacifism. At this, Bevin came to the platform and attacked Lansbury brutally for embarrassing both the party executive and the labor movement by "taking your conscience round from body to body asking to be told what you ought to do with it." The conference, despite a show of affection for Lansbury, voted overwhelmingly for sanctions: Lansbury resigned the leadership, which then passed to Clement Attlee.

The Conservatives' troubles began in the late twenties, in dissatisfaction with Baldwin's uninspiring leadership. Having launched his protectionist balloon in 1923, Baldwin was in no hurry to do it again, but protectionist sentiment in his party far outstripped him. In particular he became the target of a concerted attack in the newspapers owned by Lord Beaverbrook and Lord Rothermere, who were willing to carry their eagerness for Empire Free Trade—as it was called—into the formation of a new party. Fortunately for Baldwin, they overreached themselves; he was able to turn their campaign against them and to strengthen his image as a plain-dealing man trying his best against the machinations of selfish, power-hungry men of wealth.

At almost the same time that Baldwin put the press lords to rout in 1931, another rebellion arose to his right, a rebellion with few followers, but formidable nonetheless because it was led by Winston Churchill. Churchill had come back to Conservatism, had gained high office as an immediate reward, but still had not burned all his bridges: he remained in close contact with Lloyd George, and his devotion to free trade had not wavered; thus there always remained the possibility of a deal between Churchill and the Liberals. But the split with Baldwin came over imperial matters. Here, Churchill defended his late nineteenth-century inheritance—his father, after all, had been the first to suggest using Ulster to defeat Home Rule, and he himself had served in India, Egypt, and South Africa as a soldier and war correspondent. Baldwin's policy of conciliating India and moving steadily towards the grant of responsible government was anathema to Churchill. Over this question, brought to a head in the two round-table conferences, Churchill resigned from the shadow cabinet; he was equally pessimistic about the increasing degree of independence in the Commonwealth (a word he disliked), not least because he saw it as opening the door to a virtual denunciation of the 1922 treaty with the Irish. So deep was this breach between Baldwin and Churchill that there was no possibility of Churchill's joining the national government, and the breach became worse as Churchill became the principal advocate for rearmament and facing down the dictators. Only disaster could bring him back; when he joined Chamberlain's cabinet in 1939, it was almost the making of a coalition.

Churchill, from a past generation of political leaders, was also what no one at the time could foresee, the leader of the next generation. But another brand of Conservative leadership was also emerging in the late twenties and thirties, with which Churchill was never entirely at home and that was to dominate his second premiership and the years after. It was born in a rebellion to Baldwin's left, going beyond Chamberlain's cautious administrative interventionism to a revived Tory democracy. Oliver Stanley (a son of the Earl of Derby), Robert Boothby, and Harold Macmillan, a member of the prominent family of publishers, were its principal spokesmen in the thirties, joined towards the end by R. A. Butler, from a distinguished Cambridge academic family and connected by marriage to one of the great textile fortunes in the country. Macmillan in particular, with his pleas for the abolition of poverty, for planning, and for the coordination of public and private enterprise, might as well have found a comfortable resting place in the Labour party.

The rethinking on the left and the isolated rebels on the right in the event had little effect on Baldwin's fortunes, however chancy they seemed in 1929–1931. Baldwin and Chamberlain were the dominant figures in the national government; and when MacDonald retired in 1935, Baldwin was his natural successor. In November, 1935, the Conservatives retained 432 seats in the general election; Labour sprang back to 154. The Liberals won 21 seats, including four members of Lloyd George's family.

The main domestic event of Baldwin's third ministry concerned the Crown. Just before MacDonald's retirement, King George V had celebrated his silver jubilee. King George and Queen Mary had performed an important and valuable function for the institution of monarchy: they had democratized and humanized it to a degree unknown before. They had been assiduous in public duties during the First World War; they had toured the working-class districts; and the King became a reality in a way that none of his predecessors could have been through his annual Christmas broadcasts, which began in 1932. George's serious illness in 1927 had shown how much popular devotion there was to the monarchy, and the steady public interest in the travels and the dashing life led by the Prince of Wales promised an equal enthusiasm for his successor.

George V died on January 20, 1936. By summer, there were many rumors about the friendship of the new king, Edward VIII, with Mrs. Wallis Simpson, an American divorcée then married to a London stockbroker. Newspapers in the United States were full of gossip about the pair; the English papers printed not a word of it, and only briefly reported Mrs. Simpson's second divorce in October. But the divorce set off a round of government activity. Baldwin had tried at first to get the divorce suit withdrawn, for the fact that Mrs. Simpson was twice divorced made her unacceptable to the government as queen, and, in all probability, to most of the country as well. The government wanted the King not to marry; the King insisted on marrying and was prepared to abdicate. The matter was discussed in the cabinet in November, but not until the first week in December did it become public knowledge. Then some support for the King's position began to emerge, its most prominent figure being Winston Churchill; but most of the politicians in the country backed the government, if not on moral grounds, then on constitutional grounds — the king must accept the advice of his ministers. Baldwin announced the abdication on December 10, and the act giving effect to it was passed the next day. Under the terms of the Statute of Westminster, the Dominions followed suit, except for Ireland, which quickly removed the king from its new constitution, although he continued to be recognized as a piece of machinery (without being named) that might be needed in diplomatic relations. Edward VIII went into exile, created Duke of Windsor by his brother, King George VI. The abdication was dramatic, but historically it was transitory. It temporarily strengthened Baldwin, whose performance had been masterful; it probably permanently strengthened the monarchy by keeping it out of politics, and by bringing to the throne a king whose role as a constitutional monarch was exemplary and whose family was able to satisfy so well the insatiable public appetite for news about royal goings-on.

The Shadow of War

The abdication crisis was a brief, intense, emotional diversion from the march of events leading, as it now seems, inexorably to war in Europe. The Locarno period had ended abruptly in 1929. Both symbolically and actually, the death of Gustav Stresemann in October, 1929, marks the turning point: it removed the one powerful German advocate of reconciliation; with Briand (who stayed in office almost until his death in 1932), he was the embodiment of the Locarno spirit. But no one man could have stemmed the tide for long, however great his tactical abilities or his good will. The depression that began in 1929 and reached its depth in 1932 undercut the European economy and destroyed the reparations settlements agreed upon in the Dawes Plan in 1924 and the still more generous Young Plan accepted in August, 1929. Economic collapse in Germany brought political instability in its train, despite resort to the emergency powers granted in the Weimar Constitution. French governments found themselves increasingly immobilized by groups of extremists on both the right and the left, who challenged the very basis of the Third Republic. Given Britain's involvement in an unparalleled economic and political crisis, the paralysis of the main European democracies was complete. The ghost of Locarno hovered on for a time in one or another disarmament conference, a kind of diplomatic parlor game played for moderate stakes and with little success throughout the twenties; the last of them was wrecked by Adolf Hitler in October, 1933.

To the successive challenges of the thirties the British response was "appeasement," a word that in the light of events, and particularly of the Munich Conference of 1938, has become almost exclusively a term of moral condemnation, implying lack of foresight, nerve, and honor. In its contemporary use, however, and increasingly in historians' eyes, it was a policy of strength, imagination, and optimism. The criticisms of Keynes and the work of diplomatic historians had convinced nearly everyone in the interwar years that the peace of 1919 was unjust; the guilt that had been formally ascribed to Germany was spread or even transferred to the western powers. Moreover, no one could lightly contemplate another visitation of the horrors of war, horrors that new technology assured would be worse than in 1914–1918. Wise policy accordingly sought accommodation, redress of grievances, and recognition of the claims of national interest. Even those who later gained a reputation for "standing up to dictators" were for most of their careers appeasers too.

The first sharp challenge to these assumptions came with the Japanese invasion of the Chinese province of Manchuria in September, 1931; within a year, the conquest had been completed and the puppet state of Manchukuo set up, a loss officially conceded by China in a treaty signed in May, 1933. British policy in the Manchurian crisis was consistent and inevitable. There was much sympathy for the Japanese case: the Chinese were unable to control Manchuria; and the Japanese, whose economic interests there had been endangered, at least brought stability and order, though scarcely by creditable means. Sir John Simon, a former Liberal who was Foreign Secretary in the national government, tried to steer a middle course. At the League of Nations, he took the lead in getting the Lytton Commission appointed to inquire into the situation; sanctions were not considered, however, and the United States, despite a brief brandishing of a new doctrine of "nonrecognition" of territorial changes brought about by force, remained in isolation. Later criticism of Simon because no stronger action was taken by the League does not make the course he chose any the less sensible, considering the context in which he had to act. What the crisis proved was not the ill will or timidity of the British government, but the essential weakness of the League of Nations. Its member states, especially those large and powerful states that naturally took the lead, were preoccupied with domestic troubles; what meaningful economic or military action could have been taken is hard to imagine. And when the Lytton Commission condemned Japan and the League supported the condemnation with a vote of censure, Japan showed her contempt for mere moral gestures by withdrawing from the League in February, 1933.

The next threat arose in Germany. Adolf Hitler's National Socialist party had made startling gains in elections in 1930 and 1932, thanks to widespread economic discontent and the appeal of his narrowly nationalist slogans and panaceas—the injustice of Versailles, the futility of parliamentary democracy, the need for leadership, and especially the iniquities of the Jews. Nazi strength fell in the elections in November, 1932, but President von Hindenburg made Hitler chancellor at the end of January, 1933. In March, relying on a complaisant Reichstag elected early that month, Hitler made himself dictator. Within six months, he took Germany out of the League, withdrew from the Disarmament Conference, and took to rearming in violation of the restrictions in the Versailles Treaty. The maltreatment of German Jews, the purge of Nazi officialdom in 1934, the abortive coup against Austria resulting in the murder of the Austrian dictator Dollfuss in the same year, were watched from across the Channel with incomprehension by most, with horror by a few. Still, Germany, like Japan in 1931, could claim a degree of British sympathy: given the unfairness of the Versailles Treaty, France seemed merely stubborn in resisting the national equality that justice demanded for Germany. Among a small number of Englishmen, it is true, there was genuine sympathy with authoritarianism. In some it came to little more than a fashion for things German and a liking for the lavish entertainments at the German embassy; in others it lent more than a color of truth to later accusations of a Conservative, pro-German cabal—like the "Cliveden set," so-called after Lord Astor's house, where some of these like-minded men and women gathered. However overdrawn these allegations may be, there is no escaping the fact that there was a surge of pro-Germanism. Some of Germany's defenders were, suggestively, intellectual descendants and apostles of the late-Victorian and Edwardian authoritarianism associated with Lord Milner: sympathy for Germany came close to real power in the person of J. L. Garvin, the biographer of Joseph Chamberlain and editor of the *Observer* and, even more, in Geoffrey Dawson, the editor of *The Times*. Far more important was the widespread appeal of pacifism. Much attention was paid abroad to a famous debate at the Oxford Union, the undergraduate debating society, early in 1933, on a motion, framed with fine student bravado, that "this House will in no circumstances fight for its King and Country"; the motion carried by a wide margin. No more than symbolic, perhaps, but it deserves at least that description.

A third test of appeasement came with the Italian invasion of Ethiopia in 1935, a campaign that grew out of a border incident in the ill-defined territory between Italian Eritrea and Ethiopia in December, 1934. Mussolini had prepared his ground well. Throughout the early thirties, he had played a reasonable and conciliatory game in European diplomacy: it reached its climax in a meeting of the Italians, British, and French at Stresa in April, 1935, with MacDonald and Simon representing Britain. The three powers would agree, they said, to no unilateral repudiation of treaties in Europe, a resounding but essentially meaningless declaration that derived its main value for Italy by cementing a cordial relationship established in January, 1935, with the new French foreign minister, Pierre Laval. Laval's predecessor, Louis Barthou, who had re-erected a diplomatic barrier around Germany, had been assassinated in October, 1934; Laval's policy was to isolate Germany by accommodating Italy: to him, maintaining the "Stresa front" was crucial. Ethiopia carried its case to the League of Nations in January and again in March, when the European powers were preoccupied with Germany's successive steps towards rearmament. The British government was eager, too, to preserve the Stresa front; in June they proposed a cession of some Ethiopian territory, to be compensated for by Britain's giving up part of British Somaliland to provide Ethiopia an outlet to the sea.

By this time, however, the British public had begun to shift their attitudes, or at any rate to be aware of the magnitude of the crises developing around them. In late 1934, a group of League supporters organized the "Peace Ballot," a survey conducted by volunteers going from house to house: the results, announced in June, 1935, were pacific and internationalist; they were far from insignificant because more than eleven million people had answered the questions. Disarmament, yes; League of Nations, yes; but what was most impressive was the vote of nearly seven million to something over two in favor of supporting the League with economic and military sanctions. Buttressed by this result, the British government took the lead in encouraging League action against Italy. The League condemned the Italian invasion and voted to apply sanctions involving finance, exports, and imports. The League had not before gone so far, but it was still no great distance, for the sanctions were limited, and the British government, rather more following Laval than leading, drew back when proposals were made to strengthen them. Italy let it be known that an embargo on oil would mean war, and the risk of war the British government refused to take.

Although the government was pledged to support the League, it also repeatedly carried on negotiations outside the League; the climax to these private peacemaking efforts came when Sir Samuel Hoare (who had succeeded Simon as Foreign Secretary in a cabinet reshuffle when Baldwin took over from MacDonald) met Laval in Paris in December and agreed that Ethiopia should cede a large portion of her territory to Italy, turn over a still larger part as a "zone of economic expansion and settlement," and gain in return a corridor to the sea. The plan was leaked to the press and precipitated a violent reaction in Britain: the public's newly resolute dedication to the League's purposes had been undercut by a deal. There was no possibility of any meaningful League action after that; in May, 1936, the Italian victory was proclaimed; sanctions were withdrawn in June. Baldwin managed to survive a vote of censure in the House, perhaps partly because the Labour party's motion impugned Baldwin's honor and brought him support in his own party he might have lost on the issue itself. Rather more the victim than the perpetrator, Baldwin was nonetheless severely hurt politically, even though he forced Hoare to resign and replaced him with Anthony Eden, a young man who had made an impressive reputation as minister with special responsibility for League affairs.

Ethiopia was far away and Europe close at hand: in 1935 and 1936 a French or British diplomat had to be primarily concerned about the now open rearmament of Germany. Britain herself began, tentatively, to rearm; France carried further Barthou's reconstruction of her middle-European alliances by supporting the admission of Russia to the League of Nations and concluding a treaty of mutual assistance in May, 1935. Hitler called the treaty a violation of Locarno, using it to justify his own breaking of both the Versailles and the Locarno treaties by occupying the Rhineland, demilitarized since 1919, on March 7, 1936. To occupy territory that was unquestionably German in defiance of what was thought to be a patently unjust treaty seemed fair enough to many people in Britain, or at any rate a violation of obligations that paled in comparison with the bullying assault by Italy on Ethiopia. The British had been unwilling to give the French the military guarantees they had asked for, and the French could not, under those circumstances, attack Germany as they would have been justified in doing under the terms of the Treaty of Versailles. Looking back, one can argue that this was the point at which concerted action might well have overthrown Hitler: his generals had expected war and had advised against the occupation. But Hitler won his gamble, immediately proclaimed (as he was to do so often) that he had no further territorial ambitions in Europe, and offered deals and nonaggression pacts in all directions, except to Russia. Britain had already dealt with Hitler in 1935 in concluding a new naval agreement, an agreement that itself condoned German violation of the Versailles Treaty. The talk went on, but no agreements were ever arrived at.

The year 1936 saw a definite stiffening in British public opinion, a willingness to believe that war must come eventually. The two political figures who were coming to take an uncompromising anti-German stand — Sir Robert Vansittart in the Foreign Office and Winston Churchill in the House of Commons, remained isolated, with only scattered support from maverick politicians. But the trade unions, with Bevin in the lead, had been increasingly convinced that Hitler would have to be fought; and at the Labour party conference of 1935, as we have seen, they carried a majority of political labor with them. The left-wing intellectuals, however, stood aside. Their conversion was brought about by the emotional earthquake of the civil war in Spain, which began in the summer of 1936 between the "loyalists" supporting the legitimate coalition government of the fledgling Spanish republic and the insurgent "nationalists" led by General Francisco Franco. The British held firmly to a policy of nonintervention, to which the Continental powers also adhered— France, because her new "popular front" government under Léon Blum was prevented by internal disorder from intervening for the republicans; Germany and Italy because nonintervention could serve to mask the dispatch of weapons and of divisions of "volunteers." But large segments of British opinion outside the ranks of the official government and opposition, especially British intellectuals, were galvanized by the Spanish civil war into a militancy and a political excitement that exacerbated political divisions at home, that made war seem tolerable when fought in a right cause, and that led many of them to volunteer for service with the loyalists and led some of those volunteers to death.

The Coming of War

Shortly after the coronation of King George VI, in May, 1937, the prime minister went to the House of Lords as Earl Baldwin and was succeeded by the man long destined for the post by his abilities and his position in the party: Neville Chamberlain. With the League as good as dead, with Germany, Italy, and Japan joined together in an "axis," with British rearmament barely begun, it was logical for the government to seek "appeasement" in Europe, a word that meant pacification through the settlement of issues by negotiation and compromise. Chamberlain attached to this very comprehensible diplomatic goal a personal hatred and fear of war, a loathing of Communism, a sincere belief in rational discussion, and a confidence in personal and secretive diplomacy that led him consistently to ignore the advice of the Foreign Office. He preferred to listen to Sir Horace Wilson, a civil servant who had made his reputation in bringing employers and employees together at the Ministry of Labor.

Chamberlain's efforts to create a reasonable and friendly environment in which Germany's legitimate grievances could be redressed and differences settled peaceably were seconded by Lord Halifax, the Lord Privy Seal, and the new ambassador at Berlin, Sir Nevile Henderson. In February, 1938, Anthony Eden resigned as foreign secretary, to be succeeded by Lord Halifax. The resignation, which was later construed as grounded in firmness against dictators, with important consequences for Eden's reputation and career, was in fact mystifying, based on little more than a growing personal estrangement from Chamberlain. Still, in losing the most popular member of his cabinet, Chamberlain could seem to have capitulated to Hitler's and Mussolini's open dislike of Eden. Within a few weeks of Eden's resignation, Hitler bludgeoned his way into Austria and incorporated it into the "Third Reich." His next target was Czechoslovakia. Hitler's pretext was the existence within Czechoslovakia of a large minority of persons of German descent; although they had been outside of Germany for hundreds of years, these Sudeten Germans, concentrated in the part of Bohemia bordering on Germany, had some nationalist aspirations and some long-standing grievances against the Czechs. Under orders from Berlin, the Sudeten demands were steadily escalated. As every concession offered by the Czech government was refused as insufficient, it became clear that the Czechs would reach the point where they could not give way and maintain their national existence.

The French were allied to the Czechs, but France would not move without support from Britain, and Britain was not yet materially or spiritually ready for war; the Dominions (in the spirit of Chanak) remained in isolation. Russia had declared her willingness to aid the Czechs if the French did, but she was ignored by both the French and the British. Chamberlain, refusing to believe that Germany really threatened this new, prosperous, and militarily strong republic, declared that Britain would never go to war to defend the boundaries of Czechoslovakia: surely they could be negotiated, as readily as he had said he would give up Tanganyika, if that was Hitler's price for peace. In mid-September, 1938, Chamberlain asked Hitler if he could come to see him.

Chamberlain and Hitler met first at Hitler's retreat at Berchtesgaden on September 15; the most that Hitler would concede was the determination of the fate of the Sudeten Germans by a plebiscite, the outcome of which would be certain. When Chamberlain laid this proposal before his cabinet in London the following day, he went further: he proposed the immediate cession to Germany of all districts where more than half the population were German. The plan, which would turn all the Czech defensive fortresses over to Germany along with the Germans, was agreed to by the French; it was forced on Czechoslovakia by a joint British-French refusal to fight if Czech resistance brought down a German war on them. But when Chamberlain and Hitler met again, at Godesberg on September 22, Hitler told Chamberlain that the timetable was too slow, that German occupation had to begin within a week, a date later extended to October 1. Chamberlain was appalled—Hitler seemed to look on appeasement as a one-way street—and he returned to an England that began within hours to prepare for war.

But Hitler thought that Chamberlain might still bring the Czechs to reason; Chamberlain snatched at the chance. On the 28th, after defending his policy in the House of Commons, he dramatically announced that Hitler had asked him to come the next day to Munich for a meeting also attended by Mussolini and Daladier, the French premier. Hitler's harshest terms at Godesberg were agreed to, and the Czechs were called in and told they must accept. In a later private talk, Hitler and Chamberlain signed a statement promising that in the future all questions between their countries would be dealt with by consultation and that they would never go to war again. It was this statement that Chamberlain waved aloft when he came out of his plane in England. Recalling Disraeli's triumphant return from the Berlin Congress in 1878, he said that a second time peace had been brought back from Germany: "I believe it is peace for our time."

With Munich, argues Martin Gilbert, the traditional policy of appeasement, based on concessions from a position of strength, gave way to an emergency plan to buy peace at an enormous cost. Some aura of morality still remained, and for a little while many Englishmen thought that Chamberlain was right and he could see himself as a hero. But the criticism that had been heard from the moment of his return grew, the more so as the Czech surrender turned out to be more abject than the Munich concessions had called for, without objection from London or Paris. One blow after another seemed to follow from Munich. An accommodation was reached with Italy that failed to detach Mussolini from the Axis. The Spanish civil war dragged to its end in a nationalist victory early in 1939. On March 15, 1939, Hitler took over the rest of Czechoslovakia. The shock of that news dragged Chamberlain (with Halifax's help) into a petulant denunciation of Hitler for not having kept his word. A week later, Germany made severe demands on Poland, and on March 31, Chamberlain committed Britain to the defense of Poland's frontiers—a pledge to a country both weaker and farther away than Czechoslovakia, while Britain's military preparedness was not much greater than it had been six months before. Reluctantly and slowly, the British edged into talks with the Russians. But so did the Germans; and at the end of August, the Russians signed a treaty with Germany pledging the two powers to nonaggression against each other for ten years and carving up (prospectively) Eastern Europe. By that time, Britain was moving rapidly forward in war preparations, and some last-minute efforts at compromise (at Poland's expense) fell through. Germany invaded Poland on September 1. Two days later Britain and France declared war on Germany. ". . . Everything that I have worked for," Chamberlain told the House, "everything that I have hoped for, everything that I have believed in during my public life, has crashed in ruins." His tidy administrative genius, so precise and so successful in the ordinary day-to-day business of government, had broken on the issue of larger British interests and on fundamental questions of right and wrong.

Nor was he adequate for war. For seven months there was only a "phony war" — some losses at sea, but no bombings, no attack on the Western powers, although Poland (with Russia's help) was conquered by the Germans in three weeks. At home the early panic, generated by the coming of the war and by the hurried evacuation of mothers and children from cities, disappeared. But Britain quickly moved to a wartime regimen: high taxes, extended conscription, rationing, and blackouts. Chamberlain had reconstructed his government, bringing back Eden and sending Churchill to his old post as First Lord of the Admiralty, where he gave fullest support to the man he had so severely attacked for so long. Rapid strides were made in building up the armed forces, enough so that Chamberlain could exult early in April that Hitler, in holding off, had "missed the bus." Then on April 9, Germany invaded Denmark and Norway; to this the British responded by landing three forces in Norway that had to be evacuated within two months. This stunning reverse reinforced the general dissatisfaction with the lacklustre way in which the war was being run. In a violent debate on May 7 and 8, it became clear that Chamberlain had lost the support of the House; no one attacked him more brutally than backbenchers in his own party. One of them, L. S. Amery, fell back on the bitter words that Oliver Cromwell had used in driving out the Rump Parliament in 1653: "Depart, I say, and let us have done with you. In the name of God, go!" Chamberlain defeated Attlee's censure motion by a mere 281 to 200; 40 members of his own party voted against him and more than twice that many abstained.

Halifax was Chamberlain's choice as a successor, when it became clear that he could not persuade Labour to enter a coalition; Halifax at once refused. The King then sent for Churchill, who accepted the commission to form a government on May 10. Attlee and Greenwood of the Labour party agreed at once to cooperate and the party supported their decision on May 13. By that time the German armies were advancing rapidly through Holland and Belgium and were about to break through into France. Churchill told the House and the country that he could offer them nothing but "blood, toil, tears, and sweat" before they attained the ultimate victory.

THE LEGACY, 1918–1940

The Economy

One terrible statistic hangs over the interwar years: the United Kingdom lost three-quarters of a million men in the First World War; twice that many were wounded or gassed. British deaths in combat were only about half the number of those suffered by the French; talk about a lost generation had somewhat more meaning, statistically, across the Channel than for Britain. But no statistic can express the sense of loss that touched nearly every family in the land, nor measure memories constantly prodded by long lists of names on rolls of honor in churches, in colleges, and on village greens.

Quite apart from the First World War, the pattern of English population was changing. In no decade in the nineteenth century did the increase in population fall below 11 per cent; in the first decade of the twentieth century, it was still at 10.3 per cent. But in the next two decades the increase dropped, respectively, to 4.6 per cent and 4.7 per cent. The fall is in some ways even more remarkable than it seems, for those same decades saw a virtual cessation of the emigration that had gone on heavily in the nineteenth century, and the reduction in infant mortality that had set in after 1900 continued. The birth rate managed just to keep ahead of the death rate, and, as better housing, public health, and medicine kept people alive longer, the average age of the population rose. The main cause for the falling-off in population increase was, no doubt, deliberate restriction of births. Begun in the late nineteenth century among upper and upper-middle classes, birth control became general in the twentieth century, although contraception was by no means common practice in all classes until the Second World War.

Probably at no time before in English history had the quality of life changed so rapidly, and generally so much for the better, as in the decades between the wars. We have already seen that, in spite of the grim persistence of unemployment, the general standard of living, as economists measure it, went up. Even more striking was the impact of new departures in industry. During the Industrial Revolution, the lives of many people were drastically changed, often for the worse, at least immediately. But much of England, even of industrial England, remained relatively untouched and went its traditional and isolated ways for years. In the last half of the nineteenth century, there was a general filtering down of prosperity, through a gradual and somewhat erratic improvement in real wages rather than through fundamental changes in the ways men lived, dressed, and amused themselves. There were signs of the coming revolution, however, notably in the new department stores and multiple shops and in the expansion of the popular press.

The old staple industries on which Britain's nineteenth-century prosperity was built had provided cheap, durable, and not particularly subtle satisfactions for the needs of ordinary consumers, but in most of those industries the export market counted for much more than the home market. In the twentieth century, these priorities were reversed Britain's exports to an industrial world shifted from their old dependence on cheap cotton cloth, hardware, coal, and simple machinery to luxury goods (fine textiles, for example, or Scotch whisky) and to heavy complex machinery produced by Britain's engineering industry, the segment of manufacturing that grew most rapidly in the interwar years. The whole of industry was, moreover, undergoing a vital change in the source of power; steam was giving way to the internal combustion engine and, above all, to electricity. Except in Scotland and parts of the north of England, where hydroelectric resources existed, British electricity continued to be produced from coal, but using coal in this way was more efficient (and it became steadily more so), cleaner, and more healthful than the thousands of chimneys that made English towns their characteristic black.

One segment of the engineering industry had an impact on English life between the wars that, so far as individuals were concerned, was more revolutionary than the impact of the railway. Before the First World War, and for a time after it, the automobile was a luxury available only to the rich; but in the late twenties and thirties it spread much more widely, though by no means universally as in the United States. By the thirties very cheap (and not very powerful) cars were within reach of more prosperous workingmen. English roads did not keep pace—they still have not kept pace—and traffic jams in towns became a part of everyday life. But congestion, noise, and stench were a small enough price for the liberation the automobile made possible. Far more than the railway, the automobile and the network of country bus lines that developed rapidly after the First World War ended the isolation of the countryside; and the development of trucking gave a new flexibility to the distribution of goods. Long-distance busses (or coaches, as they are called in England) cut sharply into the railways' passenger revenue; and the coach tour became a common way to take a holiday.*

An inevitable corollary of the breakdown of isolation was the appearance of greater cultural uniformity. The full effects of that late-Victorian invention, the popular press, now became apparent. With a few notable exceptions, the provincial newspapers were steadily losing ground to the national, i.e., the London, press—most of all to papers like Lord Rothermere's *Daily Mail* and *Daily Mirror* and Lord Beaverbrook's *Daily Express*. Going to the cinema became a national pastime, still more so following the introduction of talking pictures in 1927; in the late twenties and the thirties, large motion-picture

*On the troubling aspects of the economy, see above, pp. 522–524, 528, 531–533.

theaters mushroomed throughout the country. The British film industry remained small and generally undistinguished until after the Second World War; Alfred Hitchcock was its one contribution to the art of the film. Instead, Britain relied on Hollywood, and the reliance gave at least occasion if not justification for the belief that the country was being "Americanized."

The radio, however, provided the most constant and pervasive common denominator of this new national culture. Under its authoritarian and righteous director-general, Sir John (later Lord) Reith, the BBC took on a cultural mission of rigorous respectability, doing well what had been done ineptly in another medium by the early-Victorian purveyors of "useful and entertaining knowledge." The BBC's predictable and often solemn obeisance to religion, patriotism, and established values has been much criticized; but it is likely that most listeners used their radios for mere entertainment or to fill a void and came away without being much indoctrinated. The critics are, no doubt, on firmer ground in regretting the somewhat official character of the news reports. But the alternative mode of organizing broadcasting—the sponsored programs and licensed anarchy of the United States, which British authorities were determined to avoid—has not proved to be more critical or creative than the BBC. The most important contribution of radio was its part in nationalizing culture, in creating a set of common lore, shared experiences, and famous personalities that before the First World War could have been found only in professional sports. Broadcasting, and to a lesser extent films, also began to soften distinctions in regional accents.

Catering to mass culture involved whole industries, not merely in producing the entertainments, but in manufacturing and distributing the means to enjoy them. The electrical industry was one such industry; it also contributed to the growing market for durable consumers' goods, particularly those that helped to save labor: irons, vacuum cleaners, and (for a small minority) washing machines and refrigerators. The sale of these goods, already an index of spreading prosperity, was further increased, at a risk, by the rapid increase of buying on the installment plan—called "hire purchase"—in the 1930's. Alongside expanding manufacturing and distributive industries grew the service industries, which, in terms of numbers employed, made clear gains in the interwar years, while most other industries either declined (notably agriculture, mining, and transport) or remained roughly stationary. The one service industry that declined precipitously was domestic service, a fact that reflects a sort of emancipation through greater choice on the part of the employed and that helps to explain a sense of decline felt (usually unjustly) by some of the middle and upper classes, for the first time facing a "servant problem." The texture of the economy after the First World War was infinitely richer, its range greater. A young man or woman starting out on a career in the twenties had much more to choose from, although class, education, and training were bound to limit free choice for many.

The Decline of Politics

The multiplication of alternative claims on men's time and attention, and the widening of opportunities, were two of the most important cultural themes of the interwar years, developments that had marked effects on time-honored priorities. Seen against this background, the shrinking role of politics, ironically coinciding with the attainment of full political democracy, becomes more comprehensible.

Throughout the nineteenth century, Great Britain was an intensely political country, and Westminster was in a very real sense the center of the nation's life. The gentry and aristocracy, traditionally the country's rulers, naturally gravitated there, at least in those portions of the year when their attention was not focused on their estates. For men of wealth, to become an M.P. (and perhaps at length a peer) was to set the final seal on a rise to respectability and power. For the unenfranchised, control of Parliament (and through it of government) seemed the principal way to gain their passionately held but ill-defined ends. General elections were great events: they had the excitement of color and conflict before reforms made them dull, and they were crucial in deciding the next moves in what amounted to a national sport. Even the cheap press paid what to most people today would seem inordinate attention to parliamentary debates and political gossip. The democratic electorate after 1918 did not win the vote only to ignore it: the percentage of eligible voters who turn out in a British election has remained very high. But after the First World War, politics became for most people a matter of traditional loyalties occasionally asserted, not a continuing preoccupation. Moreover, the game attracted fewer players, or players of inferior talent.

Like most interwar developments, this decline of interest had set in before the First World War, when the parliamentary process was called into question even by some of its active practitioners. The war carried things further. At least some young men who might have reinforced and enlivened political life were killed. It became a commonplace that politicians had made the war, and the notion that politics was a shabby or dirty business—never a Victorian attitude, even when corruption was in evidence—kept coming to the surface. The dreary succession of makeshifts and failures that formed the visible portion of interwar politics did nothing to lessen the revulsion. When depression and foreign affairs in the early thirties found the political parties bankrupt and immobilized by divisions, many men turned away from parliamentary politics with contempt and sought their answers in revolutionary theory and authoritarian practice.

In the nineteenth century, Parliament attracted young men not only because it was the natural summit of ambition, but because a man with a cause at heart might hope to accomplish something by being there. The gradual strengthening of party control from the 1880's, and the increasing dominance of the cabinet and especially of the prime minister, reduced the ordinary member to something like a rubber stamp. Real accomplishment was increasingly reserved to the man with the ability, drive, and luck to attain ministerial office. This is not to say that seats in Parliament lacked candidates or that any segment of government—national or local—failed to attract men eager for office; indeed considerable sacrifices were still made for political careers, for members of Parliament, though paid, were paid poorly, while much local government continued to be done by men without salary at all. But government and politics had become a less obvious goal, one among a number of competing possibilities; and for some men of ability it had become unthinkable.

The decline of politics and Parliament has usually been deplored. It is possible to argue, however, that the phenomenon was at least a mixture of good and bad. Some of the flight from politics must certainly have been due to the fact that the main business of government had become dull and routine. A highly able corps of civil servants (both nationally and locally) dealt with day-to-day matters according to a regular and largely unquestioned routine; the public might grumble about bureaucracy but had by and large become inured to it. On larger issues, too, the civil service often made the crucial decisions and so restricted the choices even of ministers. As some concerned observers saw it, this rule by professionals and the discipline imposed on Parliament threatened to bring about "the new despotism," to borrow the title of a book published in 1929 by the Lord Chief Justice, Lord Hewart: he was especially worried—and he buttressed his case with much legal learning and a fine devotion to nineteenth-century Whig history—by the increasing resort to delegated legislation and the growing number of inquiries and decisions made by administrative tribunals, outside the "rule of law" traditionally enforced by the courts. It was a lament of Victorian anti-centralizers updated: the concern has not disappeared today, nor is it without justification. But whatever abuses rose from the expansion of professional administration, the civil service was a device for the continuing solution of problems that a hundred years ago were inevitably political issues, to be dealt with at the level of legislation.

Then there was a "condition-of-England question": for all the poverty that remained in the thirties and that to some extent remains today, and for all the shortcomings or injustices men felt, and feel, in English society, that question, at least, has been answered. The flight from politics may have meant that issues able to arouse men to political action no longer existed in sufficient intensity, and for that one may be at least partly grateful. There is, however, another, less gratifying, aspect of the decline of politics. England's main problems after 1918 were pressing and difficult. But some of them were largely incomprehensible to ordinary citizens: they could be told about the balance of payments, productivity, and the weakness of sterling, but they could not be moved by them. About the things they could feel— war or peace abroad, equality at home—the initiative too often rested with other countries, or was weakened by apathy or disunion in a largely satisfied people at home. Politics had some air of futility about it.

The New Freedom

The range of possibilities in life was vastly extended by a new sense of freedom running through much of English society. It found its most obvious and perhaps even typical expression in manners. Dress became much more informal: the "lounge suit" for men went out-of-doors and to business; for women, the short skirt and the boyish look of the twenties were radical assertions of equality. Jazz, the cocktail, a new slang vocabulary, a frenzied pursuit of pleasure were nails in the Victorian coffin. The new degree of independence of women was typified in the "flapper," and the popularization of Freudian psychology underlay an easier pleasure in (or franker conversation about) sex and marriage. Divorce figures rose, and, in 1937, a private member of Parliament, in a rare triumph, carried a major bill liberalizing the grounds for divorce: the member was A. P. Herbert, independent M.P. for Oxford University, by profession a humorous writer. Homosexuality, which, except for an occasional lurid revelation, had remained all but unmentioned in the nineteenth century, escaped from concealment and ignorance but not from the threat of prejudice or legal penalties. There were bitter opponents of these sometimes frantic revolutions in taste and morals, chief among them Sir William Joynson-Hicks ("Jix"), Baldwin's Home Secretary, who moved between hounding Communists and a moral crusade and ended by leading a successful effort to prevent the Church of England from revising its Prayer Book. In the 1930's, in spite of Jix and his allies, the quest for freedom settled down into the less flamboyant forms of an accepted and permanent revolution.

Characteristically, the Victorians had sought an all-embracing explanation to satisfy the need for order and security in a world changing more rapidly than it had ever done before. Their chief recourse had been an intense and pervasive religion, or one of its many surrogates — positivism, humanitarianism, social service, even a dogmatic science. The modern world had learned to remain content with partial views and unanswered questions, and religion, already in retreat before the First World War, proved less and less able to satisfy the need to which it was once so well adapted. Until very recently, the Roman Catholic Church was an exception, its growth and prosperity perhaps related to its clear and authoritarian creeds. But the churches that had tried more completely to adapt to the forms and substance of modern thought did not fare so well. The Free Churches, the descendants of the Dissenters, suffered something not far from eclipse, at least in comparison with their great days in Victoria's reign. The Church of England, embedded in the fabric of national life, could not be overlooked, but it played at best a modest part and displayed a degree of confusion about its role.

The Church between the wars contained some able men, the most notable being William Temple, Archbishop of York after 1929 and, for a brief time during the Second World War, Archbishop of Canterbury. But at every level — national, diocesan, and parish — the Church had to expend much energy on its own institutional life. It had to raise money for charity and for the upkeep of its ancient buildings, but Church charities were as nothing to the state's social services, and cathedrals, restored at vast expense, were rather more museums than living symbols of a Christian people. In public matters, the Church no longer spoke with the force or authority natural to it in the nineteenth century. Its intellectual leaders were scholars and philosophers who wrote for their fellow professionals; occasionally descending into the popular arena with books to make abstruse matters plain. The bishops were less the stirring voice of the Church than a panel of experts on matters of conscience, giving (asked or unasked) opinions and advice in the House of Lords, in testimony before royal commissions, in public statements, or in books. The Church ministered well to a relatively small number of devout believers and to a larger number of communicants there out of a sense of civic obligation. But in most areas of public life, where by tradition the Church was central, its effectiveness, when it was not reduced to mere formality, was more critical than creative. The Church did not lack a certain residual affection, even among the indifferent, but, at best, it was usefully tangential.

Much of what had to be done in the modern world was boring and seemingly meaningless. It could hardly be justified any longer by the notion, more than a preachment in Victorian times, that men labored in the station to which God had called them. At least modern society offered means of escape—into mindless pursuits, into the vast apparatus of pleasure, into the seriousness of adult education which, under the auspices of the Workers' Educational Association, was spreading rapidly and rewardingly between the wars. The luckiest people were those who did not have to work at boring jobs, who could find satisfaction and creative enterprise in business or the professions. But business and the professions, taking them in their broadest possible definition, demanded education and training as the price of admission to their rewards; and in education England lagged most seriously behind her needs and her deserts.

English education remained sharply compartmentalized. Children of the well-to-do, or of middle-class parents who could scrape the money together, got their secondary education in the so-called "public schools," widely founded since the mid-nineteenth century (with varying results in quality) in imitation of the old foundations.* The vast majority of children whose parents could not afford or would not have thought of this kind of education were catered to by the state schools. Lloyd George's minister of education, the Oxford historian H. A. L. Fisher, had tried to raise the school-leaving age in the state schools from 14 to 15, but his plan fell to the Geddes axe in 1921; the Labour party was unable to redeem its pledge to take the step either in 1924 or 1929, and it was not done until 1947. But a first step was taken towards providing secondary education for all in the implementation of a report, made in 1926 but initiated by the first Labour government, calling for a separation of primary from secondary education at the age of eleven. During the thirties, the education authorities tried to work out some kind of general secondary education for children between eleven and fourteen.

Entrance to the universities continued to be easiest from the public schools. But the number of state-aided grammar schools—fee-paying, private foundations that gave secondary education to the age of eighteen—increased, and more free places were added; by the mid-thirties perhaps a third of university entrants came from the state-aided schools, though the proportion was smaller at Oxford and Cambridge. But the universities took in only a tiny proportion of the population as a whole, around thirty thousand students in the mid-twenties, with another ten thousand in Scotland. Although London was the largest university, Oxford and Cambridge retained their dominant positions. A few new university colleges were founded, adding to the nineteenth-century "red-brick" creations, but there

*The upper classes normally sent their sons away at the age of seven to "preparatory schools."

was no large-scale expansion. What was prophetic was the extension of government aid. In 1911, the University Grants Committee had been set up (and composed of academics) to channel government funds to the newer and poorer universities; in 1920, Oxford and Cambridge were added. And so, at least in prospect, the financial means for expansion were there. But, even allowing for the more limited English definition of a university—technical training (engineering, for example) has not normally been their business—higher education was reserved to a small proportion of the population. It was a privilege incompatible with the claims of democracy or the needs of a modern industrial society, but a privilege that between the wars was (to judge from memoirs and novels) never more attractive to those fortunate enough to gain it.

The Arts

The interwar theme of extended choice applies with force in the arts, nowhere more notably than in music. The gramophone and the radio made music available as it had never been before, and at a higher level of performance, even though at second hand. The popularity of jazz extended appreciation of musical virtuosity and imagination to many who might, even with its new diffusion, have found little appreciation for classical music. Symphony orchestras in England have always led a precarious existence. The Hallé Orchestra of Manchester was firmly established, and the BBC made a vital contribution to music in 1930 by founding the BBC Symphony Orchestra. Three years earlier the BBC had taken over sponsorship of the summer Promenade Concerts, begun in 1895 by Sir Henry Wood, concerts that were a potent and inexpensive means for music lovers to extend their knowledge and that also provided a hearing for young British composers. Unquestionably the most dynamic force in English music between the wars was Sir Thomas Beecham, the heir to a patent medicine fortune, a brilliant conductor, and a magnetic and often irascible personality. Famous before the war, he was conductor of the Hallé Orchestra for a number of years and then, after a period of retirement, founded the London Philharmonic Orchestra in 1932. No one did more to determine the patterns of present-day English musical taste.

English composers remained largely untouched by the Continental revolutions associated with Stravinsky and Schönberg. In *Façade* (1926), William Walton provided a perfect score for the reading of Edith Sitwell's nonsense verses, a musical epitome of the twenties, and his more serious works gained considerable respect: he was the best known of the younger composers until the very youthful

Benjamin Britten appeared in the 1930's. But Vaughan Williams was the only composer of the period to gain international stature.

Ballet was a virtually new art form in England, although the Diaghilev company had made some appearances in London before the First World War. It is remarkable that a country, normally derivative in its nonliterary arts, should have taken so well and so quickly to the dance, providing it with growing audiences and two important companies: the Vic-Wells Ballet (so named from two theaters) headed by Ninette de Valois, later to become world-famous as the Sadler's Wells Ballet and still later as the Royal Ballet; and the smaller Ballet Rambert, headed by Marie Rambert, which served as a remarkably productive training ground for dancers and choreographers, among them Frederick Ashton and Anthony Tudor.

British architecture between the wars hardly deserves notice. The appreciation of painting was widened by the growing interests of galleries in modern artists, notably the Tate Gallery in London, and by the development of reproduction processes which made prints of good works of art available at small cost. But British painters did not attract much notice outside of England, except for the abstract painter Ben Nicholson and, at the end of the thirties, Graham Sutherland, whose reputation was largely made after the Second World War. In sculpture, the best-known figure between the wars was the American-born Jacob Epstein, a basically conservative artist whose stylization and receptivity to primitive influences made him the archetype of "modernism" to ignorant and outraged men who knew what they liked but certainly knew nothing about art; controversy boiled about Epstein throughout the period. But by the thirties, a true modernist had emerged in Henry Moore, the most powerful and influential British artist in this century.

The theater, in most of its forms, fell victim to radio and the films; a few provincial repertory companies managed to stay alive; the music hall was in a bad way. Shakespeare continued to be played at the Shakespeare Festival at Stratford-on-Avon, where the new theater, opened in 1932, passed for modern architecture, and at the Old Vic in London, a former music hall that had been made into a remarkable cultural force by Lilian Baylis. But the great prewar playwrights had little to contribute, Shaw's *St. Joan* (1924) being the one major work. The theater remained content, for the most part, with drawing-room comedies and dramas that broke no new ground at all in either substance or dramatic technique. The film actor, composer, and playwright Ivor Novello packed in audiences in the thirties for a succession of musical romances that must be taken (sadly) as archetypes of the commercial theater between the wars, more so than the plays and reviews of Noel Coward, whose collaboration with the comedienne Beatrice Lillie was a triumph of deftly cutting yet affectionate satire.

Theater aside, the range of artistic choice grew wider, and correspondingly, the audience for literature became smaller. To some extent, writers themselves helped to make it smaller. Poetry between the wars was dominated by the figure of T. S. Eliot, an American expatriate whose spare, allusive poems caught the sense of disillusion and frustration characteristic of so many intellectuals; in *The Waste Land* (1923), one of the most important poems in the language, he offered a devastating comment on modern society that was learned, allusive, fragmentary, difficult, and all but incomprehensible to most readers.* Two novelists undertook similar technical experiments. One was Virginia Woolf, the daughter of Leslie Stephen, who tied the stream-of-consciousness technique to her exquisite sensibility; she won few sales but a distinguished reputation and justified her dominant position in the coterie known as the Bloomsbury Group, which had so far-reaching an influence on British aesthetic history. The other experimentalist, a writer of international stature, was James Joyce, an Irish expatriate whose *Ulysses* (1917) was a *tour de force* of scholarship, imagination, and verbal felicity, although its erotic aspects assured that its first reputation would be as a scandalous book. Joyce went further in the thirties in a daring but unsuccessful effort to break the bounds of language itself. *Finnegans Wake* (1939) was an example no one followed.

Of the more traditional novelists, E. M. Forster wrote his masterpiece, *A Passage to India*, in 1924 and fell silent, except for occasional essays; D. H. Lawrence wrote nothing to compare to his prewar novels, although *Lady Chatterley's Lover* (1928), another *succès de scandale*, has an important place in the history of British tolerance of sex, a place confirmed in 1960 by an opinion of the House of Lords that the book is not obscene and can be openly published in Britain after more than thirty years of clandestine circulation. The characteristic new writers of the twenties and thirties were no such giants as these: the satirists, Aldous Huxley and Evelyn Waugh, and the neo-Dickensian celebrant of the common people, J. B. Priestley. Huxley eventually became an expatriate and gave up novel-writing; Waugh, like his nonsatirical contemporary Graham Greene, became a convert to Catholicism, perhaps as a refuge from the nihilism implicit in his savage and hilarious dissection of the bright young things. They

---

*Eliot also had a profound effect on English criticism. In part, it was channeled through F. R. Leavis, a Cambridge don who was the *enfant terrible* of criticism, both literary and social. But, socially, Leavis was a radical, Eliot a high conservative. Leavis's influential periodical *Scrutiny* was published from 1932 to 1953.

were successful writers, as the literary world counts success, Priestley more popular than any of them. But the greatest popular success was reserved for the writers of thrillers (John Buchan being the most famous) and detective stories, a relatively new literary genre whose finest and most durable practitioner was Agatha Christie. And every year there was at least one new story from P. G. Wodehouse, who chronicled in prose of exquisite workmanship the exploits of Jeeves, the butler, Bertie Wooster, the rich young-man-about-town, and other denizens of an upper-class world that never was.

Science and Scholarship

The arts in the twenties at best held their own, breaking little new ground and generally inferior to what was being done on the Continent or in the United States. But in the realm of science and scholarship, British leadership was reasserted in ways that were to affect the world for years to come. Penicillin, radar, and television were three British discoveries or inventions, made at the level where pure science and technology meet; they revolutionized the world during and after the war that began in 1939. The pioneer work of Lord Rutherford in atomic physics, though less spectacular theoretically than the work, say, of Einstein, also helped to determine the shape of the world to come. English mathematicians and physicists made signal contributions to our understanding of the universe. We have already referred repeatedly to the work of J. M. Keynes, which redirected the study of economics everywhere outside the Communist world. At Cambridge, Ludwig Wittgenstein launched the systematic study of the philosophical implications of language, a concern that, particularly at Oxford, grew into linguistic analysis, a major school of modern philosophy. In historiography, the received interpretations of nineteenth-century political historians and early twentieth-century social historians were subjected to careful re-examination. L. B. Namier, at Manchester, completely recast the techniques of political history by his close analysis of the structure of politics at the accession of George III. J. H. Clapham inaugurated a similar train of investigation in economic history by his encyclopedic inquiry into the complexities of the nineteenth-century economy that defied the easy dogmatism of his predecessors; increasingly careful statistical studies, more and more informed by advanced economic theory, made economic history into a specialty of its own.

These impressive contributions — reinforced by the influx of German refugee intellectuals in the thirties — grew out of two long-range developments, the professionalization of the scholarly disciplines and the growth of the universities as centers of scholarship as well as teaching. The two processes, and many of their results, would have seemed intolerable to most Victorians. They found it hard enough to accept the truth that science was not primarily a way of proving God's wisdom and beneficence. They would have balked completely at the suggestion that philosophers or historians should (like scientists) ask simply how language or institutions work and not what lessons we can learn to make our lives or our society better.

Selected Readings

In the *Oxford History of England* there is A. J. P. Taylor's compelling and opinionated *English History, 1914–1945* (1965); and W. N. Medlicott has published an authoritative survey in *Contemporary Britain, 1914–1964*, with an epilogue to 1974 (1976). C. L. Mowat, *Britain between the Wars, 1918–1940* (1955), though now a quarter-century old, remains the best account of the interwar period.

Postwar plans are studied in great detail in Paul Barton Johnson, *Land Fit for Heroes: The Planning of British Reconstruction, 1916–1919* (1968). Mention should be made as well of the articles in which Elie Halévy, that great historian of the English liberal tradition, chronicled his progressive disillusion; they are reprinted in his *Era of Tyrannies: Essays on Socialism and War* (1938, trans. 1965). Another aspect of planning for the postwar world is traced in Henry R. Winkler, *The League of Nations Movement in Great Britain, 1914–1919* (1952). On Ireland, the background of the settlement is laid out in George Dangerfield, *The Damnable Question: A Study in Anglo-Irish Relations* (1977), covering the period from 1906 to 1921. Two further contributions to the context are Thomas E. Hachey, *Britain and Irish Separatism: From the Fenians to the Free State, 1867–1922* (1977) and Leon ó Broin, *Revolutionary Underground: The Story of the Irish Republican Brotherhood, 1858–1924* (1976). Ó Broin has also written *Dublin Castle and the 1916 Rising* (1966), and for the chief actor, B. L. Reid, *The Lives of Roger Casement* (1976). On India, G. K. Das, *E. M. Forster's India* (1977), emphasizes the turning point of the Amritsar Massacre; the novel that Forster wrote was, of course, *A Passage to India* (1924). There was scarcely an aspect of imperial and foreign policy in these years in which Jan Christiaan Smuts did not figure; his official biography is by W. K. Hancock, *Smuts:* I: *The Sanguine Years, 1870–1919* (1962)); II: *The Fields of Force, 1919–1950* (1968).

Postwar political upheaval has provoked debate chiefly about the near-demise of the Liberal party. On that subject and Liberal fortunes in the twenties, Trevor Wilson, *The Downfall of the Liberal Party, 1914–1935* (1966); Kenneth O. Morgan's interpretative essay, *The Age of Lloyd George: The Liberal Party and British Politics, 1890–1929* (1971), takes a different view, and Morgan also offers a revisionist interpretation of the much-maligned Parliament of 1918 in "Lloyd George's Stage Army: The Coalition Liberals, 1918–22," in A. J. P. Taylor, ed., *Lloyd George: Twelve Essays* (1971). The end of the coalition is the subject of Michael Kinnear, *The Fall of Lloyd George: The Polit-*

ical Crisis of 1922 (1973). See also Michael Bentley, *The Liberal Mind, 1914–1929* (1977) for an ambitious and suggestive but flawed interpretation of the Liberal decline. On the Conservatives, John Ramsden, *The Age of Balfour and Baldwin, 1902–40* (1978), is essential. R. K. Middlemas and A. J. L. Barnes, *Baldwin, a Biography* (1970), is more effective than either of the recent attempts at biographies of Neville Chamberlain, one by Keith Feiling (1946), the other by the prominent Conservative politician Iain Macleod (1961).

On the rise of the Labour party to the status of official opposition and then to power of a sort, Ross McKibbin, *The Evolution of the Labour Party, 1910–1924* (1974); J. M. Winter, *Socialism and the Challenge of War: Ideas and Politics in Britain 1912–18* (1974); Maurice Cowling, *The Impact of Labour, 1920–1924: The Beginning of Modern British History* (1971); Stephen R. Graubard, *British Labour and the Russian Revolution, 1917–1924* (1956); Richard W. Lyman, *The First Labour Government, 1924* (1957); and two major biographical studies, the first two volumes of Alan Bullock, *The Life and Times of Ernest Bevin* (1960, 1967), and David Marquand, *Ramsay MacDonald* (1976).

Ranging through the interwar years is Bentley B. Gilbert's authoritative *British Social Policy, 1914–1939* (1970). Robert Skidelsky's *Politicians and the Slump: The Labour Government of 1929–1931* (1967) led naturally to his disturbing biography, *Oswald Mosley* (1975). For a biography of Mosley's onetime associate and leftist theorist, Hugh Thomas, *John Strachey* (1973), to which should be added Neal Wood, *Communism and British Intellectuals* (1959). For a stimulating discussion of the context in which the Ottawa Agreements should be seen, Ian M. Drummond, *Imperial Economic Policy, 1917–1939: Studies in Expansion and Protection* (1974). On the emergence of the Commonwealth in these decades, R. M. Dawson, *The Development of Dominion Status* (1937). On the monarchy, Harold Nicolson, *King George the Fifth, His Life and Reign* (1953); Frances Donaldson, *Edward VIII, a Biography of the Duke of Windsor* (1976); and Brian Inglis, *Abdication* (1966).

Foreign affairs are an increasing preoccupation. For an overview, F. S. Northedge, *The Troubled Giant: Britain among the Great Powers, 1916–1939* (1966). Troubles start in the Far East, on which see Wm. Roger Louis, *British Strategy in the Far East, 1919–1939* (1971); Ian H. Nish, *Alliance in Decline: A Study of Anglo-Japanese Relations, 1908–23* (1972); and Christopher Thorne, *The Limits of Foreign Policy: The West, the League, and the Far Eastern Crisis of 1931–1933* (1972). On European troubles, A. J. Sherman, *Island Refuge: Britain and Refugees from the Third Reich, 1933–1939* (1973); K. W. Watkins, *Britain Divided: The Effects of the Spanish Civil War on British Political Opinion* (1963); and Peter Stansky and William Abrahams, *Journey to the Frontier* (1966), a study of two young martyrs to the Spanish cause from England's intellectual aristocracy. On the domestic political effects of foreign affairs, Maurice Cowling, *The Impact of Hitler: British Politics and British Policy, 1933–1940* (1975) and Robert Paul Shay, Jr., *British Rearmament in the Thirties: Politics and Profits* (1977). On appeasement, Martin Gilbert, *The Roots of Appeasement* (1966); Neville Thompson, *The Anti-Appeasers: Conservative Opposition to Appeasement in the 1930's* (1971); and D. C. Watt, "The Historiography of Appeasement," in Alan Sked and Chris Cook, eds., *Crisis and Controversy: Essays in Honour of A. J. P. Taylor* (1976). For a general account of the final debacle, Christopher Thorne, *The Approach of War, 1938–9* (1967); see also Telford Taylor's massive *Munich: The Price of Peace* (1979).

On the impact of British experience of the First World War, Paul Fussell, *The Great War and Modern Memory* (1975). Rosalind Mitchison, *British Population Change since 1860* (1977) charts the altered curve. For a general discussion of economic life, Derek H. Aldcroft, *The Inter-war Economy, 1919–1939* (1970). The cultural history of the interwar years has not been written in any general, interpretative way, but mention should be made of Asa Brigg's *History of Broadcasting in the United Kingdom* (4 vols., 1961–1978). Finally, there is the superb portrait of the country by the novelist J. B. Priestley, *English Journey* (1934).

Chapter 13
Brave New Worlds

THE SECOND WORLD WAR, 1940–1945

The Course of the War

Churchill's promise of "blood, toil, tears, and sweat" was grimly fulfilled. On May 15, Holland surrendered to the Germans. Breaking through the French fortifications at the same time, the German army reached the sea near Abbeville by May 19. On May 28, the Belgian forces gave up. With the Germans on both flanks of the British Expeditionary Force, there was no alternative to evacuation, which began at Dunkirk on May 27 and was completed on June 3, a defeat converted by the nearly total success of the operation into a kind of victory. The loss of Britain's remaining Continental ally was a matter of time. Efforts to concert action with the French broke down one after the other, and, on June 22, the French surrendered, yielding up the northern half of the country to German occupation and retaining (for a time) the southern half in a client status with a cooperative government at Vichy.

For another year, the British stood, as it is always said, alone.

Strictly speaking, the boast is not quite true. A host of governments-in-exile settled in London, as did a defiant, self-proclaimed Free French movement headed by a dissident nationalist officer named Charles de Gaulle. These exiled governments brought nothing in the way of resources, but refugees, most notably the Poles, provided men and spirit, while many of their countrymen in occupied Europe contributed greatly to British intelligence and ultimately to Allied victory by organizing resistance movements. The Dominions were at war with Germany too, and in time were to make valuable contributions. Gradually a more explicit alliance with the United States was being forged, thanks to the initiative of President Franklin Roosevelt, who managed ingeniously to find one after another chink in the legislative wall of American isolationism. The British sent vast sums to the United States to purchase war material, although it took a long time for American industry to convert effectively to producing the needed goods. Meanwhile, President Roosevelt made "surplus" American arms available to the British, and signed an agreement by which fifty overage destroyers were given to Britain in return for American rights in British bases in the Western Hemisphere. In the summer of 1941, the American Navy occupied Iceland and began to patrol more widely in the Atlantic, first encountering German submarines in September. In March, 1941, the Lend-Lease Act, agreed to in principle some time before, made dollars available to Britain for a more effective prosecution of the war.

These Allied contributions were important more in prospect than in actuality. If Britain was not quite alone, it was she who had to bear the brunt of the no longer phony war. In the summer of 1940, the Luftwaffe was assigned the task of softening up Britain for invasion; the Battle of Britain began in July. Intended at first to knock out the Royal Air Force, German bombing was soon diverted to British cities, especially London. The battle was won by the RAF, thanks to the dogged skill and courage of its pilots; to the use of the new invention of radar which, by advance detection of targets, allowed them to conserve their strength; and to the feats of British intelligence, which provided advance knowledge of German battle plans. In September, Hitler canceled plans for the invasion for that year, in effect forever: "Never in the field of human conflict," said Churchill of the RAF, "was so much owed by so many to so few." Britain was at least safe from conquest, although she was not safe from continued attacks from the air. The blitz went on in extensive German night-bombing raids, the war at sea took a heavy toll in naval ships and an even heavier toll in merchant ships on which survival so desperately depended, and Britain had to face a succession of military defeats on land.

Just before France fell, Italy entered the war, determined, in spite of her military weakness, to get in on the spoils while there was yet time. Italy's action committed Britain to a campaign in the Mediterranean and the Near East. There were many justifications advanced for it: it was to keep Hitler from the oil fields, to gain allies, and to maintain prestige; it may have appealed, too, to tradition or recent memories: the ghost of the Gallipoli campaign, waged so disastrously at Churchill's insistence a quarter-century before, hovers strangely about British strategy. But at least engagement in that area gave Britain a chance to take on, in Italy, an enemy she might have a chance of beating in the field. And so she did. From December 1940 to February 1941, British forces, based in Egypt and commanded by Sir Archibald Wavell, swept the Italians out of the North African desert as far as Benghazi in Libya, and they achieved complete success in Ethiopia, to which Haile Selassie returned in May. But the Ethiopian victory remained a solitary triumph; the successes of British arms in the desert proved evanescent. The Germans came to the rescue of the Italians, and the Afrika Korps under General Erwin Rommel threw the British back on the Egyptian bases. A British thrust into Greece, which Mussolini had invaded, was at once repelled by German forces, and in May the island of Crete was conquered within a week by a German parachute invasion. Only in the Near East did the British manage to stand secure, an area in which Hitler had no serious interest.

Shortly after this series of disasters, Britain's isolation came to an end. On June 22, 1941, the German army invaded Russia. From that moment, the main strategic question was the mounting of an invasion of the Continent that could force the Germans into a war on two fronts. The British themselves lacked the resources for so vast an enterprise. But their collaboration with the United States grew steadily closer, with at least a rhetorical climax reached in the Anglo-American adoption of the Atlantic Charter in August, 1941, a declaration of war aims including a complete and just victory over the Nazis and a vague promise of some form of collective security after the war. The United States was forced from an undeclared war into active belligerency by the Japanese attack on Pearl Harbor on December 7, 1941, and in early 1942 was forged the Grand Alliance of the three great powers — Russia, the United States, and Britain — against the Axis.

The tide was not to turn for some time. When the United States entered the war, Britain at once declared war on Japan. Within a few days, the Japanese air force sank the *Prince of Wales* and the *Repulse;* in February, 1942, the Japanese captured Singapore, the main British naval base in the Far East, soon overran all of Malaya and Burma, and seriously threatened India, where a number of extreme nationalists would have welcomed a Japanese invasion as a deliverance from the British raj. In August, 1942, a joint British-Canadian raid was launched on Dieppe in northern France, a kind of rehearsal for a second front, with disastrous results. The first successes began to come in North Africa. Wavell had been sent to India as viceroy; under his successor, General Sir Claude Auchinleck, the British fell back on their base at Alamein in the Egyptian desert, only sixty miles from Alexandria. Auchinleck was in turn succeeded by Sir Harold Alexander as theater commander, with General Sir Bernard Montgomery at the head of the Eighth Army. Rommel made his last stab at the lines at Alamein on August 30; in late October, Montgomery began a counterattack. Rommel retreated, evacuated Cyrenaica and Tripoli, and escaped. The British victory was secured on November 4; three days later, the Americans landed in French North Africa to begin the first combined operations. The Allies invaded Sicily in July, 1943, and crossed to the mainland, where Mussolini's government fell Again the Germans moved in, and in January, 1944, the Allies launched an invasion behind the German lines at Anzio that nearly ended in disaster; but by June, 1944, they had entered Rome, and the Italian campaign was won. The Mediterranean had already been open to convoys for a year.

Meanwhile, after long delays and much bickering about strategy, the second front was launched in Europe. A supplementary American landing was made in the south of France in August, but the main thrust came in Normandy on D-Day, June 6, 1944. The Royal Air Force had long been contributing to the softening-up of German-dominated Europe; ruling British doctrine since the mid-thirties had argued for extensive bombing of wide areas, a strategy that has been much criticized for its inhumanity and for the disproportion between its cost and results. The Germans retaliated, as long as the Luftwaffe was able, notably in the "Baedeker raids" of 1942 on historic English towns of no or little military significance. In 1944, retaliation took on a new form with the appearance of two secret German weapons. During the summer, the first V-bombs (V-1's) were used, self-directed flying bombs; British defenses were able to meet them and bring them down. But in September came the first rockets, V-2's, that could not be spotted and tracked like the slower buzz bombs. More terrifying because they struck without warning, the rockets caused considerable destruction, particularly in London—a severe blow to morale at just the point when victory seemed in sight. But, though they foreshadowed the warfare of the future, in 1944 they were a late, gratuitous threat. The Allied forces rolled on in Western Europe as the Russian forces spread over and absorbed

Eastern Europe. On April 29, the Italian forces finally surrendered to General Alexander—the day before Mussolini had been taken and shot by partisan forces. On April 30, Hitler committed suicide, and German surrender followed shortly. V-E Day, celebrating victory in Europe, was proclaimed on May 8. The victory in the Far East, which the British thought would be long in coming, came quickly, after the portentous dropping of two atomic bombs by the American Air Force over Hiroshima and Nagasaki on August 6 and 9. The final Japanese surrender was taken on September 2; the victory was mostly American, and the United States replaced Britain as the dominant power in the East. She did so in Europe too.

The Home Front

The administration of any war entails much improvisation; the Second World War was no exception. But the British had fuller plans, both military and civilian, for the Second World War than they had for the First. They had unquestionably a much abler group of military commanders and a structure of civil administration more responsive, flexible, and efficient than could have been possible twenty-five years before, when the apparatus of the modern state was hardly sketched out and the possibilities of state action were barely realized. In this abstract and conceptual sense the Second World War was built on the foundations of the First. Like Lloyd George, Churchill had a small war cabinet; unlike Lloyd George, his cabinet ministers were more completely subordinate, rather more in the guise of civil servants, less in the mold of Curzon, Carson, or Milner.* Churchill dominated his government even more than Lloyd George had done and extended his interest (some would have said interference) in more directions, notably into military strategy, at which he had always considered himself adept. Two ministers, however, were nearly as colorful as the Prime Minister and made extraordinary contributions to victory as well: one was Lord Beaverbrook, the press lord, who as Minister of Aircraft Production directed the almost miraculous efforts that gave the RAF the planes with which they won the Battle of Britain; the other was Ernest Bevin, who was responsible for the direction of labor under much more difficult con-

---

*Some of the ministers actually were civil servants. Sir John Anderson, for example, one of the ablest civil servants of the century, had been brought into the cabinet in 1938 (the first such shift since the creation of the modern civil service in the late nineteenth century), and became Home Secretary and Chancellor of the Exchequer during the war. Anderson was Churchill's choice for prime minister if both he and Eden were killed.

ditions than had obtained in the First World War and with infinitely less disturbance.

The regimentation of civilian life was much more nearly complete in the Second World War. Evacuation was carried out on a large scale at the very beginning of the war, but was quickly undone in the period of the phony war and, although there were subsequent evacuations during the blitz, most people stayed at home during the bombings. Air-raid shelters—many Underground stations were turned into improvised shelters in London—by no means accommodated all or even a very large percentage of the population of towns. Raids and alarms were disruptive, but in time people got used to them, and, whatever their unrecorded effects on health and efficiency, they damaged morale less than the Germans had hoped. The civilian casualties from bombing were a little under 300,000, of whom 60,000 were killed, a small enough number compared to the awful civilian casualties on the Continent.* What was perhaps most astonishing was the speed with which overtaxed facilities, such as ports and railways, were brought back into use after air raids. Rationing was much more extensive and systematic than it had been in the First World War: the threat to supplies was greater, but knowledge was more sophisticated—wartime food may have been desperately dull, but advances in the understanding of nutrition assured that the nation's diet was better balanced during the war than it had been in peacetime, when most people could follow their ordinary inherited and ignorant prejudices against what was good for them. The revolution in government finance, associated with the innovations of Keynes, assured a much more active and intelligent use of the state's armory of economic weapons, and the nation attained an unprecedented equality of sacrifice that helped to maintain unity. The improvised socialism of the First World War had made people think, somewhat innocently, about the possibilities of socialism after the war; the more extensive and sophisticated socialism of the Second World War was proof of its practical possibilities, and the determination of many to realize these possibilities was reinforced by memories of the flight from socialism in 1919-1921.

The management of Britain's external position was less successful. Far more than the First World War, the Second demanded a concentration on the war effort and a nearly complete disregard of the normal channels of the economy: no one ever thought of business as usual. Exports at the end of the war were a mere 40 per cent of what they had been at the beginning; the old staple industries, revived

*British military casualties were less than half what they had been in the First World War, 300,000 deaths as against 750,000.

with such enthusiasm in 1919 and so pessimistically rationalized in the thirties, were now finally dethroned from their historic positions, yielding in awareness as well as fact to newer industries. Britain's international financial position grew desperate. In 1946, her invisible exports were half what they had been in 1938; she had sold more than a billion dollars in overseas assets; she was deeply in debt. American aid had maintained her during the war, when, as much after Pearl Harbor as before, she was fighting America's battles. But lend-lease was abruptly terminated on the day the Japanese surrendered. Britain was once again alone, and alone in a way that was harder to comprehend or to cope with than standing solitary against enemy troops and planes.

Nor did Britain any longer have the consolation of being a great power. Churchill put much confidence in his friendship with Roosevelt, but Roosevelt was, like most of his countrymen, suspicious of British intentions. With some reason: Britain was an imperial power and the United States was not yet accustomed to the exercise of imperial power in its new forms; Britain was a competitor, whom resort to protection within the Commonwealth had labeled uncooperative; in spite of all the sentiment about Anglo-American ties, Britain was, or could be, an American liability. It probably did American egos some good to conclude that Britain was finished, and two years were to pass before it became plain that Britain needed to be rescued for more than altruistic reasons. Moreover, Roosevelt was impressed by the overwhelming power of the third member of the Grand Alliance: the Soviet Union, which made by far the largest contribution in men, material, and suffering to Germany's defeat, counted for much more than Britain's shrinking might. Many people on both sides of the Atlantic thought that Stalin's Russia would emerge from the war different, less isolated and hostile than she had been in the 1930's. The wartime strategy of the Allies was hammered out in a series of conferences, sometimes of all three, sometimes of pairs of partners. Although Churchill was the nearly indefatigable participant in all of them—Washington and Moscow, Casablanca, Quebec, Cairo, Teheran, Yalta—he rarely got all he wanted, and only the facade of equality was maintained, sometimes not even that.

Back to Politics

Politically, the First World War had been disastrous. Lloyd George had succeeded to the premiership at the head of a revolt of discontented M.P.'s, amid intrigue and infighting. Asquith and his followers were never reconciled, and as a result the coalition government was largely Conservative. Moreover, Lloyd George had himself given scant attention to the House of Commons or to the customary forms of politics. In the Second World War there was genuine bipartisanship. Once in Chamberlain's government, Churchill had been scrupulously loyal; he succeeded not by intrigue but by being the obvious choice when Chamberlain was driven from office. His own coalition was completely genuine and remarkably well balanced. When discontent arose, as it did on several occasions during the dark days of 1942, Churchill insisted on debates and votes of confidence, which he won overwhelmingly. The makeshift opposition that provided running criticism of his conduct of the war was composed of a few individuals of considerable ability and differing points of view; but acid though their speeches might be—Emanuel Shinwell and Aneurin Bevan of the Labour party were never men to pull their punches—their opposition was never less than responsible and legitimate, and never degenerated into a petty quest for partisan advantage or mere sullenness.

When the turning point was passed in 1943, the government began seriously to work on reconstruction plans. The most famous of these plans was a report made at the end of 1942 by Sir William Beveridge, a Liberal who as a civil servant had been involved in the drafting of the National Insurance Act of 1911 and who had subsequently served as director of the London School of Economics. The Beveridge Report called for an extension of social services, as the phrase had it, "from the cradle to the grave," and for the systematic maintenance of full employment, goals to which the government had committed itself fully, if somewhat hesitantly, by the end of the war. An earnest of the determination of government and country alike to make a different and better society after the war was offered in 1944 when R. A. Butler carried a major Education Act. The act finally redeemed the promises of 1918 to create a general program of secondary education: the school-leaving age was to be raised to 15 (it was actually done in 1947); and from the age of 11, children in the state system were to go to one of three kinds of secondary school, the decision depending on a much-discussed and now abandoned examination. Those who were found to have the necessary ability went to grammar schools, from which university entrance would be possible for those wishing to go still further; for the others, whose education would normally end at 15, there were technical schools or a secondary modern school, intended for general rather than strictly academic secondary teaching.

Once the Germans were defeated, the country could again begin to look to its normal political concerns. On May 18, 1945, Churchill proposed that the coalition continue until the Japanese were defeated, although he, like everyone, recognized that there had to be an early election to replace a House of Commons elected in 1935 in utterly different circumstances. The Labour party refused, and Churchill in turn insisted that the election be held as soon as possible, in July. Accordingly, he resigned on May 23, forming a "caretaker" government, mostly Conservative, to carry on during the campaign. It seemed unthinkable to the Conservatives and to Churchill himself that it would not be an easy victory, another khaki election, although to make assurance doubly sure Churchill launched some ill-advised attacks on his old coalition colleagues, including an unhappy suggestion that a Labour victory would bring with it the threat of a native Gestapo. But for all the admiration of Churchill in war, the residual distrust of Churchill in peace remained: the general strike in particular had not been forgotten. Perhaps Churchill was not, after all, the man to build the new world. To such doubters the Labour party appealed with its manifesto *Let Us Face the Future*, calling for a sweeping program of social reconstruction. The general election was held on July 5, but getting in the service vote delayed the results until July 26. Labour (with slightly less than half the popular vote) returned 393 members as against 213 for the Conservatives and their allies, 12 Liberals, and an astonishing 22 members who were Independents or representatives of splinter parties. The King sent for Attlee, who at once took Churchill's place at the Potsdam Conference, which was then sitting to determine the postwar disposition of Germany.

THE POSTWAR ERA IN PROSPECT

Labour in Power 1945–1951

Labour entered on its first majority government with a huge vote of confidence, a firm determination, and a remarkable array of talent. Hugh Dalton, once a lecturer at the London School of Economics and a leading spokesman for the moderate intellectuals in the thirties, was at the Exchequer, Ernest Bevin at the Foreign Office. At the Home Office was Herbert Morrison, the author of the bill that had led to the nationalization of London Transport in 1933 and a veteran politician whose reputation had been made in the London County Council. The left wing of the party, too, was well represented. Emanuel Shinwell, who had been imprisoned in 1919 following a general strike in Glasgow, was made Minister of Fuel and Power and later became an outstanding Minister of Defense. John Strachey, the left-wing maverick of the thirties, was Minister of Food and ultimately Secretary of State for War. Sir Stafford Cripps had returned to the party fold; he was at the Board of Trade and in 1947 moved to the

Exchequer following Dalton's forced resignation, the result of his accidentally giving advance information on the budget. At the Ministry of Health was Aneurin Bevan. A Welsh miner who had long sat for the mining constituency of Ebbw Vale, Bevan had been expelled from the party with Cripps in the late thirties; having made his peace, he became one of Churchill's most vocal critics during the war and was to be dogged for years, as Churchill was by his "Gestapo" speech, by an ill-judged but deeply felt reference in 1949 to the Tories as "lower than vermin." Presiding over a cabinet of diverse, ambitious, and idiosyncratic men was Clement Attlee, dedicated, quiet, perceptive, and tough.

The government moved quickly to fulfill the party's promises. One of its first steps was to repeal the hated Trade Disputes Act, carried by Baldwin after the general strike: the right of trade unions to join (and support) the Labour party was thus restored, subject only to the right of a member to contract out of the political levy. But there was not much time to even old scores; nor was there much time— indeed for four years there was no time—for private members to introduce legislation, so sweeping was Labour's plan and so demanding its timetable.

Of all the measures carried by the Labour government, those that attracted most attention were the moves to nationalize basic industries. Some of the legislation merely reorganized industries already in the public sector or gave formal recognition that some nominally private institutions had become in effect government departments. Thus the Civil Aviation Act of 1946 created two new government corporations, British European Airways and British South American Airways, the latter joined three years later with the British Overseas Airways Corporation, in existence since 1939; overseas cables were nationalized; and, most impressive but perhaps least meaningful of all, the Bank of England was nationalized in 1946. More important measures moved into new territory, using the old form of the public corporation in a descending scale of centralization.

Nationalization of the coal mines in 1946, nearly thirty years after it had been formally proposed by the Sankey Commission, vested the ownership of all mines and ancillary facilities in the National Coal Board, which at once became the largest employer of labor in the country. Its highly centralized administration was perhaps essential, given the serious, fragmented state of the industry and the need for both a rapid adjustment to modern market and labor conditions and a huge investment of capital to make up for decades of neglect. The nationalization of transport, in 1947, was carried out differently. The British Transport Commission became the formal holder of the assets of all the enterprises taken over—railways, trucking (except for local haulage within twenty-five miles of a company's base), canals, the already nationalized London Transport, a chain of hotels operated by the prewar railway companies, and the famous travel agency, Thomas Cook and Sons, Ltd. Each of the main categories of operation was put under an "executive," and within the Railway Executive, the interwar pattern was more or less perpetuated in six regional organizations that in time received further installments of autonomy. Electricity supply had been partially nationalized since 1926; in 1947, the generation and retail distribution of electrical power were also taken over, and the whole industry was placed under regional Electricity Boards. The regional Gas Boards, under the act of 1948, were even less closely coordinated in their policies than was the electricity industry. Finally, in 1949, when the government moved beyond public utilities to the most crucial manufacturing industry, iron and steel, the nationalized companies retained their separate identities and their historic names; the British Iron and Steel Corporation was a mere holding company.

Nearly as dramatic were the sweeping provisions for social services, the "welfare state." The National Insurance Act of 1946 redeemed the social security promises of the Beveridge Report, housing acts were passed in 1946 and 1949, and a general reorganization of relief of poverty was undertaken in 1948. The most striking statute, however, was the National Health Service Act of 1946, which came into effect in 1948 under the superintendence of Aneurin Bevan. Building on the base of Lloyd George's health insurance system of 1911, that act provided free medical care (including dental and optical treatment and fitting and all prescriptions) for everyone in the country, a service in which insurance contributions were far overshadowed by subsidies from national taxation. Hospitals, too, were nationalized, their costs borne by the Exchequer. Private medicine was retained for those who preferred and could afford it, and the National Health Service did not interfere with the patient's free choice of doctors. Still, the medical professional strongly opposed the act, although in the end only a few doctors refused to participate. In a bargain with the doctors, the state agreed to allow a quota of private beds in public hospitals, for which private patients would pay a nominal charge—an understanding that from time to time surfaced as a minor political issue.

The National Health Service changed the nature of much medical practice, especially for general practitioners, who were often overburdened (particularly in the early years of the service when the country was catching up with a legacy of medical neglect) and, many felt, increasingly reduced to serving as dispensers of pills and referral agents for specialists. But in this respect the act may only have hastened what seems to have been a long-term consequence of the increase in medical knowledge and of the growing sophistication and difficulty of its techniques; that doctors' income rose—for a time—as a result of the act is certain. There was much grumbling from patients: they faced long waits in doctors' offices, hospitals were badly overcrowded, and for many years no capital funds were forthcoming for significant extension or modernization. But no single action of the Labour government contributed more to the well-being of the country or has had more complete acceptance.

The state had many weapons to use in its struggle to right the economy and to carry out its obligations. Taxes were raised to unprecedented levels. The physical controls of wartime were retained and even extended. Much of the output of British industry was flatly denied the British consumer, either by direct prohibition or by an enormous "purchase tax," and channeled into exports. Licensing governed the availability of raw materials to manufacturers, and of resources and materials to the building industry, which was further regulated under extensive provisions for town and country planning. Direct controls were reinforced and supplemented by persuasion and cajolery. Labor was urged, even browbeaten, into restraining its wage claims, thanks in part to the relative success of efforts to control inflation and to tax profits, and in part to exhortation by the unbeatable team of Ernest Bevin and Sir Stafford Cripps.

Cripps—high-minded, puritanical, devoutly Christian, a vegetarian and a teetotaller—became the appropriate symbol of the "austerity" that was both the watchword and a precise description of British life from 1945 until the end of the decade. But increasingly the British found that their revolution seemed to lead only to a drab, depressing, and constricted life, in which travel abroad was limited, travel at home was dispiriting and difficult, restaurants (though compulsorily cheap with a five-shilling limit on meals) were dreary and bad, and one's daily round was too often a matter of queues at shops and endless shortages. The best efforts at planning seemed only to result in a series of crises of greater or lesser severity for which the remedies added up to more austerity.* Regrets were no doubt keenest among those who had been well off before the war, though some were made easier in conscience by sympathy with the goals of the new society. For those who had suffered in the thirties, even austerity could be an improvement, though a regimented improvement:

---

*The worst failure—and the best gift to the Opposition—was the Overseas Food Corporation, a government-owned body set up to increase food supplies by overseas plantations, which failed disastrously as a result of a hurried, ill-considered scheme to raise groundnuts (peanuts) in East Africa.

when the veteran social investigator Seebohm Rowntree returned for another look at the city of York he had studied at the beginning of the century and again in the mid-thirties, he found that the numbers of people living in primary poverty had fallen from over 30 per cent in 1936 to less than 3 per cent, and of that 3 per cent no one blamed unemployment.

Though much in the legacy of Labour was solid accomplishment, the warmest hopes of the party and its supporters had not been fulfilled. Yet there was apparent throughout the postwar years a genuine unity of national purpose, a surprising lack of more than the usual grumbling. Perhaps after the terrible winter of 1947, with its shortages of fuel and everything else, there was no way to go but up. Gradually, then swiftly, the physical controls were relaxed, and by the end of the decade the country was launched on what Harold Wilson, then president of the Board of Trade, called "a little experiment in freedom."

The most striking accomplishment of the postwar Labour government may, however, be found not in Britain but in India, given its independence in 1947. During the war Churchill had had to swallow some of his old dislike of the Indian nationalist movement and had grudgingly accepted the principle of dominion status for India in order to secure her wholehearted cooperation in the war. To that end, Sir Stafford Cripps was sent to India in 1942 to offer full self-government after the war, only to meet rejection inspired by Gandhi. But when the war was over the Labour government was determined to carry through its long-standing advocacy of independence. The trouble was that communalism—the division of India into religious communities—had become much more pervasive and powerful, and independence could be speedily accomplished only at the price of creating the separate Muslim state of Pakistan. The diplomacy of Lord Mountbatten, the last viceroy, did much to smooth the way for the transfer of power, for which the British had set a deadline of mid-1948; then, they insisted, they would leave, no matter what the situation in the subcontinent. Forced to act, the dominant Congress party gave in to the hated idea of partition. But the transition to independence was not peaceful. When the two dominions actually came into being, on August 15, 1948, there followed a period of communal rioting verging on civil war that left an almost ineradicable hatred between the two countries; its noblest victim was Gandhi, assassinated in January, 1948, by a Hindu fanatic. In the same year, Burma and Ceylon received their independence, without being baptized in blood; Burma chose to become a republic directly and to refuse membership in the Commonwealth. Ireland followed the same course, at last, in 1949, although the old De Valera formula of "external association" was revived in the same year at a meeting of Commonwealth prime ministers as a means of keeping India in the Commonwealth when she too chose to become a republic, as did Pakistan in 1956.

The British likewise decided to withdraw from Palestine, which they had held as a mandate since 1919. There the British found themselves in a nearly impossible situation. German efforts to exterminate European Jews during the war—successful to a horrible degree—had given new impetus to Zionism and its goal of a Jewish state of Israel; refugees flocked to Palestine. The British were pledged to the ideal of a Jewish homeland by the Balfour Declaration of 1917; at the same time, they were forced to respect the feelings of the Arabs, on whom so many British economic and strategic interests depended and from whose territory the new state was to be carved. The British thus found themselves trying to keep two hostile peoples apart, at the cost of being hated by both sides. Their decision to prevent Jewish refugees from being illegally smuggled into Palestine, while a diplomatic imperative, brought tragedy for thousands and a resort to terrorism among parts of the Jewish community already in Palestine. Again the British decided on a unilateral withdrawal as of May, 1948, leaving the problem to the United Nations and the United States. With the British buffer removed, the war that followed was won by Israel, which thereupon set about a remarkable political and economic advance that embittered the Arabs, who could do little more than bide their time until they could return to the attack.

The Economy

In 1945 the Labour Party's manifesto (or, as Americans would say, platform) was called *Let Us Face the Future*. Willingly or not, in the next five years, everyone felt caught up in a great national experiment, the creation of a new social democratic society. It can be argued, however, that Labour's program owed more to the past than it did to visions of an abstractly conceived future. Its dramatic moves in the direction of nationalization and broad welfare coverage were solidly built on precedents that ran back at least forty years and were added to piecemeal in the interval. The movements in social thought that justified abandoning individualism for collectivism were even more venerable, while the trade union movement, on which the financial and political strength of the party so largely rested, was almost a century old. Two world wars, with their crude but effective direct controls on industry, labor, and consumption, had offered glimpses of "fair shares for all." Still more potent were memories of the "bad old days" of the thirties, the long-term gains in the standard and quality of life between the wars being largely lost to view. The

Beveridge Report insisted on the maintenance of full employment, as important a postwar goal as the provision of a national minimum. Thus, the new institutions of the welfare state—allowing for some technical reorganization here and there and occasional questions about whether it all could in fact be afforded—were fully accepted by the country, and no politican dared attack them.

The cost of the programs was not, in itself, crippling. Expenditures for income maintenance after the war—all kinds of pensions, workmen's compensation, poor relief (national assistance, as it came to be called), and payments for widows, orphans, and family allowances—made up a smaller percentage of the gross national product than did similar welfare programs in the 1930's when unemployment was at a high level. Possibly the percentage spent on health was roughly equivalent to the prewar figure, though after 1948 the Exchequer took over much expenditure that had been diffused among individuals and voluntary associations in the private sector. All this—and the vast expansion of local government services and costs in health-related welfare work, education, and the like—was manageable with sharply increased taxation. Death duties, the income tax, excise taxes, and rates soared, in some instances to levels unmatched in any other country, though the redistributive effect of progressive taxation was less than was intended or than the heavily taxed rich thought was the case: there were important loopholes (capital gains, for one), and the rich and their advisers could always find ways to protect themselves, while businessmen had expense accounts, company cars, and the whole panoply of "perks."

The welfare state was, however, only one competing claim on British resources. Immediate priority had to be given to compensation for war damage and to rebuilding shattered cities; extending farther into the future was the crucial need for capital investment in houses, new towns, schools, and hospitals, and in the nationalized industries to overcome wartime deterioration and earlier failures to modernize. Moreover, Britain had an inherited position in the world that no one was prepared to abandon blithely, and that meant extensive military expenditure and at least some politically essential investment in the Commonwealth and developing nations. Such a range of commitments might have given pause to a very rich nation, and after the dislocations of two world wars, Britain was no longer rich.

Even in its Victorian heyday, Britain imported more than it exported, most years. This unfavorable balance of trade was converted into a generally favorable balance of payments by the so-called invisible exports, the money Britain earned abroad through its shipping, banking, insurance, and other services, as well as from dividends on its foreign investments.* After 1945 the pressure to import reached unprecedented heights, given long pent-up consumer demand, and the insufficiency of domestic capacity to meet the needs of the economy; to limit imports by a general policy of protection would merely worsen shortages at home and invite retaliation abroad. No longer could the invisibles be relied upon to make up the difference. At the end of the war about a quarter of Britain's overseas investments had been liquidated; her shipping capacity was down by almost the same proportion, and by the 1960's she was paying out more for shipping than she was taking in by it. Habit and reputation continued to secure Britain's pre-eminence in banking and insurance, but the United States, in this as in other aspects, was offering serious competition. Moreover, Britain was at the head of a recently constituted informal complex known as the Sterling Area, countries in the Empire and Commonwealth (Canada excluded), Asia, and the Middle East which kept their monetary reserves in London and which paid into and drew from a common dollar pool. This arrangement emphasized the importance — felt in any case by the British financial community — of maintaining the value of the pound sterling, but there was a further complication. Sterling Area countries, as well as a number of other nations, had built up credits in Britain during the war — for supplies purchased by Britain or, as in the case in India, for use of their facilities for military purposes. These "sterling balances" were blocked for the time being; that is, they could not be repatriated, but a reserve had to be maintained against the day when these balances were reclaimed.

Britain had financed the war largely from her own resources, by selling foreign investments and borrowing from her own citizens rather than from abroad as in World War I. But when the war was over and American lend-lease — of so much help during the war despite its somewhat capricious administration — was abruptly terminated, Britain could not survive on her own resources. Like the other, and even worse damaged, European industrial states, she needed American goods and the dollars to pay for them; it would take time for her export industries to recover sufficiently to earn those dollars or other foreign currencies. The immediate answer was an American loan, granted in 1946 on stringent conditions, their harshness highlighted by the more generous terms of a Canadian loan made at the same time. Between 1948 and 1950 the British, like the rest of Europe, benefited from a far more imaginative American initiative, Marshall aid, so called after General George Marshall, the

*Of course, much of the foreign investment income had been reinvested abroad. See above, pp. 385–386.

American secretary of state who proposed the plan in 1947. But these were temporary expedients. In the long run Britain had to save herself by building up her export industries to a level far beyond any earlier period to balance the demand for imports and the weakened position on the invisible account.

If exports failed to reach the required level, if British prices appeared high relative to prices elsewhere, if the international business community found its confidence in Britain's financial health seriously shaken, devaluation of the pound might prove necessary — that is, the rate at which the pound exchanged for other currencies would be lowered. This draconian step could not be taken lightly or often, for while devaluation at once made British exports more competitive in the world's markets, it also forced Britain to pay more for imports, thus restarting the inflationary spiral. And because devaluation would instantly decrease the value of balances held in London — by Sterling Area countries, businesses, serious investors, or mere speculators — the fear of it would lead to withdrawal of those funds; and if the flight from sterling proved beyond the capacity or will of the Bank of England to rectify it, it might compel the very action that was feared. Devaluation was resorted to twice — a drastic application in 1949, when the dollar value of the pound was lowered from $4.03 to $2.80; and a forty-cent cut in that value in 1967. A further decline followed (at a distance) the "floating" of the pound in 1971. To avoid such painful adjustments, governments used, wherever possible, methods of fiscal management. If the pound seemed threatened, domestic consumption (and thus imports) would be cut back by such means as increased taxes, limits on hire purchase, and raising the bank rate, which in turn would compel higher interest rates, making it more costly for British business to borrow but also attracting foreign deposits back to Britain. Such measures, however, would also slow down investment in the necessary modernization of industry and create political liabilities at home, especially if an induced recession threatened full employment. So, once a threatened crisis had passed — and it often seemed when an election loomed — controls would be relaxed to allow the economy to get started again. This alternation of restriction and expansion — "stop-go" as it came to be called — was the virtual negation of planning, but no postwar government, no matter what its political complexion, seemed able to avoid an improvisatory response to a world economy whose complexities were beyond management and to a domestic economy that would not do all that was needed of it.

Viewed in isolation, much in the economic performance of postwar Britain was admirable. The war damage was repaired, the mistakes of the post-1918 years were avoided, industry developed a new respect for science and technology, and the trade unions were fully cooperative—there were few strikes, mostly wildcat strikes against the advice of the TUC leadership, and wage increases were kept within reasonable and affordable bounds. By 1950 exports had reached the target set five years earlier, and after the Korean War in the early 1950's, the terms of trade—the ratio of what Britain paid for her imports as against what she could charge for her exports—turned in her favor; yet the British failed to keep up their position as the other European nations and Japan came into the economic arena. Elsewhere productivity—the yield per worker, whether in a single industry or in the economy as a whole—rose rapidly; in Britain it moved upward only slowly. In part this was due to the strength and conservatism of British trade unions. Cooperative though they were in the postwar years, in time appeals from union and political leaders grew less convincing and pressures for higher wages and other improvements grew among workers, often focused by militant shop stewards in rebellion against distant and bureaucratic union leadership. Strikes increased in number and, particularly in the automobile industry which had been in the forefront of the postwar export drive, began to make delivery dates uncertain. There was resistance to changes that modernization might require in traditional ways of doing things; the normal pattern of industrial relations tended to be confrontational; and there was persistent overmanning, whether from trade-union concern with security or from the desire of management to stockpile scarce skills: all these factors undercut efforts to improve productivity, despite the lessons learned and passed on by the "productivity teams" that visited American factories regularly in the late forties. There were difficulties on the management side too—a preference for selling in easy markets, like, for a time, the Commonwealth; a lack of aggressiveness and commitment; failure to provide good post-sale services or to give customers what they wanted or needed; above all, an unwillingness to invest, though here the blame must lie more with government policies than with managers, who were understandably discouraged by high individual taxation and by the impossibility of long-range planning when fiscal policy shifted so frequently.

The performance of the nationalized industries was subject to the same criticisms and more. For at least thirty years, the Labour party had looked upon nationalization as a panacea. In some cases, coal most notably, it was the quickest and only reliable way to get the necessary capital and reforms—though even there, so massive were the problems that productivity was slow to rise and absenteeism was a perpetual if understandable problem, while there was insufficient recognition of the competition that would be offered in the sixties by

oil and electricity as alternative sources of energy. But the wider expectations for nationalization were never fulfilled. There was little
more "industrial democracy" or worker control. The sheer size of
some of the industries created technical and administrative problems
not easily overcome. The device of the public corporation shielded
the nationalized industries (rightly) from detailed parliamentary interference, but occasional general debates did little to provide meaningful accountability. Nationalization did not so much socialize industry as bureaucratize it. Even though many of the manifest
difficulties were legacies from the past or inevitable features of a
transition, nationalization itself was too often blamed for dirty coal,
rising prices, late trains, or "brown-outs," the electricity shortages
caused by rapidly growing demand and insufficient generating facilities. Yet, despite the grumbling about services now publicly owned,
no demand for sweeping denationalization was heard. The mixed
economy—about 20 per cent of industry was in the public sector—
was accepted by all parties, but no one seemed capable of doing
much to better the mixed results.

A Divided World

The retreat from empire which the Labour government had so boldly
conducted in India and Palestine was not maintained. In part this
was because there was not the same agreement as to its inevitability
as there was with respect to the welfare state and the major steps in
nationalization. Winston Churchill had growled during the war that
he had not become prime minister to preside over the dissolution of
the British Empire, and when he returned to the premiership in 1951
he was no less firmly fixed in his Victorian prejudices. For much of
the time, however, the aging Churchill was only a nominal head of
his government; more considerable was a segment of Conservative
opinion, strong in the constituencies and on the back benches, that
still held to the notion that Britain's greatness lay in her imperial
mission and that firmness was the key to effective government at
home and abroad. The most respected spokesman for this point of
view was Lord Salisbury, the grandson of Victoria's last prime minister; it was strengthened by ties maintained with white settlers in the
African colonies of Kenya and Rhodesia and by the memories of a
still lively generation of military men and civil governors who had
known the Empire at its peak.

Nearly everyone in or likely to be in power agreed, however,
that the transition to independence had to be orderly and that the ultimate aim was to include the new nations in the Commonwealth,
that appealing complex of sentiment, moral obligation, and shared

assumptions. To accomplish those ends, at less cost than the bloodshed that marked the emergence into nationhood of India, Pakistan,
and Israel, meant careful preparation, constitutional apprenticeship,
and timetables. When timetables proved unacceptable and impatient
nationalists resorted to terrorism, the British united in their determination that terrorism must not be yielded to; when the incipient nation contained populations hostile to each other, on racial or religious grounds, the British felt obligated to serve as a buffer
between the warring groups until a formula for pacification could be
worked out. Decolonization turned out to be a long, arduous, costly
process. Through most of the fifties British troops were involved in
frustrating, costly, and deadly tasks — putting down Mau Mau terror-
ists in Kenya and imposing military rule on the warring Greek and
Turkish settlers in Cyprus. The ironic result was often that nationalist leaders in the colonies were imprisoned in what was deemed a
necessary show of firmness, only to be welcomed within a few years
at conferences of Commonwealth prime ministers: Kwame Nkrumah
of Ghana, Jomo Kenyatta of Kenya, Archbishop Makarios of Cyprus,
Hastings Banda of Nyasaland.

The British were not merely altruistic, not solely concerned with
saving lives or assuring constitutional rule; they were also self-interested, particularly where long-established strategic interests were
involved, as in the bases in Cyprus, Egypt, or Singapore. On this
score, too, there was substantial agreement among political leaders,
who felt the residual pull of great-power status. In fact, with China in
disarray and isolation, the postwar world knew only two great
powers — the United States and the Soviet Union. Economic interest
and self-defense, as well as sentiment, kept Britain firmly in the
American camp, despite occasionally cavalier treatment by the senior
partner in the alliance. As one of the occupying powers, Britain had
to commit a large number of troops to Germany and, as the cold war
threatened the security of Western Europe, had to keep her army
strength high, to maintain conscription when the manpower supply
was drawn dangerously tight at home, and to invest huge sums she
could ill afford in armaments. Aware that the struggle with Communism was world-wide and that her own powers were limited, the
United States expected Britain to shoulder its share of the burden of
peace-keeping not only in Europe but in the Mediterranean and in
the vast expanses east of Suez, where responsibility still came naturally to the British. Britain tried to salvage something of her great
diplomatic past by serving as a brake on Russian ambitions and as a
moderating influence on American policy. To that end, Britain
played a leading role in the North Atlantic Treaty Organization
(NATO) and in other regional defense pacts encouraged by the

United States, actively though grudgingly assisted in the rehabilitation of West Germany as a bulwark against Communism, and, when the Korean War broke out in 1950, loyally supported the United Nations action (chiefly sustained by the United States) and sent a sizeable force to participate.

Party leaders in the main agreed with a decision taken by the Labour government in 1947 to undertake the development and manufacture of an atomic bomb, which the Conservative government carried further when in 1955 it elected to develop the hydrogen bomb. The American decision in 1946 not to share atomic secrets was reversed in 1958, the year following the successful British testing of a hydrogen bomb. Despite this successful exercise of British leverage, the tragicomedy of efforts in the sixties to align British and American defense policies and weapons systems made clear how junior was Britain's status within the nuclear club.

Just as an important segment of Conservative opinion, in and out of Parliament, differed from its leadership on imperial questions, so the Labour left in the fifties and early sixties rejected Britain's role in the cold war and argued instead for a new kind of pacifism. The cold war had always been questioned by some; in the heady days after 1945 the Labour party included some serious and some mindless admirers of the Soviet Union. The notion of Soviet blamelessness did not in any significant way survive the revelations made by Nikita Khrushchev at the Twentieth Party Congress in 1954 of the horrible truths about the repressiveness of Stalin's regime or the Russian invasion that put down the Hungarian revolt in 1956—developments that robbed the tiny British Communist party of some of its best minds. But American intransigence, the often frivolous and dogmatic foreign-policy gestures of John Foster Dulles, President Eisenhower's secretary of state during the fifties, and above all the ugly phenomenon of McCarthyism, which alienated almost all British opinion, fed the long-standing anti-Americanism of the left. Their hostility to Britain's defense policies was compounded, no doubt, by frustration felt over the failure to realize full-scale socialism. Was not, indeed, the entire expenditure on war unjustified when so many social problems needed to be dealt with at home? In the mid-fifties a third of government expenditure, 10 per cent of the gross national product, went to defense. Since there was clearly no chance of persuading the two great powers to disarm, Britain, the argument ran, should voluntarily give up her nuclear arms—to save money, to protect Britain from annihilation in a nuclear war, and to gain the moral leadership of the world. The principal spokesman for this viewpoint was the philosopher Bertrand Russell, aged, arrogant, cranky, yet to some persuasive; its chief political beneficiary was

Aneurin Bevan, who headed the left-leaning dissidents from the Labour party leadership. After becoming the party's spokesman on foreign affairs in 1956, Bevan renounced unilateralism, and the movement gained a new leader in Frank Cousins, then head of the Transport and General Workers Union. At the party conference in 1960 a motion for unilateral disarmament was carried from the floor; reversed in 1961, this action was the highwater mark of the movement, but the annual Easter marches to London from the atomic energy establishment at Aldermaston continued for some years after.

On only one major area of policy was there no clear consensus at the center of British politics. Marshall aid was given on condition that there be joint planning for its use, a stipulation that led to the first organizations for European economic cooperation. Coalescing with the vision of some far-sighted European statesmen, this cooperation resulted in 1952 in the launching of the European Coal and Steel Community and in 1957, with the Treaty of Rome, in the creation of the European Economic Community—the Common Market —which came into existence in 1958, joining together for certain economic purposes the six countries of Italy, France, West Germany, Belgium, Holland, and Luxembourg. Involved, necessarily, in the early cooperative ventures, Britain stood aside from the new, more formal organizations. Fearing the federalist and, to a degree, the capitalist tendencies of the EEC, in 1959 the British organized the European Free Trade Association, in which Britain was joined by Sweden, Norway, Denmark, Switzerland, Austria, and Portugal—the "outer seven" against the "inner six." EFTA was far from a collaboration of equals, nor was it a true union—with free flow of labor and capital and coordination of industry and transport—like the Common Market; it was a customs union, no more.

Britain's economy could not easily be integrated with the economies of the Common Market countries. In some ways she was less efficient, in others a dangerous competitor. Working out a common agricultural policy had been the most difficult hurdle for the Common Market countries to surmount; how much more difficult, then, it would be to accommodate British agricultural policy, with its subsidies, relatively low prices, and ties with Commonwealth producers. Some socialists saw the Common Market as an obstacle to the national planning they still hoped to realize in Britain and which (they wrongly believed) was beyond the irredeemably capitalist countries on the Continent. Still more socialists and many Conservatives felt a deep distrust of Europe, a kind of isolationism hallowed by centuries of separation; they looked outward across the Atlantic and to the countries of the Commonwealth—to which there were, of course, protectionist ties in the Ottawa Agreements of 1932—rather than across the Channel. These deep divisions were to persist through the successive efforts in the sixties to join the Common Market and beyond the actual linkage that began on January 1, 1973.

The Shape of Politics

In the rather quiet times of the fifties, there were occasional protests against what someone called the L-shaped chamber: that on any given issue the House of Commons consisted of an alliance of the two front benches against a group of dissidents on the back benches on one or the other side.* The degree of bipartisanship — to use an American term — reflected the pervasiveness of immense problems involving the economy, the Empire, defense, and foreign policy, few of them amenable to decisive resolution by British initiative alone. At the same time, the country experienced a stability of governmental and political forms that it had not known since the days when Disraeli and Gladstone, at the heads of their respective parties, embodied what we assume to be the classic modes of a parliamentary system — at least in the English-speaking world. There were dissidents but no schisms, collaboration but no coalition, and the only third party of importance was the little band of Liberals, calling for their version of a middle way — and for voting by proportional representation, which they believed would make it possible for them to play a greater parliamentary role. In that they were probably right, for Liberals did increasingly attract a protest vote, reflecting disenchantment with the two major parties. But despite occasional dramatic upsets like the bye-election in March, 1962, when a safe Conservative seat in the London suburb of Orpington was won by a Liberal candidate, the sizeable Liberal vote never translated into more than thirteen seats, and frequently the number was far fewer.

In the Representation of the People Act of 1948 the last steps were taken to achieve the democratic principle of one person–one vote: the act abolished plural voting and the university constituencies. In the next year, to assure passage of the controversial iron and steel nationalization bill, the veto power of the House of Lords was limited to one year. In 1958 the appointment of life peers and peeresses became possible, as did, five years later, the renunciation of peerages, thus re-opening careers in the House of Commons to peers who might otherwise have been confined to minor ministerial posts in a setting of aristocratic splendor. There has been occasional talk (often among the peers themselves) of a full-scale reorganization

---

*"Butskellism" was another term for it — coined from R. A. Butler and Hugh Gaitskell.

of the upper house, limiting or entirely removing the hereditary principle; a bill was offered and then withdrawn in 1968–1969, and no agreement has as yet been reached. Meanwhile the House of Lords has become not only an assenting—and occasionally revising or delaying—chamber but one that, by virtue of its less stringent timetable and of the presence of numbers of experts brought in as life peers, can helpfully discuss principles that in the Commons would be subordinated to party requirements; the Lords have also taken special responsibility for legislation in areas of moral and social concern, like abortion or reform of the law relating to homosexuality.

The House of Commons, the center of what Walter Bagehot called the efficient part of the constitution, was kept in firm control by party discipline and, ultimately, by fear of what might happen in an election. The House of Lords, Lloyd George had sneered in 1908, was Mr. Balfour's poodle, to fetch and carry for him, bark for him, and bite whomever the Tory leader wanted bitten. It might be said that after 1945 the two sides of the House of Commons increasingly came to be their leaders' terriers—noisy, protective, but kept firmly on a lead. Harold Wilson said as much in an angry speech directed to some rebels in the Parliamentary Labour party in March, 1967: "Every dog is allowed one bite, but a different view is taken of a dog that goes on biting all the time. . . . He may not get his license returned when it falls due." Wilson's only error was in making so explicit what in fact everyone knew. In a system that was, as some maintained, increasingly presidential, voters—once, to quote W. S. Gilbert, born "either a little Liberal, or else a little Conservative"—tended to cast their ballots for the candidate who would support one or the other leader, a tendency underlined by the increasing use of television during election campaigns. With this qualification in mind, we may now turn to the stately alternation of parties and leaders as they brought their different styles to bear on issues that lay almost beyond politics.

THE FORTUNES OF THE PARTIES

Conservatism Resurgent, 1950–1955

The life of the Parliament elected in 1945 ended in 1950. In February, a general election registered the country's satiation with reform and austerity. From a majority of 146 in 1945, the Labour party sank to a majority of 6 in 1950, though it won a larger proportion of the popular vote (46.7 per cent as against 43.7 per cent for the Conservatives) than this striking drop would suggest. The burden imposed by this narrow majority was nearly intolerable, the more so as the opposition, scenting blood, gave little quarter. The ministers themselves, after five years of unprecedented legislative accomplishment, were tired; some were near death: Bevin died in 1951, Cripps a year later. A change in command was clearly in prospect, and there were signs of a change in basic policy as well.

Cripps had stepped down as Chancellor of the Exchequer, to be succeeded by Hugh Gaitskell, a university economist who spoke for the able, younger, less colorful technocrats who seemed clearly the heirs to power in the party. Under Gaitskell's superintendence, government policy shifted still more from the physical controls so natural to Labour thinking since the First World War to indirect fiscal manipulation of the economy. To the aging left wing, and to a small group of younger recruits on the left, these changes were anathema. Bevan, who said bitterly that he knew the leadership had to go to a "desiccated calculating machine," drew the malcontents about him by his oratory and emotional appeal. In 1951, along with Harold Wilson, he had resigned from office in protest over the heavy commitment to armaments in Gaitskell's 1951 budget and in particular over the nominal charge of one shilling for each prescription under the National Health Service, a modest compromise with the principle of free care to which Gaitskell had resorted to bring his budget more nearly into balance. Thus the lines were drawn for the intraparty struggles of the next decade.

Immediately, Labour could do no more than mark time until another general election. When it took place in October, 1951, Labour still commanded some 200,000 more votes than the Conservatives. But a redistribution of seats in 1949 had merged a number of safe Labour constituencies in poor areas that had been heavily bombed or from which people had fled as soon as they could, and had added seats for the fast-growing dormitory suburbs of large towns, which were likely on balance to go Conservative. Redistribution had contributed to Labour's small margin in 1950; now it gave the Conservatives a majority of 26 — not large but enough to allow a confident government, facing a Labour opposition in disarray, to survive for nearly the statutory life of the Parliament.

Churchill returned as prime minister. Not many knew that he had suffered two strokes in 1949 and 1950, and only a fourth in June, 1953 (there had been another a year before) made it apparent to most observers how handicapped he was. Determined to hold on to office, in some ways distrusting Eden (who was himself ailing), Churchill did not resign until April, 1955 — and then under pressure. For long periods he was ineffective; his mind wandered and he could not remember figures; he was in any event out of sympathy with the age into which he had survived — except in foreign affairs, which deeply concerned him, in which his reputation was deservedly great, and the shape of which, in a period of cold war, he had foreseen in his famous "iron curtain" speech in Fulton, Missouri, in 1946. Because Eden, too, was chiefly concerned with foreign affairs, the domestic leadership fell to two creative veterans of the struggle to modernize the social and industrial outlook of their party, R. A. Butler, at the Exchequer, and Harold Macmillan, as Minister of Housing and Local Government.

The Conservatives undid little that they had inherited from Labour. Most of the nationalization measures were retained: the election gave them no mandate to do otherwise, and there was by no means agreement among the party or its leaders that wholesale denationalization would be a wise step. Beyond some minor reorganization, two moves were made. Iron and steel, by far the most controversial of the Labour actions, was returned to private ownership, although the process took years and one large steel combine was never sold. Much though not all long-distance trucking, which Labour had nationalized in an effort to encourage a better coordination of road and rail services, was also returned to private enterprise. The most controversial desertion of the principle of government ownership was a breach in a state-owned monopoly created by the Conservatives in the mid-twenties; in 1954, as a concession to Conservative backbenchers and to a concerted, well-financed campaign, Parliament authorized a second television channel (the BBC had begun full-scale television transmission in the late forties) to be financed by advertising. Anathema to Labour and to everyone who cared about quality and the educational potential of the medium, commercial television became an instant success, a new means for diffusing American influence, and the overwhelming preference of viewers throughout the country.

Nothing was done to alter the basic structure of the welfare state. Expenditure on welfare rose from just under 14 per cent of the gross national product in 1951 to just over 16 per cent in 1959, and Macmillan far outstripped Labour's performance by fulfilling his seemingly rash campaign promise to build 300,000 houses in a year.* The

---

*A minister who later held the same post wrote: "I am beginning to discover. . . . that the name 'Ministry of Housing and Local Government' is an extraordinary misnomer. In fact the Ministry does no housebuilding at all. The people who build are either the local authorities or private-enterprise builders. Our Ministry is a Ministry for permissions [and] regulations. . . . Of course, Ministers in the past have always talked about housing drives and pretended to carry them out. But what they have really done is to add up the figures and take credit for the creation of houses which are largely the responsibility . . . of the Ministry of Public Building and Works, who deal with housing industry, and . . . of the Chancellor of the Exchequer, who fixes the rate of interest which largely determines how many private-sector houses are built." Richard Crossman, The Diaries of a Cabinet Minister, I (1975), p. 43.

government took office in the midst of a sterling crisis sparked by the Korean War, by the running down of reserves when Sterling Area countries spent windfall profits on imports from outside the area, and by increasing expenditures on armaments; the bank rate was raised (4 per cent now seems ludicrously low, but it had stood at 2 per cent since 1932), food subsidies were cut, and before long a sharp downturn in world commodity prices helped the situation to right itself. Another crisis in 1955 was met with an expansionary budget, which had soon to be replaced with a deflationary one. But through most of the early fifties it seemed that Conservative "freedom" was working. The remaining wartime controls were abandoned, and a wide range of goods became readily available to those who could afford them. For the first time in fifty years, perhaps ever, Britain knew true prosperity, a feeling evident in the look and spirit of the country. Though poverty persisted, especially among the old, the range of satisfactions available to most people with jobs had greatly increased: working-class families found themselves better housed, better fed, better amused (at least in some respects) than their parents had been; and to young men and women with good jobs in factories, shops, or offices indulgence became possible, at times almost a cult. The surge of well-being, coupled with awareness that Britain offered much to admire in the realms of art and intellect,* led to proud talk of a new Elizabethan age, when, on the death of her father George VI, Queen Elizabeth II came to the throne in February, 1952, and was crowned on June 2, 1953. On the day after the coronation, *The Times*, alarmed by the overconfidence, warned that the phrase was in danger of becoming "an incantation, a magician's hey presto!, as if the nation's new stature could be established merely by proclaiming it. The words are no more than a challenge. Only years of effort can turn them into a description." But there is little evidence that anyone listened.

The complacency of the fifties seems to suggest that the political passions aroused by the Labour government were only an interruption of the long-term retreat from politics in English life. Unpolitical ages are times when political parties turn in upon themselves and not infrequently fall apart. It happened in very different ways to both Labour and the Conservatives.

In one sense, Labour's difficulty was the old one of a radical party that has seen its program enacted: finding a new program consistent with its ideals. But Labour's problem was worse than that. There was disagreement about the ideals themselves, and there was the even more threatening possibility that voters were simply no

---

*See below, pp. 622–626.

longer to be wooed by appeals to socialism and social justice. The Conservative majority rose to nearly 60 in the general election of 1955 and to 100 in 1959; each victory brought a fresh crop of predictions of Labour's decline and ultimate disappearance, and a new round of internecine struggles that suggested the predictions might be right.

Attlee retained the leadership of the party until 1955, when he resigned and entered the House of Lords as Earl Attlee. His resignation brought out into the open the bitter quarrel that had developed between Hugh Gaitskell and Aneurin Bevan, a quarrel that, as we have seen, was rooted in disagreements about defense—nuclear defense in particular—and about the right means of controlling the economy and the ends to which that control was directed. Two years after Gaitskell's election to the leadership, Bevan made his peace, taking over as the shadow foreign secretary, an honorable retreat for one who had gambled and lost. In 1960 he died, mourned as much by his old enemies as his old friends. But the former Bevanites, who came to be known (from the important radical journal) as the *Tribune* group, were not reconciled.

In their eyes, Gaitskell was no socialist. In actual fact, Gaitskell had been at work on a number of schemes that, if not socialist in the old sense of the term, were certainly socialist in their emphasis on equality. As a practical politician, he saw that the old panaceas were on their way to becoming political liabilities. In this belief he moved to get the party to modify the famous fourth clause of its constitution, which called for "common ownership of the means of production," which to most people meant nationalization in the style of 1945–1949. That form of nationalization might still have its place, at least as a threat to bring a recalcitrant industry into line, but other courses might be preferable—breaking up monopolies, shareholder democracy, or "socialization" of the economy through government purchase of shares and the use of dividends for social purposes. In 1961, with little difficulty, Gaitskell got his revised clause 4, as well as a reversal of the surprise stand the party had taken in 1960 in favor of unilateral disarmament. During 1962 he built up an enviable reputation, marred only in the eyes of his admirers by his rejection of British entry into the Common Market. Suddenly, early in 1963, he died, after a brief illness. An unedifying struggle for the leadership ensued, the chief candidates being George Brown, an ebullient trade unionist and Harold Wilson, who had resigned with Bevan in 1951; as leader of the Bevanite wing, Wilson had been an advocate of unilateralism and the maintenance of clause 4. His victory in the contest promised a reversal of what Gaitskell had labored so long to bring about—or seemed to promise it to those who failed to see in Wilson a remarkably astute political opportunist.

To Suez and Back, 1955–1964

The success of the Conservatives in capturing the national mood and flattering its complacency and optimism was broken at only one point, in the Suez crisis of 1956. Although the early fifties were a period of marking time in decolonization, progress had been made in Egypt. A nominally independent kingdom since 1922, Egypt underwent a military revolution in 1952 that overthrew King Farouk and ultimately placed Colonel Gamal Abdel Nasser in power; Colonel Nasser quickly moved to assume the leadership of the Arab world and so became the principal enemy of Israel, to whose destruction the Arab countries were pledged. In 1954, the British agreed to withdraw their troops from the Suez Canal Zone and so removed the buffer between Egyptians and Israelis. But as the British withdrew, Egypt began to play the game of so many emerging states in the fifties, competitive bargaining for economic aid from the United States and the Soviet Union: the symbol of Colonel Nasser's Egypt was to be a high dam at Aswan on the Nile.

In the midst of these negotiations Anthony Eden became prime minister, schooled by long experience in foreign affairs (and correspondingly inexperienced in domestic matters) but less buoyant than he had been, through illness and, perhaps, from the long wait he had endured as Churchill's heir apparent. In 1955 John Foster Dulles offered to build the dam with British assistance, but suddenly withdrew the offer, forcing the British meekly to acquiesce. Colonel Nasser ultimately got his dam from Russia, but his immediate course was to announce that he would build the dam himself with revenues from the Suez Canal, which he nationalized on July 26, 1956, in violation of all the agreements protecting the rights of the Suez Canal Company, jointly owned by the British and French governments and a host of individual stockholders, mostly French. It was a typical nationalist expropriation, unusual only in the scale of the enterprise and the curious emotional investment among French and British alike in this hallowed "life line" to the East.

The British government set about finding expedients to undo Nasser's damage—an international conference, a Canal Users' Association to operate the Canal once Egyptian operation broke down (which it did not), an appeal to the United Nations. Eden, shocked out of all reason, was living 1938 over again. Then, at least in his own view, he nearly alone among Chamberlain's cabinet had insisted on standing up to the dictators; now he would stand up to Nasser. From the beginning of the crisis, a military plan had been concerted with the French and, in some ways, with the Israelis, whose forces invaded Egypt on October 29 and quickly defeated the Egyptian army.

France and England at once demanded withdrawal of all forces from the vicinity of the Canal, an ultimatum which Nasser rejected. French and British troops thereupon launched an invasion at Port Said. It was one of the worst blunders in British history, made by a man assumed to be a master diplomatist. Imprisoned in a historical analogy, and quite unchecked in the use of his vast powers as prime minister, Eden moved ahead, consulting only a few key ministers, informing the cabinet at the last minute, and keeping Parliament in the dark; party loyalty was enough (with a few exceptions) to gain him support when he sought it. This frankly aggressive action on an utterly disproportionate pretext tarnished Britain's reputation for probity and sound diplomatic sense. Perhaps worst of all, it distracted world attention from the Russian suppression of the Hungarian uprising that was taking place at the same time.

The old imperial nerve was touched. Much of the country supported the operation. But an intensely critical reaction surfaced in some influential circles in Great Britain, and, more important, in the United States and at the United Nations. On November 6, the invasion was called off, with a claim that it had done its work. So, disastrously, it had. British gold and dollar reserves dropped precipitously, a pipeline had been cut in Syria, the Canal was blocked by the Egyptians—and then, after all, the Canal proved to be less vital than had been thought, for the disruption of traffic between the Mediterranean and the Red Sea caused few undue hardships. In January, 1957, Eden resigned, ill and aware that his party's popularity had seriously declined, although his parliamentary majority was never in danger. The choice of a successor lay between Butler and Macmillan, and, on advice from Churchill and Lord Salisbury, the Queen sent for Macmillan.

Few politicians have had so unenviable a task; few politicians have acquitted themselves so well. Within a year, Suez seemed an almost forgotten incident in the historic past. Macmillan, though he had been involved in the Suez decisions, restored the party's morale and established his own authority in the country; in October, 1959, he won a resounding victory in a general election. Much of his success was owing to his special combination of talents. He was, as we have seen, an inventive and thoughtful political analyst, unafraid to propose steps that other members of his party might call socialist. Except for his brief tenure of the Foreign Office in 1955, he handled every ministerial assignment with distinction. He was, moreover, a ruthless politician, willing to cut down opponents or to jettison inconvenient friends and able to keep them from raising a cabal against him. The roll of his victims is impressive. His chancellor of the exchequer, Peter Thorneycroft, and some other lesser ministers resigned in 1958 to protest against rising government expenditures; Macmillan offhandedly referred as he left for a trip abroad to settling "these little local difficulties" — and Thorneycroft did not return to office until 1960 and then only to a minor post. Even the formidable Lord Salisbury, who resigned in 1957 when Macmillan decided to end the detention of Archbishop Makarios, the leader of the pro-Greek faction on Cyprus, was neutralized and never again came near to power. And when Selwyn Lloyd, an old associate of Macmillan and foreign secretary from 1955 to 1960, became chancellor of the exchequer and brought down violent if undeserved unpopularity by his proposal for an anti-inflationary "pay pause," he was sacrificed in a wholesale purge in 1962 that unceremoniously threw out seven members of the cabinet.* But with all this decisiveness went the Macmillan images, of which one could take one's pick, whether it was Supermac of Vicky's famous cartoon, or the placid, comfortable, completely unflappable Edwardian who went grouse-shooting in August wearing outlandish plus-fours. In the 1959 campaign Macmillan turned television to superb advantage: he and his party argued, and the voters agreed, that "you never had it so good."

Prior to the general election of 1959 Macmillan's skills were directed chiefly to rebuilding his party. After the election, with a comfortable majority, Macmillan undertook a series of policy initiatives that in retrospect are impressive, though at the time and since much that he did seemed improvisational. To be sure, the nagging difficulties of the economy called forth further installments of stop-go, resulting in a couple of years of stagnation; the economic growth that was increasingly the theme of the sixties — not just in Britain — eluded the government's best efforts. But new machinery was set up in 1962 to make possible in Britain the kind of planning that had been so successful in reviving the French economy. The National Economic Development Council, quickly nicknamed "Neddy," was (and is) an advisory body made up of the appropriate economic ministers and representatives of the Confederation of British Industries and the Trades Union Congress; its periodic meetings have proved useful occasions for exchange of views and, sometimes, of hard negotiations. But the heart of Neddy lay in its staff, who were to undertake studies of the best means to attain growth and of the probable consequences of the various courses available; with sound knowledge and firm advice, it was thought, management and labor

---

*When the Lord Chancellor, one of the victims, complained that he would give more notice to his cook, someone remarked that a good cook was harder to find than a good lord chancellor. John Barnes, "The Record," in David McKie and Chris Cook, eds., *The Decade of Disillusion: British Politics in the Sixties* (1972), p. 16.

would be able to make their own plans within a general outline of the best course for the nation. Moreover, Macmillan established a number of inquiries into some specific aspects of society and the economy — traffic in towns, broadcasting, company law, schools, universities, and others — and their recommendations formed the basis for much future activity.*

Perhaps the most courageous step Macmillan took was his open encouragement of rapid progress towards nationhood in the African colonies.† At the head of a party with many strong ties to white South Africa, Macmillan dared to speak on a tour of that increasingly embattled country in 1960 of the "wind of change" that was sweeping through the continent and that could not be resisted — though South Africa chose to resist, became a republic, and withdrew from the Commonwealth the next year, a loss few were willing openly to regret. As an elder statesman, Macmillan played an active role in international negotiations, trying to keep conversations going when the United States and the Soviet Union came close to nuclear war in 1962 over the installation of Russian missiles in Cuba. In the same year he brought off something of a coup in defense policy. Developing the hydrogen bomb, first exploded in 1957, had left the question of a delivery system to be solved. By 1960 it was apparent that Britain could not continue to develop her own Blue Streak system; the cost was beyond what she could afford, and the system would be obsolete by the time it was operational. The United States promised Britain that it could use Skybolt air-to-ground missiles, in exchange for American use of Holy Loch in Scotland as a base for the submarines carrying Polaris missiles — a provision that alarmed opponents of nuclear warfare and ordinary citizens worried about retaliation. Then, in 1962, the Americans cancelled their Skybolt program, and at a December meeting with President Kennedy at Nassau in the Bahamas, Macmillan extracted a promise of Polaris missiles, for which Britain would build nuclear submarines, a satisfactory ending to an unhappy episode, though an ending that made clear once again the dependence of Britain's defense policy on the United States.

Macmillan's main strategy, however, was to carry Britain into the Common Market, a goal that apparently lay behind a reconstruction of his government in 1960, when two strong Europeans were put into key positions — the Earl of Home as foreign secretary,‡ a choice

---

*The names of the heads of three of the inquiries became almost household words: Professor Buchanan on traffic, Dr. Beeching on railways, Professor Robbins on universities; on the last two, see below, 612–613, 615.
†See below, p. 616.
‡The Scottish name Home is pronounced Hume.

few would have thought possible because he was in the House of Lords, and the former chief whip, Edward Heath, as Home's deputy in the House of Commons. The Conservative party was divided, and the Labour Party was committed by its leader against joining Europe on grounds of ties with the Commonwealth and the historic separation from the Continent: Gaitskell's emotional statement in 1962 that entering the Market would end a thousand years of history allowed government propagandists to answer that the Conservatives offered not history books but the future. With strong support from key segments of industry and much of the intellectual community, negotiations were carried forward with great pertinacity by Edward Heath and seemed fairly well set for success when General de Gaulle held a press conference in January, 1963, during which he interposed a personal veto on British entry, a reflection of his fear of Anglo-Saxon hegemony and a step in his campaign to turn the Common Market into an adjunct of his nationalist reconstruction of France. Macmillan's gamble had failed.

At the end of that summer Macmillan fell ill; more than that, the magic his extraordinary personality had worked on the country in 1959 had slipped away. In part, he was a victim of the fashionable criticism of "the Establishment," a new catchword that he and his government so well embodied; his Edwardian manner made a perfect target for a group of young and sometimes amusing satirists. More seriously, unemployment had risen, not to prewar levels but high enough to be painfully evident in a country where for years jobs had gone begging, and there was discontent within the Conservative party, where the Prime Minister's cavalier treatment of colleagues was not forgotten. Hoping to stay on at least through the party conference in October, Macmillan was rushed to the hospital just as the conference opened. When his resignation came, there were hurried consultations about the succession. R. A. Butler, so long in the wings, was a natural choice, but he was old; Reginald Maudling, the Chancellor of the Exchequer, was young and able but an impression of indolence weighed against him; Lord Hailsham, the candidate of the right wing and a stirring orator, had told the party conference that he would renounce his title as a recent statute permitted, and become once again Quintin Hogg. An outside possibility was Lord Home, and Home was Macmillan's recommendation to the queen. If there had been a surprise when Home had been named foreign secretary, there was virtual consternation at the prospect of a peer as prime minister: no prime minister had sat in the upper house since Lord Salisbury retired in 1902, and Curzon's membership in that house had worked against his ambition in 1923. The tradition held: also taking advantage of the renunciation act, the new prime minister returned to the House of Commons as Sir Alec Douglas-Home.*

The choice of Sir Alec by what seemed to be an aristocratic cabal hurt the Conservative party badly, the more so as the party had already been seriously embarrassed by some compromising incidents. Throughout the fifties the country was shaken from time to time by revelations of security scandals in which British subjects of presumably unimpeachable credentials had been caught dealing with Soviet agents. In some instances, the fault lay in sloppy administrative procedures; in others, insufficient attention had been paid to routine security investigations, a carelessness that appeared to rest on the assumption that a good background, whatever personal shortcomings there might be, was a reliable guarantee of honor. But none of these revelations had the impact of a scandal that broke in 1963 when the Secretary of State for War in Macmillan's cabinet, John Profumo, admitted to having had an affair with a self-styled "model," Christine Keeler, who had also been at the same time the mistress of a Soviet naval attaché. After admitting that he had lied to the House when earlier in the year he had categorically denied reports of the liaison, Profumo resigned; a subsequent investigation by a respected high court judge set at rest rumors of a breach of security; but the moral question remained. The somewhat exaggerated outrage struck a further blow at whatever was left of the deference to "natural rulers" that Bagehot had found at the heart of English government in the nineteenth century.

The probity and transparent decency of Sir Alec Douglas-Home at least rescued his party from the worst consequences of the scandal; but he proved to be colorless and at times politically inept. When he confessed, self-deprecatingly, that he had to work out economic problems with match-sticks, it seemed less like humor than a confirmation of a growing feeling that the country needed new, vigorous leadership. This Harold Wilson, speaking for the Labour party, promised to give. In the general election of October, 1964, Labour won an ambiguous victory, with a margin of four seats. But Wilson set out to rule as though he had a solid working margin, secure in the knowledge that he was not going to be turned out in favor of a demoralized Conservative party and the return of Douglas-Home. In the summer of 1965, Sir Alec resigned as leader of his party. For the first time an election was held for a Conservative leader instead of

*After Harold Wilson made a speech in which he said that the process of democratic advance had ground to a halt with a 14th Earl," the prime minister in a television interview came up with a cutting reply: "I suppose Mr. Wilson, when you come to think of it, is the 14th Mr. Wilson."

allowing the choice mysteriously to emerge from the inner councils that guarded the party's mystique. Edward Heath was chosen, the first Conservative leader to have been educated at a grammar school instead of a public school. In March, 1966, Wilson dissolved parliament to strengthen his majority, which he managed to stretch to 96.

A False Dawn, 1964–1970

To secure that working majority in a new election was necessarily the first tactical consideration in Wilson's mind when he took office in 1964. But he and his ministers found themselves facing an economic crisis of surprising proportions, though some of the difficulty righted itself fairly quickly. The new government chose, understandably enough, to put the worst face on the situation and to blame it on the Tories. They were also able to make a great show of decisiveness, in ways especially appealing to their more militant supporters but that impressed much of the rest of the country as well. An import surcharge was at once imposed — with assurances abroad that it was a temporary expedient — along with an export rebate; a corporation tax and a capital gains tax were soon introduced, followed later by limitations on business expense accounts. After the second election, a selective employment tax, assessed on each employee but rebated to manufacturing industry, was introduced, an ingenious device that raised revenue handily but that failed in its aims of enforcing more efficient use of labor and of diverting labor from the service sector to manufacturing; what it did instead was to alienate the business community further and to damage the government's reputation with consumers as the public was made aware of how the tax pushed up prices. These steps towards stringency did not, however, deeply impress international financial circles, where restoring confidence was essential to escape from crisis, for Labour also moved to fulfill a number of its costly campaign promises — removal of the charge for National Health Service prescriptions (the issue on which Wilson had resigned in 1951), a steep but deserved increase in pensions to catch up with inflation, and, more slowly, renationalization of the steel industry in 1967.

Wilson had campaigned on the theme that only Labour could find the means and the will to manage the economy properly (Wilson had, after all, begun as an economist at Oxford) and to harness the promise of a new technological age. To that end, the government swiftly moved in 1964 to create a new Department of Economic Affairs, a Ministry of Technology, and a Ministry of Overseas Development. The first was confided to George Brown, whose flamboyant style gave the impression of great creativity. But though Brown and James Callaghan, the Chancellor of the Exchequer, worked reasonably well together, a department that threatened the economic monopoly that the Treasure had been accustomed to exercise seemed, and may have been, divisive; the DEA played a less central role once George Brown went to the Foreign Office in 1966 and was quietly abolished three years later. The other new ministries were filled by representatives of the left: Frank Cousins, head of the Transport and General Workers Union, the largest in the country, was a surprising but imaginative choice for Technology; Barbara Castle, a close associate of Wilson and a dedicated left-winger, went to Overseas Affairs; and when Cousins resigned in 1966 over Wilson's policy of wage restraint, he was succeeded by Anthony Wedgwood Benn, a former peer whose ambition had forced the passage of the renunciation act and who was to become the most vocal, clever, and consistent spokesman for the left in the Labour movement. Though it was not mentioned, much that the Labour government did was a continuation of initiatives begun in the preceding Conservative administration—use of the consultative machinery of the NEDC (to which Wilson added "little Neddies" for specific industries), the recommendations of the investigative bodies Macmillan had appointed, and the commitment to indicative planning, which culminated in a much-publicized but largely cosmetic and ineffectual National Plan published in 1965. The crisis, though occasionally easing, resisted all the efforts of an able, persuasive team. Wilson rejected the advice that came from more and more of his colleagues that the pound must be devalued once again, but in November, 1967, the step could no longer be avoided; the adjustment downward from $2.80 to $2.40, Wilson told the public, did not mean that the pound in their pockets was devalued—but of course it was, by higher prices.

Much of Wilson's effort was taken up by depressing circumstances abroad. The United States involvement in Vietnam had become full-scale war, incomprehensible to most of the English and hateful to the left, whose disenchantment grew as Wilson, with desperate skill, continued to avoid the denunciation of that war that the left wanted and that Britain's link with the United States, however strained, would not permit. The decision of the self-governing colony of Rhodesia to declare its independence in 1964, in order to maintain white supremacy over the black majority in the country, meant endless negotiations and concessions that led nowhere. In the spring of 1966, in a remarkable turnabout, Wilson announced his intention of applying for membership in the Common Market, an issue that continued to divide his party; a year later, in May, 1967, the formal application was made, only to encounter once more a firm personal rejection by General de Gaulle, the no that Wilson had said he would not take for an answer but that he had to swallow.

By far the most remarkable policy shift occurred in the area of industrial relations. It was hoped that the improvement of benefits, raised taxation on the well-off, and the stricter limitations on business perks would make wage restraint acceptable to the trade unions, and though in general the TUC gave the government support, there was increasing restiveness in the trade-union movement, and a number of left-wing leaders took advantage of it. In May, 1966, Wilson spoke out against restrictive practices; a few days later began a seamen's strike, which lasted for nearly seven weeks, resisting all Wilson's efforts at mediation and leading him to denounce the strike for blowing the economy off course; it was, he said, the work of a "tightly knit group of politically motivated men," some of them Communists. He moved to secure an early warning system, through compulsory notification, of increases in wages and prices, which the Prices and Incomes Board might hold up pending investigation; this brought the principled resignation of Frank Cousins from the cabinet. Soon Wilson resorted to a six-month wage freeze, followed by another six months of severe restraint, to be made legally binding by legislation, a step he carried, at a cost, in the party and in the Trades Union Congress. Finally, in mid-1968, the Donovan Commission, appointed three years earlier to investigate trade unions, reported. Recognizing the need for reform in the system of industrial relations, it called for an Industrial Relations Commission to supervise reforms, which the majority saw as voluntary, but which a powerful dissent argued could only be achieved by legislation. Barbara Castle, now at the Ministry of Employment, had become increasingly convinced that the minority view was correct, a view Wilson also came to share. In January, 1969, a "white paper" (a policy statement prior to legislation) was published; called *In Place of Strife*, it proposed giving the government powers to delay an unofficial strike to allow for conciliation, to order a membership ballot before the calling of an official strike, and to invoke penalties for failure to comply. The document split the cabinet and the parliamentary party and brought the National Executive Committee of the Labour party and the entire trade-union movement into the field against it. Negotiations finally brought a retreat to a possible rule change by the TUC, but when even that proved unacceptable, Wilson had to profess satisfaction with "a solemn and binding understanding" that, without changing the rules, they would be interpreted in a way consistent with the prime minister's wishes — an assurance that may have been solemn but was certainly not binding. This crushing defeat made even more apparent the heavy dependence of the Labour party on the trade unions and highlighted, as it had never been before, the position the unions had attained as, virtually, a separate estate of the realm.

A Time of Troubles, 1970–1978

Discontent with Wilson's leadership had been growing in the Labour party well before his abject defeat on the trade-union question. Surrounded by a group of personal advisers who drew much hostility from party regulars, Wilson ran his government in an extremely casual way, quarreled increasingly with the press, seemed less infallible than he had once appeared in his political judgment, and even showed a certain tiredness in his acknowledged mastery of public and parliamentary debate. Voters' disenchantment with Labour seemed clearly registered in the statistics of bye-elections and public opinion polls. But there was no obvious alternative, in the party or out of it.

There was similar dissatisfaction on the Conservative side. Edward Heath, always distrusted in his party, had failed to impress himself on the country: snobs might decry his relatively humble origins and his acquired enthusiasm for the expensive and aristocratic sport of yacht racing, but he struck most people, if he struck them at all, as dull, cold, and ineffectual—in debates in parliament, where Wilson always bested him, or on the television screen. Heath had rebuilt a shadow cabinet of relatively unknown men, who had not yet made their mark, and it was unclear how voters would react to Conservative efforts to define a genuinely alternative approach to political, economic, and social problems. At the end of January, 1970, the shadow cabinet met to hammer out a program for an election that was certain to come soon. The legislative and administrative proposals that emerged can be summed up under these heads: reform of parliamentary procedures and the committee system; tax reform, particularly a shift from direct to indirect taxation; improved pensions; tighter control of immigration, with Commonwealth and foreign immigrants treated on the same footing; support for the police in dealing with demonstrations; the reworking of housing subsidies; leaving failing firms to the mercies of the market; and an industrial relations bill, to succeed where Wilson failed. The meeting took place at the Selsdon Park Hotel, south of London. Here was a perfect target for Wilsonian scorn and threat: what had emerged from the meeting, he said, was Selsdon Man—the allusion to that famous archeological fraud, the Piltdown Man, was unmistakable—"designing a system of society for the ruthless and the pushing," leaving everyone else out on his own.

By the spring of 1970 the immediate economic future looked bleak, but the polls showed a swing away from the large lead the Conservatives had been given some time before. In an unpromising situation, Wilson chose an unpromising month, June, for the election. He expected victory and lost. With a slight lead in the popular vote, the Conservatives won 330 seats as against Labour's 287, with six Liberals and seven from other minor parties. Heath took office with a largely untried team; the two distinguished senior members were Sir Alec Douglas-Home,* the foreign secretary, and the Chancellor of the Exchequer, Iain MacLeod, whose sudden death after only a month in office removed a sophisticated, innovative mind from the party's councils. But Heath confounded his critics by moving with remarkable boldness to carry out the party's promises — and to reverse course on some of them. Negotiations were begun at once to enter the Common Market and concluded within a year, with entry to take effect formally at the beginning of January, 1973.† The bill passed the Commons by a margin of 112. Heath confidently allowed a free vote among his supporters in the Commons, losing 39 votes in his own party; though Labour whipped its members, 69 rebels refused to go along with official Labour policy of opposing entry on the Conservatives' terms. In 1972 Wilson declared that when Labour returned to office it would hold a national referendum on membership, a proposal that provoked the resignations of three of the shadow cabinet's leading Europeanists, chief among them Roy Jenkins, who had been Chancellor of the Exchequer prior to 1970. When entry actually came, the Labour party chose to boycott the European Assembly in Strasbourg, to which it was entitled to send members.

Not since 1926 had there been such a bad year for strikes as 1970; the record in 1971 was worse. In that year the Heath government carried its Industrial Relations Bill. The trade unions were offered binding and enforceable collective bargaining agreements and the compulsory disclosure by employers of certain categories of information — sweeteners for the many bitter pills; even though employers were as subject as trade unions to some of the provisions, the unionists knew that they were the principal targets. Trade unions and employers' associations were required to register so that their rules might be supervised; a code of fair industrial practices was to be drawn up; the right to join or not to join a trade union was made

---

*In 1974 Sir Alec returned to the House of Lords as a life peer, with the title Lord Home of the Hirsel.
†General de Gaulle had resigned the French presidency in 1969 and died a year later.

statutory, with safeguards against unfair dismissals for either course; the minister could order a cooling-off period and a secret ballot of the membership of a trade union in a dispute that threatened the national interest; and a new structure of labor tribunals was established, topped by the Industrial Relations Court, a new division of the High Court. With few exceptions unions refused to register and so denied themselves the advantages that would have followed; they boycotted the Industrial Relations Court — which had the almost impossible task of serving as both mediator and adjudicator — and mounted a steady personal attack on Sir John Donaldson, who headed it.

The tax structure was altered. Joining the EEC required imposition of a Value Added Tax, which replaced the older purchase tax and Selective Employment Tax; direct taxation in the higher brackets was lowered, with an eye to political advantage as well as to encouraging investment. Despite the difficulties on the labor front, the general economic outlook in 1971 was favorable: the pound was strong at about $2.60, and floating it that summer seemed no threat; there was a surplus on visible trade; reserves were high; and in early 1972 the inflation rate stood at an easily containable 6 per cent. The budget introduced in the spring was expansionist, designed to stimulate the growth the country needed (in part) to cover its mounting social costs.

The government had had to reverse itself on one aspect of immigration policy when in 1972 President Idi Amin of Uganda, whose resort to unspeakable mass killings was yet to be learned about, decided to expel Asian residents who had·dominated the economic life of the new country; defensible at the time as a move to return Africa to the Africans, the action left thousands of British subjects homeless and stripped of their means of livelihood and forced the British, as an elementary exercise in humanity, to allow some 25,000 of them to enter Britain. The proclaimed Tory allegiance to the shock therapy of the free market was also shot through with notable exceptions. In 1971, the famous firm of Rolls-Royce came to the edge of bankruptcy because of losses incurred in developing aircraft engines for the American firm of Lockheed, forcing the government to nationalize the aerospace operations of the company (though not the equally celebrated automobile manufacturer) in the interests of national defense as well as employment; and the government had to come similarly to the rescue of the Upper Clyde Shipbuilders, a combination of older firms formed with government blessing in 1968, when that troubled industry proved unable to survive against foreign, especially Japanese, competition. Heath had also insisted that, though the framework of industrial relations was to be subjected to government reorganization and supervision, collective bargaining was to remain within the ambit of economic freedom. Restraint in both wages and prices was necessary to keep inflation in check, but it was hoped that the reality of growth would make a voluntary program of limitation acceptable. But labor's unwillingness to cooperate led to direct intervention — a five-month imposed freeze in November, 1972, to be followed by a second stage of limited increases, and a third stage from November, 1973, in which increases would be supervised by a Price Commission and a Pay Board.

The government's calculations were thrown into utter irrelevance by the sharp rise in oil prices imposed by the Arab nations in the aftermath of the Yom Kippur War against Israel in September–October, 1973. Britain coped more effectively with the immediate problems posed by the oil shortage than did most of the other western nations, but the fragility of her economy could not withstand the inflationary shock of so great a distortion of the cost of energy, coupled as it was with the increasing truculence of a trade-union movement determined to make Conservative rule impossible. At the end of 1973 it was clear that Stage 3 was not going to be implemented with the help of the trade unions. Electricity supplies were already threatened by oil shortages when railwaymen imposed a ban on overtime working and the miners, crucial to the fuel supply, took the same step. A state of emergency had been proclaimed in November — with the minimum lending rate for banks raised to 13 per cent — and a month later the government announced that from January 1 industry would be limited to three days of working per week, to conserve fuel supplies. Zero growth was assumed as a consequence. With its usual unity of effort in an emergency, the country responded well to the three-day week, sharing out the sacrifices and actually increasing output. But the situation proved intolerable in the long run, and the government risked an election to strengthen its hand in the coming confrontation with the miners. On February 5, 1974, 81 per cent of the miners voted for a national strike. Two days later Heath announced the dissolution of Parliament and an election to be held on February 28. When Labour emerged with a four-vote margin over the Conservatives, 301 to 297, the balance of power in the House of Commons clearly lay with the minor parties — 14 Liberals and 23 others, mostly of various national persuasions. In the few days immediately following the election, negotiations took place between Heath and Jeremy Thorpe, the Liberal leader, but failed to produce a coalition; Heath thereupon resigned and Harold Wilson returned to office.

The immediate crisis was dealt with in a way satisfactory to the country. When the miners had struck in 1972, a public inquiry recommended a 25 per cent increase in wages, far beyond the government's guidelines but believed to be agreeable to the public as an exception. Now another exception was made: few could be found to argue that the dangerous and unpleasant work of the miners did not deserve special treatment. The settlement agreed to, the three-day week was ended on March 9, and the state of emergency came to an end two days later. The Labour government did not intend a free-for-all but pinned its hopes for wage restraint on an understanding with the unions—grandiosely (and with considerable historical violence) called the "social contract"—that wage demands would be kept within acceptable limits in return for a government guarantee of the "social wage," or benefits, and a frankly socialist policy. The latter was enforced as well by a marked increase in left-wing influence in the National Executive Committee of the Labour party, in trade-union leadership, and in the cabinet itself.

What ensued was an astonishing balancing act by a prime minister known for his riskiness and daring. Michael Foot, a superb orator, Bevan's biographer and devotee, was brought into the Cabinet as minister of employment; already there in force were Barbara Castle, Anthony Wedgwood Benn, Peter Shore, and others from the left, balanced by a group of impressive moderates headed by Roy Jenkins, now Home Secretary. A new list of proposals for further nationalization was put forward, and a National Enterprise Board was established to handle state investment in companies in need of capital (or rescue). The aircraft industry and (with some exceptions forced by the House of Lords) shipbuilding were taken into the public sector over the next two years, but it had hardly been anticipated that the principal concern of the NEB would be British Leyland. That huge combination, the result of a merger in 1968, was the only remaining British-owned company in the automobile industry, and a major employer of labor in the Midlands. Inept management, a wretched record of labor disputes, and the growing appeal of imported cars plunged the company into a cash crisis, compounding a lag in investment, from which nationalization was the only escape. The world-wide recession yielded up still more industries to government control or support, among them the largest agency marketing the popular package tours to the Continent.

The recession cut back orders for British industry but inflation shot out of control, reaching an annual rate of around 25 per cent by mid-1975. Wages for many kept ahead of prices, though they offered the simplest means of breaking out of the upward spiral, and so most of the life of the Labour government was dominated by attempts to keep the unions' demands within manageable limits. Talk about the social contract gradually disappeared, revealing it as at best a myth, at worst an exercise in self-delusion; what counted increasingly was the willingness of three key union leaders — Jack Jones of the TGWU, Hugh Scanlon of the Engineers, both from the left of the movement, and Len Murray, general secretary of the TUC — to persuade unionists into moderating their demands, for fear of bringing down the Labour government and bringing back the "union-bashing" Tories. It was a game with temporary victories, but strong pressures were building up that could in time overpower the counsels of moderation: the native militancy of some shop stewards and major union leaders; the awareness of many more skilled workers that inflation and earlier settlements had eroded the wage differentials appropriate to their superior position; the threat posed to job security by corporate mergers, the increasing dominance of multinational corporations, the growth of the state, and the insistent march of new, labor-saving technology. Some hopes were held out, both inside and outside the labor movement, for improving industrial relations by worker participation in management, a device that has had some success on the Continent and that was once before seriously discussed — in the aftermath of World War I. But reaction to the report of the Bullock Commission in 1976 suggested that management was unwilling to share its traditional prerogatives (though it was probably open to pressure) and, more significantly, that most trade unionists were unwilling to give up their prized freedom of action for shared responsibility.

In check, at least temporarily, on the labor front, the left was smartly outmaneuvered on the Common Market. Wilson's commitment to a referendum was a way of papering over a fundamental split in the party, a split reflected in the cabinet and in the prime minister's abandonment on this issue (and some others) of the traditional doctrine of Cabinet responsibility and unanimity. The promised renegotiation came up with some modification (reasonable enough under Britain's straitened circumstances) of the budgetary contribution. Accordingly, after much debate about the framing of the question, the referendum took place on June 5, 1975, asking simply, "Do you think that the United Kingdom should stay in the European Community?" With a 65 per cent turnout, the vote was two to one in favor of remaining, a margin rolled up in all parts of the country and one that left the advocates of democracy on the left no retreat other than grumbling about details (such as the mode of election of members of the European Parliament) or a minimum of sullen cooperation at the administrative level.

The economic situation, so much worse in Britain than elsewhere, was reflected in a downward slide of the pound, which dipped below $1.70 briefly at the beginning of the summer of 1976.

By the end of that year, Britain had to go to the International Monetary Fund for a huge loan. For many the specter of 1931 was once more raised; then international bankers had set stern conditions for their help, including a sharp cut in unemployment pay. But now the IMF left untouched the vast panoply of social services, whose costs had risen so sharply, and professed itself satisfied with a cutback, not in the absolute size of local government services but in the rate of increase of expenditure on them. The rather surprising moderation of the terms may have reflected political realities, but they were probably more impressive testimony to the salvation that was coming to Britain through a stroke of fortune. In the 1960's the search for oil under the North Sea began in earnest; undersea gas had become the country's sole source by the early seventies, and oil began to flow in significant quantities in 1977, with the promise (greater than originally estimated) that the supply would right the British balance of trade by 1980 and make her an oil-exporting nation for perhaps twenty years after that.

The qualified promise of the economic situation in the late seventies was not paralleled by an equal certainty on the political front. The tiny margin of Labour's victory in February, 1974, was improved in October of the same year, when Labour won 319 seats as against the Conservatives' 277; but the Liberals with 13 and the other parties with 26 continued to hold the balance, and a Labour-Liberal pact (not a coalition) assured that the more extreme proposals of the Labour party would not be carried into law. The leadership in both parties changed. Defeat in a second election doomed Edward Heath, who was blamed more and more for an error of judgment in timing the election of February, 1974. In an election held by the parliamentary party in 1975, Heath was beaten and retreated to the back benches; he was replaced by Margaret Thatcher, who had been his minister of education and science. Coming from a background very like Heath's, Mrs. Thatcher was a cool, ambitious representative of the right wing of the party, seconded, though not with notable tact, by Sir Keith Joseph, the party's principal theoretician and a former minister of health and social security. Like Heath in his period of opposition leadership in the sixties, Mrs. Thatcher made a number of tactical errors and was usually bested at the dispatch box by Wilson, but she established her ascendancy within the party as Heath had never done.

A change took place in the Labour party in the spring of 1976 when Harold Wilson suddenly resigned. His relations with many members of his party had deteriorated still further; he was snappish and impatient and his formidable debating style was declining into rudeness. The infighting among his personal staff became more apparent, and the role of his political secretary, Marcia Williams, was increasingly resented, a resentment not notably calmed when Wilson awarded her a life peerage as Lady Falkender. The honors conferred at the time of Wilson's resignation were also widely criticized, as the recipients tended to come from the new, and sometimes flashy, business circles in which Wilson seemed increasingly to find himself at home. The memories of Lloyd George stirred by this no doubt exaggerated response were overborne by another increasingly convincing parallel—that Wilson was more like Stanley Baldwin than like any other prime minister, a superb parliamentary tactician, self-consciously dedicated to compromise and healing, but without long-range goals.

Wilson was succeeded by James Callaghan, a veteran politician from a non-university, trade-union background. Almost a match for Wilson as a debater (as Mrs. Thatcher repeatedly learned) and his equal as a compromiser but with the capacity for inspiring greater trust, Callaghan carried further the isolation of the left wing at the cabinet and parliamentary level and appeared to have restored his party's capacity to survive in a general election, particularly in an improved economic climate. But divisions in the party remained. Though not distinguished by talent or depth, the left wing continued vocal and visible, particularly in the constituencies, while the moderate wing, despite its growing confidence, lost some of its most impressive members. George Brown (by then Lord George-Brown) had resigned from the party in a dispute with Wilson, and a number of older members of the party followed him into the wilderness, disillusioned and dismayed by the apparent ascendancy of the left and by what they thought trickery and shabbiness in the leadership. Other M.P.'s were driven out by constituency parties who would have no more of them—one former cabinet minister, Reginald Prentice, actually joining the Conservatives in 1977. A number of intellectuals resigned from the party in protest against a growing anti-intellectualism in the party and in its policies, notably in its neglect of, or discrimination against, the universities. The most serious loss of all was the resignation from parliament of Roy Jenkins, the most respected advocate of moderation in the party and its outstanding advocate of the European connection; Jenkins became president of the European Community, taking with him an able younger M.P., David Marquand, as his deputy.* What advantage the Labour party

---

*It is worth pointing out that Jenkins and Marquand have both made distinguished contributions to modern political biography—Jenkins with *Mr. Balfour's Poodle* and his lives of Dilke and Asquith, Marquand with his study of Ramsay MacDonald.

had came not from inherent strength but from uncertainty about the state of the opposition.

Callaghan's tactical skill and the confidence his avuncular personality evoked could not break the political and economic stalemate. While Britain's international economic position continued to improve, the parliamentary deadlock—with Labour dependent on the Liberal and on the various nationalist blocs—continued, though a working majority might in fact have done little to improve the government's performance in the unceasing struggle with inflation, unemployment, sluggish investment, and, increasingly, strikes.* The government stood firm against a long and dangerous strike of firemen, giving notice that in the public sector at least the established guidelines for wage settlements must be maintained; but the private sector was not so amenable to control or persuasion. The winter of 1978–1979, one of the worst in years, was ridden with labor disputes, including one that closed down *The Times*. Callaghan refused to call an election in October, 1978, when it was widely expected; he was certain that an improving economy would provide the basis for a Labour victory. But the polls showed a steady drain of support to the Tories. In the end, however, it was not the economy or labor troubles that brought the government down, but devolution.

The nationalist movement in Wales, resting on a widely spoken Celtic language and on awareness of a distinctive national tradition, was long-established; its focus in the early twentieth century had been on the successful campaign to disestablish the Church of England in Wales. In the 1950's, an office of Welsh affairs was combined with major cabinet-level ministries and then separated, under its own secretary of state, from 1964. The nationalist party, Plaid Cymru,† founded in 1925, drew nearly 80,000 votes in the general election of 1959 and in 1974 captured three seats in Parliament. These successes drew less attention, however, than the surprising appearance of a militant Scottish nationalism. The Scottish National party, founded in 1928, could muster only 22,000 votes in 1959, and the movement was easily dismissed as the agitation of a group of colorful eccentrics and students. But in 1964 that vote was trebled and then successively doubled in 1966, 1970, and February,1974, leveling off at something over 800,000 in the election in October of that year, with 30 per cent of the Scottish vote and 11 seats at Westminster. The movement drew strength from the relative poverty of urban Scot-

*Even so, the British record of time lost in strikes is lower than in other industrial countries.
†Pronounced "Plad Coomry." On disestablishment, see above pp. 457, 465-466.

land, from a sense of relative neglect, and from the heady prospect of fantastic riches soon to flow from oil wells in the North Sea off Scotland. By the mid-seventies there was serious talk of separation, though the practicality of that option might well be doubted. Still, having (like Plaid Cymru) effectively displaced the Liberals as the party of protest, the Scottish Nationalists cut deeply into the vote for both Conservatives and Labour and made the creation of separate assemblies for Wales and Scotland and some greater degree of control than already existed over local affairs a political necessity, though one on which the two main parties were badly split.

At the end of November, 1976, the Labour government introduced a devolution bill, providing for the two assemblies and for a separate executive for each country, though without independent revenue powers, a reservation that embittered the nationalists. Defeated on a motion to impose a timetable on debate, the government withdrew the bill, and a second attempt was made in 1978, issuing in a referendum, that extra-constitutional device that had proved so useful in resolving the equally vexed and divisive question of adherence to the Common Market. The result, in March, 1979, was a surprise to nearly everyone. The plan was overwhelmingly defeated in Wales. In Scotland, while 52 per cent of the voters approved, the turnout was only 66 per cent, and the enabling legislation required a positive vote of at least 40 per cent of all registered voters before devolution could take effect. At the end of the month, sensing a drastic alteration in the parliamentary situation, the Tories engineered a vote of confidence. The Liberals withdrew from their understanding with Labour; so did the Scottish Nationalists; and the motion of no confidence carried by a single vote, 311–310, bringing about a dissolution of Parliament and a general election. The last successful vote of no confidence was against Ramsay MacDonald in 1924.

Public opinion polls suggested that the two parties had drawn fairly close after the midwinter's discontent with Labour. But the results of the election on May 3 gave the Conservatives a majority of forty-three over all other parties; and, except for Ulster, the nationalist parties were virtually eclipsed. A solid working majority, attained despite indications that voters liked Callaghan and distrusted Mrs. Thatcher, seemed to suggest that much of the country—at least in the south where Labour representation was virtually wiped out—was ready for the change that the Tories promised in an election widely billed as the first since 1945 to offer voters a genuine choice.

Mrs. Thatcher and her colleagues had campaigned on the virtues of family, hard work, social discipline, and respect for law, an agenda that openly promised another effort to trim the power of the trade unions and to restore free bargaining within the new framework and that implied (though with decreasing emphasis) further action to restrict immigration and to encourage repatriation. Once in office, the Tories made an open show of support for the new mixed government of blacks and whites that was intended in time to carry Rhodesia into majority rule, despite the violent opposition of guerrilla forces and other African governments and the ambiguous attitude of the United States to the lifting of economic sanctions. But the real key to the government's intentions was the budget introduced in June, which drastically cut income taxes in all brackets, particularly at the top levels, in an effort to channel money into investment, making up for the loss of revenue by a sharp increase in the Value Added Tax on sales. How far this gamble will pay off, and what success the Conservatives will have with yet more perilous initiatives in the areas of immigration, labor, denationalization, and cuts in social services and local government remains to be seen: the international economy and the realities of a politics as responsive to the demand for benefits as to dislike of government interference may prove the much-maligned Butskellism to be more than a disembodied ghost from the fifties and sixties.

THE POSTWAR ERA IN RETROSPECT

Old Themes and New

The Labour government that took office in 1945 established or confirmed the main institutions and much of the official ethos of postwar Britain. A mixed economy of public and private enterprise was firmly established as the norm, but over the next thirty years the nationalized industries were subjected to some minor and some drastic alteration. Along with successive reorganizations, the BBC's television monopoly was challenged, trucking was partially denationalized, and steel was largely sold off, only to revert once more to public ownership.

The fortunes of two nationalized industries changed significantly with the altered need for their services. Coal was cut back as oil, gas, and electricity came to dominate industrial and domestic supply and as the promise of nuclear power grew; but the economic cost of the latter (and fears for its safety) and the energy crisis of the 1970's led to a renewed enthusiasm for coal, helped on by the discovery of a major new coal field near Selby in Yorkshire. After the Beeching report in 1963, sweeping reductions in rail services were made, closing down uneconomic lines and many stations; despite the social benefits of railways, especially in times of oil shortage, the private automobile and the trucking industry offered flexibilities the railways, however reorganized, could not. Although the intercity system of mainline trains had attained a good level of service by the midseventies, and although some impressive technological innovations are in prospect, the future of the railways remains clouded, not least because from the sixties the nationalized industries were expected to conduct themselves on commercial principles. An exception has been made for coal, with its vast economic and political importance: when the miners were given their exceptional wage raise in 1972, the government wrote off the Coal Board's deficit and began direct subsidies to the industry. Prices rose steadily in all the nationalized industries, but it was the railways, subject to readily available and sometimes advantageous alternatives, that suffered: declining patronage threatened a downward spiral that would be difficult to break.

Nationalization as an issue seemed virtually dead, once Labour fulfilled its obvious political obligation to renationalize steel in 1967, and it is likely that talk in the Wilson years about nationalizing the insurance industry or the large clearing banks was precisely that, talk to appease the dogmatic socialists in Labour ranks, and Conservative promises of denationalization may be a similar gesture to ideological purity. Nationalization has been more an inescapable rescue operation than the best economic and social means of organizing an industry.

The complex of insurance, health provision, and income maintenance that is summed up as the welfare state has undergone some sweeping changes. Beveridge had argued that payments into the system and out of it should be uniform, that family allowances, pensions, and similar provisions should establish a "national minimum," beyond which private arrangements would have to be made if more than basic subsistence was wanted. National assistance, as the relief of poverty was called, was a safety net to catch the unfortunate until more regular provision could be made. By the end of the fifties it was plain that the system was not working well. People were living longer and swelling the ranks of the pensionable; the numbers of unemployable would not go away and even rose, as industry became more complex and capital-intensive; and often those with legitimate claims on the system failed to exercise them, through ignorance, apathy, or pride. Moreover, the rise in the cost of living meant that pensions were too low and that in some instances national assistance was proving to be not the last resort, as had been intended, but a lucrative source of income. Labour and Conservatives alike mounted a two-pronged attack on the difficulties, though emphases varied from one government to the next: one tack was to relate pensions and other social security income to earnings, though with some redistribution from the upper levels of the earnings scale; the other was to rely more heavily on private insurance and pension plans dovetailed with the state system. And, despite Labour's professed preference for council housing—owned by local authorities—the housing market came to be dominated by the private sector, and the expanding numbers of owner-occupiers suggested that the Conservative slogan of "a property-owning democracy" was coming to have some foundation in fact. There were scandals involving slum landlords, and the overbuilding of office accommodation contrasted unfavorably in many minds with shortages in the supply of domestic housing. The problem of those who could not find homes was publicized in the seventies by charitable organizations concerned with their plight and, more dramatically, by squatters who took possession of unoccupied premises. But as a whole the nation was better housed than it had ever been, as it was also more prosperous and secure.

The same demographic problems that beset the social security and housing fields had severe repercussions on the National Health Service, where the difficulty was further complicated by swift advances in medical technology and treatment and by a staggering rise in costs. Here, too, private insurance plans flourished, allowing some patients to take advantage of private medical practice. To many on the left of the Labour party, and to the leadership of some of the unions staffing hospitals, queue-jumping for elective or minor surgery or the preferential treatment given private patients in doctors' offices was intolerable, and the seventies brought a forceful attack on private medicine, which some critics would have eliminated entirely, by, for example, denying charitable status (and consequent tax exemption) to private hospitals or building permits to establish new ones. But the real battle was fought over the maintenance of private beds in the NHS hospitals, the key concession in the compromise by which Bevan had won over the doctors at the outset. A gradual phasing out of private beds was agreed to, but how firmly the policy will stick is still unclear. The morale of doctors, at all levels of practice, has fallen—reflecting overwork (itself the consequence of insufficient output from medical schools) and the erosion of income differentials; there has been some emigration; in much of the country there is a serious shortage of doctors; and the staffing of hospitals has depended heavily on Commonwealth immigrants. Yet, however grave the financial, administrative, and political problems of the NHS, its centrality in the system of social services is unassailable.

The rise in costs of the social services has been to some extent offset by a decline in defense expenditure, but the expanding economy that could absorb these costs has escaped Britain. In other countries in Europe, where productivity and growth have far surpassed Britain's dismal record, there are more generous provisions of social services in most fields, and Britain's pioneering role in providing comprehensive social welfare has been quietly surpassed. So, too, the reality underlying the powerful political ideal of equality has proved ambiguous and difficult to interpret. Taking overall figures, the sharpest reduction in inequality of incomes occurred between 1939 and 1959, a trend that reflects the virtual elimination of unemployment in the war and the years following. Since that time, the gap has narrowed less strikingly. Many crosscurrents make gross figures difficult to interpret—a marked rise in the number of working wives, an increase in the number of pensioners living in separate households, a shift from indirect to direct taxation spreading further down the social scale, the smaller size of families.* But, whatever statistics suggest, the perception of prosperity has spread pretty widely through society, and equality is less likely to be judged in terms of income than in terms of opportunity.

This essentially psychological fact has given education its crucial place in the postwar era. The system created by the Butler Act of 1944 was hierarchical. Leaving aside the independent, or public, fee-paying schools, in the state system a selection made at about the age of eleven sent the most able students into the state-aided grammar schools, leaving the rest to the secondary modern or technical schools; a minority of grammar-school students went on to the sixth form and from sixth-formers university entrants were selected. The Robbins report on higher education, published in 1963, and the opening of a number of new universities doubled the number of students enrolled by 1970 and trebled the prewar figure, though this expanded university system still catered to a recognized elite. It is on questions of the structure and philosophy of secondary education that the two main parties have differed most profoundly. In 1965 the Labour government moved to abolish the eleven-plus examination and to order local authorities to submit plans to convert their secondary schools to the comprehensive model. This policy was reversed by the Conservatives in 1970 and resumed once more by Labour in 1974.

---

*A modest trend towards narrowing seems to emerge from the publications of the Central Statistical Office and since 1974 the reports of the Royal Commission on the Distribution of Income. The analysis in G. C. Fiegehen, P. S. Lansley, and A. D. Smith, *Poverty and Progress in Britain, 1953–73* (1977), suggests that set against a constant 1971 absolute living standard, the fifth of the population defined as poor in 1953–1954 had shrunk to a fortieth by 1973 —the accomplishment of a growing economy rather than redistribution, as the net income of the poorest fifth percentile in both years was about the same proportion of median income.

Most authorities have complied and it is a question how nearly irre-
versible the transition is; doubtful, too, is the wisdom of the move, at
least from an educational point of view. A policy of comprehensives
only, with no selection, is forcing many distinguished grammar
schools to choose whether to remain within the state system as
comprehensives or to become independent schools, able to select
their pupils and to provide an elite minority with a more traditional,
quality-oriented education.

As a world power Britain's status has fallen greatly, and its so far
idiosyncratic and scarcely assimilated role in the Common Market
suggests that the country has yet to find a new sense of its place. The
Commonwealth, which once seemed impressive, has also proved
less substantial than many had hoped. To be sure, the roll of new nations created from former British colonies testifies to the success of
British decolonization: Ghana in 1957; Nigeria in 1960; Sierra Leone,
Tanganyika (Tanzania), and Somaliland (Somalia) in 1961; Uganda in
1962; Kenya in 1963. So complete was the transition that in 1966 the
Colonial Office was absorbed into the Commonwealth Affairs Office,
and that in turn merged with the Foreign Office two years later. But
schemes for federations of some colonies came to nothing: the Federation of Rhodesia and Nyasaland, created in 1953 broke up ten
years later; in 1964 Nyasaland became Malawi, and Northern Rhodesia became Zambia, while Southern Rhodesia unilaterally proclaimed its independence to continue white rule and to present an
acute embarrassment to British and increasingly to world diplomacy.
The West Indies Federation was dissolved in 1962 after four years of
existence; Singapore seceded from the Malaysian Federation in 1965.
In many of the new nations democratic institutions have been
overthrown by single-party or military dictatorships, themselves unstable, and the benefits of parliamentary government—one of the
professed goals of the long tutelage of the colonies—have been
sacrificed for other ends. It seemed for a time in 1975–1976 that even
India was to go that route under the personal rule of Mrs. Indira
Gandhi, but the democratic parliamentary tradition was reasserted
with her electoral defeat, a victory the more gratifying for its rarity.

Redirection in nationalized industries and the working of the
welfare state, like the fever chart of the economy, profoundly affected
the lives of individuals and the fortunes of families; the changed
position of Britain in the world and in relation to its vanishing empire had less immediate impact but did alter the setting in which
most of the English saw themselves. Still, all these were themes
firmly continuous with the postwar years; they reached back, institu-
ionally and morally, for at least a century. The 1960's, however, saw
other developments that, though they may have drawn on recessive

traits in the nation's past, appeared as radical departures from settled and admired national traditions.

One of these new departures was the prominence assumed by racial tension and conflict. Britain's prosperity in the fifties and sixties served as a magnet to the poor and ambitious in colonies and former colonies in Asia, Africa, and the West Indies: it was said that a quarter of the world's population was eligible to come to live in Britain, because as residents of the Empire they were British subjects and because Britain, unlike almost all other countries, had imposed no limitation on immigrants. In the census of 1951 residents in Britain from Commonwealth countries, other than the old dominions (Canada, Australia, New Zealand, South Africa), numbered something over 200,000, about 0.4 per cent of the population; in 1971 there were well over a million, about 2.1 per cent of the population. The immigrants clustered in larger cities and particularly in the industrial towns of the Midlands — Birmingham, Wolverhampton, Leicester, Nottingham. In 1958 there were race riots in Nottingham and in the Notting Hill district of London — serious as portents if not in damage to lives or property. In 1962 the Commonwealth Immigrants Act was passed, requiring that immigrants from the Commonwealth either have independent means, a job, or useful skills and education, or qualify under a quota that the government might alter as it chose. The inflow, which had leaped to extraordinarily high levels in 1961, in anticipation of the act, was sharply cut back, though the numbers remained relatively high because of the immigration of dependents. The measure had divided the Tory leadership, and Gaitskell had set the Labour party squarely against it, but rank-and-file voters strongly approved, and when Labour came back to power, it had to abandon its principled stand and to carry a new Commonwealth Immigration Act in 1968, at a time when Asians were flooding in from the by then independent nation of Kenya. In 1965 and 1968, Race Relations Acts were carried to prohibit discrimination in public places, in housing, and in employment, and a Race Relations Board was set up. But the tensions continue.

One can, perhaps, understand public hostility when strange, alien people were intruded into a situation of economic uncertainty, especially in communities that have been by tradition tightly knit and inward-turning — though to say that is not to deny the self-evident racial cast of thinking and feeling that underlie this phenomenon, a century after the Governor Eyre controversy. What is yet more disturbing is the translation of the issue into political terms. In 1968 Enoch Powell, a second-rank Conservative politician, made a speech in Birmingham, one of the cities (like Powell's own constituency of Wolverhampton) where Commonwealth immigration had been particularly heavy; reacting against the Race Relations bill, he warned that "like the Roman, I see the River Tiber flowing with much blood." Overnight Powell became famous, and the polls showed him the first choice of many as a successor to the Tory leadership should Heath resign. The theme was one to which Powell was to return repeatedly, in carefully calculated speeches, though, in time, he was to pursue other issues — his hatred of the Common Market and his support of the Protestant cause in Ulster. An outsider, even a crank, he had no chance of real success in politics, but his legion of admirers testifies to the deep emotions aroused by the question of race, and in urging his followers to vote Labour rather than Conservative in the 1974 elections — out of hostility to the Common Market — he put and kept Labour in office. Much of the racial feeling has also gone to swell the ranks of the National Front, an extremist party formed in 1967 by drawing together a number of small right-wing groups; very strong in some parliamentary constituencies, it has drawn around 3 per cent of the vote nationally in the elections in the 1970's. Moreover, it has been regularly involved in clashes with the police and has sought confrontations with left-wing groups quite as eager for combat.*

Another aspect of the politics of the sixties and seventies that would have seemed inconceivable from the perspective of 1945 called into question the very existence of the United Kingdom through the growing strength of the Welsh and, particularly, the Scottish nationalist parties. This prospect was set back significantly by the collapse of devolution efforts and the rout of the nationalist parties in the general election of 1979. Far more serious, and tragic, was the renewed strife in Northern Ireland. Since its establishment within the United Kingdom in 1922,† Ulster was given over, economically, socially, and politically, to the ascendancy of Protestants, their fervor against Rome drawn from an old tradition enshrined in the Orange Lodges but in the twentieth century directed chiefly against absorption in the Irish Republic to the south. That very absorption was still formally the policy of the Republic and was the mission to which Sinn Fein, the outlawed political group descended from the champions of Irish independence in the early part of the century, and its military arm, the Irish Republican Army, were dedicated. The history of the province was punctuated by incidents of terrorism and violence as Catholics and Protestants clashed, and as the IRA encountered the special security forces of the Royal Ulster Constabulary. But by the sixties, relative quiet settled on Ulster, and there were signs that the

*On the Eyre controversy, see above, pp. 320–321.
†See above, pp. 500–503.

Protestant hold on the province might at last be somewhat relaxed. Ulster had from the beginning had its own legislature — a House of Commons and a Senate — known colloquially as Stormont, from the village just outside Belfast where it sat; a local administration was headed by a prime minister. Some modest gestures towards the Catholics by Captain Terence O'Neill, prime minister from 1963 to 1969, gave rise to a newly insurgent Protestantism, led by the Reverend Ian Paisley, of the Free Presbyterian Church, fundamentalist and fanatically anti-Catholic; in 1966, the Ulster Volunteer Force was formed as a Protestant militia, confronting the IRA. From 1969, when the conciliatory Major James Chichester-Clark became prime minister, violence mounted in Ulster, leading to the dispatch of British troops, back in their accustomed role of keeping apart two warring communal factions. But now the violence was closer to home than it had been in Cyprus or Kenya: television viewers across the Irish Sea could see the bombings and the bodies of victims of snipers or of vicious acts of retaliation and revenge. The IRA and its sympathizers calculated that still further escalation of violence could provoke a British withdrawal, while the Protestants resorted to violence to demonstrate their loyalty to the Crown.

In 1972 the self-governing institutions of Northern Ireland were suspended; the province was put under direct rule by a secretary of state, at the outset the able and conciliatory Conservative politician William Whitelaw. In March, 1973, a referendum produced an overwhelming vote for remaining a part of the United Kingdom. Subsequently a new constitution was instituted; it left the secretary of state in place as the custodian of the powers of the Crown, and provided for an assembly elected by proportional representation to assure "power-sharing" between Protestants and Catholics, and for an executive chosen by the secretary after consulting the parties. In December, 1973, at Sunningdale, outside London, Whitelaw got the contending groups to agree to the formation of an executive of six Ulster Unionists, four members from the Social Democratic and Labour party (which tended to draw Catholic voters), and one other member; a Council of Ireland, to promote cooperation with the Republic, was also to be established. Whitelaw's greatest coup was persuading Brian Faulkner, the last prime minister under the old constitution and a strong Protestant, to accept the doctrine of power-sharing and the office of chief executive. But Faulkner was repudiated by his party, and a general strike of Protestant workers in the spring of 1974 brought a return to direct rule.

Meanwhile, violence grew, in Ulster, in Britain, and in the Irish Republic. Specific victims might be marked out — a prominent English journalist, the British ambassador to the Irish Republic, the great military and imperial statesman Lord Mountbatten — or the terror could be random, visited on a Birmingham pub, a coachload of tourists in the north of England, London railway stations and restaurants. The British army was fighting a frustrating and deadly war. Civil wars sometimes come to an end in exhaustion and disgust, and there are signs that that may happen in Ulster: in 1976, following a particularly horrible incident in which children were killed by a careening car in a chase, two housewives organized demonstrations for peace, their courageous and continuing initiative recognized by the Nobel Peace Prize in 1977. The worst trauma of the postwar era, Ulster might be seen as the last gasp of empire, as the first move in the destruction of the United Kingdom, or as the instrument by which the twentieth-century curse of terrorism was made a part of English life, where it had been all but unknown for a couple of generations.

A third surprising element touches the nature of British politics. We have already referred to the gradual erosion of the central position of politics in English life, a trend that continued, despite commendably high polls at general elections. Official figures for individual party memberships either are not published or are misleading, but it seems likely that in both major parties membership has fallen to about half of what it was in the early 1950's. Certainly fewer people of ability are willing to undertake the arduous task of winning parliamentary seats and fighting their way to the cabinet level. Members of parliament are not well paid and are wretchedly provided with services; constituency parties are increasingly restive and, if they fall into the hands of activists of either the right or the left—those who are willing to sit out meetings and to manipulate a local machine when apathy reigns—the life of a moderate M.P. can be made miserable and his career can be cut short. But there are other problems. One is the appearance of corruption. Specific efforts have had to be mounted to root out dishonesty and bribe-taking in the once impeccable London police; entrenched local politicians have been shown in cozy arrangements with contractors and architects; and in some instances the taint has penetrated the civil service and in a rather casual way the Cabinet itself. The business world turned up many scandals, often implicating politicians: revelation of one embarrassing deal prompted Heath in 1973 to speak in the House of Commons about "the unpleasant and unacceptable face of capitalism."

Even without corruption, the immense power of ministers and the civil service could be used in a highly authoritarian manner. This was made plain in the Crichel Down affair in 1954, when a cabal of civil servants was shown to have determined on their own scheme for using an abandoned wartime air field and to have deliberately misled the former owners of the land, who had applied for its return, into thinking that their application was being seriously considered when it was not. In 1976 the courts rebuked a minister for using the test of "unreasonable" action to prevent a local authority from pursuing a politically distasteful policy. It has become fashionable to predict a dire future for Britain, and gloom among the commentators must be taken with a degree of skepticism. But it is disturbing to find thoughtful and well-informed observers wondering aloud if in fact democracy can survive a profound crisis in Britain or to find Lord Hailsham arguing that in an "elective dictatorship" protection for individuals against an omnipresent state can be found only in a written constitution and a bill of rights, not in the old reliance on administrative and parliamentary self-restraint.*

Many of the ills of Britain are readily ascribed to the persistence of a class system, which emerged in the first fifty years or so of the nineteenth century. Whatever reservations a more egalitarian age may have about that system, it worked with remarkably little friction for about a century. A powerful blow was struck against it by the failure to deal adequately (at least as most men and women saw it) with the depression of the 1930's and its social costs; a profound democratic upsurge was associated with the war and the reconstruction that followed; but the most powerful solvent was the prosperity of the fifties. There has been much talk of late about the "politics of envy," arising from resentment that prosperity has not been sufficiently shared and from the feeling that all privilege is suspect. There is something to the allegation, but it may well be that—with all the admitted continuities of style and manner from the class society of the past—we are witnessing the birth of a different principle of social organization, no longer on the basis of class but on the basis of interests.

As the outlines of a class society were shadowed forth in the old society of the eighteenth century, so the present dominance of competing interests was shadowed forth in the theory and practice of syndicalism before World War I and in some abortive efforts at institution-building after that war—the Whitley Councils and the National Industrial Council, for example.† What particularly impresses an observer today is, of course, the rapid growth and astonishing strength of the trade-union movement, to counter which, in the last couple of decades, the Confederation of British Industry has taken on new importance. But within these great economic blocs are found

*Lord Hailsham's views are most succinctly put in his Dimbleby Lecture on the BBC in 1976. *The Times* (London), October 15, 1976; the correspondence that ensued in *The Times* is worth reading.
†See above, pp. 496, 512–513.

many subordinate and conflicting interests: separate industries, managers, staff, and shareholders; differing levels of skills and trades, shop stewards, and unions at loggerheads with each other. Outside the quasi-official complexes stand the professions, themselves fragmented; pensioners; consumers; students—all with ambitions and organizations cutting across obvious class lines and offering new sources of identity. No simple pattern will ever emerge, however, if only because individuals can owe allegiance to more than one interest or can change their loyalties over time: trade unionists and managerial staff are consumers too; students grow into professionals; junior doctors turn into consultants; and everyone in time becomes a pensioner.

All ages, they say cynically, are ages of transition, but surely the mid-twentieth century is as an age of transition as were the decades in the middle of the eighteenth and the nineteenth centuries. In a post-industrial world, the accustomed categories of analysis and the old pieties and long-tested rhetoric may simply not apply.

An Island of Civilization

In 1951 a fair was held on a small site on the South Bank of the Thames in London: it was called the Festival of Britain. The gaiety and color, the ingenuity and wit of the exhibits, the awareness—for most of them the first—that visitors carried away of fanciful modern exhibition architecture offered a welcome contrast to the austerity that had not yet vanished. A hundred years earlier, the Great Exhibition had celebrated Britain's triumph; the Festival celebrated Britain's escape. But though the grimness of the world soon reasserted itself, the country could count its successes in some of the graces of life.

The vitality that has been maintained in the arts owes much to state grants channeled through the Arts Council, though that assistance has been less generous than subsidies in many Continental countries. A word must be found as well for the role of the BBC, not only in diffusing culture but in serving as patron. There are five symphony orchestras in London—one of them the BBC's—and several provincial orchestras of first rank; the capital supports two opera companies and the largest availability of concerts and recitals of any city in the world. The spread of summer festivals is also notable. The largest is that in Edinburgh, but special mention should be made of two others: Glyndebourne, dating from the thirties, with its incomparable productions of operas in a country-house setting; and Aldeburgh, founded after the war by Benjamin Britten and his friends, for the production of his operas but to which much more has been added.

Britten's fame as the finest and most fertile composer of opera in the mid-twentieth century is secure, but he worked as successfully in other forms as well. No contemporary has been able to match his skill and sensitivity in setting words to music, an art that reached a pinnacle in the *War Requiem*, set to poems by the war poet of a generation earlier, Wilfred Owen. Britten's international stature was assured; Michael Tippett's impressive contribution to opera and chamber music was less widely recognized outside Britain, but a younger generation of composers seems likely to make its mark at home and abroad, among them Thea Musgrave and Richard Rodney Bennett. The Sadler's Wells Ballet, which became the Royal Ballet, has been recognized as one of the world's great companies dedicated to classical dance. For most of the postwar years Dame Margot Fonteyn was the principal ballerina, joined in the later years of her career by the brilliant young dramatic dancer, Rudolf Nureyev, who left the Soviet Union to settle in London. The authority and versatility of Sir Frederick Ashton's choreography was matched in his generation only by the genius of George Balanchine in New York, but Balanchine's work left British audiences and most critics unaccountably puzzled when the New York City Ballet mounted its first London season in 1950, with appreciation coming only in the last few years. Britain has been an important exporter of dance, not only through the tours of the Royal Ballet but in the impact of British-trained choreographers on companies abroad—Robert Helpmann in his native Australia, John Cranko with the Stuttgart Ballet.

In sculpture Henry Moore remained the acknowledged, constantly creative master, joined in world recognition by Barbara Hepworth and Reg Butler. Among painters, in the immediate postwar years Ben Nicholson was skill active, Graham Sutherland secured his reputation, and a younger, self-indulgently terrifying painter, Francis Bacon, quickly established himself as a major artist. In the postwar years, Bernard Leach, the finest potter in the western world, became recognized as the preeminent representative of an astonishing burst of creativity in the crafts, explained in part by the excellence of Britain's many schools of art—so striking a change from the poverty of training in the arts and design of which informed Victorians complained a century earlier. The design leadership of famous turn-of-the-century firms like Liberty's, in textiles, and Heal's, in furniture, was maintained and strengthened; Continental influences grew; and by the sixties good design was making inroads even in articles for popular consumption, where it had been notably lacking. British architecture fared less well. There are some interesting and satisfying housing projects and schools and a few outstanding buildings like Sir Robert Matthew's Royal Festival Hall in London or Basil Spence's stylish Coventry Cathedral; but mostly the record is one of missed opportunities. New university construction has yielded at best mixed results. Rebuilding war-shattered towns has produced much mediocrity, and the City of London, as rebuilt, is an almost unqualified disaster, to which Christopher Wren's churches stand in elegant reproach. It is only fair to say that architects have had to work in less than favorable circumstances, caught between the sternly applied commercial criteria of their clients and a falling standard of workmanship in the building trades.

The theater has been in some ways the most exciting aspect of postwar culture. At two famous theaters the classical repertory was maintained brilliantly — at Stratford-on-Avon by the Royal Shakespeare Company (later playing in London as well) and at the Old Vic; then, in the sixties, the Old Vic became a temporary home for the new National Theatre company until it moved to its permanent quarters on the South Bank in 1976. At London's Royal Court Theater in the fifties and sixties the English Stage Company presented important new works. Britain's actors and actresses, as was true before the war, have probably been unmatched anywhere for talent and versatility, qualities encouraged by excellent training schools, and by the concentration of both theater and the film industry in London, to which television was an important and exciting addition from the fifties. Playwrights were slow to take advantage of the riches they had to work with, but in 1956 John Osborne's *Look Back in Anger* opened the way for a new, more serious drama that drew to some extent on the inspiration of avant-garde writers on the Continent, to some extent on native traditions of social protest. The old conventions, symbolized by the anachronistic official censorship of the Lord Chamberlain, were soon broken, and the censorship was put to rout. Osborne, like others among the so-called angry young men, was a bird of passage, and much playwriting, as always, became routine once the new conventions were generally accepted. Two playwrights seem destined, however, to retain a permanent place in the repertory: Harold Pinter, with his brilliantly actable plays of puzzling logic and vague menace, and Tom Stoppard, with an unmatched gift for witty manipulation of language and for wry observation of the ways of intellectuals.

An outsider must concede, with a mixture of chagrin and awe, that the British seem to write as well as ever, though the novel is less important now than it was for a couple of centuries, at least as a vehicle for major artistic expression. Two immense novelistic enterprises, of many volumes, were brought to a conclusion: Anthony

Powell's *A Dance to the Music of Time* and C. P. Snow's *Strangers and Brothers;* there was a burst of novels in the fifties and sixties dealing with provincial settings and rootless, restless young people; and Anthony Burgess has undertaken dazzling, disturbing experiments in the form, among them *A Clockwork Orange*. The novel, of course, remains supreme among popular literature, of which Britain is a heavy consumer still. It may, however, be among poets—Philip Larkin the most respected of the postwar generation—and critics that the authentic literary voice is now to be heard.

British scholarship in the social sciences and humanities has continued in strength—sound, professional, creative, if without quite the innovative grasp that characterized departures in so many fields between the wars. British science, particularly on the theoretical side, has been outstanding, and is attested to by the large number of Nobel Prizes won by British scholars. In all intellectual fields there has been some loss to positions overseas—the brain drain, as it is called—just as in the arts many of the most successful performers have been tempted to take up residence elsewhere to escape the heavy taxation that would fall on them at home. The economic crises of the seventies have caught the universities in a particularly serious way. The hopeful expansion of the sixties now threatens to become surplus capacity in the last decades of the century, and, as elsewhere, stagnation in appointments may threaten distinction of performance in some fields in the future.

The vitality in less rarefied circles has been immense. The contribution of the Beatles and their innumerable successors to the idiom of popular music can scarcely be underestimated, in Britain or abroad, as can be said also of their role in creating—along with the designer Mary Quant and the once fashionable center of swinging London, Carnaby Street—the look of the sixties and seventies. The flow of Commonwealth immigrants from India, Pakistan, and Hong Kong, preceded to some extent by an invasion of restaurateurs from Mediterranean Europe, has meant a welcome deliverance from the predictability (and often the dreariness) of English restaurant fare. And, despite limits on the availability of foreign currencies for travel abroad, the ready supply of package holidays has broken down much of the insularity of the country at nearly all social levels.

It is fitting to conclude with an allusion to the new variety and ease of access that characterize mass entertainment and enjoyment, for it has become a standard, if sometimes wearying and evasive, retort to criticisms of Britain's decline that the British are, in fact, showing the rest of the world how they can, and perhaps under less affluent conditions must, live. There is something to the argument. The celebrated German sociologist Ralf Dahrendorf—as director of the

London School of Economics an instance of a reverse brain drain — has said that England is an uninhabitable country whose inhabitants have tried to make it habitable by being reasonable to one another. Some of that admired reasonableness has dissipated. There have been bursts of violence throughout the postwar years, particularly in cities — Teddy Boys and Skinheads, racial violence, hooliganism among football crowds, and a brief spasm of home-grown terrorism at the beginning of the seventies — and there are more instances of sullenness and rudeness, expected in many other countries but the more noticeable in Britain, where it is and, happily, remains exceptional. Reasonableness, grace, and even a sense of style in an age not much given to it have survived wars, social conflict, loss of prestige, economic problems that will not go away, and a tide of criticism at home and abroad that would swamp a less secure or more sensitive people.

In the first edition of this book, the concluding sentences reflected that criticism, just then reaching its first flood, by asking what intellectual and moral sources Britain might find, not only to assure a comfortable survival, but to attain some new measure of greatness. Now, at ten years' distance, the question seems irrelevant — unless greatness is to be found in the refusal to pursue it and in the willingness to be content.

Selected Readings

The best coverage of the war is Peter Calvocoressi and Guy Wint, *Total War: Causes and Courses of the Second World War* (1972). Winston Churchill's own history, *The Second World War* (6 vols., 1948–1953), is a fascinating personal account. On the Far East, Christopher Thorne, *Allies of a Kind: The United States, Britain, and the War Against Japan, 1941–1945* (1978). Aspects of the remarkable British intelligence operations are found in J. C. Masterman, *The Double-Cross System in the War of 1939 to 1945* (1972) and F. W. Winterbotham, *The Ultra Secret* (1974). Full and authoritative accounts of the war on the home front can be found in the official *History of the Second World War, United Kingdom Civil Series*, among the most important of which are W. K. Hancock and M. M. Gowing, *British War Economy* (1949); E. L. Hargreaves, *Civil Industry and Trade* (1952); M. M. Postan, *British War Production* (1952); and R. M. Titmuss, *Problems of Social Policy* (1950). Tom Harrisson's *Living Through the Blitz* (1976) is a remarkably vivid record. José Harris, *William Beveridge, a Biography* (1977) marks the continuity in social reform from the first decade of the century to the publication, three decades later, of the Beveridge Report.

Two general accounts of postwar Britain should be mentioned: C. J. Bartlett, *A History of Postwar Britain, 1945–74* (1977), and Mary Proudfoot, *British Politics and Government, 1951–1970: A Study of an Affluent Society* (1974). The postwar economy is placed in a larger context in several studies:

A. J. Youngson, *Britain's Economic Growth, 1920–1966* (1967); Sidney Pollard, *The Development of the British Economy, 1914–1967;* and G. A. Phillips, *The Growth of the British Economy, 1918–1968* (1973). G. D. N. Worswick and P. H. Ady, eds., *The British Economy, 1945–1950* (1952) consists of essays on all major aspects of the country's economic life. Arnold A. Rogow, *The Labour Government and British Industry, 1945–1951* (1955) is a valuable study of economic controls. On the background of the first big nationalization move, M. W. Kirby, *The British Coalmining Industry, 1870–1946* (1978). Nigel Harris, *Competition and the Corporate Society: British Conservatives, the State, and Industry, 1945–1964* (1972) is a most suggestive essay. Kevin Hawkins, *British Industrial Relations, 1945–1975* (1976) is a valuable general discussion. See also Robert Taylor, *The Fifth Estate: Britain's Unions in the Seventies* (1978).

There are fewer biographies than one could wish of prominent postwar leaders; the best, by all odds, is by Michael Foot, a surviving Bevanite who has held high office: *Aneurin Bevan, a Biography,* I: *1897–1945* (1962) and II: *1945–1960* (1974). See also Bernard Donoughue and G. W. Jones, *Herbert Morrison* (1973). We do, however, have a number of memoirs and autobiographies. C. R. Attlee's *As It Happened* (1954) is characteristically terse and uninformative. R. A. Butler, *The Art of the Possible* (1971) and Lord Avon, *The Memoirs of Sir Anthony Eden: Full Circle* (1960) deal with the Conservatives in power and with Suez. The fullest autobiography is Harold Macmillan's *Memoirs, 1914–63* (6 vols., 1966–1973). Harold Wilson's massive *The Labour Government: 1964–1970: A Personal Record* (1971) is just that, and so is George Brown's *In My Way* (1971). Marcia Williams's *Inside Number 10* (1972) did not help her popularity in the party; and matters plummeted farther downward when Joe Haines, Wilson's press officer and a particular antagonist of Lady Falkender, published his recollections of the Labour government, *The Politics of Power* (1977). Richard Crossman, *The Diaries of a Cabinet Minister* (3 vols., 1975–1977) gives a candid personal assessment and a most revealing glimpse into the inner workings of the Cabinet, raising an important legal question about confidentiality of cabinet proceedings and the right to publish within the ordinarily prohibited period of thirty years; see Hugo Young, *The Crossman Affair* (1976).

Every general election since 1945 has been the subject of a book of close analysis, beginning with R. B. McCallum and A. Readman on 1945, H. G. Nicholas on 1950, and thereafter by D. E. Butler and his associates. The most interesting analysis of the political scene in Britain is Samuel H. Beer, *British Politics in the Collectivist Age* (British title: *Modern British Politics*) (1965), to which the discussion in the text is much indebted. Pauline Gregg, *The Welfare State, from 1945 to the Present Day* (1967) is an introduction. The first skeptical assessment of what had been accomplished in narrowing the gap was Richard Titmuss, *Income Redistribution and Social Change* (1964), though references cited in the text suggest considerable accomplishment, more by expansion of the economy than by state action. The remarkable expansion of higher education is discussed in Harold Perkin, *New Universities in the United Kingdom* (1969). The actual administration of the welfare state has not been much discussed by historians, but mention should be made of one case of bureaucratic highhandedness that ended in a minor scandal: R. Douglas

Brown, *The Battle of Crichel Down* (1955). Because anti-Americanism became so important in postwar Britain, important perspective can be gained from Henry Pelling, *America and the British Left: From Bright to Bevan* (1957).

Britain's changing position in the world can be noted through F. S. Northedge, *Descent from Power; British Foreign Policy, 1945–73* (1974); Andrew J. Pierre, *Nuclear Politics: The British Experience with an Independent Strategic Force, 1939–1970* (1972); Richard Neustadt, *Alliance Politics* (1970), which places the Skybolt incident in a broad political context; and Uwe Kitzinger, *Diplomacy and Persuasion: How Britain Joined the Common Market* (1973). On empire, D. Goldsworthy, *Colonial Issues in British Politics, 1945–61* (1971), and Hugh Thomas, *The Suez Affair* (1966). The effect of immigration from poorer Commonwealth countries can be traced in Clifford Hill, *Immigration and Integration: A Study of the Settlement of Coloured Minorities in Britain* (1970); Douglas E. Schoen, *Enoch Powell and the Powellites* (1977); and Martin Walker, *The National Front* (1977). On the background of the Northern Ireland situation, Martin Wallace, *Northern Ireland: Fifty Years of Self-Government* (1971) and J. Bowyer Bell, *The Secret Army: The IRA, 1916–1970* (1971).

Mary Banham and Bevis Hillier, eds., *A Tonic for the Nation: The Festival of Britain, 1951* (1976) deals with a cultural event of very considerable importance. The historical background of state support of the arts, which becomes so notable in the postwar years, can be found in Janet Minihan, *The Nationalization of Culture: The Development of State Subsidies to the Arts in Great Britain* (1977). On the pervasive influence of television, vol. 4 of Asa Briggs's history of broadcasting, cited in the previous chapter, and Grace Wyndham Goldie, *Facing the Nation: Television and Politics, 1936–1976* (1977).

Appendix 1
The Kings and Queens of England

1688–1980

House of Orange	ACCESSION	CORONATION
William III (1650–1702) and Mary II (1662–1694)	February 12, 1689	April 11, 1689

House of Stuart		
Anne (1665–1714)	March 8, 1702	April 23, 1702

House of Hanover		
George I (1660–1727)	August 1, 1714	October 20, 1714
George II (1683–1760)	June 14, 1727	October 11, 1727
George III (1738–1820)	October 25, 1760	September 22, 1761
George IV (1762–1830) Prince Regent since February 5, 1811	January 29, 1820	July 19, 1821
William IV (1765–1837)	June 26, 1830	September 8, 1831
Victoria (1819–1901)	June 20, 1837	June 28, 1838

House of Saxe-Coburg-Gotha (after 1917 House of Windsor)		
Edward VII (1841–1910)	January 22, 1901	August 9, 1902
George V (1865–1936)	May 6, 1910	June 22, 1911
Edward VIII (1894–1972) Abdicated, December 11, 1936	January 20, 1936	———
George VI (1895–1952)	December 11, 1936	May 12, 1937
Elizabeth II (1926–)	February 6, 1952	June 2, 1953

Appendix 2
Titles, Honors, and the Peerage

Royal Titles

The titles *Prince* and *Princess* are confined to the royal family. They are also comparatively recent. The king's sons — other than the eldest son, who after 1399 was usually created Prince of Wales — began to be called Prince in the reign of Henry VII (1485-1509); the use of prince and princess for daughters and grandchildren of the sovereign came about in the eighteenth and nineteenth centuries. Since 1917, the titles are limited to all of the children of the sovereign and to the children of his sons; they alone are styled "Royal Highness." Except for the eldest son of the sovereign, all royal children are commoners at law: Prince and Princess are mere courtesy titles. It is, however, the practice to confer a dukedom on a prince when he reaches his majority.

The eldest son of the sovereign, the *heir apparent,* is from birth Duke of Cornwall and so is entitled to the revenues attached to the Duchy of Cornwall; he is also Duke of Rothesay, Earl of Carrick, and Baron of Renfrew in the peerage of Scotland. The titles Prince of Wales and Earl of Chester, however, are conferred on him at the sovereign's discretion. On the death or succession of a Prince of Wales, the title disappears and must be regranted to the next heir apparent.

If the sovereign has no living son, the next person in line of succession is termed the *heir* (or *heiress*) *presumptive.*

Provided the title is not held by anyone else, the eldest daughter of the sovereign has been given the title of Princess Royal for life.

The Peerage

The distinction between nobleman and commoner was originally determined by the right of noblemen to bear arms. During the Middle Ages a further distinction grew up between the greater and lesser nobility. The lesser nobility merged with the representatives of the Commons in the lower house of Parliament and while, in technical heraldic terms, they are still noblemen, general usage does not consider them so. The law agrees with this general usage: knights and baronets may have titles, but they are commoners at law. The old distinctions of esquire and gentleman have lost almost all of their original meaning stemming from the socio-military hierarchy. Now they are at best ways of implying social distinctions of more or less subtlety. A check sent to a shopkeeper in payment of a bill would probably be addressed with the shopkeeper's name unadorned; but if the same person were soliciting the

shopkeeper for a contribution to charity, he would very likely add Esq. after
the shopkeeper's name on the envelope.

The greater noblemen, to whom the term *peerage* came to be applied,
were originally the close companions and advisers of the king. As the term
peerage implies (it comes from *pares, equals*), they were all on a social level
and had the right to be judged by their peers, not by their inferiors. The duty
of giving counsel to the king was a vital obligation in the Middle Ages—the
king was obliged to summon his barons, and the barons were obliged to attend. These councils were the germ of Parliament, enlarged in time by representatives of the lesser nobility and the commons. When the last two groups
withdrew for separate consultation and in time merged to form the House of
Commons, the peers were left to form the House of Lords, but that institution is not definitively recognizable before the sixteenth century. Although
the distinction that originally set peers apart was military and only incidentally political, the distinguishing mark of a peer now is his right to receive an
individual writ of summons to attend Parliament.

There are now few privileges left to peers. They are exempt from jury
service; and they share with members of the House of Commons the privilege of freedom from arrest in civil cases for forty days before and after a parliamentary session; they can also claim direct access to the sovereign, though
with the present size of the peerage, this is hardly a meaningful privilege.
The last really material privilege, the right to be tried by one's peers for
treason and felony (but not misdemeanors), was largely in disuse throughout
the period with which this book is concerned. It was last claimed in 1936, in a
case of manslaughter, and was abolished in 1948. Peers have no vote for
members of the House of Commons. Peers of course retain a degree of social
prestige: they are likely candidates for invitations to serve as patrons or
officers of charities and as members of boards of directors; by the same
token, the involvement of a peer in a scandal or a marital squabble that gets
into the courts will bring much more attention from the popular press than
would a similar transgression among ordinary mortals.

The members of peers' families are all commoners at law. Certain titles
are given to them by courtesy, but courtesy titles do not confer or reflect any
legal distinction. The children of peers, therefore, are eligible to sit in the
House of Commons.

In the eleventh century, the greater nobles were known simply as *barons*
(from *baro,* man), but the greatest of them were soon created *earls.* The multiplication of ranks beyond that of earl is a phenomenon of the later Middle
Ages. In descending order of precedence, the ranks of the peerage are as
follows:

Duke. The title dates from the fourteenth century and was first conferred
on a non-royal person in 1448. For a time at the end of the sixteenth century,
there were no dukes at all, but the rank was revived in the seventeenth century, and a considerable number of promotions to that rank were made in the
eighteenth and nineteenth centuries. No dukes are now created other than
among members of the royal family.

A duke is addressed as "Your Grace." His wife is a duchess. The eldest
son carries, by courtesy, his father's secondary title, and his eldest son in
turn carries another of his grandfather's titles, until his father succeeds to the

dukedom, when he will take over his father's courtesy title. Younger sons and daughters of a duke are called by their given names preceded by Lord or Lady. Thus the sixth Duke of Bedford's eldest son was known as Marquess of Tavistock, the title taken by the eldest son of every Duke of Bedford.* The sixth Duke's third son was Lord John Russell, the Victorian statesman. When Lord John Russell was raised to the peerage in his own right in 1861, he became Earl Russell; thereafter, in informal address, he was called Lord Russell, no longer Lord John Russell.

Marquess (or *Marquis*). This title was first conferred in 1385. Marquesses and all the other lesser ranks of the peerage are addressed as "My lord." A marquess's wife is a marchioness. Children's titles follow the practices for duke's children.

Earl. This title dates back to the eleventh century, and in its different Anglo-Saxon usage to the tenth century. An earl's wife is a countess. The eldest son takes a secondary title by courtesy. Younger sons are formally styled Honorable, usually abbreviated Hon. and never used in speech, with the given and family names; daughters use Lady with given and family names.

Viscount. Originally the *vice-comes* was the sheriff of a county. The title was first used as an honor in 1440. A viscount's wife is a viscountess. All the children of a viscount are formally styled Honorable.

Baron. Although baron is the original designation for tenants-in-chief of the crown, and although it became the generic term for members of the greater nobility in the Middle Ages, its use as a rank, conferred by letters patent, dates from 1387. The word baron is not used in formal address: a baron is always addressed formally and informally as Lord. A baron's wife is a baroness. All the children are formally styled Honorable.

Life Peers and Peeresses

Until recent times, all peerages were hereditary. In 1857, the government tried to create a distinguished judge a peer for life only, a move that was at least in part an attempt to accomplish a gentle reform of the House of Lords. The House of Lords would have none of it, and so the judge had to be created Baron Wensleydale in the regular hereditary peerage.† In the legislation reforming the law courts in 1873–1876 (see below, pp. 654–655), provision was made for the appointment of a number of lords of appeal in ordinary, who, with certain other high judicial officers, constitute the House of Lords when it is sitting in its capacity as the highest court of appeal. These "law

---

*Ordinarily, he would have remained Marquess of Tavistock until he succeeded his father as seventh duke. But, in actual fact, he was called up to the House of Lords in 1833, with one of his father's lesser titles, Baron Howland of Streatham. When he succeeded to the dukedom, however, this title again became one of his junior titles. Such accelerated promotion has not been very common and was last used in 1951.
†Here is a fine complication. Although, after being raised to the peerage, Parke would invariably have been addressed as "Lord Wensleydale," before his peerage he would have been addressed as "Mr. Baron Parke." But this usage stems from the fact that judges of the Court of Exchequer were called Barons of the Exchequer and has nothing to do with the rank in the peerage.

lords" have been created peers for life since 1876. In 1958 an act provided for the creation of life peers and peeresses as regular members of the House of Lords. Most creations since that time have been life peers, and in recent years no hereditary peers have been created by any government.

Women in the House of Lords

Life peeresses have been able to sit since 1958. In 1963 legislation permitted women holding hereditary peerages in their own right to take their places in the House. Some peerages, by the terms of their creation, have descended through the female line: the Dukes of Marlborough, for example, are descended through two daughters of John Churchill, the first Duke and the great general in the War of the Spanish Succession. The second daughter had married the Earl of Sunderland, whose surname was Spencer. After 1817, the surnames were combined as Spencer-Churchill, the full family name of Sir Winston Churchill, who was the son of a second son of a Duke of Marlborough. Normally, however, hereditary peerages have been limited to descent through heirs male. There is another exception. Those baronies that antedate the creation of baronies by letters patent exist by the mere fact of receipt of a writ of summons to attend the House of Lords; such baronies descend to heirs general, not heirs male, since there is no document to set out the mode of succession. If there are two or more daughters and no son, the barony will be held in abeyance until there is one surviving daughter or a sole surviving heir of one daughter. But the Crown can terminate the abeyance at any time in favor of one such heir.

The Selection of Titles

Titles are always in some way territorial. The place in question is usually associated with the peer upon whom it is conferred: it might be, say, his principal residence or the part of the country where his largest landholdings lie; military men have often chosen the sites of their victories and politicians the constituency they had represented in the House of Commons. Names of counties or of large or important towns are restricted to the higher ranks of the peerage. Dukes invariably take simple territorial titles: the Duke of Wellington, the Duke of Northumberland. But in other ranks of the peerage, a peer may decide to use his family name as a title, in which case a territorial title is appended. Thus, after his victory over the French at Aboukir Bay, Admiral Sir Horatio Nelson was created "Baron Nelson, of the Nile and of Burnham Thorpe in the County of Norfolk"; after his death, the title passed to his brother, who was raised to an earldom as "Earl Nelson, of Trafalgar and of Merton in the County of Surrey." This appended territorial designation is not used as part of the title, unless another peerage of older creation uses the same family name. Thus a Baron Curzon was created in 1794; therefore, when the Indian viceroy at the beginning of this century, George Nathaniel Curzon, was raised to the peerage in 1898, he had to be known as Baron Curzon of Kedleston. Political figures raised to the peerage have usually taken their family names as titles in recent years: thus Earl Attlee of Limehouse (his constituency for many years) or Lord Morrison of Lambeth.

A notable exception is Sir Anthony Eden, who when raised to the peerage chose the title Earl of Avon. Some Labour peers have joined their first and last names to form a title: Lord George-Brown, Lord Noel-Baker, Lord Francis-Williams.

Signatures

Peers sign themselves by title only: Wellington, Bedford, Attlee. Eldest sons bearing courtesy titles do likewise: Blandford (son of the Duke of Marlborough), Cranborne (son of the Marquess of Salisbury), Hartington (son of the Duke of Devonshire). A peeress in her own right signs like a peer, with her title only. The wife of a peer signs her given name and the title: the beautiful Duchess of Devonshire, who canvassed so persuasively for Charles James Fox in 1784 (by selling kisses for promises of votes), would have signed herself Georgiana Devonshire, although the family name is Cavendish. Children of a peer other than the eldest son sign their family name without the prefixes Lord, Lady, or Hon. Before being raised to the peerage, Lord John Russell signed himself J. Russell; after becoming a peer, he signed Russell.

Renunciation of Peerages

A peerage was once a virtual prerequisite for high political office, or at any rate a title made the attainment of high office easier. With the decline of the House of Lords, no important office will now normally be given to a member of that House. Thus a peerage today can abruptly terminate a political career or divert it into quieter channels. Throughout the 1950's a campaign was waged by Anthony Wedgwood Benn, a rising young Labour politician, for the right to renounce the peerage that one day would inevitably fall to him on the death of his father Viscount Stansgate; the same fate awaited a prominent Conservative politician, Quintin Hogg, the son of Viscount Hailsham. The battle was finally won in 1963. Both Wedgwood Benn and Hogg took immediate advantage of the opportunity provided to get rid of the peerages they had inherited; so among others did Lord Home, who became prime minister and returned to the House of Commons as Sir Alec Douglas-Home. On becoming lord chancellor in 1970, Hogg became once again Lord Hailsham—as a life peer—and Sir Alec was made a life peer in 1974 as Lord Home of the Hirsel.

Scottish and Irish Peers

After the Union with Scotland in 1707, no new Scottish peers were created. The Scottish peers elected sixteen of their number to serve in the new Parliament of Great Britain, with an election held for each parliament. In 1963 the representative scheme was done away with, and now peers holding only Scottish titles can sit in the House of Lords. A representative scheme was also adopted for Irish peers after the Union with Ireland in 1801; there were twenty-eight Irish representative peers. But Irish representative peers were chosen for life, and the other Irish peers (unlike Scottish peers) could vote for members of the House of Commons and could serve as members of that house. The most famous example is Lord Palmerston (the third Viscount Palmerston), who spent his entire political career in the House of Commons. After the creation of the Irish Free State in 1922, no machinery existed for electing representative peers; their numbers dwindled steadily and there are no representative peers in the House of Lords today.

Baronets and Knights

A baronetcy is best understood as a hereditary knighthood. Baronetcies were first conferred in the reign of James I as a means of raising money for the Crown. Titles and signatures are handled in the same way as with knights, except that the word Baronet, or abbreviation Bart. or Bt., follows the name in the formal style, though not in signatures: thus Sir Walter Scott, Bart. Baronetcies are not now much given.

Knighthood was originally a dignity conferred when a certain level of military attainment had been reached; but it is now a recognition of service to the state in almost any field of endeavor. When land dominated English society, a knighthood was a normal expectation of a landowner of considerable wealth and political power who was not powerful enough to assert a claim to a peerage. In the greater complexity of modern society, knighthoods are conferred upon senior civil servants, successful businessmen, university professors, cricket players, actors, and jockeys. The oldest and most numerous class of knights are the knights bachelor, but knighthoods can also be conferred in nine knightly orders: the Garter (the highest honor that can be conferred on any subject, limited, royalty aside, to twenty-five knights-companions), the Thistle (the corresponding order for Scotland, numbering sixteen), St. Patrick (Ireland, numbering twenty-two), the Bath (primarily military), the Star of India, the Indian Empire, St. Michael and St. George (service to the empire overseas and in foreign affairs), the Royal Victorian (service to the sovereign), and the British Empire. The last two orders may be conferred on women. Orders below the Garter, Thistle, and St. Patrick are divided into classes: Knights Grand Cross (or Grand Commanders), Knights Commanders, and Companions. The first two grades carry knighthoods, the third does not. The Royal Victorian Order and the Order of the British Empire are divided into five classes. Beyond the two knightly grades in each, there are Companions and two classes of Members in the Royal Victorian Order; Companions, Officers, and Members in the Order of the British Empire. The C.B.E., O.B.E., and M.B.E. are awarded in large numbers in each of the twice-yearly honors lists.

The formal title of a knight uses the given and family names preceded by Sir and followed by initials indicating the order, knights bachelor carrying no initials. Thus the comic first lord of the admiralty in Gilbert and Sullivan's *H.M.S. Pinafore* is Sir Joseph Porter, K.C.B. Knights sign themselves merely with their given and family names, without title or initials, and are addressed by title and first name only. Thus Sir Joseph Porter would have signed himself Joseph Porter and would have been addressed as Sir Joseph. Women who receive knighthoods use Dame as a title. Wives of knights are known as Lady, with the surname and without the given name. It is, therefore, usually possible to distinguish wives of knights from wives or daughters of peers. Sir Joseph Porter's wife would have been Lady Porter. Had her husband so distinguished himself as ruler of the Queen's Navee as to be raised to the peerage as, say, the Earl of Spithead, his wife would have become Countess of Spithead and would have been addressed as Lady Spithead. His daughter (he must have had children as well as sisters, brothers, and aunts), once (let us say) plain Violet Porter, when her father was a knight, would have been transmuted into Lady Violet Porter, when he became a peer. If she married a commoner, Mr. John Smith, the couple would have been referred to as Mr. John Smith and Lady Violet Smith.

Other Honors

The lower ranks of the Order of the British Empire, as we have seen, are quite widely distributed in honors lists. Two other orders, carrying no titles, confer much greater honor. Companions of Honor (C.H.) are limited to fifty persons who have rendered important national services. The Order of Merit was founded in 1902. It is limited to twenty-four persons who have distinguished themselves in art, literature, science, war, or public service. Among notable O.M.'s have been John Morley, Florence Nightingale, the physicist Lord Rutherford, the composer Sir Edward Elgar, the historian G. M. Trevelyan, the painter Augustus John, the poet T. S. Eliot, the choreographer Sir Frederick Ashton.

The Privy Council, which in the eighteenth century expanded far beyond its original definition as the king's closest councillors, still retains certain formal governmental functions. But it has also become an honorific reward for all those who attain high political office and has been used in the past as a more general honor. In formal address, the name of a privy councillor is preceded by the style Right Honorable (Rt. Hon.). This prefix is also used customarily in the formal style of a peer below the rank of duke and marquess (who are, respectively, The Most Noble and The Most Honorable). Thus, the Rt. Hon. the Earl of Iveagh, K.G., by virtue of his peerage and his having been awarded the Garter; and the Rt. Hon. James Callaghan, M.P. by virtue of his being a privy councillor and member of parliament.

This appendix can at best give a roughly adequate sketch of a subject highly complicated by inherent subtleties of usage and by many exceptions and arbitrary illogicalities. Whether the words "the" and "of" are used is a question that can cause endless difficulties, for example. For further guidance, there are a number of books of reference.

The great historical source is the many volumes of G. E. C. [G. E. Cokayne], *The Complete Peerage,* the publication of which extended from 1887 to 1959: it traces every peerage, whether in existence or extinct. For peerages still extant, one can refer to the annual issues of *Debrett's Peerage,* or to the now somewhat more infrequent *Burke's Peerage,* where descent is traced and much other information is given; *Burke's,* being fuller, is preferable. A clear, pleasant, and nicely opinionated introduction is given in Valentine Heywood, *British Titles: The Use and Misuse of the Titles of Peers and Commoners, with Some Historical Notes* (1951).

Appendix 3
The Church of England

JURISDICTIONS

The Provinces

There are two provinces, Canterbury and York. Each is headed by an archbishop; each has a Convocation, composed of houses of bishops and clergy. The provinces are independent, but through historical circumstances (not to say accidents), the Province of Canterbury has been larger and dominant. In 1832 there were only four dioceses in the province of York — the archdiocese of York, Carlisle, Chester, and Durham — plus the curious diocese of Sodor and Man, which came under the Archbishop of York but had its own Convocation. The richer and once much more heavily settled Province of Canterbury had twenty-two, including four Welsh bishoprics, which remained until the disestablishment of the Church in Wales in 1920. Today York has 14 dioceses, Canterbury 29.

The Dioceses

A diocese is the jurisdiction of a bishop, administered from the cathedral town from which the diocese takes its name.

Besides the archdioceses of Canterbury and York, the following dioceses existed in 1832, the number having been unchanged since the sixteenth century: Bath and Wells, Bristol, Carlisle, Chester, Chichester, Lichfield and Coventry, Durham, Ely, Exeter, Gloucester, Hereford, Lincoln, London, Norwich, Oxford, Peterborough, Rochester, Salisbury, Sodor and Man, Winchester, and Worcester, all in England.

The following English dioceses have been added since 1832: Birmingham (C, 1905), Blackburn (Y, 1926), Bradford (Y, 1919), Chelmsford (C, 1914), Coventry (C, refounded 1918), Derby (C, 1927), Guildford (C, 1927), Leicester (C, 1926), Liverpool (Y, 1880), Manchester (Y, 1847), Newcastle (Y, 1882), Portsmouth (C, 1927), Ripon (Y, refounded 1836), St. Alban's (C, 1877), St. Edmundsbury and Ipswich (C, 1914), Sheffield (Y, 1914), Southwark (in London, C, 1905), Southwell (Y, 1884), Truro (C, 1877), and Wakefield (Y, 1888).

The Welsh dioceses in 1832 were Bangor, Llandaff, St. Asaph, and St. David's; Monmouth, and Swansea and Brecon have been added in more recent times.

There are two kinds of subdivision within a diocese: the archdeaconry and the rural deanery. Formerly the archdeaconry was a subdivision for mixed administrative and judicial purposes, such as revenues and the enforcement of morals; but the archdeacon now has the function of advising the bishop on spiritual matters as well. The rural dean serves as a means of transmitting episcopal directives to the parishes and of communicating parochial needs (e.g., vacancies) to the bishop. This office fell into disuse after the Middle Ages, but was revived in the course of the nineteenth century.

The Parishes

A parish is the area served by a church. Parishes may vary widely in extent, population, and resources. The parish also became a unit of civil government and remained highly important in that respect until well into the nineteenth century; partly on that account, the subdivision of parishes to match the population explosion in the century after 1750 was a work of great difficulty.

For much of the period covered by this book, the governing body of the parish was the vestry; sometimes it was a meeting of all the inhabitants (analogous to a town meeting in New England), sometimes it was an elected or co-opted body representing the inhabitants. The vestry lost the last of its civil functions to the parish council in 1894 and its responsibility for the administration of ecclesiastical affairs to the parochial church council in 1921. The vestry survives, however, and aids in the selection of churchwardens and in certain other parochial duties.

The vestry had the power of levying a rate (a local tax) on the inhabitants for certain purposes — poor relief, highway maintenance, and the upkeep of the parish church and the churchyard. Church rates were abolished in 1868. The fixing of the poor rate was transferred in 1834 to the elected overseers of the poor in the unions created by the Poor Law Amendment Act of that year. All rates are now the responsibility of county or town councils.

Churches

The great church around which the life of the diocese revolves is called a cathedral. Medieval England was unusual in Europe in that many of its cathedrals were staffed by monks, who lived a cloistered life. But others, following Continental practice, were staffed by secular canons, i.e., a staff of priests who did not live under monastic discipline. These latter cathedrals survived the Reformation with little change; but the abolition of monasticism forced a change in the former from rule by monks to rule by secular canons. Although these monastic cathedrals were the oldest cathedrals in England, dating from Anglo-Saxon times, because of the change at the Reformation they have come to be known as "cathedrals of the new foundation." The creation of new dioceses in the modern period has often been done by raising the principal parish church of an important town to the status of a cathedral; it continues in both functions, whereas the older cathedrals have no parochial functions. In a few new dioceses, new cathedrals have been built — Liverpool, Truro, and Guildford — while one cathedral, Coventry, destroyed in the Second World War, has been replaced by a modern building.

The term "minster" is occasionally to be found. It means simply "a large church," and is attached to certain very old churches that were set up to serve parts of medieval dioceses that had grown too large for direct ministering by the bishop. Minsters were directly responsible to the bishop. But most parish churches have descended from private foundations by pious or prudent landowners.

THE HIERARCHY

Archbishops

When the English Church was founded in the sixth and seventh centuries, the intention was that the senior of the two archbishops would have primacy. In the event, the Archbishops of Canterbury secured the primacy for themselves—the Archbishop of York is called Primate of England, but the Archbishop of Canterbury is Primate of All England. In the Middle Ages, the Archbishop of Canterbury usually had legatine power from the pope—he could, in other words, act as the pope's representative—but these powers were held at the pope's pleasure and could be superseded by a specially appointed legate. In time, legatine powers were also given to the Archbishop of York to prevent Canterbury from growing too powerful, as seen from Rome. Although the legatine powers disappeared after 1534, certain papal functions that had been exercised through the papal legates survived and were conferred by Henry VIII on the Archbishops of Canterbury, notably the power to issue licenses and to grant dispensations (in both provinces).

Archbishops superintend the work of the Church in their provinces, preside over Convocation, confirm the election of bishops, and can deprive bishops of their office in case of default. The Archbishop of Canterbury crowns the king, is the chief spokesman of the Church in parliament and in public, presides over the Church Assembly, and has in recent years served as Chairman of the periodic Lambeth Conferences, so called from the palace where the archbishop lives. He is therefore the head of the world-wide Anglican communion, to which the Episcopal Church of the United States belongs.

Within their own dioceses, archbishops fulfill the functions of bishops.

Bishops

The bishop is the chief administrative officer of a diocese. Bishops in the primitive church were elected, but in the Middle Ages the election came to be confined to the cathedral chapter. In the late Middle Ages, for a time, direct papal appointment was the method of selection. But in actual fact, whatever the form of election or appointment, the real power of choice lay with the Crown, as it does today, being exercised, of course, by the Prime Minister. A *congé d'élire* is issued to the chapter ordering it to elect the government's nominee, and the chapter duly complies. In 1847 Lord John Russell named R. D. Hampden, Regius professor of divinity at Oxford, to be bishop of Hereford. As Hampden's orthodoxy was suspect to many people in the

Church, there was a violent reaction, and the Dean of Hereford wrote at length to the prime minister to explain his decision to oppose the election of Dr. Hampden. Lord John Russell replied:

> Sir,—I have had the honour to receive your letter of the 22nd instant, in which you intimate to me your intention of violating the law.
> I have the honour to be your obedient servant,
>
> *J. Russell*

Hampden was elected.

Until the multiplication of bishoprics in the nineteenth century, all bishops sat in the House of Lords. Now, while the two archbishops and the bishops of London, Winchester, and Durham always sit in the Lords, the other bishops rotate seats according to seniority, to make up the old number of twenty-six. Bishops had traditionally been close advisers and often dependents of the king: their political functions came naturally to them until the nineteenth-century religious revival raised serious questions about the effects of the tie between Church and State. Today the political function is minimal, in contrast to the eighteenth century, when it was often predominant.

Within his diocese, a bishop is responsible for general oversight of the Church; every three years he must make a visitation; and, either directly or through a deputy, he confirms children, i.e., receives them as full members of the Church on their confirming (usually around the age of twelve) the vows made for them at baptism by their godparents. He is responsible for the discipline of the clergy, and he ordains priests.

The growth of administrative responsibilities in modern times and the more serious view taken of the work of the diocese (ironically paralleled by a shrinking of the role of the Church in national life) has led to the appointment of assistant, or suffragan, bishops. Archdeacons and rural deans are subordinate officers with duties indicated above, and there are a number of lay officers in each diocese to look after aspects of Church administration. Since 1836, of course, much of the administration of the Church has been centralized in the Ecclesiastical Commissioners (now the Church Commissioners).

In the Middle Ages, bishops sat in Parliament in virtue of their being barons: the Investiture Controversy of the twelfth century revolved around the question of whether papal or archiepiscopal investiture of a new bishop with his spiritual authority should or should not have priority over royal investiture with the all-important lands. The formal style of a bishop, therefore, is analogous to that of a peer: he is "the Rt. Rev. ———, Lord Bishop of ———." A bishop signs his name by using his given name and the name (or an abbreviation, often in Latin) of his diocese. Thus the present Archbishop of Canterbury, the Rt. Rev. Robert Runcie, signs Robert.

Deans and Chapters

The dean is the head of a cathedral chapter; together dean and chapter control the cathedral, a control extending even to its use by the bishop. Since 1931 the bishop's right to preach in the cathedral and to use it for services in which he has a part (such as ordinations and confirmations) has been fully established by law: differences between dean and bishop have never been uncommon. Deans of older cathedrals are appointed by the Crown; the heads of newer cathedrals are usually called provosts and are appointed by their bishops.

The chapter consists of several residentiary canons who, with the dean, govern the cathedral and conduct the services. Cathedrals of the old foundation once had non-residentiary canons who drew income (called the prebend, hence the name prebendaries) from the cathedral revenues; this income was cut off in 1840. Prebendaries continue to be appointed, differing from the honorary canons attached to other cathedrals only by their retaining somewhat more prestige.

Priests

Although the term *priest* is technically correct, the word is used conventionally only for clergy who tend to the "High Church" or Anglo-Catholic position; Evangelicals and others are usually referred to simply as clergymen or ministers.

One of the concomitants of founding and endowing a parish was the right vested in the patron (usually the local landowner) of appointing the parish priest—the right, as it was called, of presentation to a benefice, or, more simply, the advowson. Advowsons quickly became a kind of property and could be transferred or willed. Much land and many advowsons came into the hands of monasteries in this way, when benefactions to monks were a common form of philanthropy. On the suppression of the monasteries in the sixteenth century, monastic patronage returned to the Crown or went to laymen who bought up monastic lands. Universities and colleges have acquired advowsons; and patronage is also exercised by archbishops, bishops, cathedral chapters, and the ministers of churches that have other churches dependent on them. Since the nineteenth century there have been trusts, dedicated to particular points of view (the Evangelicals being notable in this respect) who have bought up advowsons to spread more widely their own doctrinal viewpoint.

Traditionally, the priest has had two main sources of income, besides fees for services such as baptism and marriage. In the first place, once he is presented by his patron and instituted by the bishop—once he becomes, technically, the incumbent of the parish—he enters into possession of a freehold; in other words, until he dies, resigns, or is deprived for some ecclesiastical offence, he is the full owner of the benefice and the property attached to it. The property may consist of endowments and land, called the glebe, which may be farmed or let. The other source of income is tithe, originally a voluntary offering that quickly became compulsory in the Middle Ages and that by the end of the seventeenth century was levied solely on agricultural produce. Confined to one source of income and levied in kind rather than money, tithe was a grievance among farmers, and disputes with owners of tithes were frequent. Commutation of tithe into money payments was often agreed to, however, and in 1836 it became mandatory according to a complicated formula (tied to the price of grain) that has had to be revised

on several occasions since to take account of the unfortunate effects of agricultural depression. Since 1836 tithe has been collected (for the most part)
centrally and is paid as part of the rent of land; but acts of 1925 and 1936 have
provided for ultimate redemption of land from the tithe rent-charge. If all
tithe income from a parish went to the incumbent, he was known as the rector. Frequently, however, a portion of the tithe (the so-called great tithes) fell
to the patron—monastery, college, or individual; the patron (even though a
layman or secular corporation) then became the rector, while the incumbent
dependent on the rector's patronage was known as a vicar. Colloquially,
whether rector or vicar, the incumbent of a parish is often referred to as the
parson.

    Until relatively recently, a curate was a substitute for the nominal in-
cumbent when he was an absentee, so-called because he had the actual "cure
of souls," i.e., ministered to the spiritual needs of the parish. Often young
and in first holy orders (prior to ordination an intending clergyman is known
as a deacon, not a priest), curates were dependent on their superior and were
usually miserably underpaid. Since non-residence has been all but abolished, curates are now generally assistants to parish priests, and are required
to be appointed once a parish passes a certain size.

    A secured income gives a parson a degree of independence and free-
dom. It might make it possible for him to maintain a position against the
local squire (although he would be unlikely to do so if he owed his appointment to him), but it could also mean freedom to neglect his parish, a short-
coming with which bishops have had difficulty in dealing. But independence might be more nominal than real, for the income of parishes varied
greatly and still varies considerably in spite of all efforts by central church
authorities in the last 130 years to even out ecclesiastical incomes.

    It is not exactly an afterthought to mention the spiritual work of
clergymen; rather, it has been more or less taken for granted.

Church Law and Courts

The doctrinal standard of the Church is the Thirty-Nine Articles, adopted in
1562, a document open to much latitude of interpretation. The Act of Uniformity in the same year enforced the use of the Book of Common Prayer, which
sets out the forms of worship and rubrics governing vestments and fur-
nishings of churches. A somewhat revised Book of Common Prayer was
reimposed, following the Puritan ascendancy, in the Act of Uniformity of
1662; this statute governs these matters today. The Prayer Book cannot be
changed without the consent of Parliament; an effort to change it in 1928 was
defeated. Most parsons today, however, depart from the Prayer Book in
many particulars and so are technically liable to prosecution under the Act of
Uniformity. The medieval heritage of canon law has been in a state of confusion ever since the Reformation, and statutes governing discipline of the
clergy and the forms of public worship have probably introduced more confusion than clarification. Whatever the legal situation, the Church of England
is characterized today by a high degree of liberality and permissiveness.

    In the Middle Ages, the principal ecclesiastical court was the arch-
deacon's court, concerned not only with clerical matters but with moral

transgressions by the laity. Since the seventeenth century, it has had only minor functions to perform. The bishop's court, the diocesan consistory, is now the principal ecclesiastical court. The bishop has a veto over bringing any case into his court, which is presided over by his chancellor. Appeals from the bishop's court lie to the court of the archbishop of his province — the Court of Arches in Canterbury, the Chancery Court in York. Since 1874, the "official principal" who presides over these courts has been the same man, appointed by the archbishops and called the Dean of Arches. Before the Reformation, appeal lay from the Courts Christian in England to the papal curia in Rome. The restraint of appeals in 1533 left the king as heir to the Roman jurisdiction, which came to be exercised by the king in Chancery, with an *ad hoc* High Court of Delegates being appointed for each case. The Court of High Commission soon succeeded to most of these powers, but it was abolished in 1641, and the High Court of Delegates remained the highest court of appeal. In 1833, the powers of this court were transferred to the new Judicial Committee of the Privy Council, whose judgments (given by an entirely lay body) punctuated the history of the Victorian Church with crises.

At the beginning of our period, church courts had oversight not only of questions of liturgical practice and clerical discipline, but of probating wills and of all matrimonial causes. Since the Church's law on these matters was deeply affected during the Middle Ages by Roman law, a special legal practice grew up to deal with them, centered in a corporation, similar to the Inns of Court, known as Doctors' Commons. In 1857, testamentary and matrimonial causes were transferred to the civil courts, and Doctors' Commons disappeared six years later. Charles Dickens's *David Copperfield* draws a picture of the operation of Doctors' Commons in its decline.

For further information, the following books may be consulted:

Cecilia M. Ady, *The English Church and How It Works* (1940).
G. F. A. Best, *Temporal Pillars: Queen Anne's Bounty, the Ecclesiastical Commissioners and the Church of England* (1964).
Owen Chadwick, *The Victorian Church* (1966, 1970).
Owen Chadwick, *Victorian Miniature* (1960), a chronicle seen from both sides of the long-standing quarrel between a squire and a clergyman in Ketteringham, Norfolk.
Felix Makower, *Constitutional History and Constitution of the Church of England* (1895, reprinted 1960).
Norman Sykes, *Church and State in the Eighteenth Century* (1934).
Anthony Trollope, *The Clergymen of the Church of England* (1866), reprinted from a series of articles in the *Pall Mall Gazette*, a delightful set of composite portraits of the hierarchy and the parish clergy in the mid-nineteenth century.

Appendix 4
The English Courts

CIVIL JURISDICTION

The Common Law Courts

In the earlier Middle Ages, what we would call civil cases—those involving property or disputes between persons as to their rights—came before a variety of local courts, among which were the county courts, the hundred courts (the hundred being a legal and administrative unit of uncertain origin), and, in towns, the borough courts. Rights and duties involved in manorial or feudal relationships were adjudicated in manorial courts and courts baron. But from the twelfth century, these local courts rapidly lost ground to the superior attractions of the law administered by the king's justices. Instead of administering the custom of a locality, they administered one law throughout the kingdom; and as the body of this law was built up on precedents set by earlier decisions, it came to be known as the *common law*, common to the whole country: it was unwritten law as opposed to the written law embodied in statutes. In the period with which this book is concerned, civil jurisdiction had come to be highly centralized in three Common Law courts. Some survivals of the old local courts were still to be found, but they were only survivals, with few important powers.

The oldest, and in the Middle Ages the busiest, of the Common Law courts was the Court of Common Pleas, so called because it dealt with disputes between subject and subject; its separate existence was clearly recognized in the thirteenth century. This court was presided over by the Chief Justice of Common Pleas, who was assisted by a number of *puisne* (pronounced "puny") justices, five in number prior to the judicial reforms of 1873. The second, the Court of King's Bench, was concerned, as the name implies, with matters particularly affecting the king—with "great men and great causes," as Sir William Holdsworth has said—and it remained with the king (who in the Middle Ages was constantly on the move) long after the Court of Common Pleas had settled in Westminster. Only in the fourteenth century did this court gradually detach itself from the king and the King's Council, to remain in Westminster. It was headed by a Lord Chief Justice, who in time came to be known as the Lord Chief Justice of England, again assisted by puisne justices, who numbered five prior to the reforms of 1873. The third, the Court of Exchequer, began as a part of the Exchequer, the financial and accounting office of medieval England, which had settled down in Westminster in the twelfth century. The principal officers of the Exchequer, called Barons of the Exchequer, exercised both administrative and judicial powers (the distinction is a modern one that would have baffled them) in relation to financial matters; but at the end of the thirteenth century, the judicial side became separated from the financial side, and it was the departing judges who took with them the name of Barons of the Exchequer. The head of the Court of Exchequer, then, was the Chief Baron, and his assistants—also five in number—were puisne barons.

Throughout the Middle Ages, these three courts had specialized functions: civil disputes between subjects in one; great causes, questions touching the king, and criminal justice in another; revenue in the third. But in the sixteenth century, the courts of King's Bench and Exchequer took advantage of elastic procedures to encroach on the business of the very heavily used Court of Common Pleas. Often the procedures of these two courts were better or swifter, and more and more litigants resorted to them. In the period covered in this book, the three Common Law courts had no clear jurisdictional lines between them. They were also unequally used: King's Bench was overworked and Common Pleas underworked in the early nineteenth century.

The Assize Courts in Civil Actions

The advantage of centralized courts sitting in Westminster, in a time when transportation was crude and distances were great, would have been much offset by the hardships imposed on suitors, witnesses, and juries (who in the Middle Ages were always local and expected to judge from their own knowledge of facts) who had to travel from their homes perhaps several hundred miles to Westminster. From time to time, however, the king's justices were sent out on circuit with a commission to hear all pleas in that circuit. There was not much system about these *general eyres,* and their primary purpose was to allow the king and his ministers to keep an eye on what was going on and to make money from the inevitable infraction of rules or dereliction of duty on the part of local officials and subjects. The justices were also sent out from time to time with commissions to try *assizes,* cases under procedures worked out in the reign of Henry II for settling certain frequent disputes in property law; although these procedures were in disuse throughout the modern period and were abolished in 1833, the name assizes was preserved for these itinerant royal courts. The judges of assize also heard criminal cases, as we shall see, and often persons who were not royal justices were commissioned to hear assizes or to deal with criminal offenses in association with the justices. In time—the general eyre having disappeared amid the hatred of the people it had so effectively terrorized—the issuing of these commissions was regularized: throughout the modern period right down to 1972, assize courts sat regularly in the chief towns of counties or of divisions of large counties, staffed by justices of the courts at Westminster and by local officials serving as judges of assize under a commission from the king.

In the thirteenth century, a curious way was found to use these circuits through the country to mitigate the difficulties involved in centralizing civil trials of greater importance than the assizes: this was the *nisi prius* procedure. A case was begun in one of the courts at Westminster; a date would then be set for hearing the case at Westminster unless before — *nisi prius* — that date the royal justices came into the county, which in fact always happened. It should be understood, however, that while assizes were separate courts in their criminal function, in *nisi prius* cases the judges were really serving as delegates, so to speak, for the court at Westminster, where the cases would finally be decided on the basis of records of hearings. In civil matters, then, the assizes were part of the Common Law courts.

The County Courts

In 1846 the present system of county courts was created. The sentimental and distinguished aura surrounding the name of England's oldest but by then vanished courts was revived for new local courts, each presided over by a single judge from a panel responsible for five hundred districts divided into circuits having no necessary connection with geographical counties. County courts have handled small civil cases (at the outset the most important of these were cases of debt) below a certain sum in value. That sum has been steadily raised, and the number of judges increased. Only important cases come before the central courts.

Appeals

The idea of appeal from a judgment was difficult for the medieval mind to reach; indeed, a regularly organized system of appeals is a development only a little more than a century old. There were many more or less successful attempts to approach the idea of an appeal, such as accusing the jury of malice, but the most important device was to allege an error in the record, a procedure used for both civil and criminal cases. Now an error in the record of the case is a very narrow and often a trivial ground, but it was one that through fictions made possible a thriving form of litigation, heard in the Court of King's Bench. Still other devices were worked out — a motion for a new trial, for example — but they were far from satisfactory. The idea of actually rehearing a case on appeal was worked out in the High Court of Chancery but remained unknown in the Common Law courts down to their reform in 1873.

If the judges themselves had doubts about a particularly difficult case, they could refer it to other judges for a decision. Thus an assize judge could order a *nisi prius* case to be heard in the court at Westminster where, technically, it originated. There was also a court called Exchequer Chamber, which existed in a number of forms. One form of it was a meeting of all the judges, to whom difficult cases could be referred. But in other forms, Exchequer Chamber served as a court to correct errors in the Court of Exchequer and, for certain kinds of cases, in the Court of King's Bench. Finally, in 1830, the Court of Exchequer Chamber was established as a court of appeal from all three Common Law courts, the new court being composed of all the judges of the two Common Law courts other than the court appealed against.

The House of Lords

While appeals as we think of them were denied to litigants until fairly recently, the medieval litigant had another recourse. As the king was the fount of all justice, a subject who felt aggrieved could petition the king for redress. These petitions came to be directed to the king in council in parliament — the origin of Parliament, the term applying at first to an occasion, not an institution — an enlarged and so especially weighty meeting of the king's council. The lay magnates tried to keep the jurisdiction over petitions, as they were jealous of the professionals in the council, but in time the professionals won. But not entirely: the peers, who could claim to be the king's council extended, as the Commons could not, did retain a vague claim to deal with important and unusual cases, a claim that was defined and established for both original and appellate jurisdiction in the early seventeenth century. The House of Lords gave up its original jurisdiction in the late seventeenth century, but its appellate jurisdiction remained. Direct interference by the House of Lords with proceedings in the lower courts was also abandoned in the seventeenth century, but the writ of error came to take the place of the old medieval petitions, and lay to the House of Lords from the Court of King's Bench, the Court of Exchequer, the High Court of Admiralty, after 1707 the Scottish courts, and after 1800 the Irish courts. Appeal could also be made to the House of Lords from the High Court of Chancery, both in its relatively unimportant common law side and from its important decisions in equity, of which more presently. In exercising this appellate jurisdiction, any member of the House of Lords could take part, whether he was legally trained or not, although much (but not all) of the time untrained peers would not take part or would take advice from those peers "learned in the law." After 1844, however, the judicial function of the House of Lords was confined to professional lawyers who sat in that House.

Equity

The story is told of a lawyer who, having won a case for a large business firm in a city far away from the head office, telegraphed the president of the company, announcing, "Justice has prevailed." The president replied, "Appeal at once." The distinction between law and justice is important: any set of rules may create an injustice when applied to a situation unlike those foreseen when the rules were drawn up. The last medieval resort of appealing to the king had still another result than the appellate jurisdiction of the House of Lords. As the forms of the common law began to harden and the old flexibility disappeared, many petitions for redress, instead of going to Parliament to feed the claim of the House of Lords, were referred to the Lord Chancellor, the king's chief administrative officer whose office regularly issued the common law writs, and who himself was closely associated with the administration of the common law, although he was not a judge. If the Lord Chancellor saw fit, he could, as "keeper of the king's conscience," provide an "equitable" solution to the problem. By the sixteenth century, the Lord Chancellor had his own court, the High Court of Chancery, which administered a much more flexible kind of law that came to be called equity. The importance of the

High Court of Chancery increased steadily as new kinds of legal problems arose for which the now hidebound Common Law courts had no remedies — trust, for example, in which property was conveyed to one person or to a group of persons for the benefit of another person — and as special responsibilities were given to the Lord Chancellor by act of Parliament. From the sixteenth century, with one or two exceptions, the post of Lord Chancellor was always held by a lawyer, whereas in the Middle Ages, the Chancellor had almost always been an ecclesiastic.

The rules of equity began to be more firmly fixed in the eighteenth and early nineteenth centuries through the work of great chancellors like Lord Hardwicke (1736–1756) and Lord Eldon (1801–1806, 1807–1827): it became a system of law of great sophistication that often conflicted with the common law. At the same time the court was subject to serious abuses, the worst being the delays of years and even decades and the vast expense entailed by the complexities of equity both in procedure and rules: the High Court of Chancery is the villain in Charles Dickens's *Bleak House*. The Chancellor was assisted by twelve "masters," who had many duties which gradually came to be confined to assisting him in hearing cases. In the eighteenth century, the most important of these masters, the Master of the Rolls, became a second Judge in the High Court of Chancery, although his decisions were still subject to appeal to the Chancellor himself. In the early nineteenth century, one and then two more vice-chancellors were added; and in 1851 the Court of Appeal was established, consisting of two Lords Justices of Appeal in Chancery and the Lord Chancellor himself; this court stood between Chancery and the House of Lords. Some of the Chancellor's jurisdiction was transferred to other courts — notably the jurisdiction in bankruptcy. Thus the Lord Chancellor himself withdrew from hearing cases in equity in the first instance to concentrate on his administrative duties as head of the national system of justice and on his judicial and political duties in the House of Lords, over whose sittings he presides.

THE REFORMS OF THE 1870's

In 1873–1876, the entire judicial system was reorganized, following half a century and more of dissatisfaction, investigation, and piecemeal reform. When the act of 1873 came into effect in 1875, the Supreme Court of Judicature was established. This court, which absorbed nearly all the existing courts, consisted and consists today of two levels. The lower level is the High Court of Justice. Between 1875 and 1972, the judges of that court (addressed in court as "My Lord," but formally as "Mr. Justice ———") were assigned to one of three divisions — King's, or Queen's, Bench (incorporating the Queen's Bench, Common Pleas, and Exchequer divisions after 1881); Chancery; and Probate, Divorce, and Admiralty. This last association, so odd a linkage at first sight, arose from the fact that wills, marriage, and maritime matters were branches of the law deeply influenced by Roman, or civil, law. The judges of the lower-level court normally sit alone in hearing cases, although there are certain cases in which a divisional court of two or more justices is called for.

The higher level of the Supreme Court of Judicature was, and is, the

Court of Appeal, presided over by the Master of the Rolls (the only ex officio member who actually sits, although, formally, the Lord Chancellor is the head of the Court), assisted by a fixed number of Lords Justices of Appeals (formally addressed as "Lord Justice ————"). The appellate jurisdiction of the House of Lords was abolished, but in 1875–1876 it was restored, in a drastically changed form. When sitting as a court, the House of Lords now consists only of the Lord Chancellor; a group of life peers as professional judges, called Lords of Appeal in Ordinary; and such members of the House of Lords as have held high judicial office and whom the Lord Chancellor may call upon. But appeal to the House of Lords is not by right; leave of either the Court of Appeal or the House of Lords is required.

As to the law administered in this restructured series of courts, the act of 1873 provided that both common law and equity should be used, and that in case of conflict, the rules of equity should prevail.

THE COUNCIL

The Privy Council, which in the sixteenth and seventeenth centuries functioned as the central instrument of government, retained important judicial functions, which were exercised in the early modern period through a number of prerogative courts or conciliar courts— the Court of Star Chamber, the Council of the North, the Council of Wales, the Court of Requests, and the Court of High Commission. At first, this prerogative jurisdiction was highly popular because it was usually swift, cheap, and effective, but it declined in reputation in the early seventeenth century and was abolished in 1641 as an instrument of arbitrary rule. The Council still remained the body to which appeals came from territories overseas, and dissatisfaction with the High Court of Delegates, to which appeals from the Church courts lay, led to the transfer of that function to the Privy Council in 1832. The cases were dealt with by a committee, which was reorganized in 1833 as the Judicial Committee of the Privy Council, composed of a number of ex officio members, e.g., the Lord President of the Council, the Lord Chancellor, the chief justices of the Common Law courts, the Master of the Rolls, and such other persons as the Committee might require; a quorum was set at four and later reduced to three. The importance of the Church courts was greatly reduced in 1857, when the probating of wills and cases involving marriage were taken away from them and given to the new courts of Probate and of Matrimonial Causes, which were in turn absorbed into the reformed High Court system in 1873. Still, the Judicial Committee had to decide some important questions in the area of religion in the nineteenth century (see above, pp. 235–236, 406–407). In the twentieth century, its importance remained great in the colonial field, even for some Commonwealth countries that had acquired all the other trappings of independence, but that importance has now shrunk along with the Empire.

CRIMINAL JURISDICTION

By the eighteenth century some of the old medieval courts that had been set up to deal with the perennial problem of crime had decayed, the court-leet, for example, which descended from the sheriff's tourn of the twelfth and thirteenth centuries. Only one of these old courts has survived to the present — the coroner's court. This court has been shorn of nearly all its once extensive powers, retaining only the important duty of investigating unexplained deaths. For the period covered by this book, the criminal jurisdiction of the country may be considered under three heads.

Justices of the Peace

These officials emerged in the fourteenth century from a series of earlier experiments, and in succeeding centuries they were saddled with many heavy responsibilities, not only for police and the administration of justice, but for administration of local government as well. They were appointed by the Crown, once on the advice of the Lord Lieutenant of the county, later on the advice of local selection committees. The choice was usually made from the most worthy and respectable men in a county, so for most of the period of this book, the J.P.'s were drawn largely from the ranks of the gentry, with some notable assistance from the clergy. As was the case with members of Parliament, the early practice of paying the justices fell into disuse, so through our period right down to today, justices of the peace — with certain important modern exceptions — are unpaid. The other adjective usually associated with them is "amateur." They were not normally trained in the law unless their education as country gentlemen might have included some brief exposure to the law. They were advised on legal questions by the clerk of the peace, who owed his appointment to an official called the *custos rotulorum* (keeper of the rolls or records), usually combined as a purely formal office with that of the Lord Lieutenant. Since 1964 justices of the peace have been required to take training courses, and the old ex officio justices (such as mayors) have been abolished.

Summary powers to deal with minor and some not-so-minor offenses were given to the justices by statute: the number of justices in summary jurisdiction might vary from one to three, and the procedure with which these summary cases were disposed of was often informal in the extreme (often in a justice's house) and subject to considerable abuse or at least suspicion of abuse. After 1848, summary jurisdiction had to be exercised in a formal court setting; these courts came to be known as "petty sessions." The justices of the peace also had the important responsibility of seeing to the keeping of the peace before the emergence of professional police in the first half of the nineteenth century; the Riot Act of 1715 (see above, p. 26) was intended to strengthen them with regard to one aspect of these duties. They also had to make preliminary investigations to determine whether offenders should be sent for trial. Not until the nineteenth century, however, were any important safeguards provided for the suspect at this stage of proceedings: in 1836, the accused person was given the right to see all depositions sworn against him, and in 1848 it was provided that prosecution witnesses had to be examined in the presence of the accused.

The principal court of the justices was Quarter Sessions, held in each county four times a year and attended by all the justices of that county. Although much administrative business was transacted on these occasions,

Quarter Sessions was a full-scale criminal court, with a jury theoretically capable of trying any case short of treason. By custom, however, all serious criminal cases were sent to the assizes.

This easygoing amateur system was obviously less well suited to towns, where crime was a more serious problem than it was (or is) in the countryside. Some towns by their charters had the right to hold their own Quarter Sessions and to greater or lesser degrees to exempt themselves from the jurisdiction of the justices of the county. In such cases, officers of the corporation — the mayor and aldermen — would be appointed as justices, as would an official called the Recorder, almost always a trained lawyer who received a salary for his services; the Recorder became the sole judge in borough Quarter Sessions. By the Municipal Corporations Act of 1835, a number of boroughs were allowed to apply for a separate court of Quarter Sessions; if granted, those courts, too, were headed by Recorders. But the vast amount of lesser, summary business in large towns was also beyond the competence or willingness of amateurs, and so, following some eighteenth-century precedents, it became possible in 1835 to appoint "stipendiary magistrates," paid and now invariably trained judicial officers, though there are now very few of these.

Once a magistrate's preliminary investigation had led to the indictment of a suspect, the case was sent either to Quarter Sessions or to the assizes. The old rule of thumb was that Quarter Sessions could not judge cases involving the death penalty, a rule that sent an enormous amount of business to the assizes before the restriction of the death penalty in the early nineteenth century. Otherwise, the justices decided which court was appropriate, subject to the overriding supervision of the Queen's Bench division of the High Court. Both courts down to 1933 had grand juries, which reviewed the bills of indictment and decided if the case should go to trial; but this intermediate stage no longer exists, and magistrates commit directly to trial.

Assizes

Assizes, as we have seen, had an important role to play in civil jurisdiction. But justices sent out to hear the assizes in the twelfth and thirteenth centuries were also given commissions to deal with criminal cases, the commissions of *oyer* and *terminer* (to hear and determine) and of *gaol* (jail) *delivery*. From this descended the criminal jurisdiction of the assizes, where cases were heard before a single judge and a jury.

London has always presented special problems. From the fourteenth century, the Lord Mayor, the Recorder, and the Aldermen were appointed to the commissions of oyer and terminer and gaol delivery for the City of London, which by charter was a county in itself. They also heard cases from the surrounding county of Middlesex. In 1834, the Central Criminal Court was established for the whole of the metropolitan area of greater London: the Old Bailey, as it is popularly called, was an Assize Court — and is now a Crown Court — in session nearly the year around. Although the Lord Mayor and the Aldermen are still named to the court, it is really staffed by judges of the Queen's Bench division of the High Court and by the judges of the City of London — the Recorder, the Common Serjeant, and the circuit judges.

King's Bench and Criminal Appeals

As it was especially concerned with the business of the Crown, the Court of King's Bench had a natural criminal jurisdiction over which the Crown had largely asserted a monopoly of prosecution. King's Bench has never taken many cases in original jurisdiction, but it could remove cases into its jurisdiction by the writ of *certiorari,* a device that might be useful, for example, to assure a fair trial impossible in a locality.

While cases in magistrates' courts and Quarter Sessions might be reviewed in King's Bench on points of law, there was no regular system of appeals in criminal cases from the assizes, and so for more serious crimes, until the present century. Judges had often followed in criminal cases the old practice of the Exchequer Chamber in consulting their colleagues; this practice was given statutory form in the creation of the Court for Crown Cases Reserved in 1848. But this was a court for referral by a judge and not a court of appeal. The convicted criminal could only hope for exercise of the royal prerogative of mercy, delegated to the Home Secretary. Finally, in 1907, the Court of Criminal Appeal was established. It was composed of three or a higher uneven number of judges drawn from the justices of the King's Bench division; the Lord Chief Justice always sat as one member. No appeal could be made against acquittal. Any point of law could be appealed, but questions of fact could be appealed only with leave of the trial judge or the Court of Criminal Appeal; appeal against sentence could be heard only if the Court of Criminal Appeal gave leave. In 1966 this Court was merged with the Court of Appeal, which now functions in a Civil Division and a Criminal Division.

From the Court of Criminal Appeal and now from the Court of Appeal, and from divisional courts in the Queen's Bench there is an appeal to the House of Lords. But leave is required, either from the court below or from the House of Lords, to assure that only points of exceptional public importance are brought there.

THE REFORMS OF THE 1970's

In 1971–1972 a sweeping reorganization of the court structure was undertaken. On the civil side, the old Probate, Divorce, and Admiralty Division of the High Court was replaced by the Family Division, with probate functions falling to the Chancery Division and admiralty questions going to the Queen's Bench Division. Assizes were abolished; in their place are circuit courts, held at 24 centers in the provinces. The circuit courts are part of the High Court, and High Court judges are present for much or all of the time, though cases may be released to be tried (without altering their status as High Court cases) by a circuit judge or a recorder. Circuit judges constitute a new level of the judiciary, absorbing the old county court judges and certain other judicial appointments, along with a number of new appointees; they are supplemented by part-time judges called recorders. Appeal from the county courts and the High Court lies, as before, to the Civil Division of the Court of Appeal and to the House of Lords.

On the criminal side, magistrates' courts deal with minor offenses summarily and for indictable offenses conduct a preliminary inquiry, with power to commit for trial in a Crown Court. As a court of first instance, a Crown Court sits with a jury; as a court of appeal from the summary jurisdiction of the magistrates, it sits without a jury. Crown Courts may be held at over 80 centers throughout the country. The judge will be a High Court judge for serious cases; for the rest the courts are staffed by circuit judges or recorders, sitting singly or with justices of the peace. Appeals from the Crown Courts go to the Criminal Division of the Court of Appeal and to the House of Lords.

N.B. This appendix has dealt cursorily with an extremely complex subject. But it should be remembered that in Scotland the court structure is entirely different, and the law administered is Scots law, not the English common law.

For further discussions, see W. S. Holdsworth, *A History of English Law*, particularly Vol. I (1903, 7th ed., 1956), and R. M. Jackson, *The Machinery of Justice in England* (7th ed., 1978).

Appendix 5
Local Government

Legislation throughout the period covered by this book affected the structure, working, and spirit of local government, but two periods of time stand out as especially important. In the early 1830's vestries were reformed, the New Poor Law of 1834 introduced a new degree of rationality to that important area of local administration, and, in the municipal reform act of 1835, the governance of sizeable towns was removed from the old unrepresentative and unresponsive corporations and given to elected councils (see above, pp. 225–228). In 1888 a sweeping overhaul of local government was undertaken (see above, p. 428). Elected councils were provided for the counties, defined as administrative counties rather than the historic, geographical counties. This distinction was not carried through ruthlessly: the tiny county of Rutland had its council as did the huge county of Devon. But Yorkshire was divided into three administrative counties, corresponding to its long-standing division into the North, East, and West Ridings, and similar divisions were made elsewhere. More drastic was the designation of towns of over 50,000 population as county boroughs, town governments removed from the supervision of counties and made counties in themselves. The metropolitan area of London was also made into an administrative county under the London County Council; it consisted of the ancient, privileged City of London and 28 districts, drawn from the neighboring three counties of Middlesex, Kent, and Surrey; in 1899 those 28 districts were elevated to the status of metropolitan boroughs, each with its own mayor and council but under the LCC for certain overriding purposes. (The still wider area of Greater London was used for police and statistical purposes.) In 1894, subordinate units were created within the counties — urban districts and rural districts, each with an elected council — taking over a complex pattern of chiefly sanitary functions that had grown up, almost haphazardly, in earlier decades. The same legislation provided elected councils for the larger parishes.

The most fundamental principle enshrined in these various acts was that a distinction should be made between the government of urban and rural Britain, a principle that the increasing mobility and interdependence of the twentieth century made more and more irrelevant. In 1963 the old London County Council was replaced by the Greater London Council and the boroughs within this agglomeration were consolidated. In 1969, a royal commission, known from the name of its chairman as the Redcliffe-Maud Commission, reported on local government in the rest of the country.

In 1972 the Conservative government carried an act that only partly reflected the Commission's views but that did embody its main principles:

the separate government of large metropolitan areas and closer corre-spondence of local government units to population, though the old two-tier arrangement of local government was kept for the counties and, indeed, ex-tended to the metropolitan areas. The new arrangements came into existence in 1974. The new metropolitan areas, in addition to London, are West Yorkshire and South Yorkshire, based on Leeds and Sheffield respectively; Tyne and Wear (Newcastle); Merseyside (Liverpool); West Midlands (Bir-mingham); and Greater Manchester. In the interests of efficiency some his-toric counties were merged, in administrative fact if not in the hearts of their residents—Hereford and Worcester as the County of Hereford and Worces-ter, Cumberland and Westmorland as Cumbria—and one disappeared, Rutland being merged into neighboring Leicestershire, an absorption Rut-land had managed to resist in the early 1960's. The historic ridings of Yorkshire vanished, and what was left after the removal of the two metropol-itan areas was divided into the counties of North Yorkshire and Humber-side; the northern part of Lincolnshire emerged as the County of Cleveland; and the northern part of Somerset, as the County of Avon.

The twelve small counties of Wales, along with the somewhat anoma-lous border county of Monmouth, have been submerged in eight new coun-ties: Clwyd, Dyfed, Gwent, Gwynedd, Powys, West Glamorgan, Mid Gla-morgan, and East Glamorgan. Under an act of 1973, which came into effect in 1975, Scottish counties disappeared entirely, replaced by nine regions, with councils, and 53 district councils, along with three island councils for Ork-ney, Shetland, and the Western Isles.

For further information on an unusually complex subject:

Martin Minogue, ed., *Documents on Contemporary British Govern-ment*, II: *Local Government in Britain* (1977).

Lord Redcliffe-Maud and Bruce Wood, *English Local Govern-ment Reformed* (1974).

J. Redlich and F. W. Hirst, *The History of Local Government in England* (2nd ed., ed. B. Keith-Lucas, 1970).

Peter G. Richards, *The Reformed Local Government System* (2nd ed., rev., 1975).

K. B. Smellie, *A History of Local Government* (4th ed., 1968).

H. V. Wiseman, *Local Government in England, 1958–69* (1970).

Appendix 6
English Money

On February 15, 1971, Britain shifted to decimal currency. That a decimal system is inherently simpler, easier to manipulate in calculating (and easier for calculating machines), and less time-consuming to teach to schoolchildren were obvious arguments in favor of the change. The objections sprang chiefly from the familiarity of the old system and from a gloomy expectation that the change would offer an occasion for raising prices—a bit of cynicism that proved to have some foundation in the immediate transition period. But the new system was quickly absorbed, and regrets have largely vanished. As the old coins disappeared, so did the language that went with them: dozens of mostly forgotten slang words are associated with the old currency, but even the most common and persistent have now retreated to the pages of the dictionaries; and in a surprisingly radical adaptation, pronunciations one might have expected to linger on, since the words remained, have also been swept away—most Englishmen now say "two pence" and "three pence" instead of the "tuppence" and "thrippence" all but universal prior to 1971.

For historical study, however, a thorough acquaintance with the old system is essential, as is the ability to calculate in it. Old and new systems share two historic units: the *pound sterling* and the *penny*. The penny is the oldest English unit; it was in existence in the eighth century—a silver coin whose weight was defined by a certain number of seeds of wheat. By the ninth century 240 pennies were called a pound. The pound, too, is a unit of weight, as its name suggests; though, like the penny, its exact equivalent might vary from region to region, it was officially intended that one pound of silver should equal one pound of money, divisible into 240 pennies. The term *sterling*, of uncertain origin, came to be a guarantee of a high standard of alloy, 925 parts of silver out of 1000.

The term *shilling*, also of disputed origin, came after some experimentation to stand for 12 pennies (or pence, the other plural form*). The Latin terms for the three units were *libra* (pound), *solidus* (shilling), and *denarius* (penny); hence the abbreviations £, s., d., as in £6, 7s., 8d., or six pounds, seven shillings, and eight pence. Until relatively recent times, however, the shilling and the pound were merely "moneys of account," that is, used only in reckoning. Of the silver coins, the penny alone existed until 1279, when the *groat* (now long vanished) made its appearance, with a value of four pennies. *Halfpennies* and *farthings* (one-quarter of a penny) appeared in the fourteenth century to facilitate ordinary transactions in an economy

*"Pence" is only a plural: one must say one penny, not one pence.

656

increasingly dependent on money; the farthing survived, decoratively, until 1961.

Beginning in the middle of the thirteenth century, gold coinage was introduced, taking various forms. The first important gold coin for modern history, however, does not appear until 1663, when the *guinea* was minted, so called because struck from gold (marked with the elephant symbol) imported by the recently chartered company trading to west Africa, the Guinea coast. The value of the guinea varied until 1717, when, in a reform engineered by Sir Isaac Newton in his capacity as master of the mint, it was made equivalent to 21 shillings. In 1817 a gold pound, or *sovereign,* was minted, nicely symbolizing the conversion to the gold standard, which had been completed after a long revolution around the middle of the preceding century. The coinage of gold ceased in 1917, except for occasional ceremonial purposes.

Though no guineas were minted after 1813, the term maintained a fascinating after-life. It continued to be used, down until 1971, to state professional fees, rents for better premises, purses won by racehorses, auction prices, and for similarly impressive purposes. A doctor charging seven guineas for his services would have rendered the bill either as 7 gns. or as £7, 7s.; had he rendered it as seven pounds (£7, os., od.), someone sensitive to social nuances would probably have had as much doubt about the medical worth of his treatment as about his social standing.

The growth of banking from the latter part of the seventeenth century brought a profusion of paper bank notes, promises to pay in coin of the realm — promises the public came to trust, except in occasional crises of confidence. In England in the nineteenth century the Bank of England was given a monopoly of note issue, and private bank notes were suppressed; they remain, however, under certain strict limits, in Scotland and Ireland.

Divorced from fingers and toes, calculating in the old system (though it should be readily accessible to anyone introduced to sets in school) involves more dividing and carrying than a decimal system, but it offers some corresponding flexibilities. The pound divides into halves, quarters, fifths, and tenths;* the shilling into halves (sixpence), thirds (groat), and quarters (the threepenny bit). In the new system, the pound (a paper note) is equal to 100 pennies rather than 240; the coins are in denominations of 50p., 10p., 5 p., 2p., 1p., and ½p., the last a violation of strict decimalization that no doubt inflation will in time correct. The 10p. piece is a continuation of the two-shilling piece *(florin)* minted in 1849 as a first step in decimalization, two shillings being one tenth of a pound. In the nineteenth and overwhelmingly in the twentieth century, of course, checks (cheques in English spelling) supplanted notes and coins for many transactions, and bank credit constitutes the major part of available money.

A. E. Feavearyear, *The Pound Sterling: A History of English Money* (2nd ed., revised, 1963) is the standard account. The numismatic literature is vast, of course, because of collectors. C. H. V. Sutherland, *English Coinage, 600–1900* (1973) is a useful introduction.

---

*The coin for a quarter of a pound was the *crown,* issued in the mid-sixteenth century; though the crown disappeared, the *half crown* survived to the end, disputing with the farthing the affections of the public for its design.

Appendix 7
Additional Reading

The bibliographical notes at the end of each chapter survey relevant monographic studies. They also note appropriate volumes of important series,
such as the *Oxford History of England* or Elie Halévy's *History of the English
People*. This appendix contains the titles of useful works that do not fit readily into periods.

BIBLIOGRAPHIES AND GUIDES

The series of bibliographical handbooks sponsored by the Conference on
British Studies contains two pertinent volumes to date: Josef L. Altholz, *Victorian England, 1837–1901* (1970) and Alfred Havighurst, *Modern England,
1901–1970* (1976). They are handily brief and surprisingly comprehensive for
their size. More comprehensive, and extraordinarily valuable, are the massive volumes of Lucy M. Brown and Ian R. Christie, *Bibliography of British
History, 1789–1851* (1977) and H. J. Hanham, *Bibliography of British History,
1851–1914* (1976).

F. M. Powicke and E. B. Fryde, eds., *Handbook of British Chronology* (1961)
is particularly useful for lists of bishops and officers of state. P. and G. Ford,
*A Guide to the Parliamentary Papers: What They Are: How to Find Them: How to
Use Them* (1956) is indispensable, and to it may be added the same compilers'
A Breviate of Parliamentary Papers, 1900–1916 (1957) and *A Breviate of Parliamentary Papers, 1917–1939* (1951). *Whitaker's Almanac,* issued annually since
1869, is a wondrous collection of facts about everything in Britain. Another,
sometimes forgotten, historical source is the multivolumed *Oxford English
Dictionary;* constructed on historical principles, it gives examples of usage
that the compilers have determined were the earliest for each meaning.

POLITICAL, CHIEFLY

The pertinent volumes in the *English Historical Documents* series are: VIII:
1660–1714, Andrew Browning, ed. (1953); X: 1714–1783, D. B. Horn and Mary
Ransome, eds. (1957); XI: 1783–1832, A. Aspinall and E. A. Smith, eds. (1959);
and XII: 1833–1874, G. M. Young and W. D. Handcock, eds. (1956). There are
several useful collections of specifically constitutional documents: W. C. Costin and J. Steven Watson, eds., *The Law and Working of the Constitution:* vol. 1,
1660–1783, vol. 2, 1784–1914 (1952); E. N. Williams, ed., *The Eighteenth-Century Constitution, 1688–1815* (1960); H. J. Hanham, ed., *The Nineteenth-Century Constitution, 1815–1914* (1969); and the single-volume sweep through ex-

tracts from all of English history, Carl Stephenson and Frederick G. Marcham, eds., *Sources of English Constitutional History*, the most recent edition being 1972.

Useful for checking detail is Chris Cook and Brendan Keith, eds., *British Historical Facts, 1830–1900* (1975), but even more valuable because it is more focussed is D. E. Butler and Anne Sloman, eds., *British Political Facts, 1900–1975* (4th ed., 1975).

Party history still lacks a satisfactory overview of the Liberal party, but the other main parties are served well. Keith Feiling's *A History of the Tory Party, 1640–1714* (1924, rev. ed., 1959) and his *The Second Tory Party, 1714–1832* (1938), once regarded as supreme authorities, have sustained considerable critical battering, but they have now recovered some reputation and are certainly important in the historiography of the subject. The best survey of the party's subsequent history is Robert Blake, *The Conservative Party from Peel to Churchill* (1970). Two rather old books by G. D. H. Cole still hold the field for surveys on the labor side: *A Short History of the British Working Class Movement, 1789–1947* (rev. ed., 1947), a rather large book despite its title, and *British Working-Class Politics, 1832–1900* (1941). Henry Pelling takes over with *A Short History of the Labour Party* (1961, 2nd ed., 1965). Pelling has also written *The British Communist Party: A Historical Profile* (1958).

On modern political thought, nothing has yet replaced C. C. Brinton, *English Political Thought in the Nineteenth Century* (2nd ed., 1949).

ECONOMIC AND SOCIAL HISTORY

Rather old but still an excellent comprehensive survey is W. H. B. Court, *A Concise Economic History of Great Britain from 1750 to Recent Times* (1954), which can be supplemented by the briefer book by Peter Mathias, *The First Industrial Nation: An Economic History of Britain, 1700–1914* (1969). Another valuable survey is E. J. Hobsbawm, *Industry and Empire: An Economic History of Britain Since 1750* (1968). On the nineteenth century and after, pride of place goes to Sir John Clapham's vast *An Economic History of Modern Britain,* vol. 1: *The Early Railway Age, 1830–1850* (1927); vol. 2, *Free Trade and Steel, 1850–1886* (1934); vol. 3, *Machines and National Rivalries, 1886–1914* (1938) — a work of as much value for its detail as for its marking a historiographical turning point in the field. A. D. Gayer, W. W. Rostow, and Anna Schwartz, *The Growth and Fluctuation of the British Economy, 1790–1850* (1953) is statistically based, as is the broader and very important interpretation by Phyllis Deane and W. A. Cole, *British Economic Growth, 1688–1959: Trends and Structure* (1962). S. G. Checkland, *The Rise of Industrial Society in England, 1815–1885* (1964) is an impressively conceptualized survey that goes well beyond economic history. Charles P. Kindleberger, *Economic Growth in France and Britain, 1851–1950* (1964) is an important comparative study.

A stimulating interpretation based on social history is Harold Perkin, *The Origins of Modern English Society, 1780–1880* (1969), to which should be added a French view, Francois Bédarida, *A Social History of England, 1851–1975* (1980). Derek Fraser, *The Evolution of the British Welfare State: A History of Social Policy Since the Industrial Revolution* (1973) offers the best available overview of the changing forms of state intervention. For context and effect,

D. C. Marsh, *The Changing Social Structure of England and Wales, 1871–1951* (1958) and A. H. Halsey, ed., *Trends in British Society Since 1900: A Guide to the Changing Social Structure of Britain* (1972).

From 1840, the Board of Trade annually issued the *Statistical Abstract for the United Kingdom*. Interrupted by World War II, the series began again in 1948, issued by the Central Statistical Office as *Annual Abstract of Statistics*. Brian R. Mitchell (with Phyllis Deane) edited an *Abstract of British Historical Statistics* (1962); Mitchell and H. G. Jones published a *Second Abstract of British Historical Statistics* in 1971.

RELIGIOUS AND INTELLECTUAL HISTORY

In addition to the imposing general works, mentioned in the chapter notes, on the eighteenth century by Norman Sykes and on the nineteenth by Owen Chadwick, there is the ambitious study by Horton Davies, *Worship and Theology in England*, three volumes of which belong in the period of this book: vol. 3, *From Watts and Wesley to Maurice, 1690–1850* (1961); vol. 4, *From Newman to Martineau, 1850–1900* (1962); and vol. 5, *The Ecumenical Century, 1900–1965* (1965). G. S. Spinks, ed., *Religion in Britain Since 1900* (1952) is useful.

On intellectual currents, in addition to the books by Buckley and Houghton, mentioned in the chapter notes, John Holloway, *The Victorian Sage: Studies in Argument* (1953), W. R. Sorley, *A History of British Philosophy* (1927); G. J. Warnock, *English Philosophy Since 1900* (1958); J. A. Passmore, *A Hundred Years of Philosophy* (2nd ed., 1966); and two influential, argumentative books by Raymond Williams on literature and society: *Culture and Society, 1780–1950* (1958) and *The Long Revolution* (1961). H. S. Goodhart-Rendel, *English Architecture Since the Regency: An Interpretation* (1952) is a good brief introduction, while the forty-six volumes, county by county, of Nikolaus Pevsner, *The Buildings of England* (1951–1974), a monument to the industry and perception of the dean of architectural historians in England, are an indispensable guide to travellers as well as historians. The other arts are less well served than is architecture, but some useful titles are William Gaunt, *A Concise History of English Painting* (1964); Ernest Walker, *A History of Music in England*, revised by J. A. Westrup (1952); and Frank Howes, *The English Musical Renaissance* (1966).

FOREIGN POLICY AND EMPIRE

Britain in Europe, 1789–1914 (1937) by R. W. Seton-Watson is a magnificent survey, while the interplay of foreign policy and imperial themes is well set out in C. J. Lowe, *The Reluctant Imperialists: British Foreign Policy, 1878–1902* (1969). On the twentieth century, in addition to the Northedge books mentioned in chapter notes, W. N. Medlicott, *British Foreign Policy Since Versailles, 1919–1963* (2nd ed., 1968). On transatlantic relationships, H. C. Allen, *Great Britain and the United States: A History of Anglo-American Relations, 1783–1952* (1954) and J. B. Brebner, *North Atlantic Triangle: The Interplay of Canada, the United States, and Great Britain* (1945).

Useful surveys of imperial matters are C. E. Carrington, *The British Overseas* (1950) and Nicholas Mansergh, *The Commonwealth Experience* (1969).

THE REST OF BRITAIN

On Scotland, G. S. Pryde, *A New History of Scotland: Scotland from 1603 to the Present Day* (*A New History of Scotland,* vol. 2) (1962) and Christopher Harvie, *Scotland and Nationalism: Scottish Society and Politics, 1709–1977* (1977). On Ireland, J. C. Beckett, *The Making of Modern Ireland,* 1966; L. M. Cullen, *An Economic History of Ireland since 1660* (1972); F. S. L. Lyons, *Ireland Since the Famine* (1971); Patrick O'Farrell, *England and Ireland Since 1800* (1975); Oliver MacDonagh, *The Irish Question, 1840–1920* (1964); and Nicholas Mansergh, *The Irish Question, 1840–1921* (1975). David Williams has written a brief *History of Modern Wales* (1950); and Kenneth O. Morgan, *Wales in British Politics, 1868–1922* (1963, 1970) is also relevant.

PEOPLE

The temptation to list a few of the greatest English biographies and autobiographies must be resisted, but two valuable guides are: William Matthews, ed., *British Autobiographies: An Annotated Bibliography of British Autobiographies Published or Written Before 1951* (1955) and *British Diaries: An Annotated Bibliography of British Diaries Written Between 1442 and 1942* (1950). The essential comprehensive source for brief biographies is *The Dictionary of National Biography,* edited by Sir Leslie Stephen and Sir Sidney Lee, one of the great publishing projects of the late nineteenth and early twentieth centuries. For reference books relating to the peerage, see the reading list at the end of Appendix 2. Burke's has also published since 1837 a guide to the families of the landed gentry. For clergymen in the Church of England, *Crockford's Clerical Directory,* published since 1858, is the standard source. Biographical sketches of prominent persons currently living in Britain, and to some extent elsewhere, can be found in the annual volumes of *Who's Who,* and the deceased can be found in the volumes of *Who Was Who. The Times* is the most important source of obituaries, which in its pages have become a kind of minor art form. *Obituaries from The Times, 1961–1970* (1975) and *1971–1975* (1978) include indexes to obituary notices that appeared in those years and a selection of the full obituaries and appreciations of the more important and interesting persons. Countries and major towns in the British Isles are covered — and have been in varying degrees since the early nineteenth century — by *Kelly's Post Office Directory,* giving names, addresses, and occupations.

G. M. Miller, ed., *The BBC Pronouncing Dictionary of British Names* (1971), cited for place names in the reading list of the Introduction, is also valuable for names that might appear in history or the news.

HUMOR

The period covered by this book is richly documented by the work of caricaturists and cartoonists. A guide to early materials can be found in M. Dorothy George, *English Political Caricature,* vol. 1, before 1792, and vol. 2, 1793–1832 (1959). From 1841 to the present, *Punch* has offered cartoon and prose comments on every aspect of English life, weekly. Max Beerbohm, the writer, was a superb caricaturist; several collections have been published and can be referred to for visual comment on important figures at the end of the nineteenth and beginning of the twentieth centuries, as can the earlier caricatures of the great and near-great by "Spy," whose work appeared in *Vanity Fair,* and by his contemporary imitators. The finest political cartoonist of the twentieth century is undoubtedly David Low; again many collections have been published.

Most Victorian humor does not travel very well to our generation. A notable exception is the plays of W. S. Gilbert, and the music written during their collaboration by Sir Arthur Sullivan is itself a witty and elegant commentary on the subjects of the operettas as well as on musical style. Two twentieth-century works must be mentioned since they are so relevant to the interests of historical students, once enough is known to make the jokes understandable. W. C. Sellar and R. J. Yeatman, *1066 and All That* (1930, and often reprinted) is the classic nonsense history of England. A. P. Herbert, a writer for *Punch* and for a time an M.P. for Oxford University, published in *Punch* over a number of years a series of mock reports (in the form, approximately, of the law reports printed in *The Times*) of "misleading cases." Some are pure fantasy, some are trenchant comments on events of the 1920's and 1930's, and many involve Herbert's perpetual litigant and *alter ego* in the struggle against state interference, Mr. Albert Haddock. They are collected as *Uncommon Law* (1935).

Index

Abbreviations: *cr.*, created; k, knighted; D.B.E., Dame of the Order of the British Empire; Bt., Baronet; B., Baron; V., Viscount; E., Earl; M., Marquess; D., Duke. Where rank alone is given, the title carries over exactly as it is in preceding title. After 1958, B. without a number preceding indicates a life peerage.

Abdul Hamid II (1842–1918), 353–354
Abercromby, Sir Ralph (1734–1801, k. 1795), 138
Aberdeen. Gordon, George Hamilton (1784–1860, 4th E. of Aberdeen, 1801), 188–189, 303, 304, 306, 309
Aboukir Bay, Battle of, 138
Acadia (Nova Scotia), 69
Act of Security (1704), 64
Act of Settlement (1701), 35, 42, 49, 53n, 64
Act of Uniformity (1662), 34
Acton, Sir John (1834–1902, 8th Bt., 1835, *cr.* 1st B. Acton, 1869), 409
Acton, William (1813–1875), 403
Adderley, Charles Bowyer (1814–1905, *cr.* 1st B. Norton, 1878), 351
Addington, Henry (1757–1855, *cr.* 1st V. Sidmouth, 1805), 143–144, 145, 162, 165, 168
Addison, Christopher (1865–1951, *cr.* 1st B. Addison, 1937, 1st V., 1945), 507, 518
Addison, Joseph (1672–1719), 33
Aden, 359
Administrative reform, 94–104, 163–168, 180–181, 186–203, 210–222, 225–228, 319–320, 324–330, 399–400, 421–423
Adrianople, Treaty of, 189
Aestheticism, 415
Afghanistan, 314, 357, 452
Africa, 15, 440–442, 486, 567–568, 596, 616. *See also* Egypt; South Africa
Africa Company, 16
Agadir Crisis, 483
Agriculture, 110–111, 158, 173, 286–287, 375–377, 532
Aircraft industry, 606
Albert, Prince Consort (1819–1861), 285–286, 318
Aldeburgh Festival, 622–623
Alexander I, Tsar of Russia (1777–1825), 137, 147, 162, 169–170, 171
Alexander, Sir Harold (1891–1969, k. 1942, *cr.* 1st V. Alexander of Tunis, 1946, E., 1952), 568, 569
Alexandria, 364
Algeciras Conference, 483

Allan, William (1813–1874), 291, 322n
Althorp. Spencer, John Charles (1782–1845, V. Althorp, 1783, 3rd E. Spencer, 1834), 195, 216–217, 224
Amalgamated Society of Engineers, 291–292, 391
American Civil War, 318, 322
American Revolution, 86–89, 94–95
Amery, Leopold (1873–1955), 549
Amiens, Peace of, 138
Amin, Idi (c. 1925–   ), 604
Amritsar Massacre, 506
Anderson, Elizabeth Garrett (1836–1917), 404
Anderson, Sir John (1882–1958, k. 1919, *cr.* 1st V. Waverley, 1952), 569n
Andover Scandal, 248n
Anglicanism. *See* Church of England
Anglo-German Convention, 442–443
Anne, Queen (1665–1714), 42–43, 44, 49
Anthropology, 411
Anti-Corn-Law League, 212, 273–277, 292–293, 380
Appeals, 646, 652
Applegarth, Robert (1834–1925), 322n, 323
Arabi Pasha, Ahmad (1840–1892), 364
Arabs, 499, 578, 593, 605
Arbitration Act (1919), 514
Arch, Joseph (1826–1919), 392
Architecture, 9, 31, 125–126, 412, 559, 623–624
Argentina, 171, 377, 384
Argyll, Campbell, George Douglas (1823–1900, M. of Lorne, 1837, 8th D. of Argyll, 1847), 340
Aristocracy. *See* Peers
Arkwright, Sir Richard (1732–1792, k. 1786), 112, 114
Armistice, 498
Army, 48n, 138–139, 161, 346–348, 352–353, 449, 460, 507
Arnold, Matthew (1822–1888), 414
Arnold, Thomas (1795–1842), 295–296
Art. *See* Architecture; Painting; Sculpture
Artificers, Statute of (1563), 158

Art nouveau, 470
Arts Council, 622
Ascendancy (Ireland), 141, 191–192
Ashbourne's Act (1885), 436, 437
Ashburton. Baring, William Bingham (1799–1864, 2nd B. Ashburton, 1848), 304
Ashley. *See* Shaftesbury
Ashton, Sir Frederick (1906–   , k. 1962), 559, 623
Asiento, 21, 68
Askwith, George Ranken (1861–1942, *cr.* 1st B. Askwith, 1919), 475
Asquith, Herbert Henry (1852–1928, *cr.* 1st E. of Oxford and Asquith, 1925), 430, 459, 460, 461, 465, 476, 477, 478, 480, 490, 497, 511, 528, 571
Assize Courts, 59, 348*n*, 645–646, 651
Association for the Preservation of Liberty and Property Against Republicans and Levellers, 136
Aswan Dam, 593
Atlantic Charter, 567
Atterbury, Francis (1662–1732), 46
Attlee, Clement Richard (1883–1967, *cr.* 1st E. Attlee, 1955), 538, 549, 573, 574, 592
Attwood, Thomas (1783–1856), 193–194, 214, 224, 251, 253
Auchinleck, Sir Claude (1884–   , k. 1940), 568
Auckland. Eden, William (1744–1814, *cr.* 1st B. Auckland, 1789), 314
Austerlitz, Battle of, 144
Austin, John (1790–1859), 221
Australia, 92, 218, 219, 287, 356, 439, 449, 498, 535
Austria, 547, 587
Austria-Hungary, 137, 144, 147, 154–155, 169, 170, 303, 317–318, 353, 354, 355, 481–487
Automobile industry, 551, 606
Auxiliaries, 502
Avon. *See* Eden, Anthony

Bachelor's Walk Massacre, 479
Bacon, Sir Francis (1561–1626, k. 1603), 49
Bacon, Francis (1910–   ), 623
Baedeker raids, 568
Bagehot, Walter (1826–1877), 211, 218, 454, 588
Bakewell, Robert (1725–1795), 110
Balaclava, Battle of, 308, 309
Balanchine, George (1904–   ), 623
Baldwin, Robert (1804–1858), 220
Baldwin, Stanley (1867–1947, *cr.* 1st E. Baldwin, 1937), 509–511, 520, 527, 538–540, 544–545, 546
Baldwin, William Warren (1775–1844), 220
Balfour, Arthur (1848–1930, *cr.* 1st E. Balfour, 1915), 430, 433, 434, 436, 459, 462, 476, 509
Balfour Declaration (1917), 499, 578
Balfour Report (1926), 534
Balkan Wars, 483
Ballet, 559, 623

Ballet Rambert, 559
Ballot Act (1872), 210, 423
Banda, Hastings (1905–   ), 584
Bank Charter Act (1844), 268, 280
Banking, 19–22, 175–177, 267–268, 290
Bank of England, 20, 149–150, 172–173, 175–177, 202, 223–224, 267–268, 279–280, 574
Banks, Sir Joseph (1743–1820, *cr.* 1st Bt., 1781), 92–93
Baptists, 37, 129. *See also* Dissent
Baring, Sir Evelyn (1841–1917, k. 1883, *cr.* 1st V. Cromer, 1899, 1st E., 1901), 364
Barnato, Barnett Isaacs "Barney" (1852–1897), 384
Barnes, Thomas (1785–1841), 184
Baroque, 3
Barrie, Sir James (1860–1937, *cr.* 1st Bt., 1913), 464
Barry, Sir Charles (1795–1860, k. 1852), 213
Barthou, Louis (1862–1934), 544
Bartók, Béla (1881–1945), 471
Basutoland, 361
Battle of Britain, 566
Bax, Sir Arnold (1883–1953, k. 1937), 471
Baylis, Lilian (1874–1937), 559
Beaconsfield. *See* Disraeli
Beales, Edmond (1803–1881), 327
Beardsley, Aubrey (1872–1898), 415
Beatles, 625
Beaverbrook. Aitken, William Maxwell (1879–1964, *cr.* 1st B. Beaverbrook, 1917), 569
Beccaria, Cesare (1738–1794), 124, 178
Bechuanaland, 443
Beckford, William (1759–1844), 125
Bedchamber Crisis, 218
Beecham, Sir Thomas (1879–1961, k. 1916), 558
Belgium, 302–303, 382, 484, 485–486, 520, 549, 565, 586
Bell, Sir Charles (1776–1842, k. 1830), 297
Belloc, Hilaire (1870–1953), 472
Bengal, 70, 99, 313. *See also* India
Bennett, Richard Rodney (1936–   ), 623
Bentham, Jeremy (1748–1832), 123–125, 153–154, 160, 178, 181, 182–183, 185, 214
Bentinck, Lord George (1802–1848), 277
Bentinck, Lord William (1774–1839), 313
Bergson, Henri (1859–1941), 469, 470
Berkeley, George (1685–1753), 38
Berlin, Congress of (1879), 355
Berlin Conference (1885), 440
Berlin Decree (1806), 147
Besant, Annie (1847–1933), 392, 403
Bessemer process, 383
Bevan, Aneurin (1897–1960), 572, 574, 575, 586, 592
Beveridge, William Henry (1879–1963, k. 1919, *cr.* 1st B. Beveridge, 1946), 463, 572, 613
Beveridge Report, 572, 579
Bevin, Ernest (1881–1951), 515, 526, 538, 569–570, 573, 589
Bill of Rights (1689), 41, 48

Birkenhead. *See* Smith, F. E.
Birmingham, 18, 51, 116, 119, 136, 227, 424
Birmingham Political Union, 193–194, 196, 251
Birmingham riots (1791), 136
Bismarck, Otto von (1815–1898), 318, 438, 440, 452, 482
Black Country, 2, 18
Black Dwarf, 164
Black Friday, 515
Black Hole of Calcutta, 70
Black Monday, 394
Blackstone, Sir William (1723–1780, k. 1770), 87, 124
Blackwood's Magazine, 184
Blake, William (1757–1827), 126
Blandford. Spencer-Churchill, George (1793–1857, M. of Blandford, 1817, 6th D. of Marlborough, 1840), 194
Blanketeers, 165
Blatchford, Robert (1851–1943), 399
Blenheim Palace, 9
Bloemfontein Convention (1854), 360
Blomfield, Charles James (1786–1857), 232
Bloomsbury Group, 560
Blücher, Gebhard von (1742–1819), 154
Bluebooks, 261
Blum, Léon (1872–1950), 546
Board of Control, 311, 313
Board of Trade, 96, 98, 475
Boers, 359–361, 443–447, 447–448, 455
Boer War, 447–448, 455
Bolingbroke. St. John, Henry (1678–1751, *cr.* 1st V. Bolingbroke, 1712), 44, 45, 46, 62
Bolshevism, 487–488, 498, 519–520
Bombay, 70, 99, 313. *See also* India
Bonaparte, Joseph (1768–1844), 169
Bonaparte, Napoleon. *See* Napoleon I
Bonham, Francis Robert (1785–1863), 212, 260, 425
Booth, Charles (1840–1916), 390–391
Booth, William (1829–1912), 410
Boothby, Robert (1900–   , *cr.* B. Boothby, 1958), 539
Bosanquet, Bernard (1848–1923), 413, 461, 470
Bosnia, 483
Boston, 86–87
Boston Tea Party, 86–87
Boswell, James (1740–1795), 130
Botha, Louis (1862–1919), 448
Boulton, Matthew (1728–1809), 115
Bowdler, Thomas (1754–1825), 130
Bowring, Sir John (1792–1872, k. 1854), 311
Boycott, 367
Boyle, Richard (1695–1753, 3rd E. of Burlington and 4th E. of Cork, 1704), 31
Boyne, Battle of the, 66
Bradlaugh, Charles (1833–1891), 403
Bradley, Francis Herbert (1846–1924), 413, 470
Brandreth, Jeremiah (d. 1817), 165
Brazil, 170
Brewing, 25
Briand, Aristide (1862–1932), 508, 541

Bribery. *See* Corruption
Bridgewater. Egerton, Francis (1736–1803, 3rd D. of Bridgewater, 1748), 108
Bright, John (1811–1889), 274, 308, 311, 326, 327, 339, 343, 365
Brighton, 146
Brindley, James (1716–1772), 108–109
Bristol, 14, 15, 17, 119
British and Foreign Bible Society, 129
British and Foreign School Society, 159, 265
British Broadcasting Corporation, 521, 552, 622
British Commonwealth of Nations. *See* Commonwealth
British European Airways, 574
British Guiana, 445
British Iron and Steel Corporation, 575, 590
British Leyland, 606
British Medical Association, 463
British North America Act (1867), 535
British Overseas Airways Corporation, 532, 574
British South Africa Company, 443–446
Britten, Benjamin (1913–1977, *cr.* B. Britten, 1976), 559, 622, 623
Broad Bottom ministry, 63
Broad Church Movement, 406–407
Broadhurst, Henry (1840–1911), 397, 398
Brooks's Club, 212
Brougham, Henry (1778–1868, *cr.* 1st B. Brougham and Vaux, 1830), 159, 167, 180, 184, 185, 194, 196, 216, 217, 265
Brown, George Alfred (1914–   , *cr.* Lord George-Brown, 1970), 592, 599–600, 609
Brown, Lancelot "Capability" (1715–1783), 9
Bruce, Henry Austin (1815–1895, *cr.* 1st B. Aberdare, 1873), 349
Bubble Act (1720), 21, 120, 272
Buchan, John (1875–1940, *cr.* 1st B. Tweedsmuir, 1935), 561
Builders' Strike, 321, 322, 325
Builders' union. *See* Trade unions
Building societies, 290
Bulgaria, 354–355, 483, 486
Buller, Charles (1806–1848), 220
Bullion Committee, 150, 172
Bullock Commission, 607
Bunting, Jabez (1779–1858), 128
Burdett, Sir Francis (1770–1844, 5th Bt., 1797), 152, 214
Burgess, Anthony (1917–   ), 625
Burgoyne, John (1722–1792), 88
Burke, Edmund (1729–1797), 83, 86, 90, 95, 96, 98, 99, 104, 135
Burma, 314, 359, 577
Burns, John (1858–1943), 392, 394–395, 455, 460, 462, 484
Burns, Robert (1759–1796), 126
Burt, Thomas (1837–1922), 397
Burton, Sir Richard (1821–1890, k. 1885), 442
Bute. Stuart, John (1713–1792, 3rd E. of Bute, 1723), 80–81

Butler, Joseph (1692–1752), 38
Butler, Josephine (1828–1906), 404
Butler, Reg (1913–   ), 623
Butler, Richard Austen (1902–   , cr. B. Butler, 1965), 539, 572, 587n, 590, 594, 597
Butler Act (1944), 615
Butskellism, 587n, 612
Butt, Isaac (1813–1879), 366
Byron, George Gordon (1788–1824, 6th B. Byron, 1798), 127, 162n

Cabinet, 47, 49, 101, 260–261, 381, 490, 554, 569
Cabinet Council, 47
Calcutta, 70–71. See also India
Callaghan, James (1912–   ), 600, 609–610, 611
Calvinism, 65
Cambridge. George William Frederick Charles (1819–1904, 2nd D. of Cambridge, 1850), 347n, 449
Cambridge, University of, 9, 50, 185, 190, 296, 557, 558
Camden. Pratt, Sir Charles (1714–1794, k. 1761, cr. 1st B. Camden, 1765, 1st E. of Camden, 1786), 82
Campbell, John Ross (1894–1969), 519–520
Campbell-Bannerman, Sir Henry (1836–1908, k. 1895), 430, 455, 459, 460
Campo Formio, Treaty of, 137
Canada, 71, 81, 87, 102, 218, 220–222, 304, 356, 439, 449, 450, 451, 534, 535
Canada Constitution Act (1791), 102, 103
Canada Union Act (1840), 221
Canals, 108–109
Canning, Charles John (1812–1862, cr. 1st E. Canning, 1859), 315
Canning, George (1770–1827), 145, 147, 168–172, 186, 189
Canning, Stratford (1786–1880, cr. 1st V. Stratford de Redcliffe, 1852), 305, 307
Canton, 311
Cape Colony, 359–361, 443–447. See also South Africa
Cape of Good Hope, 155, 359
Cape St. Vincent, Battle of, 138
Capital, export of. See Foreign investment
Capital punishment, 178, 179, 187
Cardwell, Edward (1813–1886, cr. 1st V. Cardwell, 1874), 347–348
Carlile, Richard (1790–1843), 164
Carlisle. Howard, Frederick (1748–1825, 5th E. of Carlisle, 1758), 88
Carlisle Commission, 88
Carlos, Don (1788–1855), 302
Carlton Club, 146, 212, 425
Carlyle, Thomas (1795–1881), 249, 252, 321, 330, 414
Carnarvon. Herbert, Henry Howard Molyneux (1831–1890, 4th E. of Carnarvon, 1849), 350
Caroline, Queen (1683–1737), 62
Caroline, Queen (1768–1821), 146, 167–168

Carson, Sir Edward (1854–1935, k. 1900, cr. 1st B. Carson, 1921), 476, 477
Carteret, John (1690–1763, 2nd B. Carteret, 1695, E. Granville, 1744), 46, 62, 63
Cartwright, Edmund (1743–1823), 114
Cartwright, John (1740–1824), 94, 95, 104, 134, 163
Casement, Sir Roger (1864–1916, k. 1911), 501
Castle, Barbara (1911–   ), 600, 601, 606
Castlereagh. Stewart, Robert (1769–1822, V. Castlereagh, 1796, 2nd M. of Londonderry, 1821), 145, 147, 154, 161, 162, 168–169, 170
Cat-and-Mouse Act (1913), 481
Catherine of Braganza, Queen (1638–1705), 60
Catherine I, Tsarina of Russia (1683?–1727), 80–81
Catholic Association, 191
Catholic Emancipation, 141–142, 145, 180, 186, 190–193
Catholicism, 34, 36, 37n, 40, 66, 90–91, 141–143, 189–190, 190–193, 305–306, 408–409, 556, 618–620
Cato Street Conspiracy, 167
Caucus, 424–425
Cavendish, Lord Frederick (1836–1882), 369
Cavour, Camillo, Conte de (1810–1861), 318
Cawnpore Massacre, 315
Cecil, Lord Hugh (1869–1956, cr. 1st B. Quickswood, 1941), 476
Censorship, 41, 140
Central Electricity Board, 521
Ceylon, 577
Chadwick, Sir Edwin (1800–1890, k. 1889), 244, 245, 247, 261, 264, 294
Chalmers, Thomas (1780–1847), 236n
Chamberlain, Sir Austen (1863–1937, k. 1925), 476, 502, 508, 509, 511, 520
Chamberlain, Joseph (1836–1914), 345, 350, 352, 365, 370, 371–372, 405, 423–424, 427, 429, 432, 438, 441, 442, 443, 444–445, 446, 450, 458–459, 476
Chamberlain, Neville (1869–1940), 509, 511, 518, 522, 531, 546–549
Champion, Henry Hyde (1859–1928), 395
Chanak, 509
Chancellor of the Exchequer, 55–56
Chancery, High Court of, 56, 178, 179, 348
Chandos Clause, 198, 200
Charity, 27–28, 289, 556
Charles I (1600–1649), 40, 48, 64, 67, 80
Charles II (1630–1685), 34, 40, 68, 70
Charles II, King of Spain (1661–1700), 68
Charles X, King of France (1757–1836), 194
Charles Edward, the Young Pretender (1720–1788), 44n
Charlotte Augusta, Princess (1796–1817), 167
Chartism, 249–254, 261–263, 274, 281–282
Chatham. See Pitt, William
Chaumont, Treaty of, 154

Chesterton, Gilbert Keith (1874–1936), 1–2, 472

Chichester-Clark, James (1923– , cr. B. Moyola, 1971), 619

Child and female labor, 116–117, 159, 242–244, 263–264, 266, 280, 351, 390

Children's Act (1908), 462

China, 310–311, 359, 450–451, 542, 584

Chinese labor, 458

Cholera, 201

Christian Socialists, 290

The Christian Year (Keble), 234

Christie, Dame Agatha (1891–1976, D.B.E., 1971), 561

Churchill, Charles (1731–1764), 82

Churchill, Lord Randolph (1849–1895), 370, 425, 430, 431, 433, 450, 477

Churchill, Sir Winston Spencer (1874–1965, k. 1953), 460, 461, 462, 475, 476, 484, 488, 489, 498, 502, 520, 525, 526, 527, 531, 539–540, 545, 549, 565, 566, 569, 571, 572–573, 583, 589–590, 594

Church Missionary Society, 129

Church of England, 32–39, 128, 189–190, 229–230, 230–236, 265–266, 297–298, 405–409, 457, 556, 637–643

Church of Ireland, 216, 217, 230–233, 342–343

Church of Scotland, 236n

Church reform, 230–236. See also Catholic Emancipation; Disestablishment; Dissent

Churchwardens, 59

Cinema, 551–552

Cintra, Convention of, 148

Ciudad Rodrigo, Battle of, 149

Civil Aviation Act (1946), 574

Civil List, 57, 98, 143, 195

Civil service, 143, 298–299, 398–399, 346–347

Civil Service Commission, 299

Civil War, 2, 40, 64

Clanricarde. De Burgh-Canning, Hubert George (1832–1916, 2nd M. of Clanricarde, 1874), 427

Clapham, Sir John Harold (1873–1946, k. 1943), 400, 561

Clapham Sect, 128–129, 145, 177

Clarendon. Villiers, George (1800–1870, 4th E. of Clarendon, 1838), 306

Clarion, 399

Clarke, Mary Anne (1776–1852), 145

Class system. See Gentry; Peers; Social structure

Clayton-Bulwer, Treaty of, 451

Cleave, John (1795?– ?), 251

Clemenceau, Georges (1841–1929), 497

Clerk-Maxwell, James (1831–1879), 410

Clerks, 298–299, 389, 392, 400

Clifford, William Kingdon (1845–1879), 410

Clive, Robert (1725–1774, cr. 1st B. Clive, 1762), 70, 99

Cliveden Set, 543

Clubs, political, 212–213

Coal industry, 18, 113, 523, 525–526, 528, 551, 574, 586, 612–613

Cobbett, William (1762–1835), 153, 163–164, 214

Cobden, Richard (1804–1865), 276, 287, 308, 311

Cobden Treaty, 293

Cochrane. Thomas, Lord Cochrane (1775–1860, 10th E. of Dundonald, 1831), 152

Cockburn, Henry Thomas (1779–1854, Lord Cockburn, 1834) 136n

Cockerton Judgment, 456

Coke, Sir Edward (1552–1634, k. 1603), 87

Coke. Thomas William, "Coke of Norfolk" (1752–1842, cr. 1st E. of Leicester, 1837), 111

Cold War, 585–586

Cole, George Douglas Howard (1889–1959), 517

Cole, Sir Henry (1808–1882, k. 1875), 285

Colenso, John William (1814–1883), 407, 408

Coleridge, Samuel Taylor (1772–1834), 126, 181, 182–183

Collins, Michael (1890–1922), 502, 503

Colonial Laws Validity Act (1865), 534

Colonial Office, 219, 221–222, 616

Colonies, 83–84, 86–89, 92–94, 173, 218–222, 311–316, 458. See also Empire

Combination Laws (1799–1800), 140–141, 151, 158, 174

Committee of Council on Education, 265–267

Common law, 56, 177–178, 348, 644–645

Common market, 586–587, 592, 596–597, 600–601, 603, 604, 607, 611, 616

Common Prayer, Book of, 34, 555, 642

Commonwealth, 577–578, 580, 583–584, 586, 596, 616–617. See also Dominions; Empire

Commonwealth Affairs Office, 616

Commonwealth conferences, 458

Commonwealth Immigrants Acts (1962, 1968), 617

Communism, 498, 537, 584–585. See also Bolshevism

Company organization, 226–227, 271–273

Complete Suffrage Movement, 262, 274

Comte, Auguste (1798–1857), 410

Concert of Europe, 303

Confederation of British Industry, 621

Congo Free State, 440

Congregationalists, 33, 37, 129. See also Dissent

Connections, 54

Conservative Party, 211, 259–282 passim, 306, 316, 328–330, 349–352, 370, 424–425, 428–429, 430, 432, 436, 459, 464, 465, 497, 508–509, 511, 538–541, 573, 583, 585, 588–592, 593–599, 602–605, 611–612. See also Parties, political; Tory Party

Constable, John (1776–1837), 126

Constables, 58–59

Constantine I, King of Greece (1868–1923), 508

Constantinople, 307, 308, 314, 508, 510

Contagious Diseases Acts, 404

Continental System, 147–149
Convention Parliament (1688), 41, 42
Convocation of the Clergy, 34–35, 38
Cook, Arthur James (1885–1931), 526
Cook, Captain James (1728–1779), 92–93
Cooper, Thomas (1805–1892), 262
Cooperation, 239, 241, 290–291
Coote, Sir Eyre (1726–1823, k. 1802), 71
Copenhagen, Battle of, 138
Coram, Thomas (1668–1751), 130
Corn laws, 158, 181, 182, 188, 216, 224, 259, 273–277. *See also* Anti-Corn-Law League
Cornwall, 18, 50, 198
Cornwallis. Cornwallis, Charles (1738–1805, 2nd E. Cornwallis 1762, *cr.* 1st M., 1792), 89
Corporation Act (1661), 36, 59, 189–190, 228–229
Corporations reform, 59, 226–227
Corrupt and Illegal Practices Act (1883), 423
Corruption, political, 421–423, 620. *See also* Patronage, political
Corunna, Battle of, 149
Cosgrave, William Thomas (1880–1965), 503
Cotman, John Sell (1782–1842), 126
Cotton famine, 322
Cotton industry, 15, 112, 113–114, 114–115, 159, 173, 382
Council of Ireland, 502
County courts, 646
Coupon Election, 497
Courier, 184
Court system, 55, 178–179, 348, 422, 644–653
Cousins, Frank (1904–   ), 586, 600, 601
Coventry Cathedral, 624
Coward, Sir Noel (1899–1973, k. 1970), 559–560
Cowper-Temple clause, 345
Crabbe, George (1754–1832), 126
Cranko, John (1927–1973), 623
Crete, 567
Crichel Down affair, 620–621
Crimean War, 213n, 286, 298, 307–310, 325, 354
Criminal Law Amendment Act (1871), 346, 352
Cripps, Sir Stafford (1889–1952, k. 1930), 537, 538, 573–574, 576–577, 589
Croce, Benedetto (1866–1952), 469
Croker, John Wilson (1780–1857), 184
Crome, John (1768–1821), 126
Crompton, Samuel (1753–1827), 114
Cromwell, Oliver (1599–1658), 40, 64, 68, 341
Cross, Richard Assheton (1823–1914, *cr.* 1st V. Cross, 1886), 350, 351, 352
Cruickshank, George (1792–1878), 167n
Crystal Palace, 286, 412
Cunninghame Graham, Robert Bontine (1852–1936), 395, 398
Curwen's Act (1809), 145
Curzon, George Nathaniel (1859–1925, *cr.*

1st B. Curzon of Kedleston, 1898, 1st E., 1911, 1st M., 1921), 490, 504–505, 510, 518
Customs, 47–48, 56, 103
Cutlery industry, 112, 128, 322–323
Cyprus, 355, 359, 584
Czechoslovakia, 499, 547–548

Dahrendorf, Ralf (1929–   ), 625–626
Dáil Eireann, 501–503
Daily Herald, 516
Daily Telegraph, 319
Dakar, 71
Daladier, Edouard (1884–1970), 548
Dale, David (1739–1806), 160
Dalhousie. Ramsay, Sir James Andrew Broun (1812–1860, 10th E. of Dalhousie, 1838, *cr.* 1st M., 1849), 314, 315, 357
Dalton, Hugh (1887–1962), 573, 574
Darby, Abraham (1677–1717), 113
Darien Scheme, 64–65
Darwin, Charles (1809–1882), 317, 409, 410
Davitt, Michael (1846–1906), 366, 437
Davy, Sir Humphrey (1778–1829), 112
Dawes Plan (1924), 518–519, 541
Dawson, Geoffrey (1874–1944), 543
D-Day, 568
Death duties, 431, 579
Debt, national, 161, 524, 529
Declaration of Independence, 88
Declaration of Indulgence, 36
Declaration of Rights (1688), 41
Declaratory Act (1766), 84, 86
Defense of the Realm Act (1915), 488
Defoe, Daniel (1661?–1731), 23
De Gaulle, Charles (1890–1970), 566, 597, 601, 603n
Deists, 33
Delane, John Thadeus (1817–1879), 184
Demobilization, 496
Denman, Thomas (1799–1854, k. 1830, *cr.* 1st B. Denman, 1834), 167
Denmark, 89, 318, 549, 586
Depression. *See* Great Depression
Derby, Stanley, Edward George (1799–1869), Lord Stanley, 1834, 14th E. of Derby, 1851), 195, 196, 216, 232, 260, 276, 277n, 306, 309, 316, 327, 328, 330
Derby. Stanley, Edward Henry (1826–1893, Lord Stanley, 1851, 15th E. of Derby, 1869), 350, 355
Dervishes, 441
Dettingen, Battle of, 69
De Valera, Eamon (1882–1975), 502–503, 535
De Valois, Dame Ninette (1898–   D.B.E., 1951), 559
Devaluation, 524, 581, 600
Devolution, 611, 618
Devonport. Kearley, Hudon Ewbanke (1856–1934, *cr.* 1st B. Devonport, 1910, 1st E., 1917), 474
Devonshire, *see* Hardington
Dickens, Charles (1812–1870), 249, 317
Dilke, Sir Charles (1843–1911, 2nd Bt.,

1869), 350, 371, 372, 462
Disarmament, 585–586
Disestablishment, 463, 465–466, 479n, 610
Dispensing power, 41
Disraeli, Benjamin (1804–1881, *cr.* 1st E. of Beaconsfield, 1876), 172, 249, 277, 325, 328–330, 339–341, 349–352, 353, 354, 355, 356–357, 361, 363, 365, 370, 406, 424
Dissent, 33, 34, 36–37, 40, 41, 42, 66, 94, 95, 129, 136, 185, 189–190, 202, 213, 228–230, 265–266, 405–406, 456, 457
Dissenting Deputies, 36
Distilling industry, 25
Divine right of kings, 34, 48–49
Divorce, 167–168, 403–404, 555
Doddridge, Philip (1702–1751), 37
Dollfuss, Engelbert (1892–1934), 543
Domestic service, 389, 401–402, 552
Domestic system, 18–19, 112, 114–115
Dominions. *See* Empire
Donaldson, Sir John (1920–   , k. 1966), 604
Donovan Commission, 601
Dorchester laborers, 241
Douglas-Home, Sir Alec (1903–   , 14th E. of Home, 1951–1963, *cr.* B. Home of the Hirsel, 1974), 597–598, 603
Dreadnought (battleship), 449
Drummond, Thomas (1797–1840), 272
Drunkenness, 24, 25, 130
Dublin, University of, 200
Duckham, Sir Arthur (1879–1932, k. 1917), 513
Dulles, John Foster (1888–1959), 585, 593
Dundas, Henry (1742–1811, *cr.* 1st V. Melville, 1802), 101, 137, 144
Dunkirk, Battle of, 565
Dunning, John (1731–1783, *cr.* 1st B. Ashburton, 1782), 96
Dupleix, Joseph Francois, Marquis de (1697–1763), 70
Durham. Lambton, John George (1792–1840, *cr.* 1st B. Durham, 1830, 1st E. of Durham, 1833), 180, 195, 197, 199, 216, 220–221
Durham, University of, 296
Durham Report, 221
Durkheim, Émile (1858–1917), 469
Dutch. *See* Boers; Holland
Dyarchy, 506

Eastern Question, 353–355
Easter Rebellion (1916), 501
East India Company, 16, 70–71, 86, 99, 102, 223–224, 311, 313, 315, 450
East Indies, 15
Ecclesiastical Commission, 232
Ecclesiastical Titles Act (1851), 306
Economic Affairs, Department of, 599–600
Economical reform, 97–98
Economics, 93–94, 107–122, 123–125, 157–159, 267–277, 286–289, 411, 549–553, 578–583, 595–596. *See also* Industry; Trade; Trade unions

Eden, Anthony (1897–1977, *cr.* 1st E. of Avon, 1961), 545, 546–547, 549, 590, 593–594
Eden, Sir Frederick Morton (1766–1809, 2nd Bt., 1784), 178
Eden Treaty (1786), 102
Edinburgh Festival, 622
Edinburgh Review, 184
Education, 9–10, 159, 182, 185–186, 265–267, 295–296, 297–298, 344–345, 387–388, 455–456, 461–462, 557–558, 572, 615–616
Education Act (1870), 405
Education Act (1902), 455–456, 457, 462
Education Act (1944), 572
Edward VII (1841–1910), 350, 452, 454, 465
Edward VIII (1894–1972, *cr.* D. of Windsor, 1936), 540–541
Egypt, 138, 186, 303, 361–365, 439–440, 499, 593–594
Einstein, Albert (1879–1955), 469
Eire. *See* Ireland
Eldon. Scott, John (1751–1838, *cr.* 1st B. Eldon, 1799, 1st E. of Eldon, 1821), 162, 178
Elections, 51–52. *See also* Franchise
Elections, General, *1784,* 100; *1826,* 191–192; *1830,* 194; *1832,* 211; *1835,* 217; *1837,* 250; *1841,* 259; *1852,* 306; *1857,* 311, 326; *1859,* 316, 325; *1865,* 326, 422; *1868,* 339, 422, 424; *1874,* 349, 423; *1880,* 355, 423; *1885,* 370; *1886,* 372, 433; *1892,* 398; *1895,* 399, 432; *1900,* 455; *1906,* 455, 459; *1910,* 465; *1918,* 496; *1922,* 509–510, 516; *1923,* 511; *1924,* 516, 520; *1929,* 527; *1931,* 530, 537–538; *1935,* 540; *1945,* 573; *1950,* 588; *1951,* 589; *1955,* 592; *1959,* 592, 594, 610; *1964,* 598, 610; *1966,* 599; *1970,* 603; *1974,* 605, 608, 610; *1979,* 611
Electrical industry, 552, 575
Elgar, Sir Edward (1857–1934, k. 1904), 470
Elgin. Bruce, James (1811–1863, 8th E. of Elgin, 1841), 222, 311
Eliot, George (Cross, Mary Ann Evans) (1819–1880), 317, 414
Eliot, Thomas Stearns (1888–1965), 560
Elizabeth I (1533–1603), 49, 68, 350
Elizabeth II (1926–   ), 591
Elizabeth, Tsarina of Russia (1709–1762), 80
Ellenborough. Law, Edward (1790–1871, 2nd B. Ellenborough, 1818, *cr.* 1st E. of Ellenborough, 1844), 314
Emancipation Proclamation (U.S.), 318
Emigration, 174, 219, 219n; Irish, 279. *See also* Immigration
Empire, 356–357, 386, 439–453, 458–459, 503–506, 509, 531, 533–536, 547, 566, 572–578, 583–584, 616–617. *See also* Commonwealth; Dominions; India
Empire Free Trade, 538
Employers and Workmen Act (1875), 351–352
Enclosures, 61, 109–110, 118–119
Encumbered Estates Act (1849), 278–279

Engels, Friedrich (1820–1895), 160, 237, 238, 262, 280, 395
Engineering industry, 269, 287, 297, 400, 551
English Stage Company, 624
Entail, 11–12
Entertainment, public, 387–388, 551–552, 555. *See also* Mass culture
Entrepreneurs, 120–122, 160, 384, 390*n*, 507
Episcopalians (Scottish), 64, 65
Epstein, Sir Jacob (1880–1959, k. 1954), 559
Equitable Labour Exchange, 240
Equity, 178, 647–648
Essays and Reviews, 236*n*, 317, 407, 408
Ethiopia, 411, 543–544, 567
European Coal and Steel Community, 586
European Economic Community. *See* Common market
European Free Trade Association, 586
Evangelicalism, 128–129, 236*n*, 313, 406
Exchequer, 56, 57, 178, 348
Excise, 62, 103
Excise Bill (1733), 62
Exploration, 92–93
Exports. *See* Trade
Eyre, Edward John (1815–1901), 320–321

Fabian Society, 392, 395–397, 399, 515, 517
Factory Acts (1802, 1819), 116, 160, 242; (1833), 244; (1874), 351; (1891), 429
Factory and Workshop Acts (1867), 323–324
Factory legislation, 116–117, 159, 238, 242–245, 266, 280, 323–324, 390
Factory system, 114–117, 160, 266, 288, 383, 389–390. *See also* Industry; Trade unions
Fair trade movement, 458–459
Falkland Islands, Battle of the, 487
Family, 28–29, 401–404
Family Compact, 220
Family firms, 383–384
Faraday, Michael (1791–1867), 410
Farming. *See* Agriculture; Corn laws; Land system
Fascism, 521, 542–543, 567
Fashoda, 441
Faulkner, Brian (1921–1977, *cr.* B. Faulkner, 1977), 619
Federation of British Industries, 512, 621
Fenians, 342, 366
Ferdinand II, King of the Two Sicilies (1810–1859), 318
Ferdinand VII, King of Spain (1784–1833), 169
Festival of Britain, 622
Fielden, John (1784–1849), 214, 243
Fielding, Henry (1707–1754), 10, 13, 62
Fiennes, Celia (1662–1741), 9, 24
Finance, government, 20–22, 83–84, 86–87, 103–104, 139, 157–158, 161, 172–173, 224–225, 306, 431, 464, 575–576, 579. *See also* Taxation

First Continental Congress, 87
Fisher, Herbert Albert Laurens (1865–1940), 553
Fisher, Sir John (1841–1920, k. 1894, *cr.* 1st B. Fisher of Kilverstone, 1909), 449, 489
Fitzgerald, Edward (1809–1883), 317
Fitzgerald, William Vesey (1783–1843, B. Fitzgerald and Vesey, 1832), 192
Fitzherbert, Maria Anne (1756–1837), 146
Fitzwilliam, William Wentworth (1748–1833, 2nd E. Fitzwilliam, 1769), 142
Flood, Henry (1732–1791), 90
Florida, 81, 87, 89
Fonteyn, Dame Margot (1919–D.B.E., 1956), 623
Food and Drug Act, 351
Foot, Michael (1913–), 606
Foreign investment, 288, 289, 384, 385–386, 450, 506–507, 580
Foreign Office, 98, 347, 616
Forster, Edward Morgan (1879–1970), 471, 472, 560
Forster, William Edward (1818–1886), 345, 365, 368, 369
Fourteen Points, 498
"Fourth party," 430
Fox, Charles James (1749–1806), 83, 98, 100, 101, 134, 140, 144–145, 152
Fox, Henry (1705–1774, *cr.* 1st B. Holland, 1763), 81, 83, 98*n*
France, 13, 14, 16, 63, 68–71, 80–81, 88, 89, 134–143, 155, 169, 186, 194, 293, 303–304, 307–308, 316, 318, 353, 355, 363, 382, 438, 440, 441–442, 452, 481–487, 498, 508, 510, 518–519, 520, 543–544, 546, 547, 548, 565, 586, 594
Franchise, 50–52, 98, 194, 196, 197–200, 212, 226–228, 263, 324, 325, 326, 327–328, 346, 421–423, 427, 587; Ireland, 92–193, 199–200; Scotland, 199–200; women, 404, 479–481, 497, 521*n*
Francis Ferdinand, Archduke of Austria (1863–1914), 483
Franco, Francisco (1892–1975), 546
Franco-Prussian War, 353
Fraser's Magazine, 184
Frazer, Sir James (1854–1941, k. 1914), 411
Frederick II, King of Prussia (1712–1786), 80, 81
Frederick Louis, Prince of Wales (1707–1751), 62, 80
Free Churches. *See* Dissent
Free Church of Scotland, 236*n*
Free trade, 172–175, 273–277, 293, 458, 507–508, 538. *See also* Tariffs
Free-Trade Hall (Manchester), 275
French Revolution, 97, 134–143, 164
French Revolution, War of the, 136–138, 144, 147–149, 154–155
Freud, Sigmund (1856–1939), 469, 470
Friedland, Battle of, 147
Friendly societies, 151, 290–291, 323, 463
Frost, John (1784–1877), 253–254
Froude, Richard Hurrell (1803–1836), 234

Gaelic League, 478
Gainsborough, Thomas (1727–1788), 126
Gaitskell, Hugh (1906–1963), 587n, 589, 592, 597, 617
Gallipoli campaign, 486–487, 567
Galsworthy, John (1867–1933), 471
Galton, Sir Francis (1822–1911, k. 1909), 411
Game laws, 10, 379–380
Gandhi, Indira (1917–   ), 616
Gandhi, Mohandas K. (1869–1948), 506, 536, 577
Garibaldi, Giuseppe (1807–1882), 318
Garvin, James Louis (1868–1947), 543
Gas Boards, 575
Gay, John (1685–1732), 62
Geddes, Sir Auckland (1879–1954, k. 1917, 1st B., 1942), 513
Geddes, Sir Eric Campbell (1875–1937, k. 1916), 507
General Enclosure Act (1801), 109
General Sessions, 59, 60
General Strike, 241, 252, 253, 475–476, 514–515, 522–527. *See also* Strikes
General warrants, 82
Geneva Protocol, 519, 520
Genoa Conference, 508
Gentry, 5–13, 377–381. *See also* Social structure
George I (1660–1727), 44, 49
George II (1683–1760), 48, 62, 63, 69
George III (1738–1820), 80–81, 83–84, 97, 99–100, 101, 111, 142–143, 146, 167
George IV (1762–1830), 101, 125, 146–147, 165, 167–168, 186–187, 193
George V (1865–1935), 454, 465, 510, 511, 529–530, 540
George VI (1895–1952), 541, 591
George, Henry (1839–1897), 394
Germain. Sackville, George (1716–1785, Lord Sackville to 1770, Lord George Germain, 1770–1782, *cr.* 1st V. Sackville, 1782), 88
Germany, 155, 309, 318, 347, 353, 355, 383, 384, 438, 441, 443, 446, 449, 452–453, 481–488, 499–500, 501, 507, 510, 518–519, 520, 528, 541–542, 542–543, 544, 545, 546–549, 565–569. *See also* Prussia; West Germany
Ghana, 616
Gilbraltar, 68, 359
Gifford, William (1756–1826), 184
Gilbert, Sir William Schwenck (1836–1911, k. 1907), 413
Gillray, James (1757–1815), 167n
Gin Mania, 25
Gissing, George (1857–1907), 414
Gladstone, Herbert (1854–1930, *cr.* 1st V. Gladstone, 1910), 370, 463
Gladstone, William Ewart (1809–1898), 211, 223n, 229, 260, 271, 275, 276, 306, 316, 319, 326, 328, 329, 339–341, 341–344, 349, 350, 352–353, 354, 355, 356–357, 361, 364, 365–372, 423, 427, 431–432, 435, 436, 464

Globe, 184
Glorious Revolution, 20, 34, 40–41, 42, 48, 68
Gloucester, 17
Glyndebourne Festival, 622
Goderich. *See* Robinson, Frederick John
Godolphin, Sidney (1645–1712, *cr.* 1st B. Godolphin, 1684, 1st E. of Godolphin, 1706), 43, 44, 47
Godwin, Mary Wollstonecraft (1759–1797), 404
"Going out of Court," 55
Gokhale, Gopal Krishna (1866–1915), 505
The Golden Bough (Frazer), 411
Goldie, Sir George (1864–1925, k. 1887), 441, 442
Gold standard, 522–525, 530
Gollancz, Sir Victor (1893–1967, k. 1965), 537
Gordon, Charles George (1833–1885), 365
Gordon, George William (d. 1865), 320–321
Gordon, Lord George (1751–1793), 97
Gordon Riots (1780), 86, 96–97
Gorst, Sir John (1835–1916, k. 1885), 424, 425, 430
Goschen, George Joachim (1831–1907, *cr.* 1st V. Goschen, 1900), 340, 346, 371, 431
Gothic novelists, 125
Gothic revival, 412
Grafton. Fitzroy, Augustus Henry (1735–1811, 3rd D. of Grafton), 84
Graham, Sir James (1792–1861, 2nd Bt., 1824), 195, 197, 216, 232, 260, 266
Grammar schools, 557. *See also* Education
Grand Alliance, 567–569
Grand National Consolidated Trades Union, 241–242, 291
Grand Tour, 10
Grant, Charles (1746–1823), 195, 313
Granville. Leveson-Gower, Granville George (1815–1891, 2nd E. Granville, 1846), 340
Grattan, Henry (1746–1820), 90–92
Great Depression, *1873–1896*, 366, 375–386, 400; *1930s*, 528–529, 541
Great Exhibition of 1851, 285–286
Great Fire of 1666, 31
Great Trek (1837–1844), 360
Greece, 171–172, 189, 305, 355, 483, 486, 508–509, 567
Green, Thomas Hill (1836–1882), 413, 461, 470
Greene, Graham (1904–   ), 560
Grenville, George (1712–1770), 81–82, 82–83, 87, 422
Grenville, William Wyndam (1759–1834, *cr.* 1st B. Grenville, 1790), 144–145
Grey, Charles (1764–1845, 2nd E. Grey, 1807), 140, 180, 195, 201, 202, 203, 216
Grey, Sir Edward (1862–1933, 3rd Bt., 1882, *cr.* 1st V. Grey of Falloden, 1916), 455, 460, 483, 484
Grey, Henry George (1802–1894, 3rd E. Grey, 1845), 222, 276

Griffith, Arthur (1872–1922), 501, 502–503
Griqualand, 360–361
Grote, George (1794–1871), 214
Guadeloupe, 71, 81n
Guild socialism, 472
Guile, Daniel (1814–1882), 322n
Guizot, François (1787–1874), 303–304

Habeas Corpus Act (1679), 139, 368
Habsburgs. *See* Austria-Hungary
Haig, Douglas (1861–1928, k. 1909, cr. 1st E. Haig, 1919), 491
Haile Selassie, Emperor of Ethiopia (1891–1977), 567
Haldane, Richard Burdon (1856–1928, cr. 1st V. Haldane, 1912), 449, 455, 460, 517
Halifax. Wood, Edward Frederick Lindley (1881–1959, cr. 1st B. Irwin, 1925, 3rd V. Halifax, 1934, 1st E. of Halifax, 1944), 546, 549
Hammond, Barbara (1873–1961), 196
Hammond, John Lawrence LeBreton (1872–1949), 196
Hampden, Renn Dickson (1793–1868), 235
Hampden Clubs, 164
Handloom weavers, 150, 237, 253
Hanover, 49, 53
Hanover, House of, 34, 49
Hanway, Jonas (1712–1786), 130
Harcourt, Sir William (1827–1904, k. 1873), 399, 430, 431, 455
Hardie, James Keir (1856–1915), 398–399, 457
Hardwicke. Yorke, Philip (1690–1764, cr. 1st B. Hardwicke, 1733, 1st E. of Hardwicke, 1754), 181, 648
Hardy, Thomas (radical) (1752–1834), 135, 139
Hardy, Thomas (novelist) (1840–1928), 414
Hargreaves, James (d. 1778), 114
Harley, Robert (1661–1724, cr. 1st E. of Oxford, 1711), 43, 44, 45, 46, 47
Harney, George Julian (1817–1897), 252, 262, 280, 281
Harris, Howell (1714–1773), 39
Harrison, Frederic (1831–1923), 321, 323, 410
Hartington. Cavendish, Spencer Compton (1883–1908, M. of Hartington, 1858, 8th D. of Devonshire, 1891), 349, 371, 372, 429
Hartley, David (1705–1757), 123
Hastings, Warren (1732–1818), 93, 100
Havana, 80, 81
Hawarden Kite, 370
Hawksmoor, Nicholas (1661–1736), 31
Hay, John (1838–1905), 451
Haynau, Julius Jacob (1786–1853), 305
Hay-Pauncefote Treaty, 451
Hayter, Sir William (1792–1878, cr. 1st Bt., 1858), 299n
Heal's, 623
Heath, Edward (1916–   ), 597, 599, 602, 603, 604–605, 608

Heber, Reginald (1783–1826), 129, 313
Heights of Abraham, Battle of the, 71
Heligoland, 441, 487
Helpmann, Sir Robert (1909–   , k. 1968), 623
Helvétius, Claude Adrien (1715–1771), 124
Henderson, Arthur (1863–1935), 490, 491, 515, 517, 528, 538
Henderson, Sir Nevile (1882–1942, k. 1932), 546
Henley, William Ernest (1849–1903), 414–415
Henry VII (1457–1509), 55
Hepworth, Barbara (1903–1975), 623
Herbert, Sir Alan Patrick (1890–1971, k. 1945), 555
Herbert, Sidney (1810–1861, cr. 1st B. Herbert of Lea, 1860), 310
Herriot, Edouard (1872–1957), 518
Herzegovina, 483
Hetherington, Henry (1792–1849), 251
Hewart, Gordon (1870–1943, k. 1916, cr. 1st B. Hewart, 1922, 1st V., 1940), 554
Hicks, William (Hicks Pasha) (1830–1883), 365
Hicks Beach, Sir Michael (1837–1916, 9th Bt., 1854, cr. 1st V. St. Aldwyn, 1906, 1st E., 1915), 434
Hierarchy. *See* Social structure
High Church, 34–37, 233–236, 340. *See also* Church of England
Hill, Sir Rowland (1795–1879, k. 1860), 225, 261
Hindenburg, Paul von (1847–1934), 542
Hiroshima, 569
Historical Manuscripts Commission, 412
Historiography, 28–29, 411–412, 561
Hitchcock, Alfred (1899–   ), 552
Hitler, Adolf (1889–1945), 510, 541, 542–543, 545, 547–548, 566, 567, 569
Hoadly, Benjamin (1676–1761), 35
Hoare, Sir Samuel (1880–1959, 2nd Bt., 1915, cr. 1st V. Templewood, 1944), 544
Hobbes, Thomas (1588–1679), 24
Hobhouse, John Cam (1786–1869, 2nd Bt., 1831, cr. 1st B. Broughton de Gyfford, 1851), 181
Hobhouse, Leonard Trelawney (1864–1929), 461
Hobson, John Atkinson (1858–1940), 461
Hodges, Frank (1887–1943), 515, 526
Hogarth, William (1697–1764), 25
Hogg, Quintin (1907–   , 2nd V. Hailsham, 1950–1963, cr. B. Hailsham, 1970), 597
Hohenlinden, Battle of, 138
Holland. *See* Fox, Henry
Holland. Fox, Henry Richard Vassall (1773–1840, 3rd B. Holland, 1774), 195
Holland, 16, 20, 68, 89, 137, 143, 302–303, 310, 359–360, 549, 565, 586
Holst, Gustav (1874–1934), 470
Holy Alliance, 169, 170, 172
Home Office, 98, 227, 346
Home Rule, 366–373, 433–437, 464, 465–

466, 477–479, 500–502
Homosexuality, 555
Hong Kong, 311
Honors, 8, 49, 101, 528, 635–636
Hornby v. *Close*, 323
Horner, Francis (1778–1817), 180, 184
Horner, Leonard (1785–1864), 185, 244–245, 261
Horton, Sir Robert Wilmot (1784–1841, k. 1831, 3rd Bt., 1834), 219*n*
Household suffrage, 327–329, 427. *See also* Franchise
House of Commons, 45, 49–54, 64, 85, 86, 95, 142, 199, 200, 201, 202, 213–215, 260, 381, 422, 426, 427, 465, 588. *See also* Parliament; Reform
House of Lords, 8, 38, 45, 49, 64, 142, 179, 201, 202, 215–216, 319, 348, 463–466, 587–588, 630–635, 647. *See also* Parliament; Peers; Reform
Housing, 387, 496, 507, 518, 521, 590, 614
Howard, John (1726?–1790), 130, 178
Howell, George (1833–1910), 322*n*
Hudson, George (1800–1871), 270
Hudson's Bay Company, 16
Hughes, Thomas (1822–1896), 290, 321, 323, 327
Humanitarianism, 30, 159, 245, 280
Hume, David (1711–1776), 38, 93, 123, 125, 174
Hume, Joseph (1777–1855), 223, 227, 251
Hungary, 585, 594. *See also* Austria-Hungary
Hunt, Henry (1773–1835), 163, 165, 196, 214
Hunter, John (1728–1793), 297
Hunter, William (1718–1783), 297
Hunting, 379–380
Huntsman, Benjamin (1704–1776), 111–112
Huskisson, William (1770–1830), 174, 177, 179, 186, 195, 268*n*
Huxley, Aldous (1894–1963), 560
Huxley, Thomas Henry (1825–1895), 321, 410
Hyde Park riots, 327–328
Hyndman, Henry Mayers (1842–1921), 393–394, 395

Immigration, 119, 604, 617
Impeachment, 43, 46, 100*n*, 144
Imperial conferences, 458
Imperial East Africa Company, 442
Imperial Economic Conference, 531, 533
Imperialism. *See* Empire
Imperial War Cabinet, 490*n*
Import Duties Advisory Committee, 531
Imports. *See* Tariffs; Trade
Independent Labour Party, 399, 536–537. *See also* Labour Party
Independents. *See* Congregationalists
India, 70–71, 99–100, 102, 114, 276, 311–316, 356–359, 386, 452, 504, 506, 535–536, 568, 577–578, 616
India Act (1784), 102, 103
India Bill (1783), 99

Indian Civil Service, 504
Indian Mutiny, 286, 311–316, 356, 504
Indian National Congress, 505
Individualism, 159, 294
Industrial Arbitration Act (1919), 512
Industrialization, 107–108, 120, 160, 384. *See also* Industry
Industrial Relations Act (1971), 603
Industrial Relations Commission, 601
Industrial Relations Court, 604
Industry, 2, 107–108, 111–114, 114–117, 120–122, 150, 163, 173–174, 287–288, 382–386, 507, 523–527, 532, 550–551, 574–575, 576, 582–583, 601–602, 604–605, 606–607
Inheritance, 11–12
Inkerman, Battle of, 308–309
Inns of Court, 10
Inspection, 244, 247, 263–264, 266–267, 344–345
Insurance, 20–21, 288–289, 386, 523–524
Intellectual aristocracy, 299–300, 400
International Monetary Fund, 608
International Working Men's Association (First International), 322
Intolerable Acts, 87, 88
Iraq, 510
Ireland, 65–67, 90–92, 102, 119, 140, 141–143, 190–193, 199–200, 226, 230–233, 275, 277–279, 281, 341–344, 365–372, 433–437, 456–457, 464, 465–466, 477–479, 500–503, 534, 535, 540–541, 577–578, 618–620, 634–635
Irish emigration, 119, 450
Irish famine, 275, 277–279
Irish Land Act (1870), 343–344
Irish Land Act (1881), 368–369
Irish Parliamentary Party, 355, 372, 434–435, 437, 456–457, 459, 478
Irish Republican Army, 501–503, 618
Irish Republican Brotherhood. *See* Fenians
Iron and steel industry, 18, 111–112, 113, 288, 383, 599
Isabella II, Queen of Spain (1830–1904), 302, 304, 363
Isle of Wight, 199
Ismail, Khedive of Egypt (1830–1895), 363, 365
Isolationism, 449–453, 586
Israel, 578, 593–594, 605. *See also* Palestine
Italy, 143, 169–170, 409, 317–318, 438, 440, 441, 548, 567, 568, 569, 481–483, 486, 520, 521, 543–544, 546, 548, 567, 568, 569, 586

Jacobites, 44, 65
Jamaica, 67, 320
Jamaica Committee, 321
James I (1566–1625), 49, 63–64, 67
James II (1633–1701), 34, 36, 40–41, 42, 59
James, the Old Pretender (1688–1766), 44
Jameson, Sir Leander Starr (1853–1917, *cr.* 1st Bt., 1911), 445–446
Jameson Raid, 445–446, 447
Japan, 451–452, 486, 523, 542, 546, 567–568, 569

Java, 310
Jeffrey, Francis (1773–1850, Lord Jeffrey, 1834), 184
Jena, Battle of, 147
Jenkins, Roy (1920–   ), 603, 606, 609
Jenkins's Ear, War of, 62–63
Jenkinson, Charles (1727–1808, *cr.* B. Hawkesbury, 1786, 1st E. of Liverpool, 1796), 100
Jerusalem bishopric, 235
Jervis, Sir John (1735–1823, k. 1782, *cr.* 1st E. of St. Vincent, 1797), 138
Jevons, William Stanley (1835–1882), 411
Jews, 119*n*, 499, 543, 578
Jex-Blake, Sophia (1840–1912), 404
John VI, King of Portugal (1769 or 1767?–1826), 170
John, Augustus (1879–1961), 471
Johnson, Samuel (1709–1784), 32, 85*n*
Jolly George (ship), 498
Jones, Ernest (1819–1869), 280, 281, 327
Jones, Inigo, 31
Jones, Jack (1913–   ), 607
Jones, Sir William (1746–1794, k. 1783), 93
Joseph, Sir Keith (1918–   , 2nd Bt., 1943), 608
Joyce, James (1882–1941), 560
Joynson-Hicks, Sir William (1865–1932, *cr.* 1st Bt., 1919, 1st V. Brentford, 1929), 555
Judicial Committee of Privy Council, 235–236, 407, 408
July Revolution (1830), 302
"Junius," 86*n*
Junta, 322, 323, 325, 327, 397
Justice, 394
Justices of the Peace, 25, 36, 59–60, 227–228, 426, 650–651
Jutland, Battle of, 487

Kant, Immanuel (1724–1804), 123
Kay, John (*fl.* 1733–1764), 114
Kay-Shuttleworth, Sir James (1804–1877, *cr.* 1st Bt., 1849), 261, 265, 345
Keats, John (1795–1821), 127
Keble, John (1792–1866), 233
Keeler, Christine (1943–   ), 598
Kemal Atatürk (1881–1938), 508
Kennedy, John Fitzgerald, (1917–1963), 596
Kent, William (1684–1748), 31
Kenya, 441, 583, 584, 616
Kenyatta, Jomo (1893?–1978), 584
Keynes, John Maynard (1883–1946, *cr.* 1st B. Keynes, 1942), 239, 500, 507, 525, 529, 541, 561
Khartum, 365
Krushchev, Nikita (1894–1971), 585
"Kilmainham Treaty," 369
King, Edward (1829–1910), 406
King, Gregory (1648–1712), 5–9, 24, 30, 117*n*
King's College (London), 185
Kingsley, Charles (1819–1875), 290, 321
Kipling, Rudyard (1865–1936), 414–415, 504

Kitchener, Horatio Herbert (1850–1916, k. 1894, *cr.* 1st B. Kitchener, 1898, 1st V., 1902, 1st E., 1914), 441, 447, 490
Knitting industry, 112, 150, 158, 288
Korea, 451–452, 585
Kossuth, Louis (1802–1894), 305
Kruger, Paul (1825–1904), 443–444, 445–446, 447

Labor. *See* Working classes
Labor conditions, 116–117, 386–388, 512–515. *See also* Child and female labor; Factory system; Trade unions
Labor discipline, 116, 160, 286
Labor exchanges, 462
Labour Party, 457–458, 459, 461, 472–473, 497, 508, 509–510, 511, 515–520, 527–530, 536–538, 557, 573–578, 582, 585, 588–589, 591–592, 597, 599–602, 605–611, 612–613
Lahore, Treaty of, 314
Laissez-faire, 17, 93–94, 158–159, 265, 271
Lancaster, Joseph (1778–1838), 159
Land League, 366, 367
Land purchase (Ireland), 365–372, 436–437, 456
Landscape gardening, 9, 125
Land system, England, 10–13, 109–110, 377–381; Ireland, 343–344, 366, 368–369, 434
Lansbury, George (1859–1940), 517, 538
Lansdowne. Petty-Fitzmaurice, Henry (1780–1863, 3rd M. of Lansdowne, 1809), 195
Lansdowne. Petty-Fitzmaurice, Henry Charles Keith (1845–1927, 5th M. of Lansdowne, 1866), 452
Larkin, James (1876–1947), 478
Larkin, Philip (1922–   ), 625
Laski, Harold Joseph (1893–1950), 517, 537
Latin America, 170–171, 172, 176, 445, 451
Latitudinarianism, 38–39
Laud, William (1573–1645), 233
Lausanne, Treaty of, 510
Laval, Pierre (1883–1945), 543–544
Law, Andrew Bonar (1858–1923), 476–477, 478, 479, 484, 490, 497, 509–511
Law, William (1686–1761), 38
Lawrence, David Herbert (1885–1930), 472, 560
Lawrence, Sir Thomas (1769–1830, k. 1815), 126
Lawrence, Thomas Edward (1888–1935), 487*n*
Leach, Bernard (1887–1979), 623
League of Augsburg, War of the, 68
League of Nations, 498–499, 519, 542, 544–545
Leavis, Frank Raymond (1895–1978), 560*n*
Leeds, 17, 198, 199, 424
Leeds Mercury, 184
Left Book Club, 537
Legal reform, 177–180, 187, 348, 648–649, 652–653
Lend-Lease, 566

Leopold I, King of the Belgians (1790–1865), 303
Leopold II, King of the Belgians (1835–1909), 440
"Less eligibility", 248
Lesseps, Ferdinand, Vicomte de (1805–1894), 363
Levant Company, 16
Lewis, Matthew Gregory "Monk" (1775–1818), 125
Liberalism, 169–172, 186–203, 285–301, 340–341, 428–433
Liberal Party, 316, 325, 326, 327, 328–330, 355, 365, 370, 372, 397–398, 424, 427, 428–429, 430–431, 436, 454–466 *passim*, 490, 509, 511, 527–528, 587. *See also* Parties, political; Whig Party
Liberation Society, 405
Liberty's, 623
Licensing Act (1662), 41
Licensing Act (1904), 455, 456
Light Brigade, 308, 309
Lillie, Beatrice (1898–   ), 560
Limited liability, 272–273
Lincoln, Abraham (1809–1865), 318
Linen trade, 113
Liquor licensing, 349, 456
Literacy. *See* Education
Liverpool, 15, 223, 237, 330, 424, 474*n*
Liverpool. Jenkinson, Robert Banks (1770–1828, Lord Hawkesbury, 1796, *cr.* B. Hawkesbury, 1803, 2nd E. of Liverpool, 1808),146–147,160, 161, 168–169, 172, 181, 186, 192
Liverpool and Manchester Railway, 268–269
Livingstone, David (1813–1873), 442
Llewellyn Smith, Hubert (1864–1945), 463
Lloyd, John Selwyn Brooke (1904–1978, *cr.* B. Selwyn-Lloyd, 1976), 585
Lloyd George, David (1863–1945, *cr.* 1st E. Lloyd George, 1945), 455, 460–461, 463, 464–465, 475, 476, 489–491, 496–498, 500, 502, 506, 508–509, 511, 513, 528, 571–572
Local government, 11, 58–61, 119–120, 121–122, 225–228, 294, 346, 426, 428, 429, 496, 521, 654–655
Local Government Act (1888), 429
Local Government Board, 346, 496
Locarno, Treaty of, 520, 541
Locke, John (1632–1704), 32, 33, 87, 124
Lombe, John (1693?–1722), 112
Lombe, Sir Thomas (1685–1739, k. 1727), 112
London, 19–20, 22, 23, 31, 52, 79, 85, 96, 97, 102, 116, 119, 135, 173, 187–188, 198, 202, 227, 281, 321–322, 386, 387, 390, 401, 428, 568, 651
London, Protocol of (1830), 189
London, University of, 185, 230, 297
London Corresponding Society, 135, 140, 153
London County Council, 428
Londonderry. *See* Castlereagh
London School of Economics, 411

London Trades Council, 321–322
London Working Men's Association. 251–252, 397
Long, Walter (1854–1924, *cr.* 1st V. Long, 1921), 476, 477
Lord Chancellor, 55–56, 178, 647–648
Lord High Treasurer, 47, 55–56
Lord Lieutenant, 58, 651
Lord Mayor of London, 22
Lord President of the Council, 55–56
Lord Privy Seal, 55–56
Lords of Appeal in Ordinary, 348, 649
Louis XIV, King of France (1638–1715), 45
Louis XVI, King of France (1754–1793), 135
Louis XVIII, King of France (1755–1824), 154
Louisburg, 69, 70
Louisiana Territory, 81
Louis Phillippe, King of the French (1773–1850), 194, 302, 304
Lovett, William (1800–1877), 251, 262
Lowe, Robert (1811–1892, *cr.* 1st V. Sherbrooke, 1880), 327, 339, 344–345, 349
Loyd, Samuel Jones (1796–1883, *cr.* 1st B. Overstone, 1860), 268
Luddism, 150, 151, 163, 165, 196, 263
Ludendorff, Erich Friedrich Wilhelm (1865–1937), 510
Ludlow, John Malcolm Forbes (1821–1911), 290
Lunéville, Treaty of, 138
Lutyens, Sir Edwin (1869–1944, k. 1918), 412
Luxembourg, 586
Lyell, Sir Charles, 470
Lytton, Edward Bulwer (1803–1873, *cr.* 1st B. Lytton, 1866), 214
Lytton Commission, 542

Macadam, John Loudon (1756–1836), 108
Macaulay, Thomas Babington (1800–1859, *cr.* 1st B. Macaulay, 1857), 10, 184, 213–214
McCulloch, John Ramsay (1789–1864), 182, 243
MacDonald, Alexander (1821–1881), 397
MacDonald, J. Ramsay (1866–1937), 484, 515, 516, 517–520, 528–530, 537, 540
McKenna duties, 507, 531
Mackenzie, Charles Frederick (1825–1862), 442
MacKenzie, Henry (1745–1831), 125
Mackintosh, Charles Rennie (1868–1928), 470
Mackintosh, Sir James (1765–1832, k. 1803), 178
MacLeod, Iain (1913–1970), 603
Macmillan, Harold (1894–   ), 539, 590, 594–597
Macmillan Committee, 529
Macpherson, James (1736–1796), 126
Madison, James (1751–1836), 148
Madras, 70, 99, 313
Mafeking, 447

Maitland, Frederic William (1850–1906), 412
Majuba Hill, Battle of, 361
Makarios, Archbishop (1913–1977), 584, 595
Malawi, 616
Malaya, 310, 359
Malaysia, Federation of, 616
Malta, 137, 155, 359
Malthus, Thomas Robert (1766–1834), 118, 182, 402
Manchester, 51, 60, 108, 116, 119, 182, 198, 199, 227, 424
Manchester Guardian, 184
Manchuria, 542
Mandates, 499
Mandeville, Bernard (1670?–1733), 93
Mann, Tom (1856–1941), 392, 395, 473, 474
Manners, 130–131, 555–556
Manning, Henry (1808–1892), 235–236, 392, 409
Mansfield. Murray, William (1705–1793, *cr.* 1st B. Mansfield, 1756, 1st E. of Mansfield, 1776), 85
Marchand, Jean Baptiste (1863–1934), 441
Marengo, Battle of, 138
Maria II, Queen of Portugal (1819–1853), 302
Marlborough. Churchill, John (1650–1722, *cr.* 1st B. Marlborough, 1682 and 1685, 1st E. of Marlborough, 1689, 1st D., 1702), 9, 42, 46, 68
Marlborough. Sarah *née* Jennings (1660–1744, Duchess of Marlborough), 42
Marne, Battles of the, 485, 488
Marquand, David (1934–   ), 609
Marriage, 402–404
Married Women's Property Acts (1870, 1882, 1893), 404
Marshall, Alfred (1842–1924), 411
Marshall, George Catlett (1890–1959), 580–581
Marshall, John (1765–1845), 121, 243
Marshall Plan, 580–581, 586
Martineau, Harriet (1802–1876), 179, 182
Marx, Karl (1818–1883), 29, 118, 237, 395
Mary II (1662–1694), 40, 41
Mary, Queen (Victoria Mary of Teck, 1867–1953), 454
Masham, Abigail Lady (d. 1734), 42
Massachusetts, 86–87
Mass culture, 551–552, 555, 625
Master and Servant Laws, 351
Matthew, Sir Robert (1906–1975, k. 1962), 624
Maudling, Reginald (1917–1979), 597
Mau Mau, 584
Maurice, Frederick Denison (1805–1872), 290, 407–408
Mauritius, 359
May Committee, 529
Mayhew, Henry (1812–1887), 403
Maynooth, Grant, 275
Mazzini, Giuseppe (1805–1872), 304
Mechanics' Institutions, 185
Medical Act (1858), 297

Medicine, 24, 264–265, 297, 575–576. *See also* National Health Service; Public health
Mehemet Ali (1769?–1849), 303, 363
Melbourne. Lamb, William (1779–1848, 2nd V. Melbourne, 1829), 195, 216–218, 260, 277, 350
Mercantilism, 15–17, 21–22, 92–93, 93–94. *See also* Trade
Merchant Adventurers, 16
Merchants of the Staple, 16
Meredith, George (1828–1909), 317, 414
Metaphysical Society, 413
Methodism, 39, 127–129, 154, 405, 457
Methuen Treaty, 14–15
Metropolitan Board of Works, 227
Metternich, Klemens, Prince von (1773–1859), 154, 169–170
Mexico, 171
Middle classes, 222–228, 289, 319, 399–409. *See also* social structure
Middlesex, 59, 85, 95, 152
Midlothian campaign, 355, 361, 364, 423
Miguel, Dom (1802–1866), 170, 189, 302
Milan decree (1807), 147
Mill, James (1773–1836), 153–154, 182
Mill, John Stuart (1806–1873), 182–183, 300–301, 316, 321, 327, 343, 404, 411
Milner, Alfred (1854–1925, k. 1895, *cr.* 1st V. Milner, 1902), 444, 447, 448, 490–491
Milner, Isaac (1750–1820), 128
Milton, John (1608–1674), 32
Minden, Battle of, 88
Ministry of Health, 496
Ministry of Labour, 488, 512
Ministry of Munitions, 488
Ministry of Overseas Development, 599
Ministry of Reconstruction, 495
Ministry of Technology, 599
Ministry of Transport, 496
Minorca, 68
Minto. Elliot, Gilbert John (1845–1914, 4th E. of Minto, 1891), 505–506
Missionaries, 442
Mitchell, John (1815–1875), 281
Monarchy, 48–49, 169–170, 216–218, 629
Monitorial system, 159
Money, Sir Leo Chiozza (1870–1944, k. 1915), 513
Monmouth's Rebellion, 42
Monopolies, 222–224
Monroe Doctrine, 170
Montagu-Chelmsford reforms, 506
Montgomery, Sir Bernard Law (1887–1976, k. 1942, *cr.* 1st V. Montgomery of Alamein, 1946), 568
Moore, George (1852–1933), 414
Moore, George Edward (1873–1958), 470
Moore, Henry (1898–   ), 559, 623
Moore, Sir John (1761–1809, k. 1804), 148
Morant, Sir Robert (1863–1920, k. 1907), 455–456, 463
Moravians, 39
More, Hannah (1743–1833), 129
Morley, John (1838–1923, *cr.* 1st V. Morley, 1908), 427, 430, 455, 460, 484, 505

Morley, Samuel (1809–1886), 210
Morley-Minto reforms, 505–506
Morning Chronicle, 184
Morocco, 452, 483
Morris, William (1834–1896), 395, 413, 415
Morrison, Herbert (1885–1965, *cr.* B. Morrison, 1959), 573
Mosley, Sir Oswald (1896–   , 6th Bt., 1928), 529
Mountbatten, Louis (1900–1979, k. 1922, *cr.* 1st V. Mountbatten of Burma, 1946, 1st E., 1947), 572
Mozambique, 444
Munich Agreements, 547–548
Municipal Corporations Act (1835), 651
Murray, Len (1922–   ), 607
Muscovy Company, 16
Musgrave, Thea (1928–   ), 623
Music, 470–471, 558–559, 622–623, 625
Muslim League, 505–506
Mussolini, Benito (1883–1945), 521, 543, 567, 568, 569
Mustafa Kemal. *See* Kemal Atatürk
Mutiny Act (1689), 41
Mutiny at the Curragh, 478

Nabobs, 275
Nagasaki, 569
Nailmaking, 112, 253, 288
Namier, Sir Lewis Bernstein (1888–1960, k. 1952), 53, 54, 561
Nanking, Treaty of, 310–311
Napier, Sir Charles James (1782–1853, k. 1838), 314
Napoleon I, Emperor of the French (1769–1821), 137–138, 143, 144, 145, 147–149, 154–155, 168
Napoleon III, Emperor of the French (1808–1873), 305, 307, 316, 317–318
Napoleonic wars, 137–138, 144, 147–149, 154–155
Nasser, Gamal Abdal (1918–1970), 593–594
Natal, 360, 444
National Association for the Protection of Labour, 241
National Coal Board, 574
National debt, 62, 65, 161, 524, 529
National Economic Development Council, 595
National Education League, 345, 405
National Enterprise Board, 606
National Front, 618
National Health Service, 575–576, 589, 599, 614
National Industrial Conference, 512, 513
National Insurance Act (1911), 463
National Insurance Act (1946), 575
Nationalization, 521, 532, 574, 582–583, 590, 592, 599, 604, 606, 612–613
National Liberal Federation, 424
National Petition, 253
National Plan, 600
National Society for Promoting the Education of the Poor, 159, 265

National Theater, 624
National Union of Conservative and Constitutionalist Associations, 425
National Union of the Working Classes, 201, 239
Navarino, Battle of, 186
Navigation laws, 16–17, 66, 68, 93, 173, 177, 280
Navvies, 109, 269
Navy, 138–139, 140, 148, 161, 352, 438, 449, 487, 507
Nawab of Bengal, 70–71
Nazis, 542–543, 567. *See also* Hitler
Nelson, Sir Horatio (1758–1805, k. 1797, *cr.* 1st B. Nelson, 1790, 1st V., 1801), 138, 144, 147
Netherlands. *See* Belgium; Holland
Newcastle. Pelham-Holles, Thomas (1693–1768, 1st D. of Newcastle, 1715), 38, 54, 62, 63, 80, 81
Newcastle. Clinton, Henry Pelham Fiennes Pelham (1785–1851, 4th D. of Newcastle, 1795), 211
Newcastle Program, 352, 430–431, 457
Newcomen engine, 115
New Domesday Book, 377
Newfoundland, 69, 535
New Lanark, 160
Newman, John Henry (1801–1890), 234–235, 408–409
New Model unions, 291–292, 386, 389–393. *See also* Trade unions
New Party, 537
Newport Rising, 254
Newspapers. *See* Press
Newton, Sir Isaac (1642–1727, k. 1705), 30–31, 32, 122
Newton, William (1822–1876), 397
New Zealand, 92, 219, 356, 439, 449, 535
Nicholas I, Tsar of Russia (1796–1855), 171, 307
Nicholson, Ben (1894–   ), 559, 623
Nigeria, 616
Nightingale, Florence (1820–1910), 298, 308, 310, 404
Nile, Battle of the, 138
Nkrumah, Kwame (1909–1972), 584
Nonconformity. *See* Dissent
Nonjurors, 34, 40
North. Frederick, Lord North (1732–1792, 2nd E. of Guilford, 1790), 86, 88, 89, 91, 97, 98, 100
North American colonies, 14, 15, 83–84, 86–89
North Atlantic Treaty Organization (NATO), 584–585
North Briton, 82
Northcote, Sir Stafford (1818–1887, 8th Bt., 1851, *cr.* 1st E. of Iddesleigh, 1885), 298, 349–350, 430
Northern Star, 252
Norway, 549, 586
Norwich, 14, 17–19, 112, 119
Nova Scotia, 68–69
Novello, Ivor (1893–1951), 559
Nuclear power, 585, 596

Nureyev, Rudolf (1938–   ), 623
Nursing, 298, 404
Nyasaland, 616

Oastler, Richard (1789–1861), 242–243
O'Brien, James Bronterre (1805–1864), 251, 252, 262, 281
Occasional Conformity Act (1710), 45
O'Connell, Daniel (1775–1847), 191–192, 194, 196, 216, 217, 251, 261, 277
O'Connor, Feargus (1794–1855), 251, 252, 261–263, 274, 281–282
Octennial Act (1768), 90
Odger, George (1813–1877), 322n
Oil, 499, 605, 608, 611
Old-Age Pension Act (1908), 462, 463
Old Sarum, 51
Old Vic, 624
Oligarchy, 61–71
Omdurman, Battle of, 441
O'Neill, Terence (1914–   , cr. B. O'Neill, 1970), 619
Opium trade, 310–311
Opposition, 41–42, 53–54, 61–63, 146–147, 181
Orange Free State, 360, 361, 444, 446
Orlando, Vittorio Emmanuele (1860–1952), 497
Orsini incident, 316
Osborne, John (1929–   ), 624
Osborne, Thomas (1631–1712, cr. 1st E. of Danby, 1674), 42
Osborne judgment (1909), 473
O'Shea, Katharine (1845–1921), 371–372, 434–435
O'Shea, William Henry (1840–1905), 371–372, 434–435
Ossian, 126
Ottawa Agreements, 531, 586
Ottoman Empire. *See* Turkey
Overseas Food Corporation, 576n
Owen, Robert (1771–1858), 116n, 159–160, 181, 230–240
Owen, Wilfred (1893–1918), 623
Owenite socialism, 239–241, 290–291
Owens College, 296
Owner-occupiers, 12–13
Oxford, University of, 9. 50, 185, 190, 233–236, 296, 413, 557, 558
Oxford Movement, 233–236

Pacifism, 308, 311, 484, 543, 544, 585–586
Paine, Thomas (1737–1809), 135–136
Painting, 126, 412–413, 414, 415, 559, 623
Paisley, Ian (1926–   ), 619
Pakistan, 577–578
Palestine, 307, 499, 578. *See also* Israel
Palladianism, 31
Palmerston. Temple, Henry John (1784–1865, 3rd V. Palmerston, 1802), 195, 276, 301–305, 309, 310–311, 316, 318, 325, 326, 438
Panama, 64–65, 451
Pankhurst, Christabel (1880–1958), Emmeline (1857–1928), Sylvia (1882–1960), 480–481
Papacy. *See* Catholicism

"Papal aggression," 306
Paper duties, 319
Paris, Treaty of, *1763*, 81, 82, 84; *1783*, 89, 99; *1856*, 309, 353
Paris Commune (1871), 322
Parish government, 35–36, 58–59, 108, 230, 246–247, 638
Parkes, Joseph (1796–1865), 194, 212, 226, 425
Parliament, 8, 19, 25, 26, 40, 41, 48–54, 56–57, 87, 96, 109, 139, 140, 150, 158, 165, 173, 191, 195, 196–203, 211–212, 222, 260–261, 265, 397, 425–426, 463–466, 473, 496–497, 544, 589. *See also* House of Commons; House of Lords
Parliament Act (1911), 465–466, 476–477
Parliamentary debates, 85
Parliamentary reform, 94–96, 134–136, 151–154, 163–166, 180–181, 193–196, 196–203, 209–210, 223, 225, 228, 249–254, 273–274, 324–330
Parnell, Charles Stewart (1846–1891), 366–372, 434–435
Parnell, Sir Henry (1776–1842, 4th Bt., 1812, cr. 1st B. Congleton, 1841), 224, 273
Parties, political, 210–213, 423–425, 536–541, 587–588. *See also* Conservative Party; Labour Party; Liberal Party; Tory Party; Whig Party
Passchendaele, Battle of, 486
Patents, 112
Pater, Walter (1839–1894), 415
Patronage, ecclesiastical, 35, 231, 232, 640, 641–642; political, 8, 51, 54, 56–57, 67, 100–101, 103–104, 145–146, 194–195, 199, 210–211, 421–422, 426–427
Paxton, Sir Joseph (1801–1865, k. 1851), 286
Paymaster General, 98
Pearl Harbor, 567
Pearson, Karl (1857–1936), 410, 411
Pedro I (Dom Pedro), King of Portugal (as Pedro IV) and Emperor of Brazil (1798–1834), 170, 302
Peel, Sir Robert, the elder (1750–1830, cr. 1st Bt., 1800), 159
Peel, Sir Robert (1788–1850, 2nd Bt., 1830), 168, 172, 177–179, 180, 181, 186, 187, 190, 191, 192–193, 195, 217, 218, 232, 250, 259–282 *passim*, 340, 341, 522
Peelites, 306
Peel's Act (1819), 172–173
Peers, 5–13, 45, 49, 319, 377–381, 465, 587–588, 630–635. *See also* House of Lords
Pelham, Henry (1695?–1754), 63
Penal reform, 178–179, 187
Penny Magazine, 185
Pentrich Rising, 165
People's Charter, The, 251
People's Convention, 251–254
Perceval, Spencer (1762–1812), 146, 147
Percy, Thomas (1729–1811), 126
Periodicals. *See* Press
Persia, 452

Peter III, Tsar of Russia (1728–1762), 80
Peterloo Massacre, 165–166
Pethick-Lawrence, Frederick William (1871–1961, *cr.* B. Pethick-Lawrence, 1945), 481
Philippines, 80, 451
Phillpotts, Henry (1778–1869), 235
Philosophy, 32, 123–125, 182–183, 413, 470, 561
Phoenix Park murders, 369, 434
Piedmont, 317–318
Piggott forgeries, 434
Pinero, Sir Arthur Wing (1855–1934, k. 1909), 47
Pinter, Harold (1930–   ), 624
Pitt, Thomas (1653–1726), 69
Pitt, William (1708–1778, *cr.* 1st E. of Chatham, 1766), 17, 63, 69–71, 80, 90, 95
Pitt, William (1759–1806), 84, 92, 98–99, 100–103, 136–137, 138–139, 141–143, 143–144, 145, 190, 198, 378
Place, Francis (1771–1854), 152–153, 174, 202, 212, 251
Placemen, 56–57
Plague, 94
Plaid Cymru, 610, 611
Planck, Max (1858–1947), 469
"Plan of Campaign," 434
Plassey, Battle of, 99
Plimsoll, Samuel (1824–1898), 351
Plug Plot, 263
Pluralism, 37, 232
Plymouth Brethren, 409–410
Poincaré, Raymond (1860–1934), 508, 510
Poland, 499, 548, 549, 566
Police, 26, 151, 165, 178, 187–188, 276, 526; Ireland, 501, 618
Polignac, Prince de (1780–1847), 194
Political economy, 181–182
Political reform, 94–104, 163–168, 319–320, 399–400, 421–423
Political Register, 153, 164
Politics, 40–47, 47–54, 54–58, 58–61, 61–71, 79–86, 86–94, 94–104, 163–168, 319–320, 399–406, 421–423, 553–555
Ponsonby, George (1755–1817), 180
Ponsonby, John William (1781–1847, *cr.* 1st V. Duncannon, 1834, 4th E. of Bessborough, 1844), 197
Poor Law Amendment Act (1834), 245–249, 462
Poor laws, 26–27, 140, 227, 246–247, 261, 278–279, 346, 462, 521
Pope, Alexander (1688–1744), 31*n*, 32, 62, 103
Population, 7, 14, 117–120, 386–387, 549–550, 617
Porteus, Beilby (1731–1808), 129
Portland. Bentinck, William Henry Cavendish (1738–1809, 3rd D. of Portland, 1762), 99, 145
Portugal, 14–15, 148–149, 169, 170, 189, 302, 303, 586
Positivism, 323, 410
Postal reform, 225
Potsdam Conference, 573

Potter, George (1832–1893), 322*n*
Poverty, 24–28, 130, 140, 158–159, 390–391. *See also* Great Depression; Working classes
Powell, Anthony (1905–   ), 624–625
Powell, Enoch (1912–   ), 617–618
Poynings Law, 67
Prentice, Reginald (1923–   ), 609
Pre-Raphaelite Brotherhood, 415
Presbyterians, 37, 65, 129, 141. *See also* Dissent; Unitarianism
Press, 41, 82, 92, 94, 95, 135–136, 153, 163–164, 166, 181, 182, 184, 185, 196, 219, 233, 234, 237, 249, 252, 275, 280, 294, 301, 316, 319, 354, 394, 399, 404, 516, 537, 560*n*, 610
Pressburg, Treaty of, 144
Press gang, 25, 138
Pretoria Convention, 361
Pretorius, Andreas (1799–1853), 360
Price, Richard (1723–1791), 94, 95, 134–135
Price and Incomes Board, 601
Priestley, John Boynton (1894–   ), 560–561
Priestley, Joseph (1733–1804), 95, 136
Prime Minister, 47, 101, 260–261, 339–340, 510, 554, 597–598, 640
Primogeniture, 11–12
Primrose League, 425
Prisons, 130, 178, 179
Privy Council, 47, 346, 649
Professions, 297–298, 348, 400, 404, 556
Profumo, John (1915–   ), 598
Promenade Concerts, 358
Prostitution, 403, 404
Protectionism, 458–459, 531, 538. *See also* Tariffs; Trade
Protestant Association, 97
Prussia, 84, 89, 137, 147, 155, 169, 303, 318
Public health, 264–265, 294–295, 387, 463, 575–576, 589. *See also* National Health Service
Public Health Act (1848), 280, 294, 351
Public schools, 9, 295–296, 557. *See also* Education
Public Worship Act (1874), 406
Punjab, 314
Puritans, 37
Pusey, Edward Bouverie (1800–1882), 234

Quadruple Alliance, 169
Quakers, 37*h*
Quant, Mary (1934–   ), 625
Quarterly Review, 184
Quarter Sessions, 59, 60
Quebec, 220
Quebec Act (1774), 87, 220
Queen Anne's Bounty, 35
Queen's Bench, 348

Race Relations Acts (1965, 1968), 617, 618
Radcliffe, Anne (1764–1823), 125
Radicalism, 94–95, 104, 116, 135–136, 139–140, 149–154, 160, 163–168, 184, 185, 193–195, 196, 213, 214–215, 216,

Radicalism (*continued*)
220–221, 222, 227, 231–232, 250, 274–275, 365, 424, 426, 430–433, 484. *See also* Chartism; Socialism
Radio, 552
Raffles, Sir Stamford (1781–1826, k. 1817), 310
Raglan. Somerset, Lord Fitzroy James Henry (1788–1855, *cr.* 1st B. Raglan, 1852), 308
Railways, 268–271, 382, 383, 412, 475, 488, 507, 513, 526–527, 551, 575, 612–613
Rambert, Dame Marie (1888–D.B.E., 1962), 559
Rebecca riots, 254
Reconstruction, 157–168, 495–500, 506–508, 522–525, 571–573, 573–578
Red-brick universities, 296, 557–558
Redistribution Act (1885), 426–428
Redmond, John (1856–1918), 437, 456, 478, 484
Reform Acts (1832), 140, 196–203, 209–210, 222, 399–400
Reform Act (1867), 324–330, 421, 424
Reform Act (1884), 369, 426–428
Reform Club, 213, 425
Reform League, 327–328
Reform Union, 327
Regency Crisis, *1788–1789*, 101; *1810–1811*, 146
Registrar General, 261
Regulated companies, 15–16
Regulating Act (1773), 99
Reid, Thomas (1710–1796), 123
Reith, Sir John (1889–1971, k. 1927, *cr.* 1st B. Reith, 1940), 552
Religion, 32–39, 127–131. *See also* Catholicism; Church of England; Dissent
Reparations, 500, 508, 510, 518–519, 541
Representation of the People Act (1918), 497, 587
Republicanism, 350
Responsible government, 218–222, 356, 360, 448, 533, 536
Restoration. *See* Charles II
Revised Code, 345
Revolution of 1688. *See* Glorious Revolution
Revolution of 1848, 280–281, 304
Reynolds, Sir Joshua (1723–1792, k. 1769), 126
Rhineland, 500, 545
Rhodes, Cecil (1853–1902), 384, 442–446
Rhodesia, 443, 583, 600
Ricardo, David (1772–1823), 173, 181–182
Richardson, Samuel (1689–1761), 125
Richmond. Lennox, Charles (1735–1806, 3rd D. of Richmond, 1750), 96
Richmond. Lennox, Charles Gordon (1791–1860, 5th D. of Richmond, 1819), 195, 216, 232, 246
Riot Act (1715), 26, 57
Rioting, 25–26, 27–28, 43–44, 96–97, 136, 140, 150–151, 165–166, 168, 196, 201–202, 263, 281, 320–321, 327–328, 394, 617

Ripon. *See* Robinson, Frederick John
Roads, 108–109
Roberts, Sir Frederick Sleigh (1832–1914, k. 1878, *cr.* 1st B. Roberts, 1892, 1st E., 1900), 357, 447
Robinson, Frederick John (1782–1859, *cr.* 1st V. Goderich, 1827, 1st E. of Ripon, 1833), 173, 177, 186, 195, 216, 232
Robinson, Sir Hercules (1824–1897, k. 1859, *cr.* 1st Bt., 1891, 1st B. Rosmead, 1896), 445
Robinson, John (1727–1802), 100
Rockingham. Watson-Wentworth, Charles (1730–1782, 2nd M. of Rockingham, 1750), 83–84, 89
Roebuck, John Arthur (1801–1879), 265, 309
Rolls-Royce, 604
Roman Catholic Church. *See* Catholicism
Romanticism, 122, 126–127, 300
Rome, Treaty of, 586
Romilly, Sir Samuel (1757–1818, k. 1806), 178, 180
Rommel, Erwin (1891–1944), 567, 568
Romney, George (1734–1802), 126
Roosevelt, Franklin Delano (1882–1945), 566, 571
Rose, George (1744–1818), 100
Rosebery. Primrose, Archibald Philip (1847–1929, 5th E. of Rosebery, 1868), 432, 441, 455
Rossetti, Dante Gabriel (1828–1882), 415
Rothermere. Harmsworth, Harold Sidney (1868–1940, *cr.* 1st V. Rothermere, 1919), 538, 551
Rotunda, 193, 201
Round, John Horace (1854–1928), 412
Rowlandson, Thomas (1756–1827), 167n
Rowntree, B. Seebohm (1871–1954), 391, 577
Royal Air Force, 566, 568, 569
Royal Ballet, 559, 623
Royal Colleges of Physicians and Surgeons, 297
Royal Colonial Institute, 356
Royal Empire Society, 356
Royal Festival Hall, 624
Royal Household, 55, 56, 98, 217–218
Royal Irish Constabulary, 501
Royal Marriages Act (1772), 146
Royal Niger Company, 414
Royal Shakespeare Company, 624
Royal Society, 30, 92–93, 123
Royal Ulster Constabulary, 618
Rumania, 309, 355, 483, 486
Ruskin, John (1819–1900), 321, 395, 414, 442
Russell, Bertrand (1872–1970, 3rd E. Russell, 1913), 470, 585
Russell, Lord John (1792–1878, *cr.* 1st E. Russell, 1861), 180, 189, 194, 195, 196–197, 198, 200, 201, 203, 216, 217, 222, 228, 229–230, 239, 250, 259, 275–276, 282, 305–306, 309, 316, 324, 325, 326
Russia, 80–81, 89, 137, 144, 147, 155, 169,

170, 171–172, 186, 189, 303, 307–309, 314, 353–355, 357, 363, 438, 451–452, 481–488, 498, 504, 519, 520–521, 537, 545, 547, 548, 549, 567, 569, 571, 584–585, 593, 594, 596

Russian Revolution, 487–488, 519

Russo-Japanese War, 452, 505

Russo-Turkish War, 354–355

Rutherford, Sir Ernest (1871–1937, k. 1914, *cr.* 1st B. Rutherford, 1931), 469–470, 561

Rutland, 51–52, 654

Sacheverell, Henry (1674?–1724), 43–44, 46

Sadler, Michael Thomas (1780–1835), 243

Sadler's Wells Ballet, 559, 623

St. Albans, 422

St. Paul's Cathedral, 31

St. Petersburg, Protocol of, 171

Salisbury. Gascoyne-Cecil, Robert Arthur James (1893–1972, 5th M. of Salisbury, 1947), 583, 594, 595

Salisbury. Gascoyne-Cecil, Robert Arthur Talbot (1830–1903, V. Cranborne, 1865, 3rd M. of Salisbury, 1868), 350, 355, 370, 423, 428–429, 430, 433, 437–439, 442–443, 444

Salvation Army, 410

Samuel, Sir Herbert (1870–1963, k. 1926, *cr.* 1st V. Samuel, 1937), 525–526, 527

Sand River Convention, 360

Sandwich. Montagu, John (1718–1792, 4th E. of Sandwich, 1729), 88

Sanitation. *See* Public Health

Sankey, Sir John (1866–1948, k. 1914, *cr.* 1st B. Sankey, 1929, 1st V. Sankey, 1932), 513, 537

Sankey Commission, 574

San Stefano, Treaty of, 354, 355

Saratoga, Battle of, 88

Sardinia, 137, 155

Sargent, John Singer (1856–1925), 471

Savings banks, 290

Savoy Conference, 34

Scanlon, Hugh (1913–   ), 607

Schism Act (1714), 44, 45

Schnadhorst, Francis (1840–1900), 424

Schools. *See* Education; Grammar schools; Public schools

Science, 30, 31, 409–412, 561, 625

Scotland, 50, 63–65, 97, 101–102, 136, 139, 176, 199–200, 226, 236*n*, 610–611, 618, 634–635

Scott, Sir Walter (1771–1832, *cr.* 1st Bt., 1820), 126–127

Scottish National Party, 610–611

Scrutiny, 560*n*

Sculpture, 559, 623

Sebastopol, Siege of (1854–1855), 309

Secondary Education Act (1902), 429

"Second British Empire," 92

Second coalition, 136

Secretaries of State, 55–56, 96, 98

Secretary of State for the Dominions, 534

Secretary of State for War, 139, 347

Secret ballot, 197, 346, 422–423

Security, Act of (1704), 64

Security scandals, 598

Seditions Meetings Act (1795), 139, 140

Seeley, Sir John Robert (1834–1895, k. 1894), 357

Senior, Nassau (1790–1864), 243*n*, 245

Septennial Act (1716), 45, 57–58

Serbia, 354–355, 483–484

Settled Land Act (1852), 378

Settlement, Act of (1701), 35, 42, 49, 53*n*, 64

Settlement, Law of (1662), 27

Seven Years War, 71, 81–82

Sèvres, Treaty of, 508

Seychelles Islands, 359

Shaftesbury. Cooper, Anthony Ashley (1801–1885, Lord Ashley, 1811, 7th E. of Shaftesbury, 1851), 235, 243–244, 264, 406

Shakespeare, William (1564–1616), 130, 559

Shaw, George Bernard (1856–1950), 396, 471, 472, 559

Shaw, Richard Norman (1831–1912), 412

Sheffield, 18, 112, 322–323

Sheffield Outrages, 322–323

Shelburne. Petty, William (1737–1805, 2nd E. of Shelburne, 1761, *cr.* 1st M. of Lansdowne, 1784), 84, 89, 97–98

Shelley, Percy Bysshe (1792–1822), 127, 162*n*, 166

Shinwell, Emanuel (1884–   , *cr.* B., 1970), 572, 573

Shipping industry, 15–16, 224, 280, 376, 376*n*, 385, 506, 523, 532, 566, 604, 606. *See also* Navigation laws

Shooting, 379–380

Shop stewards, 512

Shore, Peter (1934–   ), 606

Short Time Committees, 242

Shrewsbury. Talbot, Charles (1660–1718, 12th E. of Shrewsbury, 1668, *cr.* 1st D., 1694), 44

Sickert, Walter Richard (1860–1942), 471

Sidmouth. *See* Addington

Sierra Leone, 616

Sikhs, 314

Silk industry, 112, 113, 158

Simeon, Charles (1759–1836), 128

Simon, Sir John (1816–1904, k. 1887), 346

Simon, Sir John (1873–1954, k. 1910, *cr.* 1st V. Simon, 1940), 542

Simpson, Wallis Warfield (1896–   ), Duchess of Windsor, 1937), 540

Sinclair, Sir John (1754–1835, *cr.* 1st Bt., 1786), 111

Singapore, 310, 616

Sinn Fein, 478, 501, 502, 618

Sitwell, Dame Edith (1887–1964, D.B.E., 1954), 558

Six Acts (1819), 166–167

Slavery and slave trade, 15, 21, 68, 101, 128, 145, 155, 222–224, 318, 359, 360

Small-Holdings Act (1892), 429
Smiles, Samuel (1812–1904), 294, 316
Smith, Adam (1723–1790), 29, 93, 102, 115, 123, 124
Smith, Frederick Edwin (1874–1930, *cr.* 1st B. Birkenhead, 1919, 1st V., 1921, 1st E. of Birkenhead, 1922), 476, 502, 508, 509
Smith, Sir Harry (1787–1860, *cr.* 1st Bt., 1846), 360
Smith, Southwood (1788–1861), 244, 264, 297*n*
Smith, Sydney (1771–1845), 184, 209
Smith, William Henry (1825–1891), 430
Smuts, Jan Christiaan (1870–1950), 448, 504
Snow, Charles Percy (1905– , k. 1957, *cr.* B. Snow, 1964), 625
Snowden, Philip (1864–1937, *cr.* 1st V. Snowden, 1932), 529, 530, 532, 537
Social Democratic Federation, 394–395, 399
Socialism, 160, 239–242, 393–397, 399, 516–517, 592. *See also* Labour Party; Nationalization; Radicalism
Socialist League, 395, 536–537, 586
Social sciences, 410–412. *See also* Historiography
Social structure, English, 5–30, 621. *See also* Gentry; Middle classes; Peers; Working classes
Society for Constitutional Information, 95–96, 134
Society for National Regeneration, 241
Society for Promoting Christian Knowledge, 129
Society for Propagation of the Gospel in Foreign Parts, 129
Society for the Diffusion of Useful Knowledge, 185
Somaliland (Somalia), 616
Somme, Battle of the, 486
Sophia, Electress of Hanover (1630–1714), 43
Sorel, Georges (1847–1922), 469, 472
South Africa, 359–361, 364, 439, 442–448, 498, 596
South America. *See* Latin America
Southey, Robert (1774–1843), 160, 184
South Sea Bubble, 21–22, 46
South Sea Company, 21–22
Soviet Union. *See* Russia
Soyer, Alexis (1809–1858), 213
Spa Field Riots, 165, 167
Spain, 14, 21, 62–63, 67–69, 80–81, 88, 89, 137, 148–149, 169–170, 171, 302, 303, 304, 546
Spanish-American War, 451
Spanish Civil War, 546, 548
Spanish Succession, War of the, 9, 43, 44, 68
Speaker of the House of Commons, 50, 368, 426
Specie payments, 149–150, 172–173, 175, 181

Spectator, 184
Speenhamland plan, 196, 247
Speke, John Hanning (1827–1864), 442
Spence, Sir Basil (1907–1978, k. 1960), 624
Spencer, Herbert (1820–1903), 293–294, 321, 410–411
Spitalfields Act (1773), 158
Sports, 10, 295, 379–380, 388, 552
Spurgeon, Charles Haddon (1834–1892), 409
Stafford. Leveson-Gower, George Granville (1785–1833, M. of Stafford, 1803, *cr.* 1st D. of Sutherland, 1833), 195
Stamp Act (1764), 83–84
Standard, 184
Stanhope, James (1673–1721, *cr.* V. Stanhope of Mahon, 1717, 1st E. of Stanhope, 1718), 45, 46
Stanley. *See* Derby
Stanley, Oliver (1896–1950), 442, 539
Stansfeld, Sir James (1820–1898, k. 1895), 346, 406
Star Chamber, Court of, 26, 58–59, 177–179, 348
Statistics, 120, 224–225, 230, 261, 411
Statute of Artificers (1563), 158
Statute of Westminster (1931), 534–535
Stead, William Thomas (1849–1921), 403
Steam engine, 18, 115
Stephen, Sir Leslie (1832–1904, k. 1902), 32–33
Stephens, James (1825–1901), 342
Stephens, Joseph Rayner (1805–1879), 253
Sterling Area, 580, 591
Stipendiary magistrates, 227
Stockton and Darlington Railway, 269
Stoppard, Tom (1937–), 624
Strachey, John (1901–1963), 537, 573
Stresa front, 544–545
Stresemann, Gustav (1878–1929), 541
Strict settlement, 11–12, 61
Strikes, 165, 196, 292, 321, 391, 392, 457–458, 454–476, 511, 513–515, 525–527, 582, 603, 610
Stubbs, William (1825–1901), 412
Sturge, Joseph (1793–1859), 263, 274
Sudan, 364–365
Suez, 359, 361–363, 593–594
Suffrage. *See* Franchise
Sullivan, Sir Arthur (1842–1900, k. 1883), 413
Sunderland. Spencer, Charles (1674–1722, 3rd E. of Sunderland, 1702), 46
Sunderland. Spencer, Robert (1640–1702, 2nd E. of Sunderland, 1643), 42
Superannuation Act (1859), 299
Supreme Court of Judicature, 348
Surveyor of Highways, 58
Sutherland, Graham (1903–), 559, 623
Sweated industries, 462–463
Sweden, 89, 586
Swift, Jonathan (1667–1745), 62, 90
"Swing, Captain," 196
Switzerland, 143, 586

Sykes-Picot Agreement (1916), 499
Symphony orchestras, 558
Syndicalism, 472–476

Taff Vale decision, 457–458, 463
Talavera, Battle of, 149
Talleyrand, Charles Maurice de (1754–1838), 302–303
Tamworth Manifesto, 250
Tanganyika (Tanzania), 616
Tannenberg, Battle of, 485
Tariffs, 158, 172–175, 181, 182, 188, 273–277, 287, 458–459, 524–525, 531–532. *See also* Corn laws; Protectionism
Tawney, Richard Henry (1880–1962), 513, 517
Taxation, 23, 48–49, 62, 83, 86, 103, 157–158, 164, 172, 224, 273, 319, 349, 431, 521, 529, 576, 579, 599, 604
"Taxes on knowledge," 164, 251*n*, 319
Taylor, Robert, "The Devil's Chaplain" (1784–1844), 193
Tea, 86
Tea, afternoon, 402*n*
Television, 561, 590
Telford, Thomas (1757–1834), 103, 104
Temperance, 349
Temple, William (1881–1944), 556
Ten Minutes Bill, 328–329
Tennyson, Alfred (1809–1892, *cr.* 1st B. Tennyson, 1884), 317, 321, 325*n*, 413–414
Terrorism, 619–620
Test Act (1673), 36, 189–190, 228–229
Textile industry, 18–19, 112, 113
Thatcher, Margaret (1925–   ), 608, 609
Theater, 471, 559–560, 624
Thelwall, John (1764–1834), 139
Thirlwall, Connop (1797–1875), 407*n*
Thirty-nine Articles, 35, 235
Thistlewood, Arthur (1770–1820), 167
Thomas, John Henry (1874–1969), 513, 529, 530, 537
Thompson, Charles Edward Poulett (1799–1841, *cr* 1st B. Sydenham, 1840), 195, 221–222, 224
Thorneycroft, Peter (1909–   , *cr.* B. Thorneycroft, 1967), 594–595
Thornton, Henry (1760–1815), 128
Thorpe, Jeremy (1929–   ), 605
Thurlow, Edward (1731–1806, *cr.* 1st B. Thurlow, 1778), 101
Tibet, 452
Tientsin, Treaty of, 311
Tilak, Bal Gangadhar (1856–1920), 505
Tillett, Benjamin (1860–1943), 392, 473, 474
Tilsit, Treaty of, 147
The Times, 164, 184, 610
Tin industry, 18
Tippett, Sir Michael (1905–   , k. 1966), 623
Tithes, 231–232, 429
Tobacco, 14, 15

Tocqueville, Alexis de (1805–1859), 301
Toland, John (1670–1722), 33
Toleration Act (1689), 36, 41
Tone, Theobald Wolfe (1736–1812), 142
Tooke, John Horne (1736–1812), 95, 139
Tory Party, 41–47, 146–147, 184, 202–203, 212–213, 214, 330. *See also* Conservative Party
Towns, 14–23, 59–61, 117–120, 226–228
Townshend, Charles (1674–1738, 2nd V. Townshend of Raynham, 1687), 46
Townshend, Charles (1725–1767), 84, 86
Tractarians. *See* Oxford Movement
Trade, foreign, 14–23, 91, 92–93, 288–289, 376–377, 381–383, 442, 450–451, 507, 523–524, 579–581, 582. *See also* Mercantilism
Trade boards, 462, 474
Trade councils, 321
Trade Disputes Act (1906), 463, 473
Trade Disputes and Trade Union Act (1927), 527, 529, 574
Trade Union Act (1871), 346
Trade Union Acts (1824–1825), 175
Trade unions, 140–141, 151, 163, 174–175, 239–242, 289–292, 321–324, 346, 389–393, 397–398, 457, 472, 476, 511–515, 515–516, 525–527, 538, 545, 572, 574, 601–602, 603–604, 606–607, 611–612, 621
Trades Union Congress, 393, 398, 457, 515–516, 525–527, 601
Trafalgar, Battle of, 144, 147
Trafalgar Square demonstrations, 394–395
Transvaal, 360, 361, 443–444, 446, 448. *See also* South Africa
Treason, 139, 140
Treasury, 57
Tremenheere, Hugh Seymour (1804–1893), 264, 266
Trent affair, 318
Trevelyan, Sir Charles (1807–1886, k. 1848, *cr.* 1st Bt., 1874), 279, 298
Trevelyan, George Macaulay (1876–1962), 25, 60
Trevelyan, Sir George Otto (1838–1928, 2nd Bt., 1886), 429
Tribune group, 592
Triennial Act (1694), 41, 43, 45, 52
Triple Alliance (diplomacy), 438, 452, 481–489
Triple Alliance (labor), 476, 511–512, 514
Triple Entente, 452, 481–489
Trollope, Anthony (1815–1882), 299*n*
Troppau, Congress of, 169
Tucker, Josiah (1712–1799), 93
Tudor, Anthony (1909–   ), 559
Tull, Jethro (1676–1741), 110
Tunis, 355
Turkey, 171–172, 186, 189, 302, 303, 307–310, 353–355, 363, 364, 482, 483, 486–487, 499, 508–509, 510
Turner, Joseph Mallord William (1775–1851), 126, 414

Turnpikes, 108
Two Sicilies, Kingdom of the, 169
Tylor, Sir Edward (1832–1917, k. 1912), 411
Tyrone. O'Neill, Hugh (1540?–1616, 2nd E. of Tyrone, 1585), 65

Uganda, 441, 616
Uitlanders, 444–445
Ulm, Battle of, 144
Ulster, 141–143, 341–345, 365–372, 433–437, 477–479, 500–503, 618–620
Ulster Volunteer Force, 619
Unemployment, 457, 508, 528–529, 532–533, 597
Unemployment compensation, 463, 508
Uniformity, Act of (1662), 34
Union of Democratic Control, 517
Union of South Africa. *See* South Africa
Unions. *See* Trade unions
Unitarianism, 129, 151. *See also* Dissent; Presbyterians
United Irishmen, Society of, 141–142
United Nations, 578–594
United States of America, 88, 148, 155, 170–171, 173, 304, 318, 322, 353, 382–383, 384, 445, 450–451, 487–488, 510, 523, 542, 566, 567–569, 571, 580, 584–585, 593, 594, 596, 600
Universities, 182, 183, 185, 230, 296, 297, 557–558, 561–562. *See also* Cambridge; London; Oxford; Red-brick universities
University Grants Committee, 558
Upper Clyde Shipbuilders, 604
Urquhart, David (1805–1877), 307
Utilitarians, 183, 300
Utrecht, Treaty of, 21, 23, 44, 45, 68

Vanbrugh, Sir John (1664–1726, k. 1714), 31
Vansittart, Sir Robert (1881–1957, k. 1929, *cr.* 1st B. Vansittart, 1941), 545
Vaughn Williams, Ralph (1872–1958), 470, 559
V-E Day, 569
Venezuela, 445
Venizelos, Eleutherios (1864–1936), 508
Venn, John (1759–1813), 128
Verdun, Battle of (1916), 486
Vereeniging, Treaty of, 448
Verona, Congress of, 170
Versailles, Treaty of, 497, 498, 499, 543
Vestries, 58, 226, 229, 638
Vincent, Henry (1813–1878), 253
Victoria, Queen (1819–1901), 217–218, 285, 339, 350, 453–454
Victorian Compromise, 289
Vienna, Congress of, 154–155
Vietnam War, 600
Villeneuve, Pierre de (1763–1806), 144
Villiers, Charles (1802–1898), 224
Vimeiro, Battle of, 148
Vincent, Henry (1813–1878), 253
Vitruvius, 31
Volunteers (Irish), 91, 477–479, 501
Voter registration, 199, 211. *See also* Franchise

Wages, 158, 388, 462–463, 473, 482, 512–515, 524–526, 601, 605, 606
Wakefield, Edward Gibbon (1796–1862), 218–219
Walcheren expedition, 145
Wales, 50, 253–254, 457, 463, 533, 610, 611, 618
Wallas, Graham (1858–1932), 396, 461, 470
Walpole, Horace (1717–1797, 4th E. of Orford, 1791), 79, 125
Walpole, Sir Robert (1676–1745, k. 1725, *cr.* 1st E. of Orford, 1742), 38, 46–47, 54, 61–63
Walton, Sir William (1902– , k. 1951), 558
Ward, William George (1812–1882), 234
War of 1812, 148, 450
Waterloo, Battle of, 154–155
Watson, James (1799–1874), 251
Watson, Richard (1737–1816), 37–38
Watt, James (1736–1819), 112, 115
Waugh, Evelyn (1903–1966), 560
Wavell, Sir Archibald (1883–1950, k. 1939, *cr.* 1st V. Wavell, 1943, 1st E., 1947), 567, 568
Webb, Beatrice Potter (1858–1943), 60, 322, 396, 400, 462, 537
Webb, Philip (1831–1915), 412
Webb, Sidney (1859–1947, *cr.* 1st B. Passfield, 1929), 60, 322, 396, 513, 516, 537
Weber, Max (1864–1920), 469
Webster, Daniel (1785–1852), 304
Wedgwood, Josiah (1730–1795), 102, 112
Wedgwood Benn, Anthony (1925– , 2nd V. Stangate, 1960–1963), 600, 606
Welfare state, 575, 579, 590–591, 613–615. *See also* National Health Service; Socialism
Wellington. Wellesley, Arthur (1769–1852, k. 1804, *cr.* 1st V. Wellington, 1809, 1st E. of Wellington, 1812, 1st M., 1812, 1st D., 1814), 148–149, 154, 170, 171, 186–189, 192, 193, 194–195, 201–202, 281, 295, 306, 309
Wells , Herbert George (1866–1946), 396, 471, 472
Wensleydale Case, 319
Wesley, Charles (1707–1788), 39
Wesley, John (1703–1791), 39, 127–128
West Germany, 584–585, 586
West Indies, 14, 15, 71, 81, 218, 223, 320, 616
West Indies Federation, 616
Westminster, 19, 52, 152–153, 182
Westminster Review, 184
West Riding, 17, 112
Wheatley, John (1869–1930), 518
Whig Party, 41–47, 83, 97–98, 101, 146–147, 180–181, 184, 191, 193–196, 202–203, 211, 212, 229, 250, 260, 277–278, 280, 365, 424. *See also* Liberal Party
Whistler, James Abbott McNeil (1834–1903), 413
Whitbread, Samuel (1758–1815), 180
Whitefield, George (1714–1770), 39
Whitelaw, William (1918–), 619

White's Club, 212
Whitley Councils, 496, 512
Whitworth, Joseph (1803–1887, *cr.* 1st Bt., 1869), 287–288
Wilberforce, William (1759–1833), 101, 128, 145
Wilde, Oscar (1854–1900), 415, 471
Wilkes, John (1727–1797), 82, 84–86, 95, 130
Wilkie, Sir David (1785–1841, k. 1836), 126
Wilkinson, John (1728–1808), 115
William II, Emperor of Germany (1859–1941), 441, 482, 488
William III (1650–1702), 20, 40–41, 42, 68
William IV (1765–1837), 193, 201, 216–217
Williams, Marcia (1932–   , *cr.* Baroness Falkender, 1974), 609
Willoughby de Broke. Verney, Richard Greville (1869–1923, 19th B. Willoughby de Broke, 1902), 465
Wilson, Sir Harold (1916–   , k. 1976), 577, 588, 592, 598, 599–602, 602–603, 605, 607, 608–609
Wilson, Sir Henry Hughes (1864–1922, k. 1915, *cr.* 1st Bt., 1919), 478, 502, 503
Wilson, Sir Horace (1882–1972, k. 1924), 546
Wilson, Woodrow (1856–1924), 497–498
Wiseman, Nicholas (1802–1865), 409
Wittgenstein, Ludwig (1889–1951), 561
Wodehouse, Pelham Grenville (1881–1975, k. 1975), 561
Wolff, Sir Henry Drummond (1830–1898, k. 1862), 430
Wollstonecraft, Mary (1759–1797), 404
Wolseley, Sir Garnett (1833–1918, k. 1870, *cr.* 1st B. Wolseley, 1882, 1st V., 1885), 449
Women, 263–264, 388–389, 403–404, 479–481, 497, 521*n*, 555. *See also* Child and female labor; Family; Marriage
Women's Social and Political Union, 480
Women's suffrage, 404, 479–481, 497, 521*n*

Wood, Sir Henry Joseph (1869–1944, k. 1911), 558
Wood, John (1793–1871), 242–243
Woolen industry, 15, 16, 17–19, 150, 173, 243, 287, 391–392
Wooler, Thomas Jonathan (1786?–1853), 164
Woolf, Virginia (1882–1941), 130, 560
Wordsworth, William (1770–1850), 126, 148
Workers' Educational Association, 557
Working classes, 158–159, 160, 163–168, 185, 193, 196, 236–254, 279–282, 289–292, 321–324, 386–388, 457–458, 511–515, 519. *See also* Factory system; Labour Party; Radicalism; Socialism; Trade unions
Working hours, 390, 462, 525–526, 528, 605, 606
Workmen's Compensation Act (1897), 429, 432
World War I, 481–491, 549–550
World War II, 548–549, 565–573
Wren, Sir Christopher (1632–1723, k. 1675), 31
Wyatt, James (1746–1813), 126
Wyndham's Act (1903), 437
Wyvill, Christopher (1740–1822), 96, 102

Yoemen. *See* Owner-occupiers.
Yom Kippur War, 605
York, 391
York. Frederick Augustus, Duke of York and Albany (1763–1827), 145
Yorkshire, 96, 199
Yorktown, Battle of, 89
Young, Arthur (1741–1820), 111
Young Plan, 541
Ypres, Battles of, 485, 486
Yugoslavia, 499

Zambia, 616
Zanzibar, 359, 441
Zinoviev letter, 520
Zulus, 360–361

88 89 10 9 8